GOOD NEWS TO THE POOR

SPIRIT-EMPOWERED
RESPONSES TO POVERTY

Explore these other Empowered21 Titles

Global Renewal Christianity: Spirit-Empowered Movements Past, Present, and Future. Vinson Synan, Amos Yong, general editors.
   Volume 1: Asia and Oceania.
      ISBN:978–1–62998–688–3
   Volume 2: Latin America with Miguel Álvarez, editor
      ISBN: 978–1–62998–767–5
   Volume 3: Africa, with J. Kwabena Asamoah-Gyadu, editor
      ISBN: 978–1–62998–768–2
   Volume 4: Europe and North America.
      ISBN: 978–1–62998–943–3

The Truth About Grace: Spirit-Empowered Perspectives. Vinson Synan, editor.
   ISBN: 978–1–62999–504–5, softcover; ISBN: 978–62999–505–2, ebook

Human Sexuality & The Holy Spirit: Spirit-Empowered Perspectives.
Wonsuk Ma, Kathaleen Reid-Martinez, Annamarie Hamilton, editors.
   ISBN: 978–1–950971–00–8, softcover; ISBN: 918–1–95071–01–5, ebook

Proclaiming Christ in the Power of the Holy Spirit: Opportunities & Challenges.
Wonsuk Ma, Emmanuel Anim, Rebekah Bled, editors.
   ISBN: 978–1–950971–03–9, softcover; ISBN: 978–950971–05–3, ebook

GOOD NEWS TO THE POOR

SPIRIT-EMPOWERED RESPONSES TO POVERTY

Edited by
Wonsuk Ma *and* **Opoku Onyinah**
Rebekah Bled, *Associate Editor*

ORU
PRESS
Tulsa, Oklahoma USA

Copyright © 2022 Oral Roberts University

Published by ORU Press
7777 S. Lewis Ave., Tulsa, OK 74171 USA

ORU.edu/ORUPress

ORU Press is the book-and-journal-publishing division of Oral Roberts University.

All rights reserved. No part of this publication may be reproduced, stored in a retrieval system, or transmitted in any form or by any means without the prior permission of the publisher. Brief quotation in book reviews and in scholarly publications is excepted.

Published in the United States of America with permission from Empowered21, Tulsa, Oklahoma

Empowered21 aims to help shape the future of the global Spirit-empowered movement throughout the world. This kingdom initiative is served by Oral Roberts University, www.oru.edu.

Cover design by Jiwon Kim
Composed by Sandra Kimbell
Design & Production Editor, Mark E. Roberts

ISBN: 978-1-950971-11-4 softcover
ISBN: 978-1-950971-12-1 ebook

Printed in the United States of America

Contents

Foreword	ix
Preface	xiii

Introduction   1
Opoku Onyinah and Wonsuk Ma

Part I: Foundational

1. Anointing by the Spirit and Ministry to the Poor   11
   William L. Lyons

2. Exploring Issues of Wealth and Poverty in the Gospels: 27
   A Ghanaian Pentecostal-Charismatic Reading of Luke 16
   Justice A. Arthur

3. Spirit Empowerment and Service to the Poor in Acts   45
   Trevor Grizzle

4. Pentecostalism and the Prosperity Gospel   63
   Opoku Onyinah

5. A Church with a Heart: Spirit and Praxis   83
   in Pentecostal Social Engagement
   Ivan Satyavrata

6. A Pentecostal Engagement of Economy from the Margins   99
   David D. Daniels III

7. Global Poverty and the Poor   123
   Sylvia Owusu-Ansah

Part II: Cases in Context

8. Beyond Liberation and Prosperity Gospel: A Third Way   141
   César Garcia

9. The Aimara Identity of Poor Neo-Pentecostals   157
   in Urban La Paz, Bolivia
   Marcelo Vargas

10. Building Our Home: *Balu Wala*, the Sabbatical   177
    and Jubilee Year
    Jocabed R. Solano Miselis

11.	Pentecostalism and the Spirit of Local Development *Alfred Cooper*	189
12.	*Todo lo Puedo*: The Empowerment of Children Born into Poverty through ChildHope *Mary Kathleen Mahon*	207
13.	Religious Conflict in Nigeria and Poverty Dynamics *Babatunde Adedibu*	227
14.	Civil Unrest and Poverty in Congo Brazzaville: A Personal Story *Médine Moussunga Keener*	249
15.	"Bread for Today"—Can Microfinance Respond to the Lord's Prayer in Reducing Poverty? *Irene Banda Mutalima*	261
16.	Empowering Christian Low-Fee Independent Schools: Edify's Response to Poverty *Makonen Getu*	279
17.	Responding to Human Needs: A Case Study of Yoido Full Gospel Church *Younghoon Lee*	301
18.	Pentecostal Civic Engagement in the Squatter Area *Joel A. Tejedo*	321
19.	The War on Drugs in the Philippines and the Image of Healing and Restoration in Mark 5:1-20 *Doreen Benavidez and Edwardneil Benavidez*	345
20.	Global Poverty and Transnational Pentecostalism in the Middle East *Eric N. Newberg*	363
21.	Spirit-Empowered Apostolic Ministry to the Poor: Through the Lens of Three Ministries *John Thompson*	379
22.	"I Tried Poverty": Exploring the Psychological Impact of Poverty and Prosperity in the Life of Oral Roberts *Daniel D. Isgrigg*	405
23.	A DREAMer's Journey and the Holy Spirit's Comfort: A Personal Reflection *Lemuel J. Godinez and Yasmine A. Godinez*	429

The Kingdom Comes: Postscript *Rebekah Bled*	447
Contributors	463
Select Bibliography	469
Name and Subject Index	477
Scripture Index	497

Foreword

There was a time when the gospel, as handed down from what we call the 'West,' was understood and communicated mainly as a complex of ideas surrounding the cross as a remedy for sin and guilt. Since the Reformation, 'salvation' has been centered on having the assurance that one has secured a ticket to heaven. The scholar Krister Stendahl has long pointed out that this is perhaps a function of the "introspective conscience of the West," as imaged by the penitent Puritan constantly beating his breast and ruminating on whether he is indeed saved.

The de-centering of theologies from the Christian heartlands has resurfaced biblical themes that have more congruence with the indigenous religions of the nonwestern world. One is the renewed emphasis on the supernatural dimensions of the Christian faith. Another is the recovery of the gospel as 'good news to the poor,' the thematic thread of this book.

As a collection of reflections and case studies on 'Spirit-empowered responses to poverty,' this book is a welcome effort at putting in a theological frame what at first seemed merely practical responses of Pentecostalism to various contexts of need, particularly in poorer countries of the world.

It is to the credit of the Azusa revival movement that it has once again put front and center the role of the Holy Spirit in the life and witness of the church. In the historical narratives of the church, there has always been an emphasis on the work of the Spirit in-between the first and second coming of Christ. Preaching by the Apostles and the Early Church was almost always accompanied by what we now call 'signs and wonders.' The Desert Fathers, in their isolation, battled both their internal demons and waged spiritual welfare. This vital connection with the spiritual dimension of our faith has unfortunately been glossed over since rationalism became a dominant influence in the churches' witness, as seen in the largely cognitive bias and propositional nature of our mission tools and strategies.

In these days of what the great missiologist-historian Andrew Walls has termed 'shifting centers,' we see the power of the Holy Spirit in engaging the traditional religions of the nonwestern world. Walls has proposed the thesis that it is actually the primal religions that form the substructure of whatever kind of Christianity emerges out of the engagement of the text with the cultural context. It is not an accident that Pentecostalism has seen so much success in places like Africa, where anyone speaking for God is assumed to be a man or woman of power.

Where I sit, I have come to the conclusion that the direct mediation of the power of God usually happens as a sign of divine grace among people in the margins, those who live in contexts where the usual institutions for public service are absent or inadequate.

By way of example, in the late '70s, our Institute researched the budding charismatic movement among Catholics, who are about eighty-five percent of the entire population. During this research, I interviewed a poor woman known as a healer in a community in the rural South. She said she heals mainly through prayer and a 'word of knowledge' as prompted by the Spirit. In one case, the Spirit merely asked her to write on a slip of paper a prescription for a man whose face had turned yellow and looked like he was dying because of some liver ailment. She did not know what she wrote, not having any kind of medical background. It turned out that the man had been taking the wrong medicine, prescribed by a quack doctor since our rural areas are underserved. The Spirit's prescription eventually worked and healed him.

In a local church growth study done in the '70s, when the mainline Protestants had begun to lose steam, the only surge in numbers noted was among the Pentecostal churches. When the people were asked what accounted for their conversion, eighty percent said it was because of the experience of healing.

It is Pentecostalism that seems to be tapping into this element of awe over healing and other supernatural phenomena which traditionally have been part of indigenous religions. Also, as a 'religion of the poor,' its talk of 'health and wealth' naturally has resonance with those who feel powerless in bettering themselves within the structures and systems of their societies.

The case studies in this book provide ample evidence of what missiologists call 'redemptive lift.' Spirit-led witness always leads to caring for those within and beyond reach of churches. Whether intended or unintended, the social consequences can range from the personal dividends due to ethical behavior, like no more drinking, partying, or visits to the yatiris as with the Aimara; or incremental economic progress through 'penny capitalism' as facilitated by micro-finance organizations; or a community-wide social uplift, as has happened in Guarilihue, one of the poorest rural communities in Chile.

The case of Guarilihue raises prospects of large-scale social and economic progress along the lines of Max Weber's analysis of Protestantism as a motive force in the development of Western capitalist societies. "This place is now an Eden," says a former pastor, eighty years after the Pentecostals arrived in the 1940s, reaching over eighty percent of the village population. "The remarkable thing is that there are no drunkards, even though they produce wine! Nor are there prostitutes, gamblers, thieves, no police patrol, nor local magistrates, a place of dreams and satisfaction," he adds.

It is true that in these churches, upward mobility does happen. In the US, the Afro-American Pentecostal churches functioned as a space for breaking down racial and economic barriers, as when they served as the backbone of the civil rights movement. However, there needs to be an intentional transformation of the theological and cultural mindset of the people if large-scale change is to happen.

Sheer numbers are not enough. About ninety-five percent of Filipinos count themselves as Christian; the Pew Research figures put at forty-four percent those who profess to be charismatics, both Catholic and Protestant. However, the tremendous church growth since the '80s has yet to increase the level of public justice and righteousness in the country. It is said that one out of thirteen Ghanaians is a member of the Church of Pentecost, a factor that can make it a potentially significant influence in Ghanaian society. But these numbers may simply mean that there happens to be continuity with the aspirations and ideals of the indigenous religious context. There may not be enough discontinuities, not enough reflection and theological critique that will challenge and transform systems and values that continue to consign people to poverty.

It is not to be wondered at that the so-called 'prosperity gospel' has been having traction in developing countries. In many of these cultures, salvation is in the here and now. Among our own people, the cherished goal is to move towards *'ginhawa,'* or relief from hardship and poverty now, not in some future time in the afterlife. When the first Spanish missionaries came in the sixteenth century, they noted with great perplexity the indifference of the people over their talk of heaven and hell. The existential threat of death and judgment had no power over a people who saw death simply as going over the deep river, to the Skyworld where they would be reunited with their ancestors and pretty much live as they have done on earth.

But talk of material blessing, in the Old Testament sense, can be truly good news in cultures wanting to rise from poverty. In a tribal culture up in the Cordilleras, the social ideal is *li-teng* – the indigenous equivalent of *shalom*, where there is health and wholeness and material blessing, and harmony with one's neighbor and with all of creation.

That there is hope for upward mobility within the small spaces afforded by Pentecostal churches is worth celebrating. The church, I am convinced, remains as the primary social context in which the saving power of God is made visible. Still, if we are to massify such influence, we need also to destroy 'strongholds of the mind,' those mental habits that Paul speaks of as standing in the way of knowing Christ and keep people captive to false ideologies and worldviews. (2 Cor. 10:3–5) In our messaging, we need to identify the cultural discontinuities, the ruptures that need to happen in our various contexts, even as we also affirm the continuities with our indigenous traditions. This book of reflections on the theological meaning and social significance of Pentecostal praxis is a step in this direction.

Melba Padilla Maggay, Ph.D.
Institute for Studies in Asian Church and Culture (ISACC)
President, Micah Global

Preface

Africans brilliantly teach that it takes an entire village to raise a child. So too did this book, especially since it unfolded in two distinct stages: the consultation and the book itself. The Bogotá consultation was warm in many ways: Latin American warm hospitality, collegial and thoughtful interactions among the presenters, and many unseen hands that made the gathering successful and enjoyable. The presenters deserve our special appreciation as a number of Latin American participants braved their language barriers, presenting their studies in a second or third language. The consultation organizers also wish to thank the leaders of the Misión Carismática Internacional, particularly Senior Pastor Bro. César Castellanos and the Empowered21 colleagues for serving the presenters with care and lavish comfort.

For the book stage, the editors are hugely indebted to the additional contributors who helped make this book a substantial contribution to the growing body of literature on Pentecostal-charismatic engagement with poverty. With the financial assistance of Empowered21, the young publisher, ORU Press, took the project on with passion and ingenuity. This book is a gift to those who fight poverty in the power of the Holy Spirit.

Gloria a Dios!

Editors
Pentecost, 2021

Introduction

Opoku Onyinah and Wonsuk Ma

Poverty and Christianity

The struggle to eradicate poverty has been an age-old problem. The desire has been to do away with pernicious inequalities and bring about appreciable equalities between the rich and the poor. The church has been part of this fight. However, there have been diverse expressions of Christian views on wealth and poverty. On one side of the spectrum is the opinion which considers wealth as the god of this world, which must be avoided and fought against. On the other side is the opinion which considers wealth as a blessing from God, which must be appreciated and enjoyed. These issues are pictured in the Gospel of Luke and the book of Acts where, on the one hand, the rich are challenged with a call to "sell everything [they] have and give to the poor" (Luke 18:22 NIV), and on the other hand, the poor receive special blessings and comfort.[1]

A good number of Christians assume that the intent of God for the world is abundance, as evident in his action in the creation order. In creation, God provided abundance and a conducive environment, and not the scarcity of resources. Human beings were created in the image of God with the great responsibility to procreate and manage the created world. However, human beings broke the relationship with God, which resulted in the fall of humanity, and placed the whole creation in imbalance, which brought about sin, death, and suffering. The fall manifests itself in evil in many ways, where people destroy one another, disobey God, and bring about poverty. Nevertheless, God, through his love and mercy, initiated a mission through Christ to redeem humanity from our decay and suffering and to restore creation (Col 1:13–14)—this is the mission of God. Thus, the church was established to carry out the mission of God. The world of poverty and suffering can be overcome and changed through the healing and life-giving mission of the church.

Consequently, the subject of wealth and poverty has attracted very much interest to both scholars and Christian leaders, who attempt to address the issue, especially on how Christians can help to promote sharing the wealth of the world equally. One such significant attempt was the Conference on Faith, Science, and the Future held in 1979, organized by the World Council of Churches (WCC) at the Massachusetts Institute of Technology (MIT) in Cambridge, Massachusetts, USA.[2] The conference was the fourth in the succession of key study conferences of the WCC, which were considered the "Life and Work" side of the movement. The first was Stockholm 1925, the second Oxford 1937, and the third, Geneva 1966. Concerning the MIT conference, altogether there were 900 participants, of which 405 official participants came from fifty-six countries. The conference stressed the interdependence of the issues of justice and sustainability. It claimed, "The twin issues around which the world's future revolves are justice and ecology." "Justice," it said, "points to the necessity of correcting maldistribution of the products of the earth and of bridging the gap between rich and poor countries." On the other hand, 'ecology' was seen as pointing "to humanity's dependence upon the earth." "Society must be so organized as to sustain the earth so that a sufficient quality of material and cultural life for humanity may itself be sustained indefinitely. A sustainable society, which is unjust, can hardly be worth sustaining. A just society that is unsustainable is self-defeating."[3] The conference was a call for a "Just, Participatory, and Sustainable Society."[4] The onus was placed on humanity to take the responsibility to make a deliberate transition to a just and sustainable global society.

Despite this call, the United Nations reports show that poverty is one of the major issues which is plaguing some continents, including Africa, South America, and some parts of Asia. In 2019, for example, the United Nations Development Program report on human development showed that there was inequality everywhere, and that such inequality in human development hurts societies, and weakens social cohesion and trust in government and institutions.[5]

2019 Bogota Consultation

Thus, the church, with all its challenges and failures, remains the salt and light of the world and the agent of transformation. It can be said that the church has perhaps not understood or appropriated its full mandate as commissioned by Christ. It is against this backdrop that the vision of Empowered21 fits in the issues of wealth and poverty. Empowered21 seeks to engage the global challenge of poverty from a Spirit-empowered perspective. From June 3–4, 2019, the Scholars Consultation of the Empowered21 hosted thirteen Spirit-filled scholars and practitioners in Bogota, Colombia, for presentations and sharing of knowledge on the theme, "Poverty, its impact, and the responses of Spirit-empowered communities." Particularly significant was the role of Latin American scholars leading the discussion, joined by three African, three Asian, and three North Americans. The consultation gave space for mutual learning and the sharing of lived-out experiences in specific socio-cultural contexts. The studies helped to identify challenges at work in each context, and the participants gained a deeper understanding of various socio-cultural contexts that would eventually promote the church's ministry. To aid the scholars to prepare their studies, the Consultation organizers had developed a theme description:

> Carefully chosen by leaders of the Spirit-Empowered Movement (hereafter "SEM"), this theme invites scholars in the movement (and others wishing to help) to help SEM members to address the roots of poverty, its impact, and the Spirit-empowered responses to the need. As this consultation takes place in South America and is jointly organized by the Empowered21 Global Office and the South American host, the consultation can offer to the world the gift of experiences, reflections, and lessons gained by South American SEM. They will be joined by global colleagues who can bring similar reflections but from different contexts.
>
> The following description of the theme aims to inform and guide the participants and presenters in their preparation for the consultation. Through this consultation, E21, as a movement, seeks to engage the global challenge of poverty from a Spirit-empowered perspective. The consultation is also intended to be a space for mutual learning. Case studies are actively encouraged to bring lived-out experiences in specific socio-cultural contexts. The studies would also identify challenges that are at work in each context. The result of the consultation which all the participants seek is a deeper understanding of such issues to promote effective Spirit-empowered ministry. Because of the nature of the topic, the organizing team is aware of the benefit of multidisciplinary reflections.
>
> Each study may include part or all of the following elements:
>
> **Roots of Poverty: Foundational Level:**
> Any experience of poverty is complex. As a Christian reflective exercise, the exploration of theoretical, especially biblical and theological layers of the issue, would be profitable. Poverty touches many theological and biblical

themes such as creation, sin, anthropology, redemption, sanctification, healing, and eschatology. But poverty also intersects with other disciplines such as sociology, political theory, economics, and psychology. Poverty is caused by many elements; hence its roots are diverse. The identification of the nature and root(s) of poverty in a particular context may take place by experience as much as by study. The result would be for participants to gain a deeper understanding of the biblical and theological teachings on poverty and the issues surrounding it. This foundational exercise would also help Spirit-empowered communities to design an effective response to human suffering caused by poverty.

Impact of Poverty and the Church:

The second part devotes attention to the devastating effects of poverty on various aspects of life. Since poverty is a dehumanizing force affecting every aspect of personal, family, and social life, studies could explore the resulting physical, psychological, spiritual, and moral effects on individuals. The scope of a study can be micro (local) or macro (global). The local church, as a community of God's people, embodies the kingdom of God in a real-life context. At the same time, Christians struggle with poverty caused by local challenges such as specific political, social, cultural, economic, and religious elements. In the search for the mission of God through his people, the reflection may touch aspects of ecclesiology and mission concerning the theology and practice of the proclamation of the gospel. In a given social context, each case study would identify the challenges faced by the church today. Some of the challenges may be theological in nature as the role of liberation theology and the prosperity gospel.

Work of the Holy Spirit Manifested in the Work of SEM:
For this final part, several questions may be raised: Should a Spirit-empowered believer or the movement have a tangible expression of compassion? What does "Spirit-empowered compassion" look like? This section could include case studies in which Spirit-empowered communities communicate, demonstrate, and live out in real-life situations the transforming work of the Holy Spirit. Further questions may be asked: How does the Spirit-empowered emphasis on the exercise of gifts (both "natural" and "supernatural") relate to poverty? What difference does this Spirit-empowered approach make vis-à-vis other Christian diakonia?

The Book

With the addition of the commissioned chapters, the final outcome of the consultation is what is published in this book, *Good News to the*

Poor: Spirit-Empowered Responses to Poverty. As the Consultation presenters came from across the globe, so too does the book have a wide representation. One geographical exception is Oceania-Pacific, which the organizers (and the editors) sincerely regret. The team is, however, pleased to have eight female contributors, as well as a good number of Latin Americans, in whose continent the consultation was held.

The book is divided into two parts, with twenty-three chapters. The first part provides biblical and theological as well as historical and sociological foundations. Here, there were seven presentations. One presenter examines from the Old Testament book of Isaiah 61, two central features of the "anointing" and the "oppressed" and how they currently inform Christian ministry. Two studies were done on the New Testament, drawing especially from Luke and the book of Acts, noting how Luke gives special attention to wealth and poverty. One study centers on theology by providing historical and theological reflections on the prosperity gospel. Two presenters show how pragmatic Pentecostal missions have been used as agents of social change within their societies. One chapter completes the foundational section by providing an overview of the state of global poverty at the time of this book's publication. These studies provide some useful information on the roots of poverty.

The second part devotes attention to the devastating effects of poverty on various aspects of life, such as personal, family, and social. The studies also explore the resulting physical, psychological, spiritual, and moral effects on individuals. The scope of the study here includes both micro (local) and macro (global) levels. The local church, as a community of God's people, embodies the kingdom of God in a real-life context. While at the same time, Christians keep struggling with poverty caused by local challenges, such as specific political, social, cultural, economic, and religious elements. In the search for the mission of God through his people, the discussions touched on aspects of ecclesiology and mission concerning the theology and practice of the proclamation of the gospel. Each case study identified the challenges faced by a specific society and how the Spirit-filled community responded to the experience and roots of poverty.

There are altogether sixteen chapters in this part. They were arranged by continents beginning with Latin America. There were five chapters from Latin America, which emphasize Pentecostal social engagement as an alternative to Liberation Theology and the Prosperity Gospel, engagement with the poor among society, and the assimilation of culture as empowerment in remote villages. The rest of the authors, four from Africa, four from Asia, one from Europe, and two from North America, carefully selected significant issues and challenges in the Spirit-filled communities from different parts of the globe.

Poverty has been a challenge for humanity as long as its existence. The statistics and studies portray alarming pictures, such as civil unrest, religious conflicts, and now, the global pandemic. In this devastating landscape, transformation through the Holy Spirit has been the focus of an increasing volume of studies, both by insiders and outsiders of the Spirit-empowered movement. For instance, the class study of Latin American Pentecostalism by David Martin convincingly proved that Pentecostal believers achieved upward social mobility.[6] This collection of studies, especially the case studies, takes another critical step: the empowerment of God's people to respond to struggling neighbors. They become active messengers to bring the good news of Christ to the suffering world. Indeed, they embody this good news through their own testimonies and actions in the power of the Holy Spirit, bringing liveliness and hope. In the course of this empowered activism, the church experiences a renewal of its healing and life-giving mission through the power of the Spirit.

Notes

1 Thomas Phillips, "Reading Recent Reading of Issues of Wealth and Poverty in Luke and Acts," *Currents in Biblical Research* 1:2 (2003), 231–269.
2 Roger Shinn and Paul Albrecht, eds., *Faith and Science in an Unjust World: Plenary Presentation*, vol. I (Geneva: WCC, 1980); and Roger Shinn and Paul Albrecht, eds., *Faith and Science in an Unjust World: Reports and Recommendations*, vol. II (Geneva: WCC, 1980).
3 Marcel C. La Follette, ed., "Pre-Conference Report," *Science, Technology, & Human Values* 4:28 (Summer 1979), 41–47.
4 Ronald Preston, "Review of Faith and Science in an Unjust World," *The Ecumenical Review* 32:4 (1980), 456–458.
5 United Nations Development Program, *Human Development Report 2019: Beyond Income, Beyond Average and Beyond Today* (New York: United Nations, 2019), 1.
6 David Martin, Tongues of Fire: *The Explosion of Protestantism in Latin America* (Oxford: Blackwell, 1993).

I
Foundational

1 "Anointed by the Spirit" and Ministry to the Poor: The Core Biblical Mandate to All Generations

William L. Lyons

Abstract

Most Bible readers are familiar with the moment in the Gospel of Luke when Jesus began his ministry by quoting an ancient passage from Isaiah 61: "The Spirit of the Lord is upon me, because he has anointed me. . . . Yet they are uncertain what "anointing" means and wonder why both Isaiah and Jesus chose to mention the poor in this context. This paper examines the arcane concept of "anointing" in the Hebrew Bible (HB)/Old Testament (OT), and then considers what was meant by "the poor" and the "year of the Lord's favor" (mentioned in both Isaiah and Luke). It demonstrates that anointed ministry to the poor is the core mandate for people of faith for all ages, and that vision of social reform has never changed.

Introduction

This paper considers a simple question from a well-known biblical passage: how does the "anointing" affect the ministry foreseen by the prophet Isaiah in 61:1–3.[1]

> The Spirit of the Lord GOD is upon me,
>   because the Lord has anointed me;
> he has sent me to bring good news to the oppressed,
>   to bind up the brokenhearted,
> to proclaim liberty to the captives,
>   and release to the prisoners;
> [2]to proclaim the year of the Lord's favor,
>   and the day of vengeance of our God;
>   to comfort all who mourn;
> [3]to provide for those who mourn in Zion—
>   to give them a garland instead of ashes,
> the oil of gladness instead of mourning,
>   the mantle of praise instead of a faint spirit.
> They will be called oaks of righteousness,
>   the planting of the Lord, to display his glory.[2]

Although the pericope is simple, the topic is vast and has been the focus of committed Bible readers for millennia. For Christians, the author of Luke draws attention to the passage that Jesus quoted at the beginning of his ministry (Luke 4:18–19). Luke also draws upon Isaiah 58:6 in this pericope. Luke 4:18–19 is a seminal passage in both the Old and New Testaments.[3] Each phrase and every word has been closely scrutinized, yet questions remain. Who is the speaker in Isaiah? What does it mean to be "anointed"? Why are those in most need mentioned as central to the ministry of the anointed person? Why did Jesus use this reference to begin his ministry centuries later in Luke?[4] This paper examines two central features of the passage, the words "anointed" and the "oppressed." It then considers current Christian practice in light of the prophetic message.

Isaiah 61 commences with a *hapax legomenon*, that is, a word or in this instance a phrase, that is unique in the Bible and occurs only once.[5] By writing, "The spirit of the Lord GOD," which appears only here in the Hebrew Bible, the prophet effectively captures the attention of his audience with a neologism. Among those familiar with the Bible, none had heard this specific phrase before (or at least not in biblical literature). It effectively arrests the flow of the narrative momentarily and clearly marks the beginning of something new. Thus, along with ancient readers and listeners, we read special words announcing something equally special. Additionally, it should be noted that Jesus's words quoted by Luke also harken back to the entire scope of the servant passages in Isaiah 40–55. As Brevard Childs holds, "a case can be made that [in Luke 4] Jesus himself ushers in the acceptable year of the Lord, and thus the citation of Isaiah 61 encompasses the entire mission of the servant, including his life, death, and offspring."[6]

Anointing

Following the unique reference to the Spirit of the Lord GOD, readers and listeners also learned that the speaker had been "anointed" for something unique. At its simplest, "to anoint," חשׁמ, in the ancient Near East means essentially what it means for people today: to apply some type of ointment or oil on the skin for various purposes including medicinal (Isa 1:6; Luke 10:34; John 9:6, 11; Jas 5:14), cosmetic (Ruth 3:3; Amos 6:6; Luke 7:46), preparation for burial (Matt 26:12; Mark 16:1; Luke 23:56), or even prior to cooking. It is a mundane action that here garners little attention.

Elsewhere in the Hebrew Bible or Old Testament (hereafter HB/OT), in what is called "Jotham's fable,"[7] the trees discuss who they might anoint as king over them in a vain attempt to find an appropriate leader (Judg 9:7–20, 57).

However, when used during special occasions, the act of anointing moves beyond a commonplace activity and assumes significant added nuances. In Genesis 28:18, Jacob anointed a stone pillar to memorialize the Lord's presence with him, when he "rose early in the morning, and he took the stone that he had put under his head and set it up for a pillar and poured oil on the top of it.) Similarly, the tabernacle was anointed with elaborately prepared, expensive, and unique oil *only* used for consecrating the holy place and those serving in it. Shields were also anointed prior to battle (Lev 8:10; Num 7:10; 2 Sam 1:21; Isa 21:5).[8] Bread was also anointed (usually translated as "spread" with oil, Exod 29:2; Lev 2:4; 7:12; Num 6:15), and buildings could be anointed (Jer 22:14). Additionally, in both Isaiah and the Psalms, the king is anointed with the "oil of gladness" (Isa 61:3; Ps 48:6-8; cf. Heb 1:9). Thus, in the Bible, "anointing" was conceived as the mechanism of consecrating for special service both people and inanimate objects and places.

Beyond consecration of people or places for "holy use," anointing may assume added meaning and the practice "served to convey power and ability to perform the function for which one was being anointed."[9] Early in the biblical narrative, Moses anointed Aaron as the High Priest (Exod 29:7; see also Lev 8:12) and his sons as priests.[10] Likewise, Saul was anointed to be king by Samuel (1 Sam 9:16), and subsequent kings are understood to be the "the Lord's anointed" (24:6):[11]

1) David was anointed as king by the "men of Judah" (2 Sam 2:4–7); subsequently, the "elders of Israel" also anointed him as king of Israel (5:3).
2) Absolom was similarly anointed as king (2 Sam 19:10).
3) Solomon was anointed as king by Zadok the priest and Nathan the prophet. Only here do we read of the priest: "the priest Zadok and the prophet Nathan anoint[ed] him king over Israel; then [blew] the trumpet, and [said], 'Long live King Solomon!'" (1 Kings 1:39, cf. 34 and 45). Like David, Solomon was also anointed a second time by the people, "they made David's son

Solomon king a second time; they anointed him as the Lord's prince" (1 Chron 29:22).
4) Joash is anointed as king in 2 Kings 11:12 when Jehoiada, the Priest, "brought out the king's son, put the crown on him, and gave him the covenant; they proclaimed him king, and anointed him."
5) In 2 Kings 23:30, Jehoahaz is anointed as king "by the people of the land."

As with any ancient history, biblical history must be reconstructed carefully by modern readers. These stories of anointing occur over hundreds of years and display a great variety of procedural variations. Nevertheless, we can say that these stories put "clear emphasis on YHWH's initiative, election, and commission," acting through the people to anoint kings.[12]

Although there are multiple references to anointing the kings of Israel (1 Sam 10:1; 16:3; 1 Kings 1:39; 2 Kings 9:6; 11:12), the Bible preserves only a single reference to an inaugural anointing of a prophet when Elijah anointed Elisha as his successor in 1 Kings 19:16.[13] Nevertheless, biblical prophets clearly understood their work to be anointed by God. Psalm 105:15 parallels "my anointed ones" with my "my prophets" in the context of divine protection for the people of Israel.

> Do not touch my anointed ones;[14]
> Do my prophets no harm.

The most notable prophetic reference to anointing is the focus of this paper, the anointing of the prophet for the unique tasks before him in Isaiah 61.

As 1 Samuel 10:1 attests, anointing was understood to be an act of God and served to bestow divine favor upon someone (Ps 23:5; 92:10) or to appoint someone to a special place of divine service (Ps 105:15; Isa 45:1).[15] Implicit in the act of anointing was also an outpouring of God's Spirit (1 Sam 10:1, 9; 16:13; Isa 61:1; Zech 4:1–14), and this aspect is picked up by the New Testament writers as worthy of note (Luke 4:18; Acts 10:38; and 1 John 2:20, 27).

There are only two places in the HB/OT where non-Israelites are referred to as anointed: 1 Kings 19:15 and Isaiah 45:1. In the first instance, Elijah, after being fed by ravens in the wilderness following his encounter with the prophets of Baal and Asherah (1 Kings 18), was directed to anoint Hazael as king of Aram.

> Then the Lord said to [Elijah], "Go, return on your way to the wilderness of Damascus; when you arrive, you shall anoint Hazael as king over Aram."[16]

The second instance involves Cyrus, the Persian king, who liberated the Jews from Babylonian captivity and not only allowed them to return home but also provided for their needs along the way. In this passage, an alien and pagan is called "God's shepherd (Isa 44:28) when Davidic kings fail."[17] Regarding the second reference, J. A. Motyer highlights five characteristics of the anointed person that he gleans from the passage and claims that there is "no better summary of the OT view of the 'anointed' person:"[18]

1) Cyrus was chosen by God (Isa 41:25).[19]
2) He was given dominion over the nations (45:1–3).
3) Throughout all the actions of the Persian king, the Lord is the real actor (45:1–7).
4) The king was appointed to set the exiles free and rebuild the city of the Lord (45:13).
5) Cyrus brought judgment upon the enemies of Israel (Isa 47).

Motyer is quick to note that "these five points are preeminently true of the Jesus, who saw himself as the fulfillment of the OT Messianic expectations."[20]

The phrase "the [Lord's] anointed" (or a cognate phase) deserves special attention in this study. Saul was referred to as anointed by the Lord twice in 1 Samuel 12 (vv. 3 and 5), and subsequently, when David spared his life (1 Sam 24:6). Later, when searching for Saul's successor, Eliab (then the eldest son of Jesse) was mistakenly referred to as "the [Lord's] anointed" (1 Sam 16:6). Much later, the same phrase appears in reference to David (2 Sam 19:21), and similar words appear in what the Bible calls, the "last words of David" which begins with,

> Now these are the last words of David:
> The oracle of David, son of Jesse,
> the oracle of the man whom God exalted,
> *the anointed of the God of Jacob*, the favorite of the Strong One
> of Israel (2 Sam 23:1; emphasis mine).

In the Song of Hannah, the biblical poet writes: "The Lord . . . will give strength to his king and exalt the power of his anointed" (1 Sam 2:10). In the same chapter and shortly before the death of Hophni and Phineas, the wayward sons of Eli who were priests at Shiloh, the theme of anointing continues:

> I will raise up for myself a faithful priest, who shall do according to what is in my heart and in my mind. I will build him a sure house, and he shall go in and out before *my anointed one forever*" (1 Sam 2:35; emphasis mine).

Other references to "anointed" include: Lamentations 4:20, "The Lord's anointed, the breath of our life, was taken in their pits," which is most likely a reference to the death of Zedekiah, the final king of Judah at the hands of the Babylonians. Additionally, in Habakkuk's Song, the people of Israel were anointed," when the Lord "came forth to save [his] people, to save your anointed" (3:13).

Additional passages could be cited,[21] however, these are sufficient to demonstrate that the Lord's anointing highlights a special relationship between God and his anointed person or people. This relationship carries with it the authority and power to rule or work in God's name. Notably, this person/these people would move beyond the failures of previously appointed people (see 1 Sam 2:35 above) and accomplish God's purposes for his people. With the exception of Josiah, however, no biblical king—not even David—fulfilled God's plan for his leaders. It is only of Josiah that we read:

> Before him there was no king like him, who turned to the Lord with all his heart, with all his soul, and with all his might, according to all the law of Moses; nor did any like him arise after him (2 Kings 23:25).

The biblical message on anointing is clear: anointing signifies divine blessing at the inauguration of a new initiative in the divine economy (God's plans for his people). However, it remains secondary to covenantal fidelity.[22] This study of anointing demonstrates that those who were anointed often failed. Even David, who certainly was anointed by God to be king, nevertheless failed, and his people bore the lasting consequences of his rebellious actions captured in the words of Nathan the Prophet:

> [7]Thus says the Lord, the God of Israel: I anointed you king over Israel, and I rescued you from the hand of Saul; [8]I gave you your master's house, and your master's wives into your bosom, and gave you the house of Israel and of Judah; and if that had been too little, I would have added as much more. [9]Why have you despised the word of the Lord, to do what is evil in his sight? You have struck down Uriah the Hittite with the sword, and have taken his wife to be your wife, and have killed him with the sword of the Ammonites. [10]Now

therefore the sword shall never depart from your house, for you have despised me, and have taken the wife of Uriah the Hittite to be your wife. 11Thus says the Lord: I will raise up trouble against you from within your own house; and I will take your wives before your eyes, and give them to your neighbor, and he shall lie with your wives in the sight of this very sun. 12For you did it secretly; but I will do this thing before all Israel, and before the sun." 13David said to Nathan, "I have sinned against the Lord." Nathan said to David, "Now the Lord has put away your sin; you shall not die. 14Nevertheless, because by this deed you have utterly scorned the Lord, the child that is born to you shall die (2 Samuel 12).

How someone lives when empowered by the anointing is primary. Put another way, biblical anointing never covered covenant disloyalty (or faithfulness), and the Bible looks forward to the day when the "Davidic ideal" of an anointed king who acts according to "all the law of Moses" (2 Kings 23:25) would be realized.

The Oppressed or Poor

The primary job of the "anointed one," as conceived by Isaiah (61:1) and repeated by Jesus in Luke 4, was to "bring good news to the oppressed [poor]." Other responsibilities would follow and are listed by the prophet, but the priority of position is given to ministry to the poor. There are several different words for "the poor" in the HB/OT including:[23]

1) יוֹבְאָ: the begging poor
2) דָּל: the poor farmer
3) רוֹסחָמ: the lazy poor
4) יָנָע: the economically oppressed, exploited, or suffering poor

Isaiah 61:1 uses םיִוָנֲע (derived from "d" above) and reads, "The Spirit of the Lord GOD (הִוהְי נֲדֹא חוּר) is upon me, because the Lord has anointed me; he has sent me to bring good news to the oppressed ..." Here "oppressed" may be translated as "bowed down or dejected,"[24] or in the case of Isaiah, "the oppressed poor." The HB/OT preserves different perspectives on these people:[25]

1) Biblical legal texts are concerned with the treatment of those who are poor and call for their protection (Lev 19:9–10; 25:35). Narrative literature in the Pentateuch and the Former Prophets (also called Historical Books) evinces little sustained consideration for the poor but, rather, focuses on the excesses of

the kings that do not address the needs of the poor.
2) Prophetic literature, on the other hand, focuses on the economic oppression of the poor by those who are wealthy. Isaiah chastises landowners who amass large portions of the land but ignore the rights or needs of the poor (Isa 5:8; 10:2). Similarly, Amos repeatedly draws his readers' attention to the plight of the poor, "[The people of Israel] who trample the head of the poor into the dust or the earth and push the afflicted out of the way . . ." are condemned (Amos 2:7; 4:1; 5:11).
3) Wisdom Literature sees poverty variously: (a) as a consequence of someone's indolent lifestyle (Prov 6:10–11; 10: 4, 15), or (b) as in Job, a result of political and economic exploitation. Job used his defense of the poor as an argument for his innocence (Job 29: 12, 16).
4) The Psalms repeatedly present God as a defender of the םיִנֲע (e.g., Ps 22:26).

Moreover, it is not surprising that there were three groups in ancient Israelite society that were particularly susceptible to poverty: widows, orphans, and strangers. They were totally dependent upon others to help them and thus were susceptible to the actions of unscrupulous people. Without a social network to assist them, or when legal protections designed to help them were ignored,[26] they suffered miserably, and the prophets are not averse to drawing attention to this need. Additionally, the New Testament is not silent on the issue, and the book of James is foremost in its concern for the poor:

> Religion that is pure and undefiled before God, the Father, is this: *to care for the infants and widows in their distress*, and to keep oneself unstained by the world (James 1:27 [emphasis mine]; see also, 2:6; 4:13–17).

Thus John the Baptist, Jesus, and the disciples embraced a lifestyle of poverty and it is not surprising that Jesus began the Beatitudes with "Blessed are the poor in spirit" (Matt 5:3), but Luke simply says, "Blessed are the poor" (Luke 6:20).[27] Later New Testament writings display continued concern for the poor and needy as the nascent church members sold their possessions to support those in need (Acts 2:45), and collections were received to assist the poor (Rom 15:26; 2 Cor 8–9; Gal 2:10). The very first action of the nascent church in Acts following the Day of Pentecost was to minister to a person in great need outside of the Temple

(Acts 3:1–10),[28] and in short order, it initiated an early ministry to the widows and orphans.

This trajectory did not cease with the end of the New Testament. Much later, after the Roman empire had become Christian under Constantine, Emperor Julian ("The Apostate"; ca., 360–363 CE) said: "It is disgraceful that, when no Jew ever has to beg, and the impious Galileans [the emperor's name for Christians] support not only their own poor but ours as well, all men see that our people lack aid from us."[29] By this time, the biblical mandate to care for the poor was a hallmark of faith in action.

Sabbatical and Jubilee Year

In addition to bringing "good news to the oppressed," the anointed person described in Isaiah 61 would also: "proclaim the year of the Lord's favor" (61:2). The phrase is generally understood to refer to the Sabbatical Year or Year of Jubilee mentioned in the Books of Exodus and Leviticus,[30] and may here be applying some of the core principles of the convention to the nation of Israel that lost everything during the Exile in Babylon (ca. 586–536 BCE).

Following six years of working the land, the Bible directs that it was to lie fallow for a year, and the dormant period was called a "Sabbatical Year" because "the land shall keep a sabbath" (Lev 25:2). Directives to allow the land to lie fallow appear in Exodus 23:10–11; Leviticus 25:1–7; and Deuteronomy 15:1–11. However, the special year is not mentioned again until Nehemiah 10:31, where the people forgo all debts in accordance with the biblical command.

The "Jubilee Year" was different. Following seven years with the Sabbatical Year ending each cycle, the fiftieth year was called a Jubilee Year—the land would continue to lie fallow for an additional year, and all debts were canceled. It is discussed at length in Leviticus 25:8–17 and 23–55 (See also Lev 27:16–25; Num 36:4; and perhaps Ezek 46:1). Outside the Bible, it is mentioned directly in Josephus *Ant* 3.280.3 and Sifra 8:2 (an early Jewish commentary on Leviticus). It provides for the following:[31]

1) The blast of the *shofar* on the Day of Atonement to begin the year-long observations;
2) The return of all Israelites to their ancestral lands and families;

3) All land was to remain fallow (crops were not planted, fields not "worked").
4) Prices for the sale of land (except for houses in cities) remained fixed.
5) Ancestral lands that were previously sold were returned to the original owners.
6) The Levites were granted special land regulations.
7) All Israelite debt was remitted, and slaves were set free.

Israelite society was fundamentally readjusted during these unique years. There would be no generational indebtedness or slavery. The Bible justifies the Sabbatical and Jubilee Year regulations with two important principles: (1) God owns the land and directs its use (Lev 25:23), and (2) God retains undisputed possession of all Israelites, and he may do with them as he wishes (25:55). David Lieber adds that these ancient conventions "represent a unique Israelite attempt to combat the social evils that had infected Israelite society and to return to the idyllic period of the desert union when social equality and fraternal concern had prevailed."[32] Similarly, Christopher J. H. Wright comments, the HB/OT:

> laws and moral imperatives about loans, interest, debts, slaves, land wages, and justice in general indicate that the first concern of Israel was for human need, not ownership . . . The maintenance of property and possessions must come second to human need. Israelite law favored persons over property and possessions.[33]

It goes without saying that the modern world has strayed far from these biblical directives to help those in need, and our fellow human beings suffer because of it.

How Should Modern Bible Readers Respond to Poverty?

Reiterating the words of James, this study convincingly demonstrates that "Religion that is pure . . . is this: to care for the infants and widows in their distress" (1:26). Everything else is secondary. How then should modern Bible readers respond? The Book of Deuteronomy offers a clear way forward,

> [7]If there is among you anyone in need, a member of your community in any of your towns within the land that the Lord your God is giving you, do not be hard-hearted or tight-fisted toward your needy neighbor. [8]You should

rather open your hand, willingly lending enough to meet the need, whatever it may be. . . . ¹⁰Give liberally and be ungrudging when you do so, for on this account the Lord your God will bless you in all your work and in all that you undertake. ¹¹Since there will never cease to be some in need on the earth, I therefore command you, "Open your hand to the poor and needy neighbor in your land."³⁴

Conclusion

This study of "anointing" in Isaiah 61 and the prophet's anticipated ministry among "the poor" has demonstrated that the passage is unique. Its distinctive wording, "The Spirit of the Lord GOD is upon me, . . ." captures the attention of listeners or readers to the new message that would follow. Beginning with legal texts and early biblical narratives, it is reiterated in the cries from the prophets and echoes through the Psalms and Wisdom Literature and into the New Testament writings. It is arguably *the core biblical mandate* for all generations.

"Anointing" is nothing special in itself and was used for commonplace activities, including medicinal, cosmetic, and funerary needs. Places were also anointed and thereby set aside for special use or service. The word assumes special nuances when used in the context of prophets, priests, or kings. Here it announces a new beginning, inaugurates a new position, and signifies great blessing and empowerment on an anointed person or group of people. Moreover, it highlights a special relationship between God and the anointed one(s). Despite the special nuances of being "anointed," however, the Bible is also clear: anointing is initiatory and empowering, while covenantal fidelity or obedience is primary. Many of those who were "anointed" in the Bible failed in their ministry, including judges, kings, and priests who left a sad legacy to history.

Isaiah's choice of עֲנָוִים (the "oppressed poor") for the focus of the anointed one's work is unforgettable. It would be a ministry to those in greatest need: the economically exposed, exploited, or suffering poor. This is not to say that the passage overlooks other ministry objectives, but Isaiah 61 and Luke 4 direct readers' attention first and foremost to the neediest people. As Julian the Apostate observed, caring for the poor and most needy is the hallmark expression of biblical faith. Nowhere do we see this more than in the fundamental restructuring of ancient Israelite society during the Sabbatical and Jubilee years. There, human economics meets godly design. Debts are canceled, slaves set free, and society was to be readjusted according to godly dictates. It is certainly a far-reaching ideal, but it is not by happenstance that Jesus chose this passage to inaugurate his ministry in Luke. His vision is what marked biblical faith as clearly distinctive in his world, and that vision of social reform has never changed.

Notes

1 This is a revised copy of a presentation given at the Empowered21 Latin American Congress Scholars Consultation, Bogotá, Columbia (2019). I am grateful for Jordan Micah Way's comments and input with this copy.

2 Isaiah 61:1–3, NRSV. With one exception, all biblical references are from the New Revised Standard Version unless otherwise noted and are formatted according to NRSV conventions. That exception is "Spirit," translated "spirit" in the NRSV, but capitalized in this paper as part of the longer, unique special name for God (יְהוִֹה֙ אֲדֹנָ֤י) here adopted by the author of Isaiah. If part of the name is capitalized, it seems to me that the entire name should be capitalized.

3 Mariusz Rosik and Victor Onwukeme, "Function of Isa 61:1–2 and 58:6 in Luke's Programmatic Passage (Luke 4:16–30)," *Polish Journal of Biblical Research* 2 (2002), 68.

4 The author of Luke initiates his ongoing focus on the poor and needy in Mary's Song of Praise, the Magnificat, or the Ode of the Theotokos: "He has brought down the powerful from the thrones and lifted up the lowly; he has filled the hungry with good tidings and sent the rich away empty" (1:52–53). This canticle is traditionally included in liturgical services of both the Catholic and Eastern Orthodox churches and serves as a foundation for the ongoing Lucan focus on the poor: 6:20–49; 7:22; 12:13–21; 14:13–14, 21; 16:1–13; 19–31; 18:22; 19:8; and 21:1–4.

5 Mary J. Obiorah and Favour C. Uroko, "'The Spirit of the Lord God is Upon Me' (Is 61:1): The Use of Isaiah 61:1–2 in Luke 4:18–18," *Teologiese Studies/Theological Studies* 74:1 (2018), 1. Even the conventions of English translations of this phrase are unique. Literally, the phrase should read "The Spirit of the Lord, LORD" (אֲדֹנָ֤י יְהוִֹה֙), however, a unique phrase required a uniquely distinct translation: "The Spirit of the Lord GOD" (see the NRSV and JPS translations [adopted as part of the title for this paper). The Peshitta of Isaiah 61:1 also supports this reading. Both the Septuagint (LXX) and Luke neglect the lengthier designation in the Masoretic Text and the Peshitta "Spirit of the LORD God," and simply use to the "Spirit of the Lord" (Πνεῦμα Κυρίου). For additional information on this intriguing Hebrew phrase and the varied attempts to render it accurately through the centuries see, Jason A. Staples, "'Lord, LORD": Jesus as YHWH in Matthew and Luke," *New Testament Studies* 64 (2019), 1-19. Staples notes that Ezekiel uses אֲדֹנָ֤י יְהוִֹה֙ frequently: 217 of the 319 times it appears in the Hebrew Bible (8).

6 Mark Gignilliat, "Theological Exegesis as Exegetical Showing: A Case of Isaiah's Figural Potentiality," *International Journal of Systematic Theology*

12 (2010), 229–230. Gignilliat draws this material from Brevard Childs, *Isaiah* (Louisville: Westminster John Knox Press, 2000), 519.

7   Jotham was the youngest of Gideon's many sons.

8   If anyone used the holy consecrated oil for profane purposes, they were to be excommunicated ("cut off from the people," Exod 30:33).

9   Timothy B. Cargal, "Anoint," in David N. Freedman et al., eds., *Eerdmans Dictionary to the Bible* (Grand Rapids: Eerdmans, 2009), 66.

10 Elsewhere Lev 7:36 claims that the Lord anointed Aaron's sons, thus the ancient Israelites understood that the active agent in Moses's work of anointing in Exodus and Leviticus was the Lord.

11 This list is only a selection of royal anointings in ancient Israel; many more could be added.

12 Marinus de Jonge, "Messiah," in David N. Freedman et al., eds., *Anchor Yale Bible Dictionary*, vol. 4 (New Haven, CT: Yale University Press, 2007), 778. De Jonge includes an extensive discussion of anointing in biblical and post-biblical texts.

13 Although the actual anointing process/event is not preserved, it may be assumed from the text. Attesting to the power envisioned in a prophetic royal anointing, the military commander Jehu's military leaders would not resist the anointing of their leader as king even though they abhorred the "anointer" Elisha, they nevertheless cried, "Jehu is king" (2 Kgs 9:4–13).

14 Following the previous verses, "anointed ones" in Ps 105:15 refers to the nascent people of Israel, who though "few in number, of little account, and strangers, . . . wandering from nation to nation, from one kingdom, to another people" (vs 12–13), were the object of the special attention of God, that is, "do not touch . . ."

15 J. A. Motyer, "Anointing, Anointed," in J. D. Douglas et al. eds., *New Bible Dictionary*, 2nd ed. (Wheaton: Tyndale House, 1987), 50.

16 The new Syrian king Hazael is mentioned in the Tel Dan Stele, however, as with Elisha, he actual "anointing event" is not mentioned.

17 De Jonge, "Messiah," 779.

18 J. A. Motyer, "Messiah," in J. D. Douglas et al. eds., *New Bible Dictionary*, 2nd ed. (Wheaton: Tyndale House, 1987), 764.

19 In this verse, the phrase, God "stirred up one from the north" is generally understood as referring to Cyrus (cf. also 41:1 where "a victor is roused from the east"). Persia is located east of ancient Israel, but ancient travelers would have followed the Fertile Crescent moving generally northwest from

Persia and then southwest toward Israel.

20 Motyer, "Messiah," 764.

21 The theme of the "anointed one" is expanded and elaborated upon in the Royal Psalms (2, 18, 20, 21, 45, 72, 89, 101, 110, 132, and 144). See de Jonge, 779–780.

22 This is especially clear in 1 Sam 15:22, "Has the Lord as great delight in burnt offerings and sacrifices, as [or] in obedience to the voice of the Lord? Surely, to obey is better than sacrifice, and to heed than the fat of rams."

23 J. David Pleins, "Poor, Poverty," in David N. Freedman et al. eds., *Anchor Yale Bible Dictionary*, vol. 5 (New Haven, CT: Yale University Press, 2007), 403. A lengthy study of each of these terms follows with occasional references to similar words in cognate languages.

24 "ענו" HALOT 2:855. For more on מְעֻנִּים see Bradley C. Gregory, "The Postexilic Exile in Third Isaiah: Isaiah 61:1-3 in Light of Second Temple Hermeneutics," *Journal of Biblical Literature* 126 (2007), 481–484. In his new translation of the Hebrew Bible, Robert Alter translates simply "poor," but in the notes expands upon his translation and adds that it refers "to people in a state of wretchedness" *The Hebrew Bible*, vol. 2 (New York: W. W. Norton & Company, 2019), 826. I think "destitute" accurately captures the nuances of מְעֻנִּים.

25 Patrick J. Hartin, "Poor," in David N. Freedman et al., eds., *Eerdmans Dictionary of the Bible* (Grand Rapids: Eerdmans, 2000), 1070–1071.

26 Leviticus reminds its readers or listeners: "When you harvest the harvest of your land, you shall not reap to the edges of your field, or gather the gleanings of your harvest. You shall not strip your vineyard bare, or gather the fallen grapes of your vineyard; you shall leave them for the poor [עָנִי] and the alien: I am the Lord your God" (19:9–10; see also 23:22).

27 "Poor," Hartin, 1070.

28 William L. Lyons, "Extending the Right Hand: An Important Yet Overlooked Defining Action of the Nascent Church," in Smitha P. Coffee and Donna Tracy Paul eds., *We, the Church: Studies in Mission & Evangelization. Essays in Honor of Bishop Dr. B. S. Moses Kumar* (New Delhi, India: Christian World Imprints, 2017), 167–174.

29 Julian, *Works* 157.22.430 (Wright LCL).

30 Rosik and Onwukeme: 67, 71. See also Benjamin D. Sommer, "Isaiah," in Adele Berlin and Mark Zvi Brettler, eds., *The Jewish Study Bible*," 2nd ed. (Oxford: Oxford University Press, 2014), 888. Marvin A. Sweeney, "Isaiah," in Michael C. Coogan et al. eds., *The New Oxford Annotated*

Bible: New Revised Standard Version with Apocrypha, 4th ed. (Oxford: Oxford University Press, 2010), 1049.

31 David Lieber, "Sabbatical Year and Jubilee," in *Encyclopaedia Judaica* 17:624.

32 Lieber, "Sabbatical Year," 625.

33 Christopher J. H. Wright, *Old Testament Ethics for the People of God* (Downers Grove: InterVarsity Press, 2004) [emphasis mine]. Here Wright quotes Robert Gnuse, "Jubilee Legislation in Leviticus: Israel's Vision of Social Reform," *Biblical Theology Bulletin* 15 (1985), 48.

34 Deut 15:7–11. Similar words also appear in Lev 25. *In Old Testament Ethics*, Christopher J. H. Wright offers an in-depth analysis of "Economics and the Poor" and concludes with a section on "Responses to Poverty" (172–179).

2 Exploring Issues of Wealth and Poverty in the Gospels: A Ghanaian Pentecostal-Charismatic Reading of Luke 16

Justice A. Arthur

Abstract

Against the backdrop of Jesus' actions and teachings on money, wealth, poverty, and economic justice in the gospels, some scholars portray him as a leader of a social movement, with a revolutionary economic program. In Luke, money is sometimes considered a normal part of everyday life. On the contrary, there is a negative view of riches in seven of the nine passages where the word "rich" is used in the third Gospel (Luke 16:1–13; Luke 19:1–9). This chapter examines Jesus' teachings on issues of wealth and poverty in Luke 16 from a Ghanaian Pentecostal-Charismatic perspective. It concludes that, unlike the prosperity gospel, from a Lukan perspective, wealth assumes a negative trait when its primary essence is to make more wealth at the expense of the poor, or when it occupies a central place in a person's life without regard for their neighbor's wellbeing. A positive dimension is established when money is utilized for the communal good, such as bridging the gap between the rich and the poor in society. Thus, wealth is either a tool for social justice, or it is an idol (mammon) that leads to slavery when accumulated.

Introduction

The theme of wealth and poverty is a topical issue in African Pentecostal-Charismatic Christianity because of the prevalence of the so-called prosperity gospel. This concept espouses the view that God's will is to bless the Christian spiritually, physically, and materially.[1] Nevertheless, the words "wealth" and "poverty" assume divergent meanings depending on the normative values of the cultural context in which they are used. Thus, any application of New Testament texts regarding these terms that do not consider the cultural differences of the reader can amount to a misrepresentation of the texts.[2] For many Pentecostal-Charismatic Christians in Africa, the Bible remains the primary source of their inspiration for daily living regarding issues of finances. The words and examples in the Bible serve as reference points for those who want to please God and live for him.

Although they live in a different world from the New Testament world of the eastern Mediterranean, they often take verbatim the injunctions in the Bible. Despite living in a twenty-first century world that is often assessed in terms of quantitative orientations such as Gross Domestic Product (GDP), and success in life is routinely judged by numbers in terms of a healthy bank balance, quality education, home ownership, and even clothing that complements a person's status, uncompromising faith in the Bible and its word is widespread in this strand of Christianity. To be faithful Christians in their context, they come to the Bible for moral reminders, for daily living, including the theme of wealth and poverty.

The contemporary African Christian is confronted with issues of wealth and poverty, just like any other Christian community. The subject is contentious because the New Testament's treatment of it falls short of establishing a clear set of core Christian teachings on the subject.[3] While the words of Jesus on wealth and poverty provide us with some behaviors, such as what is out of bounds for Christians, they also offer some difficulty in interpretation and application. Some of Jesus' words have been described as rather "radical" and as sometimes difficult to understand for a twenty-first century audience. Jesus' actions and teachings on money, wealth, poverty, and economic justice have, therefore, led some scholars to portray him as a leader of a social movement with a revolutionary economic program.[4] Indeed, Jesus' messages are considered radical not only for the first-century contexts but also for the twenty-first century. The reason is that his views on wealth and poverty were extremely different from the prevailing materialistic-individualistic culture. Also, his views sought to reform the prevailing institutionalized norms and practices regarding wealth and poverty.[5]

The radical nature of Jesus' messages on the theme of wealth and poverty is predominantly expressed in the Gospel according to Luke. The third Gospel's presentation of the fundamental aspects of the life and teachings of Jesus on the theme shows a problematic relationship, as well as the diverse ways Jesus approached the subject. On the one hand, issues of money and wealth are considered a normal part of life when their use does not engender disparities within the Christian community. This shows that money is not an issue when used appropriately (Luke 16:1–13; Luke 19:1–10). On the other hand, there are instances where wealth and riches are portrayed negatively (Luke 6:20; Luke 16:1–13;

Luke 16:19–31). The wealthy are often encouraged to redistribute their wealth in order to reduce the gap between the rich and the poor in society. It is against this backdrop that this chapter examines the issues of wealth and poverty in Luke 16:1–31. This assessment is done in the light of the Pentecostal-Charismatic practice of the prosperity gospel in Ghana. Thus, the call to action by Luke is analyzed relative to the core teachings of some Ghanaian Pentecostal-Charismatic prosperity preachers, namely, Mensa Otabil[6] and Sam Korankye-Ankrah.[7]

This chapter adopts the communicative approach proposed by the Ghanaian biblical scholar George Ossom-Batsa as a lens for analysis. This is a three-step approach that places the biblical text at the center of the interpretation process. It includes an analysis of the biblical text, attention to the call to action suggested in the text, and an engagement between the reality and the text.[8] Therefore, the chapter is divided into four main sections: an explanation of the choice of the third Gospel, a discussion of the prosperity gospel in Ghanaian Pentecostalism, an assessment of Luke 16, and an engagement of the biblical text and the prosperity gospel.

Wealth and Poverty in the Gospel According to Luke

The theme of wealth and poverty is a critical subject in the Old Testament, [9]ut to explore that in this chapter would be much too far afield. Instead, I will concentrate on the New Testament, specifically on the Gospel according to Luke. The subject of wealth and poverty is indeed an integral part of Luke. The evangelist sometimes uses unique material and parables that are absent in the other gospels (See Luke 6:20–24; 12:13–31; 16:1–13; 16:19–31; 18:18–23). There are several reasons why Luke seems to be the most relevant when dealing with wealth, poverty, and social justice. First, Luke is one of the most prolific writers in the entire Bible, contributing to almost 27.5 percent of the New Testament when the words of his two-volume work, the third Gospel, and the Acts of the Apostles are taken together.[10] Second, unlike the other evangelists who wrote primarily to Jews or Christians, Luke is the most likely to have the entire Greco-Roman world as his audience. Third and foremost, in contrast to the other three gospels, Luke's gospel addresses the significance of material possessions, the dangers of excessive attachments to riches, and the proper regard for the needs of the poor and marginalized. It covers the greatest abundance of material that emphasizes the proper attitudes and practices regarding the appropriate use of money and the disposition of material possession.[11]

Luke's treatment of the theme of wealth and poverty begins in chapter one of his Gospel before he even announces the birth of Jesus. Mary's *Magnificat* in Luke 1 re-echoes the theme of reversal of fortunes for the poor, a common motif in the Old Testament, as a way of championing the cause of the poor and showing the culpability of the wealthy, as well as indicating that the wealthy are under the threat of severe punishment. Then, the evangelist continues to show the corrupting influence of wealth and the proper use of affluence. In Luke 4, Jesus begins his public ministry by reading from the prophet Isaiah. He read from the scroll in the Temple. Significantly, the passage deals with the preaching of the gospel to the poor. Perhaps, Luke's view is that the poor would readily receive the gospel while the wealth of the rich would be an impediment. In Luke 6, a chapter dealing with blessings and woes, there is clear evidence that the blessings favored the poor and the deprived while the woes were synonymous with the rich.

Furthermore, when Jesus sends out the twelve and the seventy in Luke 9:1–6 and Luke 10:1–12, respectively, the disciples were to travel light and avoid luxuries. This is an indication of the skepticism towards wealth and its influence on the mission of the disciples. In Luke 10:25–37, the Good Samaritan also shows the proper use of wealth and material resources. That is, it should be used to serve others, even marginalized groups. This is followed by the parable of the rich fool in Luke 12:16–21, which cautions about the dangers of the accumulation of wealth. The parable ends with Jesus denouncing those who lay up treasure for themselves but are not rich toward God.

In line with the theme of reversal of fortunes and communal wealth redistribution, the parable of Lazarus and the rich man in Luke 16:19–31 also condemns the propensity of the rich to ignore the needs of the poor, especially when they are close.[12] Equally significant and even more direct is the story of the rich ruler in Luke 18:18–25, who came to Jesus to enquire about how to earn eternal life. The encounter ended with Jesus stating, "it is easier for a camel to go through the eye of the needle than for a rich man to enter the kingdom of God" (Luke 18:25).

Apart from the corrupting influence of wealth, Luke also offers some comments on the proper use of riches. First, Luke 16:1–13 deals with the parable of the unjust steward. While this parable clearly contains some ambiguities, it ultimately emphasizes that one cannot serve God and wealth (*mammon*) simultaneously. Second, in Luke 19:11–27, although the parable of the talents also contains a message about the use of wealth, the lesson remains unclear. It is clear from these Lukan texts that Jesus either heaps praises or blame on people depending on how they relate to wealth or how generous they are to others. The last pericope dealing with wealth and possession is Luke 19:1–10, which tells the story of Jesus' encounter with Zacchaeus. While Zacchaeus does not renounce the entirety of his wealth, Jesus commends him for promising to make four-fold restitution to those he had defrauded and for sharing his wealth with the poor. Therefore, in Luke's estimation, wealth is useful when it is shared or returned to the rightful owners; in this case, the defrauded.[13]

Nevertheless, some scholars assert that while Luke seems to comment on the theme of wealth and poverty frequently, the evangelist does not address the topic in a thoroughly systematic way.[14] Of course, Luke's gospel is not in any way intended to give a specific formula or an orderly package of injunctions on this one aspect of discipleship. There definitely exist some internal tensions in the third gospel regarding wealth and discipleship. For example, while in some instances Jesus allows some people to retain a significant proportion of their wealth, in other places, he is unequivocal about the demands of true discipleship, which is the renunciation of all their possession (Compare Luke 19:1–10 and Luke 14:25–33 or Luke 18:18–25).

The Prosperity Gospel and the Issues of Wealth and Poverty

The so-called prosperity gospel, sometimes referred to as the "health and wealth" gospel, has become an immensely popular teaching within the global Pentecostal-Charismatic Movement. Indeed, it has, in many ways, become synonymous with African Pentecostals and Charismatics, including the charismatic elements within the mainline historical churches.[15] Katharine Attanasi has described the prosperity gospel as a concept that says, "God wants to bless Christians spiritually, physically and materially."[16] It teaches that God's ongoing work in the world includes granting believers prosperity and health. This emerges from a material view of salvation within Pentecostal-Charismatic Christianity, especially in Africa, where the religious worldview that connects deities with abundant life and prosperity as part of salvation is prevalent.[17] Thus salvation in this sense is seen as having implications on the material aspect of this life and not just the world to come. Much as this doctrine has been attributed to being a means by which people have been raised from poverty in Africa and elsewhere,[18] it has also been critically interrogated for breaking the basic Christian obligation of redistribution of wealth to the wider community.[19] Because of its individualistic tendencies, some of its adherents, especially the preachers, have been described as self-seeking and exploiting the poor.[20]

In Ghana, there are two main types of prosperity gospel preaching within the Pentecostal-Charismatic setting. One is represented by preachers like Samuel Korankye Ankrah and Nicholas Duncan-Williams, and focuses on the principles of sowing and reaping, and the exercise of faith and prayer as the main prerequisite to success in life.[21] The second group, represented by preachers like Mensah Otabil, focuses on teaching success and emphasizing hard work, personal development, and education. The two groups are remarkably similar in the fundamental beliefs of the prosperity theology but differ in their approaches and emphasis to achieving success in life. While both groups teach on wealth accumulation and have similar perceptions on poverty, the latter group focuses on social development as well - albeit their shared views far outweigh their differences.

First, the prosperity gospel preached by both groups is generally targeted at the poor because it is believed that God wants to bless Christians with prosperity and not poverty.[22] This blessing is to be felt in every area of human life, especially financial prosperity, and health. In fact, poverty is seen as a disease and a curse that must be "hated." Adherents of the prosperity gospel generally employ several biblical texts (Ps 1:3; Ps 84:11; Duet 28–30; Matt 6:33; John 10:10; 2 Cor 8:9; James 4:2) in support of the doctrine, but the most popular one in the Ghanaian context is 3 John 2. According to their interpretation of this verse, it is God's will that Christians prosper in every aspect of their lives. Accordingly, three main ideas are propagated by prosperity preachers, namely, "God is ready to meet all human needs in the here-and-now; poverty is not the will of God for Christians," and "God is willing to deliver Christians from material poverty."[23] Ultimately, God is seen as one who is not delighted in poverty, since, in their view, the redemptive work of Jesus on the cross does not only save from sin but also from poverty and sickness. Additionally, poverty is seen as a product of a poor mindset because human beings are created in the image of God to have dominion; therefore, they cannot be poor.[24]

Second, the prosperity gospel espoused by both groups is also wealth-centered.[25] They believe that wealth is part of Jesus' atoning work and that wealth signifies the blessings of God. Adherents of the doctrine believe that Jesus died to pay not only their spiritual debt, but also for their financial and general wellbeing. Therefore, material wealth is considered part of the salvation offered by Christ, and wealth can be accumulated to glorify God.[26] The prosperity gospel teaches that God is a God of abundance, wealth, and riches, who gives liberally to his children who act in faith by "sowing seeds." Sowing and reaping, as presented in this doctrine, portrays God as a multiplier who is willing to give abundance to his children.[27] Therefore, seed sowing comes with the expectation of future financial, material, and health blessings. This teaching has motivated many Pentecostal-Charismatic Christians to donate generously to churches. As a result, some churches accumulate wealth and are involved in social development projects such as hospitals, schools, feeding the poor, etc., while others have been accused of using the doctrine to enrich themselves and their families at the expense of the poor. Yet others channel these resources into building other businesses to make even more money, with the profits believed to be plowed back into running the church and its ministries.[28]

Reading Luke 16

I opted to examine Luke 16 because, comparatively, it has a higher concentration of terminologies related to the theme of wealth and poverty. Scholars are not in agreement as regards the exact limits of some of the pericopes within the chapter, such as where the parable of the unjust steward ends.[29] In this chapter, I have adopted the following structure proposed by Clay Myers[30] for Luke 16:

1) The parable of the unjust steward (Luke 16:1–8)
2) Teaching on God and mammon (Luke 16:9–13)
3) Attack on Pharisees as lovers of money (Luke 16:19–14)
4) The parable of the rich man and Lazarus (Luke 16:19–31)

Nevertheless, because the delimitation of the text is not the primary concern, I have opted to link the first two, 1) and 2), in the structure. Consequently, I discuss Luke 16:1–13 jointly because they are usually discussed together as 2) basically forms the moral comments, or an application of 1).[31]

The Parable of the Unjust Steward (Luke 16:1–13)

This pericope has been variously referred to as one of the most difficult of Jesus' parables to interpret. The reason is that in the parable, a steward seems to be praised for his dishonest behavior and held up as an example for Jesus' followers.[32] Traditionally, it has been interpreted as showing a steward who defrauds his master but who is commended for his wisdom and prudence, qualities that the followers of Jesus should imitate in their use of material possessions. Nevertheless, difficulties with certain aspects of the parable mean there is no consensus on this view. In response to the question of how the master could praise dishonest and fraudulent behavior, some scholars have advanced socio-economic reasons that the steward's actions were not really unjust, such as the steward was only writing off the commission of the remuneration due him.[33]

The parable can be divided into a series of five acts. In act one, the steward's problem is that he has been relieved of his role by a "rich man" for whom he has been working (Luke 16:1–2). The reason for losing his job, according to the narrative, is that he has been wasting the rich man's possessions. Clearly, he does not protest his innocence from the accusations. Nevertheless, in act two, the steward comes up with a solution to the problem he faces. In a monologue, he recognizes the problem and reflects on two possible action plans, which he rejects outrightly: "I am not strong enough to dig, and I am ashamed to beg" (Luke 16:3). He then seems to have had a eureka moment: "I have decided what to do. . . ." (Luke 16:4). At this point, he does not state what the plan is, but the aim of the solution was to be received in the homes of his benefactors after he has lost his job. The next act describes how the steward plans to execute his plan (Luke 16:5–7). He invites his master's debtors and reduces their debt. He reduces two examples of debt: a hundred measures of oil were reduced to fifty, and one hundred measures of wheat were cut down to eighty. In act four, the master assesses the steward's actions: the master commends the unjust steward for his shrewdness (Luke 16:8). While the master praises the action of the steward, there is no evidence that he reinstates him. Therefore, the plan's success will be for the steward to get a new position with the master's debtors. The fifth act is an application of the parable, a counsel given by Jesus to his disciples (Luke 16:9–13).

The pericope is part of a larger section that covers Jesus' journey from Galilee to Jerusalem (Luke 9:51–19:27). The audience is primarily the money-loving Pharisees (16:14) and, by implication, the disciples of Jesus (16:1). The evangelist, Luke, basically advances themes in discipleship, such as God's mercy and forgiveness, by emphasizing that the kingdom of God is for the poor. Indeed, the phrase, "He also said to the disciples" (Luke 16:1) indicates a transition from the three parables in Luke15 and thus offers continuity in Jesus' teaching. Moreover, the phrase, "there was a rich man" also connects the pericope to other Lukan passages where Jesus critiques the use of riches and material wealth (Luke 9:57–62; 10:25–37; 12:13–21; 15:11–32; 16:1–13; 16:19–31; 18:18–30; 19:1–10; 19:11–27). The parable is sandwiched between two parables that deal precisely with the term "rich man" (Luke 12:13–21 and Luke 16:19–31). The first of these two warns about the dangers of accumulating material wealth, while the second reveals the eschatological punishment for not showing generosity to the poor. While the steward is praised for his prudence in the face of a crisis, the parable also offers a severe critique of the rich and unjust people, using the characters of the rich man and his unjust steward.

Overall, the parable's primary message could be summarized as follows: First, it scandalizes to attract the readers' attention to what true riches are. The parable indicates that the affluent landlords or their agents should decrease the amount the occupants owed. The reason is that by using their "unrighteous mammon" or wealth, they would make friends of the poor people to whom the kingdom belonged. Thus, the rich are considered outsiders to the kingdom of God. Ultimately, when Jesus returned and established the kingdom of God, there would be a reversal of fortunes in which the rich and, by implication, the powerful would be humbled, and the poor people would be exalted and given eternal dwellings. At that time, because their former creditors had treated them well, the poor would receive them into their heavenly abodes. The eschatological kingdom of God is here considered the true riches, and to enter the kingdom, a person needs to acquire friends, mainly the poor, the outcasts, etc., by sharing their false riches (wealth). Therefore, wealth is beneficial when it is used to serve the poor and vulnerable in society. Accordingly, the Pharisees and the disciples of Jesus are warned not only to use money to gain friends (16:1–9) but also to avoid being lovers of money (16:14). The unjust steward provides an example by befriending his master's debtors through the reduction of their debts.[34]

Second, as a manager, the steward was used to conducting big financial transactions and can be considered an example of those who control wealth. Therefore, the parable is encouraging the rich to use wealth in a similar way as the steward. Perhaps, this parable was directed toward the wealthy or those who manage their wealth.

Third, the parable emphasizes repentance and the significance of the practical actions that come after repentance.[35] Fourth, the parable affirms that the love of money leads to idolizing wealth and possession, which competes with God's place in a person's heart (Luke 16:13). This leads us to the second pericope in Luke 16.

The Money Loving Pharisees (Luke 16:14–18)

Sandwiched between the parable of the unjust steward and the parable of the rich man and Lazarus is the pericope, Luke 16:14–18, dealing with the Pharisees and their love of money. This suggests that after the parables in 15 and 16:1–13, which were partly directed at the Pharisees, they were still listening to Jesus' teaching to the disciples. It is their uneasiness towards the message of the unjust steward that led to the ridicule indicated in Luke 16:14. The message that to be a lover of money amounts to idolizing wealth and possessions (16:13) and making wise use of the wealth under their control (16:8) led the Pharisees to scorn Jesus.[36] Accordingly, Luke introduces them as "lovers of money." Perhaps it is this response from the Pharisees that finally leads to the next pericope, the parable of Lazarus and the rich man.

A Brief Analysis of the Parable Rich Man and Lazarus (Luke 16:19–31)

This is certainly one of the most popular parables in the Bible. Some scholars divide it into two parts owing to a tendency to use an Egyptian folktale as a parallel. Within this tradition, the first part is Luke 16:19–26, dealing with the theme of reversal of fortunes, and the second part, Luke 16:27–31, is considered a later inclusion.[37] Other scholars within this first tradition believe that the two parts are entirely independent of each other and are even conflicting in nature.[38] On the other hand, semiotic and literary analysis of the pericope argues for its unity. They argue that the parable is best considered as a three-part story made up of a description of the earthly life (16:19–21), a dialogue (16:22–23), and the afterlife (16:24–31).[39] Furthermore, the themes of reversal of fortunes and conversion are not viewed as contradictory. Instead, the pericope first shows the reversal of fortune, followed by instructions on how to avoid judgment.[40]

In this parable, the characters represent two opposite extremes on the socio-economic scale. On the one hand, the rich man is not only depicted by his wealth but his life of opulence, which is reflected in his daily banquet-like feasting and through his expensive clothing. Fitzmyer indicates that even among the rich, this man's clothing was not ordinary garments; they resembled royalty.[41] On the other hand, Lazarus was poor and covered by sores and was placed next to the rich man's gate, possibly a disabled man who could not move around by himself. In addition to his inability to freely move around, Lazarus is characterized by a dependence on crumbs from the rich man's table and is subjected to harassment from the dogs around the rich man's premises. Furthermore, the two characters' socio-economic difference becomes even more glaring when the rich man is said to have been buried, but Lazarus was not (16:22). Nevertheless, there is a reversal of fortunes after they both die (16:25–26). The rich man is tormented in the afterlife while Lazarus is being comforted because the former received good things and the latter experienced bad things in life.

The second part of the parable has eschatological implications where the rich man is interceding for his brothers (16:27–31). This shows the importance of repentance to the living.

First, the parable reveals that the reversal of fortunes is clearly linked with glaring social injustice and the lifestyle of the rich and powerful. The rich man's opulent lifestyle is depicted as a negative example of the use of resources and of the kind his brothers should avoid. Second, there is a misuse of wealth on the rich man's part, especially considering his neglect of the poor, which is in stark contrast to God's care of the poor. Multiple Old Testament sources show that God always comes to the aid of the poor, vulnerable, and the helpless, irrespective of their piety (Exod 22:22–23; Deut 10:18; 14:28–29). It is clearly a call to show compassion to the poor because, like the parable of the unjust steward, it affirms that wealth is useful when it is used to take care of the poor and vulnerable, not when it is exclusively spent on oneself and immediate family. Third, the parable carries a social message; it speaks against social injustices. This is depicted by the two socio-economic extremes and the reversal of fortunes closely connected to it. Among other things, the parable challenges the simplistic view that wealth and possessions are blessings from God, and poverty is a misfortune or a curse. It renders weak the idea of hastily connecting wealth to God's favor.[42] Fourth, the parable also moralizes and issues a call for repentance to the rich and their agents, in this case, the brothers of the rich man.

The Engagement of Luke 16 and the Reality of the Prosperity Gospel

Ossom-Batsa's communicative approach suggests that context is the framework within which the discussion between God and humanity occurs. The realization of the call to action suggested by the biblical text is linked to the context of the reader.[43] Accordingly, the reader's experience may lead him/her to understand certain aspects of the text clearly than other parts. A typical example may be the significance given to texts dealing with wealth in contexts where people have experienced dire poverty. Within the context of Ghanaian Pentecostal-Charismatic Christianity, the prosperity gospel occupies a central place, often defining the nature of lived Christianity. A dialogue between the Lukan teaching of wealth and poverty and the main characteristics of the prosperity preaching is therefore critical.

First of all, the prosperity preachers' perspective of the poor is markedly different from how they are represented in the Lukan teaching. The poor in Luke 16 are considered in a positive light to the extent that their condition is attributed to inequalities and injustices in society, and the rich are admonished to use their wealth to help them. In Luke 6:20, the poor are described as blessed and rightful members of the kingdom of God. In contrast to Luke's position, adherents of the prosperity gospel in Ghana perceive the poor as cursed and lacking faith in God, while poverty itself is an evil and a disease that must be detested by the Christian. But among other things, the parables in Luke 16 challenge this simplistic perception that wealth and possessions are blessings from God and poverty is a curse. For Luke, poverty is the consequence of social injustice and proof that the human community is still not God's community. Thus, poverty alleviation is a form of evangelization for Luke.

Furthermore, whereas the focus of the prosperity gospel is wealth, material possession, and health, Luke clearly cautions his audience against making wealth (mammon) their focus because of the danger of it leading into idolatry (Luke 16:13). The messages in Luke 16, in their Lukan context, are addressed primarily to the rich instead of the poor. For example, in the parable of Lazarus and the rich man, the emphasis is basically directed at the rich and their use of their resources.[44] The prosperity gospels' focus on wealth as evidence of a Christian's faith in God has the tendency to lead people into corruption, and to some wealthy people feeling a sense of superiority over the poor, which can result in discrimination, even in churches.

Additionally, for Luke, the proper use of money and possessions is to make friends and help the poor and the needy (16:1–13; 19–31). Wealth is to be redistributed to the community until there is no poor person. Therefore, bridging the gap between the wealthy and the poor in the community is central to the use of riches and possessions. On the other hand, the prosperity gospel is primarily individualistic, targeting wealth creation for individuals and their immediate families. Although it must be pointed out that within the Ghanaian context, there is now a conscious teaching within the movement towards wealth redistribution, championed by adherents like Mensa Otabil.[45]

Also, central to both the parables of the unjust steward and Lazarus and the rich man is the theme of the reversal of fortunes. This is also a prominent part of the prosperity gospel in the Ghanaian context. But, unlike the Lukan parables, which have eschatological orientations, the prosperity theologies deal with the here-and-now. There is widespread teaching on the transfer of sinners' wealth to believers here on earth, based on Prov 13:22.[46] Eschatological issues seem to be completely absent from the teachings of the prosperity gospel in Ghana.[47]

Conclusion

Generally, we see that Luke is not in any way glorifying poverty but drawing attention to the plight of the poor and the proper use of wealth so that money does not become an idol to take God's place in a Christian's life. The evangelist is concerned with proper stewardship of what is entrusted to the believer, as well as having a collective perspective towards wealth and poverty. From the Lukan perspective, wealth assumes a negative trait when its primary use is to make more wealth at the expense of the poor, and when it assumes a central place in a person's life without regard to their neighbor. It is a positive tool when used for the communal good, such as bridging the gap between the rich and the poor in society. Thus, for Luke, money is either a tool for social justice or an idol (mammon) that leads into slavery when accumulated. Also, it is clear from the reading of the text that because of its emphasis on individualism and wealth accumulation, the prosperity gospel perhaps contradicts Luke's view on the proper use of wealth: the redistribution to the community. Nevertheless, it affirms Luke's perspective that God does not want poverty - albeit, unlike the prosperity gospel, poverty is considered the consequence of social injustice in the Lukan perspective.

Lastly, and on a different note, the prosperity gospel-inspired projects such as the twenty-year development plan[48] have the potential to lift people from poverty by helping them to develop a savings culture, which is critical to the third world contexts.

Notes

1 Justice Arthur, "The Gospel of Prosperity and its Concept of Development: A Ghanaian Pentecostal-Charismatic Experience," *Religion* 51:1 (2020), 90–104.

2 Bruce J. Malina, "Wealth and Poverty in the New Testament and Its World," *Interpretation* 41:4 (1987), 354.

3 Thomas Massaro, "The Bible, the Economy, and the Poor," *Journal of Religion & Society* 10 (2014), 172.

4 Thomas E. Phillips, *Reading Issues of Wealth and Poverty in Luke-Acts* (New York: Edwin Mellen Press, 2001), 7; Obery M. Hendricks Jr., *The Politics of Jesus: Rediscovering the True Nature of Jesus' Teachings and How They Have Been Corrupted* (New York: Three Leaves International, 2007), 1; Reza Aslan, *Zealot: The Life and Times of Jesus of Nazareth* (New York: Random House, 2013), 2.

5 Bruno Dyck, *Management and the Gospel: Luke's Radical Message for the First and Twenty-First Centuries* (New York: Palgrave Macmillan, 2013), 193–194.

6 Mensa Otabil is the founder of the International Central Gospel Church and the pastor of the church's first congregation and headquarters church, Christ Temple in Accra.

7 Samuel Korankye Ankrah is the founder of the Royalhouse Chapel International (RCI), a Pentecostal-Charismatic church headquartered in Accra.

8 George Ossom-Batsa, "Interpretation of the Bible in a Communicative Perspective," T*he Ghana Bulletin of Theology* 2 (July 2007), 100–101.

9 R. N. Whybray, *Wealth and Poverty in the Book of Proverbs* (Sheffield: Sheffield Academic Press, 1990), 1.

10 Dyck, *Management and the Gospel*, 13.

11 Thomas Massaro, "The Bible," 168.

12 Esa Autero, Reading the Bible Across Context: *Luke's Gospel, Socio-Economic Marginality, and Latin American Biblical Hermeneutics* (Leiden: Koninklijke Brill, 2016), 251–283.

13 Autero, *Reading the Bible Across Context*, 301.

14 J. David Armitage, *Theories of Poverty in the World of the New Testament* (Gomaringen: Mohr Siebeck Tubingen, 2016), 1; Thomas Massaro, "The Bible," 168.

15 Justice A. Arthur, "Prosperity Theology(ies): Mensa Otabil and the ICGC," *Interkulturelle Theologie: Zeitschrift für Missionswissenschaft* 4 (2017), 401–419.

16 Katherine Attanasi, "The Plurality of Prosperity Theologies and Pentecostalisms," in Katherine Attanasi and Amos Yong, eds., *Pentecostalism and Prosperity: The Socio-Economics of the Global Charismatic Movement* (New York City: Palgrave Macmillan, 2012), 3.

17 Andreas Heuser, *Pastures of Plenty: Tracing Religio-Scapes of Prosperity Gospel in Africa and Beyond* (Frankfurt: Peter Lang, 2015), 1.

18 See Paul Alexander, *Signs and Wonders: Why Pentecostalism is the World's Fastest-Growing Faith* (San Francisco, CA: Jossey-Bass, 2009).

19 Andreas Heuser, "Trajectories into the World: Concepts of 'Development' in Contemporary African Christianity," in Kenneth Mtata ed., *Religion: Help or Hindrance to Development?* (Leipzig: Evangelische Verlagsanstalt, 2013), 51–68.

20 See Allan H. Anderson's forward to J. K. Asamoah-Gyadu, *Contemporary Pentecostal Christianity: Interpretations from an African Context* (Oxford: Regnum Books, 2013), xv.

21 Arthur, "Prosperity Theology(ies)," 401.

22 Samuel Korankye Ankrah, *The Rising of the Sun: Shining from Obscurity* (Accra: Combert Impressions, 2010).

23 Mensah Otabil, *Enjoying the Blessings of Abraham* (Accra: Alta International, 1992), 19–20; Ankrah, The Rising of the Sun, 157.

24 Mensah Otabil, *Beyond the Rivers of Ethiopia: A Biblical Revelation on God's Purpose for the Black Race* (Accra: Alta International, 1992), 18."

25 Arthur, "Prosperity Theology(ies)," 402

26 Samuel Korankye Ankrah, interview by Justice Arthur in Accra, Ghana, May 25, 2020.

27 Joseph Quayesi-Amakye, "Prosperity and Prophecy in African Pentecostalism," *Journal of Pentecostal Theology* 20 (2011), 291–305.

28 Justice A. Arthur, "The Gospel of Prosperity and its Concept of Development: A Ghanaian Pentecostal-Charismatic Experience," *Religion* (2020), 1–15; Arthur, "Prosperity Theology(ies)," 402–418.

29 Denis J. Ireland, "A History of Recent Interpretation of the Parable of the Unjust Steward-Luke 16:1–13," *Westminster Theology Journal* 51 (1989), 293.

30 Ched Myers, *From Capital to Community: Discipleship in Jesus' Parable about a Manager of Injustice* (New York: Oxford University Press, 2012), 51–68.

31 Ireland, "A History of Recent Interpretation," 293; John Arierhi Ottuh, "The Story of Lazarus and the Rich Man (Luke 16:19–31): Retold in a Nigeria Context," *Global Journal of Humanities and Social Sciences* 2:3 (2014), 59–76.

32 Dave L. Mathewson, "The Parable of the Unjust Steward Luke (Luke 16:1–13): A Reexamination of the Traditional View in Light of Recent Challenges," *Journal of the Evangelical Theological Society* 38:1 (1995), 29–39.

33 Joseph, Fitzmyer, *The Gospel According to Luke*, X-XXIV (New York: Doubleday, 1985); Mathewson, "The Parable of the Unjust Steward," 29; Ireland, "A History of Recent Interpretation," 296.

34 Delbert Burkette, "The Parable of the Unrighteous Steward (Luke 16:1–9): A Prudent Use of Mammon," *New Testament Studies* 64:3 (2018), 332.

35 See, Guy D. Nave, *The Role and Function of Repentance in Luke-Acts* (Atlanta: Society of Biblical Literature, 2002), 184–191.

36 Adeniyi Olubiyi Adewale, "An Afro-Sociological Application of the Parable of the Rich Man and Lazarus (Luke 16:19 - 31)," *Black Theology* 4:1 (2006), 28.

37 Dyck, *Management and the Gospel*, 13; Adewale, "An Afro-Sociological Application," 27.

38 Luise Schottroff and Wolfgang Stegemann, *Jesus and the Hope* (Eugene, OR: Wipf and Stock, 2009), 25–26.

39 Walter Vogels, "Having or Longing: A Semiotic Analysis of Luke," *Eglise et Teologie* 20 (1989), 27–46.

40 Vogels, "Having or Longing," 27–46

41 Fitzmyer, *The Gospel According to Luke*, 27.

42 Autero, *Reading the Bible Across Context*, 301.

43 Ossom-Batsa, "African Interpretation of the Bible in Communicative Perspective," 101.

44 Autero, *Reading the Bible Across Context*, 279.

45 Arthur, "The Gospel of Prosperity and its Concept of Development," 1–15.

46 Samuel Korankye Ankrah, interview by Justice Arthur in Accra, Ghana, May 25, 2020.

47 Joseph Quayesi-Amakye, "Prosperity and Prophecy," 291.

48 "My 20-Year Personal Development Plan," International Central Church, https://www.centralgospel.com/directory/gallery/downloads/20_Year_Plan.pdf, accessed December 17, 2020.

3 Spirit Empowerment and Service to the Poor in Acts

Trevor Grizzle

Abstract

The chapter draws attention to the fact that God's concern for the poor is present everywhere in scripture. More than any author in the New Testament, Luke gives focused attention to wealth and poverty. A tendentious bias against the rich and positive regard toward the poor is consistent with his theology in the Gospel and Acts, if less pronounced in the latter. For Luke, true kingdom discipleship is defined as and demands leaving comfort and security and faithfully following Jesus. Distribution of wealth in the service of the poor, therefore, not only serves a humanitarian purpose; attachment to it is a detriment to Christian discipleship, hence a call for its renunciation. This radical discipleship likely imbues the first believers' attitude toward wealth, exhibited in the communal sharing of goods in Acts. Chapters 2:41–47 and 4:32–37 deal with the socio-economic life of the community, depicting the starkest reality of poverty in Acts and the church's Spirit-inspired response to it. The two accounts of sharing of possessions, set against a backdrop of corporate prayer, unity, and the outpouring of the Spirit, indicate that the Christian community's compassionate response was no mere emotional, humanitarian, or philanthropic reaction to human need. It was inspired, enabled, and executed by the Holy Spirit.

Introduction

Poverty is not a recent problem; it is as old as human civilization. Most people today will agree that it is a huge problem globally, but few agree on how to solve or eliminate it. No one can read the Holy Scriptures and leave incognizant of the fact that God cares about the poor and how they are treated. Two thousand verses in scripture deal with the poor and poverty.[1] The various terms descriptive of the poor are used only about 300 times, the majority of which focus on material poverty.[2] Ron Sider's book, *Rich Christians in an Age of Hunger*,[3] highlighting the plight of the poor around the world and the parsimony of rich Christians, fell like a bombshell among Christians in the West, its concussion temporarily shattering the cool and casual indifference of Evangelical Christianity. Poverty around the world and the plight of the poor have not changed much over the years, however.

Poverty and the Church's Mission

Injunctions concerning the proper treatment of the poor in both the Old and New Testaments (e.g., Lev 19:9–10; 25:35; Deut 15:11; Prov 22: 9; Luke 12:33–34; Gal 2:10; Eph 4:28; James 1:27) are abundant and timeless in their applicability. They offer valuable insights into what the church's attitude and responsibility should be toward the poor, and enduring and relevant principles concerning how the church can minister to the poor in her midst and those in the larger global community. God's concern for the needy is enshrined in the Torah, amplified in the Prophets, intensified in the Gospels, illustrated in the life and ministry of Jesus, and demonstrated in the early church. Ministry to the poor is an integral part of the mission of the church in the world. It arises out of the *missio Dei* whose ultimate goal is universal *shalom/soteria*, the subjugation of hostile and demonic forces, and the reconciliation of all things to God.

Who are the Poor?

Of all the New Testament (NT) writings, the Gospel of Luke and the epistle of James provide the fullest treatment of poverty, giving focused attention to wealth and poverty, rich and poor, the proper use of wealth, and appropriate treatment of the poor. Modern Western society regards a strong middle class as the engine that drives and determines the strength of a nation's economy. However, the ancient world consisted largely of mainly two classes—rich and poor, separated by a huge socio-economic chasm. In the Greco-Roman world, the Greek *penes* and *ptochos* were the common monikers for the poor. The masses included in subsistence living were classified under the former, the destitute, and beggars under the latter. Poverty brought with it economic insecurity, hardship, and social vulnerability. Wealth was in the hands of the few who had the socio-economic privilege, held political power, and controlled the levers of local government, determined social stratification, and kept the poor in check.

In the NT, poor and poverty are denoted mainly under two terms: *ptochos* and the more ancient *penes*. The former, an adjective taken from the verb *ptocheuo* whose root means to "crouch," "duck," or "timid," refers to the begging poor who depend on help from strangers to survive. The state and activity of such a person is *ptocheia* (poverty). Significantly, four of the most frequently used Hebrew verbs for poor are rendered by *ptochos* (one hundred times) in the Septuagint (LXX).

Ptochos has many connotations in the LXX: the socially poor, peasants, those without land, the physically weak, beggars, and the homeless.[4] *Penes* is connected with *ponos* (burden, trouble) and refers to the working poor— "the man who cannot live from his property but has to work with his hands."[5] This person has limited means. *Penichros*, a cognate of *penes*, appears only in Luke 21:2, with reference to the widow at the temple treasury. It is of interest that the Markan parallel (12:42) uses *ptochos* to describe her.

Destitution and Discipleship in Luke's Theology

Before I explore poverty in Acts and how the early church dealt with it, I would like to briefly explore Luke's view of rich and poor and wealth and poverty in the third Gospel, which is also reflected, if somewhat muted, in Acts. The binary distinction of poor and rich, with nearly always a bias against the rich and positive regard toward the poor, is consistent with Luke's theology in the Gospel and Acts. While the most common term for poor or destitute (*ptochos*) appears ten times in the Third Gospel (Luke 4:18; 6:20; 7:22; 14:13, 21; 16:20, 22; 18:22; 19:8; 21:3) but not in Acts, Luke's Ebionite theology with its focus on the destitute and despised in society is very present in his second volume. "Poor" in Luke's writings carries a polyvalent and encompassing meaning that transcends economic deprivation.

As early as chapter one, Luke sets the trajectory for the theology that threads through his Gospel. Luke 1:5–44 contains a motif of disruption and reversal of social norms, behaviors, and disposition toward wealth and possessions, which is paradigmatic for the Gospel and the scope of the salvation the Messiah brings. True kingdom discipleship is herewith defined as and demands leaving comfort and security and faithfully following Jesus. This radical life of discipleship, if less conspicuous, is yet very present and discernible in the community life of the early believers in Acts. Proclamation of the good news to the poor, which was programmatic of the ministry of Jesus (Luke 4:16–18), continues to be the church's mission and message.

Jesus felt compassion for the poor and took a personal interest in their needs. From a common fund he established, he and his disciples dispensed money to the indigent (Matt 26:6–9; John 12:5–8; 13:29). On more than one occasion, he told "wannabe" disciples that they must first show compassion for the poor by giving them money (Matt 19:21; Luke 12:33; 14:12–14). He told a rich young ruler: "Sell all the things you have and distribute to poor people, and you will have treasure in the heavens; and come be my follower" (Luke 18:22, 23). For Luke, distribution of wealth in the service of the poor not only serves a humanitarian purpose, attachment to it is a detriment to Christian discipleship, hence a call for its renunciation.

Acts alone in the New Testament records the grim reality of poverty faced by the early church and the practical strategy the believers employed in dealing with it. In Acts alone is the plight of the neglected Hellenist widows exposed and equitably addressed (6:1–6). Acts also reports the Antioch church sending a famine relief of monetary contribution to the mother church in Jerusalem (11:27–30), Luke underlining that "the disciples, each according to his ability, decided to provide help for the brothers living in Judea" (v. 29). Christian communal action in the pooling of resources for the needy on the heels of Pentecost receives concentrated attention in chapters two and four. Rachel Coleman has noted that the two summaries in these chapters "make an explicit connection between positive response to the gospel proclamation and a community life characterized by a strikingly counter-cultural orientation toward wealth and possessions, one that is consistent with the ethic modeled in Luke's Gospel."[6]

The Church's Spirit-inspired Response to its Destitute

Caring for the poor is demonstrated no fewer than four times in Acts, the first two instances forming a part of Luke's three early major summaries which "emphasize the theme of empowered witness to the community in Jerusalem . . . and serve an apologetic function by emphasizing the community's virtue."[7] The first of Luke's mention of the community's socio-economic hardship relates the communal sharing by the Christian believers (2:42–46); the second[8] is another summary of such sharing (4:32–35). The selection of seven deacons to oversee the distribution of goods to the Hellenist widows constitutes the third (6:1–6), and Paul's practical service to the poor the last (20:32–35).

Chapters 2:41–47 and 4:32–37 deal with the socio-economic life of the community, depicting the starkest reality of poverty in Acts and the church's Spirit-inspired response to it. The two events reflect striking commonalities, communal sharing being central. Some regard such similarities as a duplication of a single tradition. Craig Keener thinks otherwise: "Luke intends to parallel the two narratives to illustrate a point he believes he has learned from this tradition: outpourings of the Spirit in response to prayer produce such results as these."[9] Keener's conclusion has contextual support: The depictions of the church community in Acts 2:42–47 and 4:32–38 come immediately after the first two major manifestations of the Spirit. As D. B. Krayhill and D. Sweetland have observed, the profane character of riches in Luke's Gospel is now in Acts "suddenly found in close proximity with the sacred," acknowledged by "the number of references to the Spirit in connection with possessions."[10]

The Christian community's singular expressions of mutual compassion and generosity were no mere emotional, humanitarian, or philanthropic responses to human need. They were inspired, enabled, and executed by the Holy Spirit. "Luke could not be clearer in forging a link between the Spirit's presence and power and the ability of the community to live with Christ-like generosity," underscoring that "one of the fundamental works of the Spirit in the life of the early Christians was the cultivation of a community that took a radically different stance toward the deployment of resources."[11] It is significant that the two accounts of sharing of possessions are set against a backdrop of corporate prayer, unity, and the outpouring of the Spirit. In 1:14, Luke informs that those who gathered to await the coming of the Holy Spirit "all joined together constantly in prayer" (see also 2:42). Similarly, in the second account, Peter and John, upon their release from custody and reporting to the church all that had happened to them, "raised their voices together in prayer to God" (4:23).

In addition to protracted prayer, there was unity among the believers. Where the NIV fails to translate the Greek *homothumadon* (1:14) and merely says that the believers "all joined together constantly in prayer," several other translations render the adverb "one accord" (NKJV, ESV, ASV), "one mind" (ISV, NET Bible, NASB), or "single purpose" (CEV, GW). For example, the ESV translates 1:14a, "All these with one accord were devoting themselves to prayer," the NASB "These all with one mind were continually devoting themselves to prayer," and the CEV, "The apostles often met together and prayed with a single purpose in mind."

This unity is again reflected in 2:1: "When the Day of Pentecost came, they were all together in one place"— "in one place," translating the Greek *homou epi to auto*. Keener draws attention to the use of *homou* in conjunction with "in one place" (*epi to auto*), noting that the phrase strengthens the "together" in *homou*. Much like *homothumadon* in Acts 1:14 and 2:46, it implies sameness—hence unity.[12] The shortened form *thumadon* derives from *thumos*, which infers a sense of "passion" or "ardor."[13]

Unity in the church is again seen in the second episode of the division of goods (4:24)—Luke once more using the term *homothumadon*, this time to mean praying in unanimity, i.e., praying in agreement. As in 1:14, many translations render the word "in one accord" or "with one mind." The God's Word Translation adopts the phrase "they were united." The church's togetherness is also expressed in the Greek phrase epi to auto, used five times in Acts (1:15; 2:1, 44, 47; 4:26). It generally speaks of shared space or the same purpose, but the tedium of translating it is reflected in the various translations. For example, in 1:15, it is translated "together in one place" (NLT), but also "among" (NIV, ESV) and "in the midst" (NASB, KJV). Chapter 4:26 is more consistently rendered "gather/gathered together" (NLT, ESV, NASB, KJV).

John Polhill concludes that *epi to auto* is notoriously difficult to translate but "seems to depict the gathered community, with a strong emphasis on their unity."[14]—the "perfect unity of mind and heart established by the Spirit" such that "only a full sharing of goods could function as an adequate expression of that interior oneness."[15] Coleman rightly describes the early believers as a "barrier-less community" and their breaking of bread together as "consistent with Luke's portrayal of the dominical teaching about life in the kingdom of God."[16]

The outpouring of the Spirit is a third factor that inspired the communal sharing of possessions in the two events in Acts two and four.

The outpouring at Pentecost (2:1) brought about the common distribution of goods (2:45). It is more than incidental that Luke states the spiritual climate in which such generosity was demonstrated: "Everyone was filled with awe at the many wonders and signs performed by the apostles" (2:43). In a similar vein, Luke notes that the Spirit's outpouring preceded the second event of communal sharing of possession: "After they prayed, the place where they were meeting was shaken. And they were all filled with the Holy Spirit and spoke the word of God boldly" (4:31). It is clear that the believers' acts of selfless generosity in both Acts two and four were more than altruistic, human expressions of compassion to a felt need. They were Holy-Spirit-inspired acts of love, which was "a way of obedience (amongst others) to Jesus' instruction or advice in Luke 12:33 to sell one's possessions and give alms."[17]

The Perils of Riches in Luke's Theology

Luke is universally known as an ardent advocate for the poor, the dispossessed, outcast, and marginalized in society. That is true in both the Gospel and Acts. In the Gospel, he often encourages the rich to relinquish their wealth to help the downtrodden (18:22), and in the Parable of the Rich Fool, he shows the unprofitability of hoarding wealth and riches for oneself (12:16–21) and announces Jesus' warning against greed and the seductive enchantment and inadequacy of wealth: "one's life does not consist in the abundance of possessions" (12:15). Luke's message of the proper use of wealth is ensconced in the early church's demonstration of liberality in Acts two and four. Further, for him, the communal sharing of goods is a mark of practical discipleship. Whatever else he may intend to teach in his stress in the Gospel on the renunciation of material and worldly things to follow Jesus, his message of the inversion of values kingdom living demands, the reassessment of life's priorities it summons, rings loud and clear and resounds in the division of goods in the early church.

Thus, after Peter, James, and John's miraculous net-breaking catch of fish, Jesus said to Peter, "Don't be afraid; from now on, you will catch men." Then Luke adds, "So they pulled their boats up on shore, *left everything*[18] And followed him" (5:11). In calling the tax collector Levi to discipleship, Luke is unique among the Synoptists in reporting that after Jesus said to Levi, "Follow me," he "got up, *left everything* and followed him" (5:28). To Matthew, whose lucrative occupation as a tax collector guarantees him a life of financial security, renouncing economic stability for the future uncertainties that attend discipleship is not easy. His resolute decision to repudiate all excessive fondness for material possessions teaches that "discipleship has a necessary cost that is expressed in the capacity to renounce exaggerated attachment to worldly things that have turned into idols that we serve."[19] Jesus' demand of total self-abnegation from his would-be disciple comes to a climax in Luke 14:33, where he declares to the multitude, "In the same way, those of you who do not give up everything you have cannot be my disciples."

The cost of discipleship that calls for a renunciation of "exaggerated attachment to worldly things" is very present in Acts two and four in the common pooling of goods for the needy believers in Jerusalem. Such repudiation exhibited in social solidarity of voluntary giving was Spirit-inspired and Spirit-enabled.

Concord and Compassion: Spirit-witness in Word and Deed

An exegetical study of destitution in these two chapters follows in the rest of this writing. Who were the poor among the believers in the first church? How is poverty to be understood in 2:41–47 and 4:32–37 and other passages in Acts? What characterized this condition? What were its dimensions? What brought on this economic hardship among the believers? Was the community of early believers a form of communism? Was there fiscal irresponsibility?

Robert Guelich points out that "the poor" encompasses more than economically deprived people. "*The poor* in Judaism referred to those in desperate need (socio-economic element) whose helplessness drove them to a dependent relationship with God (religious element) for the supplying of their needs and vindication."[20] Poverty relegated one to the bottom rung of the social, economic, and political ladder. Acts 2:42–47 records the first incident of poverty in the church and how the believers handled it:

> Those who accepted his message were baptized, and about three thousand were added to their number that day. [42]They devoted themselves to the apostles' teaching and to fellowship, to the breaking of bread and to prayer. [43]Everyone was filled with awe at the many wonders and signs performed

by the apostles. 44All the believers were together and had everything in common. 45They sold property and possessions to give to anyone who had need. 46Every day, they continued to meet together in the temple courts. They broke bread in their homes and ate together with glad and sincere hearts, 47praising God and enjoying the favor of all the people. And the Lord added to their number daily those who were being saved (Acts 2:41–47, NIV).[21]

With 2:41–47, Luke moves away from describing the phenomena of Pentecost to depicting the body politic and inner life of the fledgling church. The passage spotlights the commitment of the early believers to Christ and to each other, their deep concord, intimacy, and compassion for each other that manifested not only in spiritual exercise but also in the voluntary sharing of resources and generous distribution to all in need. As Rachel Coleman has noted, "Their shared relationship to Jesus brought them into shared physical presence with one another," and "being the community of Jesus' followers impacted their relationship with their possessions."[22] The numerical growth at the end of the passage relates to the inner vitality of the church.

According to David Peterson, "The flow of the narrative suggests that every aspect of their new life was then brought about by the Holy Spirit."[23] Recurrence of a similar event and its consequences on the community are recounted in 4:32-37 and 5:12–16 in inverted order with added details. Luke's intent here seems to be to show the progressive growth and expansion of the church through the Spirit-empowered preaching of the apostles and the type of new community God was forming. This utopian community may also serve an apologetic function for both Luke's readers and would-be critics outside the community of faith.[24]

Pentecost is about creating a new community that would begin in Jerusalem and fan out like concentric circles to the ends of the earth (1:8). This community, the church, is multi-national, multi-cultural, and multi-lingual (2:8–11), and is microcosmically represented in the fifteen nations gathered in Jerusalem. Luke Timothy Johnson remarks that "the gift of the Spirit brought about a community which realized the highest aspirations of human longing: unity, peace, joy and the praise of God."[25] This community would have an "unparalleled impact on later Christians who looked back to the Apostolic Age as the time when the Church was most perfectly realized."[26] Justo Gonzalez surmises that Paul's collection for the poor Christians (Rom 15:25–28; 1 Cor 16:1; 2 Cor 8:1–6) "is a continuation of the *koinonia* described in Acts, although now widened to include the Church in various cities."[27]

Peter's Pentecostal message in chapter two does not end with his appeal to the colossal crowd of guilt-ridden pilgrims to repent and be baptized for the forgiveness of sins and the consequential reception of the promised gift of the Holy Spirit (v. 38). Luke adds that "With many other words, he [Peter] warned them; and pleaded with them, 'Save yourselves from this corrupt generation'" (v. 39). Peter's entreaty is for more than private and individual salvation. It is for a public commitment to Jesus the Messiah and identification with other followers of his. In the words of John Stott, "Commitment to the Messiah implied commitment to the Messianic Community, that is, the church."[28] This is a huge demand on the Jewish listeners because such an undertaking entailed facing the rejection of family and the Jewish community and the giving of total allegiance to a new family and community highly repudiated—the church. But that is what Peter expected, and that is what happened. Peter's sermon yielded a harvest of 3,000 souls, and that number grew daily (v. 41).

Four elements constitute the spiritual and social life to which these new believers give ongoing commitment: instruction, fellowship, breaking of bread, and prayer. The Greek imperfect and present participle describing each of these four activities (*esan proskarterountes*, v. 42) denote continual or recurring action in past time and are used in 1:14 to describe the steadfast devotion of the waiting disciples at prayer. By itself, *proskarterountes* means to be preoccupied with or to persist at something. Such was the attitude of the early Christian community, first listening to apostolic instruction. Luke says the community "devoted themselves to the apostles' teaching" (v. 42). The believers are preoccupied with it and persist in it. As Jesus did and commanded his disciples to do (make and teach their disciples, Matt 28:19–20), so now they will instruct these new believers.

Assembly for this purpose was likely in the temple courts, yet it is not inconceivable that some may have taken place in Christian believers' homes. The early followers of Jesus were eager to learn about their new faith. Stott has well noted that "Anti-intellectualism and the fullness of the Spirit are mutually incompatible, because the Holy Spirit is the Spirit of truth."[29] Reception of the Spirit of truth does not, however, preclude the need for human teachers. As bearers of God's definitive truth, the apostles lived in closest proximity to Jesus and the divine salvific revelation now contained in the New Testament, making their teachings timeless in the application.

Fellowship is the second thing to which the early church was devoted, which "describes the enthusiasm believers demonstrated in a common bond at worship, at meals, and in the sharing of their material goods."[30] "They devoted themselves to . . . fellowship" (v. 42). Derived from the word *koinos* (common), "fellowship" translates Greek *koinonia*, which also means communion, association, close relationship, joint participation, or partnership. Paul Jeon observes that the term was used in Greco-Roman literature "to express the mutuality and commitment characteristic of marriage."[31]

Sharing of goods and communion with a god are ways it is used in secular Greek and by Paul in 2 Corinthians 9:13 and 1 Corinthians 10:16, respectively. It is the word Paul employs for the relief offering he exhorted the Gentile churches to collect for the mother church in Jerusalem (2 Cor 8:4; 9:13). Paul employs a cognate of *koinonia* in 1 Timothy 6:18 in admonishing the rich to be generous (*koinonikos*) in the use of their wealth: "Command them to do good, to be rich in good deeds, and to be generous and willing to share." In Acts 2:42, *koinonia* obviously refers to "the sort of harmony created by shared purpose . . . and working together,"[32] which outflowed in self-denying generosity— "not a surprising fruit of Pentecost."[33]

The third staple of the early church's spiritual and social life is "the breaking of bread" (v. 42). Commonly made into cakes that were brittle, thin, and hard, Jewish bread was broken rather than cut. But "breaking of bread" also referred to the breaking of a loaf with the hands followed by the giving of thanks to God (Luke 9:16; 22: 19; 24:30, 35). Some understand breaking of bread here as a technical term for the Lord's Supper, which finds early support in the Syriac. Others, like Graham Twelftree, view it as communal meal-sharing[34] as observed in the common evening-meals (Luke 24:30) and concluded with the Lord's Supper. Table fellowship was clearly a focal and vital part of community life. So closely is the practice linked with fellowship in Acts 2:42 that, in addition to its designating the Lord's Supper, it may also refer to common partaking of the ordinary food together in homes—another way of sharing possession.[35] The practice affords another window into the life of this liminal Messianic movement, which was intimate, borderless, and broke the custom of eating only with those of a common socio-economic-ethnic background.

Prayer is the fourth discipline to which the early church is devoted. The plural form (prayers) with the definite article in the Greek text may denote various kinds of prayers, which may include formal prayers made at set times and Christian prayers restricted to no formula, the Psalms, and spontaneous ones fashioned on biblical models.

The New American Standard captures the ongoing effect of the apostolic ministry on non-believers in Jerusalem, and their response to it stated in verse 43: "Everyone kept feeling a sense of awe, and many wonders and signs were taking place through the apostles." Mindful of the significance of the imperfect tense, F. F. Bruce describes the mood as "an enduring sense of awe-inspired by the consciousness of God . . . at work in their midst."[36] With two verbs in the imperfect, Luke indicates the continuing sense of dread and reverential awe felt by the people and the apostles' working of signs and wonders—both a consequence of the effusive presence of the Holy Spirit and Jesus continuing and confirming his work among the people.

In verses 44–45, Luke highlights the unity of the believers in two ways: in their regular meeting together (v. 44a) and periodic common sharing of everything (v. 44b). The latter further explained in v. 45 with two imperfect verbs which indicate regular practice: They "began selling [*epipraskon*] their property and possessions and were sharing [*diemerizon*] them with all, as anyone might have need" (NAS). Property (*ktemata*) refers to real estate, and possessions (*hyparxeis*) to personal belongings.[37] Luke's use of five imperfects in verses 44–45 leaves no doubt that the common sharing of goods was an oft-repeated practice in the community.

Luke does not inform us about what may have precipitated the critical need in the Christian community. Were there any sociological and/or economic factors? Were there political factors? Were economic and social sanctions imposed on the Jesus movement?[38] Was there fiscal irresponsibility?

Faulting the church for practicing communism or replicating the communalism of the Qumran covenanters (Essenes), as some scholars do, is a gross misreading of the situation. The church adopted neither the economic model nor the social structure of either. Communism advocates a classless society in which all property is perforce publicly owned, and each person works and is rewarded according to their needs and abilities. Full membership in the Qumran community required the surrender of all property and personal possessions to the community by the enlistee after the first year. Josephus writes concerning the Essenes, "It is a law among them, that those who come to them must let what they have be common to the whole order — insomuch, that among them all there is no appearance of poverty or excess of riches, but every one's possessions are intermingled with every other's possessions."[39]

The church was modeled neither after communism nor Essene communalism. First, contribution to the pool of goods was voluntary, not obligatory. Second, Christians did not divest themselves of all their personal estate and possessions, just certain portions of them (4:37; 5:4). Church members lived in their own homes (2:46; 12:12) and thus would have retained their own household possessions. Third, the practice was occasional—as needs arose—not permanent; it was local and never became universal.

Acts 4:32–37 recounts a second community pooling of resources for the needy believers. Just as Luke portrays the distinctive qualities of the Spirit-filled community after the first outpouring of the Spirit (2:42–47), so he does after they are again filled with the Spirit (4:32–37):

> All the believers were one in heart and mind. No one claimed that any of their possessions was their own, but they shared everything they had. With great power, the apostles continued to testify to the resurrection of the Lord Jesus. And God's grace was so powerfully at work in them all that there were no needy persons among them. For from time to time, those who owned land or houses sold them, brought the money from the sales and put it at the apostles' feet, and it was distributed to anyone who had need. Joseph, a Levite from Cyprus, whom the apostles called Barnabas (which means "son of encouragement"), sold a field he owned and brought the money and put it at the apostles' feet.

The passage clearly contains recapitulations and verbal resonances found in 2:42–47: unity and liberality, spiritual buoyancy of the new believers, and the authority of the apostles. In an effort to contrast the dissimilar attitudes and responses of two individuals toward the freewill giving, Luke, however, introduces Barnabas, whose commendable generosity is contrasted with Sapphira's avarice and deception, which will follow in the next chapter. What factor or factors may have brought about the harrowing fiscal condition among the believers?

The timeline between the first collection of goods and the second is uncertain. Some opine that the church at this time has doubled in size. What is known with certainty is the rapid growth of the church from 120 to well over 5,000 in a short time. Luke assures us here that neither passage of time nor growth has, however, affected the inner life or outward ministry of the church. Most of its members are poor, which could have created an economic drag on the community that had no financial help from the state. Further, Peterson remarks that the "progressive isolation" of the believers from outsiders "must have made the economic situation of many quite precarious."[40] The church's dire economic condition may have developed from the sale of "the goose that laid the golden egg," i.e., some of its more well-to-do members selling their property, which could have generated funds and jobs for the poor in their midst.

Paul Jeon warns that the community's practice and response to the need can be understood only with "a proper appreciation for its supernatural character which Luke is intentional to highlight again and again." He sees the "magnanimous display of selfless generosity" as the work of the Holy Spirit, whose foremost goal is not only to empower proclamation and the working of miracles but "building a holistic Christian community that reflects Christ in word and deed."[41] Luke, says Stott, "is concerned to show that the fullness of the Spirit is manifest in deed as well as word, service as well as witness."[42] Whatever may have triggered the problem, the Spirit inspired and enabled the believing community to remedy it. Christian generosity eliminated poverty—and without pressure or legislation—a "natural" outflow of "God's grace" (4:33) channeled through Christian love born of the Spirit! Christian stewardship at its best! True caring results in sharing— "nothing other than the gospel as it is confirmed by the Spirit."[43] Contemporary Christians are urged to "reckon with the fact that the simple act of sharing or consistent hospitality might be one of the most magnificent gifts of the Holy Spirit."[44]

Followers of a nonconformist messianic leader though they were, the early believers were not unfamiliar with the scripture that says, "However, there need be no poor people among you, for in the land the Lord your God is giving you to possess as your inheritance, he will richly bless you"

(Deut 15:4). What the early followers of Jesus did was an obedient and beneficent execution of Jesus' command: "A new command I give you: Love one another. As I have loved you, so you must love one another. By this everyone will know that you are my disciples, if you love one another" (John 13:34–35). At work among them is Paul's admonition to the Galatian believers: "Therefore, as we have opportunity, let us do good to all people, especially to those who belong to the family of believers" (6:10).

It would, however, be a misrepresentation to simply relegate the material *largesse* generated by the early church community to the sphere of ethics. Jesus committed to the Church two mandates: The Great Commission and the Great Commandment. The Spirit who empowers the Great Commission also empowers the Great Commandment. Pentecost inaugurated Christ's kingdom in the world in a way that transforms Christian vocation into "Spirit-empowered witness to Christ's kingdom, not only by proclamation but also by acting in accord with God's spirit of love in everyday life."[45] In this, all of the Christian's life and work can become a conduit through which the power of the Spirit flows in manifesting and advancing God's kingdom earth.

Notes

1. Anne R. Bradley and Art Lindsley, eds., *For the Least of These: A Biblical Answer to Poverty* (Grand Rapids: Zondervan, 2014), 40–41, 99.

2. Walter A. Elwell, ed., *Evangelical Dictionary of Theology*, 2nd ed. (Grand Rapids: Baker, 2003), 932.

3. Ron Sider, *Rich Christians in an Age of Hunger*, 1st ed. (Downers Grove, IL: Intervarsity, 1977). A revised and updated edition was published in 2015.

4. Verlyn Verbrugge, ed., "Poor, Poverty," *NIV Theological Dictionary of New Testament Words* (Grand Rapids: Zondervan, 2000), 1116.

5. Colin Brown, ed., *The New International Dictionary of New Testament Theology*, vol. 2 (Grand Rapids: Zondervan, 1986), 820–829.

6. Rachel L. Coleman, "The Lukan Lens on Wealth and Possessions: A Perspective Shaped by the Themes of Reversal and Right Response" (Ph.D. diss., Regent University, 2017), 198–199.

7. Craig Keener, *Acts: New Cambridge Bible Commentary* (Cambridge, United Kingdom: Cambridge University Press, 2020), 170.

8. Darrell Bock notes that by mentioning the church's communal pooling of goods more than once, Luke wants to call attention to it. See, *A Theology of Luke and Acts* (Grand Rapids: Zondervan, 2012), 356.

9. Craig Keener, *Acts: An Exegetical Commentary*, vol. 2 (Grand Rapids: Baker, 2013), 1175.

10. Donald B. Kraybill and Dennis M. Sweetland, "Possessions in Luke-Acts: A Sociological Perspective," *Perspectives in Religious Studies* 10:3 (Fall 1983), 237.

11. TOW Project, "Introduction to Acts," *Acts and Work*, Theology of Work Bible Commentary, https://www.theologyofwork.org/new-testament/acts#an-orienting-community-that-practices-the-ways-of-gods-kingdom-acts-242-432, accessed August 29, 2020.

12. Craig Keener, *Acts: An Exegetical Commentary*, vol. 1 (Grand Rapids: Baker, 2012), 795.

13. Simon Kistemaker, *Acts: New Testament Commentary* (Grand Rapids: Baker, 1990), 60.

14. John Polhill, *Acts: The New American Commentary*, vol. 26 (Nashville: Broadman Press, 1992), 120.

15. Luke Timothy Johnson, *The Literary Function of Possessions in Luke-Acts* (Missoula, MT: Scholars Press, 1977), 187.

16 Coleman, "The Lukan Lens," 202.

17 Eben Scheffler, "Caring for the Needy in the Acts of the Apostles," *Neotestamentica* 50:3 (2016), 135.

18 All italicized phrases mine. Such radical cost of discipleship is also seen in Luke 9:57–62.

19 Mario Lopez Rodriguez, *The Liberating Message of Jesus: The Message of the Gospel of Luke*, trans., Stefanie Israel and Richard Waldrop (Eugene, OR: Pickwick Publications, 2012), 54.

20 Robert Guelich, *The Sermon on the Mount* (Waco, TX: Word, 1982), 69.

21 Unless otherwise indicated, all references are from the New International Version.

22 Coleman, "The Lukan Lens," 202.

23 David Peterson, *The Acts of the Apostles*, The Pillar New Testament Commentary (Grand Rapids: Eerdmans, 2009), 159.

24 Peterson, *The Acts of the Apostles*, 158.

25 Luke Timothy Johnson, Sacra Pagina: *The Acts of the Apostles* (Collegeville, MN: Liturgical Press, 1992), 62.

26 Johnson, *Acts of the Apostles*, 62.

27 Justo L. Gonzalez, *Acts: The Gospel of the Spirit* (Maryknoll, NY: Orbis, 2001), 73.

28 John Stott, *The Message of Acts* (Downers Grove, IL: Intervarsity, 1990), 79.

29 Stott, *The Message of Acts*, 82.

30 Kistemaker, *Acts*, 110.

31 Paul S. Jeon, "Collectivism and/or Christianity: An Exegetical Study of Acts 2: 42–47 and 4:32–5:11" (Paper for Institute for Faith, Work & Economics, Tysons, VA, 2013), 3.

32 Keener, *Acts*, vol. 1, 1002.

33 Keener, *Acts*, vol. 1, 1003.

34 Graham Twelftree, *People of the Spirit: Exploring Luke's View of the Church* (Grand Rapids: Baker, 2009), 115–116.

35 Keener, *Acts*, vol. 1, 1004, and Wolfgang Vondey, *People of Bread: Rediscovering Ecclesiology* (New York: Paulist Press, 2008), 175–178 are among a number of scholars who argue that "breaking of bread" refers to both the Lord's Supper and community meals.

36 F. F. Bruce, *The Book of the Acts: New International Commentary on the*

New Testament (Grand Rapids: Eerdmans, 1988), 73.

37 Richard L. Longenecker, *The Acts of the Apostles: Expositor's Bible Commentary*, vol. 9 (Grand Rapids: Zondervan, 1981), 291 and note, 292.

38 Longenecker, *Acts*, 290.

39 Flavius Josephus, *Wars*, William Whiston, trans. (London: W. Bowyer, 1737), 2:122

40 Peterson, *Acts*, 163.

41 Jeon, "Collectivism and/or Christianity," 6.

42 Stott, *The Message of Acts*, 106.

43 Paul S. Jeon, "Collectivism and/or Christianity," 10.

44 TOW Project, "Introduction to Acts," *Acts and Work*.

45 TOW Project, "Introduction to Acts," *Acts and Work*.

4 Pentecostalism and Prosperity Gospel: Global Perspectives

Opoku Onyinah

Abstract

This chapter gives a brief historical background to the prosperity gospel from a global perspective. It argues that various indigenous Christianity has prosperity as part of it and, thus, the influence from the American preachers on a global level came to enhance what was already within various indigenous Christianity. While the paper takes cognizance of some alarming deficiencies within the prosperity gospel, it is argued that it is the responsibility of theologians to respond to these.

Introduction

In contemporary times, no aspect of theology has received as much attention from academia as the so-called "prosperity gospel." The prosperity preachers claim that faith and obedience to God's word invariably result in blessings, good health, the fullness of life, wealth, and success in life.[1] The issues raised against the prosperity gospel include hermeneutical challenges, such as the lack of a theology of suffering, misinterpretation of the purpose of giving and rewards, a misunderstanding of Jesus' teaching, predicating health and healing on giving, and also the lifestyle of some of the prosperity gospel ministers.

Despite these concerns, there is a clear indication among sociologists that the prosperity gospel is becoming the new phase of the Church.[2] While some churches in North America and Europe are declining in membership, churches that embrace the prosperity gospel are increasing, and some are the largest congregations in their communities.

The case is not any different in the global South. Thus, Michael Wilkinson rightly observes that the prosperity gospel has become "a key defining belief in the Renewalists in the Global South."[3] It is estimated that eighty percent of Pentecostals and many Christian traditions in Africa hold on to the prosperity gospel.[4] However, classifying which churches are prosperity churches is difficult because researchers are not consistent in their definitions. Some sociologists use a wide brush and identify all Pentecostals as prosperity gospel churches.[5] Others are narrower and associate the prosperity gospel with churches that preach the word of faith, seed-faith, and outright prosperity messages. Thus, the criteria for identifying a church as a prosperity gospel church is quite ambiguous.

With this confusion and uncertainty in mind, I will first provide a very brief history of Pentecostalism and then the rise of the so-called prosperity gospel within it. Ignoring this background may give a wrong perspective of the origins, making it difficult to address the challenges that come with it. Thus, a cursory review of the literature of the main characters of the prosperity gospel is appropriate. This will be followed by an outline of what attracts people to the message, with my main focus being Africa. Here, I will argue that the desire for prosperity is embedded within traditional African religions and indigenous African Christianity, and the American prosperity preachers only enhanced what was already an African belief. Following that, I will attempt to interpret the impact of the prosperity gospel in the contemporary world. Finally, I will contend that the idea of prosperity should not be jettisoned just because there are controversial preachers of it. Since there is much literature on the hermeneutical challenges of the prosperity gospel, these will not be addressed in this article.[6]

Pentecostalism: The Wind of God Blowing Wherever it Pleases

The re-emergence of Pentecostalism in the twentieth century did not come out of the blue, but, as shown by Donald Dayton, a Wesleyan historical theologian, it came through various revivals within Christian traditions worldwide.[7] Considering the roots in Lutherans, Wesleyans, Catholics, Pietists, Keswicks, and the revival preachers in North America, one nation or continent cannot claim ownership of the Pentecostal revival or movement. It is the wind of God blowing wherever it pleases (John 3:8).

What makes the Holy Spirit's outpouring in the Azusa Street revival in April 1906 significant for global Pentecostalism is the role of William J. Seymour (1870–1922) and his African American background. The worldwide attraction of Azusa Street revival was the combination of the baptism of the Holy Spirit, speaking in tongues, and the exuberant nature of the African Americans who were so empowered, most notably, Seymour.

William Faupel wrote that a local white pastor called the Azusa street revival a "disgusting amalgamation of African voodoo superstition and Caucasian insanity."[8] This African American tendency of expressing emotion after the Holy Spirit baptism was—and continues to be—a great attraction to the Pentecostal faith. Cecil Mel Robeck Jr. observes that the Azusa street experience became a staple fixture in Pentecostal churches that would follow.[9] Thus, it can be argued that African spirituality and exuberance greatly influenced the twentieth-century re-emergence of global Pentecostalism.

Why Pentecostalism? The Core Message of Pentecostalism

Pentecostalism's unique contribution to the global revival movements was the belief in and the practice of the baptism of the Holy Spirit, with the initial evidence of speaking in tongues. This experience pushed at the threshold of all the earlier revivalist movements within the faith traditions and was seeking a way to gush out. Pentecostalism provided the path. Therefore, Pentecostalism in the twentieth century can be seen as the official recognition or welcoming of the activities of the Holy Spirit back into the Church. Pentecostal spirituality triggers affections that enable one to respond to spiritual encounters with all the human faculties. Because of this, the Pentecostal movement eventually cut across all the dimensions of society, embracing the poor and the marginalized as well as the wealthy and the academic elite.

Generally, Pentecostals believe that all of the spiritual gifts, including the "miraculous" gifts, follow the baptism in the Holy Spirit and are powerful resources for Christian living and evangelism. A concurrent belief is that all the gifts continue to operate within the Church in this present age.[10] Pentecostals generally consider Jesus as Healer, Savior, Sanctifier, Baptizer in the Holy Spirit, and Soon-Coming King. Regarding the ongoing ministry of healing, Pentecostals point to all the healings in the Bible, and they teach that the gift is included in the atoning work of Christ, or put another way, that healing is part of salvation.[11]

Significantly, during the early part of the twentieth century, the emphasis was not on so-called healing evangelists but on the belief that healing would follow any believer's prayer. In fact, some early Pentecostals opposed those who attempted to make healing and deliverance a specialty.[12] This changed when the Latter Rain movement emerged in 1949.

The Latter Rain Movement

The Latter Rain movement emerged intending to revitalize Pentecostalism, since, for those who embraced this revival, Pentecostalism was becoming increasingly institutionalized and experiencing dryness of faith. The Latter Rain movement believed in the restoration of the five-fold ministry of apostles, prophets, evangelists, pastors, and teachers (Eph 4:11–12). In addition, the movement believed that the laying-on of hands by apostles and prophets followed the baptism of the Spirit and released spiritual gifts and other supernatural realities into people's lives. Latter Rain teachers also emphasized deliverance, and they opposed the establishment of "human organizations."[13] By its opposition to human organizations, the Latter Rain movement encouraged the establishment of independent ministries and churches. Some of the Latter Rain ministers became televangelists, a few of whom I will now discuss.

Televangelists and Healing

William Branham's preaching and healing ministry came primarily in tent meetings. Oral Roberts began his ministry in tents as well. However, Oral Roberts' successful use of television as a medium to preach and pray for the sick gained a wider audience, leading others to follow suit. These included Walter V. Grant, A. A. Allen, Gordon Lindsay, Thomas Wyatt, T. L. Osborn, Morris Cerullo, Kenneth Hagin, Kenneth and Gloria Copeland, Pat Robertson, Fred Price, and, in the 1980s, John Avanzini and Benny Hinn. The core teaching of all these healing ministers was that healing the sick makes the gospel complete.[14] Arguably, the four televangelists who made the greatest impact were Kenneth Hagin, Oral Roberts, and Ken and Gloria Copeland.

Kenneth Hagin was said to be greatly impacted by the teaching of E. W. Kenyon (1867–1948) on positive thinking. Kenyon had been influenced by the teaching of Phineas Parkhurst Quimby on metaphysical teachings.[15]

Notably, Kenyon and Parkhurst were not Pentecostals.[16] Hagin's core message, based upon Mark 11:23, was that the confession of God's word built faith. He declared, "Our confessions rule us. That is a spiritual law which few of us realize."[17] Hagin aimed to open people's understanding of what he thought was faith or the power of confession of faith.

Next in impact was Oral Roberts, who made the faith teaching easier for people to understand. Roberts' teaching can be summarized in the three principles of seed faith that he set up. First, recognize that God is your source (Phil 4:19). Second, give first so that it will be given to you (Luke 6:38b), and third, expect a miracle (Mark 11:23–24). Based on these, he encouraged people to give God something to work with, no matter how little it was, and sow in joy and faith, knowing that they were sowing in faith to reap a miracle.[18] Here, we realize that Roberts raised Hagin's Word of Faith up a notch. If you confess it and believe it, then you must put it into action. Putting it into action is like sowing a seed. Once a seed is sown, it will, by all means, germinate, and therefore expect it to germinate. Because God is your source, he will not fail you.

The main contribution of Kenneth and Gloria Copeland, who were heavily influenced by both Hagin and Roberts, was—and is—their explicit emphasis on prosperity. For Kenneth Copeland, "true *prosperity* is the ability to use the power of God to meet every need of mankind"—spirit, soul, and body.[19] God's covenant with his people is a covenant of prosperity. The husband-and-wife team stresses that "God's prosperity will only work in the life of the believer who is committed to the word because he loves God—not for material gains."[20] Thus the Copelands make it clear that God delights in the prosperity of his people. Failure to prosper is evidence of disobedience on the part of the believer.[21]

What must be understood about these ministers is that "word of faith," "seed faith," or "prosperity" was not all they preached about. Their messages touched on all the major subjects, which were vibrant in Pentecostal circles.[22]

The ministries of these ministers went viral. Para-church organizations such as the Full Gospel Businessmen's Men Fellowship and the Scripture Union patronized their activities. As a result, their messages spanned the globe and made Pentecostalism very popular and desirable.

The Spiritual Warfare Factor

Though for many years, the Pentecostal movement was outside the established churches, it eventually made inroads. This was most visible in the 1960s when the Pentecostal experience of the Spirit baptism "officially" began to be practiced among the traditional churches such as the Episcopalians, Lutherans, Presbyterians, and Catholics. This brought forth a new dimension into their church life, including the Pentecostal awareness of Satan, demons, and the powers of evil.

In the 1980s and early 1990s, there was an escalation in dealing with these powers through deliverance, breaking generational curses, and exorcism.[23] This teaching on demonology weakened the understanding of salvation and the baptism of the Holy Spirit because it held that a person could be under the sway of demons even if he or she had been baptized in the Holy Spirit. The ability to discern demonic power before praying was essential, and prayer needed to be done forcefully.

In the latter part of the twentieth century, the trend changed from demon possession to spiritual warfare levels. Two levels were propounded: "ground-level" warfare and "cosmic level" warfare. Two scholars who championed these teachings were Charles Kraft and Peter Wagner. Kraft championed the "ground-level" warfare,[24] While Wagner's concern was the "cosmic level" warfare, which he also called strategic-level warfare.[25] A significant difference between the word of faith/seed faith proponents and the teachers of spiritual warfare is that the former were mainly practitioners, while the latter were scholars. This new wave of warfare teaching rallied enthusiasts to intense prayer against demonic forces. Because the world is now a global village, this teaching spread quickly worldwide and was embraced by Pentecostal and Charismatic communities.[26]

The Pentecostal Faith Spread Across the Globe

In Asia

Our God is a global God. In Asia, for example, Hwa Yung established that the Pentecostal phenomena existed long before the arrival of twentieth-century Western Pentecostalism.[27] Nevertheless, despite what was already happening in Asia, the Azusa Street revival's long reach stretched into

India, China, Indonesia, the Philippines, and Korea.[28] Healing was a vital aspect of the Asian renewal. Vinson Synan and Thomas K. Matthew have clearly demonstrated that Paul Yonggi Cho of South Korea, one of the most influential ministers in Asia, received some inspiration from the writings of Oral Roberts and Kenneth Hagin.[29] Cho is not ashamed to state clearly the sort of relations and influences that he has from other people. His teachings on faith, healing, and prosperity are similar to many Pentecostal preachers across the globe who stress that simple faith in the Bible leads to miracles and blessings of prosperity.[30]

In Latin America

The first recorded Pentecostals in Latin America were the Chileans, whose revival predated Azusa Street.[31] Other countries, such as Brazil and Argentina (and Chile) have the largest Pentecostal churches on this continent. Most of these were directly or indirectly linked to the revival that broke out at Azusa Street.[32] As usual, the baptism in the Holy Spirit and healing featured heavily in these nations, too.

Latin America is one of the continents that embraced the new spiritual warfare movement and promoted it through national prayer conferences. For example, John Dawson and Edgardo Silvoso report about the growth of the church in Argentina as proof of the validity of spiritual warfare.[33] The work of Rudolf von Sinner, a Swiss Evangelical Reformed Church theologian who lectures in Brazil, shows how some Brazilian Pentecostals, especially as exemplified in the Universal Church of the Kingdom of God (IURD), have embraced the prosperity gospel. Prosperity includes breaking free from the "Africaness" within them, which they believe is demonized.[34] Thus, for them, prosperity is only possible by rooting out the ancestral African demons that frustrate and impede personal and societal progress.

In Africa

Before the advent of classical Pentecostalism in Africa, the Spirit's operation to heal the sick had been prominent in the lives of various "prophets" and in their churches that sprang up from the "historic churches."[35] These churches were the Africa Initiated Churches (AICs).[36] As these churches struggled to settle down in structure and theology, classical Pentecostalism arose.

The classical Pentecostal churches were started by a number of independent Pentecostal missionaries, who had been touched or commissioned by the Azusa Street Mission. They were followed by missionaries who were sent by newly emerging Pentecostal denominations. As with other Pentecostals in other continents, Spirit baptism and healing were the primary attraction.[37] However, more important to many Africans was the teaching that the baptism in the Holy Spirit would give power to overcome witchcraft, sorcery, and all evil powers. The Pentecostal churches grew exponentially, forcing the historic churches to adopt some of their practices and beliefs to hold on to their members, a tendency which is being described as the Pentecostalization of Christianity in Africa.

Indigenous Christianity Enhanced by Americanism

Because Westerners introduced Christianity to Africa, Western influence is not new to African Christianity. However, beginning in the 1970s, the seed-faith teaching, coupled with the spiritual warfare teaching, changed the face of Christianity in Africa and elsewhere. One preacher who contributed to this in Africa is Benson Andrew Idahosa (1938–1998) of Nigeria. Idahosa's message centered on faith and healing. Though he was not labeled as a prosperity gospel preacher as such, his "flashy" lifestyle challenged ministers of the gospel to shed the poverty mentality and embrace prosperity as an integral aspect of Christian living. He better qualifies as a precursor to the prosperity gospel preaching.

Witchdemonology

Spiritual warfare teachings led to a practice in West African Christianity, which I call "Witchdemonology." Witchdemonology is the synthesis of the practices and beliefs of African witchcraft and Western Christian teachings of demonology and exorcism. These beliefs include the acceptance of the reality of witchcraft, demons, and gods, the belief in territorial spirits and mapping them out, the belief in ancestral curses, and the identification of demonic realities and curses in both Christians and non-Christians. For people to be set free to prosper in life, special prayer sessions called "deliverance meetings" are held, either in groups or in private sessions.[38]

Witchdemonology opened the door for two types of prophetism. Emmanuel Anim, a Ghanaian Pentecostal theologian, identifies the first as the "Super-Charismatic" prophetic movement.[39] Ministers under this umbrella diagnose people's problems through words of knowledge or prophecy. This is not new; it is similar to divinatory consultation, which I consider the live wire of African Traditional Religion. Many people desire to prosper, have good health, and be protected from evil forces. Ministering to people in this way is the charismatic substitute for the old shrine practices in Africa traditional religions.

The second category is the arena of the "quasi-prophets." While the super-charismatic ministers may be genuine Christians who have been derailed by an unbiblical understanding of the spiritual gifts, the quasi-prophets are people whose identification with Christ is questionable. These are "prophets" who use all means, including asking people to fake illnesses and then claim to be healed after prayer is said for them.[40] These so-called prophets are causing lots of havoc on the continent. In other words, what is happening on the continent of Africa is a mixture of Christian and non-Christian activities, all taking place in the name of Christ. Some researchers label everything as the prosperity gospel, but many practices do not fit neatly in that category.

Why the Message Attracts People

It is important to find out why the prosperity message attracted so many followers among Pentecostals and Africans in particular. First, the majority of these followers saw the teachers of this ministry as Pentecostals like themselves. Second, some of the prosperity gospel advocates were credible scholars who had shown belief in "spiritual things" contrary to the assumption that intellectuals do not believe in spirits, demons, or witchcraft-related issues. Undeniably, the aftermath of the witchcraft persecution in the West, leading to the Enlightenment, produced the rationalistic worldview that has polarized rationalistic Westerners against other worldviews such as African and Asian. Perhaps the world has fallen into both of C. S. Lewis' two errors regarding the devil and demons: the one feeling an "excessive and unhealthy interest" in them, and the latter disbelieving in the devil.[41]

The third is the outstanding ability of the "word of faith" and "seed faith ministers" to use everyday language to explain the word of God so that ordinary Christians can understand it. Listeners and readers did not have to go to a theological seminary to understand their messages. Most of their books were sent freely, and pastors could easily read their materials and adapt them to suit their situations.

Fourth, these ministers used the Bible to address the needs of the people. Although many scholars have vigorously challenged prosperity hermeneutics, their refutations were for scholars, not pastors and ordinary Christians.[42] Thus, the prosperity gospel is unopposed in the pew.

Fifth, the teaching fell on fertile ground in Africa, since from ancient African cultures to the present, the desire for good health and wealth is embedded in African beliefs and practices where suffering and poverty are unacceptable, and relentless war is waged against these. A cursory review of socio-anthropological literature on the anti-witchcraft shrines and the AICs around the 1960s shows that the desire for good health and prosperity was reflected in all their activities.[43] Still, in the 1980s, Pamela Schmoll pointed out that the stress the "'monetarized' society" situation produces in the local population in Niger "finds expression in 'health'-related contexts."[44]

These point to the fact that health and prosperity have been part of the African people. Therefore, the teaching on "word of faith," "seed faith," and "prosperity" fell on good soil. It appealed to the African worldview and confirmed their aspirations for good health, wellbeing, and wealthy life.[45]

This view is significantly different from others, including Paul Gifford, Steve Brouwer, Rose D. Susan, and Rosalind Hackett. They have consistently argued that prosperity gospel is more of a North American invention than a traditional experience, and that it has been exported to the continent of Africa.[46] With African history in mind, it is postulated that the combination of biblical and primal spirituality has resulted in the rise of the prosperity gospel in Africa. Good health, the fullness of life, fertility, and prosperity were important aspects of those who were obedient to the Lord in the Old Testament; while wasting disease, premature death, and dire poverty were parts of curses for those who disobeyed (e.g., Exod 15:26; 23:24; Deut 11:26–32; 28:15–68). Thus, wellbeing and prosperity have been important parts of both biblical and primal spirituality.

Impact of the Prosperity Gospel

What needs to be explored then is the impact of the prosperity gospel in contemporary Christianity. First, it has helped people to find an identity. In his study of the Universal Church of the Kingdom of God (IURD) of Brazil, a church he identifies as a prosperity gospel church that has also flourished in South Africa, von Sinner made an interesting observation. Von Sinner was attracted to some writing on the church building of IURD in Cape Town, ". . . above all, people without name, without honor, without self-confidence and self-esteem have become dignitaries, honorable heads of families, skilled workers and motivated youth."[47] What else does this writing by church authorities signify apart from portraying people in search of identity?

Furthermore, the research of Bradley Koch, a North American sociologist on the prosperity gospel who tested the conjectures about class locations, race, and the giving habits of the prosperity adherents in the US, is instructive. He concluded that "the church [prosperity gospel church] offered a location for African Americans to seek alternative social networks and financial opportunity, as well as a supernatural road map to affluence absent the 'natural,' means to such wealth."[48] Thus, Koch partly agrees with researchers, such as Gifford, Dennis Hollinger, Harvey Cox, and David Edwin Harrell, who have argued that prosperity gospel may appeal to the poor because "it offers hope for upward mobility."[49] When pressed hard, this sort of finding still shows people who are in search of identity because of their social status.

On the other hand, contrary to the argument that the prosperity gospel appeals to the poor, there is also the assertion that the prosperity gospel may appeal to the rich because it provides justification for their elevated status.[50] Although this may not really be the rationale behind the rich accepting the prosperity gospel, it is important to discuss it. Kate Bowler, a North American historian, cited some examples in her work on the history of the prosperity gospel in America in 2010 that are very insightful. She revealed that the then business mogul Donald Trump (the forty-fifth president of the US) called, among others, Paula White his personal pastor. Again, she intimated the free access that a minister like T. D. Jakes had to advise American presidents. In addition, she cited Bishop Eddie Long as the minister who had the opportunity to officiate the funeral service of Coretta Scott King, the wife of Martin Luther King Jr. All of these ministers, she mentioned, are associated with prosperity preaching.[51] Thus, here one cannot limit the appeal of the so-called prosperity gospel only to the poor. It can be said that its appeal cuts across all dimensions of society, embracing the poor and the marginalized as well as the wealthy, intelligentsia, and the prominent.

Second, people may have become wealthy. As to whether the promises made by prosperity preachers work or not, researchers have their own biases. While some observed that it might foster changes in people's lives and result in upward mobility as they work harder and invest more,[52] others see the contrary. Those who take the contrary view are well represented by Koch's "mockery" of the prosperity gospel. Koch said, "Conversely, it is conceivable that the changes induced by adhering to the Prosperity Gospel (waiting for God to make them prosperous rather than working toward this themselves) make moving up less likely."[53]

Nevertheless, here, the observation made by a North American Sociologist, Robert Woodberry, needs to be taken seriously. For him, since scholars have so actively ignored Pentecostalism in empirical research, more definitive answers about the impact of Pentecostalism on the economy must wait until the future.[54] The study of Anim, Woodbery, Kate Bowler, R. Andrew Chesnut, and J. Kwabena Asamoah-Gyadu shows that, in some instances, the prosperity gospel has made some positive impact, especially the adoption of a more conservative moral social ethics.[55]

Third, churches have grown by preaching the prosperity gospel. Notably, some of the world's biggest churches are those who have, in one way or another, been accused of prosperity teaching. Those, besides the US churches, include Yoido Full Gospel Church (Korea), Universal Church of the Kingdom (Brazil), Myles Munroe Bahamas Faith Ministry International (Bahamas), The Redeemed Christian Church of God (Nigeria), and Hillsong Church (Australia).

Fourth, people have come into contact with God. From the above discussion, we cannot easily conclude that the impact of the so-called prosperity gospel with all of its wings¬¬—word of faith, seed faith, healing, deliverance, and prosperity—is just for the poor struggling for "upward mobility," or is just the result of exportation of the American gospel to the world. Rather, it depicts Christians searching for what can be identified as primal spirituality, worshiping God in a biblical way, and the desire to touch base with the Creator. This desire for "primal spirituality" is also what Cox discovered as found in Pentecostalism worldwide and, moreover, underlies original biblical spirituality.[56]

This kind of primal spirituality manifested through the African American exuberant type of Pentecostalism that sparked a revival in the Azusa Street is still manifesting in another way in the prosperity gospel. People who claim to have this spirituality often also claim to have had an encounter with the Creator. They accept the Bible as the inerrant word of God and often share their faith with others vigorously (evangelism). This type of Christianity is what Brouwer, Gifford, and Rose fear and consider as the basis of fundamentalism, and note that such fundamentalism is more energetic than Islamic radicalism.[57] However, for Africans, Pentecostalism, which was ignited by an African spirituality, is now back to Africa's soil in a more practical and relevant way. It is a cycle. This sort of "ministry" brings into fruition the missionaries' agenda of self-supporting, self-propagating, and self-governing.

Inform the Faithful, Not Just the Scholars

What then can we do about the negative aspects of the prosperity gospel? We need to consider that like any other move of the Spirit, and even in ideologies, there are excesses. The excesses are what theologians need to address. It is clear that many theologians and biblical scholars have responded to the excesses within the prosperity gospel, as has been mentioned already, which includes lack of a theology of suffering, misinterpretation of the purpose of giving and rewards, a misunderstanding of Jesus' teaching, attaching health and healing to giving, and also the lifestyle of some of the prosperity preachers. However, one thing that prevails is that biblical scholars and theologians' response is limited only to academia; it never reaches the practitioners, lay leaders, and church members. Furthermore, even if it does, they will not understand the language of the academy. This is an aspect of the work of biblical scholars and theologians that, as a practitioner, I consider woefully lacking in our scholarship—there is a great need to tailor our message to fit the ordinary church members.

Based on this, I recommend that biblical scholars and theologians write materials in less technical language and more comprehensible forms for church use. One of the main reasons the word of faith and the seed-faith teachings grew was the proliferation of easy-to-read and simple materials for the general public. What needs to be done is to teach what we think is right from sound biblical hermeneutics, in a simple manner that practitioners can easily understand. The prosperity gospel will not be the last wind of doctrine that will shake the church's objectives and beliefs or the Christian gospel. As history has taught us, new teaching will likely emerge from time to time. However, it should be the responsibility of biblical scholars and theologians to be able to analyze the issues and supply the church with basic and appropriate materials to address them. I do not think the current practice where scholars live in a different world and speak their own language apart from the church will augur well for the church and its future. This is a call for missionaries (scholars who are mission-minded) to serve between academia and the church—that is, placing academic theology at the service of practitioners.

Conclusion

This paper has sought to demonstrate that the Pentecostal movement in the twentieth century from which the prosperity gospel emerged has been the apex of the various revivals in all church traditions. It can rightly be argued that Christianity itself has been progressive; the new was built from the old, and the old borrowed much from the cultures around it. The so-called prosperity gospel has been presented to be considered along this line of reasoning—as a progression of ideas.

This study has also argued that the idea that the prosperity gospel is a North American invention that has been exported to Africa and other continents, rather than a quest emerging from a traditional experience in those contexts, is incoherent. Rather, it has been affirmed that the prosperity gospel is a progression of ideas, a mixture of good and evil, then reformulated *mutatis mutandis* to suit people's own purposes. Thus, the so-called prosperity gospel developed through the various movements within Pentecostalism, such as the Latter Rain revival, the word of faith teaching, seed-faith teachings, deliverance ministries, spiritual warfare teachings, the Charismatic-prophetic emphasis, and the explicit prosperity ministry. Within these various ministries came the quasi movements, which also threw more dust in the eyes of the public.

It was shown that in some ways, the prosperity gospel churches have been growing and responding to the early missionaries' goal of self-supporting, self-propagating, and self-governing for the missions of the Church. Other prosperity-related churches have shown good social ethics in their countries and have attracted public applause for awards. Thus, I have implicitly contented that it is not necessarily the message that God heals and prospers which was wrong. It is a coherent application of this message in light of the nature of God that was sometimes lacking. But we must not throw the baby away with the bathwater. Therefore, a call was made for biblical scholars and theologians among us to serve the church by providing materials for the use of "ordinary church members." Jesus still questions Peter, "Simon son of John, do you love me? [Then] feed my sheep" (John 21:17 NIV).

Notes

1. Emmanuel Kwesi Anim, "Who Wants to Be a Millionaire? An Analysis of Prosperity Teaching in the Charismatic Ministry (Churches) in Ghana and Its Wider Impact" (Ph.D. diss., All Nations Christian College, Hertfordshire, 2003), 66.
2. For example, see, Steve Brouwer, Paul Gifford, & Rose D. Susan, *Exporting the American Gospel: Global Christian Fundamentalism* (London: Routledge, 1996); Andrew Chesnut, *Competitive Spirits: Latin America's New Religious Economy* (Oxford: Oxford University Press, 2003); Cf. Michael Wilkinson, "Pentecostal and Methodological Issues for Global Pentecostalism," *PNEUMA* 38:4 (2016), 384.
3. Wilkinson, "Pentecostal and Methodological Issues," 384.
4. For example, see Asonzeh Ukah, "God, Wealth, and the Spirit of Investment: Prosperity Pentecostalism in Africa," in Sabine Dreher and Peter J. Smith, eds., *Religious Activism in the Global Economy: Promoting, Reforming, or Resisting Neoliberal Globalization?* (New York: Rowman & Littlefield, 2016), 73–90.
5. For example, see Brouwer et al., *Exporting the American Gospel*, 1–32, 263–273.
6. Attention will be drawn to some of these materials in the course of the paper.
7. Donald W. Dayton, *Theological Roots of Pentecostalism* (Grand Rapids: Zondervan, 1987).
8. D. William Faupel, *The Everlasting Gospel: The Significance of Eschatology in the Development of Pentecostal Though*t (Sheffield: Sheffield Academic Press, 1996), 202–205, 208, in Allan H. Anderson, *An Introduction to Pentecostalism* (Cambridge: Cambridge University Press, 2004), 40.
9. Cecil M. Robeck, Jr., *Azusa Street Mission and Revival: The Birth of the Global Pentecostal Movement* (Nashville: Nelson Reference & Electronic, 2006), 73.
10. Benny C. Aker and Gary S. McGee, eds., *Signs and Wonders in Ministry Today* (Springfield: Gospel Publishing House, 1996).
11. David Petts, "Healing and the Atonement" (Ph.D. diss., University Nottingham, 1993).
12. Stephen Hunt, "Managing the Demonic: Some Aspects of the Neo-Pentecostal Deliverance Ministry," *Journal of Contemporary Religion* 13:2 (1998), 216–217.

13 M. Richard Riss, "Latter Rain Movement of 1948," *PNEUMA* 4:1 (1982), 32–45.

14 For example, see Pavel Hejzlar, *Two Paradigms for Divine Healing: Fred F. Bosworth, Kenneth E. Hagin, Agnes Sanford, and Francis MacNutt in Dialogue* (Charleston: BiblioBazaar, 2011), 59.

15 "What is the Word of Faith," GospelOutreach.net, https://www.gospeloutreach.net/whatwordfaith.html, accessed December 12, 2017.

16 Dan R. McConnell, *A Different Gospel* (Peabody: Hendrickson, 1998), 15–56.

17 Kenneth Hagin, *Understanding How to Fight the Fight of Faith*, Fourth printing 1992 (Tulsa: Rhema Bible College, 1987), 112.

18 For example, *Oral Roberts, A Daily Guide to Miracles and Successful Living Through Seed-Faith* (Tulsa: Pinoak Publications, 1975).

19 Gloria Copeland, *God's Will is Prosperity: A Roadmap to Spiritual, Emotional, and Financial Wholeness* (Fort Worth: Kenneth Copeland Publications, 1978), 35.

20 Copeland, *God's Will is Prosperity*, 36.

21 Copeland, *God's Will is Prosperity*, 5.

22 For example, see Kenneth Hagin, *Demons and How to Deal with Them* (Tulsa: Kenneth Hagin Evangelistic Association, 1976).

23 Derek Prince, *Blessings or Cursing* (Milton Keynes: Word Publishing, 1990); Ed Murphy, *The Handbook for Spiritual Warfare*, revised and updated 2003 (Nashville: Thomas Nelson Publishing, 1996).

24 Charles H. Kraft, *Defeating the Dark Angels* (Kent: Sovereign World, 1993).

25 C. Peter Wagner ed., *Engaging the Enemy: How to Fight and Defeat Territorial Spirits* (Ventura: Regal, 1993).

26 Mike Wakely, "'Territorial Spirits,' Some Concerns Expressed by Mike Wakely,' Operation Mobilization, July 18, 1993.

27 Hwa Yung, "Pentecostalism and the Asian Church" in Allan H. Anderson and Edmond Tang, eds., *Asian and Pentecostal: The Charismatic Face of Christianity in Asia* (Oxford: Regnum, 2004).

28 Anderson, *An Introduction to Pentecostalism*, 123–143.

29 Vinson Synan, "Roots of Yonggi Cho's Theology of Healing" in *Dr. Yonggi Cho's Ministry and Theology* 1 (Seoul: Hansei University Logos, 2008), 263–284.

30 Robert Owens, "The Azusa Street Revival: Three Pentecostal Movement Begins in America," in Vinson Synan ed., *The Century of the Holy Spirit:*

100 Years of Pentecostal and Charismatic Renewal (Nashville: Thomas Nelson, 2001), 39–68.

31 Juan Sepúlveda, "Another Way of Being Pentecostal," in Calvin L. Smith ed., *Pentecostal Power: Expressions, Impact, and Faith of Latin American Pentecostalism* (Leiden: Brill, 2011), 37-61.

32 Robeck, *Azusa Street Mission and Revival*, 91.

33 See John Dawson, *Taking Our Cities for God: How to Break Spirit Strongholds* (Lake Mary: Creation House, 1989), 20.

34 Rudolf von Sinner "'Struggling with Africa': Theology of Prosperity in and from Brazil" in Andreas Heuser, ed., *Pastures of Plenty: Tracing Religio-Scapes of Prosperity Gospel in Africa and Beyond* (Frankfurt and Main: Peter Lang, 2015), 122.

35 Bengt G. M. Sundkler, *Bantu Prophets in South Africa*, 2nd ed. (Oxford: Oxford University Press, 1961).

36 John S. Pobee and Gabriel Ositelu II, *African Initiatives in Christianity: The Growth, Gifts, and Diversities of Indigenous African Churches* (Geneva: WCC Publications, 1998), 4.

37 Anderson, *An Introduction to Pentecostalism*, 106–107.

38 Opoku Onyinah, *Pentecostal Exorcism: Witchcraft and Demonology in Ghana* (Blandford: Deo, 2012), 171–230.

39 Anim, "Who Wants to be Millionaire?" 122.

40 Some claim even frequently to raise the disabled, open the eyes of the blind and open the ears of the deaf, release the mouth of the dumb, and even raise the dead. In the attempt, some have duped the rich and poor, and as a result, are placed in prison. Some of these are trending on social media.

41 C. S. Lewis, *The Screwtape Letters* (New York: Macmillan, 1961), 3.

42 For example, see J. Daniel Salinas ed., *Prosperity Theology and the Gospel: Good News or Bad News for the Poor?* (Peabody: Hendrickson Pub Marketing, 2017). See also, Anim, "Who Wants to be Millionaire?"

43 For example, see J. Melville Herskovits and William R. Bascom, eds., *Continuity and Change in African Culture* (Chicago: University of Chicago Press, 1959).

44 Pamela G. Schmoll, "Black Stomachs, Beautiful Stones: Soul-Eating Among Hausa in Niger," in Jean and John Comaroff, eds., *Modernity and Its Malcontents: Ritual and Power in Postcolonial Africa* (Chicago: University of Chicago Press, 1993), 199.

45 For example, see J. Daniel Salinas, *Prosperity Theology and the Gospel*. See also, Andreas Heuser, *Pastures of Plenty*.

46 For example, Paul Gifford, "Prosperity: A New and Foreign Element in African Christianity," *Religion* 20:4 (1990), 373–388; Brouwer, et al., *Exporting the American Gospel*, the title of the book itself says a lot; and Rosalind Hackett, "The Gospel of Prosperity in West Africa" in R. Roberts ed., *Religion and the Transformation of Capitalism* (London: Routledge, 1995), 119–213.

47 Von Rudolf, "Struggle with Africa," 121.

48 Bradley A. Koch, "The Prosperity Gospel and Economic Prosperity: Race, Class, Giving and Voting" (Ph.D. diss., University of Indiana, 2009), 21, 81–82.

49 Gifford, "Prosperity;" Dennis Hollinger, "Enjoying God Forever: An Historical/Sociological Profile of the Heath and Wealth Gospel in the USA," in P. Gee & J. Fulton eds., *Religion and Power, Decline and Growth: Sociological Analyses of Religion in Britain, Poland, and the Americas* (London: British Sociological Association of Religion Study Group, 1991), 53-66; Harvey Cox, *Fire from Heaven: The Rise of Pentecostal Spirituality and the Reshaping of Religion in the 21st Century* (Cambridge, MA: Da Capo Press, 1995); David Edwin Harrell, *All Things are Possible: The Healing & Charismatic Revivals in Modern America* (Bloomington: Indiana University Press, 1975).

50 Gordon Fee, "The New Testament View of Wealth and Possessions," *New Oxford Review* 48 (1981), 8–11; Steven Bruce, "Modernity and Fundamentalism: The New Christian Right in America," *British Journal of Sociology* 41 (1990), 477–496; Gifford, "Prosperity;" Koch, "The Prosperity Gospel," 14–15.

51 Kate Bowler, "Blessed: A History of the American Prosperity Gospel" (Ph.D. diss., Duke University, 2010), 231.

52 Robert D. Woodberry, "The Economic Consequences of Pentecostal Belief," *Society* 44:1 (2006), 29–35; Sheldon Annis, *God and Production in a Guatemalan Town* (Austin: University of Texas Press, 1987); David Martin, *Tongues of Fire: Explosion of Protestantism in Latin America* (Oxford: Basic Blackwell Ltd, 1990).

53 Koch, "The Prosperity Gospel," 15.

54 Woodberry, "The Economic Consequences of Pentecostal Belief," 35.

55 Anim, "Who Wants to be a Millionaire;" Woodberry, "The Economic Consequences of Pentecostal Belief;" J. Kwabena Asamoah-Gyadu,

"Prosperity and Poverty in the Bible: Ghana's Experience," in J. Daniel Salinas ed., *Prosperity Theology and the Gospel: Good News or Bad News for the Poor?* (Peabody: Hendrickson Pub Marketing, 2017), 99–114; R. Andrew Chesnut, *Competitive Spirits: Latin America's New Religious Economy* (Oxford: Oxford University Press, 2003); Bowler, "Blessed."

56 Cox, *Fire From Heaven*, 228, 243

57 Brouwer, et al. *Exporting the American Gospel*, 2, 265, 269.

5 A Church with a Heart: Spirit and Praxis in Pentecostal Social Engagement

Ivan Satyavrata

Abstract

The social witness of the contemporary Pentecostal movement has been minimized and underestimated in some studies due to inadequate articulation of its praxis. In actual fact, social engagement has been an integral feature of the movement and a critical factor in its missionary effectiveness since its earliest inception. In attempting to illustrate this with special reference to the Indian experience, the author draws from his unique perspective as a reflective practitioner leading a Pentecostal "Church with a Heart" in the city of Kolkata. The socially transforming spirituality that one observes among Pentecostals seems to be the result of a conscious intent to follow Jesus' pattern of ministry. The distinctive Pentecostal approach to social change thus sees transformed people empowered by the Spirit as the primary agents of change who seek to transform the world in the light of the in-breaking kingdom of God.

Introduction

Although Pentecostals have from the outset been deeply involved in works of compassion, they have, in general, been better at doing it than articulating it in statements of faith or theological formulations. Over two decades ago, Pentecostal mission theologian Doug Petersen, lamented the fact that despite the substantial contribution of the Assemblies of God to social involvement, "a certain 'gap' exists between pragmatic, compassionate outreach and an adequate understanding of biblical foundations which must guide these actions."[1] Dr. George O. Wood, Chairman of the World Assemblies of God Fellowship, and former General Superintendent of the Assemblies of God, USA, suggests the main reason for this "gap" in this telling observation: "It's probably been the nature of the Pentecostal experience that we have the experience first and then develop the rationale!"[2]

In earlier decades, most observers assumed that its theological conservatism and proximity to "other-worldly" dispensationalism in the early stages of its emergence should have caused the Pentecostal movement to have a weak social ethic. Others perhaps surmised that its strong emphasis on "saving souls," church planting, and multiplication might have resulted in the soundless impact of the Pentecostal movement's social engagement being obscured by the blaring voice of proclamation evangelism. Recent studies have shown beyond a reasonable doubt, however, that one of the best-kept secrets of the contemporary church is the extensive social engagement and impact that the Pentecostal movement has had over the last century. It would be difficult for any serious student of mission today to deny the modern Pentecostal movement's social impact.

Spirit-Empowered Social Impact

Attempts to describe Pentecostalism as though it were a single monolithic stream all over the globe tend to be reductionist in assuming implicitly and somewhat simplistically that the global Pentecostal movement has a single epicenter in North America.[3] Without minimizing the considerable influence North American Pentecostalism has exercised on the global Pentecostal movement, as recent studies have shown, the Pentecostal movement is, in reality, a complex blend of heterogeneous national, cultural, religious, socio-economic, theological, and ecclesiastical sources and streams of influence.[4]

In trying to define any broad aspect or trend within Pentecostalism, it is thus important to add the qualification that what is in focus is not, in fact, a monolithic tradition, but a broad movement consisting of multiple "Spirit" streams that share a certain family resemblance. Some distinctive features that mark this family resemblance in different expressions of the Pentecostal movement across the globe include an emphasis on the Acts 2:4 doctrine of the baptism in the Holy Spirit as a normative "charismatic" experience providing empowerment for ministry; and an emphasis on spiritual gifts, especially speaking in tongues, healing, and prophecy.[5] Thus, a definitive shared fundamental premise of Pentecostalism is that the Holy Spirit's immediate manifested presence experienced by the early church in Acts is normative for the Christian faith community today. Appropriation of that experience is a vital hermeneutical key in Pentecostal interpretation of scripture, their understanding of the Christian faith, and practice as a faith community.[6]

With this important clarification, we turn then to consider the essential impulses of Pentecostal social concern. From where does this global Spirit-movement, perhaps better known for its "soul-saving" and "other-worldly" emphasis, derive its social ethic? A common misconception in some quarters is that the case for a genuine Pentecostal social tradition is weak and not based on factual data. The main reason for this, undoubtedly, is that in the early stages of the movement, the Pentecostal emphasis on immediate experience found greater acceptance among the poor and less literate and hence tended to lean towards anti-intellectualism. As a result, the early Pentecostals were largely an oral community, with little interest in reflective theologizing or in documenting their experience and practice. As a revival movement, the Pentecostal movement was naturally less concerned about developing theology than it was about seeing the Holy Spirit infuse the church with spiritual vibrancy and a burden for world evangelization.

Furthermore, Pentecostal beliefs and practices were frequently framed in the categories of older conservative denominations and thus failed to do justice to the realities of their faith and praxis.[7] Like earlier dispensationalists, Pentecostals were driven by the fervent eschatological expectation of the imminent return of Christ, so that the main themes of their preaching and teaching focused on winning the lost and reaching the world before the end of the age.[8] The limited capacity for theological engagement they possessed was devoted to defending their distinctive beliefs concerning the work of the Holy Spirit against the theological skepticism of their conservative predecessors.

It is also important to remember that the Pentecostal movement emerged at a time when conservative Christians as a whole were reacting to the excesses of the social gospel movement. Pentecostals sought to distance themselves from liberal views of social concern, which appeared to reduce the Christian gospel to pure philanthropy. Hence, they tended to underplay and minimize their actual active involvement in social issues. Recent studies have, fortunately, attempted to set the record straight in this regard.[9]

The Pentecostal tradition of social engagement has its roots in the work of many of the early Pentecostal pioneers, who were actively involved in social transformation and works of compassion. The Bethel Healing Home, which Charles F. Parham (1873–1929) started in Topeka, Kansas in 1898, enlarged its activities to include rescue missions for prostitutes and the homeless, an employment bureau, and an orphanage service.[10] The relationship between love and the baptism of the Holy Spirit was crucial to William J. Seymour (1870–1922), the leader of the Azusa Street Mission. For Seymour, the Pentecostal experience of baptism in the Spirit was about immersion in love, with ". . . the power to draw all people into one church, irrespective of racial, ethnic or social diversity."[11] Frank Bartleman's famous one-liner summarized the impact of the Azusa Street revival, "The color line was washed away in the blood."[12]

In his *Introduction to Pentecostalism*, Allan H. Anderson observes:

> Pentecostals in various parts of the world have always had various social action programs, ever since the involvement of Ramabai's Mukti Mission in India in the early 1900s and the work of Lillian Trasher among orphans in Egypt from 1911. Early Pentecostals were involved in socio-political criticism, including opposition to war, capitalism, and racial discrimination. African American Pentecostals have been at the forefront of the civil rights movement. Throughout the world today, Pentecostals are involved in practical ways caring for the poor and the destitute, those often "unwanted" by the larger society.[13]

In his editorial article, "Pentecostals and Social Ethics," Cecil Robeck also refers to the charity works of early Pentecostal pioneers like Stanley H. Frodsham, George and Carrie (Judd) Montgomery, and A.J. Tomlinson.[14] For many Pentecostal ministries, like Gerrit Polman in the Netherlands, the Salvation Army's non-political approach of "Soup, Soap, and Salvation" served as a model for their social involvement.[15]

Early theological validation for Pentecostal social engagement may be found in the writings of one of the most respected AG missiologists of the previous generation, Melvin Hodges. Like most other evangelicals of his era who were concerned that the missionary mandate never be allowed to degenerate into a purely "social gospel," Hodges warns against the tendency to any such dilution of the gospel of spiritual conversion. However, in his *A Theology of the Church and its Mission*, he is careful to spell out his conviction concerning the church's social responsibility:

> Christians are the salt of the earth. Their presence and influence do affect society. . . . We can do no better than follow the words of Jesus and the example of the early Christians. True Christians are a force for righteousness and social betterment. We have only to look at what is happening on the mission

fields where the church has multiplied to see this process taking place. . . .The proponents of the theology of liberation are correct in insisting that the gospel is for the whole man and that Christians should not limit their interest to the souls of men and the future life. Christians must not be indifferent to oppression or injustice in the world.[16]

We need hardly say more, but missionaries like Melvin Hodges, who lived and worked in contexts of poverty and social oppression, and who witnessed firsthand the power of the gospel to transform every aspect of life, could not but make room in their missiology for a Christ-like response to the burning social needs that surrounded them. I am personally convinced that the Pentecostal movement's intrinsically missionary nature has been a key factor that helped shape its social conscience. The Pentecostal social response has been forged in the fires of the missionary encounter with the harsh social deprivations experienced by the poor masses living in the majority world.

As the Pentecostal movement has grown over the past century, its social impact has become increasingly evident. After observing earlier that "Pentecostals are increasingly engaged in community-based social ministries" and seek "a balanced approach to evangelism and social action," Donald Miller and Tetsunao Yamamori launched a four-year field study of growing churches in the developing world that engaged in significant social ministries. Four hundred experts worldwide were asked to nominate churches that satisfied four simple criteria: fast-growing, located in the developing world, with active social programs, indigenous and self-supporting. They were amazed to discover that nearly eighty-five percent of the nominated churches were Pentecostal or Charismatic.[17]

Miller and Yamamori's work provides strong evidence of the fact that social engagement and holistic mission within the Pentecostal movement is not a recent innovation: "Throughout the history of Pentecostalism, there have been examples of compassionate social service, so this is not a new phenomenon."[18] Their study also documents a wide range of types of social engagement by Pentecostals, from humanitarian responses to crises and human need (such as floods, drought, and earthquakes), to education, economic development, medical work, and other projects that focus on community development.[19] Further, their empirical data indicate a broad and growing acceptance of this holistic understanding of the Christian faith within Pentecostal churches worldwide.[20]

Pentecostal Social Engagement in India

Resources for tracing the social impact of Indian Pentecostalism, especially in its early stages, remain inadequate for the same reasons as observed above. Fueled by fervent eschatological expectation, Pentecostals were too preoccupied with evangelistic outreach, struggling for survival against opposition from older Christian denominations, feeding the hungry, taking care of orphans, and extending the compassion of Jesus in response to human need, to devote time to documenting their activity and history. Meanwhile, as Burgess notes with deep regret, vital primary literary sources remain mislaid, neglected, and destroyed, and most early Indian Pentecostal leaders have died without being interviewed.[21]

Although early Pentecostal missionaries in South India focused mostly on evangelistic work and the training of Indian evangelists and pastors, Burgess lists some Pentecostal charitable efforts: George Berg and Robert Cook, who established several schools for children; the industrial school at Shencottah, Tamil Nadu, founded by U. S. Assemblies of God missionaries, Robert and Doris Edwards; and a boy's orphanage at Junnar in Maharastra, started by Australian missionaries, later taken over by the U. S. Assemblies of God.[22]

North India saw more Pentecostal social involvement, with early Pentecostal missionaries establishing orphanages, elementary and industrial schools, leper asylums, and dispensaries. The Assemblies of God developed an extensive system of institutions, including an orphanage and girls' school at Bettiah in Bihar and a girls' orphanage at Purulia, West Bengal. Assemblies of God social outreach in the highly populated north Indian state of Uttar Pradesh included a boy's orphanage and schools at Nawabganj and Rupaidia, Minnie Abrams' work among leprosy patients at Uska Bazar, and a girls' industrial school at Siswa Bazar. The Pentecostal Holiness Church also established orphanages in Jasidih, Giridih, and Madhupur in Jharkhand, and Jha Jha in Bihar.[23]

Perhaps the best known early twentieth-century Pentecostal outpouring in India was the Mukti Mission revival in Kedgaon, near Pune, led by the famous social reformer Pandita Ramabai. It started in 1905 when hundreds of young Indian women, outcaste child-widows, who had taken shelter in Ramabai's *ashram* [community religious center], were baptized in the

Spirit, saw visions, fell into trances, and spoke in tongues.[24] Ramabai's Mukti Mission took care of child widows and orphans. Its social outreach included the blind, preschool education, vocational training, a hospital, a home for sex trafficked victims, and orphanages in several villages. The Mission is still active today, providing housing, education, vocational training, and medical services for widows, orphans, and the blind. Ramabai is still celebrated as a national icon of the Women's development movement in India.[25]

An interesting area of early Pentecostal social engagement that church historian V. V. Thomas has drawn attention to is the impact on the empowerment of *Dalits* - untouchable outcastes from the traditional social hierarchy, regarded as impure and polluted, hence socially excluded and isolated from the rest of society. One of the earliest American Pentecostal missionaries to South India, Robert Cook, was known as the missionary to *Dalits* because the focus of his ministry was among the *Dalits*. Having suffered inhuman oppression and subjugation for centuries both from caste Hindus as well as within older Christian denominations to some extent, *Dalits* were attracted to Pentecostal Christianity by the promise of equal access to spiritual empowerment and ecclesiastical egalitarianism that accompanied the twentieth-century Pentecostal expression of the gospel.[26]

The Kolkata [Calcutta] Experience

We turn now to an expression of Pentecostal social engagement in India with which this author has firsthand acquaintance. The story of the Assemblies of God Church & Mission in Kolkata [Calcutta] begins sixty-five years ago when young missionary-evangelists from North America, Mark and Huldah Buntain, came to share the good news of Jesus with the people of Kolkata.[27] When the Buntains arrived in Kolkata only a few years after India's independence and the Partition with East Pakistan [now Bangladesh] in August 1947, the city was filled with homeless and dispossessed refugees struggling for survival on the streets. The Buntains were surrounded by hunger, disease, and extreme poverty. Mass scale poverty is a reality that continues to date in Kolkata, a city with a population of over eighteen million. Of these, one-third live in slums, and close to one hundred thousand are completely homeless.

The Buntains began their ministry by doing what they knew best to do: preach the gospel and conduct evangelistic services. The crucial turning point in their ministry came one day while during a service, a hungry beggar appeared and hurled these words at Pastor Mark: "First, feed our bellies, and then tell us there is a God in heaven who loves us!" The feeding program Pastor Mark began in response was the first step in a social outreach program that eventually added a hospital and schools for the underprivileged, developing into a multi-faceted ministry that has continued to serve the poor of Kolkata for over six decades.

The Kolkata AG Church's social engagement is deeply rooted in the gospel of Christ, with its ultimate goal being the fullness of life, especially for the poor and marginalized in society. Social programs seek to provide immediate relief for the survival needs of the poor and long-term sustainability and empowerment that enables them to break out of the poverty cycle. These include a feeding program that serves over ten thousand meals each day in the streets and slums, provision of bio-sand filters for clean drinking water, free or subsidized basic health care, ten schools for underprivileged children at which children receive a hot mid-day meal, and basic education. A vocational training school offers a wide range of certified skill development courses, including catering, hospitality, computers, tailoring, and bedside nursing care, with promising job prospects for sustainable livelihood. The social ministry includes an agency to rescue and rehabilitate sex-trafficked children and girls from the red-light district. In addition, a teacher's training college provides certified training for teachers, and a nursing school supports the nursing requirements of the Mercy Hospital on the mission campus.

At the hub of this holistic social ministry wheel is a vibrant multi-ethnic, multi-lingual congregation of around seven thousand followers of Christ who worship in sixteen services on the weekend and participate in close to 250 Care Groups during the week. The health and unity of this "Church With the Open Arms" in which people from different ethnic, linguistic, social, religious, and caste backgrounds come together is, undoubtedly, the church's most convincing social witness. The benefits of the mission's social programs are offered to people of all faiths unconditionally and are never used as an inducement for spiritual conversion. But the power of Christ's love, which nourishes and propels the church's social engagement, inevitably results in people being drawn to Christ and adds to the body of Christ.

A Socially Transforming Spirituality[28]

The main distinguishing mark of Pentecostalism is its spirituality. The theme of the Holy Spirit's empowerment has always been at the heart of Pentecostal belief (Acts 1:8). Spirituality, living the life of the Holy Spirit, energizes and enables the church to witness to the kingdom through evangelization and social engagement. The believer's encounter with the Holy Spirit results in a spiritual transformation that reshapes his or her moral and social consciousness, causing them to become an instrument of social change. In this context, it is interesting to note the clear distinction Miller and Yamamori's study discerns between the Pentecostal approach to social ministries and Social Gospel or Liberation Theology frameworks of social engagement. They clearly view the Pentecostal response as intentionally patterned after Jesus' ministry model:

> Unlike the Social Gospel tradition of the mainline churches, this [Pentecostal] movement seeks a balanced approach to evangelism and social action that is modeled after Jesus' example of not only preaching about the coming kingdom of God but also ministering to the physical needs of the people he encountered.[29]

Furthermore, in contrast to these older approaches, Miller and Yamamori observe that Pentecostals do not attempt to reform social structures or challenge government policies but rather take "an incremental approach to social change," addressing social problems, one person at a time.[30] To that extent, the Pentecostal project engages social issues at a more subversive level, attempting to construct an alternative social reality grounded on certain core kingdom values: that all human beings are made in the image of God; that all people have dignity and are equal in God's sight, and consequently have equal rights whether they are poor, women or children.[31]

The distinctive Pentecostal approach to social change thus sees transformed people empowered by the Spirit as the primary agents of change who seek to transform the world in the light of the in-breaking kingdom of God. We will now examine how Pentecostal spirituality shapes Pentecostalism's social response as we look at five key features of Pentecostal spirituality. [32]

Prayer/ Worship

Individual and corporate prayer and worship experience are vital features of Pentecostal spirituality. Prayer is really the "cry" of the kingdom in response to Jesus' exhortation to his disciples to pray for the coming of the kingdom (Matt 6:10), and is critical in missionary engagement of the powers of evil that hinder the advance of the kingdom. It is God's kingdom by nature: God's gift and work. Believers do not construct the kingdom, but rather ask for it and welcome it. It comes by grace and grows within us by the power of the Spirit. Prayer empowers us and compels us to strive for just and loving relationships among people, family, community, and society. Pentecostals' corporate worship experience is an important element in the shaping of Pentecostal spirituality and is a crucial element in social engagement when directed towards kingdom advancement and in opposition to the powers of evil.

Liberation

The Pentecostal experience of Spirit baptism is basically one of empowerment. The overwhelming reality that this experience opens to believers is liberation from captivity to the powers of evil that keep them from the fullness of life. It is liberating to those existing in the shadows, marginalized from society's economic and social center, whose poverty leaves them feeling helpless and disempowered. Powerful, intimidating, and destructive forces that hold the poor captive must yield to the power of the Holy Spirit.

The liberating experience of the power of the Holy Spirit counters the negative experience of power as an inescapable descending spiral. The gifts of the Spirit empower their recipients "to do" and "to be," negating the significance of popular prerequisites to power, education, wealth, and other status symbols. Those who are of no consequence in society find themselves part of a rapidly growing alternative society in which they are highly esteemed and appreciated because of their giftedness once they come into the church. This experience of liberating empowerment has become the basis for the upward mobility of Pentecostals in society.

Healing

The belief and practice of divine healing have been vital components of Pentecostal spirituality since the movement's inception and is the earliest indisputable pointer to the movement's holistic concern. Pentecostals departed early from the theology of their evangelical and fundamentalist predecessors when they sought to apply the benefits of the atonement of Christ to the whole person, body, soul, and spirit, and is why they have naturally and easily been moved to respond to the felt physical needs of the poor. It was impossible to believe that God's "real presence" manifested through the power of the Spirit could miraculously heal sick bodies while not being concerned with responding to the felt physical and social needs of the poor and dispossessed.

Community

One of the signs of the Holy Spirit's empowering presence is *koinonia*. The word *koinonia* is used eighteen times in the New Testament and denotes that fellowship among believers, which the Holy Spirit creates (2 Cor 13:14; Phil 2:1). The *koinonia* of the Holy Spirit involves a sharing of common life within the church (Acts 2:42–46; 5:42) and is illustrated in its description as the body of Christ (1 Cor 12). This means that the members of the body have an obligation within the body to "one another," and these obligations constitute hallmarks of *koinonia*, marks or signs of the distinctive kingdom lifestyle, such as love, unity, justice, healing, godliness, and other gifts and fruit of the Spirit.

The *koinonia* of the Spirit enables the church to demonstrate what the reign of God is like and to incarnate the values of the kingdom that Jesus taught. Thus "witnessing" was not something the early church did: it was a function that flowed out of the church-as-community's common life and experience. The concern they showed for the poor, widows and strangers, was not a separate activity but rather an extension of their worship and witness.

Spirit-inspired *koinonia*, patterned after the early church model, has been a powerful agent of social transformation since the beginning of the Pentecostal movement. The strong sense of community helps Pentecostals find a new sense of dignity and purpose in life, and results in the emergence of communities that function as empowering social alternatives to oppressive structures. Their solidarity gives them a sense of equality and causes them to challenge inequality in the treatment of minorities, women, and the poor. Thus, during a time when racial and gender inequality was endemic, Pentecostals welcomed black and white, male and female, rich and poor.

Hope

Pentecostals view their experience of the Spirit in eschatological terms, offering a present foretaste of a promised future (Eph 1:14). They believe that they have been called by God in the "last days" (Acts 2:17) to be faithful witnesses of Christ in the power of the Spirit, through word, works, wonders, and life. Fervent hope in the imminent coming of the Lord has sustained Pentecostals during persecution, harassment, imprisonment, and martyrdom during the last century. Pentecostals today continue to believe that intense hope will continue to be necessary for endurance, healing, and engagement of the forces, both social and spiritual, which oppress and violate people.

Karkkainen points out that for many Pentecostals, eschatological hope has brought optimism about the work they are doing to bring about social transformation. They view their efforts as visible "signposts," evidence that the kingdom of God has pressed into the present.[33] Miroslav Volf adds further theological validity to this perspective based on the assertion in Rom 8:21 that the liberation of creation cannot occur through its destruction but only through its transformation. He argues that kingdom-oriented social projects have eschatological significance, and eschatological continuity between God's present reign and the reign to come "guarantees that noble human efforts will not be wasted."[34] The significance of such eschatological continuity is well articulated in the words of a leading Pentecostal social ethicist: "Expressions of Christian social concern that are kingdom-signifying deeds of anticipatory transformation are the kinds of human effort that God preserves, sanctifies and directs teleologically toward the future age of God's redemptive reign."[35]

Conclusion: Heavenly-Minded and Socially Engaged

The Pentecostal message is very good news among the poor; it answers their immediate felt needs and often unleashes powerful redemptive forces resulting in the upward social mobility of believers, providing powerful spiritual impetus and community support for a better life. The genius of Pentecostalism has thus been its relevance to the powerless by its ability to penetrate the enslaving power structures of the socially and economically marginalized. It is thus not accurate to caricature Pentecostals as those who view persons as "souls with ears," rather, in Miller and Yamamori's words: "Instead of seeing the world as a place from which to escape, they want to make it better, especially by following Jesus, who both preached about the coming kingdom and healed people and ministered to their social needs."[36] Pentecostals offer not only spiritual refuge from the problems of this world but concrete and authentic social engagement alternatives; they have, in fact, done so from the very beginning as a natural extension of their passion for extending God's kingdom.[37]

Notes

1. Douglas Petersen, "Missions in the Twenty-First Century: Toward a Methodology of Pentecostal Compassion," *Transformation* 16:2 (April 1999), 54.
2. George O. Wood, Letter to Dr. Joseph Dimitrov, March 29, 2010.
3. Ivan Satyavrata, *Pentecostals and the Poor: Reflections from the Indian Context* (Baguio: APTS Press, 2017), 7.
4. For instance, see Donald Miller and Tetsunao Yamamori, *Global Pentecostalism: The New Face of Christian Social Engagement* (Berkeley: University of California Press, 2007), 19.
5. Satyavrata, *Pentecostals and the Poor*, 9.
6. Harvey Cox, *Fire from Heaven: The Rise of Pentecostal Spirituality and the Reshaping of Religion in the Twenty-First Century* (Cambridge, MA: Da Capo Press, 1995), 71.
7. Wolfgang Vondey, *Pentecostal Theology Living the Full Gospel* (New York: Bloomsbury, T & T Clark, 2017), 2–3.
8. Frank D. Macchia, "The Struggle for Global Witness," in Murray W. Dempster, Byron D. Klaus, and Douglas Petersen, eds., *The Globalization of Pentecostalism: A Religion Made to Travel* (Carlisle, U.K.: Regnum, 1999), 9.
9. See Miller & Yamamori, *Global Pentecostalism*.
10. Gary B. McGee, "Tongues, The Bible Evidence: The Revival Legacy of Charles F. Parham," *Enrichment* 4:3 (Summer 1999), n.p.
11. Iain MacRobert, "The Black Roots of Pentecostalism," in Jan A. B. Jongeneel ed., *Pentecost, Mission and Ecumenism Essays on Intercultural Theology* (Frankfurt am Main: Verlag Peter Lang, 1992), 9.
12. Frank Bartleman, *Azusa Street* (South Plainfield, NJ: Bridge Publishing, 1980), 54.
13. Allan H. Anderson, *An Introduction to Pentecostalism* (Cambridge: Cambridge University Press, 2004), 276–277.
14. Cecil M. Robeck, Jr., "Pentecostals and Social Ethics," *Pneuma* 9:2 (Fall 1987), 105–106.
15. Cornelis van der Laan, "Treasures Out of Darkness: Pentecostal Perspectives on Social Transformation," (Spirit and Struggle: Beyond Polarization Symposium, Amsterdam, the Netherlands, October 12, 2009), 2.

16 Melvin L. Hodges, A Theology of Mission: *A Pentecostal Perspective* (Springfield, MO: Gospel Publishing House, 1977), 96.

17 Miller & Yamamori, *Global Pentecostalism*, 42–43.

18 Miller & Yamamori, *Global Pentecostalism*, 211–212.

19 Miller & Yamamori, *Global Pentecostalism*, 213.

20 Miller & Yamamori, *Global Pentecostalism*, 3, 212.

21 S. M. Burgess, "Pentecostalism in India: An Overview," *Asian Journal of Pentecostal Studies* 4:1 (2001), 98.

22 Burgess, "Pentecostalism in India," 92.

23 Burgess, "Pentecostalism in India," 93.

24 Allan H. Anderson, "Spreading Fires: The Globalization of Pentecostalism in the Twentieth Century," *International Bulletin of Missionary Research* 31:1 (January 2007), 9.

25 Satyavrata, *Pentecostals and the Poor*, 11–12.

26 V. V. Thomas, *Dalit Pentecostalism, Spirituality of the Empowered Poor* (Bangalore: Asian Trading Co., 2008), 152–153.

27 Various portions of Mark and Huldah Buntain's story may be found in several biographies, the threads of which are brought together in Julie Ma, "Touching Lives of People Through the Holistic Mission Work of the Buntains in Calcutta, India," *International Bulletin of Missionary Research* 40:1 (January 2016), 72–79. In fulfilment of Mark Buntain's vision for indigenization, the AG Church in Kolkata [Calcutta] transitioned to and functioned under national leadership as of April 2006.

28 Murray A. Dempster, Byron D. Klaus, and Douglas Petersen, eds., *Called and Empowered: Global Mission of Pentecostal Perspective* (Peabody: Hendrickson Publishers, 1991); Cecil M. Robeck Jr., "Pentecostals and Social Ethics," *Pneuma* 9:2 (Fall 1987), 103–107; Richard J. Mouw, "Life in the Spirit in an Unjust World," *Pneuma* 9:2 (Fall 1987), 109–128; Murray W. Dempster, "Pentecostal Social Concern and the Biblical Mandate of Social Justice," *Pneuma* 9:2 (Fall 1987), 129–153.

29 Miller & Yamamori, *Global Pentecostalism*, 212.

30 Miller & Yamamori, *Global Pentecostalism*, 216.

31 Miller & Yamamori, *Global Pentecostalism*, 4–5.

32 This section, with minor edits, reviews my treatment of this theme in Satyavrata, *Pentecostals and the Poor*, 50–56.

33 Veli-Matti Karkkainen, "Truth on Fire: Pentecostal Theology of Mission and the Challenges of a New Millennium," *Asian Journal of Pentecostal Studies* 3:1 (2000), 48.

34 Miroslav Volf, "On Loving With Hope: Eschatology and Social Responsibility," *Transformation* 7 (July/September 1990), 29.

35 Murray W. Dempster, "Christian Social Concern in Pentecostal Perspective" (Presidential address, Conference of the Society for Pentecostal Studies, Lakeland, Florida, November, 1991), 36.

36 Miller & Yamamori, *Global Pentecostalism*, 30.

37 Douglas Petersen, *Not by Might Nor by Power: A Pentecostal Theology of Social Concern in Latin America* (Oxford: Regnum Books, 1996), 233; Paul N. Van der Laan, "Towards a Pentecostal Theology of Compassion," *Journal of the European Pentecostal Theological Association* 31:1 (April 2011), 36–52.

6 A Pentecostal Engagement of the Economy from the Margins

David D. Daniels III

Abstract

The margins of the economy are the focal point of most Pentecostal engagement of the economy because, while the Spirit-empowered movement includes people from all income brackets, the poor and working poor are a sizeable percentage within global Pentecostalism. This essay will argue that progressive Pentecostalism consisted of two perspectives with each being marked by a social ethic. These two perspectives will be discussed as pragmatic currents that emphasize entrepreneurship by cultivating financial skill-building. After discussing these two currents, the essay will examine how a Pentecostal concept of economic justice and economic democracy could strengthen the Pentecostal engagement of the economy from the perspective of the margins by advocating the restructuring of the economy towards economic justice.

Introduction

Progressive Pentecostalism, reflected in the agencies and social ministries sponsored by the Spirit-empowered movement, is part of what the urban theorist Mike Davis, has identified as an emerging feature of Pentecostalism, becoming "the largest self-organized movement of urban poor people." On the margins of the economy, they "[give] self-help networks for poor women; offering faith healing as para-medicine; providing recovery from alcoholism and addiction; insulating children from the temptations of the street; and so on." According to Davis, these ministries have built a "government of the poor" and, it could be added, an economy of the poor through its networks.[1]

The social ministry of the Spirit-empowered movement operates in an arena where the eight largest global Pentecostal social agencies have contributed goods and services valued at more than 3.1 billion US dollars and impacted 250 million people in over one hundred countries between 1980 and 2010. These Pentecostal social agencies include Latin American Childcare, Save Africa's Children, Convoy of Hope, Operation Blessing

International Relief and Development Corporation, COGIC Charities, Apostolic Christian World Relief, and World Assemblies of God Relief and Development Agency.[2]

These social ministries resonate with the concept of progressive Pentecostalism as coined by Dr. James Forbes, professor emeritus at Union Theological Seminary, during the late 1970s. It is attuned to the Holy Spirit "moving in the shadows of sacred places and the structures of secular institutions." Forbes would later stress that progressive Pentecostalism possesses "a strong emphasis on [the] Spirit, but deep commitment to transformative social action." Progressive Pentecostalism more often seeks to empower the poor, women, and marginalized peoples rather than solely engage the rich, men, and social elites.[3]

In the co-authored book *Global Pentecostalism: The New Face of Christian Social Engagement*, Donald Miller and Tetsunao Yamamori acknowledge that during the early 2000s, progressive Pentecostalism promoted the social responsibility of Pentecostals to the society. The emphasis on social responsibility reflects a move towards the historic Protestant ethic and away from a totally other-worldly orientation. This Pentecostal social orientation resembles the Protestant ethic of Max Weber with its accent on religion as an agent of social change within the society.[4]

Progressive Pentecostalism and the Economy on the Margins

There are at least two wings of progressive Pentecostalism. There is a progressive wing of classical Pentecostalism with its emphasis on salvation holiness, the baptism of the Holy Spirit, balanced living, and charismatic gifts. There is also a pragmatic progressive wing of the prosperity gospel movement with its emphasis on salvation and charismatic gifts, as well as health and wealth as a blessing for all Christians.

Adoyi Onoja credits the Pentecostal movement, especially prosperity doctrine preachers, with a pragmatic emphasis, for initiating within various African countries an "attitudinal change" in regard to the economy.[5] These followers of a pragmatic Pentecostal message on every continent, especially among the poor and working poor, seek to enter the economy as entrepreneurs rather than laborers. They are optimistic rather than fatalistic about their economic futures as Christians. Key to the potential success of the adherents to this pragmatic Pentecostal message is financial skill-building, ranging from learning entrepreneurship, management, realistic goal setting, appropriate borrowing and saving strategies, and investment strategies. These skills are connected with attitudinal changes that address fear, sloth, and greed. These Spirit-empowered ministries sponsor several avenues of training and conversation on economic matters as well as launching new businesses and investing in various economic ventures. Ogungbile adds that job creation has been a by-product of the new businesses, media outlets, universities, medical facilities, and hotels that have been started by this Pentecostal economic cohort.[6]

Progressive Pentecostalism and its Economic Ethic

The emphasis on entrepreneurial talents reflects a move towards the historic Protestant ethic and away from a thaumaturgical orientation, the economic narrative of the classic prosperity gospel. According to Hans Baer and Merrill Singer, thaumaturgical is the term of wonder-working, capturing the instrumental role that religion can play in manipulating the spiritual arena to achieve the purposes of the religious agent. This narrative reflects a world that stresses God's agency while noting the demonic or anti-life forces' activity and downplaying human agency. In this narrative, the supernatural overweighs economic forces. Even when human agency is highlighted, the human agent intervenes or assists God through spiritual practices such as prayer, tithing, or seed faith. A large spiritual drama serves as a backdrop to the economy. God exercises primary agency in the economic world scripted by prosperity gospel preachers and adherents.[7]

The stressing of divine agency, demonizing of debilitating economic forces, and devaluing of human agency fits well with the thaumaturgical approach to the classic prosperity gospel. Baer and Singer identified the thaumaturgical or manipulationist orientation as one of five types of sectarian religious organizations. An expressive strategy of religious rituals is joined to a positive stance toward the dominant cultural patterns ("financial prosperity, prestige, love, and health"). Baer/Singer distinguish between how churches engage in expressive strategy; for the prosperity gospel, right speech and giving are central.[8]

The pragmatic prosperity approach recognizes the pivotal role that business skills and financial strategies can play when coupled with God's financial blessings; therefore, human agency is seen as consequential in the divine-human equation. The pragmatic prosperity gospel introduces a grammar of causation and an economic narrative that reflects a world that holds divine and human agency in a creative balance. In this world, the supernatural still plays a role among economic forces, necessitating the pivotal role of prayer and spiritual discernment. In addition to human agency engaging in the spiritual practices of prayer, tithing, or seed faith, there is the need to learn business practices, especially practices that resonate with biblical principles. While a spiritual drama still serves as a backdrop to the economy and God exercises primary agency in the economic world, there is much to learn from entrepreneurs and business gurus, especially those who are Spirit-filled Christians.

Consonant with the scholarship of David Maxwell, I will build upon Maxwell's articulation of what Peter Berger calls the "ingredients of the Protestant ethic." Maxwell states:[9]

> what Peter Berger describes as the ingredients of the Protestant ethic: a rational attitude to the world, a systematic approach to economic activity, individual agency as a religious mandate ("vocation"), a sober lifestyle implying delayed gratification and saving (Weber's inner-worldly asceticism), a foregoing of wider kinship ties in favor of the nuclear family and last but not least, a high regard for education.

Maxwell contends that there is yet a resonance between the "modern Pentecostals and Puritans," the exemplars of the Protestant ethic. However, Maxwell quotes Ezekiel Guti of Zimbabwe to offer an African interpretation of the prosperity doctrine with an accent on "basic security" rather than wealth, success, or excess. "Financial blessing is when you have enough to give to God through your church and enough to have your needs met not with a credit card. True prosperity is not money all the time. True blessing is to have enough to eat. The key is peace of mind, peace in the heart, peace in the family and good health."[10] Maxwell remarks that the prosperity doctrine within certain context operates within the "penny capitalism" of poor countries; it is a "'staggered advancement' within a hierarchy of inequality."[11] In this context, the teaching of a pragmatic prosperity doctrine launches "indigenous business" within the informal economy by engaging in microenterprise: homemade clothing, resale, and cooked food items. In addition to microenterprise, Ezekiel Guti, for instance, encourages his members to enter the larger formal economy through his Professional and Business Network, established in 2010, which provides financial services through Kingdom Asset Management, a financial and investment firm.[12]

Progressive Pentecostalism can be interpreted as a practice of ministry based "on the principle of justice," seeking to address the "perceived underlying circumstances of inequality" and to "locate systemic solutions to social problems" in the words of Elizabeth Lynn, Susan Wisely, and Paul Ylvisaker. Key are the efforts to advance structural changes— changes in social conditions—that address the underlying causes of poverty, gender disparities, racial disparities, and so forth. A distinction is to be made between reforms that work within the current economic and political system and restructuring as reforms that work towards and participate in the transition to a new economic or political system.[13]

Progressive Pentecostalism and the Economic Ministry of A Classical Pentecostal Denomination

In Ghana, for instance, the Church of Pentecost, as a progressive wing within classical Pentecostalism, launched social ministry during the late twentieth century. It was more than a decade prior to the expansion of civil society in Ghana; in a way, the denomination anticipated the changes that were to occur within the larger society. While the social ministry of the Church of Pentecost commenced in 1979, civil society in Ghana began expanding during the 1990s as the government transitioned from military to civilian rule. Like other faith-based organizations within Ghanaian civil society, the social ministry of the Church of Pentecost has made a positive impact on society. Its social ministry can be credited as being one of the factors in cutting the poverty rate in Ghana by fifty percent between 1990 and 2010.[14]

In its initial entry into social ministry, the Church of Pentecost shifted from conceiving of social ministry as relief in 1979, to welfare in 1980, and to social services in 1983. In 1994, the Church of Pentecost deemed social ministry as a way to demonstrate the love of God. It has cast its social service ministry as a sign of its embrace of social responsibility and holistic development, with holistic development seriously promoting "spiritual, social, and political wellbeing." The Church of Pentecost has embraced a rich vocabulary to express its commitment to economic justice: poverty alleviation, empowerment, development, and partnership. These social initiatives have often served as lifelines to at-risk communities. They have reflected the call of Christians to serve the "least of these" as demanded in Matthew 25, those who live on the margins of the economy.[15]

The social responsibility of the Church of Pentecost has been framed in terms of "partnership[s] with governments, communities and other like-minded organizations." The set goal is to empower poor communities to reach economic sustainability.[16]

In 2008, according to Daniel Okyere Walker, Opoku Onyinah, upon being elected as the chairman of the Church of Pentecost, submitted to the church a proposed revision of the mission statement. His goal was to better frame the expanded practice of social ministry in the Church of Pentecost. In the Vision 2018 document, the Church of Pentecost recognizes its ecclesial responsibility to contribute to the national development of Ghana as a country. Since "the church exists within a nation, it needs to play its prophetic role effectively in order for peace and tranquility to reign in the nation." Since "approximately one of every thirteen Ghanaians is a member of The Church of Pentecost," the denomination collectively is a significant factor in Ghanaian society.[17]

Especially in at-risk urban and rural communities lacking key functioning institutions, social efforts directed by the Church of Pentecost provide vital services, especially efforts related to capacity building and community development. As early as 2003, the Church of Pentecost Social Services (PENTSOS) began to partner with UNICEF and Geneva Global, a US-based faith-based organization, in "supporting 109 orphans and widows at Bolgatanga in the Upper East region." PENTSOS sponsored "income-generating activities including guinea fowl rearing, cloth weaving, soap and pomade making, and batik, tie and dye to enhance their incomes."[18]

PENTSOS has partnered with the HONEY Project in order to advance entrepreneurship among youth and young adults in selected secondary, vocational, and technical schools. The partnership with PENTSOS provided "technical training" aiming at developing young entrepreneurs and providing opportunities for the generation of sustainable income generation for the secondary schools as well.

The business schools at Regent University College, Central University, and Pentecost University introduce Pentecostals to ways to enter the formal economies. For instance, Pentecost University's School of Business sponsors a business periodical called *Pentvars Business Journal*, an international refereed journal begun in 2006. The journal publishes articles on subjects ranging from microfinance, management, and banking, to monetary policy. The authors have degrees from business programs in the Netherlands, such as Maastricht School of Management, and the United States, such as the University of Illinois, as well as Ghana's School of Business at the University of Cape Coast. Pentecost University's School of Business offers standard courses in marketing, finance, consumer behavior, entrepreneurship, supply chain, and management. In addition to a Bachelor of Science degree in business subjects, they offer master's degrees in commerce and in business administration (MBA). The faculty hold doctorates from various universities. Key to the Pentecostal business education is an emphasis on "Christian values of integrity and honesty" throughout all courses. Additionally, these business schools offer courses that include mission statement writing, feasibility study, pricing, sales and selling, human resources, accounting, financial literacy, and negotiation strategies. The major writing project for the program is drafting a comprehensive business plan.[19] Some even understand entry into the business arena as part of their vocational calling as Christians.

An article co-authored by Charles O. Kwarteng and Hannah Emma Acquaye highlights social ministries akin to those of the Church of Pentecost. Specifically, the micro-financing ventures of credit unions are defined as a means to confront poverty. Credit unions that offer microfinancing to the working poor provide the poor with "soft credit facilities . . . either to start up or expand their businesses."[20] In 2009 micro-finance and other initiatives were sponsored through the formation of credit unions. PENCO became the acronym for the Cooperative Mutual Support and Social Services Society Limited of the Church of Pentecost. Among the objectives of PENCO has been building "the capacity of members in entrepreneurship in order for them to succeed in their business."[21] Providing start-up capital and expansion funds has been key to the vision of PENCO. In conjunction with other developments in the Ghanaian economy, social ministry efforts like those of the Church of Pentecost, as noted above, have "helped cut the poverty rate in half."[22]

Walker noted that "PENTSOS is engaged in poverty alleviation programs amongst women with the support of UNICEF and Geneva Global, a U. S. based Christian NGO." It also partnered with the HONEY Project Global Outreach, as noted above, which focuses on addressing "social and economic disparities in emerging nations and communities" by alleviating poverty through various initiatives.[23]

Progressive Pentecostalism promotes what David Maxwell has called "penny capitalism" of poor countries as a "'staggered advancement' within a hierarchy of inequality" alongside bourgeois capitalism. Penny capitalism focuses on "indigenous business" within the informal economy that engages in microenterprise: homemade clothing, resale, and cooked food items. Bourgeois capitalism inserts Pentecostals into the formal economy.[24]

Through its social ministry and philanthropy, the Church of Pentecost has participated in the efforts that have "helped cut the poverty rate in half" within Ghana. From providing start-up capital and expansion funds for small rural and urban businesses.

Progressive Pentecostalism and the Economic Ministries of Two Prosperity Gospel Congregations

In addition to the approach of the progressive wing of classical Pentecostalism and its social ministry and economic ministries, there are currents within the Spirit-empowered movement in which the prosperity doctrine has developed a pragmatic prosperity emphasis. The pragmatic prosperity doctrine also resembles the Protestant ethic of Max Weber with its accent on greater human agency and offers business education as an essential element within the reframing of this revised prosperity gospel. These developments have proponents in the United States and Nigeria with Dr. William "Bill" Winston of Living Word Christian Center in the United States, and Rev. Samuel Adeyemi of Daystar Christian Center in Nigeria who both, as prosperity gospel preachers, stress entrepreneurship within their reframing of the prosperity gospel.

When business education joins prosperity doctrine, a pragmatic form of prosperity gospel emerges. With an emphasis on entrepreneurship and other business skills, this pragmatic form of prosperity teaching interjects a new divine-human agency equation, personal responsibility for learning business skills requisite for "realizing" prosperity, blending of business and biblical knowledge, and an educational apparatus to disseminate a prosperity doctrine-oriented business education. The pragmatic approach also shifts the economic behavior of prosperity gospel adherents from consumption to entrepreneurship. This pragmatic approach consequently interjects a new sector within the economic arena spawned by prosperity gospel ministries.

In addition to the classic type of prosperity gospel made popular by televangelists such as Kenneth Hagin, Benson Idahosa, Dag Heward-Mills, and Paula White, there is what Ogungbile calls a "middle position," or what I call a pragmatic prosperity gospel. Bill Winston is a proponent of this pragmatic prosperity gospel, as demonstrated through his founding of the Joseph Business School in 1998. The Joseph Business School's vision is to "Eradicate Generational Poverty," and its mission is to use:[25]

> Practical and biblical principles to empower adults to develop indispensable skills as successful entrepreneurs and business leaders thus equipping them to eradicate poverty in their lives and communities . . . [and] to develop successful Christian entrepreneurs who will create income and employment opportunities for others, through the wealth and job creation that entrepreneurship and vocational training can provide. This, in turn, will assist in the rebuilding of the inner cities.

As a former executive with IBM, Bill Winston learned first-hand about the business world from his work experience. His pragmatic approach recognized a resonance between sound biblical principles and solid business principles. Rather than focus on teaching about prayer or positive confession alone, Winston established the school to train a new generation of Christian entrepreneurs. Through this new class of Christian entrepreneurs, wealth will be generated, and jobs will be created. Additionally, the Joseph Business School would offer a program in vocational training in order for the school to be able to reach students from all educational backgrounds and interests. The faculty of the Business School consists of Spirit-filled Christians who are drawn from the ranks of business executives, entrepreneurs, and professionals that are graduates of elite business programs such as Harvard University's Graduate School of Business, University of Pennsylvania's Wharton School of Business, the University of Chicago's Booth Business School, and Northwestern University's Kellogg School of Business, and additional internationally renowned research universities.[26]

Winston grounds the vision of the Joseph Business School in Isaiah 48:17 (KJV): "teacheth thee to profit." The use of the word profit in Isaiah connected with Winston's previous profession of being a corporate executive prior to his entry into full-time ministry in the 1980s. As a word associated with the corporate world, it jumped out of the biblical text at him. According to Deloris Thomas, vice-president of Joseph Business School, Winston received a prophecy that ministry wasn't just for the pulpit; there were to be marketplace ministers like Joseph and Daniel in the Bible; marketplace ministers were business people who advanced the kingdom of God and its message in the marketplace. In response to the prophecy, Winston began holding business workshops. He taught people "how to use their money to advance the kingdom, how to use their finances for the good of the kingdom." Workshop participants started asking Winston to teach them not only about prosperity in an inspirational way, but also teach them in practical terms about entrepreneurship, financial literacy, and other related topics.[27]

Winston recruited Deloris Thomas and her husband to launch this new initiative. The Thomases were executives in different major corporations and graduates of MBA programs (University of Chicago and Harvard). They discovered Kathy Ashmore and an Ohio State University initiative, Program for Acquiring Competency for Entrepreneurship (PACE). The Joseph Business School would build upon the Ohio State University program. Dr. Winston wanted the Joseph Business School to target those who were excluded from the economy: high-school dropouts, welfare moms, and the underemployed. He wanted to reach those who were left out of the economy, the disenfranchised. Dr. Winston thought that by reaching this population with the gospel through the Joseph Business School, these converts would be powerful testimonies of transformed lives. As living testimonies, they would attract others to the church. He wanted the Joseph Business School to focus on "people who could learn that they could achieve, that they were actually endowed with wisdom (Exod 31). His goal was that JBS would teach them how to generate one million dollars in three years."[28]

The Joseph Business School is a business and entrepreneurship program that can be completed in nine months. The academic year consists of three terms. Students complete over thirty classes, attending class each term for about eleven Saturdays, comprising 161 contact hours; this is the equivalent of one semester of college classes. Within its nine-month format, there are courses that clearly reflect the Christian orientation of the Joseph Business School, such as Christ and the Corporation, Life as a Christian Entrepreneur, and Prayer. Other courses would fit into any business school program: Time Management, Marketing, Intro to eCommerce/eBusiness, Business Management, Financial Analysis, and Business Plan Preparations. In the Christ and the Corporation course, the specifically Pentecostal focus is expressed in the course description, which seeks to inculcate "the wisdom and understanding of being an anointed entrepreneur called and appointed by God" as well as introduce the student to "learn how to hear the voice of God." In the Life as a Christian Entrepreneur course, students will study biographies of "entrepreneurs who operate under the anointing and direction of God." Whereas in the Prayer course, students "learn what, why, and how to pray for their businesses." Additionally, course subjects include mission statement writing, feasibility study, pricing, sales and selling, human resources, accounting, financial literacy, and negotiation strategies. The major writing project for the program is drafting a comprehensive business plan.[29]

In addition to the campus program, the Joseph Business School sponsors an online program, making the curriculum available through the internet. According to Deloris Thomas, a high percentage of graduates have become successful business people. The Joseph Business School combines the teaching of "biblical principles to business management and entrepreneurship." The business curriculum was "developed by the Joseph Business School in conjunction with the Program for Acquiring Competence and Entrepreneurship, the Center on Education and Training for Employment, and Ohio State University (PACE-CETE/OSU)." The Joseph Business School campus program has received approval from the Illinois Board of Higher Education Division of Private Business and Vocational Schools and accreditation from the Accrediting Council of Continuing Education and Training (ACET), an accrediting agency recognized by the U.S. Department of Education.[30]

The Joseph Center, an affiliate of the Joseph Business School, was founded in 2005 and includes a Small Business Development Center (SBDC); it was "one of the first faith-based SBDC's in the United States." The SBDC receives matching funds from the U. S. Small Business

Administration through a partnership between the federal office of Small Business Administration and the Illinois Department of Commerce and Economic Opportunity. The federal funds are then matched by funds raised by the Joseph Center. This program offers the following services: "professional business consulting, business training, workshops, and assistance in obtaining business loans." It offers "individualized, confidential business consultations at no cost" related to patent/new product development, business acquisition, business start-ups, and market analysis and strategies. Workshops cover topics such as intellectual property and government procurement.[31]

Additionally, the Joseph Center hosts an incubator for business start-ups through sponsoring continuing education workshops titled, "Starting a Business." In these workshops, the students learn about patents, business certification, basic accounting, social media use, eCommerce, intellectual property, and business plan components, along with other topics. For a "nominal rental fee," the incubator office provides secretarial support and space for start-up businesses to operate administratively. It "offers a wide array of business support resources including fully-furnished, large and small office spaces, voicemail and mailbox service, furnished workstations and conference rooms fully equipped with internet services, presentation boards, LCD projectors, audio conferencing and more." The Joseph Center offers its business start-up clients "business coaching, as well as assistance." Thomas states that, at the center, students are introduced to equity or debt funding as well as potential financial partners from the government and the private sphere who are interested in minority business and women's business enterprises.[32]

The Joseph Business School also sponsors a vocational program for high school graduates with certificates in information technology, health care services, food services, environmental services, and transportation services. These training programs are co-sponsored by companies or labor unions in order to make the graduates readily employable. The business school's various programs promote the pragmatic approach to teaching the prosperity doctrine with its dual emphasis on human and divine agency in operating within the economic arena.[33]

The Joseph Business School Global Network was formed to introduce this pragmatic approach to prosperity doctrine to Africa as well as other continents. Participants in the Global Network are affiliates of the school and are not satellite programs. The Joseph Business School also has an online e-learning program, which is available to students outside of the United States. Through participation in the Global Network, congregations, schools, or colleges can have access to select academic offerings of the Joseph Business School: syllabi, online classes, and webinars.[34]

In 2014, there were sixteen affiliates of the Joseph Business School (JBS) on four continents, including three campuses in Africa. There are two affiliates in South Africa: (Durban and Johannesburg) and one affiliate in Uyo, Nigeria. The affiliates use the JBS curriculum, but they recruit and employ their own faculty. Each affiliate is based in a congregation. In Zambia, Swaziland, Ghana, and Zimbabwe, Joseph Business School has sponsored workshops to introduce participants to entrepreneurial training from a biblical perspective. Annual economic summits have been held in South Africa since about 2007.[35]

According to Eddie Kornegay, a Christian ethicist and the Dean of Continuing Education and Professional Development at the Joseph Business School, [36]

> Dr. Winston has a huge vision for education. He dedicates resources to it. He has a heart for the community and a concern for youth. He began with a vision for a Bible College. His heart is for those with little or no education. He envisions that JBS creates the model and replicates it throughout the city, the state, the nation, and the globe. He wants to create a hub-and-spoke system.

For Dr. Kornegay, prosperity is understood in the context of the Holy Spirit bringing or producing prosperity. The Holy Spirit is seen as bringing the resources for the Christian to use. The task of the graduate of the Joseph Business School is to use these resources to manifest God's kingdom and reflect God's glory. This is a spiritual endeavor. Echoing the mission statement, Kornegay adds that prosperity doctrine "uses practical and biblical principles to empower adults [to be] successful entrepreneurs and business leaders."[37]

With over 450 alumni/ae, the Joseph Business School has interjected a new element into the teaching of the prosperity gospel in North America and in Africa: a focus on skill-building in addition to its message of faith. Some of the alumni of the Joseph Business School testify that they learned how "to use the anointing to reform or elevate one's skills, gifts, and education. To elevate us above what the world's standards limit us.

Bring from heaven the power of the principle to prosper the work above one's own strength."[38]

Parallel to the layering for the prosperity gospel with entrepreneurial skill development and business education as developed by Bill Winston and the Joseph Business School is the ministry of Samuel Adeyemi of Daystar Christian Centre and of Success Power International. Danny McCain, in his study of Pentecostalism in Nigeria, recognizes a similar shift in the teaching of the prosperity gospel that resembles the pragmatic emphasis that I have been noting.[39]

McCain quotes Paul Adefarasin to make this point: "In the old days, prosperity was postulated as a miracle of giving and receiving, and it didn't require much responsibility from the individuals. It was a 'bless me' cup." McCain explores similar developments in Daystar Christian Centre, a Lagos congregation pastored by Samuel Adeyemi, where Adeyemi has turned the first of his four Sunday services into a class on entrepreneurship. Additionally, Adeyemi's congregation sponsors Daystar Leadership Academy, which offers classes in "financial management, project management, systems development, organizational growth, entrepreneurship, and building an excellence-oriented organization." McCain notes that other ministries in Nigeria have followed the shift.[40]

Located in Lagos, Nigeria, Adeyemi's ministry includes Daystar Leadership Academy, which offers a business education program. Adeyemi was inspired by Sunday Adelaja, a Nigerian pastor of a megachurch in Ukraine, and his History Makers Training. Adeyemi is able to transmit his ideas on radio and television through his broadcast, Success Power. He is the author of *Parable of Dollars; Success Is Who You Are; Multiply Your Success; We Are the Government*; and other books.[41] Adeyemi envisioned that through relevant biblical teaching, the church could impact the government, the economy, and local neighborhoods. Adeyemi saw the need for a shift in the preaching of the prosperity gospel. He said:[42]

> Generally, I see that people in the society are getting tired of the so-called prosperity message for a few reasons. One, the idea that everybody will become millionaires after believing that for ten, fifteen, twenty years, some people are getting weary of that. Secondly . . . the money [raised] is not even used to improve the infrastructures of the church so that the church members enjoy it, not to talk about not even being used to affect the society. So, church members become suspect. So, I think that people are getting tired of the over-

emphasis on money. At the same time, I see now that there are some of us who want to come through again with the wholesome thing, that it's spiritual prosperity, mental development, and security development.... I think that the balance is now beginning to come in.

Through Daystar Christian Centre, Adeyemi has led efforts that have renovated five public schools in 2001, built science labs and donated science equipment and other supplies to public schools, and donated medical equipment and pharmaceuticals to public hospitals. Danny McCain, professor at the University of Jos in Nigeria, characterizes this shift in the teaching of the prosperity gospel as a shift toward "more stress on human responsibility in acquiring prosperity" biblically. According to Adeyemi, "There is no substitute for hard work in the school of success." Adeyemi contends, "For a long time, people in the church thought that by praying and fasting alone, they could manipulate God into giving them a powerful breakthrough. It does not work that way.... Prayer and fasting are necessary, but they cannot take the place of skill."[43]

With the Daystar Leadership Academy, the courses taught include financial management, entrepreneurship, time and life management, problem-solving, delegation strategies, and organizational growth. In addition, there is a course on the supernatural. On the faculty are instructors with accounting degrees as well as with Master of Business Administration (MBA) degrees. They earned degrees from universities in Nigeria, the Netherlands, and Great Britain.[44]

With this pragmatic shift reflected in the prosperity gospel ministries such as those of Bill Winston and Samuel Adeyemi, prosperity doctrine has been reframed as a doctrine with ingredients drawn from the Protestant ethic, a grammar of causation with a greater accent on human agency, and the introduction of entrepreneurial education as a key component of the teaching with its melding of biblical and business knowledge. The pragmatist innovation in prosperity teaching also entails a shift in the economic behavior of prosperity gospel adherents, from consumption being the focus to entrepreneurship being the goal.

The pragmatic approach to the prosperity gospel with its shift from consumption to entrepreneurship has interjected new economic behavior on the religious landscape of Black America and Africa. Surveying these prosperity gospel ministries and their impact on the religious landscape in order to ascertain the extensiveness, density, and variety of the economic activity these have generated might be an initial way to chart their presence in the economy.

Educational institutions such as Joseph Business School and the Daystar Leadership Academy sponsored by prosperity gospel ministries reinforce currents in the wider Pentecostal and Charismatic movements in Africa and Black America spurred by business degree programs based at Pentecostal universities and business journals sponsored by these universities. The pragmatist innovation in the teaching of the prosperity gospel by megachurch and televangelists, such as Bill Winston and Samuel Adeyemi, illustrate the ways that African Americans and African Christians are contextualizing the prosperity gospel as well as impacting the economic sectors of their respective economies through their different pragmatic prosperity gospel of entrepreneurship.

Progressive Pentecostalism and a Pentecostal Concept of Economic Justice and Economic Democracy

Economic justice has been a concern of Black Pentecostal activist-pastors since the mid-twentieth century, such as Bishop Smallwood Williams, who worked with Martin Luther King Jr. during the Civil Rights movement, and Bishop Herbert Daughtry, who campaigned around economic issues during the post-Civil Rights era as well as during the early twenty-first century. Black Neo-Pentecostal activist-pastors include clergy such as Randolph L. Jones of Philadelphia. A leading Black Pentecostal scholar, Keri L. Day, an ethicist who is a professor at Princeton Theological Seminary, engages economic justice in her scholarship. Her perspective would resonate with the concept of economic democracy that Martin Luther King Jr. advocated. King and Day advocate a restructuring of the economy to advance economic justice and promote a flourishing economy. Rather than focusing on alleviating poverty, economic democracy addresses the structural causes of economic inequality and elements of economic justice.[45]

A Pentecostal commitment to economic justice should introduce the concept of economic democracy which emerges out of marginalized Pentecostal communities as the "government of the poor" as places that have "challenged the dominant institutional political space by crafting alternative counter-publics [and economies] out of which they articulated possible futures of love, care, and democratic living." Such a concept should foster Pentecostal economic analysis as inquiries into how power works in our economy and how it could better work to end poverty. More than ending poverty, economic democracy pursues a just economy by lobbying to secure a living wage, adequate health care, decent housing, a solid public education system, etc. It also provides "a better distribution of wealth" and demonstrates a moral use of capitalism. Central to a Pentecostal economic democracy is the need for parity between the interests of capital and labor.[46]

While the economy is reformable, it lacks the capacity to reform itself or correct itself on its own in order for the economy to perform in a moral way. By design, the current US economy, as well as those in other countries, privileges capital, and the capital sector. The capital sector also possesses a disproportionate amount of power to influence the economy in its favor. The capital sector represents the economic interests of the top one percent of the population.

The exploitation of labor and the marginalization of the poor within the economy are the marks of unrestrained and unchecked capital, as well as an immoral form of capitalism. The goal of economic democracy is economic security for all people, so that all people, especially the poor, are treated with dignity and afforded a humane standard of living. To achieve economic security for all, full employment and a federal guaranteed minimum income are often proposed.

In order to create economic security by countering the economy's orientation to benefit the capital sector, labor and the citizenry have to be organized and mobilized to counterbalance the privileges of the capital sector. Without such a counterbalance, ordinary people will continue to be underserved by the economy. As noted, labor and the citizenry need to serve as a counterbalance. More than organized labor alone is needed to counterbalance the capital sector. Organized and mobilized sectors of citizens, consumers, congregations, and civil society groups need to leverage their power on corporations and the federal government to restructure the economy, shifting the economy towards economic justice and erect a just economy. As the electorate, the citizenry stands as a counterforce to unrestrained capitalist interests. It pressures legislators to pass legislation that secures and expands "prosperity for all." Within an economic democracy, citizens come first; the citizenry has precedence over capital and labor. The citizenry provides oversight and, through legislation, pivots the economy towards economic justice.[47]

Without introducing a viable counterbalance to the power of the capital sector in the economy, large populations of the society, especially the poor, will be abused and marginalized by the economy. In addition to serving as a counterbalance to the capital and labor sectors and redistributing the power relationship between labor, capital, and the citizenry, the parity between the interests of capital, labor, and the citizenry play a role in fostering "a conscience" within the economy. When the right of capital is balanced by the right of labor and of the citizenry, the right of capital can act with a conscience; capitalism can be used in a moral manner.[48]

In a democratic economy, the economy operates more humanely, productively, and profitably when the recognition of the right of the citizenry to be on par with capital and labor. According to Keri Day:[49]

> Justice, love, and care are not merely regulative ideals, but concrete actions that foster redemption and renewal in *this* world toward a more just, compassionate society. They "radicalize" hope. The possibility of loving and trusting communities is not only a future horizon, but all need to be prefigured in the here and now. . . . Radical hope offers the conditions that give rise to alternative social worlds out of which beloved communities can emerge and flourish.

A Pentecostal concept of economic democracy can embrace "radical hope," open "new horizons," and extend "the frontiers of democracy" towards a just society.

Conclusion

A Pentecostal engagement of the economy from the margins offers new ways to pursue economic justice through a Spirit-empowered embrace of economic democracy. A Pentecostal concept of economic democracy proposes a restructuring of the economy towards economic justice. In this exploration of progressive Pentecostalism, pragmatic currents within classical Pentecostal and the Prosperity Gospel movement offer a focus within Pentecostal economic ministries in which both emphasize entrepreneurship through the cultivation of financial skill-building. This Pentecostal pragmatic orientation resembles the classic Protestant ethic with its accent on religion as an agent of social change within the society.

Whereas a Pentecostal economic ethic engages a grammar of causation and an economic narrative that reflects a world that holds divine and human agency in a creative balance, a progressive Pentecostal economic ethic would address economic hierarchies of inequality, eradicate economic disparities, and envision a just economy. By interpreting Pentecostal economic ministries as part of a Pentecostal "economy" and "government of the poor," these ministries provide context for the development of a Pentecostal concept of economic justice and economic democracy. Thus, Pentecostal communities on the margins of the economy can generate new horizons and pathways to a just economy marked by parity between citizens, labor, and capital as well as radical hope.

Notes

1 Mike Davis, "Planet of Slums," *New Left Review* 26 (March-April 2004), 84–85.

2 Operation Blessing International Relief and Development Corporation, FY11 *Annual Report* (2011), 2: Between 1978 and March of 2011 "OBI has touched the lives of more than 249 million people in more than 105 countries and fifty states, providing goods and services valued at over $3.1 billion." See also, David D. Daniels III, "Future Issues in Social and Economic Justice: The Social Engagement of Pentecostals and Charismatics" in Vinson Synan, ed., *Spirit-Empowered Christianity in the 21st Century* (Lake Mary, FL: Charisma House, 2011), 339–355.

3 James Forbes, *The Holy Spirit and Preaching* (Nashville: Abingdon, 1989), 15.

4 Donald Miller and Tetsunao Yamamori, *Global Pentecostalism: The New Face of Christian Social Engagement* (Berkeley: University of California Press, 2007); also see Daniels, "Prosperity Gospel of Entrepreneurship in Africa and Black America" in Andreas Heuser, ed., *Pastures of Plenty; Tracing Religio-Scapes of Prosperity Gospel in Africa and Beyond* (Frankfurt am Main: Peter Lang, 2015), 265–278.

5 Adoyi Onoja, "The Pentecostal Churches: the Politics of Spiritual Deregulation Since the 1980s," in Julius O. Adekunle ed., *Religion in Politics: Secularism and National Integration in Modern Nigeria* (Trenton, NJ: Africa World Press Inc, 2009), 263–273.

6 David Ogungbile, "African Pentecostalism and the Prosperity Gospel," in Clifton Clarke, ed., *Pentecostal Theology in Africa* (Eugene, OR: Wipf and Stock, 2014), 145.

7 Hans A. Baer and Merrill Singer, "Toward A Typology of Black Sectarianism as a Response to Racial Stratification," in Timothy E. Fulop and Albert J. Raboteau eds., *African-American Religion: Interpretative Essays in History and Culture* (New York & London: Routledge, 1997), 268–269, 257–276.

8 Baer and Singer, "Toward a Typology of Black Sectarianism," 263, 268–270.

9 David Maxwell, "Social Mobility and Politics in African Pentecostal Modernity," in Robert W. Hefner ed., *Global Pentecostalism in the 21st Century* (Bloomington, IN: Indiana University Press, 2013), 95.

10 Maxwell, "Social Mobility and Politics," 96.

11 Maxwell, "Social Mobility and Politics," 98.

12 Maxwell, "Social Mobility and Politics," 106.

13 Elizabeth Lynn and Susan Wisely, "Four Traditions of Philanthropy," in A. Davis and E. Lynn, eds., *The Civically Engaged Reader* (Chicago: Great Books Foundation, 2006), 210, 212, 213; Ylvisaker quoted in Lynn and Wisely.

14 Akosua Darkwa, Nicholas Amponsah, and Evans Gyampoh, *Civil Society in a Changing Ghana: An Assessment of the Current State of Civil Society in Ghana* (Accra: CIVICUS and GAPVOD, 2006), 20, 24.

15 Church of Pentecost's website, https://thecophq.org/pentsos/, accessed February 23, 2021; Okyere Daniel Walker, "The Pentecost Fire is Burning: Models of Mission Activities in the Church of Pentecost" (Ph.D. diss., University of Birmingham, 2010), 116, 25. "Widows and Orphans Receive 400 million-cedi Fund," Ghana Web, April 24, 2006, https://www.ghanaweb.com/GhanaHomePage/NewsArchive/Widows-and-orphans-receive-400-million-cedi-fund-103141, accessed February 23, 2021.

16 Walker, "The Pentecost Fire Is Burning," 24.

17 *Vision 2018 Five-Year Vision for the Church of Pentecost Covering the Period 2013–2018: Impacting Generations* (n.p.: General Council of the Church of Pentecost, 2018), http://www.pentecost.ca/wp-content/uploads/2013/03/vision-2018.pdf, accessed February 25, 2021.

18 "Widows and Orphans," GhanaWeb Regional News.

19 *Pentvars Business Journal* (International Refereed Journal) 6:2 (April–December 2012); See also, www.pentvarsjournal.com; Pentecost University College Graduate School Master of Commerce and Master of Business Administration catalogue for 2013.

20 Charles O. Kwarteng and Hannah Emma Acquaye, "The Role of Ghanaian Churches in the Financial Rehabilitation of the Poor: Implications for Revisiting the Social Mission of Religious Institutions," *Journal of Financial Services Marketing* 15 (March 2011), 305.

21 "Pentecost Co-operative Mutual Support and Social Services Society Limited (PENCO)," https://pentsos.org/penco/, accessed February 25, 2021.

22 Darkwa, Amponsah, and Gyampoh, *Civil Society in a Changing Ghana*, 10.

23 Walker, "The Pentecost Fire Is Burning," 122.

24 Maxwell, "Social Mobility and Politics," 95.

25 The Joseph Business School brochure 2014; tour to the Living Word Christian Center complex and the Joseph Business School on Sunday, January 11, 2015, as well as attendance at the Sunday worship service and the Joseph Business School Graduation, on Saturday, January 10, 2015.

26 See faculty page of the Joseph Business School website, https://www.jbs.edu/jbs-faculty/, accessed January 11, 2021.

27 Phone interview of Deloris Thomas, Vice President, Joseph Business School on January 7, 2015 by David D. Daniels III.

28 Phone interview of Deloris Thomas.

29 The Joseph Business School brochure, 2014.

30 Phone interview of Deloris Thomas.

31 Joseph Center brochure, 2014.

32 Phone interview of Deloris Thomas.

33 Phone interview of Eddie Kornegay, Dean of Continuing Education and Professional Development at the Joseph Business School on August 22, 2014 by David D. Daniels III.

34 Phone interview of Deloris Thomas.

35 Phone interview of Deloris Thomas.

36 Phone interview of Eddie Kornegay.

37 Phone interview of Eddie Kornegay.

38 Phone interview of Eddie Kornegay.

39 Danny McCain, "The Metamorphosis of Nigerian Pentecostalism: From Signs and Wonders in the Church to Service and Influence in Society," in Donald E. Miller, Kimon H. Sargeant, and Richard Flory, eds., *Spirit and Power: The Growth and Global Impact of Pentecostalism* (Oxford, UK: Oxford University Press, 2013), 160–181.

40 McCain, "The Metamorphosis of Nigerian Pentecostalism," 166–168.

41 McCain, "The Metamorphosis of Nigerian Pentecostalism," 177.

42 Interview of Rev. Samuel Adeyemi on June 9, 2011 by Danny McCain of the University of Jos; the interview is used with permission from Danny McCain, which was granted by email on December 25, 2014.

43 Danny McCain, "From Idahosa to Adeyemi: The Evolving Theology of the Prosperity Gospel in Nigeria," (paper presented at the 42nd Annual Meeting of the Society of Pentecostal Studies, Seattle, WA, 2013), 14, 19, 21; quotes from the paper are used with permission granted by Danny McCain on December 25, 2014.

44 See the faculty page of the Daystar Leadership Academy website, https://dlaonline.org/faculty/, accessed January 11, 2021.

45 David D. Daniels III, "Against Poverty: The Holy Spirit and Pentecostal Economic Ministries," in Antipas Harris, ed., *The Mighty Transformer: The Holy Spirit Advocates for Social Justice* (Irving, TX: GIELD Academic Press, 2019), 30–53; Keri Day, *Religious Resistance to Neoliberalism: Womanist and Black Feminist Perspectives* (New York: Palgrave MacMillan, 2016); David D. Daniels III, "Economic Democracy, Martin Luther King Jr., and the Black Church Tradition," Telos: *Critical Theory of the Contemporary* 182 (Spring 2018), 29–45.

46 Day, *Religious Resistance to Neoliberalism*, 161; King, "Paul's Letter to American Christians," (A sermon delivered at Dexter Avenue Baptist Church, Montgomery, AL, 1956), https://kinginstitute.stanford.edu/king-papers/publications/knock-midnight-inspiration-great-sermons-reverend-martin-luther-king-jr-1, accessed January 11, 2021.

47 Martin Luther King, Jr. "Twenty-fifth Anniversary Dinner, United Automobile Workers Union, Cobo Hall, Detroit, Michigan, April 27, 1961," in Martin Luther King Jr., Michael K. Honey, ed.,*"All Labor Has Dignity"* (Boston: Beacon Press), 29.

48 King, "AFL-CIO Fourth Constitution, Americana Hotel, Miami Beach, Florida, December 11, 1961," in Martin Luther King Jr., Michael K. Honey, ed.,*"All Labor Has Dignity"* (Boston: Beacon Press), 35–36.

49 Day, *Religious Resistance to Neoliberalism*, 161.

7 Factors Perpetrating Global Poverty and Its Eradication: The Role of Christianity

Sylvia Owusu-Ansah

Abstract

The subject of global poverty is discussed here from three dimensions: identification of the poor, the causes of poverty, and God's provisions for the poor. The study looks at poverty as a global concern from the perspective of the United Nations (UN) and the Millennium Development Goals (MDGs) and explores the primary sources of poverty. In the introductory session, the generic and working definitions of poverty and the poor are examined from both the sociological and theological spheres. The causes of poverty, especially the human factors such as institutions, systems, authorities, and policies that translate into injustices and exploitation, as well as human attitudes perpetuating the circle of poverty, are discussed. Finally, the biblical provisions for the poor are also examined with regard to God's attributes as the father of the fatherless, the husband of the widow, and the defender of the poor and the outcast, with much emphasis on the marginalized and neglected members of the human community. Observations and recommendations are made regarding the Christian attitude towards the poor, poverty, and how to eradicate or minimize the effect and impact of poverty in the world's communities. The study aims at contributing to the sustainable development goal agenda.

Introduction

The word "poverty" and/or "poor" is from the Latin word *pauper* and has its roots in the words *pau-* and *pario* meaning "giving birth to nothing," referring to unproductive livestock and farmland.[1] "Poverty amid plenty is the world's greatest challenge."[2] This paradoxical statement by James D. Wolfensohn, President of the World Bank, is the reality we currently face in this century. The first Sustainable Development Goal (SDG) of the 2030 Agenda is to end poverty in all its forms in all countries.[3] This then raises the question, who exactly are the poor, and how do we free them from this condition? Identifying the poor at different levels of society, such as the individual, household, community, district, and regional level, is key. This is because, in order to take action (planning and policymaking) that favor the poor, social classes need to be defined using attributes such as gender, ethnicity, religion, and culture, location and livelihood status, as well as the type of household. That is the number of members, their age distribution, and the gender of its head.[4]

Identifying the Poor

Several definitions have popped up to provide a comprehensive meaning of poverty. One may come across terms such as income or monetary poverty, multidimensional poverty, absolute poverty, and relative poverty. Basically, poverty can be defined as "a situation in which someone does not have enough money to pay for their basic needs."[5] A person is classified as "poor" if their earnings cannot provide for their "basic needs" in a given area.[6] According to the Encyclopedia Britannica, "Poverty is said to exist when people lack the means to satisfy their basic needs."[7] In this context, the identification of poor people first requires a determination of what constitutes basic needs. These may be defined narrowly as "those necessary for survival" or broadly as "those reflecting the prevailing standard of living in the community."[8] The United Nations defined poverty in 1998 as "a violation of human dignity whereby humans are denied from having choices and opportunities."[9] The Organization for Economic Cooperation and Development (OECD) defines poverty as the inability of people to meet economic, social, and other standards of wellbeing.[10] Another definition by The World Bank depicts poverty as a pronounced deprivation in wellbeing.[11] It goes further to describe deprivation as a lack of food, shelter, clothing, health care, and education. In addition, poor people suffer injustice from state institutions and society, and often, they are rendered voiceless.[12]

Who are the Poor?

Recently, two modifications have been made to the 2030 Agenda. The first change is that poverty is now perceived as both a lack of sufficient income (income poverty) and as deprivation in several dimensions of life (multidimensional phenomenon). Secondly, the Agenda focuses on reducing poverty not just at the national level, but also within specific population groups.[13] Income poverty is measured as the proportion of people living on less than USD 1.90 a day.[14] Poverty, which comprises different dimensions of deprivation relating to human capabilities (consumption and food security, health, education, rights, security, decent work), must be addressed in the context of environmental sustainability. Also, reducing gender inequality is important to all dimensions of poverty because poverty is not gender neutral.[15] Moreover, women play a crucial role in realizing all the SDGs.[16]

Gender inequality is experienced differently by men and women in different societies. Kinship rules determine the extent and manifestations of gender inequality to a considerable degree. Female poverty is more prevalent and typically more severe than male poverty. This is even more so when these rules are heavily in favor of men.[17] Women and girls in poor households usually find themselves at a disadvantage when it comes to private consumption and public services. They are victims of violence by men on a large scale and are more likely to be uneducated. They are often excluded from political and social affairs and are therefore unable to overcome poverty the same way men do in most situations. Women are instrumental in catering to the basic needs of poor households. Therefore, gender inequality is a major cause of female and overall poverty.[18] Jonathan Haughton and Shabidur R. Khandker state that "poverty may also be tied to specific types of consumption; for example, people could be house poor or food poor or health poor. These dimensions of poverty often can be measured directly, for instance, by measuring malnutrition or literacy."[19]

Addae-Korankye agrees to the submission that, "Poverty is hunger; poverty is lack of shelter; poverty is being sick and not being able to see a doctor (. . .); poverty is losing a child to illness brought about by unclean water; poverty is powerlessness, lack of representation and freedom."[20] The Bible looks at poverty in a slightly different way. Calvin Fox suggests that the biblical definitions for poverty refer to people who are destitute because of natural disasters such as fire, accident, or flood, as well as to those who once had property but have lost the property and means of sustenance so are not able to make ends meet. Fox maintains that the Bible attributes the main cause of poverty and destitution to oppression caused by invading armies or the behavior of the rich and powerful people.[21] The rich and powerful take advantage of the poor and needy, widows and orphans, and violates their rights. Examples of oppression include injustice, exploitation, defrauding, and denying workers their due wages. God is on the side of the oppressed. Fox argues that to eradicate poverty caused by oppression, oppression must be removed. He adds, "If the oppression is systemic and institutionalized, those systems and institutions must be confronted by the law. Such opposition calls for brave action, even resistance, from individuals, churches and the community at large."[22]

Poverty Reduction as a Global Agenda

Augustin Kwasi Fosu explains that the:

> Goal One of the Millennium Development Goals (MDGs) of halving poverty by 2015 enjoys a major emphasis in the international discourse and has consequently made the talk about poverty a subject of global interest. Hence, the question; "has Goal One of the Millennium Development Goals (MDGs) of halving poverty by 2015 been achieved?" The World Bank's report indicated that, "since the 1980s, the poverty rate has been trending considerably downward globally." [23]

Recent research conducted on approximately fifty low and lower-middle-income countries found that "poverty is still a big problem, especially in sub-Saharan Africa, and interventions succeeding in alleviating income poverty are not necessarily effective in reducing multidimensional poverty."[24] The study "highlights the need for new labor market policies in Africa, which could increase both the quantity and the quality of employment, together with a minimum wage."[25] It also found that most of the poor reside in rural areas. Efforts on poverty alleviation should, therefore, concentrate on improving the status and lives of people living in rural areas.[26] Grant notes that "poverty is not only a national phenomenon that has reached crisis proportions; it is also a global one."[27] "The UN Food and Agriculture Organization estimates that 239 million people in sub-Saharan Africa were hungry and undernourished in 2010 due to poverty."[28]

Types of Poverty

Sarlo distinguishes between absolute and relative poverty. He explains that while absolute poverty describes an unhealthy lack of basic necessities, relative poverty refers to a condition of being unequal rather than a situation of insufficiency.[29] This implies that a person is poor not because they actually lack anything that is considered a necessity, but rather because there is a wide gap between what they have and what most others have in the society regardless of their standard of living.[30]

Absolute poverty is further divided into extreme poverty and overall poverty. Extreme poverty refers to the lack of income required to meet the basic food needs, whereas overall poverty represents the lack of income required to meet both food and non-food needs.[31]

Cyclical poverty refers to poverty that may be "widespread throughout a population, but the occurrence itself is of limited duration."[32] Collective poverty "involves a relatively permanent insufficiency of means to secure basic needs—a condition that may be so general as to describe the average level of life in a society or that may be concentrated in relatively large groups in an otherwise prosperous society."[33] People who are affected by concentrated collective poverty, like generalized poverty, "have higher mortality rates, poor health, low educational levels."[34] Economically they are usually unemployed and underemployed. They are unskilled and have job instability. Affected individuals and communities can be helped by creating new opportunities for employment in new industries, encouraging small-scale industries and businesses, and training to acquire high levels of skills to facilitate better employment opportunities.[35]

Case poverty refers to people or families who are unable to meet basic needs even in social surroundings of general prosperity. This situation may be caused by a chronic disease or affected individuals may be emotionally or physically challenged.[36]

Causes of Poverty

Causes of poverty include corruption, education, political instability, wars, and civil wars, natural and geographical characteristics, ineffective governance, and government policies.[37] Most literature on poverty, however, classify the causes into two main categories, namely: structural causes and behavioral causes.

Structural Causes

In this section, I will discuss the structural causes in relation to education, ineffective government policies, and economic causes. The structural causes of poverty refer to systemic factors that reduce opportunity and increase economic insecurity. These include discrimination on the grounds of race and gender, which are deeply rooted in our institutions and markets; low wages and thirst for profit; poor investments in education, health care, and bad economic structures such as social insurance and low wage income. Zechariah 7:10 admonishes us not to oppress the widow or the fatherless, the alien or the poor (NKJV).[38] "The failure to correct and accommodate the natural differences between people results in an uneven playing field and promotes the creation of poverty."[39] It is the duty of every nation to protect the basic human rights of its citizens by ensuring that they have access to a level of goods and services that promote their health and wellbeing.[40] Ecclesiastes 9:16 declares, "Wisdom is better than strength. Nevertheless, the poor man's wisdom is despised, and his words are not heard." The poor are usually deprived of their voice, power, and independence. Consequently, most poor people are treated rudely and subjected to humiliation, inhumane treatment, and exploitation at the hands of the institutions of state and society. They are especially oppressed in places where there is no rule of law, and the lack of protection against violence, extortion, and intimidation. "Unaccountable and unresponsive state institutions are among the causes of relatively slow progress in expanding the human assets of poor people."[41] David. A. Bessler notes that in some instances, "It may be sufficient to say that living in poverty is a matter of chance, related to the circumstances of one's birth or the outcomes of nature or world events beyond individual's influence."[42] The Bible cautions rulers about God's dislike of corruption. Isaiah 10:1–4 states:

> Woe to those who decree unrighteous decrees, who write misfortune, which they have prescribed to rob the needy of justice, and to take what is right from the poor of my people, that widows may be their prey, and that they may rob the fatherless. What will you do in the day of punishment, and in the desolation, which will come from afar? To whom will you flee for help? And where will you leave your glory? Without me, they shall bow down among the prisoners, and they shall fall among the slain. For all this, his anger is not turned away, but his hand is stretched out still.

Education can be used as a tool to increase income, quality of jobs, and improve the quality of life. Unfortunately, most poor countries face a continuous rise in poverty due to a lack of training skills, productive knowledge, and good education. Without the respective skills and knowledge needed in the work environment, one is left with very few options, and most find themselves in low-income jobs. Education directly supports the wellbeing and emancipation of people, while indirectly stimulating social change and economic production.[43] Jesus Christ mentioned in Luke 4:18, "The Spirit of the Lord is upon me because he has anointed me to preach the gospel to the poor." Jesus also stated in John 8:32, "And you shall know the truth, and the truth shall make you free." To know is to be taught or to learn, and knowledge is the beginning of freedom. The Bible states that it is the lack of knowledge that makes people perish (Hosea 4:6). "Education can be a life empowering experience for all, and what the poor need most is empowerment."[44]

An analysis made by Michael Lipton in 1977 reports on what he calls poverty, saying that ineffective governance and government policies play a major role in perpetuating et al. One problem in developing countries is the neglect of rural areas by governments. According to Lipton, elites, who mostly live in urban areas, have a stronger voice and greater power resources to oppose governments. On the other hand, people in rural areas are less educated and not well connected. Therefore, they do not have the power to affect policymaking at the national level. As a result, governments tend to adopt policies that favor the urban regions, such as special subsidies and lower taxation.[45]

What developing countries need most is responsible governance to help mitigate or eliminate poverty. A good legal and institutional governance framework is key in increasing opportunities for both women and men to escape poverty. Policies and incentives, such as debt relief, increased market accessibility, increased foreign direct investment, sustained support for civil society, especially the underprivileged, amongst others, are necessary to fight poverty:[46]

> Governments need to recognize gender exclusion when shaping legal, institutional, and policy frameworks, for instance, in allocations of public expenditure. In several countries, household crop production, children's health and education, and birth rates have all improved as a result of gender-specific national budgets.[47]

Other factors that cause poverty include political instability, wars, and civil wars. The nation's resources are channeled into war efforts instead of productive activities, and investments are reduced.[48] Natural and geographical events may also cause a nation to experience poverty. Geographical features and natural events such as earthquakes, floods, and drought are all elements outside of human control:[49]

> Climate change and exposure to natural disasters are distinct risks that threaten to derail international efforts to eradicate poverty by 2030. With increasing temperatures, many of the world's poorest and most vulnerable people will face growing risks of more intense or longer droughts, extreme rainfall, flooding, and severe heat waves.[50]

Another factor constituting global poverty is the subject of low "living wages" emerging from poor economic structures. Laura Stivers and others opine that poverty has increased in recent times and that "By ethnicity, twenty-four percent of the homeless are Hispanic American."[51] Living wage, as defined by the Catholic Education Service, "is an independently calculated hourly wage rate designed to pay employees enough to cover their basic living needs (e.g., cost of food, housing, and basic needs)."[52] A great percentage of the global working force does not receive wages meaningful enough to reflect the hours they spend working. That is to say, the minimum wage of the average worker globally is insignificantly low, rendering them the inability to provide for themselves, families, and dependents, irrespective of the number of hours they invest working. Even in the notable richest nations, we still find people poor and unable to make ends meet because of low wages though they work full time.[53] In the United States, for instance, "many full-time working Americans cannot meet their basic needs" and are "often forced to choose between feeding their families or heating their homes."[54] They lamented, "If you work full time, you should not be poor. . . .No one should be working poor."[55] Attesting to this statement, the Unitarian Universalist Association professed, "jobs should lift workers out of poverty, not keep them there."[56] Fosu concurred that "the lower the level of income, the more likely that [one] will fall below basic needs and put the individual into poverty."[57]

It is argued that behavioral and personal differences are major root causes of poverty in modern society. The term "poverty culture" is used to refer to a set of attitudes and behaviors that are passed down from parents to children and promote bad, self-defeating decisions that lead to poverty. Attitudes that conflict with attributes such as self-control, confidence, hard work, resilience, honesty, a positive attitude, and perseverance can influence the opportunities one may have and life outcomes. "The critical attributes that are most important to human fulfillment and success can be cultivated."[58] The Bible encourages the development of integrity, hard work, and other beneficial attributes that would help someone to live a fulfilled life. Proverbs 6:9–11 cautions against laziness: "How long will you slumber, o sluggard? When will you rise from your sleep? A little sleep, a little slumber, a little folding of the hands to sleep—so shall your poverty come on you like a prowler and your need like an armed man." Proverbs 13:18 cautions against rebelliousness: "Poverty and shame will come to him who disdains correction, but he who regards a rebuke will be honored." Proverbs 14:23 warns against idleness: "In all labor there is profit, but idle chatter leads only to poverty." Proverbs 21:5 warns against mediocrity: "The plans of the diligent lead surely to plenty, but those of everyone who is hasty, surely to poverty." Proverb 23:20–21 warns against harmful habits: "Do not mix with winebibbers, or with gluttonous eaters of meat; For the drunkard and the glutton will come to poverty, and drowsiness will clothe a man with rags."

God's Provision for Poverty

In battling global poverty, the provisions that God has made for the poor in the Bible come into focus. The Christian faith has, since time immemorial, demonstrated a positive attitude in combating poverty, particularly global poverty. The Old Testament explicitly defines God's mind and intentions concerning the poor and the needy. Numerous biblical references discuss how the poor and needy are to be treated, including the consequences of neglecting God's instructions concerning them. The term poor and poverty are sometimes used in conjunction with widows and orphans, expressing the nature of the ordeal and challenges common to them.[59] The reason why widows and orphans are used in connection with the poor and poverty is that they are considered the most vulnerable. They are also the most neglected people in all societies.

The meaning of these terms as used in the Old Testament often depends upon the context. There has been emphasis concerning fair treatment of the poor in Exodus 23:6. The poor are not to be denied justice, and they are also to be treated equitably as part of God's covenant with his people. God commanded the Israelites in Deuteronomy 15:11 to give to the poor and needy dwelling in the land. In Luke 14:13, Jesus Christ tells his followers that when they give a feast, they are to invite the poor, the maimed, the lame, and the blind. Throughout the Bible, God cares greatly about the poor and needy, the oppressed and marginalized in society. Christians are admonished to care for and love them without discriminating, to attract the blessings of God (Psalm 41:1; Prov 22:9; 28:27). Doing otherwise would incur the wrath of God who treats all mankind equally. 2 Corinthians 8:9 declares, "For you know the grace of our Lord Jesus Christ, that though he was rich, yet for your sakes, he became poor, that you through his poverty might become rich" (Provide Version). This implies that God does not want the poor to remain poor. The poor and needy persons were also to be treated with respect. Deuteronomy 24:10–11 notes they were to be supported and not to be charged with interest (See also, Exod 22:25; Lev 25:35–38). Special provisions were to be made for the poor and needy and strangers (Lev 19:9–10; 23: 22; Deut 24:19–22). The widows, orphans, especially the fatherless, strangers, and the poor were to benefit from the gleaning laws and other provisions. The poor, the strangers, and hired workers were also permitted to eat freely from the lands that were allowed to lie vacant:

> When you reap the harvest of your land, you shall not wholly reap the corners of your field when you reap, nor shall you gather any gleaning from your harvest. You shall leave them for the poor and stranger such as cleaning laws silly chickens I am the Lord your God (Lev 23:22).[60]

Other benefits included debt cancellation for the poor at the end of every seven years (Jubilee, Deuteronomy 15:1–9) and the total freedom during Jubilee for Hebrews who had become slaves because of poverty (Lev 25:39–41; Lev 25:54). That God is on the side of the poor and the needy means that God is on the side of justice. The poor are often taken advantage of and denied justice. Deuteronomy 10:18 declares, "He administers justice for the fatherless and the widow, and loves the stranger, giving him food and clothing." The Bible portrays God as the supplier and provider of the poor and needy. For example, Isaiah 41:17–18 states:

> The poor and needy seek water, but there is none,
> Their tongues fail for thirst.
> I, the Lord, will hear them;
> I, the God of Israel, will not forsake them.
> 18 I will open rivers in desolate heights,
> And fountains in the midst of the valleys;
> I will make the wilderness a pool of water,
> And the dry land springs of water.

Not only is God fighting for the poor to administer justice on their behalf, but God also rewards those who consider and assist the poor and needy. Psalm 41:1 declares, "Blessed is he who considers the poor; The Lord will deliver him in time of trouble." Regarding the issues of fair wages, both the Old and New Testaments "speak specifically about the just treatment of laborers, and the equitable payment of wages."[61] Throughout the Torah, there are specific instructions on the proper treatment of workers. These scriptural texts are believed to have been "generally framed by a reminder from God that we know how it is to be slaves, and we must therefore show both justice and compassion for those who labor on our behalf."[62] In Deuteronomy 16:20, the Bible advocates the pursuance of justice; "Justice, justice, shall you pursue." The Bible has advocated strongly for structural economic justice in Leviticus 19:13 and Deuteronomy 24:14–15.

It is clearly evident that throughout history, people of the Christian faith have been intimately connected to the specific issue of justice regarding the payment of wages. Like the Christian faith, other faiths such as Judaism, Islam, and Buddhism, have demonstrated similar enthusiasm against economic injustices, which contribute enormously to combating global poverty. The Islamic faith teaches that the notion of justice is founded on equality and human dignity.[63] It expounds that "God has enjoined justice and righteousness for all humans in all matters including but not limited to family matters, workers issues, trade, and all relationships."[64] In addition, it teaches that "the employer-worker relationship must be based on justice and mutual consent honoring the dignity of the worker."[65] The Buddhist work ethic suggests that employers are required to respect their employees by assigning them to work according to their ability, supplying them with food and with wages, tending them in sickness, sharing with them any delicacies, and granting them leave at times.[66] In the same way, servants and employees are also required to serve their masters and employers by showing compassion to them in five ways: they rise before him, they go to sleep after him, they take only what is given, they perform their duties well, and they uphold his good name and fame.[67]

Justice and fairness to all humans characterize God's approval of human relations on earth. Efforts aimed at eradicating poverty are, therefore, in line with God's desire for fairness and equitable treatment of the poor and the marginalized.

Conclusion

The study has looked at the global issue of poverty and its effect on the nations of the world. Poverty is seen as a concern needing urgent attention at the global level. Poverty is no longer evaluated in monetary terms only, but in a multidimensional form affecting every area of human endeavor. Poverty affects not only the physical wellbeing of an individual but their emotional and psychological wellbeing as well. The Sustainable Development Goals (SDGs) give much attention to how to eradicate poverty in all its forms. Sustainable development calls for the reduction or eradication of poverty.[68] However, the multidimensional nature of poverty has created a lot of debate about who the poor really are, how to measure poverty, and what is the best approach to tackle poverty. The interconnection between deprivations makes poverty a complicated problem to tackle. On the other hand, it means addressing any one of the factors that may cause a chain reaction among the others.

Poverty is caused by exploitation, injustice, natural disaster, corruption, mismanagement, and laziness. It is true that the poor suffer many levels of deprivation. This may range from low income to a lack of access to relevant training and education for personal development to discrimination and social exclusion. The poor are mentioned over 300 times in the Bible. This is a clear indicator of how much God cares for them. Christians are not only encouraged to share their resources (including time and energy) with the poor but also the gospel of Christ (see Luke 4:18 and Matt 11:5). James 2:5 indicates that God has chosen the poor of this world to be rich in faith and heirs of his Kingdom (Luke 6:10). The gospel brings hope, and hope is something the poor need. In the end, what God requires of mankind is to do justly, to love mercy, and to walk humbly with Him (Micah 6:8).

Eradicating poverty means dealing effectively with the different levels of deprivation while involving all the necessary drivers of change, such as institutions, authorities, systems, and government policies. Systems and institutions must be put in place to work toward eradicating poverty. Payment of fair wages and equitable treatment of all people, including the poor, the strangers, and the vulnerable, is admonished in the Bible. Human structures and institutions that play a role in perpetuating poverty should be stopped, and policies that negatively affect the poor and maintain a cycle of poverty should be curtailed.

Notes

1 Alex Addae-Korankye, "Causes of Poverty in Africa: A Review of Literature," *American International Journal of Social Science* 3:7 (2014), 147.

2 The World Bank, *World Development Report* 2000/2001: Attacking Poverty (Oxford University Press, 2001), v.

3 The World Bank, *Attacking Poverty*, v.

4 OECD, "The DAC Guidelines: Poverty Reduction," OECD Publications Service (2001), 4.

5 Michael Rundell, *Macmillan English Dictionary for Advanced Learners* (Oxford: Macmillan, 2002), http://www.macmillandictionary.com/dictionary/british/poverty, accessed October 6, 2020.

6 R. Ram, "The Role of Real Income Level and Income Distribution in Fulfilment of Basic Needs," *World Development* 13:5 (1985), 589–594; N. L. Hicks and P. Streeten, "Indicators of Development: The Search for a Basic Needs Yardstick," *World Development* 7:6 (1979), 567–580.

7 Adam Augustyn, "Poverty," *Encyclopedia Britannica*, Encyclopedia Britannica Inc., 2020, https://www.britannica.com/topic/poverty, accessed September 20, 2020.

8 Augustyn, "Poverty."

9 Alex H. H. Ng, Abdul G. Farinda, Fock K. Kan, Ai L. Lim, and Teo M. Ting, "Poverty: Its Causes and Solutions," *International Journal of Humanities and Social Sciences* 7:8 (2013), 2471–2479; David Gordon, "Indicators of Poverty for Youth" (United Nations Expert Group Meeting on Youth Development Indicators, New York, 2005), 3–4, cited in Ng et al., "Poverty," 2471.

10 OECD, "Poverty Reduction," 4.

11 The World Bank, *Attacking Poverty*, 37.

12 The World Bank, *Attacking Poverty*, 15, 37.

13 Francesco Burchi, Daniele Malerba, Nicole Rippin, and Claudio E. Montenegro, "Comparing Global Trends in Multidimensional and Income Poverty and Assessing Horizontal Inequalities" (Discussion Paper, German Development Institute, 2019), 35. 14   Burchi et al., "Multidimensional and Income Poverty," 1.

15 OECD, "Poverty Reduction," 2.

16 United Nations Women, "Women and Sustainable Development Goals," (2016), 3, https://sustainabledevelopment.un.org/index.php?page=view&type=400&nr=2322&menu=1515, accessed November 25, 2020.

17 The World Bank, *Attacking Poverty*, 118.

18 OECD, "Poverty Reduction," 40.

19 Jonathan Haughton and Shahidur R. Khandker, *Handbook Poverty and Inequality* (Washington DC: World Bank Publication, 2009), 1.

20 Addae-Korankye, "Cause of Poverty in Africa," 148.

21 Calvin Fox, "Biblical Definition of Poverty, of 'The Poor'" Re/Formed Living, April 10, 2016, http://www.reformedliving.org/index.php?option=com_content&id=660:the-new-biblical-definition-of-poverty-of-the-poor&catid=64:justice&Itemid=57, accessed December 27, 2020.

22 Fox, "Biblical Definition."

23 Augustin Kwasi Fosu, "Inequality, Income, and Poverty: Comparative Global Evidence," *Social Science Quarterly* 91:5 (December 2010), 1432–1445; Augustin Kwasi Fosu, *Global Monitoring Report* (Washington, DC: World Bank, 2006), 3–4.

24 Burchi et al., "Multidimensional and Income Poverty," 37.

25 Burchi et al., "Multidimensional and Income Poverty," 37.

26 Burchi et al., "Multidimensional and Income Poverty," 37.

27 Jacquelyn Grant, "Poverty, Womanist Theology, and the Ministry of the Church," in Paul Plenge Parker, ed., *Standing with the Poor: Theological Reflections on Economic Reality* (Cleveland: Pilgrim Press, 1992), 48.

28 Frank Kabuya, "Fundamental Causes of Poverty in Sub-Saharan Africa," IOSR *Journal of Humanities and Social Science* 20:6 (2015), 78–81.

29 Christopher A. Sarlo, "The Causes of Poverty," Fraser Institute, March 26, 2019, https://www.fraserinstitute.org/studies/causes-of-poverty, accessed April 6, 2021.

30 Sarlo, "Poverty."

31 Udaya Wagle, "Rethinking Poverty: Definition and Measurement," *International Social Science Journal* 54:171 (2002), 156.

32 Augustyn, "Poverty."

33 Augustyn, "Poverty."

34 Augustyn, "Poverty."

35 Augustyn, "Poverty."

36 Augustyn, "Poverty."

37 Ng, et al., "Poverty," 2472–2475.

38 Scriptural quotations are from New King James Version (NKJV), unless indicated otherwise.

39 Sarlo, "Poverty."

40 Mona Mowafi and M. Marwan Khawaja, "Poverty," *Journal of Epidemiology & Community Health* 59:4 (2005), 260.

41 The World Bank, *Attacking Poverty*, 35.

42 David. A. Bessler, "On World Poverty: Its Causes and Effects," (November 2002), 2, http://agecon2.tamu.edu/people/faculty/bessler-david/webpage/poverty.pdf, accessed October 4, 2020.

43 Ng et al., "Poverty," 2474.

44 Ng et al., "Poverty," 2474.

45 Burchi et al., "Multidimensional and Income Poverty," 19.

46 Ng et al., "Poverty," 2477; OECD, "Poverty Reduction," 2477.

47 OECD, "Poverty Reduction," 49.

48 Ng et al., "Poverty," 2475; The World Bank, *Attacking Poverty*, 50.

49 The World Bank, *Attacking Poverty*, 50; Ng et al., "Poverty," 2475.

50 Eva Ludi, "Poverty Brief – Understanding Poverty," (Paper written for poverty-wellbeing shareweb and the Swiss Agency for Development and Cooperation, 2013), 6, https://www.shareweb.ch/site/Poverty-Wellbeing, accessed September 10, 2020.

51 Laura Stivers, Christine E. Gudorf, and James B. Martin-Schramm, *Christian Ethics* (Maryknoll: Orbis Books, 2012), 105.

52 Paul Barber, *A Catholic Guide to the Living Wage* (London: Catholic Education Service), 2020, 2.

53 H. Sklar, and P. Sherry, "Wages and the Word: A Scriptural Approach to Minimum Wage Policy," Let Justice Roll Living Wage Campaign, www.letjusticeroll.org, 2009, 45.

54 Sklar and Sherry, "Wages and the Word," 45.

55 Sklar and Sherry, "Wages and the Word," 45.

56 Peter Morales and Bill Schulz, "Joint Statement on Raising the Minimum Wage: A Moral Imperative," Press Release, Unitarian Universalist Association, 2013,

http://www.uua.org/pressroom/press-releases/joint-statement-raising-minimum-wagemoral-imperative, accessed August 20, 2020.

57 Fosu, "Inequality, Income, and Poverty," 2010, 4.

58 Sarlo, "Poverty."

59 Robert D. Spender, "Poor and Poverty, Theology of" in Walter A. Elwell ed., Baker's Evangelical Dictionary of Biblical Theology (Grand Rapids: Baker Books, 1996), https://www.studylight.org/dictionaries/eng/bed/p/poor-and-poverty-theology-of.html, accessed April 4, 2021.

60 D. E. Stedman, *God's Message to all People* (Katunayake: New Life Literature, 1999), 303.

61 Sklar and Sherry, "Wages and the Word," 45.

62 Jack Moline, *Labor on the Bimah: A Special Resource for Synagogues* (Chicago: National Interfaith Committee for Worker Justice, 2000), 3.

63 Hussam Ayloush, *Labor in the Minbar: Muslim Readings and Prayers* (Chicago: National Interfaith Committee for Worker Justice, 2000), 1.

64 Ayloush, "Muslim Readings and Prayers," 1.

65 Ayloush, "Muslim Readings and Prayers," 1.

66 Narada Thera, trans., "Sigalovada Sutta: The Discourse to Sigala, DN 31," *Access to Insight* (November 2013), https://www.accesstoinsight.org/tipitaka/dn/dn.31.0.nara.html, accessed August 20, 2020.

67 Thera, "Sigalovada Sutta."

68 United Nations, "Transforming Our World: The 2030 Agenda for Sustainable Development," sustainabledevelopment.un.org A/RES/70/1, accessed March 24, 2021.

II
Cases in Context

8 Beyond Liberation Theology and Prosperity Gospel: A Third Way

César García

Abstract:

This chapter[1] addresses the issue of poverty from the perspective of the Anabaptist Tradition.[2] How have Anabaptists taken up poverty as an essential mission issue? How do they distinguish themselves in their response to poverty in contrast to other Christian Traditions? What insights does their perspective bring to the broader Christian discussion on this topic today? What is the role of the Holy Spirit in motivating the Anabaptist response? These and other questions will be addressed here from the perspective of a Latin American Mennocostal.[3]

Introduction

One of the most disturbing experiences for many pastors in Colombia is to be identified as a Christian minister. Someone once asked me, "Are you a pastor?" "That's right," I nervously responded. As I feared, the immediate response was, "Then you rob people of their money! You likely have a brand-new car, a very luxurious house, and many bodyguards to protect you from everyone else, right? Tell me, what else do you do besides getting rich and abuse others?" Ouch! How could I respond in the face of the overwhelming abundance of cases that support the validity of such claims and line of questioning?

Unfortunately, there are many Colombians who have been cheated and hurt by ministers in Christian congregations. Somebody even said to me recently that the prosperity gospel in Colombia only works for pastors. Why is this issue of money and church so crucial in Colombia? Understanding some realities of the Colombian context may give us some insight.

Colombian Context

Amnesia is a hallmark of the Colombian people, who have an immense need to forget and escape their reality. *"Colombia se derrumba y nosotros de rumba*" (while Colombia collapses, we party) is a popular saying that sums up the tendency to want to ignore the suffering that afflicts us. Sports, soap operas, and beauty pageants are some ways how we try to escape our context as Colombians.[4]

The leading Latin American historian, Marco Palacios, explains that "Colombia offers one of the worst pictures of income distribution in Latin America, and therefore the world."[5] Economic inequality, political exclusion, and land distribution are historical problems that afflict Colombia. Shortly after gaining independence in 1810, the country's elites—descendants of the Spanish *conquistadores*—secured control over virtually all political and economic power. These traditional political parties have continued to dominate the elections in Colombia. This has allowed the same families of elites to hold on to their positions of privilege and power.[6]

This pattern of political inequality and economic injustice has truncated opportunities for development by the Colombian people, resulting in heightened levels of social conflict, frustration, and desperation. Colombian cities have large areas of illegal settlements where people exist in subhuman conditions. Meanwhile, the rural areas have traditionally suffered from total neglect by the government. These obstacles, plus the lack of opportunities, have been one of the reasons for the formation of revolutionary and guerilla groups since the middle of the last century.[7]

Thousands of political leaders have been assassinated over the last fifty years, and millions of people have been displaced. According to the National Historical Memory Centre, more than sixty thousand people have disappeared in violent ways.[8] However, it is important to note that violence is not limited to armed conflict. Violence permeates every sphere of society in domestic relationships (e.g., the violent discipline of children and spousal abuse), schools (e.g., gangs, bullying), business (e.g., emotional and power abuse), and politics (e.g., violent polarization and offensive political speech). The frequent massacres and assassination of social leaders and human rights activists amplify this reality.

Therefore, in this context, many people use churches as an escape mechanism. In the same way of movies, beauty pageants, and sports, worship services, and other religious activities work as a distraction; a vehicle to forget the immense suffering caused by violence. This situation gets even worst when, according to the Colombian Catholic theologian Jaime Laurence Bonilla, the response to the suffering and needs of others in countless churches is one of indifference.[9] With few exceptions, the megachurches of the large cities have no social programs and do not provide support to people in extreme need.[10] They give little if any attention to issues of social justice. The first change in one's life that these churches frequently promise is instant financial success. Yet, this promise is for individual success that does not take into account the importance of holistic transformation for the person and their immediate environment.

The Pew Research Center explains: "When asked what they think is the most important way for Christians to help the poor, Catholics in nearly every Latin American country point most often to charity work. By contrast, pluralities of Protestants in many countries say that 'bringing the poor and needy to Christ' is the most important way to help."[11] This understanding of the church's role concerning society results in delegating the church's responsibility to charity agencies, spiritualizing that responsibility, and even supporting political parties without being aware that these political organizations may ignore or even contradict Christian values. I have described so far a typical protestant, evangelical, and Pentecostal response to poverty in Colombia that is even worse when it takes place under the framework of the so-called "prosperity gospel." Let me then detail this a bit more.

Two Ways
Prosperity Gospel
This way of doing theology has led churches to numerical success in Colombia. Churches that promote a gospel of prosperity have become an important religious force in the country. However, this approach has several problems. First, the use of marketing strategies has given a consumerist flavor to this movement. It offers an individualistic gospel that helps Colombians avoid their context of violence and suffering.

Second, the pursuit of social justice is almost non-existent in the majority of churches that use this theological method. They do not preach the necessity of changing our present situation based on the future that God reveals as his will for the human race. The only change they offer is individual, egocentric, and immediate financial growth, without the possibility of a new integral beginning for the community based on the new creation. In this way, a prophetic voice is reduced to predictive Biblical prophecy and moralistic messages against abortion, immoral sexuality, etc.

Finally, this methodology's strong personal leadership style emphasizes the Colombian *caudillismo*, ignoring the biblical concept of servant-leader. In these churches, hierarchical structures are so strong that they resemble military patterns of obedience to their leaders.[12] They do not accept criticism of leadership. Leaders are considered to have a privileged position before God, which makes him or her untouchable. As a consequence, anarchy and fragmentation have been common in these movements.

Argentinian theologian René Padilla, argues that these churches have adopted the "mass empire" culture, since they use business strategies and marketing techniques to reach their numerical goals, offering material prosperity, making people feel good, and emphasizing entertainment.[13] Thus, these churches tend to measure God's presence in an individual by his or her capacity to consume. For that reason, these churches pursue the same objectives as Colombian consumerist society, such as having a nice car, fine clothes, and a great education.[14] Preaching a prosperity gospel is not the only way Colombian churches respond to poverty issues in their context. Some churches have promoted Liberation Theology. However, this approach to poverty also brings its challenges.

Liberation Theology

Liberation Theology is a distinct form of theology, with Latin American origins in the 1960s and 1970s. It is oriented toward the poor and oppressed, affirming that God is on the side of the poor. Liberation Theology calls for critical reflection on praxis, asserting that real knowledge of God comes in and through a commitment to the cause of the poor.[15]

This way of doing theology is apparently very relevant in Colombia. Its emphasis on memory may help Colombians not to forget the tragedies of murders and injustices and to work for the transformation of these realities. Because this methodology prioritizes experience above knowledge, it is very attractive for people who are searching for authentic new life and values. Furthermore, in a country with such inequity, the call for justice and economic balance is more than necessary; it is a Christian imperative.

Among the contributions of this theological style in the Colombian context, we might mention: its stress on praxis as the point of departure for theology; its focus on the poor and suffering, which emphasizes the importance of a social and prophetic gospel; its call for the hermeneutic of obedience as a condition to understand the Scriptures.

However, I find significant weaknesses in Liberation Theology. For example, the personal dimension in our relationship with God is sometimes lost in Liberation Theology, but this is very important in the Colombian context. Even though some liberation theologians such as Gustavo Gutiérrez have tried to add a spiritual emphasis in their work, in Colombia, Liberation Theology, as practiced by some churches with a liberal inclination, tends to diminish the necessity of spiritual or mystical experiences.

Liberation Theology is a captive of the Constantinian synthesis[16] because it assumes that it is possible to bring justice only by changing political structures, which presupposes the Christianization of the state through revolution. In opposition to this, I prefer to believe in local communities where justice and equality are possible in the voluntary and personal decision to follow Jesus. I will get back to this issue later. In Colombia, this theology has developed a rational emphasis that is characteristic of the socialist, Marxist positions.[17] In addition to the focus on praxis that this method embodies, Colombian churches also borrow an ideological platform from Marxist philosophy to justify their work. That requires a socialist and philosophical knowledge that sounds foreign to most of the Colombian poor, many of whom lack access to education. In this oral and visual culture, Liberation Theology does not engage Colombian culture as successfully as the Pentecostal movements do.

In Colombia, a theological style that only looks for justice without emphasizing forgiveness and reconciliation is not adequately relevant to the people. Moreover, it can be harmful in our context of conflict and violence. This method places the pursuit of freedom and the struggle for justice at the center of the Christian social agenda. This approach, in the words of the Croatian Anglican theologian, Miroslav Volf, is favored by some Christian activist groups. Volf affirms:

> Such groups have effectively left the message of reconciliation to otherworldly "pietists" and taken up the pursuit of liberation as the most appropriate response to social problems. The process of reconciliation between

persons and peoples, they believe, can commence only after liberation is accomplished; peace will be established only after justice is done.

The pursuit of liberation and the struggle for justice are indispensable; they are integral to Christian social responsibility. But if they are understood as tasks preceding the process of reconciliation and independent of it, rather than as indispensable aspects of a more overarching agenda of reconciliation, they are beset with two major problems. First, designating liberation and justice as the primary categories of Christian social responsibility divorces the character of social engagement from the very center of the Christian faith—from the narrative of the cross of Christ, which reveals the character of the triune God. On the cross of Jesus Christ, God is manifest as the God who, though in no way indifferent toward the distinction between good and evil, nonetheless lets the sun shine on both the good and the evil, the God of infinite and indiscriminate love who died for the ungodly in order to bring them into divine communion, the God who offers grace to the vilest evildoer and justifies the unjust.

Second, the primary stress on liberation is suited only to situations of manifest evil in which one side is unambiguously the victim—in the right—and the other unambiguously the perpetrator—therefore in the wrong. Most situations, however, are not so clean. Especially in conflicts with a longer history, each party, for good reasons, sees itself as the victim and perceives its rival as the perpetrator. As a consequence, each side can see itself as engaged in the struggle for liberation. If social responsibility is organized around liberation, the Christian faith ends up dangerously reducing the moral complexity of the situation and feeding into the self-righteousness of each party by assuring them that God is on their side. The primary role of the Christian faith is then to motivate and legitimize the struggle. Reconciliation is not even attempted—at least not until "our" side has won. Unless liberation has been integrated into the larger agenda of reconciliation, it becomes unclear why reconciliation should be attempted after victory. [18]

A Third Way

Challenges related to poverty are, of course, older than either the prosperity gospel or Liberation Theology. Catholic and Orthodox churches were responding to these issues for one thousand five hundred years before the Reformation and have continued doing so until today. However, I would like to focus on how Anabaptism—a movement that started in the sixteenth century as part of the Reformation—has responded. This movement is represented today by Mennonites, Brethren in Christ, and other Anabaptist groups that share the same historical roots with what is known as the Radical Reformation.

For the Anabaptists of the sixteenth century, the response of faith led immediately to fellowship in a community of believers through baptism. The voluntary decision to follow Christ was demonstrated through baptism, which was, simultaneously, the point of entry into the church. "The doctrine of the church was central to Anabaptist theology. The church was to be the visible body of Christ," explains the Anabaptist historian Arnold Snyder.[19] Of course, that implied that the church consisted of believers who had voluntarily decided to form a new community.

This way of understanding Christian faith and church required the existence of freedom to make religious choices. It also implied that there would be people who would choose not to follow the Christian way. To ensure the presence of the church, there must be freedom and the possibility of saying "no" to the Christian faith, Christian values, and a Christian lifestyle. Without liberty and a guarantee of freely living out decisions about faith, there won't be a true church.

In contexts like Colombia, our churches need to recover this vision. We often find people speaking about Colombia as a "Christian" country or promoting the approval of laws that reflect Christian values but are oppressive for people who do not share the same convictions. Although Christians are called to promote morality in society, this cannot be done by imposing Christian values over others. Otherwise, the freedom of Christians to practice Christian values could be threatened if the majority of society were not Christian.

Safeguarding the freedom of all minorities guarantees the freedom of Christians as well. That is a reason why I do not share the idea of imposing economic, social justice from the top-down as Liberation Theology proposes it. The concept of redistribution of wealth has to be a voluntary decision lived out practically in the new creation known as the church. Generosity, economic self-denial, and sacrificial giving for the sake of the community must be the result of personal conviction and the work of the Holy Spirit in the new believer.

Anabaptists understood that, according to the book of Acts, a consequence of been filled with the Holy Spirit is financial sharing in the community of the Spirit. In addition to prophecy, miracles, and other mystical experiences, a life of generosity and sharing of wealth has to be a fruit of the Spirit. Only God's presence can overcome the natural human tendency towards egocentrism and self-satisfaction. Only God's presence overcomes consumerism and materialism, creating, in that way, an alternative community to the society.

Anabaptists in the sixteenth century opposed the idea of a unified Christian state, pointing instead to the need for a new society—a voluntary society—which, in contrast to a secular society, would show without coercion God's will for humanity according to the Christian faith. Part of that will have to do with giving generously out of love and self-denial for the poor's wellbeing and not giving out of self-interest or the search for financial blessings.

In the words of the American Baptist historian, William R. Estep, "The Anabaptists were not interested in constructing a church through coercion, either by infant baptism or by the power of the magistrate (*Obrigkeit*). . . . They were concerned with gathering a church of believers who had freely responded to the proclamation of the gospel."[20] This way of thinking rejects the idea of depending on human governments to promote Christianity or looking for ways of getting legal, religious privileges over others.

According to the Mennonite theologian John Howard Yoder, "The primary social structure through which the gospel works to change other structures is that of the Christian community."[21] It is the church—not just local but also global—that is called to be an alternative community, which, by its existence and practice of mutual financial support, denounces injustice and inequity. The Christian church does so by living out a new kingdom of justice and bringing hope when it demonstrates that a new and different society is possible in dependence on the Holy Spirit.

Only if economic and financial differences are overcome in the church will we have anything to say on this matter to the societies that surround us.[22] As long as indifference or individualism instead of interdependency is daily realities among our churches, we will not be effective in our advocacy or support for those who suffer. As long as the church relies on Christian politicians to promote their religious values, and oppresses minorities by imposing Christian values, societies like Colombia will continue rejecting the message of a crucified God who invites us—without coercion—to love God and love each other. Therefore, an Anabaptist response to poverty today can be characterized as follows.

A Center-on-God Response

As a church, we want to follow the words of the apostle Paul that served as a base for Anabaptist leaders: "For no one can lay any foundation other than the one that has been laid; that foundation is Jesus Christ" (1 Cor 3:11). Our actions as a church are done as the body of Christ, in the spirit of following and imitating his character and life. The church depends on the Holy Spirit rather than on secular achievements.

Any support we offer to those in suffering must be motived by God's love and Jesus' focus on the vulnerable in society; those who are victims of systemic injustice and violence.[23] As the experts in Human Rights and religion, John Witte and Frank Alexander affirm, "the Bible is fundamentally concerned about the poor, the widow, the orphan, the sojourner, and the needy in our midst."[24]

Our undoing of injustice, or better, our pursuit of justice, begins in God's heart. It is the fruit of our communion and relationship with him. Once we love God above all things, the love for our neighbor comes naturally. It is impossible to love God and to ignore who he loves at the same time. "I, the Lord, love justice!" says Isaiah 61:8. Economic justice cannot be built without God, and it is not possible to proclaim God without doing justice.[25] The experience of God is inseparable from a commitment to justice. "God is over and over characterized as just, as doing justice, and as loving justice,"[26] states the American philosopher and liturgical theologian Nicholas Wolterstorff.

It is love for justice that motivated Jesus to protest injustice and hypocrisy and to call for social change.[27] It is love for justice that served as a base for biblical passages that demanded justice from rulers in the Old Testament: "As we see in Psalm 72, the good king delivers the needy, defends the cause of the poor, and saves the weak and needy from oppression and violence,"[28] says Wolterstorff. It is love for justice that made Jesus' life of action more than mere advocacy on behalf of oppressed humanity. It is love that motivated Jesus to give up all of his advantages to secure the final benefit of those he came to serve.[29] As the German martyr Dietrich Bonhoeffer affirmed through his life and thought, one's Christology and ethics are inseparable.[30]

A Center-on-the-Church Response

As stated above, Anabaptists affirm the centrality of the church in God's strategic plan of social transformation. As the theologian Stanley Hauerwas says, "this church knows that its most credible form of witness (and the most 'effective' thing it can do for the world) is the actual creation of a living, breathing, visible community of faith."[31] As we can see in the scriptures with the creation of Israel, the biblical method of social transformation had to do with the formation of an alternative society that lives out a new way of ethics and values that—like a magnet—would attract others (Deut 4:5–8). In the words of the Mennonite theologian Alain Epp Weaver, "by embodying an alternative way of life through faithful practices, the people of Israel attract others to God's vision of shalom for the world."[32]

It follows that this social ethic of transformation has to do more with a communal witness embodied by God's people than with a top-down exercise of power, control, and imposition. That may be a reason why Jesus, in his use of the Scriptures, identified himself with Daniel more than with King David—with the Israel of the Exile more than with Israel's kingdom.[33]

Israel's tradition of wisdom, nonconformity, and mission in exile was the preferred model used by Jesus, rather than the monarchy or the exodus. The Israel of the exile was a people without land or nationalism. It was a community of displaced people, a confessional community more than a political kingdom. In this context, Israel becomes a resistant community with a strong identity that has many important lessons for the church in this post-Constantinian era. It was a community that shared their financial needs, taking care of the poor that lived in their midst, and practicing mutual generosity and communal financial support. Living and offering a real social alternative is the way of survival in our current consumerist Babylon.

Jesus' example invites us to look for ways of transforming our societies from the bottom upwards. "The world cannot be set right from the top,"[34] says Yoder. It requires the witness of a vulnerable community that is not in charge of financial resources, that exercises a radical dependence on God alone. As Yoder affirms, "those who . . . seek to gain power in order to implement their religious vision have chosen (probably consciously) a strategy hardly reconcilable with that of the New Testament church."[35]

The centrality of community in the Mennonite faith experience leads to a new society and an alternative to promoting individualism. Relationships in this community are marked by compassion and forgiveness, as witnessed in the person of Jesus. That also leads us to care about the needs of those around us, whether they belong to our community or not. In contexts such as Colombia, Mennonites not only offer an alternative society, they are also actively involved in the search for society's wellbeing in general, understanding this as part of their witness to God's love for the world.

A Center-on-the-Poor Response

Concerning social development ministries, Anabaptists in Colombia have embraced a preferential option for the poor. Most congregations in this country can be found amid vulnerable populations located in low-income areas. Many of them are made up of people who have been displaced by the violence or have been directly affected by the civil war that has plagued Colombia for over five decades. Colombian Mennonites have founded church agencies that specialize in community development. Even so, the social responsibility of churches continues to be lived out via soup kitchens, free education, microloans, cooperatives, senior care, etc., that they provide in their communities. They cultivate the gift of service and seek to involve the whole community in social service, especially during times of natural disaster. Mennonites in Colombia understand that all social work is rooted in a personal relationship with God, that the Holy Spirit guides it, and that the goal is to bless people in need regardless of whether they accept Christ or not, and to offer this service without promoting a specific church.

Colombian Anabaptists frame their ministry in terms of a theology of the cross, where they depend on the presence of the Holy Spirit to reject the drive to accumulate wealth and the dominance of money that is present in consumerist societies. Mennonites understand that all they have are God-given gifts that, first and foremost, are to be used for the wellbeing of the community. The simplicity that Jesus preached through his life continues to be a relevant challenge in contexts marked by economic inequity, such as Colombia.

The examples that I have mentioned from Colombia are also present on a global scale. Mennonites in Paraguay are well known for their cooperatives and credit unions. Anabaptists in the USA and Canada have developed banks, cooperatives, social development agencies, and health organizations that benefit their communities and societies.[36] In Africa, Asia, and Europe, there are countless ministries of service that express generosity and love for the poor in local congregations and secular societies.

Conclusion

According to Mennonite theologian John Driver, the gospel of salvation in the New Testament comes to us from a position of socioeconomic and political weakness rather than a position of economic affluence and human power.[37] That implies that our mission, if it has Jesus as its center, must be framed by the form and content of Christ's message.

According to 2 Cor 5:17–19, "if anyone is in Christ, there is a new creation." It is in this sense that Driver reminds us, "The church not only proclaims the kingdom of God, but also is the community of the kingdom, anticipation (modest but authentic) of the kingdom."[38] In the church, the new creation, the *eschaton*, has already begun. Therefore, the church is called to live—here and now—in a new paradigm of life, this is, according to God's will for the world, as it was evidenced in Jesus' words and life. This new life implies a radical departure from secular values that glorify egocentrism, consumerism, and social class separation. Churches must be recognized by their generosity, compassion, simple life, and service to the poor rather, than by the abuse of power or accumulation of wealth.

Churches need to offer an alternative community to the societies of this world where refugees, displaced, immigrants, and other unprivileged minorities are welcomed and treated with the dignity that God has given to us as humans. The world needs to see churches that do not ignore realities of violence and poverty; churches that practice reconciliation and forgiveness among enemies; churches that experience financial equity by the joyful, voluntary, and creative sharing of possessions through programs or entities of mutual aid.

I pray for a church able to be salt and light in places of financial inequality and poverty. I pray for a church to which the world may look in its search for alternatives to end injustice. Let's be that church, built on the power and dependence on the Holy Spirit.

Notes

1. Parts of this article appeared in my essay, "Mennocostals in a Contextual Way," in Martin William Mittelstadt and Brian K. Pipkin, eds., *Mennocostals: Pentecostal and Mennonite Stories of Convergence* (Eugene, Oregon: Pickwick, 2020), 1–13; and "Perspectives on the Reformation and its Impact on Freedom of Thought and Conscience from a Mennonite Perspective," in Bettina Krause ed., *A Conversation on the Reformation, Christian Identity, & Freedom of Conscience: A Commemoration of the 500-year Anniversary of the Protestant Reformation* (Public Affairs & Religious Liberty, General Conference of Seventh-day Adventists, Silver Spring, MD, 2017), 40–47.

2. I grew up in Colombia and served as a pastor in that context. I now serve as the General Secretary of Mennonite World Conference, a global communion of Anabaptist-related churches representing 107 national churches, comprising 10,000 local congregations in approximately sixty countries.

3. Today, many descendants of the Anabaptist movement of the sixteenth century may be identified as Mennocostals. "Mennocostal" – Pentecostal Mennonites – is the best characterization of the majority of Anabaptists in the Majority World today. Martin William Mittelstadt first used "Mennocostal" in his writing "My Life as Menno-costal: A Personal and Theological Narrative," in Paul Alexander, ed., *Pentecostals and Nonviolence: Reclaiming a Heritage* (Eugene, OR: Wipf and Stock, 2012), 316–334. "Majority World" refers to what in other contexts might be called the Global South. The "Majority World" includes Asian and European countries that do not strictly belong to the Global South geographically but would if considered from an infrastructure and economic position.

4. Marco Palacios, *Between Legitimacy and Violence: A History of Colombia, 1875–2002* (Durham: Duke University Press, 2006), 239.

5. Palacios, *Between Legitimacy and Violence*, 218.

6. Thomas E. Skidmore and Peter H. Smith, *Modern Latin America*, 6th ed. (New York: Oxford University Press, 2005), 253.

7. Álvaro Camacho Guizado and Alberto Valencia Gutiérrez, *Álvaro Camacho Guizado: Violencia y Conflicto en Colombia* (Bogotá: Universidad de los Andes, 2014), 268.

8. Centro Nacional de Memoria Histórica, *Hasta Encontrarlos: El Drama de la Desaparición Forzada en Colombia* (Bogotá: CNMH, 2016), 74.

9. Jaime Laurence Bonilla, "Teología de la Prosperidad, Neoliberalismo, y Esperanza Cristiana," in Andrés Eduardo González Santos, ed., *Memorias Primer Congreso Internacional:Diversidad y Dinámicas del Cristianismo en América Latina* (Bogotá: Editorial Bonaventuriana, 2007), 153.

10 William Mauricio Beltran Cely, *De Microempresas Religiosas a Multinacionales de la Fe: La Diversificación del Cristianismo en Bogotá* (Bogotá: Universidad de San Buenaventura, 2006), 190.

11 "Religion in Latin America," Pew Research Center, November 13, 2014, http://www.pewforum.org/2014/11/13/religion-in-latin-america/, accessed November 22, 2016.

12 Beltran Cely, *De Microempresas Religiosas a Multinacionales de la Fe*, 199.

13 Milton Acosta, "Power Pentecostalisms: The 'non-Catholic' Latin American Church is Going Full Steam Ahead—But Are We on the Right tTack?," *Christianity Today* (August 2009), 40–42.

14 Ana María Bidegaín Greising and Juan Diego Demera Vargas, eds., *Globalización y Diversidad Religiosa en Colombia* (Bogotá: Universidad Nacional de Colombia, Facultad de Ciencias Humanas, 2005), 277.

15 lister E. McGrath, *Christian Theology: An Introduction*, 25th Anniversary, 6 ed. (Malden, MA: Wiley Blackwell, 2017), 74–75.

16 "Constantinian synthesis" is the period (represented in several generations) in which the church became identified with the power structure of its context. It is related to the emperor Constantine's time in the fourth century, when the church passed from being a persecuted minority to the empire's religion. It implied a change in ecclesiology, eschatology, and Christian social ethic. See John Howard Yoder, *The Priestly Kingdom* (Notre Dame, IN: University of Notre Dame, 1984), 135–147.

17 Jean-Pierre Bastian, "Pentecostalismos Latinoamericanos: Lógicas de Mercado y Transnacionalización Religiosa," in Ana María Bidegaín Greising and Juan Diego Demera Vargas, eds., Globalización y Diversidad Religiosa en Colombia, Colección Sede, (Bogotá: Universidad Nacional de Colombia, Facultad de Ciencias Humanas, 2005), 341.

18 Miroslav Volf, "The Social Meaning of Reconciliation," *Interpretation: A Journal of Bible & Theology* 54:2 (2000), 162–163.

19 Arnold Snyder, *Anabaptist History and Theology* (Kitchener, Canada: Pandora Press, 1997), 155.

20 William Roscoe Estep, *The Anabaptist Story: An Introduction to Sixteenth-Century Anabaptism*, 3rd ed. (Grand Rapids: Eerdmans, 1996), 245.

21 John Howard Yoder, *The Politics of Jesus: Vicit Agnus Noster*, 2nd ed. (Grand Rapids: Eerdmans, 1994), 154.

22 Yoder, *The Politics of Jesus*, 150–151.

23 C. Norman Kraus, *The Jesus Factor in Justice and Peacemaking* (Telford, PA: Cascadia, 2011), 113.

24 John Witte and Frank S. Alexander, *Christianity and Human Rights: An Introduction* (Cambridge: Cambridge University Press, 2010), 320.

25 Rafael Gutiérrez Cuervo, *Cristología y Moral: El Seguimiento de Jesucristo Como Compromiso con la Justicia* (Bogotá: Pontificia Universidad Javeriana, Facultad de Teología, 2004), 93–94.

26 Nicholas Wolterstorff, "Seeking Justice in Hope," in Miroslav Volf and William H. Katerberg eds., *The Future of Hope: Christian Tradition Amid Modernity and Postmodernity* (Grand Rapids, MI: Eerdmans, 2004), 85.

27 Kraus, *The Jesus Factor in Justice and Peacemaking*, 117.

28 Wolterstorff, "Seeking Justice in Hope," 89.

29 Witte and Alexander, *Christianity and Human Rights*, 324.

30 Dietrich Bonhoeffer, *Ética*, trans. Lluís Duch (Madrid: Trotta, 2000), 23.

31 Stanley Hauerwas and William H. Willimon, *Resident Aliens: Life in the Christian Colony* (Nashville: Abingdon Press, 1989), 47.

32 Alain Epp Weaver, *States of Exile: Visions of Diaspora, Witness, and Return* (Scottdale, PA: Herald Press, 2008), 33.

33 Jesus used the term 'Son of Man' as his favored description for himself, eighty-three times in the New Testament. He used this rather than 'Son of David,' which was a title given to Jesus by others and associated with hierarchy and royalty. The term 'Son of Man' located him in the Daniel tradition (see Daniel 7).

34 Yoder, *The Politics of Jesus*, 151.

35 John Howard Yoder, *The Christian Witness to the State* (Scottdale, PA: Herald Press, 2002), 27.

36 One example of these institutions is Everence. See John D. Roth, *Where the People Go: Community, Generosity, and the Story of Everence* (Harrisonburg, VA: Herald Press, 2020).

37 John Driver, "Messianic Evangelization," in Wilbert R. Shenk, ed., *The Transfiguration of Mission: Biblical, Theological & Historical Foundations* (Scottdale, PA: Herald Press, 1993), 200.

38 John Driver, *Contra Corriente: Ensayo Sobre Eclesiología Radical*, 3. ed. (Santafé de Bogotá, Colombia: CLARA, 1998), xv.

9   The Aimara Identity of Poor Neo-Pentecostals in Urban La Paz, Bolivia

Marcelo Vargas

Abstract

Neo-Pentecostal experience has a profound effect on the life of the Power of God Church (PoG) affiliates while mirroring deep-rooted features of Aimara cultural tradition. Innovative interaction of these two convenes a new identity. Their new identity is still predominantly Aimara. Indigenous worldview exerts a permanent influence, but neo-Pentecostal Christianity has significantly influenced identity and worldview in urban Aimara places. They have incorporated both radical change and continuity into their indigenous lifestyle and identity because they are not moved by the conflict of bipolarity but by their three-dimensional logic, that is, their way of perceiving reality and determining how they relate with the supernatural both of Aimara and neo-Pentecostal beliefs.

Introduction

An interactive encounter of meanings is taking place in the La Paz religious scene, where the Power of God (PoG) Church makes use of its flourishing marketing style, with practices adapted to both old and new, urban and Aimara cultures.[1] This meeting of meanings creates conflict and generates new identities. For Aimara neo-Pentecostals, this new identity involves new beliefs, while maintaining indigenous elements, synthesized rituals, contextual social relationships, and re-interpreted ethical norms. Pentecostalism has become a socio-religious expression that questions the traditional hegemonic monopoly of the goods of salvation and social and cultural behavior up to this point in history, both by those who have adopted institutional Catholicism mixed with Aimara animism and by conservative evangelical protestants. Marginalized urban populations in La Paz are turning to different religious practices, creating a heterogeneous religious scenario.

Pentecostalism in Latin America has been described as the Protestant version of populist Catholic religiosity.[2] It is populist not only because it attracts the poor but also because it molds people's day-to-day way of life.

The growth and influence of neo-Pentecostalism in Bolivia occur in the midst of increased poverty for millions of people who are finding that the neo-Pentecostal church apparently identifies with their world of suffering and their socio-religious world. If the role of fiestas or festivals within populist urban Catholicism is looked at, it can be found that they fulfill a dual function. While being an outward expression of devotion to a "saint" or "virgin," they are also a mechanism for promoting someone within the social hierarchy. In other words, these religious *fiestas* are a mechanism for identifying and integrating the inhabitants of a given area while also allowing the wealthy social elite to show off their social, cultural, and economic superiority. Work-related *fiestas* serve to recreate the identity of those who have immigrated to large cities. On studying the syncretism of *fiestas*, Xavier Albó distinguishes between a religious syncretism linked with Andean tradition and another type of syncretism related to power groups. Writing about the first, he says:

> Just as it is difficult to distinguish Christian aspects within the fiesta, it is also complicated to isolate the purely Andean elements that have been transformed or neutralized by two complementary factors: the historical factor of their Christianization and the more recent urbanization factor. [3]

Populist Catholicism, therefore, combines beliefs and rituals, integrating and adapting traditional Catholic and Aimara values to powerfully attract the urban multitudes of the city of La Paz, as expressed in *fiestas*. It promotes socioeconomic structures based on the form and logic of reciprocities associated with power, affection, rights, and obligations. It influences family, kinship models, the rules that govern friendship, traditional unionism, and the relationship between neighbors, following a concept closely linked to past and present countryman religious practice. In doing so, it redefines and rebuilds identity.

While some tend to relate Pentecostalism to urban modernity, seeing conversion to a new religion as an effective means for adopting a Western lifestyle, others see it as an idealized reconstruction of traditional, indigenous society.[4] In other words, for the uprooted, disorientated masses attempting to build new socio-cultural patterns in cities, Pentecostalism offers a substitute community that offers effective answers and solutions for the construction of a new identity. However, instead of separating the trend towards modernity from the trend towards the traditional indigenous world, Pentecostal practice and message have both elements of continuity and discontinuity with people's forms of cultural and religious expression.

What, then, are the characteristics of neo-Pentecostalism that explain its identity and work? What is happening specifically in the PoG Church? This Neo-Pentecostal form of Bolivian Pentecostalism is operating mainly in urbanized sectors of La Paz that are poor and marginalized, who have strong indigenous roots. The poor people who attend the PoG in La Paz live in areas where life is precarious and, in recent years, has become even more insecure and worthless. How does the church handle the daily challenges faced by its members and leaders?

Power of God Church in Cultural Context

> Pentecostalism, rather than being a doctrine, proposes a particularly intense experience of God, capable of offering a "road to salvation" – new meaning to life – radically different from the biographic opportunities offered by society in general. . . . It opens doors to an experience of God, without the need for mediation. . . . It communicates a known, verbal and non-verbal language. . . .The subject being announced is also a man of the people. . . . It is nourished by the incorporation of a community of people that shares the experience and celebrates it in affective, effective solidarity with new believers. [5]

The context of the people and the church is peculiar to the majority in the biggest city in the indigenous and poor country. Located in the busiest, highly populated area of La Paz, with high demographic density, the PoG's main arena for generating a harvest for its evangelizing work is the *La Casa de Dios in Riosiño* square. This area is in the northwestern hillside of the Bolivian capital city, distinguished as the most densely populated area. This area is also home to participants of *Señor del Gran Poder Fiesta*, the main religious expression of populist Catholicism, held annually in May.[6] The parallelism between the names of the church, "Power of God," the geographic area, "Great Power," and the well-liked, urban catholic *fiesta* name, "Lord of Great Power," are probably not a coincidence, but reveal a prevalent thread that unites cultural, religious, geographic, and social aspects of the Aimara people who live in this context.

The PoG's favorite action ground is the *Gran Poder* area. People come from many different poor neighborhoods to attend the meetings. Very needy social sectors; a neglected, abandoned population; a context marked by crisis, conflict, and contrasts, with low-income levels, precarious employment, limited access to basic services – this is the reality lived in this part of La Paz, and, in turn, by the congregation.

Power of God Worship Service Experience

The first of the six Sunday services held in the PoG (Power of God) start early, just as the life of the Aimara people living in La Paz and the Sunday street sellers in the *Gran Poder* area begin before dawn. The main church building is open while it is still dark, its doors opening to allow the people already arriving at 4:30 a.m. A worship and praise time starts before 6:00 a.m., by which time the building is packed with standing room only. In fact, the building is set up for the congregation to stand to allow the maximum number of people to attend each service. Four rows of seats are laid out on the right-hand side of the colorful building, earmarked for the elderly and those in poor health. Otherwise, people stand throughout the services, which usually last for over three hours. The most popular service with both congregation and pastor is the early Sunday morning service.

Here, the soloist who leads the music gradually moves from quiet invitations to worship, to more lively praise songs set to rhythms based on Latin pop, then, to Bolivian and Colombian *cumbia*-style music, the singing growing increasingly louder and more effusive. This progressive preparation lasts for ninety to one hundred and twenty minutes, building up to the moment of Pastor Guachalla's appearance. His arrival is the focal point of everyone's attention. It signals the beginning of two of the most important parts of the service: the appeal for tithes and offerings and the delivery of the message.

During the last half-hour of the praise time, about fifty uniformed ushers, both men and women, stand with their backs to the stage like a squadron of soldiers. They line up, ready for their work to begin as soon as the pastor appears. Fifty ushers are quite a high percentage for a congregation of five to six hundred, but their role is to move through the untidy rows of people, passing out the blessed offering and tithe envelopes printed with the church logo and motto, making sure that no one refuses to receive one.

Pastor Guachalla's church motto is a short phrase taken from the Bible, which he sprinkles liberally throughout his appeals and sermons, often in crescendo tones, like a talisman capable of stirring the congregation to feverish heights. "Because nothing is impossible for God," the pastor says. "Because nothing is impossible for God," the congregation repeats effusively.

The pastor adorns his motto with phrases that create a collective sense of comfort, excitement, stupor, and absence of any critical spirit. The church building appears to become the only place on earth for the congregation, and the pastor knows he has them where he wants them.

The pastor knows from experience that by eight o'clock in the morning, he has prepared the ground for his malleable flock. He subsequently moves straight to the point; he asks them for their offerings using two symbols from the Aimara worldview — reciprocity and retribution for the *yatiri* or traditional religious healer.[7] At this crucial point in the Sunday morning services, he makes use of the practices of this Aimara religious agent to ask for cash contributions from the church members. He ties the giving of offerings to the people's understanding of native cultural performances.

One member is already waiting near the platform to be invited to join the pastor, who then embraces him and commends him for his offering of one thousand United States dollars (USD). The pastor has the money in his right-hand pocket, and he now takes it out, holds it in the air, then counts the green notes slowly one by one: "100, 200, 300 . . . 800, 900, 1000."

Pastor Guachalla then tells the congregation: "For his generosity, this brother will receive a crown of gold in heaven. Do you want to receive a crown of gold? Or maybe one of tin or, even worse, one of paper?" He asks them how much they plan to give this morning, then asks them to give more. He teases them, urging them to give more if they do not want the congregation to laugh at their crown. He warns that the donor of one thousand U. S. dollars will laugh from his seat in heaven on seeing that they do not have a golden prize. With his words, his mimicry, and through using different types of voice, the pastor now has everyone laughing. The message is clear: the more you give to the PoG, the more you will receive under the Aimara principle of reciprocity. The more you give to the church, the more you will receive from God. This is the backbone of the Aimara communal and religious cultural belief in reciprocity.

The crowds' response is slow. Some begin to open their blessed envelopes to add a little more cash. The pastor reminds those who own the homes that God gave them that gift without them doing anything to deserve it. He tells those who live in a rented property that God gave them that roof over their heads. He ends by asking if they, who have homes to live in, will leave God without resources. This is another appeal that penetrates the fibers of the native worldview. If God has given to us, will we not, in turn, give to him?

Pastor Guachalla suddenly stops speaking to the standing congregation, now doing some mental arithmetic to see if they can afford to give more, and turns his eyes to the roof building to show that he is addressing God to make clear what he has said. He prays for those who do not believe, for those whom the devil has blinded so that they will not give sacrificially, for those who have quickly forgotten how much they have received, and for those who could still receive a crown of gold! He then interrupts his communication with God to hold a final ritual before the ushers collect the offerings.

Imitating a *yatiri*, Pastor Guachalla orders everyone to put their envelopes on the left-hand side of their chest close to the heart. In my field research, I saw the testimony of an Aimara man, who described how before asking for payment, the *yatiri* asked him to put the money close to his heart to show that his decision to give is made with all of his feelings. If they want and seek great things, they must give sacrificially to receive the best.

Here, the pastor makes a short parenthesis to explain that the "House of God" construction in one of the city's most densely populated areas costs approximately two million U. S. dollars. "Because nothing is impossible for God," is chorused by the congregation. When the uniformed ushers return on their tortuous route through the standing faithful, they have collected what will be the first of five bountiful Sunday collections.

The PoG Church has become rich and powerful, adopting and adapting the indigenous channels of reciprocity and relationality regarding the transcendent by using syncretistic practices of how divine religious favors are paid, using the Aimara language and worldview as powerful tools.

The PoG owns a network of radio stations in each capital city and a television network that broadcasts nationally, especially in prime areas that are easy for the population to access. Although nobody is forced to give, the church services use mechanisms to exploit people's innocence and lack of information. The church uses an abusive induction. The same method is used in mass media meetings or musical concerts. The masses are manipulated using emotionalism and exploitation of their ignorance, belief system, and their poverty.

Before starting his sermon, the pastor allows a few people to give testimonies of healing miracles. Though the time for the remainder of the service is now short, the much-awaited message has yet to come. First, there are testimonies. One shares about healing from chronic anemia that stopped him from walking or even thinking. Others talk of the desperate urban misery experienced since moving to the city. Upon leaving the church building after three-and-a-half hours of intensive performance, church members encounter additional cases of chronic anemia and extreme poverty in the corridors. People in need are lying on the pavement looking for an opportunity for a pentecostalized animist help or solution to their problems.

Interviews with Leaders and Members

Field exploration demonstrates that the ordinary church members and intermediate-level leaders in the PoG, both young people and adults, adopt new forms of thinking, which are reflected in their identity and their duty to fulfill the church's task and objectives. They have changed their daily routine as a result of conversion. Now all converts submit to church structure and leadership and consider themselves sent and empowered to look for new converts.

This section's qualitative analysis is based on twenty-nine in-depth interviews with fifteen intermediate-level leaders (cell groups and worship) and fourteen ordinary PoG Church members. Each interview lasted for about an hour and focused on the following five areas, with open exchange and discussion between the interviewer and interviewee:

1) Perception of the personal conversion experience
2) Experience related to the mission of the believer
3) Concepts about the mission of the believer
4) Experiences in evangelization and discipleship
5) Opinions about integral mission

Members' Perception of Conversion[8]

After conversion, PoG members experience metamorphosis, profound change in their lifestyle and concept about life. The reconstruction of mental, emotional, and spiritual concepts as a result of approaching and joining the PoG Church is a perception shared by ordinary members and intermediate leaders. Ordinary members born in rural areas talked about emotional states, such as looking for happiness or feeling drawn into the urban fury of drunkenness and parties. People with Aimara roots but who were born in urban areas had a different perspective about their conversion. Several had joined the PoG after being baptized in other evangelical churches. Some had been Baptists or part of another large Neo-Pentecostal church in La Paz, *Cristo Viene* (Christ is Coming), where, they said, the Holy Spirit was absent, and there was a bad testimony. For both groups, conversion had meant no more drinking, no more participation in parties, and no visits to Aimara religious men, like *yatiris*. The following testimony was shared by a woman, an ordinary PoG church member, who has been attending the church for more than two years:

> I was going through a tough time in my family. I was thinking about committing suicide. Someone invited me to church, and I accepted Jesus there. That was in December 2000. My life changed. Now I don't participate in the dance groups any longer. I went to talk to my relatives to ask for forgiveness and to forgive. I never used to do that because I was too proud. I share about my conversion with other people. I tell them about what I was going through before. I share in my work with relatives and with people whenever I get the chance.

In talking about their conversion, interviewees emphasized both physical healings received as well as their lifestyle prior to conversion. Their reasons for belonging to the PoG were often associated with healing miracles, which they themselves or close relatives, such as spouses and children, had experienced. After conversion, there is dynamic combat between the old and new worldview. This amalgam is not unchangeable and rigid, but flexible, under constant revision and restructuring. It forms an identity that is not entirely new that but differs from the old one while still being built on indigenous ethnicities.

Leaders' Perception of Conversion

How does a young Aimara intermediate leader describe his conversion experience? He belongs to a worship group and Andean music group. Let us see what he says, remembering that he has been in the congregation for a long time:

> I received Christ in 1999. My mother talked to me about the word. It was a miracle. I never knew what a miracle was before, but since I met God, I learned that only God could do miracles. Before, things went badly for me at work; now, they don't. Since then, lots of things have changed, for example, my character. I used to be very rebellious with my mum; I never obeyed her. I liked dancing. The year I was converted, I was about to participate in a folkloric parade, but I didn't. I never consulted *yatiris*, but I visited the Socavón [mine entrance where people worship the Virgin and the devil] in the *Oruro Carnival* parade, and I used to pray to the saints.

When talking about their conversion experience, young leaders focus on changes in character and conduct. They talk about the fact that they no longer participate in religious festivals or attend social gatherings where alcohol is served. They emphasize the sentimental aspect of their conversion, the change of heart. Adult leaders, on the other hand, focus on new moral values. Those with prior experience in grassroots organizations practice their leadership skills learned outside the church–in unions, mothers' clubs, or neighborhood associations–by working within the church helping the administration, as soul-winner cell group leaders, or in radio programming. Another generational difference is the relationship with Aimara Andean beliefs and religious agents post-conversion. The young people tend to adhere much less than the adults to the Aimara worldview and animistic rituals, adopting the globalized vision transmitted in urban centers. In both groups, male and female adults and youth all express that sharing the testimony of their conversion with friends and relatives is a powerful instrument for disseminating their new faith.

Members' Perception of Mission

The new Neo-Pentecostal faith clearly gives each convert the unavoidable responsibility to share and expand its particular way of understanding and living their faith as if it were unique and superior. All of the people interviewed expressed that they had found a meaning for life, a greater purpose, which they described as "serving the Lord," "preaching," "telling people to repent," "talking about the Lord," "winning souls from hell," "God heals, I tell them. . . ." Each testimony is part of a concept and mission experience that applies to men and women, young and old.

Although all of those interviewed include in their new perception the desire to share their new worldview in the areas where they live, in the country, and in the world, new converts accept this challenge without joining neighborhood associations or other socio-political groups. On the other hand, older converts, both men and women, are much more open to participating in grassroots organizations.

Both groups, however, separate the practice of their faith from any form of serving others. Their physical and spiritual energy, financial resources, and personal assets are for their own and the church's use rather than for meeting others' needs. Apart from praying for divine healing, the PoG tends to defer material needs to a secondary plane. In the following testimony, one member describes his understanding of the mission of the believer:

> Since my conversion, my life's purpose has been to serve the Lord and tell everyone about the gospel. I do not have any specific plans for my family, just for them to know the Lord and not to suffer in this world. My plan is that everyone in my neighborhood converts to the gospel, and I share with all types of people in order to reach that goal.

Other activities described by the interviewees as part of their mission include handing out tracts, ushering at church services, prayer, fasting, evangelizing in the streets and public squares, and hospital visitation. Their new lifestyle often earns them criticism and rejection from relatives and neighbors.

Leaders' Perception of Mission

One phrase repeated by the interviewees, young and old, when referring to their mission is "saving souls." This, they say, is their life's purpose. Through teaching in "Soul Winners" groups, worship group leaders' choice of music, and soul-winner cell group leaders clearly specify that their priority focuses on people's souls. Young leaders show complete indifference to the social aspects of their faith, limiting themselves to give an example of solidarity and honesty in the workplace. Adults who have previous experience in grassroots organizations, on the contrary, talk about having been, and in some cases still are, part of neighborhood or shop-owner organizations, and share that they participate in campaigns to give used clothing and other articles to the poor. Again, the following testimony from a young Aimara leader reflects the focus of his mission:

My life's purpose is to save my soul. There would be no sense for me to have a profession or wealth if I do not save my soul [because] I would not go to be with God. In the short-term, I want to have a profession (usually taken to mean finishing a university degree) so that I can give my brothers and sisters what my parents couldn't give them. In the medium-term, I want to have a family and preach the word of God, and in the long-term, I want to have a ministry but always guided by my pastor. Plans for my neighborhood include holding campaigns, and activities to win them: dinners, food, show films. . . reach places where [the gospel] has not reached. The church has a mission and a vision. The mission is to win souls; the vision is to convert them to God.

The mission described by these respondents seems to be isolated from their social, political, and economic environment, even isolated from the religious scenario, as it fails to take any other type of faith into consideration. It is a mission almost exclusively focused on spiritual aspects, effectively practiced inside the nuclear and extended family. Almost all of those interviewed talked about successfully sharing their new way of life and faith with family members and workmates.

Members and Evangelism

The commitment to evangelize is deeply rooted in all of those interviewed, whether they have been in the church for a long or short time. However, what does evangelism mean for these people? Evangelizing for them means guiding others to go to church to hear the gospel, telling friends, relatives, neighbors, and workmates about how to know the good news of Jesus Christ. Convincing men and women to attend church, or to hear Radio Sol or watch TV Channel 45, is the main goal. In addition to mass media, PoG members also contribute to church growth by telling others about the miracles, both inside and outside the church. One Aimara woman, born in the rural area, said: "I share the gospel with everyone all the time. I have guided many people to take the first steps. I don't remember how many because I no longer have any contact with them." Another young indigenous woman, also born in the country, said: "I share the gospel with everyone and give out tracts, but I've never done any follow-up with anyone." One married man born in the rural area said: "I share the gospel at work with my workers at break time. Sometimes they have problems, so I preach to them. I also talk to my relatives about the Lord." Another woman, born in the city, said: "I always preach when I get the chance because that is my job. I share with my customers, my colleagues in the market, relatives, and neighbors."

Believers, who have been part of the congregation for less than two years, appear to invite a much larger circle of friends and acquaintances. Their new faith makes them more daring and less selective about who they invite. On the other hand, older believers tend to prefer sharing with a more intimate circle of relatives and close friends or workmates. Newer converts are more intense about "sharing" their faith, while older believers show more perseverance and strategy in their mission work.

Leaders and Evangelism

The head of church administration, also the leader of the "Soul Winners" cell groups, and leader of a local shopkeepers' organization, said the following in talking about evangelization and discipleship:

> I constantly share the gospel with my family, friends, people I don't know. The doors are always open for everyone to the people who come to church and ask for help, whether they're Christians or not. I tell them that there's a God who can change our lives, who can help us be born again and be new, but in Jesus Christ. We go out to the streets with the pastor to preach the word in the squares, hospitals; everyone must do it because they want to without any conditions. I guide the new converts into "Soul Winners" groups and the meetings I have with shopkeepers. Each experience is important to me because each one is another life for God. In every experience, my pastor helps me.

Cell group leaders and adults who previously belonged to grassroots organizations say they have led many people to conversion. This is not the case with worship group leaders and adults who have never participated in social organizations outside of the church. All of them, however, are committed to bringing new people into the PoG. One phrase used frequently in the interviews is "saving souls from hell." This seems to project their own need before conversion, their own sense of having been in hell. Even those who had been members of conservative, evangelical churches before joining the PoG – churches with little preaching about miracles, ecstatic experiences, and the gifts of the Holy Spirit – talk about only truly knowing God when they felt his power in the PoG Church.

> I have only shared the gospel with my brothers and sisters. I have had no experience with friends and people who are not Christians. Neither have I had the opportunity to guide a new convert in taking the first steps because I

still have much to learn. I need to know more about the word; I need to have a stronger foundation in the word. I will do it when I have acquired more knowledge. . . .The church should not only work to save souls from hell so that everyone can be saved.

As with ordinary members, intermediate PoG leaders also share the good news about miracles, first with their extended families and then their friends and workmates. But they also go further, talking to neighbors, mothers' clubs, schools, and universities. They talk about what they believe God has done through supernatural deeds, sharing in the streets, in the church, with people they do not know, with drug users, the sick, couples contemplating divorce; they share every day and everywhere. Discipleship is basically understood as the continuous indoctrination of the convert. It is rarely practiced or even mentioned, compared with convincing people to attend church or share a testimony of healing. The purpose of their life is to "win souls," which implies making that initial decision without worrying too much about what comes after.

One young worship group leader said:

I share the word at all times, whether at work, with neighbors, family, strangers. I talk to them about the word of God, telling them my testimony and talking to them about the Bible. In the word of God, it says, "This gospel will be preached to every creature." That is an order from Jesus, and I obey it without looking for anything in return. Any reward I get is God's blessing on my business and the experience with people who are just becoming Christians. You can share it with them, and usually the results are good. Those who are converted are always in the church.

Members and Integral Mission

"We have to enhance the Aimara culture without accepting idolatry and traditions;" "we should think about the country's development;" "we must recover things in the culture;" "Aimara culture is of the devil;" "the pastor has told us not to get involved in politics." These, sometimes contradictory opinions, were expressed by individual church members regarding integral mission and would appear to be spontaneous, changeable, and paradoxical observations rather than ongoing, well-thought-out reasoning or reflection.

Church members intrinsically understand the identification with the poor and sensitivity to the cultural context expounded as vital for integral mission[9] because they are or have been poor, and they come from the Aimara culture. The sensitivity and concern felt by poor Christians about the unemployed, the hungry, the poor, who are vulnerable to and often exploited by the injustices of a segregationist system does not seem so much from a reflective awareness about these issues as from empathy for having shared the same suffering and the same indigenous identity. Their Neo-Pentecostal commitment and the process of change occur within this indigenous, socioeconomic reality. An elderly woman, born in the rural area, said: "I have very little money, but if I had some, I would help all the children and poor people so that they do not suffer." A new convert also said: "The church should work to save souls and seek God first, and then it should worry about society, the poor and the orphans, and work for them, but our faith should be founded on Christ alone."

New converts seem to make a temporary clean break with politics, culture, and any activity that implies participation in society. An older convert, on the other hand, said: "We can participate in the neighborhood committee by choice." Another woman expressed the belief that "the church should contribute to the country's development and the Aimara culture, but condemn idolatry," meaning that they must leave the worship of images, saints from a Catholic background, ancestors, and gods from Aimara religion. These opinions reflect a substantial shift from the initial emotional charge experienced on the threshold of conversion.

Older converts, both male and female, expressed a desire to strengthen, improve, and recover aspects of their Aimara culture while emphatically rejecting idolatrous practices. They share aspirations of betterment, improvement, and rescuing the Aimara culture. This could reflect either a desire to preserve something precious and intimate or reflect the need for continuity and preservation.

Leaders and Integral Mission

Very few middle-level leaders still believe that the church's mission is only "to save souls from hell" or that "the Aimara culture of the devil." Although they acknowledge that the church does not address social issues, choosing to prioritize soul-saving, they recognize the importance of balance in the Christian mission, which clearly separates saving souls and the church's social responsibility. Evangelization is most important, but the believer should also contribute to Bolivia's progress, enhancing

Aimara culture with the gospel, engage in helping the poor, working for a better future for Bolivia, and eliminating class discrimination. This radical separation between evangelization and social issues, relegating the latter to an inferior plane, is justified using the following explanations: "By evangelizing we form good people who value life;" "Winning souls is development for the country;" "It is helping so that many people are not living in the streets;" "It is getting people out of vice so that they are useful for society."

Although the concept of an integral mission says that the Christian faith impacts every part of human lives, that may cause a Western dichotomy between what is spiritual and what is social. The Aimara members of the PoG Church don't have such dichotomy in everyday life. By talking about integral mission, they identify with their ecclesial context because they are poor people from indigenous communities. Young and adult intermediate leaders almost unanimously agree that they should value their Aimara culture, speak their language, reject some of the negative customs, and retain solidarity, companionship, music, and traditional dress. The Aimara culture is part of them, and they believe the church should recreate that culture. The following testimony gives some insight into the Christians' vision of their Aimara culture:

> The pastor teaches us that speaking Aimara is not a sin. Indigenous people indeed consult *yatiris*, have contact with them, but in my church, we will change that. There are lots of Aimara-speaking people who go to the church; they are going to change that.

Conclusion

The beliefs and actions at PoG Church are an indigenous answer to existential anxieties experienced as a result of broken roots, poverty, and social and personal limitations. PoG members get psychological and spiritual strength from the church's ritualistic performances, obtaining confidence in their own vernacular terms, in other words, in live, pre-existing, internal substructures.

With the change in social relations in migrating from rural areas or adjusting to constant urban changes, religious beliefs are transformed or weakened, forcing people to take a long look at the prearranged social and religious system. At first glance, the PoG Church seems to be in the front line of changing people's lives and culture, but a more careful examination reveals that sometimes the opposite is true. By choosing the PoG Church, people would appear to be accepting its system, which represents not only social conditions and life patterns but also the existing indigenous Aimara identity.

The diverse approaches to the selected interviewees – new and old converts, youth and adults, urban and rural-born, ordinary members and intermediate leaders, male and female – show that they are all involved in the PoG scenario in an open, cooperative fashion that masks an indigenous system that is over and above the church structures. Conflicts, often unconscious, incongruous, and autonomous, occur in the conventional logic systems that actively guide people's actions. The standard logic is centered on rational thought, measured common sense, and arguments based on what is good and bad. But the indigenous native system prevails, disqualifying rationality and focusing on feelings and the spirit.

The cultural Aimara vitality is also observable in inward manifestations through the perception of personal conversion, concepts, and experience of mission, especially evangelization and discipleship, and the opinions about integral mission obtained from the interviews of ordinary members and intermediate leaders.

Conversion brings these people a flexible fusion of old and new, channeling an identity formatted by indigenous ethnicity that is, therefore, not entirely new. For the young, the change is a change of heart sentimentalizing their perception; its conversion is focused on feelings. For adults, the transformation has more to do with moral values shaped by the native worldview.

Within Neo-Pentecostal belief, mission is an unavoidable duty. This is a mission exclusively focused on "winning souls." The responsibility of sharing and spreading its particular way of living the Christian faith is understood to be the major purpose of life. All the interviewees expressed this emphasis on spiritual matters, with spiritual needs as a priority and material needs as secondary. Mission, therefore, is disintegrated from the socio-political-economic context.

New believers adopt the gospel of Jesus Christ with an intense commitment combined with an unselective attitude about people and places. It is not important for them to share their testimony with relatives;

there is a wider openness, including a range of people and influence. Older PoG believers, on the other hand, strategically persevere with their extended family and friends. All of them practice their Aimara communality when evangelizing or multiplying disciples. Intermediate leaders proselytize more willingly just to introduce people to the new faith. Pastor Guachalla, as a maximum leader, has a distinctive role of initiating others into the Christian faith that mirrors many of the features of the traditional *yatiri*.

The global system exerts its uncontrollable power within Neo-Pentecostals at the PoG church, shaping its identity on the one hand, while also reaffirming the Aimara legacy. Obvious westernized features can be observed but within the framework of traditional, indigenous customs. Western Europe, Africa, and Asia have responded to the homogenization of humankind and democracy by splitting into more officially recognized countries. Never before in history have as many national divisions been seen as are now present in contemporary times. The parable of the seed and the plant pot, the incarnational paradigm, or the principle of acceptance and separation that Paul applied have been taken on board by Pentecostals, not as a response to a rational understanding of the Bible, but as a consequence of their own indigenous nature.

Notes

1 The Aimara, or Aymara, is a sizable indigenous population comprising several people groups. Numbering about 3.5 million, the Aimara live in the Alitplano region of the Andes with significant numbers in Peru and Bolivia, and a smaller concentration of people in Argentina and Chile. El Alto, Bolivia has been called the Aimara capital of the world. A traditionally agricultural people group, their traditional animism includes a deity called Pachamama, which translated, means "Earth Mother." See *Encyclopedia Britannica Online*, s.v. "Aymara People," accessed November 26, 2020, https://www.britannica.com/topic/Aymara; See also, Minority Rights Group International, "Highland Aymara and Quechua," *World Directory of Minorities and Indigenous Peoples*, updated January 2018, https://minorityrights.org/minorities/highland-aymara-and-quechua/, accessed November 26, 2020.

2 Juan Sepúlveda "Pentecostalism as Popular Religiosity," *International Review of Mission* 78:309 (1986), 80–88.

3 Xavier Albó and Matías Preiswerk, *Los Señores del Gran Poder* (La Paz: Centro de Teologia Popular, 1986), 241.

4 Virginia Garrard-Burnnet, "Identity, Community and Religious Change Among the Maya of Chiapas and Guatemala," *Journal of Hispanic Latino Theology* 1:6 (1998), 61-79; Frias Mendoza and Victor Hugo, Mistis y Mokochinches: *Mercado, Evangélicos y Política Local en Calcha* (La Paz: Editorial Mama Huaco, 2002), 102–108.

5 Germán Guaygua and Beatriz Castillo Herrera, *Identidades y Religión: Fiesta, Culto, y Ritual en la Construcción de Redes Sociales en la Ciudad de El Alto* (La Paz: Instituto Superior Ecuménico Andino Teología, 2008), 77.

6 Albó and Preiswerk, *Los Señores del Gran Poder*, 5, 113.

7 See, Tomás L. Huanca, "The Yatiri in Aymara Communities" (Master's Thesis, University of Florida, 1987), https://www.worldcat.org/title/yatiri-in-aymara-communities-with-complete-text-by/oclc/23734619.

8 All interviews are taken from Aimara primary sources during fieldwork in 2003 and 2006, in La Paz, Bolivia. In 2003, there were seven focus groups comprised of thirty-eight members of the Power of God Church, including fifteen men and twenty-three women. From these focus groups, there were transcripts as well as twenty-two hours of recorded videotape. In 2006, I held in-depth personal interviews with twenty-nine people including fifteen intermediate level leaders and fourteen ordinary members of the Power of God Church. The participants in 2006 were eighteen men and eleven women. All interviews were conducted in confidence and the name of the

interviewees are withheld by mutual agreement. All the subsequent direct quotations are from the interviews.

9   René Padilla defines the church's integral mission thus: "Evangelization and social responsibility are inseparable. The gospel is the good news about the kingdom of God. Good works, on the other hand, are the signs of the kingdom for which we were created in Jesus Christ. Words and actions are indissolubly united in the mission of Jesus and his apostles, and we should keep them together in the church's mission, in which Jesus' mission is prolonged until the end of time," *Mision Integral: Ensayos Sobre el Reino y la Iglesia* (Buenos Aires: Nueva Creación, 1986), 191.

10 Building Our Home: *Balu Wala* and the Year of Jubilee

Jocabed R. Solano Miselis

Abstract

The *Balu Wala* is a Gunadule ancestral story sung by grandparents in the Gunadule congress house. The story represents the system of oppression suffered by the marginalized and impoverished, and their liberation that arises from the felling of the tree by those who have been dispossessed themselves. This chapter will weave together the story of the *Balu Wala* with the scriptural command for the Year of Jubilee. Through this interwoven framework of indigenous stories and scriptural commands, we will look at the concept of ecological justice, concluding that both scripture and indigenous wisdom have much to say to us on this pressing issue.

Introduction

In a day like any other day, the people of the Gunadule[1] nation get up early in the morning before the sun rises in order to do their daily chores. You can hear the grandfather getting up to go to the fields and cultivate the land. You hear the voices of your brothers who are preparing themselves to go fishing. And then you can hear someone whispering in the kitchen; grandma preparing breakfast. It is dark still, but everybody at home knows that they have to get up early in the morning to be ready for the day. They have heard generation after generation that one must get up before *Dad Ibe* (the grandfather the sun comes out), so he may give us energy and find us ready for the task of the day. "Because if we are not ready," says grandma, "then laziness will trap us."

There are stories that form or distort ways in which we understand and live life. The Gunadules have many stories, symbols, dances, and songs, which have formed the Gunadule people and formed their way of living on one of the most important ethical pillars that the Gunadule people hold highly, the sense of community. Not everything started in harmony, the grandfathers and grandmothers tell us. There was a time when chaos prevailed in our communities, when we did not want to live in a community with each other. Therefore, God taught us, the Gunadule, through the Earth, and through brothers and sisters how to live in the community. Thus, the stories of the Gunadule people are full of characters that represent the Gunadule life and how this life has been built through the passage of time. These stories also show how the people have resisted the process of violence, such as the violent conquest by the Spanish to *Abya Yala*,[2] which caused the greatest genocide in human history, as well as the current colonizing processes that continue to exist today, manifesting in different societal features. For example, the epistemicide[3] that continues to open the wound in the heart of the *Abya Yala* people. Epistemicide, to put it in simple words, is the attempt to kill the Indigenous spirit, in this case, the spirit of the Gunadule nation.

Development and Ancestral Models

The manifestation of violence against minorities is clear in national plans such as those offered by "development" models. As Nicolas Panotto says:

> When the Western societies talk about development, they generally refer to urbanization, capitalism, economic systems, new technologies, and globalization. Development and underdevelopment are placed as opposites. Development implies that conditions in core nations are replicated in the third world. As a result, the idea of development becomes a sociocultural concept that not only means the difference between two opposites, but also creates a dynamic of submission of one opposite to the other. In sociocultural and geopolitical terms, we see these same concepts of domination and underdevelopment applied to Indigenous nations. The geopolitical position of the small nations within the larger nation-state is that of the amplest inferiority.[4]

These models "benefit" some people, but oppress others. Such an approach increases the gap between those who are privileged and those who are vulnerable in our societies. There are economic models sustained by the labor of Indigenous people, peasants, afro descendants, immigrants, etc., those who do the hard work but collect minimal benefits. Similarly, such models exploit and abuse the land, causing the death of animals, forests, and biodiversity. They are found in the jungle, alongside the wisdom of the plants, which are not found in other places. And the indigenous peoples know of them well. Likewise, such models bring death to humanity at the global level, directly affecting the most vulnerable beings, though it is the most vulnerable in our current system, who cause the least damage to this nega (home), which we also call earth.

Amidst this reality, there are ancestral models, from time immemorial, in the Indigenous nations of *Abya Yala*, who have been living in harmony with the earth. One of these models is that of the Gunadule nation. This text will briefly discuss the importance for our current society to be exposed to Indigenous knowledge, as well as to recognize it as valuable and learn from it. These models make significant contributions to humanity, not just as a current tendency of including persons who have been traditionally marginalized, but also as legitimate models with plans that can bring hope amidst our current crisis. If we do not start working on this plan with intentionality and a sense of urgency, then humanity will face significant losses. With the extinction of Indigenous languages, the knowledge of plant medicines is also lost, as well as other ways of knowing in regard to relationships between nature and humanity. This loss affects us all equally. With these urgent challenges, I would like to knit a land-based perspective in regards to the year of jubilee from an Indigenous point of view, as the daughter of the Gunadule nation. This is one of the stories of the Gunadule nations, the *Balu Wala*, and the biblical text for the year of Jubilee is Exodus 23:10–11.

Stories that Form and Stories that Distort

For centuries, the Gunadule people have maintained their social, economic, and political life in a holistic manner, based on their spirituality. Spirituality is their search for God, which has been called *Bab Igala* (God's way) or *Anmar Dadgan an Nangan Daniggid* (the path that our grandfathers and grandmothers have walked). This path has been paved with learning; our grandfathers and grandmothers walked through chaos, lamentations, suffering, celebration, joy. We have learned from *Nabgwana* (the heart of the earth), whom we call mother because she has fed us, taken care of us, and we the Gunalude people have respected and learned, we have listened, observed, touched, felt her heart. From her, we learned how to relate with each other, how to live in harmony and balance. "God gave to the earth, to *Nabgwana*, her image," the grandfathers sing while in the hammock, in a *nega* (home), which we call *Omagged negga* (house of the Gunalude council). "She gave us joy and knowledge."

The songs of the Gunadule provide the foundations of the narratives of our people. These narratives allow us to learn from the memories, from the realities that we currently live, from the *Nabgwana* (the heart of the earth), from God. We have been formed through the act of observing, listening, and feeling the Earth. This has been our formation. In this chapter, I will share with you one of the stories that talks about how the Gunadule nation has been formed to remember that the greater good should be for all. You will hear this song in the context of one of the most sacred places of the Gunadude people, the *ommaged nega* (house of the Gunalude council).

The Story of the *Balu Wala*

The *Balu Wala* is one of the stories told by the Gunadule leaders to educate the people. Memory is transmitted orally: those who sing are specialists that study for years so that they can sing and share their stories. This is an excerpt from the *Balu Wala* story, "In the beginning, *Abya yala* was perfect and very beautiful. *Oloabiagundiwala*[5] showered her peacefully. At that time, *Abya yala* had not yet experienced the weight of those who were going to make her feel sorry. Later on, Biler[6] and Bursob[7] showed up, then their children. Thereafter, many others came down. Subsequently, Ibeler[8] and his siblings appeared: Oller, Wigaliler (Wigabibbiler), Olosunnibeler, Buudur, Gwadgwaddule, Bugasui (Igwaoginyabbiler), and Olowagli. Ibeler was the eldest.[9]

When they arrived, *nana Olobibbirgunyai* suffered under the whipping of the storms; the steppes and hills got cloudy. Violent hurricanes unleashed their power and tornados of different colors, blue, red, black, and white. Sacred places (*gulu saglagan*) were desecrated. Ibeler saw this, and it hurt him; he suffered from the trees falling: the *igwawalagan*, the *isberwalagan*, and the *naggiwalagan*.[10] Amidst so much dispair, Ibeler started to look for the causes of such disaster. He confined himself in *surbanega*,[11] to dig deep from there to the different levels and aspects of the Earth, and thus, unveil the deep waves of evil: Where are these rainstorms coming from? Who is shaking the trees? Step by step, Ibeler came closer to a humongous tree. The tree was *igubwala*.[12] It was also called *ibsanwala* or *baluwala*. Ibeler found that in the highest treetop of *igubwala* there was the origin of all the cyclones. From the treetop, the allies of Biler threw blue and red rainstorms and also yellow and black rainstorms.

Ibeler then looked for a way to know what was happening in the gigantic tree, then he sent a louse to *amma* (aunt) Guggurdili's scalp, without her knowing. She was the only one that came back and forth from that tree. Thereafter, Ibeler took the louse that had been attached to *amma's* scalp. The louse said the following: "Across the path, great cyclones roar, they blow terrible hurricanes, and that is how we arrived at the highest treetop. There I have seen an extensive banana, yam, and cocoa plantations; there is abundance. Over there, the people seem to not suffer; they have plenty." The louse continued, "In the tree, in the highest top, there is an immense branch, which is pointing towards the sunrise. Also, where the branch starts, there is a community of people with a lot of power. They are unleashing the storms that are destroying it all. They are lifting cyclones and are throwing them to the ocean. They bring out the blue, red, and yellow cyclones, and make the big trees fall over the great mother Earth. They frighten us with typhoons and deprive us of the goods of *Balu Wala*. Full of fear, we are unable to see their opulence. Typhoons fall over us, frosts fall over us, and they amuse themselves at our fear and our death."

Right after Ibeler learned about all the details of the big tree of salt, he set out to treat it. Ibeler had convinced himself that only by treating the great tree; there would be a relief for the pain of *Nabgwana*. Ibeler knew that only from the fallen tree, peace will arrive. He also saw that there was a necessity to gather the goods that would come up from the *Balu Wala*.

Analzyng the Story of the *Balu Wala*

The story tells us that at the beginning, the earth was compact; there were no continents, the earth as a unit. This talks about the period of the earth that was many moons back, but the story also tells us the characteristics of that particular time. The Earth was perfect, and there was justice. There was a balance between the land, humanity, and the cosmos, given that the beings that lived on it, lived in harmony. The perfection can be seen present in the loveliness of *Abya Yala*.

The story continues unraveling and points us to generations with the names of some characters that appear in the story as Biler,[13] Bursob, and their children. These characters represent evil. The evil lay in the possession of the tree, *Balu Wala* only for themselves. As one listens to the story being sung, then other characters appear in the scene. Some of those are Ibeler[14] and his siblings, who represent goodness. They did not know what was happening to *Abya Yala*; they did not know the reason for the many storms, hurricanes, the violation of sacred places, or why there was scarcity. Other characters that come to the scene are Biler, Bursob, and their children, who took power. They represent evil; they appropriated the highest top of the tree, *Balu Wala*, where there were all kinds of riches and abundance.

One day, Ibeler had a dream, because they did not know what had happened to *Abya Yala*. It had turned from being lovely and perfect to chaos, and now it was a whole disaster. In the dream, Ibeler saw the tree, *Balu Wala*, and saw the top of the tree, where natural phenomenon formed, which then were thrown to those who lived under the tree. He wanted to find out who was causing all this harm. Then he reflected and sent an animal spy, a louse, and put it in a grandmother's hair. This grandmother was the only one that came up and down in the tree. When the louse came back, he told Ibeler, "In the treetop, there are a lot of riches, pleasures, power, and opulence." He told them that up there, the production of corn, plantain, and yam is controlled. And those who are up there throw crumbs to those who are under the tree.

Those who were down below were terrified, they were afraid of the hurricanes and the storms. Therefore, those who were below were paralyzed, they did not get to see the sources of injustice and the inequity in which they were living, though they were very afraid. However, when the louse spy told them what was happening, Ibeler and his siblings had an idea. What to do so all the riches being monopolized could be distributed for all? They thought that the best strategy was to cut the tree. For eight days, the strategists cut during the day, but they rested at night. When they got up and went to see the tree, they found out that *Balu Wala* looked intact, brand new.

It seems that some animals such as the serpent, the frog, and the deer came at night and licked the wounds of the tree, leaving the tree as if it was brand new. Ibeler analyzed the situation and strategized. He called for conversations, dialogues among the communities. He made allies with other groups and prepared safe food and poisonous arrows. The fight was not going to be easy. Finally, well-organized and with an understanding of the situation, they went back to cut the tree, the *Balu Wala*. Each wound that the tree was given fell to the ground in pieces, and the skin would turn into crabs, fish, and other animals. Finally, after a lot of concerted efforts, they were able to knock down *Balu Wala*, and so much wealth fell as well, in the spiritual, animal, plant, and mineral forms. This allowed for the strengthening of the community, and then they could live in peace because the balance was restored, and there was equity for all.

When I hear this song, to my mind, the moments of oppression return, the pain and the fear that humanity has lived through in different moments of history. The ambition and the selfishness, the desire to accumulate power and riches just for ourselves has brought us a lot of sorrow and has cost us thousands of lives which have perished, and many other thousands that suffered alienation, scarcity, oppression, enslavement, and pain because of the greed and the dehumanization of those who enrich themselves at the expense of those who are the most vulnerable. On the other hand, there are systems in crisis because those are not sustainable for the majority of humanity. The reality in which we live today is also reflected in the memories of the Bible, showing what reality we would live in when selfishness prevails, and thus, we stop thinking about the greater good.

The Year of Jubilee

We can see one of these moments when God says to the people of Israel the importance of practicing the year of the jubilee, the sabbatical year, with urgency. When we are being called to do something, it is precisely a result of us not doing it. In this passage, we can see some of the consequences of what we are not doing. "For six years, you are to sow your fields and harvest the crops, but during the seventh year, let the land lie unplowed and unused. Then the poor among your people may get food from it, and the wild animals may eat what is left. Do the same with your vineyard and your olive grove" (Exod 23,10-11). This is the oldest text about the sabbatical year.

The implications of what is not being done are present when one hears what one has to do. What we notice first is that God invites the people of Israel to seriously consider the land. The relationship with the land, as found in Genesis, is an invitation to cultivate the land, to take care of it. It is clear in this passage, once more, the importance of planting, but also the importance of letting the land rest. This relationship frees the people from the instrumentalization of land, and also shows us God's loving relationship with the land, inviting us to have such a relationship as well. It is necessary to deepen this affective relationship in the current climate crisis. It is necessary to rethink a theology of the land. Moreover, another important element to be analyzed is that the land is not always to be cultivated; it needs to rest. In that way, the poor who do not have land can eat from the harvest. The sabbatical year lies in justice and equity for all, from beginning to end, because the owner of the land is God (Ps 24:1)

This justice and equity is not only for the poor but also for the animals. It is a way of living in which there is care for creation as a whole. Whoever has vineyards and olive groves is the rich. And it is for those who have the riches, whose challenge is to recognize that they belong to the land, and the one inviting us to the land is the owner. The accumulation of land is denounced when we are told what to do in the scripture passage. Pablo Richard[15] says that the very *dejar descansar* (to let rest) literally means "to let free." The human has the right to work the land and harvest its bounty, but God also defends the rights of the land for rest and freedom.

Interweaving the *Balu Wala* and the Year of Jubilee

Nations have stories that, as I have noted, form or distort ways in which we understand and live life. The Gunadule people have many stories to challenge and to invite others to live in harmony with the cosmos, the land, and humanity. Both in the search for a fulfilled life and in regard to how to live in a relationship with others, the Gunadule people have resorted to their stories and how these stories have been constructed. Their stories regarding their relationship with God, with the land, with the Gunadule community, and recently, relationships with other peoples. The Jubilee, the sabbatical year, the sabbath have the intention of finding a fulfilled life for all humanity, a fulfilled life which is is found in God's Shalom.

When we interweave stories, we can see some points in common. When we hear or read both stories completely, we see such stories come from God. The story of the *Balu Wala* mentions that Ibeler knew that everything that was created by *Baba and Nana* (God) has not been created just for a single group of people; instead, it was created for all the children of mother earth. The sabbatical year, the jubilee, the origins come from God. Both stories mention that the bounty of the earth is for all. In the story of *Balu Wala*, the point is to protect humanity. In the year of jubilee, the point is to protect the tribe. In the *Balu Wala*, the land is not anyone's property. The jubilee and sabbath year remind us that the land and people are God's property, a direct contrast with the royal tribute system where the land and people were considered property of the king. In the year of jubilee, agrarian reform is enacted so that all families who have had economic problems can return to work their ancestral lands.

The year of jubilee keeps the utopia of the origins alive against the tributary system. Once the ram's horn was heard, there was jubilance, celebration, restitution, the time of freedom in which everything could replenish. In the *Balu Wala*, one can learn about the pain of the land when it is appropriated. In the jubilee, the joy of life is expressed: the joy of the enslaved, of the exploited, of all those who have been oppressed. In the *Balu Wala*, cutting the tree so there could be equity was a "disgrace" for those who had amassed riches (material, spiritual, mineral). For those for whom the tree was cut, such a situation was a source of celebration. The year of jubilee shows us the power of God and his goodwill for all of us. Both stories give us a lot of insights for us to continue analyzing.

In what way do the systems in which we live today need a jubilee, a sabbatical year? In what way do such systems need *Balu Wala*, so that we are freed from greed and the vices that oppress and bring pain to my siblings? What systems are keeping those oppressed who do not have the wellbeing that I enjoy? Because if I have it, then they do not have it; therefore, it is a privilege. As followers of Jesus, we are called to live a lifestyle that reflects the ethic of justices, love of the jubilee, of the sabbatical year, love of *Balu Wala*. What are the implications of the requests that God is making for us in the jubilee? How should we respond to these implications that apply today in the political, economic, and social system in which we live?

Conclusion: A Lament

> Woe those corrupt governments and those who are power drunken in their palaces! They think they are the highest amongst the nations, which will turn against them. Oh, corrupted house due its own greed!

I passed by and saw your way of governing in the church, in the communities, that are to be spaces to worship God. Look if those spaces are better than these kingdoms. If their ways are better than our ways.

You that are waiting for the unpleasant day and bring the chair of inequity. You sleep in prominent spaces, eat potato, corn, and coffee from the hand of the indigenous people, the peasants, the workers. You eat from their sweat, you hurt them, and you are accomplices of such injustice. You dance at the rhythm of the music of your land, you claim, "We love our land and our flag;" to the rhythm of the traditional music you say, "we are from this land," but in reality, you hate, you bring death, and destroy the land and the people of the land.

You drink the most exquisite drinks and dress with the best attires, which are the latest fashion; also you use the most expensive perfumes. Yet you do not grieve over the poverty of the people.

Woe to those who mock the vulnerable, woe to those who feel better than others because they come from other origins, have a different skin color, or speak another language! And for that they believe that they are superior.

Woe to those who rape and exploit the land! With their hand, they attempt to rip her heart out, the heart of Mother Earth. They want to leave the forests' lungs with no air. They want to leave the jungle without eyes and without hands. They are making *Abya Yala* bleed! Murderers! Their hands are full of blood!

Woe to those who kill the Indigenous leaders when these are defending their territory, their land! They amuse themselves while their blood is being spilled!

Woe to those who make their wealth out of evil habits! At the expense of the vulnerable, they enrich themselves!

Woe for those who rejoice and say, "Have not we acquired power by our force?"

Woe to those who do not cry with the one who suffers and who celebrate the pain of the other!

Woe to those who mock the symbols of the Indigenous peoples, because they believe that their own are better.

Oh, brothers and sisters, woe to us if we do not know how to read God's message through the Indigenous people of *Abya Yala* (the Americas).

Notes

1 Gunadule is an indigenous nation that exists in an ancient way within the territory that is now Panama and Colombia.

2 *Abya Yala/Abia Yala* is the name given by the Gunadule to the continent most people know as America. The Gunadule culture maintains that there have been four epochs in the evolution of Mother Earth. Each epoch has a different name: *Gwalagunyala, Dagargunyala, Yaladinguayala*, and *Abya Yala*. The latter name refers to a "land redeemed, favored, and loved by Baba and Nana (*yala a bonodadi*)," and according to its fuller meaning, is a "mature land, land of blood," Aiben Wagua, *En Defensa de la Vida y su Armonía* (Panama: Proyecto EBI Guna / Fondo Mixto Hispano Panameño, 2011), 12.

3 Destruction of people's own knowledge, caused by European colonialism, coined by Boaventura de Souza Santos, *Epistemologies of the South: Justice Against Epistemicide* (Milton Park, UK: Taylor & Francis, 2014).

4 Nicolás Panotto, "Post-development, Difference, and Socio-cultural Identities: The Divine in-between as a Contribution to the Epistemology of Ecotheology," in Oikotree Movement, *Life-Enhancing Learning Together* (Daegu, Korea: Less Press & Life in Beauty Press, 2016), 312–331.

5 The sacred river of the Gunadule people that irrigated Abia Yala.

6 Biler is a character that symbolizes evil and disorder in Gunadule stories. He is the first man that had been created to take care of mother earth.

7 Bursod is the first woman on earth.

8 Ibeler is a central character in the Gunas treatises, symbolizing the liberation of mother earth; the good.

9 Eight brothers who liberate the earth, which was subjected to the cruelty of Biler and his allies.

10 The name of some trees found in the Gunadule territory.

11 Surbanega is the enclosed space or enclosure where medicine is bathed, or a ceremony is held.

12 Igubwala is the same as baluwala and is a tree of salt, which represents the system of oppression suffered by the marginalized and impoverished, and their liberation that arises from the felling of the tree by the dispossessed themselves.

13 Biler is a character that symbolizes the evil and disorder in Gunadule stories.

14 Ibeler is a character who represents in the Gunadule stories the good, the liberation of Mother Earth, from the dispossessed. It is also a symbol of the unity and harmony of the cosmos.

15 Pablo Richard, "Ya es Tiempo de Proclamar un Jubileo: Sentido general del Jubileo en la Biblia y en el Contexto Actual," RIBLA: *Revista de Interpretación Bíblica Latino Americana* 33 (1999), 8.

11 Pentecostalism and the Spirit of Local Development

Alfred Cooper

Abstract

"This place is now an Eden," is the way ex-Pastor Daniel Figueroa refers to Guarilihue, eighty years after the Pentecostals arrived in one of Chile's poorest agricultural communities in the central valley's Coelemu district. "The remarkable thing is that there are no drunkards, even though they produce wine! Nor are there prostitutes, gamblers, thieves, no police patrol, nor local magistrates, a place of dreams and satisfaction," he adds. This case study seeks to tell the story of how the Pentecostal revival in the 1940s reached over eighty percent of the population of Guarilihue, raising spiritual, oral, and developmental standards, overcoming local poverty, becoming "an Eden" in ex-Pastor Figueroa's words.

Introduction

Guarilihue, known as the "Pearl of Itata," is a tiny community that was last registered in the 2002 national census at slightly more than 700 inhabitants:[1] 407 men and 337 women in 235 homes averaging 3.16 inhabitants per home. Today's figures at the Municipality of Coelemu show a population that varies between 1,200 to 1,500 to date. Taking in Upper Guarilihue, there may even be an existent population of circa 2,000 people. Social worker, Valentina Sanhuesa Martel, daughter of present-day Pastor of the Iglesia Evangélica Pentecostal, Apolonides Sanhueza, confirms these statistics.[2]

My question for this community is this: Is the transitional development of what was in the 1940s, the very poor community of Guarilihue in becoming a very prosperous community in a period of eighty years, due, in fact, to the arrival of the Pentecostal gospel in 1939? The Weberian theory would hope the answer is "yes," and I will seek to construct and confirm this thesis from the testimony of the church members and local statistics.

Focus of study

My approximation to the study of Guarilihue embraces the Weberian concept of development through the Protestant work ethic,[3] salvation, thrift, re-investment, and work as a contribution and service to God and community as observed in post-Reformation, Calvinist, Northern Europe. Moreover, Weber's special focus on how Protestant communities, and what he denominates as "sects" (here, the Pentecostal church, Iglesia Evangélica Pentecostal de Chile) can inter-relate in a network of "honorability" that in the United States produced a culture of prosperity.[4] When applied to this obscure, isolated, and little-known community, there emerges a classic picture of development from extreme poverty in 1939 to remarkable prosperity in 2019. I was, therefore, able to focus my study on a specific time period of eighty years. My wife and I arrived at the church of over 700 members on the exact day of their eightieth-anniversary celebrations.

Through a series of twenty-nine semi-structured interviews of fourteen people over two days, I was able to acquire enough primary material to trace the history of this remarkable Pentecostal church, its development, and its undoubted influence in the community. From the first-hand testimonies of the interviewees, I was able to gather adequate material to support my work. These include the pastor and his wife, key church members who have the memory of the earliest stages of the Christian and local community, several young professionals who comprise the present generation with their particular updated perspectives of social transition, and the one non-Pentecostal in the village that I was able to find who gave me an "outside" critical appraisal of the church and its community involvement.

A Brief History of Guarilihue

The first records, mostly handed down by word of mouth, would suggest that the sector known as Guarilihue was only sparsely inhabited by indigenous peoples who lived in *ruca* (reed huts) and mostly lived off farming and livestock. The Spaniards who arrived found small trails and few signs of habitation and land that seemed propitious for the planting of vines. The lands were empty for many decades "without an owner" according to oral tradition, and therefore officially belonged to the king of Spain. During the nineteenth century Chilean wars of Independence, the area was used to move armies from both sides and by outlaws who took refuge in the hills. A famous bandit, José Miguel Neira, operated from the area of Guarilihue, and it is thought that some of his descendants made the area their home. Several of the church members still bear his surname, for example, and there is a wine from this region named after him.

A Choice Area for Wine

Guarilihue is situated in the middle of the *Ruta del Vino*, the wine route which was both its undoing and its development boon. In a recent article on the town in Chile's main newspaper, *El Mercurio*, Hernán Liñan explains why the local grape has become so valuable over the years, stating,

> In fact, today, the revaluation of heritage strains is in fashion, and in that matter, Guarilihue is at the top of the list, with Semillón, Aramón, Moscatel de Alejandría, and País strains. So Guarilihue is one of Chile's choice wine-growing areas, and yet it has been almost entirely cultivated by Pentecostal families who never touch a drop of wine! [5]

Another article in a viticulture magazine says something similar:

> The evangelical church is disproportionately large. In the middle of that small street that people here call the "town" of Guarilihue, this church slaps you in the face with its columns, its thick cement walls, its two floors of cream-painted concrete. The signboard reads, "Templo de la Iglesia Evangélica Pentecostal." Then I find out from the wife of Don Omar, a producer of grapes and one of the notables of the town, that "eighty percent of the inhabitants of Guarilihue are evangelicals." Occasionally a Catholic priest comes by, but he merely walks around, because, he is told, they have known the gospel for many years now, and that they number seventy percent of the town; that there are no robberies in the place, there are no drunks, there is no crime even though, imagine, there is so much wine.[6]

Visitors to the area will note the area is now enormously prosperous. On either side of the one road and up on the hills of Guarilihue Alto, one discerns large, luxury homes with swimming pools; homesteads with vineyards dotted haphazardly among them. In the distance are the pines, the new source of prosperity that the locals have bought into. The homes of the brethren are large and comfortable, like the houses of the upper middle sectors in Santiago. Each family, it seems, sports two or three large vans and pick-up trucks. The setting tells of past poverty but of present prosperity and comfort. The present economic shift from wines to timber with the advent of the *Celulosa Arauco y Constitución*, a Chilean wood pulp, engineered wood, and forestry company in Nueva Aldea, some twenty miles away, has brought more prosperity to local farmers, despite the evidenced ecological damage that is mounting against the company's policies. It was this originally inhospitable land that became known for its drunkenness, carousing, and abject poverty that was to later become the "Pearl of Itata."

A Prophesy

Recounting a prophecy about the future of Guarilihue, Miguel Sanhueza had this to say, "Everyone remembers how a brother, Nuñez, got up in a meeting forty years ago and said, 'There will be roads, one day, where now there are only river tracks and carts. These tracks will rise up, and this valley will become roads that will be filled with vehicles.'" To a man and woman, the community all confirm that this transformation is due to the gospel.

Remembering Guarilihue of the past, Don José Martel, one of the oldest surviving members and the father-in-law to Pastor Apolonides, says:

> I remember it being very poor. Very poor . . . I was born in Guarilihue, and I remember there were no roads, only tracks by the river, small rucas (reed huts built in the indigenous style). As a child, I wore *chalas* (car tires with string). Every Saturday, there would be *fiestas* where they would gamble and drink. The drunkenness caused miserable poverty. Cards and drinking. We grew up very poor, eating a little wheat and potatoes where we could get them. There was great violence in the home, and the women were much more patient than they are today, as they would wait after a beating until the husband got over the drunken state, and then they would go back to him.

The Iglesia Evangélica Pentecostal

The gigantic white Pentecostal church that measures almost 150 square meters seats up to 1000 members when the upstairs gallery is opened for special occasions and seems to take up the entire block of surrounding land that has been bought up by the brethren. It looks out of place in this rural setting. It is larger than many city church buildings, or "temples" as they call them. These believers are the direct inheritors of the now-famous Chilean Pentecostal revival of 1909.

Pentecostalism in Chile

Willis Hoover (1858–1936) tells his own story of how the Methodist Church in Valparaiso sought God fervently after hearing of the Azusa style Pentecostal outpourings in India under Pandita Ramabai's school for orphaned girls in Mukti,[7] at a time when Protestants numbered a small fraction of the population. Various National Census readings give percentages for the population of Protestants/*Evangélicos*, in 1920 at 1.45%,[8] at 5.6% in 1960,[9] later 15.14% in 2012, reaching 16.62% in 2017.[10] Out of a national population of 17,574,003 Chileans, 2,145,092 called themselves *evangélicos*. Eighty percent of the *evangélicos* in Chile, by the same census readings, are Pentecostal.

After coming to Chile with his wife as Methodist missionaries under William Taylor[11] in 1889, Willis Hoover tells of how, in 1909, successive outpourings upon their Methodist holiness-styled churches led to full-blown revival that eventually led them out of the Episcopal Methodist church. His book extensively details the ways in which the baptism of the Holy Spirit brought new manifestations to their experience, leading to a wave of Pentecostal revival and growth.[12] Valparaiso, Chile, thus became one of the first manifestations of the Pentecostal revival of the twentieth century. Because, as Juan Sepúlveda has expounded,[13] it was an isolated revival and therefore developed particular indigenous characteristics, it is a particularly interesting example to study.

The Baptism of the Holy Spirit

As has been noted, Hoover was a Methodist and had already been privy to experiences in the Holy Spirit holiness in that tradition. But what he now sought was the Azusa-style Baptism of the Holy Spirit with "manifestations," including tongues as the initial evidence. This they received in a period between June and September 1909.[14] With this breakthrough, Hoover established the first Pentecostal church in Chile, initially called *La Iglesia Metodista Pentecostal*. This church split over leadership squabbles in 1932 and formed *La Iglesia Evangélica Pentecostal*.[15]

Evangelism

Giving his reflections in a Pentecostal newspaper in 1932, some thirteen years after the revival had commenced and only seven years before the gospel reached Guarilihue, Hoover lays out reasons for the success of the revival. After listing the many characteristics of the classic Pentecostal manifestations that they had enjoyed, he further, and very tellingly says:

> Perhaps one of the secrets of the growth is the intense evangelism that has taken place. It can truly be said of the brothers that they are all occupied and occupied all of the time. A congregation will form a group of brothers who organize themselves into groups of "volunteers," choose a leader, often the pastor himself, and begin to work regularly. They preach on the streets and venture into new territories where the gospel has not been heard before, cycling to villages or nearby cities whereby they start up new works. When these new communities are formed, the volunteers will continue to visit them on a weekly basis even though they be twenty, thirty or forty kilometers away. These new congregations that are thus started up with so much sacrifice will, in turn, continue the work of evangelism themselves.[16]

Pastor Polo

Today, the pastor of the *Iglesia Evangélica Pentecostal* in Guarilihue (from here on referred to as IEP) is Apolonides Exequiel Sanhueza Neira. Pastor Polo (given this nickname for short, and because he is a "local kid") is now their sixth pastor. A humble and godly man, who punctuates his phrases with "only by the grace of the Lord" or "for his glory," confirmed to me the key characteristics of the IEP Pentecostalism that had led to such growth in Guarilihue. "Undoubtedly, the baptism of the Holy Spirit is the great secret for us Pentecostals. And then the evangelism that follows as you can see for yourself."

The earliest groups of evangelists were workers named by Pastor Hoover himself, such as Pastor Venegas from Concepción, and after him, Juan Arias Bravo, who came to work the sectors around Concepción pioneering new *locales* (mission localities). One such local was Guarilihue.

Eightieth Gospel Anniversary

On November first, 2019, the Guarilihue IEP church was celebrating eighty years since the gospel had arrived in the area. They were also honoring their elderly members, many of whom had clear memories of the beginning of the revival that had eventually swallowed up, it seems, practically the entire local populace. Currently, on any given Sunday, the congregation of 650 to 700 people arrives for the evening service from where they would have attended their morning Bible Schools in their eight local groupings in Tomé, Rahuil, Magdalena, El Castaño, El Canelo, Checura, Carrizal, Tinajacura. These represent a roughly twenty-mile radius

When I asked Pastor Polo if he and his wife ever had a day off, he explained that it was difficult because on Sundays, there was work all day. In the morning in the eight *locales* (above), where the *guías* (lay workers in charge of teaching the Bible classes at the locales) would visit. At these places, as well as in the Central Temple where he was responsible, there were Bible classes on Sunday mornings. Then on Mondays, the Dorcases (women workers) would pray, and on Tuesdays, the Dorcases work preparing for local charities. Thursdays were dedicated to going out preaching in the localities. On Fridays, he had to prepare the Bible class for his *guías*. Saturday started with a prayer meeting, followed later by the cyclists and preachers going out to all the neighboring towns and villages. Added to this was the monthly vigil on Friday from 8:00 p.m. to 12:00 a.m., "or until the Spirit leads. We plan the hour of entry, but he plans the hour of the exit!"

Furthermore, since the days of Pastor Hinojosa, the work of the pastor has been so influential that the pastor had become a leader for the entire community. He was a judge to help solve family problems, a social worker, even an ambulance driver to nearby Coelemu when ladies were about to give birth (he had recently had five such runs in one of his three pickup trucks). He told me he has a personal, private prayer habit, three times a day; in the morning, at midday, and at night. "There is never any rest," he smiled seriously, "because the Holy Spirit never rests! Of course, I train deacons so that they can carry the burden with me and so that the people don't get bored with listening only to me!"

The Hinojosa Years

Time is measured by pastoral tenure in Guarilihue. Their timeline, therefore, looks as follows:

Froilán Hinojosa Venegas: 1957–1975. Built the first church in 1969.
Luis René Zambrano Tapia: 1975–1989.
Aldo Exequiel Córdoba Muñoz: 1989–2003. Built the present church in 1997.

José Morales Osses: 2003–2004.
Daniel Figueroa Godoy: 2004–2016.
Apolonides Exequiel Sanhueza Neira: 2016–present.

I was able to discern without too much difficulty that the really major revival work and fruit had begun under Pastor Froilán Hinojosa, the first established pastor in Guarilihue. Before him, they had only been a large *local* and a Sunday School. I was eager to talk with his three children, Daniel, Joel, and Esther, who are all now successful traders in wines with some of the largest wine companies in Chile like *Concha y Toro* and *De Martino*. I wanted to get to my main question: Why did the community prosper as it has?

The Poverty of the Early Mission Years

Esther explained how there were fifteen children in the family and how she was sixteen when their mother died, leaving their pastor father a widower. He never married again and gave himself entirely to the development of the church and the community. She became the mother for the children, and she says she was able to raise them all and be her father's church helper at the same time:

> Sometimes visitors would arrive, and there was nothing in the home but bread, and my father would say, "Serve the bread, daughter. And the wheat coffee." At other times when the construction workers would come, we would have to go and sleep on the hay, as they needed to sleep in the house with their machines. We would put the same chicken bones back into the pot to make soups. We would go without when the visitors came.

Then she pointed at the eightieth-anniversary festivities and noted, "And see today how this is a banquet, like an expensive wedding ceremony! So, God has prospered us over these eighty years!"

Esther's reflection was an intelligent appraisal of what had happened over the eighty years, especially since she lived the difficult but fruitful years when the revival truly burst over Guarilihue under the ministry of her father, Pastor Hinojosa:

> I remember how the politicians would come when there were elections as they knew we held many votes. We are around eighty percent of the community. Frei and Jorge Alessandri[17] came and my mother, I remember, prophesied to him: "Don't worry you will be President of Chile," which of course came

true! My father would visit everyone, the sick and troubled, nicely dressed up. Later, God gave him a car, once he had made a great effort so that roads would be built and we no longer had to walk along the river edges. It was Joel here who would be the ambulance driver when he had to take people to the hospital. Everyone loved him for these things.

And then God began to prosper us. . . . we had been very poor but now God began to teach us to look after our money, to reinvest our profits to buy more land and sow more vines, to make the best wines, even though no brother or sister ever touches a drop of wine. You see that in this *Valle de Itata* we have the oldest vines in Chile and also the best. We were able to bottle over a million liters and so we were able to sell, thank God, at the best prices.

Because of all the wine, drunkenness was everywhere. When the gospel came, people were completely delivered from alcoholism and began to be prospered with their money and families. Our family now owns over seventy hectares of vineyards. Nowadays, we only sell grapes. We no longer bottle the wine. And what happened, in the end, was that the Catholics began to fall behind. You see, God prospers us with health and plenty. They began to want to copy the [Pentecostal] Christians so they could also prosper and use their money better. The [Pentecostal] Christians would help their neighbors and also invite them to church.

The Gospel Arrives

The earliest knowledge of the gospel arrived from Tomé in 1939, some twenty-three miles away from Guarilihue, sent from the IEP in Concepción. These preaching groups would walk for miles, following the riverbeds and reaching the small villages and communities on the way. "Hoover's preachers of this Pentecostal gospel arrived with powerful, anointed preaching, invitations to come to the services where 'God will transform your lives,'" remembers eighty-three-year-old José Martel Torres, as he recalled the way drunken and miserable Guarilihue was gradually awakened to Christ's transformation:

> The preachers first came from Tomé in 1939, and soon there was a little local gathering in the wine storehouses, next to the vats where wine was produced. We could smell the wine all the service. We were taken to the services by an aunt. But later, when my Dad was converted to the Lord from his drunkenness, he began to preach, himself, with great power. We started another small gathering (called locales) in Tinajacura. I would accompany him, preaching outside, and soon it became like doves flocking to their roost. Many began to arrive.

The question begs an answer: why did the neighbors arrive in this distant, rural, inhospitable, vice-ridden, violent place of poverty?

The Power of Transformation

Repeatedly, those interviewed would use two phrases that for them explained the impact on the local population. *"Dios hace el trabajo"* (God does the work), and *"Dios los transform"* (God transformed them). There was clearly a perception of supernatural encounters with the living God. It was also clear that the divine intervention had a transformational effect on those who came to the meetings and eventually believed. José tells of his own father's conversion:

> My father was converted from extreme poverty. He had eight children and would drink all of his money. One day he went out looking for someone to give him some bread, and no one gave him a crumb. With great sadness, he went up into the hills to pray and ask if what the *evangélicos* preached was true. He went up twice to pray and felt nothing. But on the third time, God was waiting for him. . . . he felt God's reprimand and received faith. From there, the blessing began. He never drank again, and he became one of the most faithful workers of the church. His name was Fidel Segundo Martel. I used to accompany him preaching. I wanted to preach, so I practiced preaching to the bulls.

The factor that most appears to have impacted and brought the community to join the IEP *locales* was this transformation from alcoholism and family abuse into honorable, sober citizens who began to work hard, look after their families, and develop their work; even work related to the production of wine. Emblematic of this transformation was the testimony of don Miguel Sandoval who appears to have been something of a Gadarene in the community:

> I own the shop *El Manatial* beside the church. I had a loudspeaker next to me all day when they preached! I sometimes felt that fire was burning me up as I listened. We were Catholics with no life change. I got ill with peritonitis. Doctors told me I had three days to live. Death came and said to me, "I am coming for you." I cried out to God finally and asked for his forgiveness. At 11:00 at night, again, death came for me. I was taken up to what looked like a giant fence where no sin could go through. That was when I heard the Lord say, "Your sins are forgiven" and "I am going to heal you." He also said, "Through your words, many will come to this salvation." And so, it was. I was healed, and then ministry began with my wife, who also was

saved. Later, with Pastor Zambrano, I was appointed to be president of the "volunteers" who went out preaching. I have never stopped working for the Lord, and many have come to him.

Indeed, many refer to Sandoval as a key figure in the conversion of the community, much like the Samaritan woman who took many to see Jesus (Acts 4:39).

The Supernatural Element

José remembers the great power of the meetings when the Holy Spirit would manifest:

> In the meetings, we children would sometimes be terrified. When the men were taken by the Spirit, they would begin to dance and whirl, worshiping God, crying *Aleluya*, speaking in tongues sometimes. Because they worked in the wine presses, they wore clogs with nails on the soles. These nails would strike the stone floor, and sparks would fly. The wooden crates that served as benches were piled up so that the people could dance unhindered, and we children would scamper up onto them and watch the sparks fly! Sometimes, people would fall as though smitten to the ground, four or five at a time, and the ladies would have to cover them with blankets.

La Iglesia Evangélica Pentecostal Community Influence

The following are influences on the community.

Number: The three days we were able to share with the IEP left us astonished at the fact that numerically they have won practically their entire community to their church, and at the all-pervasive impact of the gospel on the present-day culture of the town.

Frugality: The biblical Pentecostalism (Protestantism, as Weber would see it), in fact, did teach the newly incorporated members to begin to use their money wisely, to reinvest in more land, to take care of their families, to "save and prosper," as Esther explained.

Holiness: Their emphasis on holiness is seen everywhere. The women, dress in the old-style Pentecostal way, long skirts (no trousers!), decently showered and clean, hair worn in a bun mostly and never cut, the men in suits and ties for church, always respectfully attired, such that a modern observer could think he is in an Amish town.

Morality: Morally, they are, of course, the majority and prevailing influence. The all-pervasive embrace of family values makes for sound co-existence. These values include loving relationships, respect for authority, submission to the law, obeying kingdom values in obedience to God, helping neighbors, respect for private property, and keeping all vice at bay, including alcohol (of course!), internet pornography, drugs, and violence.

Ecology: There is visible ecological consciousness. There was hardly a paper to be seen on the streets because they take order and tidiness very seriously. When I found a beer can and some paper wrappers on the ground at the top of a neighboring hill, I was surprised. It was later explained to me that a group of bikers had breezed through the town and had gone up the hill.

A Catholic Opinion

It was important for me to find at least one person who would give me an outsider interview, one who could give a different perspective on the massive evangelical presence and influence on the town. It was remarkably difficult, but, by chance, I came across Edith Ulloa, who managed the local grocery shop. I had expected her to be an *evangélica* since the shop was called *El Manantial* (the Spring of living water). I later learned that it belonged to an IEP member, and she rented it from him (the owner was Miguel Sandoval, of course!). She told me she had lived all her life in Guarilihue, was a Catholic, and yet coexisted happily with the many IEP brethren all around her. "Tell me," I asked, "Is it healthy that a town is made up of seventy-five percent *evangélicos*?" "It's not seventy-five percent but ninety percent," she retorted frankly. She continued:

> This big church next door is the IEP, and they are seventy-five percent of the town. But there are other evangelicals: the Methodist Pentecostals, the Wesleyans, the *Iglesia Pentecostal de Dios*, put together with the Catholics, who make up ten percent of the population. We are all Christians! There is good and bad in having so many *evangélicos*. The good is that we are a peaceful community all the time, there is no crime, no drunkenness, no swearing, the schools are full of well-behaved children, and the police have no work to do here. In fact, the Captain of Coelemu police some years back complained that the local police never sent in any reports, not even of some drunk wandering the streets as in the other towns.

She later informed me that there was one known drug user in the school, who was influenced by friends from other cities, but that the whole community was aware of his problem and that it was an example of where the IEP should also help.[18] She continued that there was another man whose transformation was very impressive. She then told the story of Miguel Sandoval, whose testimony is recorded earlier in this chapter. According to her, many in the community joined the church because of him. She then described those she considered as separatists:

> They have been very separatist in the past, although now that Polo, a fellow from Guarilihue is the pastor, I notice they are getting better. They could help the community more! They could build a Fire Station, for instance, or an old peoples' home. We seriously need both. Or help in the Teacher Parent associations, but they were forbidden to take part in politics or other social interactions with the community by some of their pastors. This is not good. They are so influential! Look, before, Pastor Hinojosa (Froilán Hinojosa Venegas, 1957–1975) was a great influence. He made contacts with Coelemu and became President of the committee that built the roads, he was always helping everyone whether they were from the church or not, and he even had a bridge named after him!

Further Questions

Several questions began to form in my mind as I interviewed the older members. Did this "old time religion" with buns and long dresses have a sell-by date? How could the fast pace of change in Chile, a globalizing culture, be kept out? Was this Protestant work ethic, clearly successful during these eighty years, still a working framework for the future Guarilihue community? These inquiries were especially pressing as during those very days of our visit, as in Santiago and most major cities in Chile, huge unrest and criminal ravaging was going on, ostensibly on the theory that "this neo-liberal economic model is now dead!" I needed to interview the youth to find out their perspective on the future.

How the Youth see the Future

Hector Neira Martel (a descendant of the famous bandit from earlier days) is from Guarilihue but went to Concepción to study Psychology. He began the conversation by confirming the Weberian theory behind the remarkable development in Guarilihue. But his interest lay mainly in explaining why so many of the IEP young people remained firm in their faith and Christian testimony even though now most parents help them go to study at university, and they no longer want to take on the family wine business. There are many serious professionals among them now. Martel said, "it used to be ten percent of the youth who went on to higher education, but now it is eighty or ninety percent." He understood that the young people receive such a healthy formation and community identity while at the Guarilihue church that later they step naturally as believers with a faith in God into their various professions like doctors, dentists, and teachers.

As the conversation progressed, Martel revealed weakness and danger I can discern among the Pentecostal youth in Chile generally, "In my case, I had to separate the naturalistic aspects of my studies with the spiritual. As my studies questioned my values or premises, I learned to separate these so that I studied psychology as a discipline separate from my faith. I took the understanding but didn't let it invade my faith."

When I suggested he read up on philosophy and apologetics, he immediately retorted that he would love to and that it is only recently (over the last twenty years?) that these subjects have been allowed for the youth to study by pastors reared on the dictum that "the letter kills." This is, of course, an aging community, and most youths want to emigrate. Martel explained:

> Wines made us prosper, and they are now world-famous, but here youth want to work at other things, and not just in their family industry. You know, so much work and prosperity has affected us. We are tending to be a little more insular. The farmers have never developed a cooperative system, for instance. They have helped one another out, and the community but not wanted to organize themselves further than that. Here is a challenge for the future of our community—more collectives in working schemes.

Pastor Polo's daughters, Valentina Sanhueza Martel (age twenty-four), a social worker from Santo Tomás University and INACAP technical college, and María José Sanhueza Martel (age twenty-one), a teacher in the local state school, held to much of what Martel said. "Youth remain faithful to their basic faith premises mostly because they contrast their very stable and peaceful IEP culture with what they meet at the University 'outside.'" They also confirmed that youth want to leave, though they take their values with them when they do leave:

> The Guarilihue church prospered with the wines, but then the prices have dropped, and youth want to leave. Yes, they are convinced that the grounding they received in the church has stood them firm, and we want to bring up our children in the same way. We all speak the same language, and there is only one drug offender here influenced from outside.

At the school, María José tells of how sixty percent of the children are IEP and that half of the teachers are also. They respect secular state rulings for the school but find that since they share a church as well as a classroom, they will often sing Christian songs together and pray. She said:

> When our kids go off to college, their faith gets a blow at first and tends to wane as their eyes are opened to all that there is out there, but usually, they contrast the lifestyles and end up returning to the faith of their church. We realize that the family is breaking down in our Chilean society, and we must help with our testimony hold it together.

Conclusion

Clearly, the Pentecostal gospel with the baptism of the Holy Spirit, and its biblical ethos and lifestyle, brought capitalism and prosperity to Guarilihue. The youth discern that, despite the community church spirit, their capitalist enterprises could now enter a new collaborative phase, although they find it hard to see how it would occur. Weber's "networks of honorability" have operated from the start, as a Pentecostal was always a trustworthy person to do business with, and later the Catholic community emulated the Pentecostal way. "And, quite honestly, there seems little incentive to change the way things have been run so successfully up until now, apart from the migration of the youth to other activities," says Héctor Martel.

Can the globalizing world shift be kept at bay as they seem to do for now? Will the youth who are beginning to paint their nails and cut their hair maintain their Pentecostality, even if they are to lose the more external aspects of their IEP Pentecostalism? Let Pastor Polo's last words to me leave the incognitos in the air and focus us on the task, "It is so wonderful how the Lord continues to work and win souls here in Guarilihue! There still is so much work to do!"

Notes

1. "Los Censos de Población en Chile (1813-2002)," MemoriaChilena: Biblioteca Nacional de Chile, http://www.memoriachilena.gob.cl/602/w3-article-31530.html, accessed April 3, 2021.
2. All interviews were held in Guarilihue, Chile, from November 1–3, 2019.
3. Max Weber, *The Protestant Work Ethic and the Spirit of Capitalism* (New York: Scribner, 1958).
4. Max Weber, *Sociología de la Religión* (Mexico City: Colofón, 2010), 132–159.
5. "Economía Y Negocios," *El Mercurio* (February 10, 2019).
6. Patricio Tapia, "Guarilihue Vinorama," November 5, 2017, http://guarilihue.blogspot.com/2017/11/guarilihue-vinorama.html, accessed April 4, 2021.
7. Willis Collins Hoover, trans., Mario G. Hoover, *History of the Pentecostal Revival in Chile* (Santiago: Ebenezer Publishing, 2000).
8. "XII Censo General de Población y I de Vivienda," MemoriaChilena: Biblioteca Nacional de Chile, http://www.memoriachilena.gob.cl/archivos2/pdfs/MC0055466.pdf, accessed April 4, 2021.
9. "Censo Población, 1960," Instituto Nacional de Estadística, https://www.ine.cl/docs/default-source/censo-de-poblacion-y-vivienda/publicaciones-y-anuarios/anteriores/censo-de-poblaci%C3%B3n-y-vivienda-1960.pdf?sfvrsn=38205f0d_2, accessed April 4, 2020.
10. "Memoria Censo 2017," Censo Instituto Nacional de Estadística, https://www.ine.cl/docs/default-source/censo-de-poblacion-y-vivienda/publicaciones-y-anuarios/2017/memoria-del-censo-2017/libro_memoria_censal_2017_final.pdf?sfvrsn=2f7aa860_6, accessed April 4, 2021.
11. A well-known Methodist mission promoter who brought Methodist missionaries to Chile at the end of the nineteenth century and founded schools in Chile.
12. Hoover, *History of the Pentecostal Revival*.
13. Juan Sepúlveda, "The Power of the Holy Spirit and Church Indigenisation: A Latin Perspective," in Néstor Medina and Sammy Alfaro, eds., *Pentecostals and Charismatics in Latin America and Latino Communities* (New York: Palgrave Macmillan, 2014).
14. Hoover, *History of the Pentecostal Revival*, 29–38.
15. Hoover, *History of the Pentecostal Revival*, 246.
16. Willis Collins Hoover, "Pentecostés en Chile," *Fuego de Pentecostés* 54 (1932), 1.

17 Presidential candidates who visited Pentecostal churches seeking their votes in the 1940s and 1960s.
18 I had to marvel at the fact that there was only one.

12   *Todo lo Puedo*: The Empowerment of Children Born into Poverty through ChildHope: A Case Study

Mary Kathleen Mahon

Abstract

Poverty in Latin America is marked by severe economic disparity, the effects of which are especially damaging to children, negatively impacting their opportunities for the future and marring their sense of identity. Poverty is a form of powerlessness which is intensified in the lives of children. The ministry of ChildHope is a compassionate response to the needs of poor children that provides education and Spirit-empowered transformation. This essay discusses ways in which Spirit-empowerment is expressed within the community of the ChildHope schools.

Introduction

The severe economic disparity that is characteristic of poverty in Latin America is particularly damaging to children's development, hindering their opportunities for the future, and marring their sense of identity. Poverty is a form of powerlessness, which is intensified in the lives of the vulnerable, especially children. For children who are born into poverty, it is difficult to imagine a future that is distinct from the reality in which they live. This powerlessness produces hopelessness, which results in children who are unable to realize the potential with which they have been created. The ministry of ChildHope is a compassionate and intentional response to the needs of poor children, providing quality education and Spirit-empowered transformation.

This essay discusses five ways in which the Spirit-empowerment of the children is expressed within the community of the ChildHope schools. These are: the teachers' belief in the potential success of the children; the students' assertions that they believe they can make something of their lives, often citing the verse "I can do all things through Christ"; an experiential spirituality that reframes the negative social influences affecting the children; the transformation of the children's sense of identity; and narratives or sacred stories which empower the children to envisage a place for themselves in the world.

Poverty in Latin America

Latin America cannot seem to pull itself out of poverty. Although at first glance, the region of Latin America and the Caribbean is classified as a region of middle income by world standards, a closer study shows poverty rates that are much higher than would be expected in light of their high GDP per capita.[1] This excess poverty is due to high levels of inequality in the distribution of resources. It is at the expense of the poor strata that the wealthier classes get richer in the region.[2] Quality educational access for the poor is one of the strategies listed by the World Bank to combat the deep-rooted inequality in Latin America.[3] It is only through education that the poorer classes can hope to pull themselves out of the trap of poverty.

The 2005 United Nations Report on the World Social Situation identifies the development of an equitable society as the key to the reduction of poverty worldwide.[4] As seen in the case of Latin America, overall economic growth alone cannot guarantee the eradication of poverty. In recent decades, as the economies in Latin America have grown, the chasm between the rich and the poor has remained great, or even widened.[5] In order to see a sustained change in the indices of poverty, the problem of inequity in the region must be tackled. The United Nations report further states that increased opportunities are provided by equal access to public services—in particular education and healthcare—which is essential to decrease the great level of intergenerational transmission of poverty and inequality.[6]

In its global initiative of Sustainable Development Goals, The United Nations notes that education provides upward mobility and is key to escaping poverty.[7] This global initiative comes on the heels of the Millennium Development Goals, which made strides in raising the overall statistics of primary school enrollment. However, the final report noted that the poorest children in the world are still excluded from access to education.[8] Furthermore, mere access to elementary education is not enough to help people pull themselves out of poverty; secondary education is essential.

The salaries of the undereducated in Latin America perpetuate the disparity between rich and poor.[9] Although statistics vary from nation to nation, generally, in Latin America, those who have completed a sixth-grade education are able to earn fifty percent more than those with no education. Those with twelve years of education make twice as much as those who have no education.[10] This inequity of education leads to inequity of income as well as inequities in healthcare, power, and social integration. The connection between the lack of education and poverty is so intertwined that many studies assess poverty level in the region based on the educational culture of the home. A study by the Inter-American Development Bank, noting that insufficient education sets the course for poverty throughout the life cycle of the individual and across generations in Latin America, classifies homes as poor based on the educational level of the head of household.[11] A household is considered poor if the head of household did not complete primary education or sixth grade. According to this study, a child born into poverty who earns a secondary education is considered to have escaped or made a break from the intergenerational transmission of the poverty cycle in Latin America. Only one out of five students from families in poverty are able to complete secondary school.[12]

Primary education alone will not affect the inequality in Latin America. Furthermore, the poorer sectors in Latin America show higher dropout rates, higher repetition of grade levels, and poorer attendance in classes. A study by the Economic Commission for Latin America and the Caribbean (ECLAC) of the United Nations suggests that at least a tenth or eleventh-grade education is needed for people not to fall into poverty in the region. In addition, two years less of education implies twenty percent less income during a lifetime.[13]

Identity and Poverty

Poverty is a multidimensional phenomenon that encompasses more than a mere lack of income.[14] Among other factors, the poor lack the social power needed to improve their situation. It is this powerlessness that mars the image of God in the poor.[15]

The Construction of Self-Concept

The construction of self begins early on in a child's life. When children are born, they have no identity. Children are not born with social roles or self-representations to define themselves. Their identities are developed as they grow and interact with others in various social settings. Yet, once these identities are formed, they play a crucial role in the control and management of everyday life.[16] The development of a child's identity takes place within a cultural context.

This construction of self occurs as the developing child participates in social interactions within a particular cultural-historic situation.[17] The self helps to maintain the permanence of the culture, as well as react to its own evaluation of the culture. Bruner compares the self to a barometer, which, in essence, responds to the local cultural weather.[18] The self also has the capacity to overcome the negative aspects of the culture. By using its capacity for reflection and imagining alternatives, the self is able to reframe what the culture is offering and envisage a better future.[19] This agentive nature of self must be developed in order to help children break away from the culture of poverty.

Agency and Powerlessness

The quality of agency within the construct of self is particularly important in the empowerment of the individual. A sense of agency over the world and one's self includes a recognition of the individual's control over his or her own destiny.[20] Agency refers to the capacity of the individual to initiate and carry out activities, and thereby implies skill and know-how.[21] Because the school community is a child's earliest exposure to social institutions outside his or her home, the school and the educational process play a critical role in the formation of self.

Nobel laureate Amartya Sen, notes that individual agency is essential to development, although it is constrained by social, political, and economic opportunities.[22] While organizations such as the United Nations and the World Bank assess poverty in Latin America and the Caribbean by looking at the big picture, using national studies and statistics to gauge opportunities, the child born into poverty has a much different perspective. The statistics that indicate greater access to education and high Gross National Product (GNP) per capita are eclipsed by the reality of their day-to-day existence. This is the population that the ministry of ChildHope serves.

A child is in the unique stage of being and becoming. In this process of development, the child constructs a theory of self in order to make sense out of his or her world and experiences.[23] A child born into poverty experiences the reality of the powerlessness of the world in which he or she lives. His or her agency is constrained by these realities. Jayakumar Christian explains the powerlessness of the poor as captivity in a web of lies. It is a "world of flawed assumptions and interpretations."[24] For a child born poor, these lies influence his or her worldview and can negatively affect the development of self. The powerlessness of the poor is perpetuated by the worldview of the people in a poverty community.[25] The powerlessness of the poor is not only a current reality, but also a continuous disempowerment in the lives of the children.[26] In this context, a child's dreams for the future are very limited.

Children's Spiritual Development

Children's spirituality and spiritual development is a current focus of research that overlaps multiple disciplines within the social sciences.[27] While earlier research focused on areas of religious education and used cognitive and moral development stage methodologies to determine a child's grasp of concepts about God, current research is based on the theory that spirituality is an innate aspect of the developing child and not culturally constructed. Rather, spiritual awareness is biologically structured in human beings and expressed culturally.[28] Therefore, spirituality is a universal feature of humanity regardless of religious beliefs or lack thereof.

This essay studies the empowerment of children within the cultural context of the ChildHope schools. ChildHope is a ministry that partners with local Pentecostal Assemblies of God Churches within poor communities in Latin America and the Caribbean to bring about transformation in the lives of poor children through education and ministries of compassion. While the philosophical foundations of the schools are based on Christian and biblical values, students are not required to attend any particular church. Chapel services are held weekly, and each academic day begins with Bible reading, devotional reflection, and prayer. God and spirituality are an integral part of each day for the teachers and students.

Several key religious and spiritual formation theorists will be reviewed to provide a basis for the understanding of spirituality within the lives of children. James Fowler was a pioneer in faith development, being the first to study how a person's concept and understanding of God evolves.[29] Robert Coles listened to the stories of children, many of whom were facing great difficulties, as they applied their spirituality to provide meaning to what was happening around them.[30] These two laid the foundation for David Hay and Rebecca Nye's concept of spirituality that will be used to evaluate the spirituality in the ChildHope schools.[31]

James Fowler

In the area of religious and spiritual education, James Fowler's research provided a shift away from the study of the development of religious concepts to the study of faith development. His work integrated theories of psychosocial, cognitive, and moral development to identify six stages of faith development that span a person's lifetime.[32]

Faith development theory defines faith in both a functional and structural way that includes many faith traditions as well as secular ideologies.[33] Faith is understood in an inclusive sense and is qualified as the foundation for beliefs, values, and meaning, which provides an essential centering process giving direction to human beings, assisting them as they relate in community, and empowering them to deal with the challenges of life and death.[34]

Robert Coles

Robert Coles avoided paradigms and labels as his research evolved, and he listened to children's stories, noting an innate spirituality that promoted a resiliency among children living in challenging circumstances. Rather than assessing what a child is able to understand regarding spiritual matters based on his or her capacities within a structured situation, Coles spoke directly to children and allowed them to lead the flow of many of the conversations. Coles assumes that all human beings possess awareness or consciousness, and it is through language that people, children, and adults alike, attempt to understand and express what they learn to others.[35]

In his research with children, Coles noted a connection that children drew between meaning and spirituality. He observed that children draw upon their religious experience and spiritual values in order to understand what is happening to them and the reason why.[36]

David Hay and Rebecca Nye

The work of David Hay and Rebecca Nye identifies the core of children's spirituality as the construct of relational consciousness. The simple basis of children's spirituality seems to lie in a relational consciousness from which arise religious experiences that are aesthetic and meaningful, responses to mystery, and moral insight.[37] Spirituality, in this sense, refers to the consciousness that a child always expresses within the context of a relationship. The spirituality of children presents itself as a profound and detailed thought process that can be termed consciousness, all the while confined within a clearly relational realm.[38]

Hay and Nye identify three categories of spiritual sensitivity that provide a foundation to the study of spirituality and are believed to be part of any person's spiritual experience.[39] Awareness-sensing is more than involuntary alertness or focus of attention. It is also a reflexive process in which the child is aware of what he or she is experiencing.[40] Awareness–sensing of children's spirituality is expressed in the experiences of here and now, tuning, flow, and focusing.

Mystery-sensing is the transcendent aspect of spirituality. It refers to the awareness of incomprehensible experiences in the person's life.[41] In the expression of spirituality in children, mystery-sensing is seen in the constructs of wonder, awe, and imagination. Value-sensing, a term first coined by Margaret Donaldson in 1992, is the third category of spiritual sensitivity and refers to the moral expression of children's spirituality. Value-sensing is conveyed through delight and despair, ultimate goodness, and meaning. The qualities of relational consciousness as defined by Hay and Nye inform this case history by providing a definition of spirituality in the students.

Classical Pentecostalism

The belief system and practice of the ChildHope schools are aligned with Classical Pentecostalism. An emphasis on experiences with God and personal narratives or testimonies is encouraged in the classroom and chapel services. The three-fold expression of spirituality as relational consciousness: awareness-sensing, mystery-sensing, and value-sensing can help define the Pentecostal practice and experience of the students in the ChildHope schools.

The scientific data provided by the research supports the view that spirituality is entirely natural and grows out of a biological disposition. Although spirituality is innate in the biology of human beings, it can be dimmed or enhanced by culture.[42] Spirituality is essential to culture, providing the foundation for individual and societal contentment. Children have a rich capacity for spirituality that is merited to their psychological qualities and biological make-up. Spirituality naturally flows through the life of a child regardless of whether they can define or not. Their understanding of spirituality and experience is not based on religious knowledge or moral rules that they have been taught.[43] Additionally, Hay and Nye's research show the importance that a child be aware of his or herself as a subject in order to encourage the interpretation of the world in relational terms.[44]

The Child Born into Poverty

In light of the above, what is life like for a child born into poverty? Statistically, the future looks dim. To be able to pull themselves out of poverty, they must exceed their parents' level of education, and the motivation to do so must come from within. Economic stresses on the family pressure children to drop out of classes at the end of primary school to contribute, either by working to financially support the needs of the home or by caring for younger siblings, so the adults are free to work.

Life is also emotionally difficult. The births of most of the children born into poverty were not planned by the mother, and that message is communicated to the children. They feel that they are a mistake and a burden to the family. As they observe their lives, families, and communities, they find it difficult to imagine a better future for their lives. They experience the powerlessness of poverty. They often feel hopeless.

Agency is a concept that is essential in the development of self in a child,[45] and, I would argue, the key to Spirit-empowerment in the life of children born into poverty. Agency can be defined as the ability to decide to do something and carry it out. This idea is quite revolutionary in the life of a child who feels that he or she is an object rather than a subject in his or her life. For the children born into poverty, life merely happens to them. They do not feel like they have a choice that can affect their future.

For my doctoral research, I conducted a study of what teachers can do to foster agency in children born into poverty. The setting of the study was a ChildHope school in Costa Rica. If we look at the results of my research through a Pentecostal lens, we see that in most cases, the agency expressed in these students was an expression of Spirit-empowerment. While I conducted the research several years ago, my findings continue to be confirmed through my discussions with school personnel, in teacher forums, and conversations with children in the ChildHope schools.

ChildHope

The work and ministry of ChildHope trace its roots back to 1963 in the country of El Salvador. In 1963, a Christian school was founded by Assemblies of God Missionary John Bueno in response to the needs of poor children in San Salvador. The ministry grew throughout the nation, and in 1977, Latin America ChildCare (LACC) was founded with a threefold purpose. First, there was a desire to encourage the vision in other nations in Latin America and the Caribbean and to share the concern for marginalized children. Second, Latin America ChildCare sought to provide philosophical and theological guidelines to the new programs fomenting the priorities of evangelism and social concern. Finally, LACC was established to provide a channel by which interested donors in the United States and Canada could partner with the ministry and help individual children.[46]

The ministry of ChildHope (previously known as Latin America ChildCare) has spread throughout the region and currently reaches approximately 100,000 children in nearly 300 schools in twenty countries.[47] The mission of ChildHope is to transform the lives of children born into poverty through the good news of Jesus Christ, education, and ministries of compassion.

In my initial doctoral research and subsequent interviews with students in ChildHope schools, I have identified five ways in which Spirit empowerment is expressed in the lives of children as a result of the ministry within the ChildHope Schools.

Teachers' Belief in the Potential Success of the Students

Spirit-empowerment is cultivated in the lives of students when teachers communicate their belief in the potential success of the students, in spite of the low educational culture within the home. ChildHope teachers are aware of the social problems within the community and the complications in the students' home lives and are concerned that these external influences could have a negative impact on the students' learning. The teachers help the students deal with the negative social and familial influences.

In addition to an understanding of the community culture and its effect on the students' motivation for learning, the teachers are aware of the negative messages that many students receive at home from their own family members. Cognizant of the adverse influence of the students' realities at home, the teachers expressed their struggle to keep their students motivated. This motivation transmitted by the teachers results in the students feeling empowered. A third-grade girl expressed this principle when talking about her teachers: "She tells us that someday she will have to go the clinic and she will run into us. We will be old, and we will be working there as doctors."[48] One school communicated the belief in the students' potential success with a banner that was hung in a prominent location. At the top was printed *Todo Se Puede Lograr*, which means, "Anything can be accomplished." This is a title of a song that the children's choir sang at chapels and assemblies. On the banner were photos of previous students who were now professionals. There was a doctor, an administrator, a bishop, a teacher, and other professionals. The last frame was empty and included the text, "This space is for your photo."

Although the culture of the community and even the children's own homes are filled with hopelessness for the future, the community of the ChildHope school provides hope for the children by expressing belief in the students' potential for success. This hope, in turn, empowers the children to be able to envision a better future for themselves.

The Students' Assertions that they "Can do all things through Christ."

Luis Gonzalez Brenes is a graduate of a ChildHope school. He is currently a pastor and professor at both a Seminary and a Christian University in Costa Rica, and he holds multiple advanced degrees in education and theology. He earned a doctorate in education and recently completed his doctoral studies in theology. When Luis was ten years old, the ministry of his school had a competition. Children were challenged to memorize sixty verses from the Bible. The student who could recite all sixty would receive a brand-new, shiny bicycle. Luis wanted that bicycle and worked hard to memorize the verses. Although he was very prepared, Luis was nervous the day of the competition. He quite clearly recalls the Holy Spirit speaking to him and saying, "you can do this" in an audible voice. The verse "I can do all things through Christ who strengthens me" (Phil 4:13, NKJV) came to his mind. Luis felt empowered by the Spirit. He stepped forward and recited all sixty verses and won the bicycle.

At the time, Luis said he was very excited about winning the bike. As he reflects on the experience now, he realizes it represented much more for his life. He realized he had God-given talents to memorize and the ability to speak publicly. His teachers and the director of the school recognized his talent. Each time there was a need for a student to give a speech or preach a sermon, Luis was chosen. He believes this was God's Spirit empowering him for his future ministry both in the pulpit and in the classroom.

Nine-year-old Abagail, a current ChildHope student, shared her story of being empowered by the Spirit:

> God will help me to accomplish things. He came to earth to save us; he is real and wants to be with us. When I think of this verse, "I can do all things in Christ who strengthens me," it makes me think I can do anything. I wasn't going to participate in the Arts Festival - not in any competition in the school because I felt like I can't win, and I thought it wasn't worth it if I couldn't win. But then I read that scripture, "I can do all things . . ." so I decided to sing and I'm in the school choir. God gave me that verse, and now I do something I love to do - sing - in the school choir. [49]

Experiential Spirituality Reframes Negative Social Influences

The spirituality expressed in the school is of an experiential nature. Few references are made to doctrine or theology in the discussions of God in classrooms or in chapel services. The focus is on the Bible, God's presence, and his involvement in the everyday lives of the children. This methodology reframes the child's understanding of his or her circumstances and difficulties of life within a spiritual perspective and, in turn, empowers the students.

The values that are taught and practiced in ChildHope schools emerge from a Christ-centered, biblically-based faith and are linked to the experiential spirituality taught in the schools. The values held by the educational community provide a structure in which to reframe the negative social influences in the lives of the students. In addition, the

218 Good News to the Poor

Christian values taught in the school provide a context within which to interpret negative social influences in a manner in which students are able to respond to these influences.

Coralia Bonilla, the Director of Linda Vista ChildHope school, who has served for twenty-six years, explains the importance of values in the empowerment of children:

> The spiritual values are super important because in their families, they do not receive these; in fact, they receive anti-values. And for the children that have emotional problems or psychological problems, it is with values that we empower them that they are somebody, that they have value. It doesn't matter if they came from a home of poverty or extreme poverty. Or if they don't know their father, or if they don't even know who their father is, or if they have been given away by their mother. They know that there is someone—who is God—who loves them above all.[50]

In chapel services and in the daily devotional times within the classrooms, students are able to share the realities of their home lives in the form of the prayer request. Students request prayer for family members who are involved in drugs and violence, even those who are victims or perpetrators of serious crimes. The children are very aware of what happens in their community. The prayer times help the children to reframe the trauma of their own reality. They come to understand the role that Satan plays in trying to destroy the community and their families. They understand that God's presence is real and will help them through the difficulties. They learn that these events do not define them and that they do not need to follow the same path. The Spirit will empower them to have a different future. Tears are often shed, and burdens are left at the metaphorical altar.

The Transformation of the Children's Sense of Identity

In the lives of children born into poverty, empowerment is expressed in the ability to act, to make a decision for one's own life, and to carry it through. Children who have been born into generational poverty often feel like objects rather than subjects in their own lives. Poverty has been defined as powerlessness, and this powerlessness is intensified in the lives of children.[51] They often believe their future is set, and they are destined to live a similar life to those of their family members and others they observe in their community. Their world can be very small. Statistics paint a grim future for these students.

Often these children grow up aware that they were not planned, and they consider themselves a biological error. The vulnerability of childhood, combined with the belief that one's birth was neither planned nor desired within a context of the intergenerational transmission of the poverty cycle, can deeply mar a child's identity. Spirit-empowerment is seen in the lives of the children when the educational community of ChildHope intentionally molds the identity of the children with the word of God.

Coralia Bonilla recognized the crisis of identity of her students. She sought the Holy Spirit's guidance to lead her to scriptures for the children to memorize. She first required the teachers to memorize the scriptures. Then, the students would learn the verses weekly. The verses became a part of the identity of the children as they declared the truth of the Word of God.

Maria was a girl in a ChildHope school in Costa Rica. When she was in third grade, the teachers and director began noticing disturbing behavior in the little girl; she began acting seductively toward adult men. Soon it was discovered that Maria's sister was a sex worker and worked from home. Her brother was a drug dealer and also ran his business out of the house. Maria's mom also made her living by manipulating men. Maria was a beautiful and likable child. Her family began priming her to be able to someday pull them out of poverty. They told her someday a rich man would take her to live with him and she could help her family. The Director and the teachers at the school began working with Maria to help her understand her value, having been created in God's image. Maria's understanding of her identity changed, and she was empowered. By sixth grade, she was a spiritual leader among the girls. She understood that her identity and future were not determined by the choices and actions of her family, but by the empowerment of God in her life.

Narratives or Sacred Stories which Empower the Children to Envision a Place for Themselves in the World

Bruner notes that narrative provides cohesion to culture and structuring to individual lives. An individual can construct his or her identity and create a place of belonging within a culture through narrative.[52] The narrative is a key component in the lives of the students and the teachers at ChildHope school. In many instances, the narrative takes the form of personal sacred stories or testimonies. In this way, the difficulties of life's realities are reframed in a spiritual context, producing clarity, comfort, and hope in the lives of the students. Snyder defines hope as "a cognitive set involving the self-perceptions that one can produce routes to desired goals (pathways), along with the motivation to pursue these goals (agency)."[53]

Students are encouraged to use narrative to bring meaning and hope to their reality through prayer and the sharing of sacred stories or testimonies. In the daily prayer times and in the chapel services, students are encouraged to share prayer requests and the answers to prayers that they experienced in their lives. This practice helps the students to bring meaning to their lives by reframing the negative social influences and giving them hope and empowerment. In addition, as the children tell their stories, they are becoming a subject in the narrative.

A fifth-grade boy named Carlos shared his story. His mother was very sick. This concerned the boy and his siblings because the mother not only cared for them, she was also the primary breadwinner. He came to school with a burden for his mother. He and the other students prayed for his mother in the chapel. Carlos said that he felt the Holy Spirit and cried and cried during the service. His mother was healed. A few months later, they thought his brother had cancer, so Carlos and his brother "prayed really hard," and the brother was healed. The telling of the story empowered Carlos. The hearing of the story by Carlos' classmates empowered them to trust God in their lives.

As the children hear stories of God's intervention in the lives of their fellow students, they are able to see themselves in the stories and are given hope for their own difficulties in life. Students are empowered to create a place of belonging within the faith community and build the agency to turn to God when they are burdened. In turn, they are able to envision a better future for themselves, having been empowered by the Spirit.

Conclusion

There is a common practice in one of the schools that always moves me. It illustrates what Spirit-empowerment looks like in the faith communities of the ChildHope schools in the lives of children born into poverty. Each time a student, even those in preschool, stands up in a group to give a presentation, or make a speech, or lead in prayer, he or she will follow the same pattern: "Good morning. I am a child of God, and my name is Dillon."

I believe that phrase encapsulates the message of the school and is the foundation of the empowerment that I see expressed in the students of the ChildHope schools. I am a child of God; it doesn't matter if my father abandoned me. I am a child of God, and I am important to him; it doesn't matter what my family may say of me. I am a child of God created with a purpose in his image; it doesn't matter what my community thinks of my future. I am a child of God; it doesn't matter what statistics about poverty predict for my life. I am a child of God, and I can do all things through Christ who strengthens me.

Notes

1. United Nations, *The Inequality Predicament: Report on the World Social Situation 2005*, http://www.un.org/esa/socdev/rwss/docs/2005/rwss05.pdf, 49, accessed April 13, 2019.
2. John W. Sherman, *Latin America in Crisis* (Boulder, CO: Westview Press, 2000), 176.
3. David De Ferranti, Francisco H. G. Ferreira, Guillermo E. Perry, and Michael Walton, *Inequality in Latin America: Breaking with History?* World Bank Latin American and Caribbean Studies, World Bank Group, 2004, http://documents.worldbank.org/curated/en/804741468045832887/Inequality-in-Latin-America-breaking-with-history, 310, accessed August 15, 2020.
4. United Nations, *The Inequality Predicament*, 135.
5. In Latin America and the Caribbean, the bottom forty percent of the population receive 14.5% of the region's wealth while the top twenty percent consumes 53.2%. UNICEF, *The State of the World's Children 2019: Children, Food and Nutrition: Growing Well in a Changing World* (UNICEF, New York), 239, https://www.unicef.org/sites/default/files/2019-12/SOWC-2019.pdf, accessed August 15, 2020.
6. United Nations, *The Inequality Predicament*, 27.
7. UN Sustainable Development Goals, https://www.un.org/sustainabledevelopment/sustainable-development-goals/, accessed April 13, 2019.
8. United Nations, *The Millennium Development Goals Report 2015*, https://www.un.org/ millenniumgoals/2015_MDG_Report/pdf/MDG%20 2015%20rev%20(July%201).pdf, 26, accessed April 13, 2019.
9. Samuel A. Morely, *Poverty and Inequality in Latin America* (Baltimore, MD: Johns Hopkins University Press, 1995), 48.
10. United Nations, *The Inequality Predicament*, 76.
11. Ricardo Morán, Tarsicio Casteñeda, and Enrique Aldaz-Carroll, "Family Background and Intergenerational Poverty in Latin America," in Ricardo Morán ed., *Escaping the Poverty Trap: Investing in Children in Latin America* (Washington, DC: Inter-American Development Bank, 2003), 15–60.
12. ECLAC, *Social Panorama of Latin America* (Santiago, Chile: Economic Commission for Latin America and the Caribbean, 2010), 87.

13 Ernesto Ottone, "La Equidad en América Latina en el Marco de la Globalización: La Apuesta Educativa [Equality in Latin America in the Framework of Globalization: The Educational Bet]" in Sergio Martinic & Marcela Pardo, eds., *Economía Política de las Reformas Educativas en América Latina* [Economic Policies of Educational Reforms in Latin America] (Santiago, Chile: CIDE, 2001), 81.

14 John Friedman, *Empowerment: The Politics of Alternative Development* (Cambridge, MA: Blackwell 1992), 66.

15 Jayakumar Christian, *God of the Empty Handed: Poverty, Power and the Kingdom of God* (Monrovia, CA: MARC, 1999), 194.

16 Richard M. Ryan and Edward L. Deci, "On Assimilating Identities to the Self: A Self-determination Theory Perspective on Internalization and Integrity within Cultures," in Mark R. Leary and June Price, eds., *Handbook of Self and Identity* (New York: Guilford Press, 2003), 253.

17 Jerome S. Bruner, *Acts of Meaning* (Cambridge, MA: Harvard University Press, 1990), 107.

18 Bruner, *Acts of Meaning*, 110.

19 Bruner, *Acts of Meaning*, 110.

20 Daniel N. Stern, *The Interpersonal World of the Infant* (New York: Basic Books, 1985), 123.

21 Jerome S. Bruner, *The Culture of Education* (Cambridge, MA: Harvard University Press, 1996), 34.

22 Amartya Sen, *Development as Freedom* (New York: Anchor Books, 1999), xi.

23 Susan Harter, *The Construction of the Self: Developmental and Sociocultural Foundations*, 2nd ed. (New York: Guilford Press, 2013), 1.

24 Christian *God of the Empty Handed*, 161.

25 Christian *God of the Empty Handed*, 160.

26 Christian *God of the Empty Handed*, 157.

27 David Hay and Rebecca Nye, *The Spirit of the Child*, rev. Ed. (London: Fount, 2006); Donald Ratcliff, ed., *Children's Spirituality: Christian Perspectives, Research and Applications* (Eugene, OR: Cascade Books, 2006); E. C. Roehlkepartain et al., eds., *The Handbook of Spiritual Development in Childhood and Adolescence* (Thousand Oaks, CA: Sage, 2006).

28 David Hay, Helmut K. Reich, and Michael Utsch, "Spiritual Development: Intersections and Divergence with Religious Development," in E. C.

Roehlkepartain et al., eds., *The Handbook of Spiritual Development in Childhood and Adolescence* (Thousand Oaks, CA: Sage, 2006), 50.

29 James W. Fowler, *Stages of Faith* (New York: Harper and Row, 1981).

30 Robert Coles, *The Spiritual Life of Children* (Boston: Houghton Mifflin, 1990).

31 Hay and Nye, *The Spirit of the Child*.

32 Fowler's stages of faith development are (a) intuitive-projective (toddlerhood and early childhood), (b) mythical-literal (middle childhood and beyond), (c) synthetic-conventional (adolescence and beyond), (d) individuative-reflective, (e) conjunctive faith, and (f) universalizing faith, Fowler, *Stages of Faith*.

33 J. W. Fowler, and M. L Del, "Stages of Faith from Infancy through Adolescence: Reflection on Three Decades of Faith Development Theory," in E. C. Roehlkepartain et al., eds., *The Handbook of Spiritual Development*, 43.

34 Fowler and Del, "Stages of Faith," 36.

35 Coles, *The Spiritual Life*, 22.

36 Coles, *The Spiritual Life*, 100.

37 Hay and Nye, *The Spirit of the Child*, 109.

38 Hay and Nye, *The Spirit of the Child*, 109.

39 Hay and Nye, *The Spirit of the Child*, 65.

40 Hay and Nye, *The Spirit of the Child*, 109.

41 Hay and Nye, *The Spirit of the Child*, 75.

42 Hay and Nye, *The Spirit of the Child*, 141.

43 Hay and Nye, *The Spirit of the Child*, 93.

44 Hay and Nye, *The Spirit of the Child*, 109.

45 Most studies of the development of self focus on the evaluative nature of the self, such as self-esteem, self-efficacy, self-image. However, before a child can evaluate how he or she feels about him or herself, agency must be present and developed. A child must be empowered to make decisions and be empowered to carry them out. The children in the study rarely mentioned an evaluative assessment of themselves, rather what they valued were teachers who believed they could do something.

46 For an extensive history of the program of Latin America see Douglas Petersen, *Not by Might, nor by Power: A Pentecostal Theology of Social Concern in Latin America* (Oxford England: Regnum Books International, 1996).

47 Statistics gleaned from the ministry website, childhopeonline.org, accessed May 18, 2019.
48 Personal interview, San José, Costa Rica, February 8, 2019.
49 Personal interview, San José, Costa Rica, February 8, 2019.
50 Personal interview, San José, Costa Rica, September 26, 2013.
51 Judith Ennew and Brian Milne, *The Next Generation: Lives of Third World Children* (Philadelphia: New Society,1990), 22.
52 Bruner, *The Culture of Education*, 42.
53 Chris. R. Snyder, "Measuring Hope in Children," in Kristin A. Moore and Laura H Lippman, eds., *What do Children Need to Flourish?: Conceptualizing and Measuring Indicators of Positive Development* (New York: Springer, 2005) 61.

13 Religious Conflict in Nigeria and Poverty Dynamics in Northern Nigeria

Babatunde Adedibu

Abstract

Nigeria is perhaps one of the most diverse, multi-ethnic, multi-religious, and extremely volatile nations in Africa. This is due to ethnocentrism, politics, and religious idiosyncrasies, despite being a secular state constitutionally. Interestingly, the Nigerian federal state, despite being the largest economy in Africa with an estimated Gross Domestic Product (GDP) of $400 billion, though classified as a lower-middle-income country by the World Bank, is plagued by poverty. Moreover, it has been observed that in Nigeria, geography and religious incidents seem to have a positive correlation. An overview of the mapping of the religious crisis in Nigeria points to a preponderance of these events in the Northern states of Nigeria. This might reinforce Karl Marx's assertion that religion is the "opium of the people" in Northern Nigeria. This development has led to a resurgence of interdisciplinary research by scholars of religion, sociology, politics, and humanities in general on the effects of the environment on religious psychology and inclination to violence. It is pertinent to note that the ethno-religious crisis in Nigeria can be traced from the pre-colonial era based on previous scholarship assertion. However, this study provides a different perspective from other studies on the religious crisis in Nigeria by not only focusing entirely on causes of religious crisis, but also on the contributions of religious crisis to poverty in Northern Nigeria. The methodologies employed are observation and secondary sources that are relevant to the subject matter. This study will, among other things, examine how religious crisis is contributing to the continued impoverization of the inhabitants of Northern Nigeria.

Introduction

Nigeria is a vast and diverse country consisting of about 924 kilometers with a teeming population of about 190 million people as estimated in 2017.[1] It is the seventh most populous nation in the world.[2] In the last three decades, Nigeria has, to a large extent, been intricately linked with various polarizing factors, which include nepotism, ethnocentrism, and religious bigotry and terrorism as of late. However, it might be apt to note that the prevailing religious extremism and ethno-religious crisis in Nigeria is part of the global kaleidoscope of religious extremism that was accentuated after the September 11, 2011 attack on the World Trade Center and the Pentagon buildings, which killed thousands of people.

It is perhaps apt to note that the emergence of the Nigerian state in 1914 was fraught with challenges due to its highly diverse and multi-ethnic conglomeration of over 350 ethnic groups. Interestingly, the diversities of these ethnic groups in Nigeria, rather than being a unifying factor, to a large extent now ride on ethno and religious sentiments that seem to be tearing the seams of the unity of the country apart. The intriguing yet observable malady within the Nigerian space is the endemic corruption of the leadership of the Nigerian state over time.[3] Corruption is the hydra-headed monster that has succeeded in redefining the country as one of the major causes of the ethno-religious crisis.[4] The implosion of religious crisis in Nigeria since the 1990s has invariably led to it being classified in the Global Index on Terrorism. For four consecutive years (2013–2018) Nigeria has occupied the third position on a list of 138 countries, according to the 2018 ranking on terrorism. Nigeria was Africa's most terrorized nation in 2018, according to a report released by the Australia-based Institute for Economics and Peace. Apart from 2014, when Nigeria was ranked fourth, it has remained in the unenviable third position in the Global Terrorism Index (GTI) ranking since 2001.[5] This is apparent with the upsurge of various ethno-religious crises across the nation, particularly the *Boko Haram* sect[6] and the Fulani herdsmen in the Northern part of Nigeria.

Religious sentiments and active patronization of religious institutions by state functionaries is the norm despite Nigeria being a secular state as enshrined in Section 38 (1) and (10) of Nigeria's 1999 Constitution, which guarantees freedom of religion and prohibits the declaration of the state religion.[7] Nevertheless, in practice, such a provision is not the reality, as the Nigerian Nobel laureate winner, Professor Wole Soyinka, berated the role of religion in Nigeria. Soyinka said, "The sitting president of this nation, [Retired] General [Mohammadu] Buhari, once said: 'If you don't kill corruption in this nation, corruption will kill us. I would like to transfer that cry from the moral zone to the terrain of religion. If we do not tame religion in this nation, religion would kill us.'"[8] Soyinka's perspective on the role of religion in the balkanization and gradual mortification of the Nigerian state might stem from an insider's perspective as a Nigerian stymied in the battle of ethno-religious crisis. Soyinka's view on the role of religion resonates in Wilson's attempt to buttress Karl Marx's conception of religion as an opiate, but he noted that ". . . [Religion] is much deadlier than opium. It does not send people to sleep; it excites them to persecute one another. . . ."[9] Thus, within the Nigerian context, it might be imperative to note that religion seems to be "amphetamine."[10] Igboin captures this argument when he posited that ". . . religion generates and sanctions wars, strife, tyrannies, oppression, suppression of the truth and the like. It stands to reason that its functions are unfavorable to peaceful human coexistence, particularly in an unequal society."[11] From the philosophical perspectives, the likes of Lenin,[12] Bertrand Russell,[13] Wilson,[14] and a host of contemporary scholars have contributed to the Marxian theory on religion which has been critiqued by other scholars. However, since the purview of this study is not a philosophical perspective of religion, much attention is devoted to the religious crisis, which has become part of the everyday life of Nigerians living in the Northern part of the country.

Statement of the Problem

Religious crisis in Nigeria is a major fault line made up of social, economic, and political discontinuities that are seemingly tearing apart the bond of unity of the country. Previous scholarship examined the motivations for religious conflicts, rising religious fanaticism, and the political correctness of Nigeria's leaders' attempt to address this social challenge. Much attention has been placed on the causes of religious crisis in Nigeria, but this study examines the contributions of religious crisis to poverty in Northern Nigeria, particularly in the North-eastern zone, which can be described as the theatre of religious violence, and where poverty is extreme.

Mapping of Religious Crisis in Nigeria

The amalgamation of the Northern and Southern protectorates by the British Colonial administrator Lord Luggard redrew the entity of Nigeria. Various views have been expressed with respect to the rationale of the contraption of the two protectorates into a nation despite the huge cultural, religious, and ethnic diversities, as well as the educational disparities between them. The political landscape during the agitation for independence was straddled with ethnocentrism and religious colorations. The first Prime Minister of Nigeria, the late Alhaji Tafawa Balewa, speaking in the Northern House of Assembly in 1952, echoed his reservations about the amalgamation of the country. He said that:

> ...The Southern people who are swarming into this region daily in large numbers are really intruders. We don't want them, and they are not welcome here in the North. Since the amalgamation in 1914, the British Government has been trying to make Nigeria into one country, but the Nigerian people are different in every way including religion, custom, language, and aspiration. The fact that we're all Africans might have misguided the British Government. We here in the North, take it that "Nigerian unity" is not for us.[15]

From the above assertion, it is obvious that the current religious and ethnic crisis dated back to the pre-colonial era.[16] This was accentuated by the forced contraption of the Northern and Southern protectorates to form Nigeria by the blurring of ethnic and cultural markers, in order to fuel the continued imperialistic drive of the British colonialists.[17] In view of the pluralistic nature of Nigerian states, the dominant religions are Islam, Christianity, and traditional religions. These three principal religions are quite diverse in liturgy, ritual, doctrine, beliefs, and religious idiosyncrasies. Igboin, however, noted that religious conflict in Nigeria is politically motivated particularly in the Northern part of the country. He thus further averred that in "Nigeria, geography and religious phenomena and events have appeared to have symbiosis."[18] Igboin anchored his assertion in the fact that the Northern part of Nigeria, which is predominantly Muslim, has experienced more violent demonstrations irrespective of the causative factor, whether religious or political, in comparison to Southern Muslims.[19] Thus, within the Nigerian context, there seems to be a positive correlation between geography and religious violence, as evidenced by various religious conflicts in the country.

Maitatsine Sect

The outbreak of the Maitatsine[20] riots in Northern Nigeria in 1980 was perhaps the climax of the mushrooming sect that had its antecedents of a Cameroonian migrant, Mohammadu Marwa, to Kano, who was jailed in 1962 and deported, but then immigrated back to Nigeria. The growth in membership of the Maitatsine sect was not overnight, as the sect continued to attract adherents through their doctrinal persuasion. However, the state security apparatus exhibited ignorance until the riot of *Sabongari* in 1972, with increasing religious upheaval amongst the members leading to the Kano riot of 1980. The Maitatsine sect proliferated due to the departure from basic Islamic orthodoxy. This departure is reflected in antagonistic views and interpreting the Quran in a questionable manner, with their leader calling himself a Prophet. This was summed up by Sheikh Gumi, a renowned Islamic scholar in Nigeria, who faulted the theological positions of the sectarian movement, "[Maitatsine is] a trail of one-track minded Malams versed only in the recitation of the Quran by heart, and not fully comprehending what it contained."[21]

Mohammadu Marwa and his members rejected Western education and technology.[22] Jos experienced the first Maitatsine riot on September 2, 1980, when members of the sect confronted and overpowered over 300 police officers, but left for Kano, which was the hub of the Maitatsine movement.[23] The Kano Maitatsine's riot of December 18–19, 1980, heralded a new era in the history of religious conflict in Nigeria with the death of over 4,177 people and wanton destruction of properties across Kano municipality.[24] Bulumkutu, a hamlet near Maiduguri, was attacked from October 26–30, 1982, leaving over 3,350 dead. Religious intolerance reared its ugly head again as some Muslim students in Fegge, Kano, fomented trouble over the construction of a church near a mosque leading to the death of three people. Maitatisine effectively raised various cells in different parts of Northern Nigeria. At the same time, some of their members regrouped in towns like Sokoto, Yola, Gombe, and a host of other cities to continue their sectarian ideals.

The city of Jimeta, Yola, in the former Gongola state, was ravaged by the Maitasine sect on February 27, 1984, while Musa Makanaki sought refuge in Gombe, his hometown after the Yola conflict was ravaged. Apart from Boko Haram, Maitatsine is perhaps the only religious sect that had devastating effects on the socio-religious, economic, and political life of Northern Nigeria. However, the growth of this movement is predicated on the fact that:

> the problem goes beyond the distribution of wealth within society. The Maitatsine movement has flourished in the eighties, amid the package of economic ills - high prices, scarcity, retrenchment, and unemployment— which Nigerians call "austerity." This is, in part, the legacy of the profligate politics of the Second Republic. [25]

Other Ethno-Religious Crises

Other ethno-religious crises prior to 1999 included the Tiv and Junkun[26] communal clashes in 1991, Zango Kataf and the Hausa-Fulani crisis in the 1990s, and the Kafanchan riot of 1987. Likewise, there was a massive religious crisis due to the advertised crusade of Reinhard Bonnke arising from the non-issuance of a visa to Uztas Ahmed Deebat, a Muslim cleric from South Africa for an evangelistic crusade in Kano. The introduction of Shariah Law in 1999 by the former Governor of Zamfara State, Alhaji Sani Yerima, led to arson and destruction of properties of Christians and their churches in Northern Nigeria. Although some observers noted such a development inevitably undermined the integrity of the Nigerian state,[27] others, including Chukwu, argue that it was politically motivated to disrupt the government of President Olusegun Obasanjo, a Christian from the South.[28] Despite various views expressed by proponents of Sharia law[29] and vice versa, it is apt to posit that the introduction of Sharia law in some Northern states further polarized the already strained Muslim-Christian relationship since many Christians were attacked and lost all their economic livelihood as religious zealots ruptured the fragile peace in many of these states.

From the foregoing, the Northern part of Nigeria seems to be the amphitheater of religious and ethnic crisis. The table below gives an overview of the religious crises in Nigeria and their causes from 1999–2018. It is apt to note that the religious crisis in Nigeria, which has already led to the untimely death of thousands of Nigerians and the destruction of private and public properties, might continue unabated.

Table 1:   Cases of Religious Crisis in Nigeria, 1999-2018

S/N	DATE	TOWN/STATE	NATURE OF CRISIS
1	July 1, 1999	Sagamu, Ogun State	The crisis between Yoruba traditional worshippers and Hausa groups as a result of the killing of a Hausa woman by the Oro Masqueraders for violating traditional rites.
2	Dec 20, 1999	Ilorin, Kwara State	Muslim fundamentalists attacked and destroyed over fourteen churches, properties worth several millions of naira destroyed.

3	Feb 28, 2000	Aba, Abia State	The religious crisis that led to the killing of over 450 persons.
4	Feb 21-22, 2000	Kaduna, Kaduna State	Crisis over the introduction of Sharia; an estimated 3000 people died.
5	Oct 12, 2001	Kano, Kano State	Religious crises in protest of U.S. invasion of Afghanistan over Osama Bin Laden: over 150 persons were killed.
6	Sept 7-17, 2007	Jos, Plateau State	The religious crisis between Muslims and Christians: Mosques, churches, and several properties were damaged.
7	Nov 16, 2002	Kaduna, Kaduna State	Attack of Christians by the Muslims over an article written by Isioma Daniel on Miss World, over 250 people were killed, and several churches were destroyed.
8	Feb 14, 2004	Numan, Adamawa State	The religious crisis between Christians and Muslims over the location of the Central Mosque close to Bachama Paramount ruler's palace: over seventeen persons killed.
9	Feb 18, 2006	Maiduguri, Borno State	The religious crisis between Christians and Muslims over the Danish Cartoon of Prophet Mohammed in Jyllansposten Newspaper: over fifty persons killed, thirty churches, over 200 shops, and fifty houses destroyed, and one hundred vehicles vandalized.
10	Mar 22, 2007	Gombe, Gombe State	Religious crisis over the killing of a Christian teacher for allegedly desecrating the Qur'an while attempting to stop a student from cheating in an examination hall.

11	Nov 28, 2008	Jos, Plateau State	The religious crisis between Muslims and Christians over the controversial results of the local election: over 700 people killed.
12	July 26-30, 2009	Bauchi, Borno, Kano and Yobe State	The religious crisis unleashed by Boko Haram sect on Christians: over 700 people killed 3,500 persons internally displaced, 1,264 children orphaned, over 392 women widowed, and several properties destroyed.
13	Mar 7, 2010	Jos, Plateau State	Attacks by Fulani Moslems on Christian-dominated villages of Dogo-Nahawa, Shen, and Fan: thirteen persons killed.
14	Apr 11, 2010	Gombe, Gombe State	Attack on a Christian village by Fulani herdsmen: Three houses and six vehicles were torched.
15	Jan 5-6, 2012	Jos South, Plateau State	Gunmen stormed a Deeper Life Church, shooting indiscriminately at worshippers. The Boko Haram Islamist sect claimed responsibility for the shooting.
16	Jan 5-6, 2012	Mubi, Adamawa State	Suspected Boko Haram militants stormed a gathering of Igbo Christians and shot sporadically, killing over twelve persons and injuring others.
17	May 2016	Padongari, Niger State	The religious crisis that left four persons dead.
18	June 8, 2016	Kakuri, Kaduna State	A Christian man was stabbed for not joining Ramadan Fast.
19	Mar 14, 2018	Abuja [Federal Capital Territory]	Protest by Muslim groups rocks National Assembly on the Public Hearing over Amasa Firdus, Law School student Hijab controversy.

Source: Sampson in Olabimtan Apuwabi[30]

Boko Haram

From the table above, it can be noted that numerous religious conflicts have taken place in Nigeria, and one of the most lethal since its emergence in 2002 is Boko Haram. The group was founded by Mohammed Yusuf and it is committed to imposing a *sui-generis* Islamic regime based on Sharia in opposition to democratic principles in Muslim-dominated Northern Nigeria. The members of this movement refer to the movement as *Jama' at ahlis Sunnah lid Da'wat wal Jihad*, whose English translation means "people committed to the propagation of the Prophet's teachings and jihad." However, the literal translation in Hausa language, which is the language of one of the three major ethnic groups in Nigeria, Boko Haram means "Western education is sinful." Boko Haram militancy can be traced to the capture and killing of its founder by the Nigerian police in 2007. Due to this development, the group has claimed responsibility for various arsons, bombings, deaths, and destructions of properties in promoting its sectarian ideologies.[31]

Borno State caught the world's attention on April 14, 2014, when 276 schoolgirls from the government-owned Chibok Secondary School were kidnapped by Boko Haram. Boko Haram perpetrated two-thirds of the conflict events in the six states of North East Nigeria: Adamawa, Bauchi, Borno, Gombe, Taraba, and Yobe.[32] Since 2009, the Boko Haram insurgency has affected over fifteen million people.[33] For instance, in the North East of Nigeria, Boko Haram:

> ... has triggered an acute humanitarian and forced displacement crisis, with devastating social and economic impacts on the population, further deepening underdevelopment and regional inequalities. The most affected states are the Borno, Adamawa, and Yobe. The most affected groups are women, children, and youth. Boko Haram's tactics have included multiple modes of attack, including suicide bombings, seizure and destruction of entire villages, forced displacement, abductions, sexual violence targeting women, and forced recruitment of men. Although Boko Haram-held territory has reduced in size over the last few years, the group continues to perpetrate consistent attacks in North Eastern states.[34]

The insurgency of Boko Haram in other North Eastern Nigeria pales in comparison to North Central region, which comprises of Benue, Kogi, Kwara, Nasarawa, Niger and Plateau State, as well as the Federal Capital Territory (FCT). However, Jos, the capital of Plateau State, has been the focal point of religious conflict of Fulani herdsmen and their Islamization agenda through violence and displacement of original settlers in several communities around Jos municipality.

The next section considers how the religious crisis in Northern Nigeria has contributed to poverty.

Nigeria's Paradox: Poverty in the Midst of Wealth

Poverty is a very fluid concept that has been defined from various perspectives by developmental agencies, global financial institutions, and scholars. It is often associated with limited choices, poor living conditions, and inability to afford basic necessities of life such as housing, feeding, and decent income. However, United Nations defines poverty as:

> A denial of choices and opportunities, a violation of human dignity. It means lack of basic capacity to participate effectively in society. It means not having enough to feed or cloth a family, not having a school or clinic to go to, not having the land on which to grow one's food or a job to earn one's living, not having access to credit. It means insecurity, powerlessness, and exclusion of individuals, households, and communities. It means susceptibility to violence, and it often implies living in marginal or fragile environments, without access to clean water or sanitation.[35]

The above definition is encompassing in terms of the various facets of human needs. Furthermore, the World Summit for Social Development held in Copenhagen in 1995 states in its Program Action that:

> Poverty has various manifestations, including lack of income and productive resources sufficient to ensure sustainable livelihoods; hunger and malnutrition; ill health; limited or lack of access to education and other basic services; increased morbidity and mortality from illness; homelessness and inadequate housing; unsafe environments; and social discrimination and exclusion. It is also characterized by a lack of participation in decision-making, and in civil, social and cultural life.[36]

It is clear from these definitions that poverty in Nigeria is a reality as the various manifestations and consequential characteristics of poverty are prevalent. Ironically, Nigeria is the largest economy in Africa, with a gross domestic product (GDP) of $400 billion, while the country constitutes seventy-one percent of West Africa's GDP and twenty-seven percent of the continent's GDP. GDP per capita is $2,123.00, and Nigeria is classified as a lower middle income nation.[37] Nevertheless, despite being the "fifteenth largest oil producer in the world in 2016," with the "ninth largest oil reserves,"[38] the country was recently declared the poverty capital of the world, overtaking India with over 87 million estimated to be living in poverty. Fifty percent of the population is living below $1.90 per day, according to World Poverty Clock.[39] The poverty rate in Nigeria between 1980 and 2010 rose:

> by 153.6 percent (or 62.76 percent if $1.25 USD/person/day 2005 PPP line is used). The equivalent number of poor people rose from 39.2 million to 112.47 million (see Figure 1). This is despite a rise in the country's GDP per capita by roughly nineteen percent and over seventeen percent decline in the level of inequality (measured in terms of Gini index).[40]

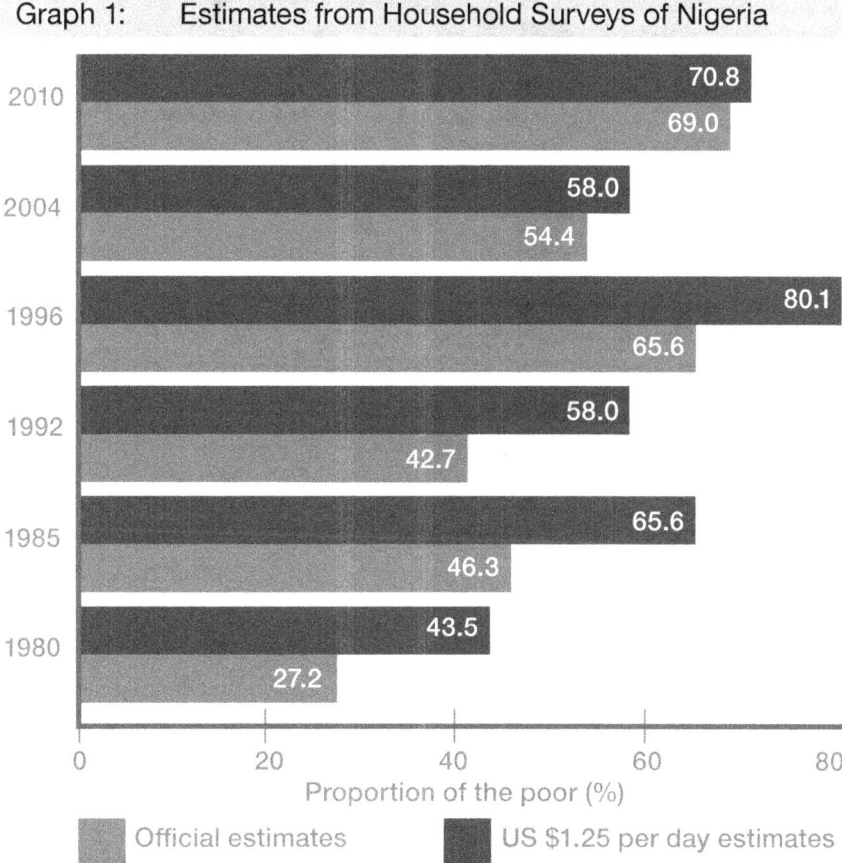

Graph 1: Estimates from Household Surveys of Nigeria

Source: National Bureau of Statistics[41]

As of 2010, the World Bank assessment of absolute poverty as $1.25 USD per person per day (equivalent to 360 Naira) means that seven out of ten Nigerians were considered poor by this standard. Despite the fact that Nigeria was classified as the poverty capital of the world in 2019, it has been observed that there exists disparity in terms of poverty between Southern and Northern Nigeria. The disparity is exemplified in Table 2 below.

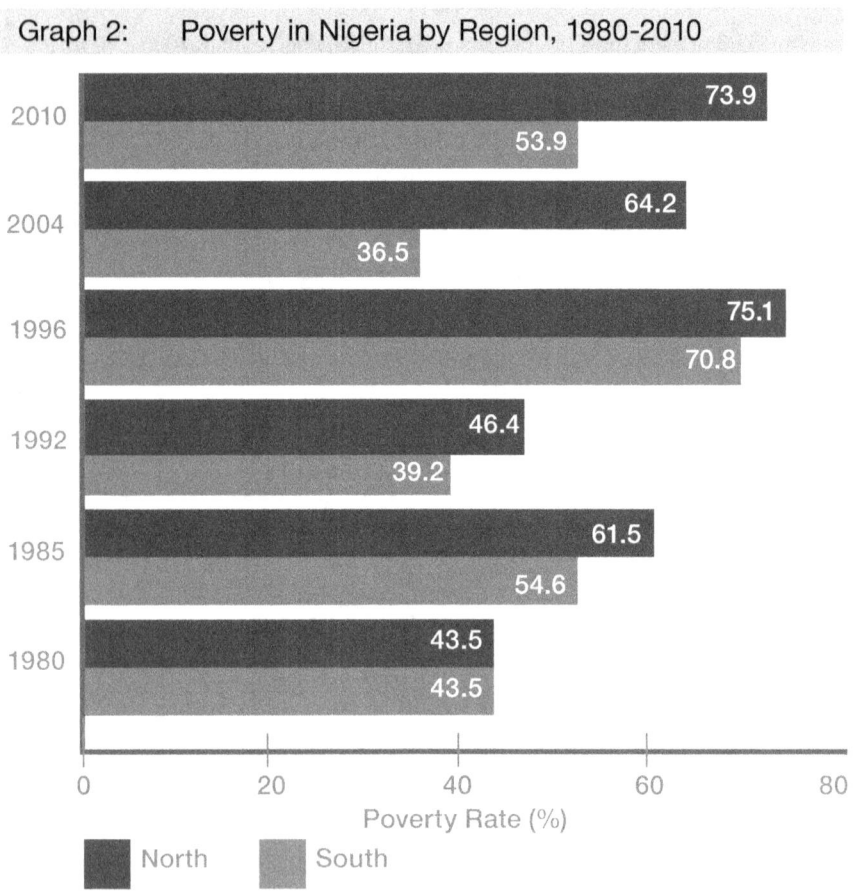

Graph 2: Poverty in Nigeria by Region, 1980-2010

Source: Author's calculation using household surbeys of Nigeria, 980-2010
Source: National Bureau of Statistics[42]

From graph two, the disparity in poverty between Southern and Northern Nigeria is obvious. This development raises salient questions about what could be responsible for such a disparity, especially against the backdrop that more Northerners have ruled the country than Southerners. This analysis is hinged on the fact that ethno-political patronage has been raised to a dogma. Does that imply that the challenge of nepotism and statutory policy such as Federal Character or quota system are not contributing to the amelioration of poverty?

As of 2012, poverty is almost pervasive across all geo-political zones of the North. The "North West has 77.7% of its population living in relative poverty, the North East came second with 76.3% of its population living in relative poverty while the North Central States has 67.5% of its population living in relative poverty."[43]

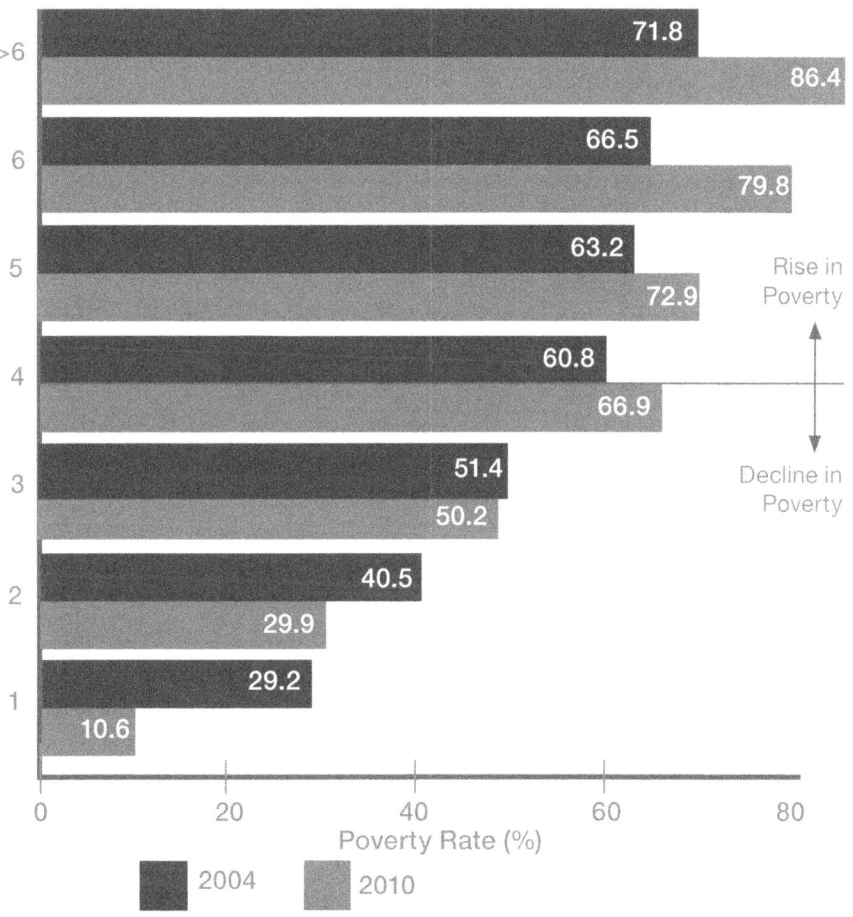

Graph 3: Northern States Ranked Highest in Poverty and Household Size

Source: Zuhumnan Dapel calculation using 2004 and 2010 household surveys of Nigeria[44]

It is apt to posit that leadership ineptitude and fiscal corruption of the ruling class is a major causative factor of poverty in North Eastern Nigeria.[45] This position is reinforced by political recklessness, mismanagement of public funds, and insecurity due to the incessant problems of religious crises, particularly the menace of Boko Haram in North Eastern Nigeria. The precarious poverty in North Eastern Nigeria might inform the commitment of the Nigerian states to ensuring the security of life and properties with the aim of initiating and sustaining a global model for post-conflict initiatives in the North East.

Likewise, the state with the largest household size based on Graph 3 also has the highest poverty rate. This dichotomy might be because:

> the North-South divide widened during the 1960s and 1970s despite the political dominance of the North. The latter's growing economic inferiority may have been at the root of the reluctance of the Northern elite to rely upon market mechanisms or to relinquish control over the distribution of oil revenue.[46]

Another reason for the poverty divides is the literacy level. Northern Nigeria is noted to have a high illiteracy level compared to the South, and this seems to have a positive correlation with poverty. The 2010 National Literacy Survey of the National Bureau of Statistics indicates that "adult literacy rate was 56.9 percent, with huge variations between states (Lagos 92.0 % and Borno only 14.5%), regions (urban 74.6 % and rural 48.7 %) and sex (male 65.1% and female 48.6%)."[47] This definitely has a multiplier effect on various facets of development such as skilled manpower, industrialization, and wealth creation. It is pertinent to note that the illiteracy level as of 2017 was very high, and this is reflected in the willingness of the United States, under President Donald Trump's administration, to invest $117m in Sokoto and Bauchi States.[48] The continued illiteracy level is probably exploited by the few elites to create class structure and perpetuation of poverty. They do this through the exploitation of the poor and through religious deceit through *zakah*, which is a form of almsgiving treated in Islam as a religious obligation or tax, which, by Quranic ranking, is next after prayer (*salat*) in importance.

The third reason for this North-South disparity is the religious crisis, which has turned the region into an amphitheater of violence. Religious conflicts have affected the socio-economic and infrastructural development of Northern Nigeria, particularly North Eastern Nigeria, due to cases of sectarian insurgency such as *Maitatsine* of the 1980s, *Yan Izala*, and *Boko Haram*. These have contributed in great measure to the continued impoverization of Northern Nigeria. Other reasons for the dichotomy include household size, which is higher in the North in comparison to the South, as depicted in Graph 3 above.

How Religious Crisis contributes to Poverty in Northern Nigeria

The effects of the religious crisis cannot be over-emphasized in any society, Nigeria inclusive. The socio-economic, political, educational, and religious spaces are inherently violated due to religious extremism in any context where the religious crisis occurs. Since the 1980s, the Northern Nigerian context has experienced massive human, fiscal, industrial, and cultural losses. Religious crisis leads to an unconducive environment for prospective investors from within and outside the country. The associated economic losses of capital investment and infrastructural destructions that have characterized sectarian insurgency in the North will put any investor to flight. To the international community, such development leads to the classification of such communities as potentially high-risk investment areas due to lack of security of lives and properties. Foreign Direct Investment flow into Nigeria, particularly the North, will be curtailed as the opportunities for job creation, employment, per capita income, and higher standard of living are truncated by a religious crisis.[49]

Secondly, the high illiteracy in the North is both the effect and conveyor of poverty in the North. In Northern Nigeria, many people, particularly of school age, are traditionally sent to traditional Quranic School under the tutelage of a *Mallam*. These protégées, most times, are expected to be discipled by the *Mallams*. Ironically many of these Islamic teachers do not have adequate welfare support such as housing, feeding, and clothing for their disciples. The protégées of the Mallams thus resort to alms begging from the members of the communities, since they are to live with their mentor and learn the tenets of Islamic faith that, incidentally, might be averse to any form of Western education. The protégées are referred to as *Almajiri* (singular), derived from the Arabic word *Al-muhaajirun* which is, by inference, a learned *Mallam* that propagates the peaceful course of Islam. From the experiential perspective of a researcher who lived in Sokoto, Nigeria, for seven years, these *Al-muhaajirun* are vulnerable to social vices, social exclusion, and abuse, and are employed by sectarian movements to cause inter- or intra- religious conflicts against other Islamic sects or Christians. *Almajirai* (plural) in Northern Nigeria are estimated to be over 7 million. The human capital, lost through illiteracy and rejection of Western education, constitutes a major blockage to alleviating poverty in Northern Nigeria.

The religious crisis poses a major challenge to education in many affected parts of Northern Nigeria. Sectarian movements like Boko Haram that are averse to Western education have plundered and destroyed educational institutions, kidnapping and abusing female students. The kidnapping of 276 Chibok girls is still very fresh in the hearts of many Nigerians. Education is vital to any sustainable development plan of a nation. However, the closure of schools, insecurity, intimidation, and fear of the unknown create major constraints to learning, not only to students, but also to parents. With the North presently educationally disadvantaged, the continued religious crisis will aggravate the illiteracy level of this part of the country.

The continued subscription by Northerners to Islamic education without recourse to Western education dates as far back as the colonial era when the Southerners embraced Western education and its attendant attractions. Nevertheless, Islamic education need not be averse, causing the detriment of Western education, which is largely required for the human development of the populace. It is also important to state that religious capital contributes to the holistic development of a community through the appropriation of social capital within the religious space. However, any religious education that is unable to address the material and existential realities of humanity should be reviewed.

Religious crisis in Northern Nigeria, particularly the North Eastern region, has led untoward humanitarian crises in the region due to the pre-existing poverty and worsened by lack of political will by successive governments to be committed to the sustainable development of the region. The North Eastern Nigeria is experiencing "one of the biggest humanitarian crises in Africa, with an estimated 13 million people in areas affected by Boko Haram violence," particularly Adamawa, Borno, and Yobe states.⁵⁰ The economic and health demographics of the North Eastern Nigeria is appalling. Obasanjo summarizing the "November 2016 Report produced by United Nations Office for Coordination of Humanitarian Affairs" (OCHA) noted:

- Food security: From January to October 2016, about 880,700 people had to receive food assistance to survive.
- Protection: An estimated 1.8 million people are in need of protection and assistance against gender-based violence (GBV) and HIV/AIDs, which is on the increase among Internally Displaced Persons (IDP).
- Education: Protective space is unavailable. In Adamawa State alone, about 6 million is needed for a massive infrastructural investment in some affected local governments.
- Food insecurity: An estimated 5.1 million people experience food insecurity in Adamawa, Borno, and Yobe States.
- Health: 5.9 million people are in need of health assistance. In Borno State, over fifty people were reported to have died as a result of malaria, while in Adamawa State, malaria and chest infections are the most prevalent diseases in the camps.
- Water Sanitation Hygiene: Water provision remains critically low. Some 3.65 million people are in need of water, sanitation, and hygiene (WASH) assistance.⁵¹

The implications of the above facts illustrate the magnitude and multifaceted nature of the challenges of poverty in the North Eastern part of Nigeria. If the religious crisis caused by *Boko Haram* is sustained by the movement, the North Eastern Nigeria crisis will worsen and ultimately lead to more loss of lives and suffering of indescribable proportions to the inhabitants of the communities.

It is quite obvious that Islamic fundamentalism is intricately linked with the religious crisis in Northern Nigeria, which has been noted to be a major cause of religious riots and poverty in the region. However, with the preponderance of seemingly religious bigotry, poverty might be changed through the intentional evangelistic outreach by Christian denominations focusing on the transformation of individuals, which has a holistic impact on the socio-economic and religious worldviews. Although it is an undeniable fact that Northern Nigeria is a largely Muslim dominated area, Christian evangelistic initiatives should be channeled through social initiatives with a distinctive Christian ethos, addressing educational and economic disparities within the Northern Nigerian contexts.

Conclusion

Although most religious adherents view religion as an instrument of peace and unity, religion in its practical reality is ambivalent. It is capable of inciting both violence and peace. But more often than not, and most especially in Northern Nigeria, I have argued that there is a correlation between incessant religious violence and poverty. Statistics examined have shown that Northern Nigeria, which is more prone to religious extremism and violence, is correspondingly poorer. Again, despite the fact that the North has produced more political rulers since independence in 1960, in an ethno-political context where political patronage is largely ethnic-based, the North is yet poorer than the South. I have shown that education plays a critical role in poverty management and alleviation. But in a context where Western education is forbidden and only Islamic education is embraced, which more often than not is dogma-inclined, a large cache of an army is waiting to be cheaply recruited by religious extremists and insurgents, as is being witnessed in the case of Boko Haram. Thus, as extremists destroy human and material capital, so does poverty multiply.

In order to address this situation, it has become imperative to suggest the need to invest heavily in education, Western education in particular. Ironically, the hegemonic aristocrats of the North send their children to the best schools in the country and abroad to acquire Western education. The fact that this class of people does not solely patronize Islamic education is an impetus for the government to encourage Western education in the North. In addition, employment opportunities should be created for the teeming population, rather than the hand-outs given to youth as rewards for political solidarity. Further research is recommended, however, to examine how interest in Western education can be stimulated in the north.

Notes

1 Ngozi Okonjo-Iweala, *Fighting Corruption is Dangerous: The Story Behind the Headlines* (Cambridge: MIT Press, 2018), 1.

2 Associated Press, "Nigeria to Pass the U.S. as World's 3rd Most Populous Country by 2050, UN Says," NBC News, June 22, 2017, https://www.nbcnews.com/news/world/nigeria-pass-u-s-world-s-3rd-most-populous-country-n775371, accessed May 10, 2019.

3 Babatunde Adedibu, "Corruption Conundrum: A Call for the Awakening of the Prophetic Role of Nigerian Pentecostal Church Leaders," in Igboin Benson ed., *Corruption: A New Thinking in Reverse Order* (Oyo, Nigeria: Ajayi Crowther University Press, 2018), 148–163.

4 Beloveth Nwankwo, "Rhetorics and Realities of Managing Ethno-Religious Conflicts: The Nigerian Experience," *American Journal of Educational Research* 3:3 (2015), 292–300.

5 Abdur Rahman Alfa Shaban, "Nigeria, Somalia: Africa's Most Terrorized Countries in 2018 – Report," AfricaNews.com, June 12, 2018, https://www.africanews.com/2018/12/06/nigeria-somalia-africa-s-most-terrorized-countries-in-2018-report//, accessed May 16, 2019.

6 The name of the group means "'Western,'" or 'non-Islamic' education is a sin."

7 Shari'a and the Nigerian Constitution, https://www.hrw.org/reports/2004/nigeria0904/13.htm, accessed May 15, 2019.

8 Emma Ujah and Levinus Nwabughiogu, "Nigeria: If We Don't Tame Religion in Nigeria, It Would Kill Us – Soyinka," AllAfrica, https://allafrica.com/stories/201701130279.html, accessed May 17, 2021.

9 Karl Max, cited in Ian S. Markham, *Understanding Christian Doctrine* (Hoboken, NJ: Wiley, 2017), 16.

10 Amphetamine is a central nervous system stimulant that is used in the treatment of attention deficit hyperactivity disorder, narcolepsy, and obesity. The use of religion and religious extremism has redefined the continued existence of Nigeria, particularly, between Christians and Muslims in various parts of Nigeria, and particularly in Northern Nigeria.

11 Benson Ohihon Igboin, "Karl Marx on Religion: The Perspective of Boko Haram in Nigeria," *Journal of Religious Culture* 183 (2014), 4.

12 Ted Peters, God - *The World's Future: Systematic Theology for a New Era*, 2nd ed. (Minneapolis: Fortress Press, 2000), 378.

13 Bertrand Russell, *Why I am not a Christian and Other Essays on Religion and Related Subjects*, ed., Paul Edwards (New York City: Simon & Schuster, 1957), 19.

14 Andrew N. Wilson, *Against Religion: Why We Should Try to Live Without It* (London: Chatto & Windus, 1991), 48.

15 Tafawa Belewa, cited in Adisa Adeleye, "Amalgamation of 1914: Was it a Mistake?" *Vanguard Newspaper*, May 18, 2012, https://www.vanguardngr.com/2012/05/amalgamation-of-1914-was-it-a-mistake/, accessed March 11, 2021.

16 K. Kazah-Toure, *Ethno-Religious Conflicts and Human Rights Violations in Nigeria* (Kaduna: Human Rights Monitor, 2003), 21.

17 J. A. Sangosanya and P. Sha, *Ethno-Religious Conflicts and Human Rights Violations* (Jos: Niri Press, 2005), 12.

18 Igboin, "Karl Marx on Religion," 4.

19 Igboin, "Karl Marx on Religion," 4.

20 This was his alias which evolved as a result of his faltering linguistic skill. "Hausa Maitatsine" developed because Marwa would say in halting Hausa, "*Wanda bata yarda ba Allah ta Tchine*," meaning "May Allah curse the one who disagrees with his version"—thus, *Mai Tachine*, later pronounced more accurately as Maitatsine.

21 Sheik Gumi cited in an interview in *The New Nigerian*, November 7, 1982, paragraph 41.

22 These features resonate with the Boko Haram sects that have wreaked havoc in Northern Nigeria, and seems to be a reoccurring decimal among sectarian Islamic movements. For instance, during the colonial era, there were few sectarian movements as well as literary evidence of poets who warned against the use of goods from the Western world. For further reading see Mervyn Hiskett, *The Sword of Truth, the Life and Times of the Shehu Usman Dan Fodio* (New York: Oxford University Press, 1973), 164–165.

23 A. N. Aniagolu, "Report of Tribunal of Inquiry on Kano Disturbances" (Lagos: Federal Government Press, 1981), paragraphs 42, 55, and 227.

24 Emefie Ikenga-Metuh, "Two Decades of Religious Conflicts In Nigeria: A Recipe For Peace," *Bulletin of Ecumenical Theology* 6:1 (1994), 69.

25 Elisabeth Isichei, "The Maitatsine Risings in Nigeria 1980-1995, A Revolt of the Disinherited," *Journal of Religion in Africa* 17:3 (Oct. 1987), 201.

26 Kabir Kura, "Muslim-Christian Cooperation for Conflict Prevention/Management, Peace Building and Reconciliation in Northern Nigeria"

(Conference on Muslim-Christian Cooperation in states of Nigeria, October 2010, Kaduna, Nigeria).

27 Matthew Kukah, *Human Rights in Nigeria: Hopes and Hindrances* (Aachen, Germany: Missio, 2003), 24.

28 Cletus Chukwu, "Religion as a Factor in Nigerian Political Culture," in Peter I. Gichure and Diane B. Stinton, eds., *Religion and Politics in Africa: Theological Reflections for the 21st Century* (Nairobi, Paulines, 2008), 62.

29 For further reading see, Abdulalahi A. An-Na'im, "The Future of Shariah and the Debate in Northern Nigeria," in Philip Ostien, Jamila M. Nasir, and Franz Kogelmann, eds., *Comparative Perspectives on Shariah in Nigeria* (Ibadan, Spectrum, 2005), 327.

30 Olabimtan Apuwabi, "The Effects of Religious Crisis on Economic Development in Nigeria," *International Journal of Academic Research in Business and Social Sciences* 8:6 (2018), 325–326.

31 Zach Warner, "The Sad Rise of Boko Haram," *New African* 1 (April), 38–40.

32 Abul Azad, Emily Crawford, and Heidi Kaila, *Conflict and Violence in Nigeria: Results from the North East, North Central, and South South Zones* (Washington D. C.: The World Bank, 2018), 8.

33 Azad et al., *Conflict and Violence in Nigeria*, 8.

34 Azad et al., *Conflict and Violence in Nigeria*, 8.

35 "The Statement for Action to Eradicate Poverty adopted by the Administrative Committee on Coordination in May 1998," quoted in the "Report of the Independent Expert on Human Rights and Extreme Poverty," E/CN.4/1999/48, accessed May 6, 2019. See also, David Gordon, "Indicators of Poverty and Hunger" (Expert Group Meeting on Youth Development Indicators, New York, December 2005), www.un.org.esa/socdev/unyin/documents/YdiDavidGordon_poverty.pdf, accessed May 6, 2019.

36 United Nations, "PAWSSD, Chapter 2," Department of Economic and Social Affairs: Social Inclusion, 2019, paragraph 19, https://www.un.org/development/desa/dspd/world-summit-for-social-development-1995/wssd-1995-agreements/pawssd-chapter-2.html, accessed May 18, 2019.

37 Okonjo-Iweala, *Fighting Corruption is Dangerous*, xvi.

38 Cited in Okonjo-Iweala *Fighting Corruption is Dangerous*, xvii.

39 Bukola Adebayo, "Nigeria Overtakes India in Extreme Poverty Ranking," CNN World, June 26, 2018, https://edition.cnn.com/2018/06/26/africa/

nigeria-overtakes-india-extreme-poverty-intl/index.html, accessed May 6, 2019.

40 Zuhumnan Dapel, "Poverty in Nigeria: Understanding and Bridging Poverty Between the North and the South," Center for Global Development, April 6, 2018, https://www.cgdev.org/blog/poverty-nigeria-understanding-and-bridging-divide-between-north-and-south, accessed May 6, 2019.

41 The official estimate is used by National Bureau of Statistics, while the author Zuhumnan Dapel, uses US$1.25. See Dapel, "Poverty in Nigeria," for detailed analysis.

42 Author's calculation is based on household surveys of Nigeria, 1980–2010. For detailed analysis see, Zuhumnan Dapel, "Poverty in Nigeria."

43 Terwase Ngbea and Hilary Chukwuka Achunike, "Poverty in Northern Nigeria," *Asian Journal of Humanities and Social Studies* 2:2 (April 2014), 268.

44 Dapel, "Poverty in Nigeria."

45 Olusegun Obasanjo, "Liberation Theology and the Crisis in North Eastern Nigeria," in Samson Adetunji Fatokun, Jacob Kehinde Ayantayo, Solomon Makanjuola Mepaiyeda, et al., eds., *African Christianity in Local and Global Context* (Ibadan, Nigeria: Baptist Press, 2018), 57.

46 *Dapel*, "Poverty in Nigeria."

47 UNESCO, "Action Plan: Nigeria" (High Level International Round Table on Literacy, Paris, September 2012).

48 Friday Olokor, "Why Literacy Rate Remains Low in the North," PUNCH News, March 3, 2017, https://punchng.com/why-literacy-rate-remains-low-in-the-north-us/, accessed May 25, 2019.

49 A. C. Owwumah, "Communal and Ethno-Religious Crises and their Implications for National Development in Nigeria," *Developing Country Studies* 4:17 (2010), 118–125.

50 Obasanjo, "Liberation Theology," 56.

51 Obasanjo, "Liberation Theology," 56–57.

14 Civil Unrest and Poverty in Congo Brazzaville: A Personal Reflection

Médine Moussounga Keener

Abstract

In this chapter, I share about the toll poverty takes on people forced into it by harsh circumstances. I will focus on occurrences that I witnessed or experienced as a refugee during an ethnic civil war in my country, Congo Brazzaville, including hunger, sexual exploitation, disease, and death.

Introduction

Located in west-central Africa, The Republic of Congo, also (and hereafter) called Congo Brazzaville, is surrounded by neighbors Cameroon, the Central African Republic, the Democratic Republic of Congo, Gabon, and Angola, and is home to a diverse population. Congo Brazzaville's population is estimated at four million, over half of which live in the two major cities of Brazzaville and Pointe-Noire.[1] The Encyclopedia Britannica notes, "urban in-migration has long been an important demographic trend. During the colonial era, the new colonial cities, and Brazzaville in particular, attracted African migrants. Demographic trends have also been linked to local and neighboring patterns of conflict."[2]

Four primary ethnic groups comprise about ninety-five percent of Congo Brazzaville's population. The largest of these is the Kongo or Bakongo. The Kongo people group is largely located in the southern region, is comprised of many subgroups, and represents about half Congo Brazzaville's population. The other three major ethnic groups live in the northern region. They include the Sangha, who make up about twenty percent of the population, the Teke, who represent approximately seventeen percent of the population, and the M'bochi, who make up about twelve percent of the population.[3] Approximately seventy-five percent of the country is Christian, with thirty percent of Christians identifying as Roman Catholic. The Protestant streams of Christianity in Congo

Brazzaville include the Evangelical Church of the Congo and African Independent Churches, such as the Kimbanguist Church. There is a small Muslim community located in the urban centers of Brazzaville and Point-Noir and comprised of foreigners.[4] According to the World Bank, the poorest sixty-five percent of Congolese citizens live in the six regions in the south of the country, where social protection programs cover less than five percent of these.[5]

This study intends to present civil unrest as a significant root of human suffering, including poverty. In civil conflict, the consequences of suffering are far-reaching, felt beyond those direct actors in the conflict itself, and far outlasting the moment that history places as the end date. The suffering caused by war is no respecter of cease-fire negotiations, ethnicity, or socio-economic status. War displaces and destroys; in a civil war, those who are displaced and destroyed are citizens of the same country. The devastation such conflicts cause affects everything from available drinking water and food supply, to sexual violence, to death from diseases that would have been preventable if the country's existing infrastructure was not dismantled. Such was my experience. In this paper, I will look at the effects of civil unrest and war on displaced civilians through the lens of my own story. This chapter is an offering, drawing from the resource of personal experience as a refugee of civil conflict in my country, Congo Brazzaville.

The 1990s: A Decade of Civil Conflict

According to the United Nations, ten percent of the world population still lives in extreme poverty, surviving on less than $2.00 a day. Most of these people live in sub-Saharan Africa, the part of the world where I am originally from. The Republic of Congo, where I grew up, was one of the main oil producers of sub-Saharan Africa. Despite inequalities in wealth distribution, the country was relatively safe, and many people had a better life. In the 1980s, the Republic of Congo was the fourth leading oil country in Africa. Unfortunately, by the end of the 1990s, due to corruption in political rulers, civil wars, and conflicts, poverty spread. As a result, "nearly half the population now lives in poverty."[6]

The University of Michigan defines a civil war as "an internal conflict that involves at least one thousand combat-related deaths, with each side incurring at least five percent of these deaths."[7] Development economist, Paul Collier, takes this definition and looks further into the twin issues of civil unrest and poverty, asking whether poverty leads to civil war or if civil war leads to poverty. "In fact, both relationships hold simultaneously."[8] Collier pinpoints three specific economic characteristics that make a country prone to civil war: low income, slow growth, and dependence upon primary commodity exports:[9]

> Suppose a country starts its independence with [these three economic] characteristics. . . . It is playing Russian roulette. That is not just an idle metaphor: the risk that a country in the bottom billion [of global GDP] falls into civil war in any five-year period is nearly one in six, the same risk facing a player of Russian roulette. Once a war has begun, the economic damage undoes the growth achieved during peace. Worse, even aside from this economic damage, the risk of further war explodes upward.[10]

Such was the case in Congo-Brazzaville as the country entered the 1990s. Having secured independence from France in 1960, three decades later, Congo Brazzaville was an economy heavily dependent upon oil production and "experienced an almost continuous decline in per capita income between 1985 and 2000."[11] The civil war of 1993-1994 over the disputed elections caused two thousand casualties and displaced tens of thousands,[12] thus setting the stage for the civil wars of 1997 and 1998-99. Again, Collier is poignant:

> Of course, war is much worse than just a prolonged economic depression: it kills people. Overwhelmingly, the people who die are not killed in active combat but succumb to the disease. Wars create refugees, and mass movements of the population in the context of collapsing health systems create epidemics. . . .Both economic losses and disease are highly persistent: they do not stop once the fighting stops. Most of the cost of civil war, perhaps as much as half, accrue after the war is over.[13]

In Congo Brazzaville, once the civil war of 1997 began, government soldiers and militia, as well as the opposition militia, participated in pervasive extortion and mistreatment of civilians. Civilians were killed, beaten, and detained because of their ethnicity. Both sides targeted densely populated areas with armed violence. Soldiers and militias participated in heavy looting, causing immense property damage. As a result, thousands of people, mostly civilians, were killed, and hundreds of thousands were displaced.[14]

My Story

Poor people have always existed. Deuteronomy 15:11 says, "There will always be poor people in the land. Therefore, I command you to be openhanded toward your fellow Israelites who are poor and needy in your land."[15] There are many reasons people find themselves shackled in poverty, including lack of education, poor health, poor infrastructure, unemployment, and bad religious teaching. Sometimes people are coerced into that state by tragic circumstances like war. That is my story.

When I was a teenager, Ngoma Moise, an evangelist full of the Spirit, gave my father a prophecy for me: "I see Medine, like a shining star, going to a foreign country to study." What good news! They praised God and celebrated. Then the man of God was troubled as he continued, "I see her coming back to Congo, but there is war, and she has disappeared." That drove my father to his knees, praying for my safety. Many years later, I went to France and the United States to study. After I defended my Ph.D., I booked a flight, ready to go home, even though the war had started back home. On the day of my flight, I was told at the airport that there was no flight going to Congo Brazzaville that day, so I rebooked for the next week. When I finally got home, I learned that on the day that my first flight was canceled, there was heavy fighting in Brazzaville (the capital of Congo), and there were many casualties around the airport. I then remembered the prophecy and realized that God heard my parents' prayers of protection over me many years before and protected me.

But that was not the end of the war in Congo. A few years later, war broke again, and I was trapped. If I had known that becoming a war refugee would automatically make me poor, that my basic human needs for food, safe water, adequate housing, health care, and adequate clothing would not be met, that my nephew and niece would not have access to education, I might have asked for different testing. Then again, we do not get to choose.

People prosper when there is stability, peace, and opportunities for growth in a healthy environment; war brings the opposite. Stability and peace were never more than illusions during the war; things were constantly changing, and rumors abounded. We were not safe anywhere, even in our own homes. On December 26, 1998, my cousin was killed by Angolan soldiers who had occupied our small town. One of the soldiers wanted his girlfriend, and my cousin defended her. The soldier shot him. As my cousin cried out in pain for help, no one came to his rescue because people were afraid to intervene and lose their own life. He died in the street, not far from his home, a couple of hours later.

Living on the Run

Most poor people do not have adequate housing. When war drove us out of our home, we did not have a safe place to call home for almost two years, being on the run so many times. Following the day we left our home because we were running for our lives, we did not have a decent place to sleep for weeks. We spent the night in abandoned schools or hospitals or churches. All the windows in these places were just openings without coverings. Those places did not offer any shelter against thieves, malarial mosquitoes, germs, etc. I remember one night we spent in an abandoned hospital where hordes of mosquitoes assaulted us. I tried my best to protect my young son by offering my body as a buffer. When morning came, I saw that his head was very dark and wondered if he had grown more hair. When it became clearer, around 6:00 a.m., I realized, to my horror, that his head was covered with mosquitoes!

Hunger is a constant companion when people live in poverty. We barely had enough to eat during the war, feeding ourselves once a day from what we could get. For days, we ate ferns that grew by the riversides. Even though they were so bitter that one felt like gagging, they were free and had some nutrients to help us. Occasionally we were happy to get some protein from rats and snakes (for those who ate them). In those circumstances, the temptation to sell oneself short to satisfy the gnawing hunger was ever-present. One day as we sat by our temporary housing, my niece bounded in carrying a plate of food, and she was very happy about it. My niece was turning into a beautiful teenager, and I knew what the soldiers were already thinking about her. She told us that one of the soldiers had bought the food for her from the women selling wild meat on the street. After hearing this, I marched her back to the seller and asked her to give it back. Of course, she was very upset because that plate of food was yummier than the fern and rats we were eating. I squatted to her eye level and asked her to name the kind of food she ate before the war. I also told her that the price she was going to pay for that tasty meal was to acquiesce to the sexual favors that would ensue later. Many soldiers and other men offered food in hopes of getting sex in return. I told her the story of the young woman who accepted food from a soldier only to be asked to have sex afterward. Although she was afraid of contracting AIDS, it was too late; she had eaten the food.

Poverty, Illness, and Death

As a result of poor housing and poor nutrition, we frequently got sick with malaria, typhoid, hemorrhoids, fever, diarrhea, and the like. Because we were poor, we could not go to the hospital; the first thing they would ask is for us to pay.

I remember the day I almost lost my son. He had malaria and started to convulse. I did not have the money to go to the local hospital. So uttering desperation prayers, I ran to a little private clinic that belonged to a friend of my brother's who worked in the medical field and had opened a small place to treat patients and get few coins to feed his family. When we got there, my son was cold and was losing his voice. He told me that I was lucky because he had not had anyone come all morning, and he was about to close for the day. I was doubly lucky because there was just one injection against malaria left. He did not ask me for money. He just injected my son, David, with the medicine and told me to pay as soon as I had some money. He saved my son's life, and I am always grateful to God and to that man. The next day, someone I knew lost her son to malaria. My son's life that day was worth $2.00, the amount of money needed to pay the hospital to get treatment. But in the eyes of God, his life was worth much more, and Jesus spared his life.

Being poor made us vulnerable and powerless in the face of sickness and death. One additional source of misery for us was the lack of decent clothing; we were reduced to wearing rags, which did not protect us from the chilly evening, scorching sun, and all sorts of insect bites. That also made us vulnerable to illness. The lack of healthcare opportunities contributed to the loss of many lives. Death could have been avoided if people had access to medicine. And death did happen a lot among poor people. One such example is a teenager who was pregnant during the war. On Saturday, August 14, 1999, Bouna gave birth to twins. One of the twin babies died a few hours after birth, and Bouna herself was in a critical condition; her stomach started to swell. There was no money, no real medication, no antibiotics to help her. We collected what money we had, but it was not enough because people did not have much. The next day Bouna died. The despair in our hearts and faces was heavy.

Our only recourse was to cry out to God. And God did answer his children. During one of the malaria episodes I experienced during the war, I was so sick that I was hallucinating, and my family was worried about my condition. As I laid there sick, unable to do anything or eat any of our tasteless meals, I prayed, asking God for his mercy. My family tried concocting whatever kind of tisane they could. A lady stopped by with the only quinine injection they could find. All these things were not enough to help me. I felt like I was wasting away. Then by God's grace, I started to get better slowly. Four or five days later, a family stopped by and asked my father how I was doing. He replied that I was better and wondered if they had been out of their hiding place in the forest for a few days because that's the only way they would have known that I was very sick. The man said that God showed him in a dream that I was sick and urged him to pray for the daughter of Moussounga Jacques. In response to his people's prayers, God restored my health. For many poor people, health is truly a gift from God!

Power and Powerlessness

Living in poor conditions also meant living in a kind of lawlessness, where those who were more in need were taken advantage of, having no one to fight for them. During the war in Dolisie, my family was visited by soldiers from our own region, the ones who were supposed to protect us. They came into our home searching for "spies." They looked around, and one of them concluded, "this old man is rich, he has provisions, a TV, a telephone, a stove . . ." So they asked us for 300000 CFR francs, a little over $500 USD. Of course, we did not have that much money. When my Mom handed them $6.00, one of them was so angry that he yelled insults and cursed at us, then fired his gun. Thank God, the bullet went between my father and brother. The bullet ricocheted on the cement ground and hit a window with a loud noise. We ended up handing them most of what we had, which was $60.00. We were all physically and emotionally exhausted. When they left, some of us were consumed with fear that prompted a physical reaction of fever and diarrhea.

It was a recurrent event to see soldiers who were supposed to protect their own people turn on them, plunder them, and abuse them. Being poor is a kind of zoo where the strongest ones crush the weak ones. Women are especially vulnerable in a vicious way; rape is rampant among poor people. During the war, two of our greatest fears were for women in our family to be raped by men and for our men to be gunned down by soldiers.

In Moubotsi village, a young woman from the north of Congo was raped by eleven soldiers. I felt so useless and helpless because I could not save her from her tormentors, who had guns. Her only fault was to belong to the wrong tribe and region in the war. Even in refugee camps, women were not protected. Melanie, one of the refugees who found refuge in the refugee camp in the neighboring country, Gabon, was defiled by the one who was supposed to protect her:

> One evening, Melanie had a headache and was not feeling well. A Congolese priest who worked in the pharmacy saw her and asked her to follow him to the pharmacy where they kept medicine. Once in the pharmacy, he locked the door. Melanie did not suspect anything wrong because this was the same priest who was helping sick refugees—one of the priests who had pleaded for her registration. Maybe he would talk with her, give her medication, and pray for her to get well, she thought. But, suddenly, he turned toward her and forced himself upon her. She was in a locked room, in a part of the building that was empty in the evening, so nobody heard her cries as she was weakened by sickness and disgust. . . . He used his position as "a man of God" to rape an innocent and helpless victim.[16]

Many times, the lives of those living in poverty are not valued. I faced that reality one day in March of 1999 when my brother, Emmanuel, was mistaken for someone else and found himself with a gun pointed at his chest. The soldier who was getting ready to shoot him had red eyes, a sign that he was under the influence of a drug. Standing there, helpless and silently crying to God for his intervention, I realized how someone's life could be snatched in an instant. Emmanuel was saved because a high official knew that Emmanuel was not the other man and told his soldier to put his gun down. But many did not have a high official to save them and so lost their lives.

I've heard people use stereotypes when referring to poor people, and one that I have often heard is laziness. I know that lazy people are everywhere, but most of the poor people I knew were hard-working people. We trekked for miles to get food during the war, walking through swamps and forests infested with army ants and snakes, carrying heavy loads of firewood and root vegetables on our heads and backs. I still suffer from back pain because of all the heavy loads that I carried during the war so that my family could eat.

The Church's Response

In the midst of all the chaos our lives were thrown into, we found solace in God and God's people. The love of Jesus made a difference in the way we were treated as war refugees. In my "war journal," there are two villages: the evil village (Tao-tao) and the good village (Moubotsi). The difference was due to the people we encountered. In the first village, we met with non-Christian people. They did not show us any compassion. For example, when we were searching for drinking water, we were directed to a well of dirty water for washing, and we drank that water until a mute boy tried to explain to us using his hands that that water was very bad. Food was costly here, and the village people did not mingle or converse with us.

On the other hand, the second village welcomed us with open hands, and that's because most of the people we met there were Christians. They helped us find places to bed down and took us to their private gardens so we would have food to eat. The presence of Jesus in the lives of these people made a big difference for us as refugees. When the church remembers that Jesus was a refugee himself (Matt 2:13–15), then we can serve best those who are suffering.

Conclusion: A Christian Response to the Legacy of Civil War

Right after the war, my country was impoverished. A family of five subsisted on about $4.00 for food for the whole day. Poverty also bred a host of other difficulties. In the aftermath of the war, Congo was plagued by poor infrastructure. Most roads were in appalling conditions, which led to accidents and loss of life, especially in rural areas. Electricity was spotty in the whole country; only two water dams provided energy in the country, and the rest came from the neighboring country, the Democratic Republic of Congo. Power cuts led to a shortage of drinking water. People used rainwater, wells, and streams to meet their supply. Unfortunately, many contracted cholera, typhoid, and other diseases because the land was not cleaned of the decomposing bodies of humans and animals resulting from the war. Additionally, for most people, a water filter was a luxury they could not afford. My mother suffered from typhoid during the war and for many months after the war was over. She died of a stomach ulcer after her husband, my father, passed away. My friend Clementine suffered greatly and died of breast cancer. People could hear her crying out in pain from miles. If my parents and friend had had access to the sort of medical technology and medicine found in the West, they might still be with us today. High infant mortality due to poor nutrition and lack of healthcare was another strain on society. Mothers, like one of the teenage moms in a Sunday school I taught, died during childbirth. Poor housing and unemployment contributed to poor health and unhealthy sexual relationships. Many women exchanged sexual favors for food, rent, or clothing.

The last part of Deuteronomy 15:11 says, "Therefore I command you to be openhanded toward your fellow Israelites who are poor and needy in your land." We are called to be proactive in helping our brothers and sisters in need, to lend a listening ear and comfort in any way we can. Poor people are people like you and me. They need to be seen and heard. Like the churches that helped us during the war, we can also help according to our means. Even if you help one person, you have helped. The more we give, the more we receive. Let us never grow weary of praying; after all, we are in a spiritual battle, and the weapons have been provided.

Notes

1 "People," Embassy of the Republic of Congo, http://www.ambacongo-us.org/en-us/aboutcongo/peopleculture/people.aspx, accessed November 23, 2020.

2 *Encyclopedia Britannica Online,* s.v. "Republic of the Congo: Demographic Trends," by Dennis. D. Cordell, https://www.britannica.com/place/Republic-of-the-Congo/Demographic-trends, accessed November 23, 2020.

3 *Encyclopedia of the Nations,* s.v. "Congo, Republic of the (ROC): Ethnic Trends," https://www.nationsencyclopedia.com/Africa/Congo-Republic-of-the-ROC-ETHNIC-GROUPS.html#:~:text=Congo%2C%20Republic%20of%20the%20(ROC)%20%2D%20Ethnic%20groups,in%20the%20high%20forest%20region, accessed November 23, 2020.

4 *Encyclopedia Britannica Online,* s.v. "Republic of the Congo: Religion" by Dennis. D. Cordell, https://www.britannica.com/place/Republic-of-the-Congo/Religion, accessed November 23, 2020.

5 The World Bank, "Republic of the Congo: Overview," The World Bank in the Republic of the Congo, updated October 21, 2019, https://www.worldbank.org/en/country/congo/overview, accessed November 23, 2020.

6 BBC News, "Republic of Congo Country Profile," Africa, January 8, 2018, https://www.bbc.com/news/world-africa-14121191, accessed November 30, 2020.

7 Paul Collier, *The Bottom Billion: Why the Poorest Countries are Failing and What Can Be Done About It* (Oxford: Oxford University Press, 2007), 18.

8 Collier, *The Bottom Billion,* 32.

9 Collier, *The Bottom Billion,* 32.

10 Collier, *The Bottom Billion,* 33.

11 Rina Bhattacharya and Dhaneshwar Ghura, "Oil and Growth in the Republic of Congo," International Monetary Fund Working Paper, African Department, August 2006, https://www.imf.org/external/pubs/ft/wp/2006/wp06185.pdf, accessed November 23, 2020.

12 Wikipedia, "Republic of the Congo Civil War (1993-1994)," updated June 24, 2020, https://en.wikipedia.org/wiki/Republic_of_the_Congo_Civil_War_(1993%E2%80%931994), accessed November 23, 2020.

13 Collier, *The Bottom Billion,* 28.

14 "Republic of Congo 2nd Civil War," Military, GlobalSecurity.org, https://www.globalsecurity.org/military/world/war/congo-b.htm, accessed November 23, 2020.

15 Unless otherwise indicated all Bible references in this paper are to the New International Version (NIV) (Grand Rapids, MI: Zondervan, 1984).

16 The full story of Melanie can be found in Medine Moussounga Keener, "The Cost of War on Women," *Priscilla Papers* 26:1 (Winter 2012), 4–7.

15 "Bread For Today"—Can Microfinance Respond to the Lord's Prayer in Reducing Poverty? A Case Study in Zambia

Irene Banda Mutalima

Abstract

The fight to end poverty has vexed humankind for decades, seemingly without long-term solutions. With increasing populations, poverty poses a threat of ensconcing its debilitating effects across generations. Often, however, poor people have limited information and capacity to develop structures that can help them ascertain options to guide them in charting their way out of poverty. Yet within these communities are structures that can provide leadership towards sustainable livelihoods. The Church is one of those structures, which is already active within most communities where poor people reside. Picking on the aspects of Acts 6:1–7, this paper works on the hypothesis that achieving sustainable livelihoods is a complex undertaking, requiring appropriate structures and foci to achieve set goals. The study does not provide a conclusive position but lays out the beginnings of an action research process with selected communities and willing churches within the North-Western Province of Zambia.

Introduction

"There should be no poor among you, for the Lord your God will greatly bless you in the land he is giving you as a special possession" (Deut 15:4 NLT).

"There were no needy people among them, because those who owned land or houses would sell them and bring money to the apostles to give to those in need" (Acts 4: 34–35 NLT).

One imagines a whole host of undesirable human conditions whenever poverty is mentioned. It could be a life of squalor and deprivation, or merely being unable to afford a decent meal. It could be benchmarked against the perception of the observer with a set standard of what a life devoid of poverty should look like, or it could be an individual or community identifying themselves with life conditions below what they would consider acceptable. Thus, there is a variety of contexts that qualify an understanding of poverty. What is important to note is that poverty describes human living that is substantially below an accepted standard. This assessment is important because ensuing interventions will often be aimed at bridging the gap that will reduce or expunge the state of being poor among affected people. Poverty, therefore, is one of the key descriptors of people's livelihoods. How we think about livelihoods will influence the design of solutions to ameliorate those conditions.

The Context

In the last fifty decades, poverty has been acknowledged when people earn less than $1 or $2 a day (depending on the preferred indicator); when people are unable to find employment in order to earn enough money to sustain themselves, or when people are living in conditions of famine, hunger, poor nutrition, or malnutrition. This classification, whose origins are mostly external to the people experiencing poverty, has over the years influenced the design of interventions that were used, a good number of which were actually successful in alignment with initial classification. The achievement of some of the Millennium Development Goals (MDGs 2000–2015) is testimony to this.

The Success of the Millennium Development Goals (MDGs)

According to the then UN Secretary General Ban Ki-Moon, "The MDGs helped to lift more than one billion people out of extreme poverty, to make inroads against hunger, to enable more girls to attend school than ever before, and to protect our planet."[1] He, however, acknowledged gaps in critical areas with great inequalities still evident. Success is evident in these areas: life expectancy at birth, mortality rates for every 1000 births, and increased literacy, given the increased populations. However, areas of concern that have a bearing on livelihoods include: high numbers of youths not engaged in progressive activities, especially in medium and low human development countries; low enrollments into tertiary institutions for youths of tertiary going age; high numbers of the population experiencing multidimensional poverty,[2] also as juxtapositioned to the diminished percentage of income that the poorest forty percent of the population holds; worrying numbers of gender-based violence against women by their intimate partners. These are among issues that raise questions about the propensity of poverty among low-income populations, and therefore what needs to be done and by whom. In this context, we look at what a sustainable livelihood approach should take into account when designing interventions. We also examine the role of the Spirit-filled church in creating sustainable livelihoods and, in so doing, lessening the effects of poverty.

What are Livelihoods?

Livelihoods are about how people assure themselves a living in the present and for the future. Livelihoods are complex and can comprise various and disparate factors all at once. However, at the core of livelihoods are people, and often commonly understood in the sense of a household or people belonging to the same house, though it can also cover communities collectively. In defining livelihoods, Chambers and Conway highlight three factors that are key in appreciating their complexities:[3]

What Livelihoods Consist Of

These include the capabilities and assets that people possess and the activities required to convert those capabilities and assets into means of living. A shortfall of capabilities and or assets can easily lead to poverty. However, even where usable capabilities and assets are available, the inability to develop actions that lead to a means of living can also introduce poverty. Thus, the identification and activation of requisite capabilities and assets become an important element in ensuring livelihoods.

The Factors that Make a Livelihood Sustainable

Livelihoods are prone to various stresses and shocks whose impacts often lead to deprivation. Some examples are the onset of a drought or a flood that affects crop yields, sickness or death in the family that requires cash utilization, or the death of a breadwinner. Thus, sustainable livelihoods need to have embedded in the mechanisms for coping and recovery in such a way that lessons learned can enhance existing capabilities for future endurance. Such a mechanism should also create opportunities for future generations.

The Result or Long-Term Impact of a Sustainable Livelihood

Given the complexity of livelihoods, actions that lead to means of living should generate impacts that are grounded for net benefits beyond the affected household. For example, cutting down trees for charcoal, while bringing income to the family concerned, is an environmental concern whose adverse effects have far-reaching consequences beyond the benefiting family. The following diagram aims to capture the various factors that need to be taken into account when designing initiatives for sustainable livelihoods.

Sustainable Livelihoods Framework
MEANS TO ATTAINING A LIVING

Capabilities
- What people can do
- How adaptable those capabilities are
- What opportunities/willimgness exists to improve/enhance capabilities

Assests:
- *Resources:* land, water, tools, livestock, equipment, etc
- *Stores:* savings, food, items of value, etc
- *Claims:* support structures in times of stress/ shocks- welfare system, Church, NGOs
- *Access:* opportunities to know about/ use resources, stores, etc- transport, education, radio, TV, information technology, etc

Appropriate Actions leading to means of living

A LIVING

SUSTAINABLE LIVELIHOODS

Factors for Sustainable Livelihoods
- Mechanisms for coping and recovery from shocks and stresses
- Mechanisms for improving and enhancing capabilities
- Ability to create opportunities for future generations

Long-term Impact
- Designed to benefit intended households
- Net benefits to accrue beyond affected households- locally and globally

Adapted from Chambers and Conway 1992

A deficit in one or more of the above factors has the potential of keeping people in poverty or reversing any gains that have been made in moving them out. This diagram is our working hypothesis and will be fully tested as we work with potential community leaders able to implement this within their communities.

Poverty, therefore, inhibits a large number of poor people from enjoying the richness of human life as it reduces their choices and opportunities. A World Bank study summarized the perspectives of the poor by stating that they experience voicelessness, powerlessness, and exclusion, as they have very limited access to and influence over decisions that affect their lives. [4]It is for this reason that, to a large extent, interventions that are meant to help poor people and are driven by external forces, end up thwarting the voices of the intended beneficiaries: poor people. Yet even where they have notional space for their voices, poor people will often fail to negotiate their way out of poverty due to limited capacities. This is where we think community leadership can play an important role. The church has a very strong presence in areas of Zambia where incidences of poverty are high. They are also, by their very mandate, expected to prefer poor people.

Defining a Spirit-Empowered Church

The word of God tells us that the spirit of God gives the power to act as one is led. Jesus told his disciples to wait until they had received that power. They were not to rush into anything until they had been empowered. In Luke 24:49, Jesus says, "... but tarry in the city of Jerusalem until you are endued with power from on high" (NKJV). Jesus clarifies this instruction after he had risen from the dead in Acts 1:8, "But you shall receive power when the Holy Spirit has come upon you; and you shall be witnesses to me in Jerusalem, and in all Judea and Samaria, and to the end of the earth" (NKJV). The story of the Pentecost in Acts 2 marks the birth of the Spirit-empowered or Spirit-filled church:

> When the Day of Pentecost had fully come, they were all with one accord in one place. And suddenly there came a sound from heaven, as of a rushing mighty wind, and it filled the whole house where they were sitting. Then there appeared to them divided tongues, as of fire, and one sat upon each of them. And they were all filled with the Holy Spirit and began to speak with other tongues, as the Spirit gave them utterance (Acts 2: 1–4 NKJV).

A change had taken place. This change was necessary for the work that was expected of this new Church. Without this empowerment, the Church would not have been able to be and to do the things they subsequently did. This group of people that were already of one accord received utterance and started speaking with other tongues. After explaining this strange occurrence, Peter concludes by saying, "Therefore, let all the house of Israel know assuredly that God has made this Jesus, whom you crucified, both Lord and Christ" (v. 36 NKJV).

The boldness, with which Peter and the disciples displayed as a result of the Holy Spirit's empowerment, enabled them to add about 3,000 new members to this new fellowship. It is important to note that for the longest time, the temple in Jerusalem was the locus for worship and the church, as the Psalmist declares in Psalm 27:4, "One thing I have desired of the LORD, that will I seek: That I may dwell in the house of the LORD. All the days of my life, to behold the beauty of the LORD, and to inquire in his temple" (NKJV).

Pentecost hailed a new dispensation, and the space for worship had moved from a building to the person (2 Cor 3:16). This new church displayed some interesting characteristics: they were filled with the Holy Spirit, and the boldness was evident; they were united and prayed together; they worshiped and praised God together; they exhibited great generosity and had common property; they had power as evident in work and miracles that followed them. Pertinent to this paper is that the day-to-day livelihood needs were cared for as well.

The new Spirit-filled church developed a way of living: they were united in purpose and action. Those who had the property sold it and brought cash to the apostles, which was then distributed according to the needs among them. Echoing the spirit of Deuteronomy 15:4 that highlighted the need for relief from poverty, the new Spirit-filled church made sure there were no needy persons among them (Acts 4:32–37). There was an evident transformation in their lives that they willingly sold their properties in order to share with those who had little or none. The Spirit-filled church became a place where members belonged, the good news was shared and preached, and members found relief for their livelihood deficits.

Furthermore, leadership structure enabled those who felt aggrieved to locate a place that they could take their grievances. Thus, when the

Greek-speaking Jews among them noticed that their widows were being neglected in the food-distribution process, they raised the matter with the apostles (Acts 6:1–6). This necessitated a re-think on how they (apostles) were providing leadership to the new gathering of believers, and a process emerged. In coming up with this process, the apostles considered two important factors. First, that the problem was real and needed to be resolved without compromising the important duty of doing the ministry of the word of God. Second, that the problem was important enough to warrant a defined process that would take on the full responsibility of ensuring that these daily needs were met.

In coming up with this process, the scripture tells us that the twelve apostles gathered all the disciples and acknowledged the problem. They were, however, emphatic that they would not neglect the ministry of the word of God in order to pay attention to the problem at hand and proceeded to propose a more long-term solution. They required the disciples to select seven men from among them who they knew to be full of the Spirit and wisdom.

Evidently, a committee of seven Spirit-empowered men was appointed, and the apostles laid their hands over them and prayed, thereby creating an internal structure to serve the needs of the church members. While scriptures do not go into detail on how this structure worked, it is clear that consequently, "the word of God spread, and the number of disciples multiplied greatly. . . ." (Acts 6:7 NKJV).

It can be argued that the indwelling of the Spirit brought about a transformation that introduced a new ethic of doing things, along with higher integrity. These men could be trusted. After all, the new church had just witnessed the death of Ananias and Sapphira as a result of their dishonesty to the Spirit (Acts 5:1–11).

Lessons for the Local Church

The modern church has gone through a period of uncertainty regarding whether its role should extend beyond evangelism to include social action. Ronald Sider is one of the church leaders who agonized to find balance. He talks about his interaction with a certain James (not his real name):

> Brother James needed someone to tell him about Jesus. No social programs could have restored the brokenness at the center of his being, but he and his

family also desperately need better employment and education systems. . . . [Sider lamented] Why can't there be thousands and thousands of churches all across our world that meet the needs of the whole person in the name of the Lord whom we worship and follow?[5]

Persistent reflection over the scripture has highlighted that by relegating social action, the church would effectively be neglecting the very essence of God's heart towards poor people. While evangelism would always remain the core focus, increasingly, the church has taken on more and more social interventions. In relation to the church of Act 2, Garrison notes that as a result of the outpouring of the Spirit, the church was able to function in important areas that form the comprehensive strategic plan whose implementation can only be possible through the empowerment of the Spirit.[6] Garrison describes these functions as follows (Acts 2:42–47).

1) Connecting with God and one another: The members were able to connect with God in all aspects of their lives while building spiritually strong bonds of fellowship with one another. Both spiritual and physical needs were met.
2) Spiritual growth: The presence of the Holy Spirit enabled a strengthening of belief in God and changed behaviors towards God and one another. Many heard the word of God and became disciples, and relationships were strengthened. In such an environment, it is not surprising that there was an intentional focus on ensuring no one was in need.
3) Willingness to serve: As members of the church matured in the things of God, they not only began to identify with the different gifts they had, but willingly gave themselves to serving one another, building up the Spirit-filled church and caring for the community.
4) A strong focus on worship: This new way of life and a willingness to serve was done through corporate praise, prayer, teaching and singing.

The modern-day Spirit-filled church has pursued these four ideals and largely continues to bring about transformation wherever the church has grown.

Poverty and Church Action in the Zambian Context

The Zambian Constitution establishes the nation as Christian, with eighty-five percent of the population professing some form of Christianity. It is, however, the Pentecostal churches popularly known as "born agains," who emphasize the work of the Spirit through charismatic gifts, such as speaking in tongues, healing, and manifestations of miracles. They are often associated with the indwelling of the Spirit. This perception does not imply that other churches are not experiencing the move of the Spirit and are not functioning as Spirit-empowered churches.

Over the years, the church in Zambia has been known as a serious actor in dealing with societal issues, including the provision of health, education, and taking on justice issues. The expectation is that the Pentecostal churches in Zambia will have a similar impact. A number of Pentecostal churches have feeding programs, schools, health activities, and financing activities that have a societal impact.

While these efforts are laudable, they have not broken the chain of poverty so as to enable poor people to participate in their own development. Statistics show that Zambia has a population of 17.4 million people and is classified as a medium human development country.[7] However, for the period 2007–2018, 53.2% of the population was experiencing multidimensional poverty, and only 8.9% of total income was in the hands of the forty percent who comprise the poorest population. Country-specific reports show rural poverty in 2015 at 76.6%.[8] The economy has largely depended on the mining industry, though fifty-eight percent of the 39 million hectares of land is potentially good for agriculture. There is, therefore, the real potential to boost agriculture that could benefit rural folk.

The North-Western Province of Zambia

The North-Western Province covers an area of 125,826 square kilometers with a population of 833,818. Of this population, 72.8% are in rural area with limited infrastructure.[9] Despite improvement in recent years, typical indicators of development such as per capita income, employment, and access to water and electricity are all still much lower in North-Western Province, compared to, for instance, the Copperbelt Province.

The province is home to three large mines that together produce up to forty percent of Zambia's total annual copper production. The presence of these large mines has led to significant infrastructure built, including the new airport building and runway in Solwezi (the Provincial capital), public roads, classrooms in government schools, market stalls for traders, and an entire purpose-built residential area, with some of the best constructed homes in Solwezi. More significant, however, is the direct impact the mines make simply by doing business with local companies. In terms of support to poor communities, the mines run various activities for women and youths through their corporate social responsibility (CSR) budgets. These contribute to poverty reduction.

Despite these efforts, the province still faces serious challenges. School infrastructure and access to education, health service delivery, and clean water remain huge challenges to local communities. There is a general poor state of the road network, which leads to high transportation costs, and poverty incidences are high at 66.4%, with 48.4% being classified as extremely poor. The highest poverty rates are recorded among small-scale farmers, which stand at 78.9%.

Working with Farmers: The Pilot Project

My company, TUCUZA Associates Limited, decided as part of our mission to support small-scale farmers in North-Western Province, with a view to creating pathways out of poverty while meeting shareholder expectations. We decided to run a pilot project in the 2016–2017 farming season, which runs from October to May. In seeking local leadership, we worked with one of the mines that gave us access to the farmers they had supported before. 148 farmers participated in the pilot, and we provided bean seeds and fertilizer. We chose common beans for the pilot because this is a crop that is well understood in the area and would not require any learning on the part of the farmers. The pilot was meant to help us understand how we could work with the farmers. The farmers performed well, and we were able to market their produce. We learned several key lessons.

First, that it was possible to mobilize small-scale farmers onto our out-grower scheme. We could also increase the numbers to upwards of 20,000 over time. We recognized that it was these small-scale farmers who mostly experience poverty. This fits well with our mission.

Second, that there is a large enough market for mixed beans locally and in the East/ Southern African region. However, we could also explore other cash crops. Third, that with proper training and coordination, we could introduce the idea of a demand-driven focus to our farmers. This means that we could explore markets locally and beyond and opt for optimal cash crops to match market needs.[10]

These lessons led to the decision to have a local presence in the form of an anchor farm that would manage the out-grower scheme as it functioned as a stand-alone business in its own right. We had sought and acquired farmland to serve as a stand-alone, sustainable business while managing an out-grower scheme that would spur an increasing number of small-scale farmers into demand-driven farm production.

The out-grower scheme would serve to bring small-scale farmers into a market system where they would have better chances of increasing their incomes as they chart their way out of poverty. These farmers would have an option to replicate on their own pieces of land, whatever we produced on the anchor farm, to meet market demand. In planning for this, we had full control of what would happen at our farm and the underlying reasons. We could make informed choices that would be beneficial to informed stakeholders. We, however, had no way of knowing, or indeed, of influencing activities that would contribute to the factors necessary to create sustainable livelihoods for the small-holder farmers. It is for this reason that we saw the need to partner with local leadership whom we felt would ensure that the work actually contributed to sustainable livelihoods.

In this first year, we focused on developing our base on the farm. We, however, felt the need to onboard some farmers onto the out-grower scheme. We had lost touch with the farmers who participated in the pilot phase, so we had to look elsewhere. We had to go back again to the mine for access to the farmers they had worked with before. Through that effort, we were able to onboard 211 farmers.

Defining the Theory of Change

We have set up an anchor farm to manage an out-grower scheme. Using the farmer out-grower model, the intention is to have an increasing number of farmers produce for known markets (demand-driven) to be assured of incremental incomes, which would, in turn, help them chart their way out of poverty. The theory of change that we articulate describes the steps and underlying assumptions that should lead us to our long-term goals of creating social impacts in the community while assuring shareholder value.

Problem

We identified the problem that we felt we could help address as low household incomes due to low productivity and a lack of market. We felt that if we partnered with these communities, we could catalyze demand-driven productivity. To get to this point, we would have engaged with viable markets, thereby connecting the small-scale farmers to the markets. Hopefully, this would lead to quality and quantity production that would then constitute sustainable income streams.

Strategies

We split our strategies into three phases: the pilot phase, the proof-of-concept phase, and the expansion phase. In the pilot phase, we confirmed the need to move forward and establish a presence in the area. We are now in the second phase, where we are establishing the anchor farm and the management protocols of the out-grower scheme. This is the phase that will be important in ensuring we collaborate with strong and long-term community leadership. The conversations with churches to do that have started. The expansion phase will be a consolidation of lessons learned, and growing the initiative, should results so dictate.

Activities and Outputs

We started with the anchor farm and the out-grower scheme including documenting the processes and ensuring the systems work. Some of this work has already started and is on-going. We envisage that the outputs will include sales from the anchor farm and from the out-grower scheme. These sales should enable servicing of all and any loans we will have arranged to finance production. The sales should also culminate in net incomes. Community leadership will need to have been trained to ensure this happens within the communities. It will be a process that removes the farmers from dependency mode to generating their own incomes.

Outcomes

As indicated above, we envisage incremental net incomes for the anchor farm and for the smallholder farmers. We also hope to be able to meet the needs of the markets that we will be serving to the intended extent.

Impact

As incomes increase, we hope that this will enable farmers to make choices that improve their livelihoods and enhance coping and recovery mechanisms in the event of shocks and stresses. We will also pay attention to the environmental effects of the work we do. Through this work, we will be able to contribute towards the first five sustainable development goals: the end of poverty, food security, well-being and health, gender equity, and economic growth.

We are very mindful that without partnering with local leadership, all the above will be difficult to achieve. We are, however, confident that should we collaborate with local leadership that is selfless and truly want to see changes in people's lives, we can make progress. This is where we see the role of the Spirit-empowered church.

Local leadership would be key to ensure appropriate assessments towards sustainable livelihoods. They are the ones who would navigate such issues as: What capabilities and assets exist in the community? What optimum capabilities and assets are needed, and how do we bridge the gap? What mechanisms need to be in place to deal with shocks and stresses? We, therefore, see the need to work with established leadership and, where needed, help to develop their capacity to provide community leadership.

Courting the Spirit-Filled Church in North-Western Province

As we settled in the area, we sought to engage with both the local traditional leaders and church leaders. With the traditional leaders, we found ourselves with a challenge we had not previously been aware of. The presence of the mines and development NGOs in the area and their support to the communities had created a perception that was different from what we were proposing. We realized that the community leaders expected us to provide them with food and some form of allowances for participating in meetings. Some of the leaders told us this was the norm. While we did not check with the mines or the development NGOs, we were sure that this approach would not sit well with our model. Furthermore, we did not have the resources to take that route. Our model was based on supporting the community to drive its own development agenda.

We interacted with some church leaders and found a willingness to partner with us. At the same time, they acknowledged their lack of capacity to provide the type of leadership we envisaged. The following are thoughts I received from some of the church leaders we interacted with:

> . . .Your passion is really overwhelming, and worthy praying for and supporting. From my little experience, the church in North Western hasn't done enough in combating poverty, apart from small, isolated projects like school projects, poultry, and crop farming in some rare cases. For me, the greatest challenge I have seen is church leadership, more especially pastoral leadership. Much is needed to help build their capacity if the church is going to rise to this challenge.[11]

> As church leaders, we acknowledge that approximately eighty-two percent of the arable lands available in Zambia are located in the remote part of the country where there is only basic infrastructure. . . . The church, in general, is involved more in evangelism and church planting more than empowering its members in agriculture. A few church leaders have started teaching the importance of land and agriculture to their congregants. A few members have received the message well and are farmers. A few churches and Christian organizations have begun to farm.[12]

> The church has good stories going back to our missionary days as to how they assisted members and communities to deal with poverty in the region. The setting up of Mutanda Centre was exactly to do that. We have had some farming activities dotted around the country; Kalende in Mufumbwe, Itimpi in Kitwe, Mununga farm in Mpika, and Kaindu in Mumbwa are examples of ECZ poverty alleviation agenda. How successful these have been is another issue, and this depended so much on personnel. So, the Mandate of Mutanda Centre[13] was to go flat out to make the area (region) food secure, and at some point, it worked so well. However, the current situation needs much to be desired. . . . As indicated, the major challenge has been a human resource for us as a church. We have had very good provision from the Lord through various cooperating partners, but we have simply failed to manage these assets. We are trying to revive these efforts by re-constituting and placing the right managers to help us manage these assets for their intended purpose.[14]

As we are already establishing ourselves in the area, we are progressing these conversations to come up with processes that help develop the capacity of the local church to provide the needed leadership. Building their capacity may not necessarily fall within our mandate, but as we craft these partnerships, we will explore ways of ensuring that the capacity is built.

Conclusion

Looking at the Sustainable Livelihoods Framework discussed above, the role of the Spirit-filled church would start with determining what capabilities communities under their care have, how adaptable those capabilities could be, and an understanding of what opportunities exist to improve or enhance those capabilities. Such a church would also need to conduct an audit of what assets are at the disposal of the community. These assets would include resources like water, land, tools, livestock, and equipment; stores such as savings, food, and items of value; claims such as welfare systems and hospitality programs within the church to mitigate stress and shocks; and access to useful information. These would enable the crafting of appropriate actions that would utilize capabilities to exploit existing assets in the process of generating sustainable livelihoods.

It can be argued that the church of Acts 6 had a sense of the assets available to them and the capabilities to convert those assets into useful livelihoods. Members of this church were united in purpose and action. Furthermore, this unity compelled those who had property to sell it for the benefit of the community as a whole. The proceeds from the sale were brought to the leaders and distributed in an equitable way. In so doing, they made sure that there were no needy persons among them (Acts 4:32–37). The Spirit-filled church became a place where members belonged, such that when problems arose, resolutions were possible.

Our interactions with the Spirit-filled church in the North-Western province of Zambia highlight challenges that negate a progressive approach to sustainable livelihoods. Church leaders are themselves experiencing livelihood challenges that their members experience. Collective assets are few, just as there are very few individuals who might, like Barnabas of the early church, sell their land for the common good. The helplessness that comes from not having money overshadows the utility value of other existing assets like land, water, and livestock that could contribute to sustainable livelihoods using existing capabilities. Yet, it is not a hopeless situation.

This is the beginnings of a work that not only presents an opportunity for the local church to extend their relevance to the total person, but also has the potential of reaching many poor farmers to improve their livelihoods. The church would need to introspect on the following questions: How should the church equip itself to meet the needs of its community of members? What structures would respond to the livelihood needs of their members? What capacity building activities will be required for the church to provide livelihood solutions to their members without neglecting their core mandate of evangelism? With a huge portion of the population being classified as poor, and a good number frequenting the Spirit-filled church, this is a relevant intervention.

Notes

1 "Were the Millennium Development Goals a Success? Yes- Sort Of," World Vision International, July 3, 2015, https://www.wvi.org/united-nations-and-global-engagement/article/were-mdgs-success, accessed March 30, 2020.

2 Multidimensional poverty definition identifies overlapping deprivations that poor people experience across their standard of living, health, and education, and tries to measure the average number of deprivations that each person experiences at the same time. This is called the Multidimensional Poverty Index.

3 Robert Chambers and Gordon R. Conway, "Sustainable Rural Livelihoods: Practical Concepts for the 21st Century" (Discussion Paper, Institute of Development Studies, East Sussex, 1992), 5.

4 Deepa Narayan, Robert Chambers, Meera Kaul Shah, and Patti Petesch, *Voices of the Poor: Crying Out for Change* (Oxford: Oxford University Press, 2000) 2.

5 Ronald Sider, *Evangelism and Social Action-in a Lost and Broken World* (London: Hodder and Stoughton,1993), 23.

6 Alton Garrison, "A Spirit-Empowered Church: The Process and Plan of the Acts 2 Church," *Influence Magazine*, 2015, https://influencemagazine.com/en/Theory/A-SpiritEmpowered-Church, accessed April 3, 2020.

7 "Beyond Income, Beyond Averages, Beyond Today: Inequalities in Human Development in the 21st Century," Human Development Report 2019, United Nations Development Program, http://hdr.undp.org/sites/default/files/hdr2019.pdf accessed March 28, 2021.

8 "2015 Living Conditions Monitoring Survey Report," Central Statistical Office, https://www.zamstats.gov.zm/, accessed April 4, 2020.

9 "2015 Living Conditions," Central Statistical Office.

10 TUCUZA Associates Limited Newsletter 1:1 (March 2020), 2.

11 Bishop Charles Mapuranga (Pentecostal Holiness Church, Solwezi), email, March 7, 2020.

12 Bishop Fortune Mwiza (Deliverance Church, Lusaka), email, March 19, 2020.

13 Mutanda Centre is a mission centre in North-Western Province. It has structures for the church to support social action in the area.

14 Bishop Paul Mususu (Evangelical Church in Lusaka), email, March 25, 2020.

16 Empowering Christian Low-Fee Independent Schools: Edify's Response to Poverty

Makonen Getu

Abstract

It is now commonly recognized that with the help of efforts made during the last thirty years, particularly after the implementation of the Millennium Development Goals (MDGs), the rate of global extreme poverty has been halved. The Sustainable Development Goals (SDG)s of 2015–2030 are expected to help the remaining 600 million escape poverty and lower the rate of extreme poverty to a single digit. The paper argues that poverty is multi-dimensional and is a matter of material scarcity and sin-caused broken relationships and concludes that its alleviation happens when both material and spiritual deficiencies are simultaneously addressed. The fight against global poverty is an undertaking in which the Sprit-empowered community should and must participate in response to the kingdom mandate. This paper does two things: discusses how education tackles the different aspects of poverty and provides a case study of Edify as part of the Christian response, showing how supporting low-fee independent Christian schools contributes to poverty alleviation.

Introduction

The definition of the term poverty is as varied as the worldview of the people defining it. Even those who adhere to the same worldview might have different ways of defining poverty. The same goes for the differences in the analyses of the causes, remedies, and measurement of poverty. Human-centered (secular) and Jesus-centered (biblical) worldviews are considered here. The purpose of this paper is to look at global poverty from a biblical perspective with a special focus on the Christian response to poverty alleviation using the Edify as a case study.

In 1995, the United Nations (UN) defined poverty as "a condition characterized by severe deprivation of basic human needs, including food, safe drinking water, sanitation facilities, health, shelter, education, and information. It depends not only on income but also on access to services."[1]

Human beings have consistently endeavored to free themselves from the bondage of poverty by developing technology, organization, systems, and structures to produce and exchange more and better things necessary for meeting their needs and improving their standard of living at different points in time. The Industrial Revolution that took place in the West was a major leap in the generation of wealth at an unprecedented scale. Agricultural economies were transformed into manufacturing, and production became mechanized. The result was increased abundance and improved living standards. In the words of North and Thomas, "The affluence of the Western man is a new and unique phenomenon. In the past several centuries, he has broken loose from the shackles of a world bound by abject poverty and recurring famine and has realized a quality of life which is made possible only by relative abundance."[2] It is not so in the rest of the world yet. In Africa, particularly Sub-Saharan Africa, most economies are predominantly agricultural, and the production methods applied are still traditional. Mechanization is limited, and industry is rudimentary in quality and small in scale resulting in a low rate of wealth generation and widespread poverty.

Global Effort to Tackle Poverty

Ever since the end of World War II, the United Nations (UN), the World Bank, the International Monetary Fund (IMF), bilateral development agencies, and charity organizations have been fighting poverty in a concerted manner by supporting national development efforts through multilateral, bilateral, and private aid. The two major global efforts that stand out as having made remarkable achievements in tackling global poverty alleviation include the Millennium Development Goals (MDGs) and Sustainable Development Goals (SDGs).

In the year 2000, 191 UN member states and twenty-two international organizations committed eight goals, each with specific targets to:

1) Eradicate extreme poverty and hunger
2) Achieve universal primary education
3) Promote gender equality
4) Reduce child mortality
5) Improve maternal health
6) Combat HIV/AIDS, malaria, and other diseases
7) Ensure environmental sustainability
8) Develop a global partnership for development

These MDGs were to be achieved by 2015. Astonishingly, at the end of 2010, poverty rates were halved. The number of people surviving on less than $1.25 a day fell from thirty-six percent to twelve percent between 1990 and 2015. The total number of people living in poverty was then estimated at 736 million.[3]

As the MDGs culminated in 2015, the SDGs were initiated and signed by 193 UN member countries to end poverty by 2030. The number of goals was more than twice those of the MDGs. These goals consisted of:

1) No Poverty
2) Zero Hunger
3) Good Health and Well-being
4) Quality Education
5) Gender Equality
6) Clean Water and Sanitation
7) Affordable and Clean Energy
8) Decent Work and Economic Growth
9) Industry, Innovation, and Infrastructure
10) Reducing Inequality
11) Sustainable Cities and Communities
12) Responsible Consumption and Production
13) Climate Action
14) Life Below Water
15) Life On Land
16) Peace, Justice, and Strong Institutions
17) Partnerships for the Goals[4]

The seventeen SDGs are interrelated and together have 169 targets and 230 indicators compared to the eight MDGs, which were broken into twenty-one targets and sixty indicators. The SDGs commenced in January 2016 and are now in their fifth year of implementation.

In addition to this, the "End Poverty" campaign of the 2010s engaged all types of people and organizations, including schools and religious establishments, as well as private businesses across the globe. Nelson Mandela was one of the statesmen who campaigned and rightly spread the idea that poverty was manmade, and it could therefore be unmade by man. The "End Poverty" campaign not only raised mass awareness and passion, but also elicited a huge response both in advocacy and aid money globally. Artists like Bono and Bob Geldoff campaigned shoulder to shoulder with prominent anti-poverty leaders like Jeffrey Sacks, multi-and bi-lateral agencies, heads of states, charities, and private businessmen such as Bill Gates.

The Geography of Poverty

Despite the decline in poverty numbers achieved under the MDGs and during the last eighteen years of the SDGs, poverty still persists, exerting crushing power on hundreds of millions of people. Using the World Bank rate of $1.90/day as a measure of extreme poverty, the World Data Lab estimated in January 2019 that 600 million people lived in extreme poverty across the world. Although the UN target is to reduce the number of people living in extreme poverty to below three percent by 2030, the World Bank estimates that Sub-Saharan Africa has little or no chance of achieving the stated target.

About seventy-five percent of the forty-three countries with poverty rates above eighteen percent are in Africa. It is also estimated that seventy percent of the world's poor are in Africa, which is up from fifty percent in 2015. In 2023, this ratio is expected to rise to eighty percent, which is up from sixty percent from 2016, rising to ninety percent in 2030. It is also estimated that by 2030, nine of the ten countries with the greatest number of poor people in the world will be located in Africa. With over 110 million citizens in extreme poverty, Nigeria is estimated to be the poverty capital of the world. According to the World Bank, the number of people living in poverty continues to decline in South Asia, but no matching decline is expected to happen in Sub-Saharan Africa.

Christian Response to Global Poverty through Education

To cities filled with the homeless and impoverished, Christianity offers charity as well as hope. To cities filled with newcomers and strangers, Christianity offers an immediate basis for attachments. To cities filled with orphans and widows, Christianity provides a new and expanded sense of family. To cities torn by violent ethnic strife, Christianity offers a new basis for social solidarity.[5] God cares about poverty and the people who languish in poverty. As his image bearers, the desire in human beings to fight poverty originates from God.

God's anti-poverty response started when he saw that Adam and Eve, who rebelled against him and joined arms with Satan, were covering their naked bodies with the fig leaves they sewed together. God made tunics of skin and clothed them (Gen 3:7, 21). In this first instance of scarcity for human beings, God responded with kindness and provisions. He also commanded humans to love their neighbors and respond to the needy in society.

Overview

Since then, human beings have responded to the needs of the poor, the broken, and the hopeless in different ways. Jesus himself demonstrated how important this response was through both word (proclamation) and deed (social action). In fact, he equated responding to the needy, stricken by poverty, with responding to his need, as described in Matthew 25.

In pursuit of God's mission to set the poor free from the bondage of poverty, Christians have been involved throughout history in tackling both local and global problems by engaging in various poverty-alleviating socio-economic interventions, of which education stands out as the most vital one. Pre-eighteenth-century records show that individual Christians and the church were at the forefront of education. Not only did the church initiate and run most of the kindergarten, primary, and secondary schools, but it also established some of the world-renowned universities like Oxford, Cambridge, Bologna, Freiburg, Sorbonne, Harvard, Yale, Princeton, and Stanford, among others, all of which have drifted from their original Christian mission.[6]

Add to these the hundreds of thousands of Christian schools, colleges, and universities across the globe that have been and are currently serving societies by providing access to pre-university as well as under-and post-graduate university education as part of God's global mission. Add the many Christian development organizations as well, such as World Vision, Catholic Relief Services, Christian Aid, Tearfund, Opportunity International, Hope International, Adventist Development and Relief Agency, Ecumenical Church Loan Fund, Lutheran World Federation, Business As Mission, and many more local entities which all run programs aimed at community development and wealth generation among the poor of the world. Local and international churches also play a significant role in fighting global poverty in various ways, including education.

Why Education?

The Commonwealth Education Hub states:

> The narrow focus of the MDGs has been replaced by an integrated and all-encompassing agenda, which emphasizes poverty eradication, inclusive growth, environmental sustainability, equality, and a people-centered agenda within seventeen goals and 169 associated targets. Education plays an important role across all SDGs, driving progress towards sustainable development.[7]

In a similar way, a joint survey, undertaken by Educate A Child and FHI, asserts:

> In addition to serving as the focus for SDG4 ("ensure inclusive and equitable quality education and promote lifelong learning opportunities for all"), education directly contributes to the goals addressing poverty reduction and reduced inequalities, health and nutrition, economic growth and labor market opportunities, as well as peacebuilding and the promotion of democratic institutions. Primary education, in particular, is recognized as a catalyst to meeting many of the most important development challenges that exist today.[8]

Generally speaking, education has been regarded and upheld as a powerful tool for personal and national development in all societies, even before it was given in formal ways through institutions. In its multi-dimensional nature, poverty is comprised of, among other things, material shortage, poor health, political and social exclusion, lack of freedom and gender equity (powerlessness), lack of peace and security, absence of opportunities for creativity and critical thinking, environmental degradation, and spiritual oppression. Education contributes to the alleviation of all these dimensions of poverty directly or indirectly by enhancing development that alleviates material poverty, political empowerment, and gender equity that result in participation and inclusion, health, peace and stability that ensure security, creativity and critical thinking, environmental care, and spiritual freedom through faith in Christ.

The general global view is that education has an inherent quality of generating better citizens, families, communities, and nations. Jekayinfa and Kolawale quoted in Ohaniydo, state that education seeks "to produce a useful citizen. A useful citizen is useful both to himself and the society in which he lives and generally, to the world community."[9] Sultana asserts that there is no development without education. He says, "Beyond any doubt, education plays a pivotal role in the development of any country. In a developing country, education gains even more importance. . . . No education no development."[10] In other words, no development without education and no poverty alleviation without development.

Edify's Response and Contribution to Global Poverty Alleviation

Edify shares the global view of the role of education in enhancing development and alleviating poverty by generating citizens equipped with skills and knowledge that enable them to become employable and income earners. This constitutes part of Edify's rationale for the choice of education as its method of response. While recognizing the role of education in personal and national development and the legitimacy of this pursuit, Edify holds that this is only a partial solution and not the entire solution to global poverty.

The secular worldview sees poverty as a lack of resources to meet basic needs, i.e., not having adequate money to have access to food, shelter, clothing, education, and health services. Yes, economic exploitation, including corruption, inequality, and uneven distribution of resources and unfair terms of trade, as well as political oppression, social exclusion, lack of freedom and opportunities, causes poverty resulting in all forms of vulnerability and powerlessness.[11] Edify brings another important factor to the equation: broken relationships caused by sin. In fact, sin resulting in broken relationships is the mother of all poverty.[12] All the other factors constitute the symptoms rather than the causes of poverty.

The solution to multi-dimensional poverty, therefore, lies in both the generation of wealth and the restoration of relationships between humankind and God, humans and humans, and humankind and the environment, through faith in Jesus Christ, the son of the living God, which leads to salvation. Consequently, this comes through the knowledge and acceptance of the values and principles expressed in the Bible. Edify's program is about facilitating the simultaneous pursuit of both income generation and spiritual transformation (character formation) through education. Therefore, the education Edify promotes is value-based and seeks to enhance character development in such a manner that people are freed from both material and spiritual poverty.

The next section is devoted to presenting Edify's program and discussing how it contributes to poverty alleviation.

History

Edify is a not-for-profit Christian NGO based in San Diego, California, USA. It was co-founded by Chris Crane and Tiger Dawson in 2009.[13] The vision of Edify is flourishing, godly nations. Edify aspires to contribute to the building of nations in which people live, fulfilling what God requires of them: "Do justice, love mercy, and walk humbly with God" (Micah 6:8). In other words, nations that are led by God-fearing citizens, and where an environment is created in which human beings live in communion with God, one another, and the environment.

The organization's mission is to improve and expand sustainable Christ-centered education globally.[14] This relates to supporting low-fee independent (private) schools (LFIS) owned by Christian social entrepreneurs and/or churches providing Christ-centered primary and secondary education in marginalized communities. In general, Edify doesn't support government schools and private schools. In the latter case, only LIFS, which are already undertaking, or are willing to undertake, Christ-centered education as part of their school curricula, are included in Edify's program.

In its first year of operation, which was in 2010, Edify began serving in two countries: Ghana and the Dominican Republic. Today Edify operates in eleven countries across Africa, Asia, and Latin America. Seven of these are in Africa, three in Latin America, and one in South Asia.[15] The focus on Africa is a reflection of the higher rate of poverty and poorer quality of education than the other two regions.

Products and Services

The main products and services offered by Edify consist of loan capital to improve and expand school facilities, training to equip school leaders and develop sustainable Christ-centered schools, and education technology to enhance learning outcomes and employability.

Let us consider how these products and services are provided and how they are applied in the promotion of Christ-centered education that contributes to the alleviation of global poverty.

Access to and Quality of Education

Despite the increased access to education created by the Universal Primary Education (UPE) following the MDGs, education in List Income Countries (LICs) in general, and Africa in particular, still suffers from poor quality and limited capacity to absorb all school-age children. According to UNESCO, "About 263 million children and youth are out of school. The total includes 61 million children of primary school age, 60 million of lower secondary school age, and includes the first ever estimate of those of upper secondary school age at 142 million."[16]

Lack of access to education is more chronic in marginalized and poor communities. Some of the reasons include limited or no availability of public (government) schools and limited capacity of LFIS. The latter are constrained from enrolling more children because they cannot expand their physical classrooms, because they lack the capital needed to do so. They are unable to borrow from commercial banks and other financial institutions in the capital market because they lack collateral and sufficient borrowing history.[17] The very purpose of their existence, providing educational access to disadvantaged children to help them unleash their potential and escape poverty, is put at risk.

During its nine years of operation, Edify has provided a total of $27 million in loan capital to Christian LFIS schools. This has mitigated the capital constraint through the provision of loans. Edify has removed part of the capital constraint faced by Christian LFIS and empowered them to improve and expand their educational facilities. As a result, LFIS have been able to create more opportunities for children in socio-economically marginalized communities to access education.

School loans are not only used for expansion. They are also used for improvement. Edify's loan capital helps LFIS to increase their enrolment following the physical expansion of educational facilities and the overall improvement in the general learning environment. This includes improvements in ventilation, lighting, classroom equipment like furniture and learning aides, toilets for boys and girls, safe drinking water, canteen, and play/sport grounds. An improved learning environment creates a more conducive atmosphere for teaching and learning, which in turn leads to higher quality education. With improved quality comes improved academic performance, which also results in increased enrolment.

By giving loan capital to Christian LFIS to improve and expand their school facilities, Edify contributes towards the provision of more access and higher quality education to children in poverty. More children who would otherwise have been out of school have been afforded the opportunity to receive education in schools that have accessed Edify loans. By creating opportunities for more children to attend school, Edify's program has played a vital role in alleviating educational poverty both in quantity and quality. So far, about 4,000 Christian LFIS have benefited from Edify's lending program and have been able to serve over 1 million students.[18]

Income/Wealth Generation Through School Entrepreneurs

Christian LFIS are social businesses. School fees constitute the core source of income. This is positively correlated with the level of enrollment. The higher the enrollment, i.e., student population, the larger the income. Increased enrollment means increased fee income and profitability, which leads to sustainability. Both access (quantity) and improvement (quality) to education result in increased enrollment and therefore increased income. Edify's loan capital helps Christian school owners to achieve both and boost their profitability.

In addition to increased enrollment, the rate of income generation among school entrepreneurs is enhanced by business and accounting training and those applying Quickbooks,[19] facilitated by Edify. School entrepreneurs have acquired financial skills which they did not have prior to their partnership with Edify and have applied them to improve their financial health, including the rate of fee collection, record keeping, budgeting and planning, as well as profit and loss calculations. This has brought improved financial discipline and stewardship, and hence profitability.

Still, another contributing factor lies in the improvement of staff recruitment and retention schools have made following Edify's intervention. Initially, most of the schools supported by Edify did not have adequate experience in human resources (HR) management. Poor HR skills led to frequent attrition, creating interruptions, parental disappointment, student withdrawals, and recruitment expenses resulting in revenue declines. The leadership and HR training provided by Edify helps school entrepreneurs to improve their recruitment, retention, compensation, staff care, and performance appraisal policies and practices, thereby mitigating these problems and stabilizing their revenue stream.

Also, some of the school entrepreneurs who have installed computer labs with the loan from Edify use these as income centers. By making their computer labs available for use by the public outside of school hours at reasonable rates, the schools generate additional income.

As a result, many of the almost 4,000 school partners have experienced increased personal as well as business income leading to increased consumption, savings, and investment. Edify's intervention has helped them to reduce the impact of income poverty on their personal and business lives. The diagram below shows how Edify's products help LFIs increase income.

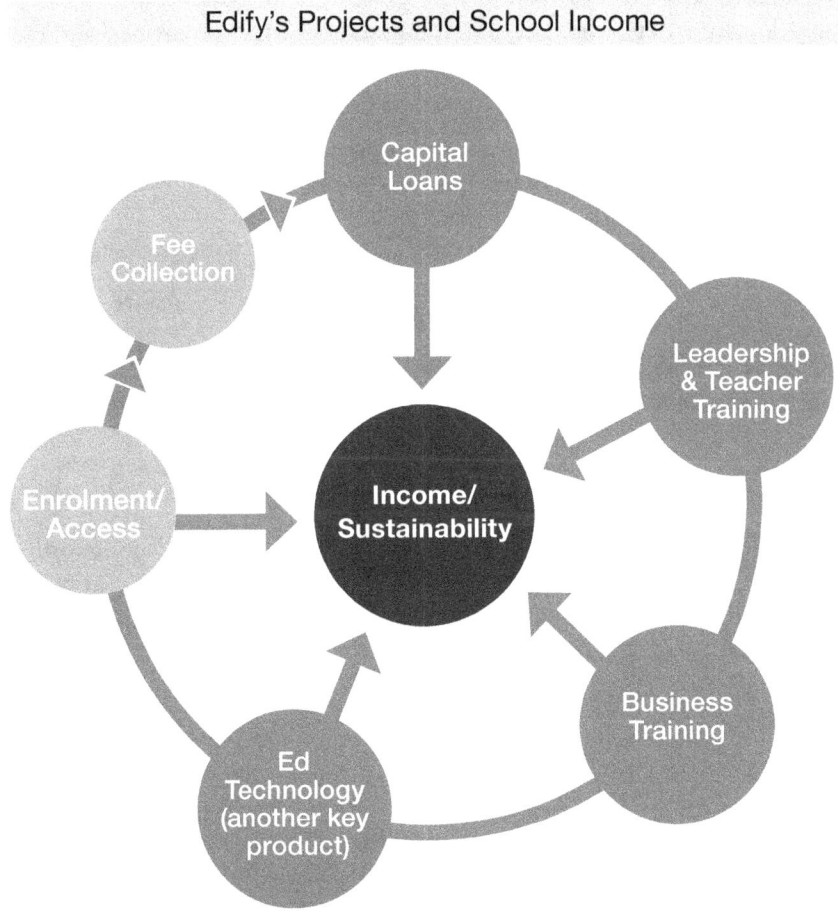

As shown in the diagram, the capital loans, leadership and teacher training, business training, and education technology services provided improve efficiency, accountability, and stewardship as well as enrollment, thereby increasing the rate of fee collection and profitability. As a result, school owners earn relatively more with the propensity to save more and improve their standard of living.

Teachers and Support Staff

Not only are schools enabled to retain their existing teachers and support staff, but they are also able to recruit new staff as they grow following Edify's interventions. Without those interventions, some of the schools benefiting from Edify's program would have closed, and many teachers and support staff would have lost their jobs. This would have affected many families negatively due to increased unemployment and income poverty.

In addition, teachers are trained in Christian values and principles, which include the Christ-centered worldview regarding the role of money and good stewardship. This is another output resulting from Christ-centered training activities facilitated by Edify. Teachers serve to their best abilities as unto the Lord to retain their employment. They also manage money God's way so that they don't lack. In other words, Edify's program contributes to poverty alleviation by enabling schools to sustain and create jobs for teachers and support staff and inculcate Christ-centered values and principles regarding money. A total of about 14,000 teachers and school leaders have benefited from Edify's program.[20]

Lending and Training Partners

One of the many strong attributes of Edify is its policy of collaboration and serving in unity. Edify doesn't seek to foster competition. Rather, it chooses to partner with others. This is the best way of building the body of Christ and exercising good stewardship.

The two core programs of lending and training facilitated by Edify are implemented in partnership with other like-minded organizations. Edify doesn't find it necessary to create its own microfinance structure to run its lending programs. Rather, Edify partners with existing local Christian Microfinance Institutions (MFIs), which become responsible for managing all lending activities. Local financial institutions receive loan capital from Edify and lend it to Edify's school partners using their own structures and regulations. The interest income earned goes to the MFIs, although they are also expected to contribute part of it towards transformation training activities for the schools. The loan from Edify enables the partner MFIs to grow their program and income as well as their capacity to create and sustain employment. These partnerships are other contributions by Edify towards poverty alleviation.

Likewise, Edify transformational trainings are implemented in partnership with Christian training organizations with local and/or international affiliations. Edify organizes training events given by training partners. Edify also buys training materials and other Christian literature from training partners for distribution in schools. Edify pays fees, transport, and food expenses incurred by training facilitators. These partnerships also contribute to fellow like-minded institutions to alleviate poverty.

Communities and Nations: Present and Future

At present, one of the main poverty alleviation contributions to communities and nations resulting from Edify's program is the tax income generated from the increased income attained by school entrepreneurs and their employees, partner organizations and their employees, as well as related suppliers and producers. Prior to Edify's partnership, the level of tax paid by Christian LFIS was much lower for two reasons. First, many schools were making low or no incomes, with many of them operated at a loss. Second, many schools were not properly registered as part of the regular tax system. Their partnership with Edify has boosted their income and thus the amount of tax paid. Those who were not paying were trained to fulfill their national obligation on a regular basis and register their entity, which they have done. This means increased community and national revenue meant to be used for common public purposes.

Edify's programs help schools generate employable citizens by offering computer and other skills through education technology and by enhancing academic excellence, i.e., learning outcomes among students. This will enable their students to be engaged in gainful and well-paying jobs, and hence move from being dependent on their families to being independent sources of economic support to their parents and extended family members. It also means an increase in the number of tax-paying individuals, resulting in higher tax revenue to communities and nations.

Character Development

Participants in Edify's program grow in a special type of character development. This character development is rooted in Christ-centered values and principles as written in the Bible. Such character comes from following the teaching of God's word as part of the education provided in schools. In the beginning, education was given in the presence of God. He was the first teacher, and Adam and Eve were his first students in the first school, the Garden of Eden. There, he taught them about himself, his creation, their role, and the rules that mattered, including relationships and marriage. That order remained until reason, rationalism, and humanism appeared, and God was taken out of school. Thus, education was offered in two parts, divided into the secular and the sacred instead of taking it as a whole. As a result, education has focused on generating future citizens with skills and knowledge, but very little character.

As mentioned above, Edify program(s) facilitate education that produces future citizens with both academic and character excellence with a desire to build flourishing, godly nations. The education Edify supports and seeks to generate citizens with a new mindset of serving and not lording over others. Citizens who put others first and themselves second follow the example of Jesus, who came to serve and die for others. Edify seeks to bring God back into education, into the school, into the classroom, and ultimately, into the minds and hearts of children so that they leave schools equipped with both the secular and biblical knowledge of the world and are prepared for the good work. How does character development contribute to poverty alleviation? For the sake of being brief, let's examine three specific areas.

Oppression

Broken relationships are the cause of poverty; sin is the cause of broken relationships. The beginning of all genuine freedom is, therefore, freedom from the bondage of sin through salvation. Sin cripples, binds, and imprisons. Sin imprints and nurtures the scarcity mindset in people and, through them, entire communities and nations. Sin inculcates hopelessness. The "I-don't-have," and "I-cannot," or "I-am-unable" perceptions that hold people from unleashing their potential have their origin in sin. By facilitating Christ-centered education that leads children to salvation and/or strengthens their faith in Jesus, developing Christ-like character, Edify contributes to the generation of future leaders who serve communities and nations with a mindset of abundance. The "I-am-able," the "I-have," and the "I-can-do-everything-through-Christ-who-strengthens-me" perspective. They become people who not only see potential in themselves as God's image bearers, but who also count on and build on God's promises as an asset. The scarcity mindset is oppressive and constraining and thus causes poverty. The abundance mindset is liberating and releasing and thus results in poverty alleviation. Herein lies Edify's contribution.

The other form of oppression is the oppression of man by man. Because of sin, there are the "haves" and the "have-nots." The "haves" are those in power who pursue their self-interest first and exercise injustice, exploitation, and inequality against their fellow citizens. Landlessness, unemployment, financial exclusion, exorbitant loans, lack of freedom of movement, lack of opportunities, lack of democratic rights, deprivation of basic capabilities, etc., are part of the oppression, the "unfreedoms" suffered by the "have-nots." These constraints hinder people from doing their best in unleashing their potential and flourishing, and alleviating poverty.[21] The Christ-centered education facilitated by Edify seeks to generate citizens who follow Jesus in doing justice, loving mercy, and walking humbly with God. In the world they serve, there is no Jew nor Greek, male nor female, servant nor master. They are all one in Jesus. There is mutual love, care, and respect in that no one will be above the other. No one will be left behind to live in poverty. There will be equal people, loving, sharing, and serving one another; no oppression, no poverty.

Corruption

> Corruption, which has always existed, is today an obstacle to effective good governance. In many parts of the world, corruption in the form of public misconduct has led to illegal and morally crooked practices such as bribery, misallocation of resources, and the misuse of power and influence for personal or corporate gain at the expense of the wider society. . . . Linked with drug trafficking, money-laundering, illegal trade of arms, and many other forms of

criminality, corruption is harmful to economic growth. [22]

Corruption is defrauding, cheating, embezzling, and stealing, practiced by people who abuse their positions for dishonest personal gain. It is the drive for self-enrichment and disregard for the interest of others that causes people, particularly those in power and influence, to commit such criminal activities in betrayal of the trust they have been given.

The Christ-centered education facilitated by Edify promotes honesty, transparency, integrity, loyalty, accountability, responsibility, sharing, and generosity according to the teaching of Jesus. After learning about Christ-like character traits, students stop lying, stealing, cheating, harassing, and bullying others for personal gain. Deeply transformed people are likely to avoid practicing corruption: instead, expose and condemn corruption. They do good for their people, for their countries, and for their God. The lower the corruption rate is, the more available public resources will be for the common good. Resources that would have ended up in the bank accounts of corrupt individuals for hoarding and accumulation will now be allocated to poverty alleviation.

Witchcraft

Belief in witchcraft and witchcraft-induced jealousy is very strong among Africans. Some people are said to be preoccupied with trying to bring down those who seem to be doing better than them, while such potential victims avoid the appearance of doing well in order not to stir the jealousy of witches.[23] In Zambia, for example, I heard Mr. Naboth Ngulube, an official from the Ministry of Labor and Social Services, sharing that people believed that they would be bewitched and would risk their lives and property if they were seen to be radically improving their socio-economic status. To look better and more self-sufficient than their neighbors was viewed as inviting troubles. To be safe, he continued, people preferred to keep in line with their neighbors and practice dependency even when it was not necessary. The accepted rule, he said, was: "even if you have salt at home, ask your neighbor to lend you some and pretend that you are struggling."[24] I personally witnessed this in a village in Luapula Province where World Vision was implementing a health project. A retired teacher moved to his original village and, using his savings, built a modern house. The villagers fled, believing that they would be bewitched by his witchdoctor. With reference to witchcraft and business, Buckley writes:

> There may be much more than a lack of finance, skills or demand that is preventing African micro-entrepreneurs from expanding. . . . In many cultures, success in business is put down to the wielding of malign supernatural powers, and the entrepreneur can be isolated rather than admired in his or her community. . . . The supernatural – the ancestor, the spirits, traditional medicine, superstition, and so on – is at the heart of African cultures and plays a central role in explaining life. . . . For example, in Accra, the Ga people who dominate fishing believe that they see gods walk on the sea on Tuesdays; they, therefore, refuse to fish on this day. Others . . . will spend what little money they have on concoctions or the advice of spiritualists. For people like these, the supernatural is real and its effects cannot be ignored.[25]

We see here how witchcraft practices tend to hinder people from making self-improvement while causing them to spend the little money they have vainly believing an investment in witchcraft brings better fortunes. In both cases, witchcraft undermines people's efforts to come out of poverty. Indeed, it aggravates poverty. The Christ-centered education facilitated by Edify makes students aware of the animistic and harmful nature of witchcraft practices. As they learn and become grounded in their knowledge of the values and principles of Jesus, they reject such harmful practices. This results in personal, physical, and spiritual development, courage, and savings. People cease being intimidated by witchcraft and evil powers. They become bold and defy the pressure to conform to animistic worldviews. Instead, they choose to transform themselves by the renewing of their minds the Jesus way, thereby flourishing both spiritually and materially.

Conclusion

The world identifies global poverty with material scarcity and its solution with material abundance. The common response seeks to increase the rate of growth measured by per capita income with the belief that increased income enables those struggling to meet their socio-economic needs and escape poverty. The more money people have, the greater the opportunities for buying more and better-quality food, shelter, and clothing, and for accessing non-physical goods and services. While recognizing the role of material scarcity in poverty, abundance in poverty alleviation, and the difference increased income makes, the Christian worldview, i.e., the Spirit-empowered school of thought, holds that this is only one part of the whole equation in poverty alleviation. The root cause of poverty is sin, which is the source of broken relationships: humankind to God, human to human, and humankind to environment. Human beings do not only suffer from material poverty, but also from spiritual (character) poverty. Global poverty is, therefore, made up of material and spiritual poverty. As increased income is key to material poverty alleviation, so salvation is to spiritual poverty alleviation. The two components go hand in hand and have to be addressed simultaneously in response to multi-dimensional poverty. Investing in material poverty alleviation and leaving or rejecting any effort that is geared towards spiritual poverty alleviation, as the world does, results only in an incomplete response.

The Spirit-empowered response to global poverty should stand for a truly holistic transformational development approach. No matter the cost, Spirit-empowered Christians should uphold that the only true solution to global poverty is the simultaneous application of the material-spiritual (bread-word) principle; not one or the other on its own. In research, debate, advocacy, wealth generation, evangelism, and education, Spirit-empowered Christians should speak out about this truth and make their voices heard. Dealing with the monopoly of secular ideas as the source of defining the cause and solutions of global poverty by promoting Spirit-empowered ideas on all fronts is a sure way of addressing global poverty.

This is what Edify is doing in the field of education: instilling God's ideas and Christ-centered values and principles in the leaders of tomorrow, while they are still young and full of imagination. Edify's approach stands in stark contrast to the secular ideas and values, resulting in God-ignorant and God-opposing future leaders. Edify counteracts its scheme through powerful partnerships with Christian schools and other like-minded organizations to bring God back into the classroom. This makes it possible to raise God-fearing future leaders who are equipped to build flourishing godly nations so that inequality, oppression, and exploitation will vanish. These future leaders will bring, instead, the abounding abundance and the absence of scarcity, where multi-dimensional poverty (material and spiritual) becomes history. Materially, employment is enhanced, thereby increasing productivity and production, leading to increased personal, community, and national income (wealth generation) and increased consumption (improved standard of living). Politically, justice, equality, peace, and security are established. Spiritually, sin loses its grip, leading to the restoration of broken relationships, love, kindness, honesty, and humility. This is the ultimate impact of Christ-centered education promoted through Christian LFIS with the support of Edify: Flourishing godly nations empowered by the Spirit of the Holy Spirit.

Notes

1 "Report of the World Summit for Social Development 1995," United Nations Department of Economic and Social Affairs, https://www.un.org/development/desa/dspd/world-summit-for-social-development-1995.html, accessed March 21, 2021.

2 Douglas North and Robert Thomas, *The Rise of the Western World* (Cambridge: Cambridge University Press, 1973), 1.

3 See, "Millennium Development Goals: 2015 Progress Chart," Statistics Division, Department of Economic and Social Affairs, United Nations, https://www.un.org/millenniumgoals/2015_MDG_Report/pdf/MDG%202015%20PC%20final.pdf, accessed March 21, 2021.

4 "Transforming Our World: The 2030 Agenda for Sustainable Development," United Nations, https://sustainabledevelopment.un.org/content/documents/21252030%20Agenda%20for%20Sustainable%20Development%20web.pdf, accessed April 23, 2019.

5 Rodney Start, *The Rise of Christianity: A Sociologist Reconsiders History* (Princeton. Princeton University Press, 1996), 161.

6 Charles Malik, *A Christian Critique of the University* (Downers Grove, IL: Intervarsity Press, 1982), 29–32.

7 "Education and the SDGs," The Commonwealth Education Hub, https://www.thecommonwealth-educationhub.net/practice-centre/find-tools-and-resources/education-and-the-sdgs/, accessed April 26, 2019.

8 Educate A Child and FHI 360, "Education and the SDGs" (Occasional Paper Two, October 2016), https://educationaboveall.org/uploads/library/file/2a8e15847d.pdf, accessed April 29, 2019.

9 Chinedu Ohanyido, "The Pivotal Role of Education in Africa's Development" (Global Education Conference Network, July 2012), https://www.globaleducationconference.org/profiles/blogs/the-pivotal-role-of-education-in-africa-s-development, accessed on April 29, 2019.

10 Seher Sultana, "Importance of Higher Education in Developing Countries," Ezine Articles, January 14, 2010, https://ezinearticles.com/?Importance-of-Higher-Education-in-Developing-Countries&id=3578101, accessed April 29, 2019.

11 Robert Chambers, *Rural Development: Putting the Last First* (London: Longman Group, 1983), 110.

12 Bryant Myers, *Walking with the Poor: Principles and Practices of Transformational Development* (Maryknoll, NY: Orbis Books, 2000),

67. See also Darrow Miller, *Discipling Nations: The Power of Truth to Transform Cultures* (Seattle: YWAM Publishing, 1984), 63.

13 For bios see https://www.edify.org.

14 The core values include, "Christ-like service (special emphasis to the needy), commitment to prayer, operate with high integrity, all things done with excellence, applaud entrepreneurial spirit, best idea wins, and be joyful, be thankful and have fun," Edify Core Values, https://www.edify.org/core-values/, accessed March 22, 2021.

15 The eleven countries include: Burkina Faso, Dominican Republic, Ethiopia, Ghana, Guatemala, India, Liberia, Peru, Rwanda, Sierra Leone, and Uganda.

16 "263 Million Youth and Children Are Out of School," UNESCO, July 15, 2016, uis.unesco.org/en/news/263-million-children-and-youth-are-out-school, accessed May 5, 2019.

17 Makonen Getu, "The Role of Edify in Promoting Christ-centred Education Through Low-fee Independent Schools," *Transformation* 35:3 (July 2018), 168.

18 "Edify Annual Report 2019," 1, 5, https://www.edify.org/financials/, accessed April 2, 2021.

19 Quickbooks is an accounting software used to improve record keeping and reporting.

20 "Edify Annual Report 2019," 5.

21 Amartja Sen, *Development As Freedom* (Oxford: Oxford University Press, 1999), 3–34.

22 Jean-Marie Hyacinthe Quenum, "The Root Cause of Widespread Corruption in Sub-Saharan Post-Colonial Nation-States," *Asian Horizon 6:1* (March 2012), 103–108.

23 Jim Harries Kima, "Witchcraft, Culture, and Theology in African Development," *Africa Nebula* 2 (September 2010), 143.

24 Naboth Ngulube (Speech, Nordic Technical Assistance Seminar, Lusaka, Zambia, 1988).

25 Buckley Graeme, "Superstition, the Family, and Values in Microenterprise Development," *Small Enterprise Development* 7:4 (1996), 13, 16.

17 Responding to Human Needs: The Case of Yoido Full Gospel Church, Seoul, Korea

Younghoon Lee

Abstract

The first half of the twentieth century was a difficult time for Korean society and the Korean church. The Japanese colonial period and the Korean War made the society unstable in many aspects and made the lives of Koreans extremely poor.[1] Hundreds of street refugees struggled to survive each day, and poverty and disease prevailed. In this situation, the Korean church had to be contextualized to meet the desperate needs of the Korean people. This context of poverty and suffering has remained a very important influence on the direction of the ministry of Yoido Full Gospel Church (hereafter YFGC) in particular.[2]

Introduction

YFGC's ministry started in a tent church in 1958 in a poverty-stricken area called Daejo-Dong, an outskirt of the capital of war-torn South Korea. People were not interested in a message of eternal salvation because of the daily reality of suffering they were experiencing. Allen H. Anderson states that for David Yonggi Cho, the founding pastor of YFGC, the message of Christ and the power of the Holy Spirit was "a present contextual message" that provided hope to those who were in despair. Anderson continues, "This context of poverty and suffering has remained a very important influence on Cho's preaching and is the basis of the theology he developed for a despairing and hopeless people."[3] In the first part of this article, we will present the thought that the Pentecostal movement was a movement for the socially and economically marginalized. Then we will deal with the contribution of YFGC's social ministry for the lower class and the underprivileged. In the final section, we will discuss the crucial question of the theological motivations which drew YFGC's attention to suffering, the poor, and the socially and economically marginalized.

Pentecostal Historical Considerations

The Pentecostal movement has been considered "the religion of the poor" because the movement had started among poor, lowly, and despised. However, a recent study does not view the people who started this movement as stuck on the bottom rungs of the social ladder. After analyzing the social status of early Pentecostal members, Grant Wacker suggested that the people who participated early twentieth-century Pentecostal movement were "well-dressed, intelligent and the best people of the town."[4] Pentecostal scholar Robert Anderson challenges Wacker's idea of viewing the Pentecostal movement as the best people's movement. According to Anderson, members of the Pentecostal movement were mainly the lower classes. Anderson states that the people and churches who participated in the Pentecostal movement participated in social ministry.[5] For example, Amy Semple McPherson, founder of the International Church of the Foursquare Gospel, set up a large distribution center in Los Angeles, CA, in 1927 during the Great Depression, providing food and clothing to 1.5 million people. In 1931, a huge cafeteria was built to provide daily lunches for the unemployed, women, and children.[6] Sociologists Donald E. Miller and Tetsunao Yamamori add their voice, pointing out that historically, the Pentecostal movement was an important force for the socially and economically marginalized. However, this is not just a historical fact, but also a present reality. According to Miller and Yamamori, eighty-five percent of the churches that are currently most actively involved in the social ministry and transformation are members of the Pentecostal denomination or similar denominational churches.[7]

Pentecostal Churches and Social Engagement

See, for example, the case of Florence Muindi and Addis Kidan Baptist Church in Addis Ababa, Ethiopia.[8] Muindi, a Pentecostal believer and public health professional, works with the church to establish community-wide health and hygiene practices. The result of this development-focused approach is a movement away from treating the symptoms resulting from poor hygiene that were rampant before this form of social engagement. Miller and Yamamori questioned Muindi on her views about the best organization for utilizing her public health background. Muindi's answer is telling, and perhaps representative, of Yoido Full Gospel Church, and indeed, the global body of Spirit-empowered believers:

> When we quizzed Florence on why she thought the church was the appropriate institution for expressing her medical skills, she said that she had turned down a lucrative job offer from the United Nations. While secular NGOs may have their place, she said that they come and go, whereas churches are stable institutions with deep roots in the community. In contrast, a secular NGO is typically an outside institution, imposing an external agenda, and it is often controlled by people who do not live in the community. Given her public health model of community organizing and empowerment, she believes that churches are well positioned to effect long-term change in the community. But more important, it is the job of the church, she says, to be "Christ's hands and feet in the world."[9]

Another example of a Pentecostal church on the front lines of social engagement is in Kolkata, India. The Kolkata Assembly of God Church takes a systematic approach to both poverty relief and development. The church seeks to meet the urgent needs of the moment, serving more than 10,000 meals a day, providing bio-sand filters to purify otherwise non-potable water, and offering a basic health care clinic. The church is also intentional about raising the long-term prospects of those they serve through providing education, basic health care, and hot lunches to students at ten schools for underprivileged students, and through providing certifiable vocational skills training which lead to job prospects and a better future. Senior Pastor of Kolkata Assemblies of God Church, Ivan Satyavrata explains:

> The benefits of the social programs are offered to people of all faiths unconditionally and are never used as inducement for spiritual conversion. But the power of Christ's love that nourishes and propels the church's social engagement inevitably results in people being drawn to Christ, for which evidence is available in abundance. [10]

Korean Pentecostal scholar Wonsuk Ma notes that this kind of social engagement finds its roots in Pentecostal theology. "There are several key Pentecostal beliefs that encourage response to social challenges."[11] Ma lists these key beliefs as "1. Called: God touches us! 2. Empowered: The Holy Spirit baptizes us! 3. Commissioned: We are story-makers!"[12] Ma continues, "Pentecostals firmly believe that social action begins with a personal experience of God's grace and power."[13]

For a Pentecostal believer, the experience of God's touch is not for the sake of that believer alone. "Almost every family of Pentecostalism believes that the Holy Spirit empowers God's people for bold action."[14] Empowered for bold action, able to make meaningful differences as Spirit-empowered change agents in both their own stories, and in the stories of others, Pentecostal believers are unleashed into social engagement in some of the most desperate places in the world. Yoido Full Gospel Church is no exception.

Social Needs and Yoido Full Gospel Church's Response

Yoido Full Gospel Church's ministry is a leading example of serving those who are socially and economically marginalized. Pastor Yonggi Cho has always been interested in social issues such as ministry to the socially and economically marginalized. From the beginning of his ministry, Cho embraced the impoverished and directed his church to share God's blessings with the socially marginalized through helping meet needs and sharing with others. Yoido Full Gospel Church has grown up with Korean society, and Cho proclaimed absolute hope to those who were in absolute despair.[15] Cho's compassion and orientation towards those who were suffering came from a place of authenticity:

> Poverty is a curse from Satan. God desires that all His people prosper and be healthy as their soul prospers (3 John 1:2). Yet much of the world has not really seen poverty as I have seen it. Especially in the Third World, people live their lives in despair, struggling to survive for one more day. I am from the Third World. I know first-hand what it is not to have anything to eat.[16]

A Foundation of Social Engagement

Beginning as a tent church with five members, all of whom were economically marginalized, including Yonggi Cho himself, "Pastor Cho Yonggi called out to God for messages appropriate for such harsh reality."[17] Serving as a pastor among the poor, Yonggi Cho sought to discern what answers scripture provides for those whose next meal is uncertain. Through this search, Yonggi Cho came up with the principle of the three-fold blessing as an interpretation of 3 John 2; the blessing of the soul, the spirit, and the body, which has been a hallmark of his ministry, and the ministry of YFGC.[18]

Yoido Full Gospel Church's Theological Response

While YFGC makes significant economic, material, and practical impact through their ministries for the poor, which shall be discussed in the second part of this chapter, the empowerment people in poverty experience via the healing and the positive message of hope based on Pentecostal theology is considered by many as the most forceful contribution to YFGC's ministry to the poor. Sebastian C. H. Kim categorizes this type of theology as kibock sinang, or "seeking blessings," saying that it is one of the two primary contextualizations of Korean theology in response to the issue of poverty.[19] Kim explains:

> *Kibock sinang* is not new to the Korean church, nor is it unique to Korean religiosity as it is a common phenomenon of people who profess any form of religion known as *do ut des*: I will do this in the expectation of receiving something from gods. What is interesting in the particular context of the post-war Korean church was that there was a shift in thinking from the early revival phenomenon of emphasizing "spiritual blessings" in the eschatological dimensions to include the material manifestation of those blessings. This was in line with the government campaigns for economic growth at all costs and the rise of the *jaebul*, Korean family-run mega-companies. In the midst of it all, the Korean church experienced rapid growth in numbers and produced megachurches.[20]

One of the primary blessings included in David Yonggi Cho's three-fold blessing is that of divine healing. Being divinely healed from tuberculosis as a young man, the call to preach divine healing as part of salvation came intertwined with Yonggi Cho's call to ministry. "While Cho was reading about divine healing in the Bible, he was touched by it and repented for not having fully believed it. He prayed and fasted for three days. On the third day, he had a vision of Jesus in which he was called to dedicate his life to preaching the gospel."[21] Indeed, for those in poverty, ailing from disease as Yonggi Cho once was, supernatural healing is frequently the only solution. Yonggi Cho and YFGC take the expression of health in 3 John 2 seriously, and divine healing is considered one of the primary evidence of the empowerment and activity of the Holy Spirit in their midst. Naming 3 John 2, "a scripture passage that is central to understanding Cho's ministry," William W. Menzies notes that it "is emblazoned on the wall in the reception area of the great Yoido Full Gospel Church."[22] Menzies continues:

It is critically important to keep in mind, as one evaluates the teaching of Cho, the situation into which he came. The Korean nation had suffered terribly. The Christians had suffered. Many were very discouraged and had lost all hope. It was into the dark night of post-war Korea that God raised up Yonggi Cho to elevate the horizons of his people. His message was the announcement of hope, of the victory there is in Christ, of the available empowering of the Holy Spirit. He saw the practical blessings of salvation embracing not only the spiritual dimension of mankind, but also the physical and the material dimensions, as well. It was this emphasis that caused Cho to be criticized, not only by non-Pentecostal Evangelicals, but by many Pentecostals, as well. [23]

Regarding such critics of this "seeking blessings" or *kibock sinang* theology, Kim is incisive. "It may be relevant to those who have already received material blessings to preach about suffering and the Cross, but the poor who are already suffering wish liberation from it."[24]

Cho's empowering preaching also includes healing for the worldview of discouraged and downtrodden people. With unwaveringly positive messages, Cho does not ignore the realities of life in poverty but instead, focuses on the biblical hope we have as believers in Christ who live according to the word of God. Christ heals us from both disease and discouragement as we follow him.

Kibock sinang has harnessed the people's desire for *kum* [dream or hope] in the present context. In Korean religiosity, the desire for something better, both spiritual and material, is expressed as seeking blessings. It is the humble desire of those who have not experienced the fullness of life and who are constantly facing despair and poverty. [25]

The legacy of Cho's preaching is a transformation of the worldview which empowers those whose conditions of existence left them without the freedom or ability to dream of a better or different future. The impact of this message reaches far beyond Korea. In their book, *Global Pentecostalism: The New Face of Christian Social Engagement*, Donald E. Miller and Tetsunao Yamamori note that there are three consistent and important variables that influence the nature and character of the social ministries of Progressive Pentecostals:

the size of the congregation, the theological views of the pastor and people, and the social and political context of the country in which the social ministry is being implemented. Religious ideas never stand alone; they are always influenced by their social location, including the character of the organization that is promulgating them.[26]

As the largest church in the world,[27] the theology of David Yonggi Cho and YFGC is well-positioned to impact and empower the downtrodden across the globe. The rest of this chapter will focus on YFGC's specific social engagement in Korea and beyond.

Elim Welfare Town

YFGC has practiced Christian love by extensive social work for the lower class and the underprivileged for the last sixty years. As the church grew rapidly during the 1970s, YFGC participated in social ministry by serving low-income households and people in slum areas.[28] Elim Welfare Town was built in 1986 as the biggest Christian welfare center in Asia. This town is named for the oasis of Elim in Exodus 15:27, which reads, "Then they came to Elim, where there were twelve springs and seventy palm trees, and they camped there near the water,"[29] and exists as an oasis in Seoul for the young, the unemployed, and the homeless elderly, providing practical resources for each of these groups. Elim Welfare town has vocational training for young people and the unemployed in order to give them proper guidance, and to support their self-reliance based on the spirit of the gospel and the love of Christ. This training provides professional skills for furniture design, green automobile and building repair, digital design, lacquer nacre, cooking, electrical work, jewelry design, landscape management, and hair design.[30] For the elderly, there is a state-of-the-art living facility and a team of caregivers, including members of YFGC who volunteer as hospice care members at the health center in Elim Welfare Town.[31] Elim Welfare Town began with a committed budget of fifteen million USD, "a sign of [YFGC]'s commitment to serving the community beyond the four walls of the church."[32]

Generosity as Intercession

When the economic crisis hit the nation in the late 1990s, the national economy badly needed international short-term loans. Upon receiving such loans from the International Monetary Fund (IMF) the entire economic system came under the IMF's supervision and austerity measures. Koreans remember this as the "IMF crisis." YFGC participated in the nation's effort to counter the deep economic recession during the

IMF crisis by collecting the gold of church members.[33] Because of the devaluation of the national currency, the government was struggling to service the debt of these IMF loans. Gold became an important new currency to service the debt, as the price of gold in Korea was not as seriously affected by devaluation as the national currency. Therefore, in 1997, the government pleaded to the nation for people to donate or sell their gold to the government. In response, YFGC, which was already engaged in several prayer programs and practicing austerity measures as a community, ran a large-scale campaign as part of its prayer for the nation in order to set a good example as a Christian by practicing thrift and saving. The result of this nationwide participation, combined with the restructuring of the financial and business sectors, was that Korea was able to "graduate" from under the IMF supervision earlier than predicted.[34]

Providing Medical Care

The Full Gospel Medical Center opened in July of 1981 as a medical mission affiliated with the businessmen's fellowship division of YFGC, and in January of 2003, the clinic was expanded as a church organization, while retaining the name of the Full Gospel Medical Center. Now YFGC supports the medical project, medical service in domestic, rural churches, overseas medical mission, health consulting for church members, emergency treatment, and physical checkup for new believers. In 1999, the church's relief and development NGO, Goodpeople, founded medical volunteer teams made up of both non-medical professional church members as well as medical professionals, who do home visits to give medical care to those with disabilities, the isolated elderly, migrant and international workers, the homeless, and others who may be struggling socio-economically. Further, when there is an accident or natural disaster, "Goodpeople sends medical groups consisting of doctors, nurses, social workers, and volunteers to expediently provide medical assistance as well as damage restoration."[35]

Building Homes

Habitat for humanity with love is a movement to provide simple and comfortable residential places for neighbors living harsh lives in undesirable conditions due to poverty and disease. It gives them hope for independence, so that they can be healthy members of the society to which they belong. The habitat movement began in the United States in

1976, and later, in August 2004, YFGC church started this movement with forty young adults from YFGC's Pneuma Youth Mission, carrying out the campaign of house repairing at Somang Village in the city of Chuncheon, Shinbuk-eup Chunjun-ri.[36] A Habitat for Humanity homeowner, Jung-bae "remembered the landscape well when he was building his new home in the west of South Korea. . . . Just think about it – there was nothing but rice fields here. But we built our houses in this place!"[37]

Giving Food

Boxing Day originated from the medieval times, where the church distributed boxes of daily necessities to the poor during the harsh winters. Since 2012, YFGC and Goodpeople have held this annual event, and about 73,000 boxes of hope with basic food and hygiene supplies have been delivered to neighbors in need so far. These boxes of hope have been a warm comfort and great strength for the people in poverty. They include the elderly who live on their own, socially and economically marginalized, single-parent families, and multicultural families struggling with financial difficulties.[38] Not only YFGC, but also other Korean local churches have been a social network, providing a safety net for the socially marginalized. For example, the Korean church has long practiced what is called "Love Rice" (or *sungmi*). "When cooking any meal, most Christian women set aside a small amount of rice for those who were needy. Once a week the rice was brought to the church for the use of those who were needy within the church as well as for the local community."[39] In addition, the Korean church established an organization called the "South-North Sharing Campaign" in 1993, after hearing that North Koreans were suffering from food shortages. Through this organization, the Korean church, which transcends denominations, has especially helped the children of North Korea by giving food such as powdered milk, flour, and soymilk.[40]

International Engagement and Aid

YFGC's social ministry is not limited to South Korea. Goodpeople, an International Relief Development NGO, is an organization that was established in 1999 in order to let the world know the reality of global neighbors who are exposed to life-threatening dangers such as poverty, diseases, and disasters due to their social alienation. They also provide systemic and professional help that transcends borders, praying that each person's act of sharing will allow their global neighbors' hopes to become a reality. For this reason, Goodpeople actively carries out diverse ministries with the goals of development of marginalized areas, eradication of poverty, child protection, education, disease prevention and treatment, emergency relief, and one-to-one sisterhood relationship with children, especially in domestic and overseas areas where minority groups live without civic or government protection. Goodpeople has provided relief for those suffering from hunger, disease, and war all over the world, including the Philippines, Sri Lanka, Bangladesh, Indonesia, Vietnam, and Afghanistan. For instance, Goodpeople has constructed a fifteen-kilometer pipeline for the Maasai in Kenya. This pipeline is designed to provide the major water source for the Elim farmland, which helped the Maasai, pastoral nomads, settle down in the Elim area.[41]

In 1999, the Goodpeople Emergency Relief Organization was established as a support system for Kosovo refugees, Paju flood damage, and Turkish victims. Goodpeople not only sent a search-and-rescue team for disaster relief, but they also provided medical services, anti-epidemic efforts, water purification work, and orphanage building projects to restore the affected regions as quickly as possible.

In the Philippines, a municipal hospital was built for minorities. The municipal hospital consists of internal medicine, dentistry, pediatrics, obstetrics, and gynecology, providing high-quality medical services such as comprehensive medical care and emergency procedures to the Kapaz citizens and Aeta people who do not receive medical benefits.[42]

Intercultural Ministry in Korea

Currently, Korea is rapidly changing into a multicultural society, having about two million international residents. YFGC established a multicultural center in Ansan, conducting various programs, including Korean language education for foreign workers and multicultural families. Through the establishment of the Multicultural Mission Organization in 2008, YFGC's social ministry has been expanded to focus on the international people who increasingly migrate to South Korea. For example, after the Sewol Ferry Tragedy of 2014, YFGC started "Medical Service of Love" to deliver hope-sharing boxes to traditional market merchants and multicultural neighbors in Ansan, a region that suffered great loss as a result of the tragedy.[43]

In March 2013, Yoido Full Gospel Church announced that one-third of the church budget would be used for the ministries to the socially underprivileged and marginalized. So far, this promise has been kept, and Yoido Full Gospel Church has set an example to Korean society and other churches.[44]

Theological Motivation for Social Ministry

An important question we will discuss in this chapter is, what theological motivation led to YFGC's keen attention to suffering, poor and socially and economically marginalized? The purpose of this chapter is to provide an answer to this question and show that theological motivation for social ministry lies in the theory of the gospel of blessing, the faith of sharing, and holistic salvation.

Communal Blessing

First of all, the basic theological motivation for social ministry lies in Yonggi Cho's theory of the gospel of blessing, which emphasizes communal blessing. Regarding the gospel of blessing, Yonggi Cho suggests that "We should enjoy the blessing Jesus has given us and share this blessing with others." According to Yonggi Cho, sharing blessing is the will of God and the way to honor Jesus Christ.[45] Because of sin, human beings were fallen and had to live in a land filled with thorns and thistles. God, however, sent Jesus Christ to this world in order to save human beings. When Jesus was born, he was wrapped in cloth and was placed in a manger. Herod was searching for Jesus to kill him, so his parent escaped to Egypt and lived in a poor environment. Jesus moved from town to town, valley to valley, and had no place to lay his head. He lived from hand to mouth. Some insist that we must become poor because Jesus lived in a poverty-stricken life. However, Yonggi Cho notes that such a biblical view fails to see why Jesus became poor. Yonggi Cho makes an insightful observation about 2 Chronicles 8:9:

> 2 Chronicles 8:9 clearly explains why Jesus became poor. It says, "For your sake, he became poor, so that you through his poverty might become rich." This message is clear, so much so that it cannot be interpreted in different ways. Through Christ, we are redeemed not only in eternal sin but also in poverty. If we do not enjoy the blessings of God, we make the life of Jesus worthless. Therefore, we must enjoy the blessings Jesus completed, and share the blessing with others.[46]

The key to Yonggi Cho's doctrine of blessing is not to store the blessing of God, but to share with people around us. This is not a selfish, individualistic doctrine; rather it is a communal blessing that focuses on sharing one's blessing. As we live for the poor and marginalized, we can truly enjoy God's blessings.[47]

Faith Sharing

The second theological motivation for social ministry is clearly described in YFGC's theory of the faith of sharing. Faith of sharing is faith that returns blessings to God and distributes them to our neighbors. The faith of the full gospel is not a selfish faith, but it is both a God-centered faith and a faith for others. Bible clearly describes that the apostles in the early church made an effort to the distribution of food and sharing (Acts 4:32–37), Cornelius and Dorcas, who always did good and helped the poor, were blessed (Acts 9:36, 10:2), and Macedonian churches were highly commended for rich generosity (2 Corinthians 8:1–5). Daniel advised King Nebuchadnezzar to do what is right, and to be kind to the oppressed as a way to be blessed (Daniel 4:27). In our life of faith, blessing and serving the poor are inseparable. God is with the individual, society, and nation that practices sharing and serving.[48]

Holistic Salvation

YFGC's social ministry is closely related to Cho's understanding of holistic salvation. Holistic salvation has social features precisely because the redeeming work of the Spirit involves the physical and material dimensions of human life.[49] Korean churches have two different positions on social participation and soteriology. The first position argues that social change comes naturally as a result of individual salvation, and the latter position insists that we cannot think of individual salvation without social salvation. It is true that the theory of the Five Gospels emphasizes the salvation of souls, but this does not mean that this theory neglects social participation.[50] Social participation and salvation of soul are simultaneous. Yonggi Cho's three-fold blessing is not only related to life-to-come but also to this present life, such as the real problems of life, healing of disease, saving from poverty, and sharing of blessing. Therefore, according to Cho's theological point, the salvation of soul and the salvation of society should be in harmony.[51]

It is interesting to note that Yonggi Cho and YFGC did not first set up a social theology and then forge a matching social agenda. Amos Yong describes it thus: "Rather a socially sensitive mission emerged out of a pneumatologically rich understanding of the saving work of the Spirit. It is precisely such socially empowered mission and praxis that funds, nurtures, and sustains a potent socio-political theology."[52]

Yoido Full Gospel Church's Legacy of Social Engagement

Traditionally, the Pentecostal movement has been regarded as a non-social and non-political movement. According to Robert Anderson, the 1918 split in the Assemblies reflected a difference within the Pentecostal movement from its earlier years between the revolutionary potential of all millenarian movements and conservative elements.[53] Since the Pentecostal movement was originally composed mainly of lower-class people, there was a possibility for the movement to grow into a social transformation movement. However, under the influence of fundamentalism, it transformed into a non-social conservative movement. Despite Anderson's claim, however, there are plentiful records of serious social concerns and participation of the Pentecostal movement in social ministry.[54] Yoido Full Gospel Church has also participated in social ministry both internally and externally for the past sixty years. Moreover, YFGC's social ministry has been expanded to a cosmic horizon by Pastor Yonggi Cho's reconsideration of biblical text John 3:16. Cho defines that God's love contains not only the salvation of mankind but also the salvation of society and the ecosystem.[55] In the process of putting this theology into practice, Yoido Full Gospel Church established Christian Greenmovement Mission (C.G.M.) to prevent the pollution of the ecosystem, and to recover the order of creation. Furthermore, the church has protected the environment by carrying out a campaign to recycle waste paper and milk cartons.[56] And when the Taean coastal area of South Korea was suffering from a serious oil spill in 2007, about 6,000 members of Yoido Full Gospel Church participated in volunteer work to remove the spilled oil.[57]

Conclusion

In this article, we began our discussion with sixty years of the social practices of Yoido Full Gospel Church. Since YFGC was established in the post-war milieu of poverty, the church gave hope to suffering and destitute people. Moreover, YFGC taught people to share God's blessings with the socially marginalized. In the second part, we have tried to answer the question of theological motivation for social ministry. We have attempted to build YFGC's theological motivation on the theory of the gospel of blessing, the faith of sharing, and holistic salvation. Yonggi Cho's theory of blessing is the key to sharing and serving others. This is related to the theory of the faith of sharing. The third theological motivation lies in holistic salvation, which emphasizes the harmony of the salvation of soul and society.

Christ is the head of the church, and the church is his body. The church is established by Christ and guided by Christ. The Bible says that the church is a letter from Christ (2 Corinthians 3:3) and the salt and light for the dark world (Matthew 5:13). In other words, the church finds its value and direction only when it exists for the world, not for itself.[58] Christianity has an important mission to serve the socially and economically marginalized. One of the main issues raised in today's Christianity is closely tied with the "rich-poor gap." As the economic crisis continues all over the world and the distance between financial inequalities, the "rich-poor gap" increases constantly, the dimensions of the problem of situational poverty are also amplified in the globalizing society.[59] YFGC's efforts in dealing with poverty in the world are regarded as a critical issue.

The Yoido Full Gospel Global Network (YFGN) was founded to support YFGC's missions work abroad through sixty years of Full Gospel's missionary work through exchanges between local churches and pastors and influential Korean churches and institutions all integrated into one global network. YFGN helps send out local pastors into Asia and holds Asia Leaders' Summit with Christian coalition leaders in Asia, as well as Korean church leaders' gatherings. By encouraging and developing the Pentecostal movement, YFGN has formed a launching pad for world missions that target marginalized people in the world. It seeks to secure its role based on the Pentecostal movement offer a new direction in carrying out missions. Furthermore, YFGN provides Spiritual Formation Leadership Seminars (SFLS) and Osanri Christian conference in Korea (OCCK) to local pastors around the world that wish to learn the pastoral ways of the Yoido Full Gospel Church. The SFLS is a comprehensive international program that combines the core educational programs of Yoido Full Gospel Church that cover the theory of blessing, holistic salvation, and the faith of sharing.

I suggest that Yonggi Cho's theory of blessing, holistic salvation, and YFGC's theory of the faith of sharing point to a rich theological framework for the social ministry of churches. YFGC's ministry for the socially and economically marginalized not only plays an important role in guiding Christianity to the right direction, but also sets a good example for churches both in Korea and throughout the world. However, it is very significant to set the right direction in order to maximize the effectiveness of serving socially and economically marginalized. Churches in Korea should be in dialogue with churches in the world in order to solve challenging topics like economic poverty relief and social problems.

Notes

1 Yoido Full Gospel Church, *60th Anniversary with the Holy Spirit* (Seoul: Yoido Full Gospel Church Press, 2018), 27.

2 Younghoon Lee, *The Holy Spirit Movement in Korea* (Oxford: Regnum Books International, 2009), 137.

3 Allan H. Anderson, "A Time to Share Love: International Pentecostalism and Social Dimension of Youngsan," *Journal of Youngsan Theology* 17 (2009), 30.

4 Grant Wacker, Heaven Below: *Early Pentecostal and American Culture* (Cambridge: Harvard University Press, 2001), 199.

5 Robert M. Anderson, *Vision of the Disinherited* (Peabody, MA: Hendrickson Publishers, 1992), 195.

6 Edith Blumhofer, *Aimee Semple McPherson: Everybody's Sister* (Grand Rapids, MI: Eerdmans, 1993), 269.

7 Donald E. Miller, and Tetsunao Yamamori, *Global Pentecostalism: The New Face of Christian Social Engagement*, trans. Sunggun Kim and Jonghyun Chung (Seoul: Church Growth Institute, 2008), 255.

8 Donald E. Miller and Tetsunao Yamamori, *Global Pentecostalism: The New Face of Christian Social Engagement* (Berkley, CA: University of California Press, 2007), 40.

9 Miller and Yamamori, *Global Pentecostalism*, 41.

10 Ivan Satyavrata, "The Feeding of 10,000," in Wonsuk Ma, "When the Spirit Comes Down," *Sojourners* (January 2017), 4.

11 Ma, "When the Spirit Comes Down," 1.

12 Ma, "When the Spirit Comes Down," 1–5.

13 Ma, "When the Spirit Comes Down," 3.

14 Ma, "When the Spirit Comes Down," 2.

15 Younghoon Lee, *The Cross on Calvary: The Theological Foundations of the Full Gospel Faith* (Seoul: Church Growth Institution, 2011), 272.

16 David Yonggi Cho, *The Fourth Dimension*, vol. 2 (Alachua, FL: Bridge-Logos, 1983), 137–138.

17 "1958-1961, The Early Years - The Tent Church," Full Gospel Church of Serving, http://fgcos.org/xe/TentChurch, accessed December 16, 2020.

18 See David Yonggi Cho, *Threefold Blessing* (Seoul: Yongsan Publications, 1977).

19 Sebastian C. H. Kim, "The Problem of Poverty in Post-War Korean Christianity: Kibock Sinang or Minjung Theology?" *Transformation* 24:1 (January 2007), 44.

20 Kim, "The Problem of Poverty in Post-War Korea," 44.

21 Younghoon Lee, "Life and Ministry of David Yonggi Cho and Yoido Full Gospel Church," in Wonsuk Ma, William W. Menzies, and Hyeon-sung Bae, eds., *David Yonggi Cho: A Close Look at His Life and Ministry* (Baguio, Philippines: APTS Press, 2004), 4, quoting Nell L. Kennedy, *Dream Your Way to Success: The Story of Dr. Yonggi Cho and Korea* (Plainfield, NJ: Logos International, 1980), 118–121.

22 William W. Menzies, "David Yonggi Cho's Theology of the Fullness of the Spirit: A Pentecostal Perspective" in Wonsuk Ma, William Menzies, and Hyeon-sung Bae, eds., *David Yonggi Cho: A Close Look at His Life and Ministry* (Baguio, Philippines: APTS Press, 2004), 36.

23 Menzies, "David Yonggi Cho's Theology," 36.

24 Kim, "The Problem of Poverty in Post-War Korea," 45.

25 Kim, "The Problem of Poverty in Post-War Korea," 45.

26 Miller and Yamamori, *Global Pentecostalism*, 53.

27 Murray Rubinstein, "New Religious Movement: Korea," Encyclopaedia Britannica Online, https://www.britannica.com/topic/new-religious-movement, accessed December 16, 2020.

28 Lee, *The Holy Spirit Movement in Korea*, 98.

29 Unless otherwise indicated all Bible references in this paper are to the New International Version (NIV) (Grand Rapids, MI: Zondervan, 1984).

30 Yoido Full Gospel Church, *60th Anniversary with the Holy Spirit*, 84.

31 "Sharing Love: Full Gospel Hospice Care," Yoido Full Gospel Church, http://english.fgtv.com/a04/05.asp, accessed December 5, 2020.

32 Victor Lim Fei, "Korea Study Tour Day: 4," citynews.sg, January 29, 2009, https://www.citynews.sg/2009/01/29/korea-study-tour-day-2/, accessed December 5, 2020.

33 Gold became an important new currency to service the debt, as the price of gold in Korea was not as seriously affected by devaluation as the national currency. See Lee, *The Holy Spirit Movement in Korea*, 116.

34 Lee, *The Holy Spirit Movement in Korea*, 116.

35 "Health and Medical Care Program: Medical Volunteer Group" Goodpeople, https://eng.goodpeople.or.kr/business/domestic/medical.php, accessed December 16, 2020.

36 Younghoon Lee, *Yoido Full Gospel Church: A Little Seed of Infinite Possibility Growing in the Heart of God* (Seoul: Yoido Full Gospel Church Press, 2018), 41.

37 "In Top Form," Habitat for Humanity: Asia-Pacific, https://www.habitat.org/ap/stories/top-form, accessed December 16, 2020.

38 Lee, *Yoido Full Gospel Church: A Little Seed of Infinite Possibility*, 38.

39 Lee, *The Holy Spirit Movement in Korea*, 115.

40 For more details see http://sharing.net/document/pg6.

41 Lee, *Yoido Full Gospel Church: A Little Seed of Infinite Possibility*, 38–39.

42 Lee, *60th Anniversary of the Assemblies of God of Korea with the Holy Spirit* (Seoul: The Assemblies of God of Korea, 2013), 334.

43 Lee, *60th Anniversary of the Assemblies of God*, 306; See also, Martin Fackler, "A Year After Sewol Ferry Tragedy Peace is Elusive for South Korean City," *The New York Times*, April 15, 2015, https://www.nytimes.com/2015/04/16/world/asia/sewol-ferry-disaster-anniversary-finds-south-korean-city-still-bewildered.html, accessed December 16, 2020.

44 Lee, *60th Anniversary of the Assemblies of God*, 322.

45 Yonggi Cho, *Five-Fold Gospel and Three-Fold Blessing*, 188.

46 Yonggi Cho, *Five-Fold Gospel and Three-Fold Blessing*, 187–188.

47 Yonggi Cho, *Five-Fold Gospel and Three-Fold Blessing*, 189.

48 Lee, *The Cross on Calvary*, 246–247.

49 Amos Yong, "Salvation, Society, and the Spirit: Pentecostal Contextualization and Political Theology from Cleveland to Birmingham, from Springfield to Seoul," *Journal of Youngsan Theology* 17 (2009), 47.

50 Yonggi Cho lists the five tenants of the Five-Fold Gospel as the Gospel of Regeneration, the Gospel of the Fullness of the Holy Spirit, the Gospel of Healing, the Gospel of Divine Healing, and the Gospel of the Second Coming of Christ, "Core Messages: The Five-Fold Gospel," David Cho Evangelistic Mission, http://www.davidcho.com/neweng/bb-1.asp, accessed December 7, 2020.

51 Lee, *The Cross on Calvary*, 248–249.

52 Amos Yong, "Salvation, Society, and the Spirit," 52.

53 Robert M. Anderson, *Vision of the Disinherited* (Peabody: Hendrickson Publishers, 1992), 195.
54 For more details see Dukman Bae, *A History and Theology of the Pentecostal Movement* (Daejeon: Daejanggan, 2012), 167–169.
55 Mun Chul Shin, "Eco-Theology of Youngsan," *The Holy Spirit and Theology Journal* 22 (2006), 120.
56 Yoido Full Gospel Church, *60th Anniversary with the Holy Spirit*, 111.
57 Yoido Full Gospel Church, *60th Anniversary with the Holy Spirit*, 145.
58 Lee, *The Cross on Calvary*, 246–247.
59 J. Stavros J. Baloyannis, "The Poverty Under the Light of the Neurosciences," *Journal of Neurology & Stroke* 10 (2020), 44.

18 Pentecostal Civic Engagement in the Squatter Area of Baguio City, Philippines

Joel A. Tejedo

Abstract

Pentecostals are frequently considered to be on the sideline of civic engagement with less participation in public life due to their preoccupation with other-worldly eschatology and one-way ticket evangelistic efforts. This study[1] does not share the above observations but instead argues that Pentecostal civic engagement[2] has been increasingly recognized as one of the resource capitals that empowers the lives of the poor. Research, however, about the civic engagement of Pentecostals in South-East Asia, particularly in the Philippines, remains understudied and invisible in much of the literature on civic engagement. This paper attempts to investigate the impact of Pentecostal-Charismatic religion on civil society and to ask what contribution the study of the "Spirit-empowered" religion makes to our understanding of the role of religion in human society. This study utilizes both quantitative and qualitative approaches of inquiry to flesh out empirical evidence that reveals what Filipino Pentecostals believe and practice about civic engagement. We provide a case study of our findings to further point out that Pentecostals in the Philippines are not on the "sidelines" of civic engagement, but one of the religious players in the creation of a just and loving society.

Introduction

The family of Joseph and Elma is one of the 142 families residing in the squatter area of Lower Rock Quarry who were forced to leave the small farm they were tilling in Pangasinan due to poverty and financial scarcity. The insufficiency of their livelihood to augment their daily needs challenged them to migrate and find a better life in Baguio City.[3] Joseph and Elma have three children residing in a small *barong barong* (shanty house) with seven other families' homes attached to their small house. Joseph is working as a scrapper in a shop, and Elma most of the time serves as a housekeeper. Elma was put in touch with the local Pentecostal church when her children came to the feeding project, a ministry that Pentecostal believers started in the area. Her three children were the first attendees among the twelve children that Pentecostal believers fed in 2010.

When these Spirit-filled believers started skills and livelihood training to provide an income-generating livelihood to the most indigent families, Elma joined the training and also became interested in studying the Bible. Through this training, Elma was awarded a livelihood and began to earn money for her family. Known as unwed couples, Joseph and Elma were one of the twelve couples who were the recipient of the mass wedding conducted by the church to help and assist unwed couples in the area. Through this civic participation, Joseph and Elma became church members to the newly pioneered church in Lower Rock Quarry (LRQ), serving as staff in feeding the children and managing the small store established by the church in their area.

Review of Literature

Context of the Study

Studies reveal that people living in the squatter areas or *"barong barong"* are mostly the informal and casual workers whose wives live and maintain their household without jobs and livelihood. They are the residents of peripheral and low-income settlements who depend much on band-aid assistance from the government and non-government organizations during typhoon seasons. They are, of course, the "homeless" and "illegal settlers" who illegally live in a property owned by landowners, waiting for eviction and demolition from police authorities. Under Presidential Decree Number 772, made during the Marcos Administration, an illegal settler can be defined as:

> Any person who, with the use of force, intimidation or threat, or taking advantage of the absence or tolerance of the landowner, succeeds in occupying or possessing the property of the latter against his will for residential commercial or any other purposes, shall be punished by an imprisonment ranging from six months to one year or a fine of not less than one thousand nor more than five thousand pesos at the discretion of the court, with subsidiary imprisonment in case of insolvency.[4]

During the administration of Gloria Arroyo, the allocation of 3.2 billion every year for ten years for the socialized housing unit for illegal settlers was justified by her administration because, according to the report of the

Metro Manila Inter-Agency Committee on Informal Settlers (MMIAC), one out of five families is a squatter. This report also found that there are 544,609 households of informal settlers in Metro Manila, representing twenty-one percent of the total population of 2.6 million households.[5]

Costello's question of whether migrants tend to amass in the slum area to initially adjust in the urban life is worth pursuing. The assumption that migrants flock to the urban squatter areas as necessary entrepots, "or 'zones of transition'" to adjust the urban life raises some implications. Squatter areas are basically disorganized and lack basic government services like electricity, water supply, etc.[6] Social researchers find that not all migrants are attracted to the squatter areas due to the ability of Filipinos to absorb peripheral members of the family such as servants, lodgers, and extended kin.[7]

Filipino attitudes toward illegal settlers in the Philippines are mixed with apathy and sympathy. The affluent and middle-class Filipinos criticized the government for their lenient implementation of the rule of law and babying the illegal settlers by allowing them to live in a land funded by the hard work of someone. Using the word of Srinivas, this perspective views squatter settlements as the invasion of the masses to these private and public properties as a "social evil" that needs to be eradicated, without taking seriously the basic question of "adequate housing for all."[8] Srinivas observes that there are three defining characteristics that provide a framework for understanding squatter settlements. First, squatter settlements, because of their illegal status, have inadequate services and infrastructure with little dependence on formal authorities and formal channels. Second, illegal settlers belong to the low-income group who are predominantly migrants, either from rural to urban or urban to urban locales. Third, they are made up of settlers who lack ownership of the land they built their houses or those who temporarily rent from private individuals or families with an informal or quasi-legal arrangement.[9]

Many Filipinos are now fed up with the illegal settlers and believe that they are the cause of why the Philippines cannot reach its highest potential to become a business hub in Asia. The burgeoning number of squatters does not serve favorably in the eyes of foreign investors. In addition to being perceived as out of control, the squatters have no respect for the property rights of others and totally disregarded the welfare of the environment and other people.

Civil societies such as non-government organizations and the religious sector, however, believe that the misery of the people in the squatter areas is due to the inability of the political sector to implement programs of empowerment. People in the squatter areas are perceived as "political capital," being used and having their votes purchased during election times. Thus, non-government organizations and the religious sectors are sympathetic to their miseries and advocate their rights through various interventions.[10] Based on the studies of Tendero, there is an increasing movement of civic engagement done by religious NGOs in the country because of the increasing poverty and exploitation experienced by the poor. These organizations are providing moral and values education for the impoverished children, providing jobs and resources for the indigent, and advocating their welfare and rights through emancipation and contextual education.[11]

Civic Engagement as a Part of Christian Missiology

Over the years, discussion regarding contextualized Christian mission among the poor has been raised and brought into the center of discussion by few Asian scholars. Wotsyn and De Mesa, Catholic theologians, warn mission practitioners that mission "divorced from reality is irrelevant and meaningless."[12] Asian scholars like Wonsuk Ma and Julie Ma encourage Pentecostals to always translate the gospel in the local context of the people they serve.[13] Ma strongly argues the ideal model of truly Asian theology is a real interplay of the text and in the given context. Hwa Yung urges Asian scholars to search for an authentic theology that is contextual with respect to the sociopolitical realities of the communities, pastorally and evangelistically engaged, takes the issue of contextualization seriously, and is affirmed by biblical witness and tradition.[14] Melba Maggay, a social anthropologist from the University of the Philippines, calls for Filipino Christians to develop a new model of mission, perhaps different from the colonial and economic power imported by Spanish-American mentors; a mission model that is incarnational and that comes from the context of the poor and powerless.[15] Ed Lapiz, one of the few voices of Christian nationalism in the country, challenges Filipino churches to make Christianity become Filipino in form.[16]

Without a doubt, the International forum of Evangelical scholars recognizes poverty as a major problem of many nations, and one that is caused by many complex issues created by unjust structures by social, political, religious, and economic institutions.[17] In a case study done for the World Council of Churches (WCC), Michael Taylor describes poverty as a complex reality that has "many images." These images are often characterized by a lack of basic necessities such as income deprivation, shortfalls in consumption, inadequate nutrition, and poor access to education. These images of poverty are about vulnerabilities and coping with incapacities.[18] Because poverty is caused by oppressive structures, it demands that individuals, governments, and non-government organizations collectively participate to become responsible for the restoration of the human dignity of the poor.[19]

Civic Engagement to the Poor is at the Heart of Prophetic Ministry

This study acknowledges that the fall of man became a tragic case that established the alienation of the human being from God and all his other relationships (e.g., neighbors and creation). Evidently, this can be traced back to Satan, the enemy of human beings and God. Poverty is caused by ecological, social, and economic exploitations. The Bible clearly states that poverty can come from famine such as drought, shortage of food, through insect plagues or locust (Gen. 12:10; 26:1; 45:1; 1 Kings 17:1–16; Exod 7–12; Joel 1), natural disasters such as hurricanes, tornados, lightning, fire, or earthquake (Job 1:18-19, 16; Gen 19:24–29), and sudden illness, forced migrations, and social exclusion (Ruth 1:6; 2 Kings 4:1–7). The Bible reveals when famine takes place, God raises up prophets and leaders to create political and social reforms that defended the rights of the poor (Gen 47:20–26).[20]

Another form of alienation that results from the fall is the social exclusion of people from their neighbors. When neighbors are in enmity with each other, war and oppression emerge, which becomes a social and economic blow to the people. This can be seen in the social life of the Israelites in their relationship with their neighboring communities (2 Kings 6:24–7:20; Isa 2:1–5; Mic 4:1–4). When their neighboring nations were led by socially elite, corrupt leaders who were insensitive to the welfare of their own people, they created colossal poverty among the people (Eccles 5:8; Neh 5; Mic 3:1–4, 9–12; Ezek 22:23–31; 34).[21]

In other cases, poverty is linked to the breaking of the covenant between a person and God by means of idolatry (2 Kings 14:26, 17, 21:1–18, 24–25), breaking the sabbath commandment (Isa 58:13–14), neglect of the temple's ministry, like failing to pay tithes, offerings, and provide care for the poor (Mal 3:6–12; Prov 3:9–10; Isa 58:13–14; Neh 13:15–18). The wisdom literature also mentions many things about laziness and slothfulness as causes of personal poverty (Prov 6:6–11, 10:4, 19:15, 20:13, 24:30–34, 28:19). This comes when a person is addicted to alcohol (Prov 23:19–21, 21:17) and extravagance of lifestyle (Prov 13:18, 21:5).[22]

The Old Testament writers, who refuse to forsake the poor, describe poverty as an involuntary social evil to be abolished; therefore, they do not tolerate poverty. God's people should not harden their hearts to the poor, but rather, should be generous by providing for their basic needs without charge. In the same way, Yahweh stipulated God's people to give their tithes, not only to support the religious institution, but also to help the aliens, the widows and orphans. Although the support of the indigent poor was the obligation of family members, Yahweh instructed his people that they should be allowed to share in the tenth of the agricultural harvest every third and seventh year (Duet 24:14, 16:19). Yahweh also instructed his people that the indigent were to be paid promptly for their labor, the same day it was earned.[23]

The Old Testament has much to say about the powerless poor. The powerless poor are the people who are oppressed through political and social exploitation. In the studies done by Thomas Hanks regarding the etymological understanding of oppression, poverty is characterized by many forms of oppression, which are often described as injustice (*ashaq*) that comes through an unjust and cruel exercise of power and authority by some political or religious structures.[24] Whenever such injustice occurs, the poor become enslaved or are reduced to slavery (*yanah*) that consequently animalizes (*nagas*) and crushes (*ratsats*) their lives. Poverty coming through oppression and exploitation will not only humiliate the victims, but also create hostility and conflict, which will consequently result in impoverishment and killings.[25] Yahweh instructed the political and religious leaders in the Old Testament to execute impartial justice and maintain the rights of the poor by advocating for their welfare. Prophets were the well-known champions and defenders of the poor. They powerfully and poignantly condemned injustices done to the poor, especially when they were exploited (2 Kings 21:1–10), and when their rights were trampled upon through bribery (Amos 2:6, 5:1). Furthermore, the Bible describes some as the "humble poor" who, due to oppression and their helplessness, come to Yahweh for mercy and vindication. These humble poor are depicted as the "meek" and "contrite in spirit" that tremble at God's word (Zeph 2:3, 3:12; Isa 66:2, 49:13). The Psalmist describes them as the "afflicted and lonely" that wait patiently for God's vindication. These poor were given the assurance that they will "eat and be satisfied" and they will inherit the land in the age to come (Ps 5:6). Psalms 19:18 shows the needy and the afflicted are the object of God's care. They have the promise that God will not forsake them (v. 10) and that he remembers their prayers. Those who show acts of mercy and care toward the poor are blessed by God (Ps 41:1; Matt. 5:7). And also, this is an act of worship to God. On the other hand, oppression of the poor is an act of contempt to God (Prov. 14:31).

Methodology

The research methodology employed for this study was a combination of multiple approaches. First, a quantitative survey questionnaire was given to pastors, church workers, Bible school students, and church members to understand the perceptions of Pentecostals about poverty. The survey is comprised of twenty-eight questions with five sets of questions in each domain. The questionnaire is divided into four parts: the demographic information of the respondent, the perceived problems of the respondent in the community, description, and causes of poverty, and the church attitude and approaches toward the poor/poverty. It is the central goal of the questionnaire to look at the mission endeavors of the respondent's church and to examine it carefully to see if there is a positive movement and ministry from the local church toward poor people.

The majority of the respondents in this study are from two groups of selected local Pentecostal churches in Northern Luzon: the Ilocano and Cordilleran Pentecostals. The Ilocano Pentecostals are identified as the people of Ilocos Region and Cagayan Valley. Among the lowland Ilocano Pentecostals, there are 123 respondents represented by twenty-one local churches, ninety-one respondents came from the Assemblies of God, and twenty-seven came from Independent Pentecostal charismatic members.

Among the Cordilleran Pentecostal churches, there are 121 respondents, of which eighty-three came from the Assemblies of God, and 38 from independent Pentecostal churches. Cordilleran people are comprised of many tribal groups, mainly the *Kankanaey, Isneg, Itneg, Kalanguya, Igorot,* and *Ibaloi.* They are the people in the mountains who can speak *Ilocano,* the regional dialect of Northern Luzon, but also have their own dialect and cultural distinctive, which differ from the Ilocanos. The Ilocanos and Cordilleran people in Northern Luzon were labeled and sometimes perceived as "Ilocanos" among the Tagalogs and Cebuanos.

This research process was done through personal visits to these selected local churches to interview local pastors and members and to observe their existing ministries. The process by which the questionnaire is given to the respondents is through personal participation in a collective meeting of ministers, with the voluntary assistance of selected research staff who administered the survey, letters, and emails, and through conducting collective interviews with group respondents such as church members or theological students.

Findings and Summary of Results

Issues and Problems in the Community

In the first domain, under the issues and problems in the community, the respondents were asked which they think are the most prominent problems in their community. The question was comprised of eight issues the community was facing: health, nutrition, housing, water sanitation, basic education, income, employment, or peace and order. The purpose of the question was to identify and construct the image of poverty in the respondents' communities. This is also to set the context of this study to understand the perceived issues of the respondents' communities.

Based on the findings, unemployment is perceived by Ilocanos and Cordilleran Pentecostal churches to be the most pressing problem in their community. Next is insufficient income, leading to a food shortage and living below the poverty line. Moreover, health issues like pregnancy-related deaths, children's mortality rate, and other health-related problems beset the community members. These could be caused by problems in the water, sanitation, and lack of nutrition. Furthermore, there are also peace and order, and housing problems in the community.

The Asian Development Bank (ADB) studies conducted in 2005 reveal at least seven causes of poverty from a broader perspective, such as macroeconomic problems, employment issues, rapid population growth, low agricultural productivity, governance concerns including corruption, armed conflict, and physical disability.[26] However, Arsenio Balisacan, an expert economist specializing in poverty issues in the Philippines, admits although the causes of poverty in the Philippines are multidimensional: employment and income, the twin problems of individuals, remain the prime struggle of the majority of Filipinos. He reveals the inability of Filipinos to find jobs and earn a substantial income is caused by a lack of capabilities in terms of educational achievement and health.[27]

This observation is quite similar to the findings of Medalla and Monsod, that the failure of households to fuel economic resources triggered hunger, health issues, and malnutrition of their family members. In the context of rural areas, lack of employment and income "breed regional unrest, armed conflicts, and political upheavals, undermining the progress in securing sustained economic growth and national development."[28] In addition, the disparities in access to reliable water supplies, electricity, and especially education predict the occurrence of armed conflicts.

Nature of Poverty

With respect to the nature of poverty, respondents in this section were asked how they view a poor person. They were given five choices based on scholar's definitions of poverty. In a study conducted by developmental workers such as Bryant Myers, poverty was defined as social realities: that a person is considered poor when he/she has a lack of resources,[29] lack of freedom to grow,[30] lack of access to social power,[31] or are victims of the disempowerment,[32] and lack of power and all its relationship.[33] With respect to the results of the nature of poverty, in general, both the Ilocano and Cordilleran Pentecostals agree that a person is considered poor if he lacks basic needs such as food, shelter, clothing, and employment. A poor person, as perceived by the respondents, is one who is spiritually and financially bankrupt, with no permanent house, and who lacks training and opportunities. Cordilleran Pentecostals added that a poor person is one who has been abandoned by his relatives and has become needy and a beggar. Another respondent from Cordillera added that natural calamities (e.g., typhoons, earthquakes, and flash floods), illegal logging, lack of social and health services, and lack of educational and economic opportunities are other major images of poverty in Cordillera.

Causes of Poverty

In this section, respondents were asked for their perceived assumptions of the causes of poverty based on the findings of social scientists. It is the purpose of the researcher in this section to know if poverty is caused by the poor themselves, the irresponsibility of political leaders who are stealing the money of the people by means of graft and corruption, the national oligarch or bureaucratic capitalists in the country, the lack of political will of the government to implement its pro-poor programs, or the fragmented culture of the Filipinos. While the researcher admits there are varied studies regarding the causes of poverty, this study chose these five major realities to test the perceived assumptions of Ilocano and Cordilleran Pentecostals.

The results of the study indicate that Ilocano and Cordilleran Pentecostals agree, with a mean of 3.16 and 3.04 respectively, that graft and corruption, disunity among the people, and lack of self-reliance cause poor people to become poorer. Moreover, the respondents strongly agree that the rich do business to enrich themselves alone, and the country lacks the political will to implement some of its programs to alleviate the conditions of the poor. This observation reveals that, aside from the lack of the initiative of the poor families to get out from poverty, the business and political sectors are contributing to the disempowerment of the poor.

The recent findings of Clarke and Sison clarify the findings above (the case of political patronage, bureaucratic capitalism, and the inability of the government to enforce a pro-poor program in the country) contributed to the widening of the gap between the rich and poor due to the unequal distribution of wealth and power.[34] Nevertheless, both Ilocano and Cordilleran Pentecostals, aside from the causes mentioned above, believe that poverty is experienced because of laziness, failure to save money, natural crisis, vices, inability to start a business venture, and lack of employment.

Combating Poverty

This section asked the respondents about the role and the task of local Pentecostal churches in combating poverty. Respondents were asked if they strongly believe that Pentecostal churches are seriously combating poverty when the church becomes a prophetic community by denouncing systemic evils in the community, by organizing local churches to be the center of education for social concern, by restoring human dignity and self-worth through Spirit-filled worship and *koinonia* ministry, by establishing compassion ministries that become a healing community, or aggressively evangelizing the people. The Ilocano and Cordilleran Pentecostals strongly agree, with means of 3.27 and 3.31, that Pentecostal churches have a significant role in seriously helping to combat the issue of poverty by: emphasizing the lordship of Jesus through aggressive evangelism, and letting people accept Jesus as Lord and Savior; making the local church a center of education for social concern through teaching the values of the kingdom and denouncing systemic evils in society; fostering authentic fellowship and worship that restores human dignity; and becoming a healing community by providing refuge and compassion ministries to the poor. This observation reveals that there is an increasing awareness by the Ilocano and Cordilleran Pentecostals of enforcing and developing a contextual, holistic ministry to the poor communities. The mean reveals a high level of awareness which signals the Pentecostals to become agents of social change in their respective communities.[35] Although the political and business sectors perceive the church, in general, as only a reservoir and dispenser of spiritual teaching and values, recent trends show the burgeoning of social ministries to the poor accomplished by Pentecostal churches.[36]

When inviting suggestions from the respondents as to how to combat poverty, Ilocano and Cordilleran Pentecostals strongly recommended that local churches should set up a separate department in the church which deals with the issue of poverty, providing skills and livelihood training that fuel sources of income for those who have no capital. While the Cordilleran Pentecostals do not negate the suggestions above, they feel it is necessary for the church to overhaul its entire ministry, making the local church an advocate of holistic ministry by addressing the social concerns of the people by teaching people to become resourceful through working diligently, investing their resources creatively, and saving money for their future. Cordilleran Pentecostals also suggest that local churches have a long-term plan for the poor and avoid a kind of "dole out" ministry. If distributing finances are necessary, the church should put up church-based micro-financing that allows their poor members to borrow money with little interest.

Means of Fighting Poverty

In the next domain, respondents were asked which alternative and viable options they recommended for the church to combat poverty. While this research acknowledges different approaches to combating poverty, this study provided five viable options currently practiced by the government and non-government organizations, such as advocacy groups and Christian churches. Since forty percent of the country's workforce is in agriculture, respondents were asked if it is necessary for Pentecostal churches to be engaged in livelihood farming. The purpose of the first question was to discover if Pentecostals believe agriculture can be a potential tool to get the economy going again. Another option practiced by different organizations is the utilization of church-based microfinancing projects for the poor in the community. Both Ilocano and Cordilleran Pentecostals were asked for their perceptions on the importance of using micro-enterprise as a way of building poor communities. The popularization of micro-financing as an alternative for the poor is practiced by the government and Christian organizations as a prime method of empowering the poor.

Respondents were also asked the importance of establishing church-based learning centers that meet the holistic needs of children in the community. The increasing numbers of vulnerable children as one of the images of Philippine poverty was also brought to the discussion, asking Pentecostals what alternative options they can offer and whether they believe it necessary for Pentecostal churches to establish church-based schools that provide quality education for the poor. Included in the question was the importance of creating training workshops to privide skills and livelihood for the unemployed in the community. In addition, respondents were asked if it is necessary for Pentecostals to exert efforts to protect the environment.

Ilocano and Cordilleran Pentecostals agree, with a means of 3.19 and 2.90 for Ilocano and Cordilleran respectively, that a Pentecostal church combats poverty when the members engage in livelihood projects and the church provides training and micro-financing schemes for livelihood programs, the church subsidizes learning centers and feeding programs for the children and establishes non-formal education, and the church helps in organizing cooperative stores, and protects the environment. To determine whether there is a significant difference between the perceptions of the Ilocano and Cordilleran Pentecostal church members, the t-test was used. The finding shows that at the five percent significance level, there is no marked difference between the two groups as indicated by the t-statistic of 0.493, which is lower than the tabular value of 2.447. This implies the Ilocano and Cordilleran Pentecostal church members have similar levels of theological and philosophical understanding of poverty.

This observation reveals the statistical similarity between the two groups of respondents even though the Cordillera provinces like Abra, Ifugao, Mt. Province, and Benguet are included in the lists among the top twenty poorest provinces, compared to the Ilocano Region (IR), which is not included in the list of poorest provinces. Pentecostal perceptions of poverty have never changed. This implies that both Ilocano and Cordilleran Pentecostals acknowledge the majority perception that poverty is intractably linked to graft and corruption, and the widening gap between the rich and the poor remains as the prime challenge facing Filipinos.

A Case Study of the Civic Engagement of Sambayanihan Ministries International Inc. in Lower Rock Quarry

Lower Rock Quarry (LRQ), also known as "Lagoon," is one of the 128 villages of Baguio City. It has a population of 1,800 and is mostly inhabited by the *Kankana-ey*, the *Ilocanos*, the *Pangasinanse*, and some 200 Muslims in the south. LRQ is known as the "Little Tondo" of Baguio City because, according to social observers, the village is the most depressed and poorest village among the *barangays* of Baguio City. The extreme poverty in the village is caused by unemployment, lack of income, and sometimes the recurring flood in the area (due to heavy rain and narrow drainage of the village). Most of the inhabitants are poor migrants from the lowland; farmers who are tilling the vegetable garden in the middle of the village, and some Muslim families who are working as vendors in the city of Baguio City. LRQ is the home of much of the city's garbage because it is a place where all the garbage is dumped during the rainy season. While there are many children in the village, the community lacks daycare centers and elementary and high schools for the children. As a result, there are many out-of-school youths in the village. Some of the families don't have enough supply of clean water and electricity. LRQ is populated by unchurched people. Although the city is populated by Catholic, Protestant, and Pentecostal churches, as well as paganism, no religious groups dare to build a chapel in the village because of the recurring floods in the area. So, the spirituality of people in the village is dependent on the church centers and fellowships in the city.

History of Assimilation in the Community

Laying the work in the slum area is a product of corroborative network and partnership with the local government and other organizations in the civil society. The Tejedos took seriously the mandate of Jesus to bring the gospel to the poor, and interplay that passion by taking the inputs of the local people. Before they started a ministry of intervention, they coordinated and partnered with the local officials. The local officials who know well the social conditions of the people serve cannot be bypassed. The ministry of Pentecostal Assemblies of God (PAG) in the village was started five years ago when the International Praise Center, the church of international students of the Asia Pacific Theological Seminary, challenged Joel and Carolyn Tejedo to start a ministry for the indigent families in LRQ. Out of the couple's obedience to the command of Jesus to bring the good news to the poor, they started meeting with the local officials to see how the church could be of help to the poor families within their constituents. After series of conversations with the local officials, they started surveying and understanding the demographic information of the village and identifying the needs that could be used as an entry point of bringing transformation in the community. After identifying the indigent families in the area and discovering that the twin problems of the village are characterized by "empty pocket" (*laman ng bulsa*) and "empty stomach" (*laman ng tiyan*),[37] the Tejedo's launched a skills and livelihood training and organized a feeding program in the village. The first training was attended by twenty women from the indigent families in 2011, and the feeding program was attended by twelve children in the same year.

There are at least three rationales why these two legs of ministries were started by the Tejedos. First, to translate the love of God into concrete action, second, to create economic awareness in the community, and third, to start empowering the lives of the poor. As a result, the Tejedos started the *Sambayanihan* Ministries International Inc. (SMII), a non-profit and faith-based organization with civic concern, especially for the poor children and indigent families in LRQ. SMII is a transformational ministry, providing holistic development for children and skills and livelihood training for local people to empower them to significantly increase their livelihood performance and expand the capability to experience human dignity and wholeness.

Intervention and Approaches

The ministry of Pentecostals at LRQ is a product of participatory engagement of religious organizations, faith-based NGOs, local government, media, academia, indigenous people, and other organizations in the civil society. Without the sharing of skills and resources of these organizations, PAG would not be able to spearhead pro-poor activities that empower the lives of the poor in the area.

Participatory Interventions

Since the ministry of PAG in the area, there have been significant interventions that affected and transformed the lives of the poor. The social engagements include:

- Providing micro-enterprise and church-based micro-financing for indigent families, funded through donations from the International Praise Center
- Skills and livelihood training and women's empowerment through the *Kumikitang Kabuhayan ng Kapamilyang Kristiano*
- Free mass wedding for the twelve unwed couples who were unable to finance their weddings
- Medical and dental mission for the whole village
- Provided other medical services for the one-hundred Muslim and Christian children
- Free haircuts and hygiene kits for the one-hundred children
- Secondhand clothing and school supplies distribution every year for the impoverished children in the area
- Provision of sewing machine for poor migrant widows who do not have capital and sustainable income
- Street cleaning done by church youth and university students
- Feeding program on a regular basis for the one-hundred children in the area
- Mass children's dedication for the twenty-three infants and young children

Holistic Child Development

Children are taught to fear God and obey his commands. Without a personal relationship with their creator, there can be no transformation. In LRQ, the Tejedos are ushering these children to experience transformation through personal relationships with God and Spirit-filled worship. Central to the children's worship is the regular study of God's word. God's word builds community.

In many cases, the children at LRQ are malnourished and do not have adequate access to food. Children are physically weak, without proper hygiene or nourishment. So, the priority of the Holistic Child Development program, in partnership with the families and the *barangay*, is to ensure that these children are fed regularly. Therefore, the Tejedos feed the children on a regular basis. Often, the Tejedos also conduct medical missions to assist families in their health condition.

Children need to not only be fed physically, but they also have to be mentally and morally equipped, armed with the values of the kingdom of God. So, the Tejedo's program includes this non-formal education of the children. They teach them science, mathematics, character building, and value formation. This program is integrated into their Saturday feeding and health program. In addition to these, they allocate time to play sports and develop musical skills. Their hope is for a Christian daycare center to be built in LRQ to increasingly empower these poor children to reach their highest potential in life.

Skills and Livelihood Training

Though the parents are living in the slum area of LRQ, income and unemployment is also prevalent in the village. We do not need to measure the pervasiveness of poverty; it's one of the obvious characteristics of the village. Families of these children are living in squatter houses with a lack of economic access, without electricity, and sources of clean water. The ministry of SMII regularly provides training to the unemployed people in LRQ. The training center serves as a venue to empower men and women to acquire skills and income-generating livelihood such as making organic noodles, peanut butter, bread, and cookies from root crops, etc. The goal of this training is to enable unemployed men and women to become spiritually and economically responsible, providing financial assistance to those who are unable to produce sustainable income due to financial shortage.

One of the livelihoods of the families in the squatter areas of LRQ is gardening. The village is inhabited by multicultural groups living in the middle of the village, with small portion of land tilled by the families. The church encourages these families to plant vegetables using organic fertilizers as a way of preserving the environment and encouraging local people to patronize organic vegetables. The vision was born from the frugal wisdom of Joseph to till the land and store food for the coming famine and poverty (Gen 41).

The central idea of this holistic program at LRQ is to build a Spirit-filled church that empowers people to experience healing and wholeness in the name of Jesus. All the projects and programs above serve as points of entry for the poor to experience freedom in Christ. The ministries of SMII are just tools helping to bring them to fundamental transformation. With these programs, the ministry envisions raising up Spirit-filled worshippers in the LRQ community, so that these worshippers may become empowered witnesses in the society.

Impact

Social transformation and change can be possible when civil society works hand in hand to create a better society. But such transformation cannot be achieved without spiritual transformation, and without bringing the people into a pedagogical process that changes the worldview and values of the people. Children are the next generation that shape society, so at the forefront of Christian ministry, children must be taught to love God and love their neighbors.

Establishing a personal money management program by providing seminars on biblical economics and basic accounting for the poor in the squatter areas enables them to have freedom from debt and/or financial difficulty. To this end, SMII teaches the ten-twenty-seventy principle of handling money and earnings from their sales. Once they are awarded a livelihood, it is the requirement of our organization to encourage them to give ten percent of their earning, save twenty percent of it, and then use the seventy percent to add to their capital.

Providing livelihoods for the people will not only create economic awareness among the poor, but save them from addictive vices and chaotic lifestyles, re-engage with education, improve behavior and behavioral results, improve the sense of wellbeing, reduce anti-social behavior, and enable safer streets, reduce re-offending, reduce hunger, and improve physical health, improve family life, and eradicate homelessness. In the program, they will incrementally learn the value of stewarding their bodies, skills, and their families. The goal is to make these people spiritually, socially, and economically responsible citizens in the community.

Missiological Implications

Pentecostal ministry, in its very nature, is characterized by the passion and willingness to interject the gospel into every situation. This Pentecostal involvement depends on the challenges which emerge from a given context. While it is true that Pentecostals are accused of being socially irresponsible because of their futuristic attitude, this concept is rather inconclusive. How can we be certain that our civic engagement is in touch with the context of ministry toward the poor without presuming so?

First, since endemic poverty is what characterizes the majority of the Filipino communities, Filipino Pentecostal civic engagement must responsibly correspond to the pressing needs of the poor people in the rural areas. Any serious civic participation of local church endeavors must not fail to ask what the issues are that the people themselves are asking.

Second, due to massive poverty in the rural and urban communities, Pentecostal civic engagement should be holistic. A local church is holistic in its mission when it increases social awareness of the church, as shown by its discussion of wider local and national issues rather than just the usual moral issues. The church, in corresponding to the socio-political realities, must be able to integrate in its bible studies, preaching, and other discipleship programs concern for holistic development. This can be seen in its responsiveness to the needs of its immediate locality, its participation in local and national affairs, and its advocacy both for local and national concerns with representation and participation in the formal political structures.

Third, because massive poverty is caused by unemployment, Filipino Pentecostal civic engagement must participate in church-based or community-based programs/ projects that advocate programs dealing with these kinds of human survival issues. Filipino local churches must be reminded that the Philippines is rich in natural resources, and

Filipinos as people should be naturally able to create sources of income that are organic to the Philippines. The issue here is resourcefulness and creativity in the approach to using natural resources God has provided for the Filipinos.

Fourth, because the concept of social capital known as civic engagement is almost foreign Pentecostal believers, local churches and theological schools as well as Pentecostal organizations should increase awareness at the local, regional, and national level, whereby research and training should be conducted and disseminated. Fundamental to the development of a Pentecostal form of civic engagement, the task of positioning the local church as a center for social concern should be practiced and implemented within the local churches. Pentecostal local churches should not be understood as mere caretakers and dispensers of spiritual truth and values, but they should also creatively integrate into their training and Bible studies the importance of educating the members to participate creatively in the regeneration of their local communities.

Conclusion

Pentecostal civic engagement, as this chapter states, is indeed a social resource to rebuild the lives of the poor. When Pentecostals are not afraid to work and partner with other organizations in civil society, they will not only build communities, but acts as a mechanism to produce a just and loving society. As long as the church translates its witness in the production of the common good in society, the church will increasingly transmit its worldview and values in the community. Pentecostal civic engagement, however, is costly because it demands genuine solidarity with the poor and involves Christian discernment as to how to translate our Christian faith and spirituality into the lives of the poor. For Christian practitioners of civic engagement, it involves genuine humility and creativity in working with other organizations in the civil society. Triumphalist spirit has no place in partnering with other organizations.

Notes

1 This paper was first presented at the Study Group on Social Theology, at the Tyndale Research Center in Cambridge, England, on July 1–3, 2015.

2 Civic engagement can be defined as a citizen's right to participate in the decision process that involves them in the economic, social, cultural, religious, and political process that affect their lives. It is also focuses on the increasing of their capabilities and skills in the civil society to participate and engage in decision making processes that hold the state accountable.

3 Baguio City is one of the cities in Northern Luzon, Philippines, which is located at the top of the mountains of the Cordillera Administrative Region. Baguio City has 129 villages and has a population of 300,000. Among the 129 villages, Lower Rock Quarry, according to the social observers, is the poorest and the most depressed village in Baguio City.

4 "Penalizing Squatting and Other Criminal Acts," Presidential Decree 772, President of the Philippines, September 4, 1975, https://thecorpusjuris.com/legislative/presidential-decrees/pd-no-772.php, accessed March 25, 2021.

5 Norman Bardadora and Alcuin Papa, "Metro Squatters Relocation Costs 32 Billion Pesos," *Philippine Daily Inquirer*, October 19, 2009.

6 Michael L. Costello, "Slums and Squatter Areas as Entrepots for Rural and Urban Migrants in Less Developed Society," *Social Forces* 66:2 (December 1987), 428–429.

7 Costello, "Slums and Squatter Areas," 430.

8 Hari Srinivas, "Urban Squatters and Slums: Defining Squatter Settlements," Concept Note Series E–036, Global Development Research Center, April, 2015, https://www.gdrc.org/uem/squatters/define-squatter.html, accessed March 24, 2021.

9 Srinivas, "Urban Squatters and Slums."

10 Sierry Soriano Tendero, "The Practice of Empowering the Urban Poor by Four Non-Government Organizations in Metro Manila: Grounding for Emancipation Education" (Ed.D. Diss., Asia Graduate School of Theology, 2006), 11.

11 Tendero, "The Practice of Empowering," 11.

12 Jose M. De Mesa and Lode L. Wotsyn, *Doing Theology: Basic Realities and Processes* (Quezon City, Philippines: Claretian Publications, 1990), 16–17.

13 Julie Ma, *Mission Possible: Biblical Strategies for Reaching the Lost* (Oxford: Regnum, 2005).

14 Hwa Yung, *Mangoes and Bananas? A Quest of an Authentic Asian Christian Theology: Biblical Theology in an Asian Context* (Oxford: Regnum, 1997), 52, 56, 62, 77.

15 Melba Padilla Maggay, "Early Protestant Missionary Efforts in the Philippines: Some Intercultural Issues," in Wonsuk Ma and Julie Ma, eds., *Asian Church and God's Mission* (Caldwell, NJ: OMF Literature Inc. 2002), 29–41.

16 Eduardo Lapiz, *Paano Maging Filipinong Kristiano* (Becoming a Filipino Christian) (Quezon City: KALOOB, 1998), 5.

17 Herbert Schlossberg, Vinay Samuel, and Ronald Sider, *Christianity and Economics in the Post-Cold War Era: The Oxford Declaration and Beyond* (Grand Rapids, MI: Eerdsmans, 1994), 20–21.

18 Michael Taylor, *Christianity, Poverty, and Wealth* (Geneva Switzerland: WCC Publications, 2003), 3.

19 Taylor, *Christianity*, 21.

20 Taylor, *Christianity, Poverty, and Wealth*, 21.

21 Taylor, *Christianity, Poverty, and Wealth*, 35.

22 Taylor, *Christianity, Poverty, and Wealth*, 235.

23 Taylor, *Christianity, Poverty, and Wealth*, 235.

24 Thomas D. Hanks, *For God So Loved the Third World: The Biblical Vocabulary of Oppression* (Maryknoll, NY: Orbis, 1983), 5–7.

25 Hanks, *For God So Loved the Third World*, 15–17.

26 Karin Schelzig, "Poverty in the Philippines: Income, Assets, and Access," (Southeast Asia Department, Asian Development Bank, 2005), 87.

27 F. M. Medalla and K. R. L. Jandoc, "Philippines: GDP Growth after the Asian Financial Crisis: Resilient Economy or Weak Statistical System?" (Discussion Paper, University of the Philippines School of Economics, Quezon City, 2008), 5.

28 S. Monsod, "Philippine Poverty: Situation, Trends, Comparisons," (Quezon City, Philippines: UP School of Economics, 2008), n.p.

29 At the formative stage of developmental transformation, some practitioners define poverty as "lack of things" like access to physical, material and economic resources. This approach tends to identify and provide the "missing things." This definition assumes that when these things like food or shelter are provided, then the poor will no longer be poor. However, because people tend to also lack information and critical survival skills, it attempts to provide this information and living skills by acquainting the

poor with a learning environment. Christians tend to use the knowledge of the gospel to "fill" that information.

30 Robert Chambers, "Rural Poverty Unperceived: Problems and Remedies," *World Development* 9:1 (January 1981), 7–18. This view is upheld by Robert Chambers, a prominent scholar of poverty issues. who views the poor as living in a "cluster of disadvantage," who live in the "poverty trap" in six areas: material poverty; physical weakness; isolation; vulnerability; powerlessness; and spiritual poverty.

31 John Friedman, *Planning in the Public Domain: From Knowledge to Action* (Princeton, NJ: Princeton University Press, 1987), 56. He argues that the poor should be entitled to five social avenues for creating social space and influence to move out from poverty: social networks; livelihood; social organization; knowledge and skills, defensible life space; and financial resources.

32 Jayakumar Christian, *God of the Empty-Handed: Poverty, Power, and the Kingdom of God* (Monrovia, California: MARC, 1999), 16–25. Building his arguments from Chambers and Friedman, Christian sees the poor household "embedded in a complex framework of interacting systems" such as the personal, psychological, social, physical, and religious spiritual systems. The poor, according to Christian, find themselves trapped inside a system of disempowerment made up of these interacting systems. Each part, according to Christians, contributes to the disempowerment of the poor through the deceptive practice of the non-poor. These non-poor practices what Christian calls the god complexes" and can be traced to the deceptive "principalities and powers."

33 Connie Harris Ostwald, "A Deeper Look at Poverty: Challenges for Evangelical Development Workers," *Transformation* 26:2 (April 2009), 130–145; 131.

34 Gerard Clarke and Marites Sison, "Voices from the Top of the Pile: Elite Perceptions of Poverty and the Poor in the Philippines," *Development and Change* 34:2 (May 2003), 60. For instance, Clarke and Sison reveal that the majority of legislators in the congress are from the richest families: the national oligarchs in the Philippines, who are clothed with political dynasties, own big business firms, and are closely linked to the reigning political parties in order to protect their business interests.

35 See Douglas Petersen, *Not by Might Nor by Power: A Pentecostal Theology of Social Concern* (Oxford: Regnum, 1999). Petersen argues that Pentecostals, by virtue of their pneumatic praxis grounded on their charismatic theology of the Holy Spirit, are beginning to develop a social praxis that is instrumental in accomplishing social change.

36 Joseph Rommel Suico, "Institutional and Individualistic Dimensions of Transformational Development: The Case of Pentecostal Churches in the Philippines," (Ph.D. Diss., Oxford Centre for Mission Studies, Oxford, England, 2003). See also, Tendero, "The Practice of Empowering the Urban Poor."

37 I discovered these facts after interpreting the results of the data that I collected from the local people of Cordillera and the Ilocos Region.

19 The War on Drugs in the Philippines and the Image of Healing and Restoration in Mark 5:1–20: Contrasting Perspectives on the Worth of the Human Being

Doreen Benavidez and Edwardneil Benavidez

Abstract

Rodrigo Duterte's war on drugs in the Philippines has criminalized and dehumanized drug dealers, pushers, and users, resulting in a bloodbath. In this paper, we look at the narrative Duterte seems to espouse and propose a counter-narrative through which to view and respond to the issue of drug users in the Philippines.

Introduction

Before the 2016 Presidential election, Rodrigo Duterte had already declared during his campaign that one of the problems that he would solve once he won is the Philippine drug problem. He promised to solve it in six months' time. Even at that time, he promised that he would use any means necessary, even killing all the 3 million people involved in illegal drugs, to achieve his goal. We foresaw that there would be a bloodbath. Our fear came to pass. What saddens us is the support of the majority of Filipinos on Duterte's war on drugs, even though thousands have already fallen victims to it. We feel that the value of human life has been reduced to almost nothing. In this paper, we acknowledge the power of stories. We believe that this may explain this phenomenon that we are wrestling with. We also hope to provide a way to regain the dignity of people trapped in drug addiction.

The State of the War on Drugs in the Philippines

President Duterte's "war on drugs" has claimed thousands of lives from poor communities, mostly male breadwinners, leaving children as orphans and families at much greater risk.[1] According to the Philippine Drug Enforcement Agency (PDEA), 5,281 suspects involved in illegal drugs were killed during the 123,441 operations conducted from July 2016 to February 2019.[2] These deaths, PDEA claims, were casualties of their operations, explaining that drug suspects were killed because *nanlaban*—they "resisted arrest" and were involved in a shootout against police officers.[3] However, the Philippines Commission on Human Rights (CHR) has documented hundreds of cases where witnesses and evidence point to summary execution by the police rather than death caused by a shootout.[4] Human rights groups also assert that the number of victims during police operations is higher than what PDEA claims, reaching up to 12,000.[5] This number does not include the close to 23,000 deaths related to the war on drugs which the Philippine National Police (PNP) labels as "homicides under investigation" (HUI).[6]

Human rights groups, however, believe that these were extrajudicial killings (EJKs) rather than HUI. They explain that when drug-related police operations came under scrutiny, execution-style deaths, including torture by unidentified men in plainclothes of those suspected to be involved in illegal drugs, became reoccurring.[7] CHR believes that these are police officers who became involved in vigilante killings or extrajudicial killings (EJKs).[8] Rights groups also identify that seventy-four minors were among those who have been killed during police operations and vigilante killings (as of December 2017).[9] While authorities claim that they were collateral damage, the Children's Legal Rights and Development Center asserts that the children victims were targeted suspects, as was the case of Kian delos Santon.[10]

On August 16, 2017, Kian delos Santos, seventeen years old, was shot dead in an alley by three policemen who claimed that Kian shot them during an operation (*nanlaban*), forcing them to shoot back.[11] They also claimed that they recovered a .45 caliber gun and two sachets of suspected shabu from the boy.[12] However, CCTV footage showed that Kian was dragged by the cops to a dark alley and a witness stated that Kian was on his knees begging for his life before the series of gunshots.[13] This evidence created a public uproar calling for justice for Kian. On November 29, 2018, more than one year after Kian's death, the three cops were convicted of murder and were sentenced to life imprisonment without the possibility of parole.[14] However, as observed, Duterte's drug war continues, and no other police officer has been convicted other than those in Kian's case.[15]

These killings paint a horrifying picture of the war on drugs. However, according to a survey in 2017, eighty-eight percent of Filipinos support the President's war on drugs, even though seventy-three percent believe that EJKs are taking place.[16] In the same survey, fifty percent of Filipinos do not believe the police accounts that the victims were involved in illegal drugs or that they "resisted arrest"—*nanlaban*. Further, respondents felt "many victims were falsely identified by their enemies as drug users and pushers, and then killed by police or shadowy vigilantes."[17] In addition, some believe that the drug syndicates are the ones killing each other and not the police. In an interview with a supporter, the respondent stated, "They (the killings) aren't really EJKs. . . . It's the *narcos* who are killing their own people."[18] Others consider the news reported by the mainstream media to be an exaggeration or even fake news because they are controlled by elites and by political opposition who want to discredit the President and regain power and influence.[19] In another survey in 2018, the majority of Filipinos (seventy-eight percent) are satisfied with the anti-illegal drugs campaign of the government and classified it as "very good."[20]

In a news article attempting to understand why the majority of Filipinos support the drug war, a pro Duterte interview respondent stated, "It really hits a nerve when I hear about those deaths. It's painful. But I think that violence of that kind is unfortunately inevitable when there's a struggle for power, especially when drug gangs are involved."[21] This statement echoes the President's claim that the drastic measures and violence were necessary and unavoidable. In the same article, another respondent said, "Criminals are using human rights groups as a shield. . . . They were given fair warning, and if they want to avoid violence, they can just turn themselves in."[22] In this mindset, the deaths were the victims' fault. The then Justice Secretary Aguirre, when asked to comment on the Amnesty International report, said, "The criminals, the drug lords, drug pushers, they are not humanity. They are not humanity . . . In other words, how can that be when your war is only against those drug lords, drug addicts, drug pushers. You consider them humanity? I do not."[23] A pro-administration Senator Sotto, defending Sec. Aguirre's statement said, "Humanity, which is about 7 billion people, cannot be compared against a hundred, or 200, 300 million people involved in drugs. You cannot compare that. . . . Humanity is greater than those involved with illegal drugs. That is the interpretation that I understand."[24]

Both these statements of high-ranking government officials place drug addicts, drug pushers, and drug lords in the same category, describing them as not human.

The Power of Stories

The above characterization of people involved in illegal drugs resonates with how President Duterte characterizes them in his stories in his speeches (elaborated below). Police and police actions toward drug addicts, drug pushers, and drug lords also resonate with Duterte's characters in his stories, within which the views and actions expected of law enforcers and law-abiding citizen are to kill them.[25] Barrera points to the power of stories in explaining the effects of Duterte's stories. For Barrera, "Stories compel actions. They act as selection/evaluation systems that hail people to assume identities, and they make life social – grouping and disconnecting people."[26] Acknowledging that Duterte is also caught up with the stories he has heard and told, Barrera argues that "they are responsible for why Duterte declared his war on drugs, adopted identities that outraged some, and connected and disconnected him from alliances."[27]

The Story of the War on Drugs in the Philippines

Barrera argues that "Duterte has been caught up in a heroic saga characterized by apocalyptic stories."[28] Barrera observes that in Duterte's heroic saga story, he characterizes himself as the hero and the only savior fighting against the dark forces of the evil of society – drug and the addicts, pushers, and drug lords. However, Barrera points out that Duterte's story does not follow a romantic genre in which the hero brings salvation through legal means, but rather, it is an apocalyptic one, "where legal means must be set aside to restore order."[29] Barrera explains that an apocalyptic genre, while having the same upward plot progression of events with the romantic genre, deviates from it in terms of "its extreme polarization between the protagonist and antagonist, ideal motivations of the hero, and extraordinary objects of struggle."[30]

The People Involved in Illegal Drugs

Drugs and people involved in illegal drugs are characterized as "the persona of 'evil' and 'enemy'" who is destroying the lives of the children and youth, families, and the future of the Filipinos.[31] Duterte's stories characterize drug addicts as "worse than slaves,"[32] hopeless in the sense that they cannot be rehabilitated,[33] and he says they are not his countrymen. They are instead criminals, a menace to society that will destroy the future of the Filipinos,[34] and are therefore outside of the protection of the state and deserve to be killed.[35]

This characterization of people involved in illegal drugs was intensified by the spectacle of violence of the war on drugs. Reyes explains that in Duterte's spectacle of violence, people involved in illegal drugs are humiliated, not only while living, but also when dead.[36] Killings happen in the homes of suspects, traumatizing their family and their community. Bodies of drug suspects are found dumped in alleyways, garbage collection bins, bushes, and rivers, with placards strapped around their necks or laid beside the bodies that read *pusher ako* ("I am a drug pusher"). Add to these the media coverage and depiction of the dead suspects. According to Reyes, the bodies of suspects are objectified and utilized for political purposes sending a strong message that those that the president decided were "the persona of 'evil' and 'enemy'" will be killed.[37]

Law-Abiding Filipinos and the Police

The law-abiding Filipinos are characterized as victims of the evils of drugs and the people involved in illegal drugs. Duterte's stories describe the drug predicament as an extraordinary object of struggle; one so severe in its depth and scope that it affects the whole country and the future of the nation.[38] As the protagonist, Duterte commissions the law-abiding citizens and the police "who are just doing their job" to be with him as his main supporting protagonists against the antagonists – drugs and people involved in illegal drugs. Duterte empowers them to kill the criminals, the antagonists, if given the opportunity, and promises to have their backs and even reward them for it.

President Duterte

Duterte, as the hero in his stories, characterized himself as a law-abiding and God-fearing Filipino who is going to save his country. He is the protector of the police, which he characterizes as "just doing their job." Duterte claimed that his war on drugs is motivated by his love for his countrymen and that he is willing to die (or kill) to save and protect the

Filipino people. Barrera observes that Duterte's stories are "peppered with internalized motivational fidelity to higher ideals, which are given more importance than legal procedures."[39] These ideals may provide justification for the sacrifice of the many lives in Duterte's war on drugs. Barrera observes that Duterte characterizes himself as having been endowed with the power to neutralize the drug problem and protect his countrymen, while at the same time claiming powerlessness because of the depth of the drug problem.[40] Barrera points to this as an example of a power paradox; "power permits while powerlessness compels violent interventions."[41]

Response of Law-Abiding Filipinos

In spite of international pressure from the United Nations and the European Union as well as criticisms from the Catholic Church in the Philippines and human rights groups, President Duterte pledged to continue his war on drugs and is even willing to kill more. The majority of Filipinos support Duterte's campaign against drugs and believe that there has been an improvement in law and order. However, in surveys taken in 2016, seven out of ten Filipinos want suspects to be alive,[42] and eight out of ten Filipinos fear being killed because of the drug war.[43] While the families left behind of the victims of the drug war can be considered law-abiding citizens, they are excluded in Duterte's stories.

What Filipinos Lost

While the victims of the drug war can be considered lost, people under the spell of Duterte's stories see them as hopeless criminals who are not humans, therefore deserving of their fate. In this perspective, what was lost is the sense of humanity.

Alternative Stories

Mohammad and Fulkerson suggest that if people would change their existing paradigms on the drug problem, the dominant drug policies can be changed.[44] To do this, Frank proposes that alternative stories may be provided to stand in contrast with the other.[45] Barrera explains, "People can orchestrate a narrative ambush on dominating stories. As people are capable of narrative inflation – from low mimesis to the apocalyptic genre—they are also capable of narrative deflation: talking down the risk associated with the apocalyptic genre by using low mimetic discourses."[46] The succeeding two sections present two stories that stand in contrast to the war on drugs narrative. These two stories may have the potential to ambush the dominant story. Faith/religion has a strong influence upon Filipinos, and the first story is drawn from scripture, an authority in matters of faith/religion. The second story is a success story, something that the war on drugs cannot claim, because of the fact that the problem of drugs has not been solved three and a half years after the six months promised by the Duterte administration.

The Gospel Story: Mark 5:1–20

There are basically three prevailing interpretations of the story of Jesus and the Gerasene demoniac. One is "traditional" in that it demonstrates Jesus as a miracle worker. The second interpretation suggests that the story was Mark's subversive manner of uniting the people to stand up and reject the Roman occupation; that this story in particular and Mark's Gospel, in general, were political manifestos aimed at reminding the Jewish community that Jesus had come to free them from the bondage of the Roman occupation. Meyers has taken this Markan story and used it to turn the entire gospel into what is basically a liberation theology position.[47]

The other liberation view of this story focuses on the mental state of the possessed man. A number of recent journal publications have focused on this aspect of the story. One of the more compelling articles relates the story to broken lives caused by mental illness.[48] O'Day notes that the community demonstrated a lack of compassion and that they had given up on this man.[49] In modern terms, the possessed man had "suicidal tendencies," he was beyond hope, and his suffering was unabated. By yielding to the grace present in God's mercy through Jesus, the man acknowledges his lack of independence. It is by that same grace and mercy that he is able to live again. Jesus' power to expel hatred and re-establish love is the most extraordinary power there is; its power overcomes death with life.[50] It is this reading of Mark that perhaps comes closest to what we want to focus on in this paper.

It is our contention that Jesus had crossed the Sea of Galilee intentionally in order to begin his mission to the Gentiles. The episode begins as Jesus has stilled the storm and rebuked the disciples for their lack of faith as they crossed the lake and encountered a storm (Mark 4:35–41). Jesus has stilled the seas, demonstrating his control over the chaotic forces of nature, and his actions become a symbol of divine power.

They have crossed the boundary, landing on "the other side" (5:1) in the land or region of the Gerasa. There has been a great deal of scholarly debate over the name of the town or village to which Mark is referring to. Regardless of the location, Mark is more interested in "articulating geo-spatial 'space' in terms of narrative symbolic than actual place names."[51] The point of the narrative is that Jesus has purposefully entered Gentile territory.

The Demoniac Man

As Jesus leaves the boat, he is approached by a man who has been living among the nearby tombs. The man is possessed by an unclean spirit. The man lived among the tombs (v. 3), he cut himself, and he lived among unclean animals (v. 11). The text would lead the reader to conclude that the man had been exiled from his community to the tombs. Repeated attempts to shackle him with chains had all been unsuccessful; nobody had been able to subdue him (v. 4). This man is physically strong, and the spirit that has possessed him has made him even stronger.

The possessed man is also bruising himself or cutting himself with stones. This is often seen as an indication that the man suffered from some type of mental illness, and ultimately his healing is a sign of hope for those who suffer from a similar illness. Mark has carefully painted a bleak outlook for the possessed man that evokes a great sense of sympathy, even empathy, toward him. The man personifies self-destruction and social isolation.[52] No matter how you want to diagnose the condition of this man, it is evident that here was a man who is wretched and hopeless; human abnormality at its worst.

The People of Gerasa

The problem of the people of Gerasa is that they do not know what to do with the man. How hopeless the people of Gerasa were! How hopeless we always feel in the presence of a wretched person. We examine the conditions and concluded that nothing could be done with such people. This resulted in repressive actions. They tried chains and shackles. If we cannot cure abnormality, we can shackle it. This is what the people of

Gerasa did to the man. What society does is to lock people in prison and asylums. What enormous effort has society spent in the task of preventing the abnormal from doing harm to others?

Jesus

As Jesus and the twelve advance up the shore, they see this poor man rushing to meet them. The man, or the demon possessing him, knows who Jesus is. Jesus and the disciples are facing the same problem that of the people of Gerasa, which is, in some form or other, the supreme problem of society: human abnormality. In contrast to how the people of Gerasa treated the man, this story shows the method of Jesus.

Jesus is fully aware of the problem before him. How does he meet the case? Jesus sees himself as the agent of the cure, and he believes that the man is deserving of that cure. In Jesus, there is no such thing as a hopeless case. The man, seeing Jesus from afar, runs to him and prostrates himself before Jesus. The man cries out to Jesus, repeating the same statement made by the demon in 1:24. Mark is clearly using this to parallel the two exorcisms, the first on Jewish soil and the second on Gentile soil.[53] Addressing Jesus as "Son of the Most High God" further represents an acknowledgment by the man that Jesus is of superior power and he is expecting to be subject to punishment. Jesus never showed fear of the man. He was calm and inquired of the man's name, giving a name to the face. Then Jesus commanded the evil spirit to come out of the man.

In 5:9, Jesus speaks for the first time in the narrative. Engaging the demoniac, he asks the possessed man, "What is your name?" The answer is, of course, "My name is Legion; for we are many." The man is possessed by a great number of demons. The demons beg and bargain with Jesus not to drive them out of the land. They beg Jesus to let them inhabit a group of pigs grazing on a nearby hillside. Therefore, unclean spirits enter unclean animals. Jesus grants their request, sending them out to the pigs. As the demons leave the man and enter the pigs, eventually killing themselves, we see the full restoration. The man is clothed, seated with Jesus, speaking normally, and he has left the tomb. He is fully restored.

The People of Gerasa and their Response

The people tending the pigs leave the area and begin telling, or announcing, what had happened in the city and the surrounding countryside (v. 15). The people of the region come to see what has happened; two thousand pigs jumping off a cliff didn't happen every day. The crowds see Jesus and the once-possessed man who is now clothed and speaking normally. It is obvious to them that he has been cleansed of the demons. Unlike those near the exorcism in Capernaum who were "amazed" (1:27), these people are afraid. So frightened are they that they plead with Jesus to leave the area. The people of Gerasa plead with Jesus to leave the area because of the destruction of their property, i.e., the pigs. By asking Jesus to leave, they are saying that they are comfortable with their lives and are rejecting the life that Jesus offers, even if it means living with demons.

The disregard of the cost is an important element in the method of Jesus. Jesus did not apologize for the loss of the pigs. It did not matter to him how many pigs were killed. A man was saved. Jesus did not count the cost, but people do. The people tending the pigs fled to the city with the news, and the people who had tried to restrict the man saw a wondrous sight. There was the man, clothed, restored, and in his right mind. When the people heard what happened, they pleaded for Jesus to leave. It is the only instance in Jesus' ministry where people asked him to go away. It is the only instance where his ministry cost the people everything because Jesus left. Society is ready for reforms, but they cost too much. At Gerasa and today, people like the demoniac man will continue to exist because a property is esteemed above humans. This halts all possible reforms. This story of the pigs demands that we ask the question – are we willing to pay the cost of salvation and reform? There is really a cost.

What the People of Gerasa Lost

That day, the people of Gerasa lost a strong, good man who has more worth than pigs. The man became a social being. He is ready to go with Jesus. The man an hour before would have attacked Jesus. He has not only ceased to be a menace to society but desires to enter into social relations. Jesus obliges the people, and as he is about to leave, the formerly possessed man pleads with Jesus to allow him to "be with him" (v. 18). The man begs to be part of the group following Jesus in the same tone when the demons begged not to be sent out of the region and that the people of the region used to plead with Jesus to leave the area.[54] Jesus denies the man's request. Instead, the man is instructed to go back home and tell his family what Jesus had done for him and how the Lord had bestowed his mercy upon him (v. 19). The man goes throughout the Gentile region proclaiming what had happened to him just as Jesus had instructed him. Apparently, the man was quite a successful missionary as well, as the story concludes by noting that "all were amazed," presumably by the story he told about Jesus' work and God's mercy (v. 20). The man becomes an apostle of salvation. He is willing to take the ministry among his friends. He becomes active in the undertaking of which he was himself the beneficiary.

The healing of the demoniac may suggest possibilities of meeting the misery of people today. It warns us that we must be prepared for the costs and, when we are willing, it cheers us with the assurance of untold gain. Jesus is indeed a liberating figure through exorcism or healing. The once-possessed man in Gerasene bears witness that each of us, whether possessed by demons or whatever other baggage we might have, are capable of restoration through the extraordinary power of Christ's love that leads us from death into life.

The Story of the War on Drugs in Bogo City [55]

Amid widespread claims that police have been killing suspected drug users, one police officer has taken a different track and proven that a bloodless campaign can help solve the country's drug problem. Chief Supt. Byron Allatog of the Bogo City Police Station in the Province of Cebu chose to give drug pushers and addicts a chance to live and change their ways.

The Philippine Drug Enforcement Agency (PDEA) conferred a drug-free status on Bogo City in July 2017. What is noteworthy is the fact that this was achieved with zero deaths. While ordinary police officials conducted their war against drugs with a high level of harshness, Chief Supt. Byron Allatog, with the help of the city mayor, other local officials, and the community, preferred the humane way by focusing on rehabilitating drug addicts. His strategy apparently worked, as this city had not recorded a single killing since the 39-year-old policeman assumed his post in December 2016 until the city was declared drug-free in July 2017. Bogo also became the first city in Central Visayas and the second in the country to be declared drug-free by the PDEA.

People Involved in Illegal Drugs

In 2016 when Chief Supt. Byron Allatog was assigned in Bogo City, almost all *barangays* were infested with drugs. But in just eight months, the city was declared drug-free. According to Allatog, "Human life is important. Some people may say, 'He's a drug addict, nothing but trash.' But do these people even consider the fact that these drug addicts have families? I want people to know that killing is not the final solution to the problem of illegal drugs,"[56] he explained. For him, drug addicts need help to change.

The People in Bogo City

Allatog recalled going to every *barangay* in Bogo City to get people behind what he calls the "whole-of-community" approach.[57] He said that he told one group after another that the drug war is not just a matter for the police but for every *barangay* captain and all the members of the community.[58] He told them that they all had to acknowledge that there was a problem and that everyone must help to fix it.[59] He said, "It is a shared responsibility, sharing and sacrificing time and resources because it is our moral obligation and responsibility to protect our town because my family lives here, I work here, and my children study in this community."[60]

Chief Supt. Byron Allatog

Chief Supt. Byron Allatog considers human life sacred and believes that everyone, even the worst criminal, deserves a second chance. His respect for life may be traced to his parents' teachings and his roots as a member of the Bontoc tribe of Mountain Province, a province in the northern part of the Philippines. In his tribe, anyone who kills another human being, he said, must offer prayers and three pigs to atone for this sin in a ritual called "*chaw-es*."[61] When he became a policeman in 2001, Allatog lived by what he learned as a child—the value of human life. But the government's brutal war on illegal drugs tested his beliefs, he admitted.[62] He was with the Criminal Investigation and Detection Group as assistant regional chief of Calabarzon in July 2016, when President Duterte took over the reins of government. He recalled, "I told my men, if it is not necessary to kill, then why do it? Of course, we have to defend ourselves when the call arises. But as much as possible, I want the suspects to live."[63]

The People in Bogo City and their Response

The people of Bogo city were convinced that the community-based rehabilitation program is still the best approach to dealing with the drug problem. The Mayor of Bogo city, the city officials, the *barangay* officials, and the community people joined and supported the vision of Allatog.

What the People in Bogo City Gained

In July 2017, the PDEA declared all twenty-nine *barangays* in Bogo City "drug-free." From July 2016, at least 1,955 users in the city had surrendered to the police, while forty-five drug pushers had been arrested in different police operations. The city had been rid of drug pushers, yet no one was killed.

The police chief is also active in the local government's community-based drug rehabilitation programs that have so far helped more than 200 drug surrenderers. Included in the three-month rehab programs are seminars and physical activities.

The Center for Family Ministries (CEFAM) of the Catholic Church launched "The Lost Sheep Initiative" (TLSI). The Lost Sheep Initiative aims to provide centralized support to independent community-based rehab initiatives by way of funding, soliciting volunteers, and coordinating curriculum development. TLSI believes that those who have had trouble with drugs are our brothers and sisters who may have lost their way but not their humanity. They need to be gently guided to find their way back onto their own paths, with dignity and respect, rather than being forced onto someone else's like prisoners.

TLSI believes that addiction is a disease of the mind and spirit and must be treated as such, using a combination of science and spirituality, as global best practice suggests. TLSI has been collaborating with the Philippine National Police (PNP), the Department of Health (DOH), and Philippine Drug Enforcement Agency (PDEA), and local government officials in the community. TLSI volunteers include church officials, priests, businessmen, and laypersons.

Conclusion

Other countries who have fought their own costly drug wars have found a public health-based approach to be the only sustainable long-term solution, notably Colombia, and most radically, Portugal. No country has succeeded in entirely eradicating drugs from their societies, but with public health approaches, some countries have reduced drug use significantly, and perhaps more importantly, reduced drug-related crime even further.

In this paper, we described the bloody scene of the war on drugs in the Philippines. Drawing from Barrera, we explained how President Duterte, his government, the police, his supporters, and the people involved in illegal drugs and their families have been caught up in a heroic saga characterized by apocalyptic stories. In this story genre, the people involved in illegal drugs were dehumanized and objectified, and illegal forms of action were justified. With the hope of orchestrating a narrative ambush on the dominant story, we propose two stories that may be considered as alternatives, the story of the demon-possessed man in Mark 5:1–20 and the story of Chief Supt. Byron Allatog. In both stories, we learn that if we acknowledge the value and dignity of every human being, however wretched he or she is, there is no hopeless case. Also, both stories show how non-violent approaches can work, resulting in transformation. In the biblical story, the power of Jesus to transform lives, and in the story of Allatog, the power of collaboration and community participation is clearly evidenced.

Notes

1. Zigor Aldama, "How Rodrigo Duterte's War on Drugs Has Become a War on the Poor," South China Morning Post, January 20, 2018, https://www.scmp.com/magazines/post-magazine/long-reads/article/2129538/how-philippines-war-drugs-has-become-war-poor, accessed April 7, 2021; Reuban James Barrete, "Children Paying Grim Price for Duterte's War on Drugs," South China Morning Post, April 16, 2017, https://www.scmp.com/comment/insight-opinion/article/2087714/dutertes-war-drugs-leaving-children-pay-price-not-asking-why, accessed April 7, 2021.

2. Anna Felicia Bajo, "Latest Drug War Death Toll: 5,281 Killed, 176,021 Arrested as of Feb. 2019," GMA News, https://www.gmanetwork.com/news/news/nation/689368/latest-drug-war-death-toll-5-281-killed-176-021-arrested-as-of-feb-2019/story/, accessed June 2, 2019.

3. Vina Salazar, "War on Drugs: 'Nanlaban,'" Rappler, http://www.rappler.com/nation/144592-war-drugs-nanlaban, accessed June 3, 2019.

4. Krixia Subingsubing and Mariejo S. Ramos, "'Nanlaban' Victims Unfazed by Legal Hurdles," Inquirer News, https://newsinfo.inquirer.net/1012901/nanlaban-victims-unfazed-by-legal-hurdles, accessed June 2, 2019.

5. Roy Narra, "Death Toll in Duterte Drug War up to 5,176: Real Numbers PH," The Manila Times, https://www.manilatimes.net/death-toll-in-duterte-drug-war-up-to-5176-real-numbers-ph/518667/, accessed February 28, 2019

6. "World Report 2019: Rights Trends in Philippines," Human Rights Watch, https://www.hrw.org/world-report/2019/country-chapters/philippines, accessed December 28, 2018.

7. Subingsubing and Ramos, "Nanlaban."

8. Subingsubing and Ramos, "Nanlaban."

9. Jhesset O. Enano, "Group Finds 74 Minors in Drug War Body Count," Inquirer News, April 6, 2018, https://newsinfo.inquirer.net/980513/group-finds-74-minors-in-drug-war-body-count, accessed June 3, 2019.

10. Enano, "Group Finds 74 Minors."

11. Jodesz Gavilan, "TIMELINE: Seeking Justice for Kian Delos Santos," Rappler, November 28, 2018, https://www.rappler.com/newsbreak/iq/timeline-justice-trial-kian-delos-santos, accessed November 18, 2020.

12. Gavilan, "TIMELINE."

13. Jessica Bartolome, "The Kian Delos Santos Case: A Timeline," GMA News, November 29, 2018, https://www.gmanetwork.com/news/specials/content/24/the-kian-delos-santos-case-a-timeline/, accessed November 18, 2020.

14 Bartolome, "The Kian Delos Santos Case."

15 Rambo Talabong, "3 Years After Kian's Death Killings Continue Under Duterte," *Rappler*, August 16, 2020, https://www.rappler.com/nation/third-death-anniversary-kian-delos-santos-killings-continue, accessed November 18, 2020.

16 "Nine out of 10 Filipinos Support Duterte's Drugs War," *South China Morning Post*, October 16, 2017, https://www.scmp.com/news/asia/southeast-asia/article/2115585/nine-out-10-filipinos-support-dutertes-drugs-war, accessed April 7, 2021.

17 "Half of Filipinos Dispute Police Accounts of Drug War Deaths," *South China Morning Post*, September 27, 2017, https://www.scmp.com/news/asia/southeast-asia/article/2113111/half-filipinos-dont-believe-police-accounts-drug-war-deaths, accessed April 7, 2021.

18 "Why so Many Young Liberal Filipinos Support Duterte's Drug War," *South China Morning Post*, April 19, 2017, https://www.scmp.com/news/asia/southeast-asia/article/2088621/dutertes-drug-war-horrifically-violent-so-why-do-many-young, accessed April 7, 2021.

19 "Why so Many Young," *South China Morning Post*.

20 Helen Flores, "78% of Pinoys Satisfied with Drug War – SWS," *The Philippine Star*, September 24, 2018, https://www.philstar.com/headlines/2018/09/24/1854162/78-pinoys-satisfied-drug-war-sws, accessed June 3, 2019.

21 "Why so Many Young," *South China Morning Post*.

22 "Why so Many Young," *South China Morning Post*.

23 "Criminals Are Not Human – Aguirre," *Inquirer News*, February 1, 2017, https://newsinfo.inquirer.net/867331/criminals-are-not-human-aguirre, accessed June 4, 2019.

24 "Sotto Explains Why Drug Users 'Not Part of Humanity'," *ABS-CBN News*, February 5, 2017, https://news.abs-cbn.com/video/news/02/15/17/sotto-explains-why-drug-users-not-part-of-humanity, accessed June 4, 2019.

25 Christina Mendez, "Duterte to PNP: Kill 1,000, I'll Protect You," *The Philippine Star*, https://www.philstar.com/headlines/2016/07/02/1598740/duterte-pnp-kill-1000-ill-protect-you, accessed June 4, 2019, "'Go Ahead and Kill Drug Addicts': Philippine President Rodrigo Duterte Issues Fresh Call for Vigilante Violence," *South China Morning Post*, July 2, 2016, https://www.scmp.com/news/asia/southeast-asia/article/1984193/go-ahead-and-kill-drug-addicts-philippine-president-rodrigo, accessed April 7, 2021.

26 Dan Jerome Barrera, "Drug War Stories and the Philippine President," *Asian Journal of Criminology* 12 (2017), 341-359.

27 Barrera, "Drug War Stories," 359.

28 Barrera, "Drug War Stories," 359.

29 Barrera, "Drug War Stories," 352.

30 Barrera, "Drug War Stories," 353.

31 Barrera, "Drug War Stories," 355.

32 Rodrigo Duterte, "Drug Addicts Are Worse than Slaves," ABS-CBN News Channel Youtube, January 17, 2019, Youtube video, minute 0:36, https://www.youtube.com/watch?v=yJ_wNC-B944, accessed May 21, 2019.

33 Rodrigo Duterte, "Rodrigo Duterte on Drugs, Death and Diplomacy: Talk to Al Jazeera," *Al Jazeera English*, October 15, 2016, Youtube video, minute 2:46-23:09, https://www.youtube.com/watch?v=S2KtLTXXej8, accessed 22 May 2019.

34 Rodrigo Duterte, "Full Video: Rodrigo Duterte's State of the Nation Address (SONA) 2018," Inquirer.net, https://www.youtube.com/watch?v=BGkRWHwT2JE, accessed 22 May 2019.

35 Danilo Andres Reyes, "The Spectacle of Violence in Duterte's 'War on Drugs,'" *Journal of Current Southeast Asian Affairs* 35 (December 2016), 111–137.

36 Reyes, "The Spectacle of Violence," 120–123.

37 Reyes, "The Spectacle of Violence," 117.

38 Barrera, "Drug War Stories," 355.

39 Barrera, "Drug War Stories," 354.

40 Barrera, "Drug War Stories," 355.

41 Barrera, "Drug War Stories," 355.

42 Eimor P. Santos, "Filipinos Satisfied with Duterte's Drug War, But Want Suspects Alive - SWS," CNN, October 7, 2016, http://cnnphilippines.com/news/2016/10/07/SWS-Duterte-war-on-drugs-survey.html, accessed June 4, 2019.

43 "8 of 10 Pinoys Fear Dying in Drug War," *The Philippine Star,* December 20, 2016, https://www.philstar.com/headlines/2016/12/20/1655209/8-10-pinoys-fear-dying-drug-war, accessed June 4, 2019.

44 Fida Mohammad and Gregory Fulkerson, "The 'War on Drugs': A Failed Paradigm," in Marten W. Brienen and Jonathan D. Rosen, eds., *New Approaches to Drug Policies: A Time for Change* (London: Palgrave Macmillan UK, 2015), 229–249.

45 Arthur W. Frank, *Letting Stories Breathe: A Socio-Narratology* (Chicago: University of Chicago Press, 2015).

46 Barrera, "Drug War Stories," 359.

47 Ched Myers, *Binding the Strongman: A Political Reading of Mark's Story of Jesus* (Maryknoll, NY: Orbis, 1988), 191.

48 Gail R. O'Day, "Hope Beyond Brokenness: A Markan Refection on the Gift of Life," *Currents in Theology and Mission* 15:3 (1988), 244–251.

49 O'Day, "Hope Beyond Brokenness," 244.

50 Susan Garrett, *No Ordinary Angel* (New Haven, CT: Yale University Press, 2009), 134–135.

51 Meyers, *Binding the Strong Man*, 190.

52 Brendan Byrne, *A Costly Freedom: A Theological Reading of Mark's Gospel* (Collegeville, MN: Liturgical Press, 2008), 96.

53 John R. Donahue and Daniel J. Harrington, *Sacra Pagina: The Gospel of Mark* (Collegeville, MN: The Liturgical Press, 2002), 164.

54 Donahue and Harrington, *Sacra Pagina*, 167.

55 See, Ador Vincent S. Mayol, "Bloodless: This Cop Chief Gives Pushers, Addicts Chance to Live," *The Inquirer*, October 15, 2017, https://newsinfo.inquirer.net/937947/war-on-drugs-drug-killings-extrajudicial-killings-bogo-city-police-station-byron-allatog-pdea#ixzz5pqH3yENa, accessed April 7, 2021.

56 Mayol, "Bloodless."

57 "A Start Up Approach to the Drug Problem," *Makati Business Club Forum* 2 (2018) 3.

58 "A Start Up Approach," *Makati Business Club Forum*, 3.

59 "A Start Up Approach," *Makati Business Club Forum*, 3.

60 "A Start Up Approach," *Makati Business Club Forum*, 3.

61 Mayol, "Bloodless."

62 Mayol, "Bloodless."

63 Mayol, "Bloodless."

20 Global Poverty and Transnational Pentecostalism in the Middle East

Eric N. Newberg

Abstract

Driven by the impact of global poverty, large numbers of documented and undocumented workers from South Asia and Africa have migrated to countries in the Middle East.[1] The highest share of the migrant population is located in the Middle East. Many of these workers are Pentecostals. Migrants tend to alter the religious makeup of the countries in which they settle and construct new forms of transnational family life with global chains of care. The paper will provide an overview of Pentecostal evangelization in the Middle East and report on the findings of ethnographic research on transnational Pentecostals in the Maghreb, the Levant, and the Arabian Peninsula.

Introduction

Global Poverty and Transnational Migration

Today, we are witnessing a heightened consciousness concerning transnational migration as a driving force of globalization. Transnational migration has increased exponentially in response to the pressures of global poverty.[2] As a means of escaping poverty, millions in the global South are migrating to wealthier nations in search of more gainful employment as domestic workers.

According to Diana Myers, global economic forces in countries with a large deficit of decent work (LDDW) requires people to choose between staying in place with every expectation that deprivation will worsen over time, or opt for transnational migration despite its attendant risks in the hope of gaining a secure livelihood. Myers holds that globalization, like its colonial antecedents, condemns people to severe lifelong poverty.[3] Extremely poor people migrate out of desperation. In their study of migration from Egypt and Ghana, Rachel Sabates-Wheeler, Ricardo Sabates, and Adriana Castaldo found that for the poor in these countries, migration was an effective strategy for mitigating or escaping poverty.[4]

Yet severe poverty is not the only reason why people migrate from LDDW countries. Few would migrate if it were not for demand for certain types of labor in destination nations.

Migration research has demonstrated that migration involves inherent tensions. On the one hand, migration can be seen as an expression of agency. Migration decisions, choice of destination, adaptation, and incorporation, and transnational relations are linked with family ties and bonds. Migrants bring higher income and more opportunities. Migration is often grounded in one's sense of responsibility to the family. Migration scholars observe the emergence of a new transnational form of family life. They define transnational family life as social reproduction across borders. Transnational families live separated from each other much of the time, yet remain together united by collective welfare and unity, a process termed "familyhood across national borders." On the other hand, migration can also lead to disconnection. Family separation can lead to disruption, emotional and psychological costs for children, spouses, and the elderly, causing a plethora of social problems and breakdown of social norms. In the place of an absent mother or father, someone has to fill the gap. Fathers rarely take over child-rearing responsibilities when mothers migrate. Instead, other family relatives often step in to address the care deficit.

There is little doubt that voluntary migration from a poor to a rich country almost always benefits the individual migrant, who may easily find himself or herself earning in an hour what he or she earned in a day in the country of origin. International migrants typically send remittances to family members in their country of origin. Nonetheless, many experts believe that labor migration does not significantly improve the development prospects of the country of origin. Far from being productive, remittances may increase inequality, encourage consumption of imports, and create dependency. They are often delivered with stunning inefficiency; as much as twenty percent of their value is said to disappear, commonly through high transfer fees and poor exchange rate offerings. Source countries have had great difficulty in converting remittance income into sustainable productive capacity. Remittances may not constitute a rising tide that raises all boats, but they do have a very important effect on the standard of living of the households that receive them, constituting a significant portion of household income. They are an important social safety net for poor families, possibly reducing additional out-migration in particularly difficult times.

According to the International Labor Organization (ILO), there are 11.5 million migrant domestic workers in the world. Most of these workers are transnational migrants occupied with household labor. Domestic work includes a wide range of jobs typically dominated by men, such as gardeners, drivers, and security guards. However, the majority of migrant domestic workers are women, leading scholars to characterize this phenomenon as the "feminization of migration." In the Arab States, six in ten women are employed as migrant domestic workers. Labor migration and domestic work are intimately tied in the Arab states, which host 17.6 million migrant workers, representing over thirty-five percent of all workers in the region.[5]

Normally there are three ways in which domestic workers migrate to the Middle East: via connections with relatives and friends; through recruitment agents; and as refugees smuggled by boat. In the absence of a livable wage in their countries of origin, migrants come seeking job opportunities abroad. Since the 1970s, the employment of foreign women as domestic workers has rapidly grown, first in the oil-rich Gulf States and later among the new middle class in Lebanon, Jordan, and Yemen. As indigenous Arab women enter the workplace, the need for domestic help has been met through migrant workers. In the Middle East, migrant women face a number of restrictions. Migrants cannot work and reside legally without having a "sponsor" (*kafil*), who is in most cases their employer. In most cases, migrant domestic workers are required to reside in the house of their sponsor/employer. The drawback is that the home is considered the private sphere, not covered by local labor law. They may be confined to homes in which they work, have their passports confiscated, their residency status downgraded, and suffer harsh treatment such as no day off or sexual harassment. In return, they hope to acquire sufficient money with prospects of a better standard of living. In many cases, the harsh treatment impels a worker to escape and find work on her own as a freelancer without a contract. Legally, migrants in the Middle East cannot work as freelancers, and if they are caught, they face detention and a heft departure fee. Despite the risks, a large proportion of the migrant workers in the Middle East have opted for freelancing.

From the point of view of migrant domestic workers, being legal is not seen as a great advantage. The move toward freelancing needs to be seen in terms of the context in which being legal entails limited agency and burdensome obligations. Freelancers benefit materially from freedom of movement. They can exercise agency in finding access to networks of friends, educational opportunities for language acquisition, financial resources, means of communication, support of a church community. Such networks are a dominant feature of Pentecostal evangelization in the Middle East, to which we now turn.

Overview of Pentecostal Evangelization in the Middle East

The presence of Pentecostalism in the Middle East is significant, among other reasons, because this region includes the lands of the Bible. The beneficiary nations listed in Acts 2 include residents of two countries in North Africa–Egypt and Libya, as well as Arabs (Acts 2:9, 11). Although the earliest Christians might not have used the expression "Pentecostal," they perpetuated the dynamic of the Christian Pentecost as the source of the growth and empowerment of the church.[6] The primary stimulus of the growth of Pentecostalism today is to be found in its recipients' experiences of the Holy Spirit, resulting in a capacity for cross-cultural transmission and cross-cultural transplantation, a phenomenon that Lamin Sanneh calls the "translatability of the gospel."[7]

We can distinguish at least two categories of Pentecostalism in this region: indigenous Pentecostal groups that operate under a veil of secrecy due to constraints imposed by Islam and those founded as branches of Pentecostal groups from abroad. The indigenous Pentecostal groups are largely constituted as house churches and do not hold publicly announced meetings. Those planted by missionaries and expatriates include the Assemblies of God, the Church of God (Cleveland), the Foursquare Gospel Church, the Full Gospel Businessmen's Fellowship International, YWAM (Youth with a Mission), and Christ for all Nations. Churches in the former group are typically independent and hardly ever rely on external assistance, while many groups in the latter category rely on outside funds, literature, and sometimes personnel from mission headquarters in the West. The indigenous Pentecostal groups have embarked on their own mission activities, planting branches in host countries and in other parts of the world by means of a reverse mission process.

Albeit in relatively small numbers, people in the Middle East are attracted to become Pentecostals by two common features, namely, emphasis on a personal religious experience of spiritual rebirth and manifestations of charismatic gifts such as speaking in tongues, prophecy, healing and miracles. Most Pentecostal groups emphasize "holiness" (moral purity). Across the board, they are intensely interested in religious experience rather than in ritual or formal liturgy. Pentecostals in this region, as elsewhere, are noted for preaching a "prosperity gospel." Some have assimilated prosperity ideas from North American Pentecostalism. Yet, the commitment to the gospel of prosperity fits in well with the values of indigenous cultures, where talismans such as the evil eye are displayed in plain sight to ensure prosperity, health, and protection from malevolent spiritual forces. Expatriate African Initiated Christian groups, such as the prophetic churches, have expanded in the Middle East as part of the new African Diaspora. These Pentecostal groups attract people because they are seen to be helping people in their everyday lives.

Modern Pentecostalism was introduced to the Middle East by missionaries associated with Classical Pentecostalism.[8] According to Michael Wilkinson, "Pentecostal mission work is animated by a pneumatology that emphasizes the calling and empowering of the Spirit, the ongoing leading of the Spirit, and signs and wonders to authenticate the work of the Spirit."[9] As with other Western missionaries, Pentecostals in North Africa and West Asia largely failed to gain adherents from non-Christian peoples and gained most of their converts by proselytizing Orthodox and Catholic Christian communities rather than by evangelizing non-Christians. Even today, leaders of the historic indigenous churches of the Middle East express resentment toward Pentecostals and Evangelicals for weakening their communities against Islam. At present, there is no formal cooperation between the Middle East Council of Churches and any Pentecostal body in this region of the world.[10]

Pentecostalism came to the Arabian Peninsula later than to the Maghreb and the Levant. Currently, the presence of Pentecostalism in the region has increased due to economic migration related to globalization. Many countries in this region, especially the Persian Gulf countries, have great wealth from oil but acute labor shortages, which they have met by means of foreign workers. Transient migrant workers make up two-thirds of the labor force in these countries. South Asians constitute the largest non-Arab expatriate community in the Gulf States. Temporary migrants are accorded no political representation. Their wages are less than their Western or Arab counterparts. Compelled by the pressures of globalization, these migrants find better economic prospects as contract workers than they would as free laborers in their home countries. In the 1960s and 1970s, multiple Christian congregations were established in several Gulf States, primarily in urban centers. The rulers of the Gulf States have been very tolerant toward expatriate Christians, even donating land for the construction of church edifices. Every Friday, thousands of Christians gather to worship the God of the Bible, often at the same time as Muslims meet for Friday prayers in their mosques. Pentecostal churches are among the several expatriate groups of Christians in the Arabian Peninsula.[11]

Regional Survey

How transnational Pentecostals relate to the Islamic states and societies of the Middle East can be surmised from a survey of the Pentecostal presence in selected regions. Like all branches of Christianity in this part of the world, Pentecostal evangelization has had to contend with the obstacles imposed by Islamic hegemony.

Maghreb (North Africa)

In terms of visible appearance, Pentecostals are few and far between in the Maghreb, aside from Egypt. In Algeria, there is only one officially recognized Pentecostal congregation affiliated with the Assemblies of God. However, the Pentecostal presence in Algeria might be more robust, judging from a 2006 law establishing "conditions and regulations for the practice of non-Muslim services."[12] This law was aimed specifically at Evangelical and Pentecostal preachers who had gained conversions among indigenous Berbers. Many of these converts remain "secret believers."[13]

Prior to the outbreak of war in Libya in 2011, more Christians lived in Tripoli and Benghazi than in any other city in North Africa, aside from Egypt. Since Muammar Qaddafi's fall in 2011, Islamist groups have harassed Christians and forced them to convert. A small indigenous Christian community does exist. However, most of the Christians in Libya are foreigners working in the country. A sizeable number of Pentecostals in Libya are migrant workers in the oilfields from sub-Saharan African countries.[14]

The Assemblies of God have a substantial presence in Egypt. These churches continue to support the orphanage established by the pioneer Pentecostal missionary Lillian Trasher, in Asyut and a small prenatal clinic in a poor section of Cairo. Febe Armanios reports that in the past fifty years, a charismatic renewal movement has emerged among Egypt's Copts:

> especially within communication outlets, narratives of healing and the miraculous, prayer and worship styles, evangelization and social services. Coptic believers have been actively searching for multiple ways to harvest the redemptory powers of the Holy Spirit and to feel directly connected to/touched by the divine.[15]

Coptic clergy and laity have turned to charismatic Christianity, mostly couched in familiar Orthodox terminology, in order to strengthen belief, spirituality, and communality.[16]

Levant (Israel, Lebanon, Jordan, Syria, and Iraq)

Pentecostals occupy a small yet vital and growing sector of the Christian space in Israel, Lebanon, Jordan, Syria, and Iraq. Pentecostal churches in Israel include local branches of international denominations (the Assemblies of God, the Church of God, the Church of God of Prophecy), independent charismatic ministries (Cornerstone, Voice of Healing, Congregation of the Lamb on Mount Zion, House of Bread Church, Christ to the Nations), African Initiated Churches (Church of Pentecost, Resurrection Power, Living Bread Ministries International, Beth-El Prayer Ministry), independent local churches in the West Bank (Immanuel Church) and Messianic churches in Israel (King of Kings Assembly). Of these churches, the two most vital indigenous congregations are the King of Kings Assembly in Jerusalem and Immanuel Church in Bethlehem.[17]

Large numbers of non-indigenous Christians, compelled by global poverty, have migrated to Israel. Many of these workers from Eastern Europe, Asia, and Africa are Pentecostals. Much to the dismay of the Israeli government, a growing number of African migrant Pentecostals have established themselves in Israel. They found their way to Israel between the late 1980s and early 2000s, coming mostly from Ghana, Kenya, and Nigeria.[18] The opportunity for migrant labor emerged as a result of the first Palestinian *Intifada* (Uprising) in 1987–91. In response, the Israeli government retaliated by erecting checkpoints in order to control the movement of Palestinian workers into Israel. This resulted in a wholesale exclusion of non-citizen Palestinians in the West Bank and Gaza from working in Israel, causing dramatic changes in the Israeli labor market. Whereas Palestinians constituted four and a half percent of the Israeli labor force in 1993, and migrant workers accounted for just over one and a half percent, by 2000, the proportion of Palestinians had dropped to 3.3 percent, and that of migrant workers had risen to 8.7 percent. By 2003, the number of migrant workers had increased to ten-twelve percent of the labor force. About half of the migrant workers came to Israel as documented laborers, the other half as undocumented. The number of government permits issued to employ overseas workers increased from 4,200 in 1990 to 9,600 in 1993, and then tenfold to 103,000 in 1996. By 2000, the Israeli economy had become heavily dependent on transnational workers.[19]

In the same period, other pathways were available for African migration to Israel, some legal and others illegal. Large numbers of Ethiopians came to Israel seeking asylum from political and military conflict, and others came under the right of *aliyah*.[20] In addition, growing streams of undocumented migrants made their way to Israel by means of what has been termed the "tourist loophole."[21] Given Israel's profound archaeological, biblical and religious significance for several world religions, the Holy Land attracted pilgrims, some of whom extended the period of stay allowed by their tourist visas and slipped unnoticed into the Israeli economy as undocumented workers. This loophole facilitated the entry of tens of thousands of migrants from West African and other countries. The African migrant workers replaced the newly excluded low-paid, low-skilled Palestinian workers from the West Bank and Gaza, cleaning houses and offices, serving in restaurants and hotels, caring for children and the elderly, and performing other low-wage, physically demanding jobs. The majority of the African migrant workers settled in the most affordable neighborhoods of Tel Aviv, especially around the old Central Bus Station, where they found relatively cheap housing, discount shops and food markets, good bus transportation to all parts of the city and country, and the company of other migrant workers, including Africans.[22]

Most African migrants to Israel joined a church made up of fellow Africans. These churches tended to be Pentecostal and/or affiliated with the African Initiated Christianity (AIC) movement. The Africans in Israel derived spiritual, social, economic, and political benefits from their churches. In fact, the African churches became the center of the lively African community in Israel. At their peak, more than forty such congregations were meeting in the southern part of Tel Aviv. Theologically, the African churches in Israel can be identified with all three types of AIC churches: African-Ethiopian churches, Prophet Healing churches (also called Spiritual or Zionist churches) and neo-charismatic churches. Most of the Africans interviewed by Galia Sabar in her ethnological research described their churches as "Pentecostal."[23] The African migrant churches emphasize the power and gifts of the Holy Spirit: the experience of the Holy Spirit in trances, healing, and deliverance; the existence of witches and spirits; narrative theology; and the prosperity gospel. As with Pentecostal churches worldwide, the services in these churches provide a release and a feeling of community and togetherness. The churches functioned as an extended family in providing support for members by means of rites of passage for marriage and death. Most African churches maintained their connection with Africa by offering lectures and seminars on political issues in their home countries. Church leaders assumed a political role in lobbying for improved living conditions and legal status. The churches provided not only a sense of belonging but also practical assistance. Church members helped new arrivals find housing and work, explained the bus routes, taught housecleaning skills, and shared tips about wages, hours, work conditions, and how to get along with Israelis. Finally, the vitality of the African churches in a Jewish state with a small Christian minority augments the importance of the African churches.[24]

In Lebanon, there are three Assemblies of God congregations and a Muslim Background Believers church with fifty congregations. Many of the Pentecostals in Lebanon are migrant workers from Africa and the Philippines, some of whom are undocumented. In her research on Ethiopian Pentecostal churches in Lebanon, Bina Fernandez found that these churches afforded migrant female domestic workers with a sense of support, community, and agency that functioned as a means of resisting domination by oppressive Muslim employers. More than 5,000 people from many nationalities attend an annual festival of Pentecostal churches in Lebanon for a weekend in March. According to Fernandez, the Pentecostal churches have created a safe space for migrant workers, in which forms of mutual support create a counterculture, empowering their members to navigate the underground world of undocumented workers.[25]

In Jordan, there are sixteen Assemblies of God congregations. Emphasizing conversion and baptism of the Spirit, these congregations are concentrated in the Amman area and are foreign-led. They operate a healthcare clinic in Amman. One Pentecostal congregation with one hundred adult members is affiliated with the Church of God (Cleveland). This congregation is Holiness-Pentecostal, emphasizing conversion, sanctification, and baptism of the Spirit. It is expatriate-led.[26]

In Syria, the only known Pentecostals are a network of house churches that meet secretly. Prior to the American invasion of Iraq in 2003, there was a substantial Pentecostal community in the country. However, the unintended consequences of the invasion have been devastating for all the Christian communities and many Pentecostals are among those who have fled from the country.[27]

Arabian Gulf

Many who come to the Gulf States for work as domestic workers are Pentecostals. In Saudi Arabia, they play a conduit role in connecting other domestic workers with Pentecostal fellowships. Pentecostals have excelled at attracting expatriate workers of Chinese, Ethiopian, Korean, Filipino, and South Asian extraction. In many instances, Saudi employers confiscate the passports and identity papers of their domestic workers and allow them to leave home only once a week to go to church. In these cases, Pentecostal churches function as sanctuaries for undocumented workers who have freelanced to escape oppressive conditions.[28]

More than half of Kuwait's population does not hold citizenship. Of these, most are foreign workers from the Levant, South Asia, the Philippines, and Ethiopia. Foreign workers comprise a large part of the membership of the churches in Kuwait. Two Arab Pentecostal churches in Kuwait are known for effective evangelism.[29] The government of Bahrain allows expatriate Christians to worship freely as long as they do not evangelize Muslims, which is illegal. No Bahrainis admit to being Christians, but there are a considerable number of secret believers. Most of the Christians are expatriate workers from India, the Philippines, the United Kingdom, and the USA. House churches are active, particularly among Filipino expatriate workers.[30] Although no outreach to the indigenous population is officially permitted in the United Arab Emirates, religious freedom is enjoyed by Christian groups. The ruling families have loaned land to Christian communities and allowed the construction of compounds for church meetings. Immigrant workers constitute the strength of Christianity in the United Arab Emirates (UAE).[31] Oman tolerates (and is mildly supportive of) the religions of its foreign workforce. Christian proselytism of Muslims is forbidden; therefore, virtually all of Oman's Christian population is foreign. Since 1973, expatriates have been freely allowed to worship according to their religious affiliations, build religious compounds, and proselytize, among other expatriates.[32] In Qatar, the government recently adopted a policy of allowing expatriate Christians to worship in public and construct church buildings. Qataris who accept Christian faith outside of Qatar have faced ostracism by their families when they publicly acknowledge their conversion. There are practically no indigenous professing Christians in Qatar. Almost all of the Christians in Qatar are expatriate workers.[33]

The Yemeni constitution stipulates that proselytizing Muslims is strictly prohibited. If a Muslim seeks information from another religion, this is considered apostasy, punishable by death. Nonetheless, it is thought that there are some secret believers in Yemen. The national Christians that exist are crypto-Christians. Although churches are not officially recognized in Yemen, non-Muslims are allowed to practice their religion under strict restrictions. Most Christians in Yemen are migrant workers of Middle Eastern, Ethiopian, Indian, and European extraction. An Ethiopian Cultural Center is located in Sana, where Ethiopian domestic workers can make connections, celebrate cultural and religious occasions, and find help with housing and work.[34] There are no known Pentecostal churches in Yemen.[35]

Conclusion

A growing number of African migrant Pentecostals have ensconced themselves in the Maghreb, the Levant and Arabian Peninsula, coming mostly from Ethiopia, Ghana, Kenya, Nigeria, and the Philippines. Compelled by the pressures of globalization, these migrants find better economic prospects as contract workers than they could as free laborers in their home countries. Every Friday, thousands of Christians gather for worship, often at the same time as Muslims meet for Friday prayers in their mosques. Pentecostal churches are among the fasting growing expatriate groups of Christians in the Middle East.[36]

Most African migrants affiliate with a church made up of fellow Africans. The African migrant churches emphasize the power and gifts of the Holy Spirit; the experience of the Holy Spirit in trances, healing, and deliverance; the existence of witches and spirits; narrative theology; and the prosperity gospel. As with Pentecostal churches worldwide, the services in these churches provide an emotional release.

African transnational Pentecostals derive spiritual, social, economic, and political benefits from their churches. Church members help new arrivals find housing and work, explain the bus routes, teach housecleaning skills, and share tips about wages, hours, and work conditions. These churches function as a matrix of the lively African community in Diaspora, affording migrant workers with support, community, and agency, functioning as a means of resisting domination by oppressive local employers. Pentecostal churches have created a safe space for migrant workers, creating a counterculture of mutual support and empowering their members to navigate the underground world of undocumented workers.

Pentecostalism in the Middle East does not share the bright prospects for growth projected for the movement worldwide.[37] The demographic status of Pentecostalism in this region corresponds to that of other segments of Christianity. According to the Pew Research Center, the Middle East-North Africa region is home to less than one percent of the world's Christians. Only about four percent of the region's residents are Christian.[38] Although Christianity began in this area, it now has the lowest overall number of Christians and the smallest share of its population that is Christian. Christians are a minority in every country. Almost half of the Christians in the region live in either Egypt or Lebanon. Pentecostals represent a relatively small segment of the Christian population in this region and are faced with formidable obstacles to the growth of their movement due to the spread of Islamic extremism. Yet, we can conclude based on our findings that at the margins of the societies of this region, a growing number of people continue to encounter the Spirit of God and experience profound transformation, evidencing the markers of Pentecostal spirituality.

Notes

1 For current literature on migrant workers in the Middle East, see Bina Fernandez, "Household Help? Ethiopian Women Domestic Workers' Labor Migration to the Gulf Countries," *Asian and Pacific Migration Journal* 20:3–4 (2011), 433–457; Bina Fernandez and Marin de Regt, "Making Home in the World: Migrant Domestic Workers in the Middle East," in Fernandez and de Regt, eds., *Migrant Domestic Workers in the Middle East: The Home and the World* (New York: Palgrave Macmillan, 2014), 1–26; Ninna Nyberg Sorenson and Ida Marie Vammen, "Who Cares? Transnational Families in Debates on Migration and Development," *New Diversities* 16:2 (2014), 89–108, http://newdiversities.mmg.mpg.de/wp-content/uploads/2015/01/2014_16-02_07_Sorensen_Vammen.pdf.

2 Kathleen Newland, "Migration as a Factor in Development and Poverty Reduction," Migration Information Source, Migration Policy Institute, June 1, 2003, https://www.migrationpolicy.org/article/migration-factor-development-and-poverty-reduction, accessed May 26, 2019.

3 Diana Tietjens Myers, "Rethinking Coercion for a World of Poverty and Transnational Migration," in Diana Tietjens Myers, ed., *Poverty, Agency, and Human Rights* (Oxford: Oxford University Press, 2014).

4 Rachel Sabates-Wheeler, Ricardo Sabates, and Adriana Castaldo, "Tackling Poverty-Migration Linkages: Evidence from Ghana and Egypt," *Social Indicators Research* 87:2 (June 2008), 307–328.

5 Maria Gallotti, "Migrant Domestic Workers Across the World: Global and Regional Estimates," International Labour Organization, 2015, http://www.ilo.org/wcmsp5/groups/public/---ed_protect/---protrav/---migrant/documents/briefingnote/wcms_490162.pdf, accessed May 26, 2019.

6 J. Kwabena Asamoah-Gyadu, "Pentecostalism and the Transformation of the African Christian Landscape," in Martin Lindhardt, ed., *Pentecostalism in Africa: Presence and Impact of Pneumatic Christianity in Postcolonial Societies* (Leiden: Brill, 2014), 105.

7 Roswith Gerloff and Abraham Ako Akrong, "Independents, 1910–2010," in Todd M. Johnson and Kenneth R. Ross, eds., *Atlas of Global Christianity*, 1910-2010 (Edinburgh: Edinburgh University Press, 2009), 76.

8 Allan H. Anderson, Spreading Fires: *The Missionary Nature of Early Pentecostalism* (Maryknoll: Orbis, 20017), 4.

9 Michael Wilkinson, "Charles W. Chawner and the Missionary Impulse of the Hebden Mission," in Peter Althouse and Michael Wilkinson, eds., *Winds from the North: Canadian Contributions to the Pentecostal Movement* (Leiden: Brill, 2010), 52.

10 Cecil M. Robeck, Jr., "Christian Unity and Pentecostal Mission: A Contradiction," in Wonsuk Ma, Veli-Matti Karkkainen, and J. Kwabena Asamoah-Gyadu, eds., *Pentecostal Mission and Global Christianity* (Oxford: Regnum Books International, 2014), 206.

11 T. V. Thomas, "South Asian Diaspora Christianity in the Persian Gulf," in H. Chandler Im and Amos Yong, eds., *Global Diasporas and Mission* (Eugene: Wipf & Stock, 2014), 119–121.

12 Matthias Riemenschneider, "The Situation of Christians in the Middle East and North Africa," *KAS International Reports* (Konrad Adenauer Stiftung, 2011), 12, http://www.jstor.org/stable/resrep09942, accessed May 26, 2019.

13 Tom Heneghan, "Christian Missionaries Stir Unease in North Africa," *Reuters*, December 15, 2008, http://blogs.reuters.com/faithworld/2008/12/15/christian-missionaries-stir-unease-in-north-africa/, accessed May 26, 2019; Riemenschneider, 12.

14 Paul-Gordon Chandler, "Turmoil in Tripoli," *Christian Century* 128:7 (May 2011), 11; Fredrick Nzwili, "Christians in Libya Uneasy about Move to Sharia Law," *Christian Century* 131:4 (February 2014), 216; Riemenschneider, 7.

15 Febe Armanios, "The Coptic Charismatic Renewal in Egypt: Historical Roots and Recent Developments," (International Association of Coptic Studies Quadrennial Congress, Rome, Italy, September 2012), http://www.orthodoxchristianity.net/forum/index.php?topic=55503.40;imode, accessed January 30, 2016.

16 Allan H. Anderson, "'Stretching Out Hands to God': Origins and Development of Pentecostalism in Africa," in Martin Lindhardt, ed., *Pentecostalism in Africa: Presence and Impact of Pneumatic Christianity Postcolonial Societies* (Leiden, Brill, 2014), 57.

17 Christians represent a mere two percent of the population of Israel. Christians in Israel amount to 161,000 out of a total population of 8,345,000. Of these, 127,000 are Arab Christians. About forty-five percent are Catholic, forty percent are Orthodox, and forty percent fall under the category of "other." Jewish Virtual Library, https://www.jewishvirtuallibrary.org/jsource/Society_&_Culture/newpop.html, accessed May 9, 2015. It is estimated that from 6,000 to 15,000 Israelis are adherents of Messianic Judaism, some of whom are Pentecostals. See Paul A. Pomerville, *The New Testament Case against Christian Zionism* (Seattle: CreateSpace, 2015), 150. In Palestine there are about 50,000 Christians in the West Bank and 1,000 in Gaza out of a total population of approximately 4.5 million. Christians comprise approximately two percent of the population of the West Bank and one percent in Gaza. These estimates

cannot be verified because the Palestinian Authority does not use a census to obtain population statistics. Christian groups in the West Bank and Gaza include Eastern Orthodoxy, Oriental Orthodoxy, Catholicism (Eastern and Western rites), Anglicanism, Protestantism, and Pentecostalism, concentrated mainly in East Jerusalem, Ramallah, Nablus, and Bethlehem. See also "Palestinian Christians in the Holy Land," Institute for Middle East Understanding, http://imeu.org/article/palestinian-christians-in-the-holy-land, accessed May 9, 2015.

18 Sarah S. Willen, "Introduction," in Sarah S. Willen, ed., *Transnational Migration to Israel in Global Comparative Context* (New York: Macmillan Palgrave, 2013), 9.

19 Willen, *Transnational Migration*, 11.

20 Steven Kaplan and Hagar Salamon, "Ethiopian Jews in Israel: A Part of the People or Apart from the People?" in Uzi Rebhun and Chaim I. Waxman, eds., *Jews in Israel: Contemporary and Cultural Patterns* (Lebanon, NH: Brandeis University Press, 2004), 118.

21 Willen, *Transnational Migration*, 12.

22 Dafna Strauss, "The Black Diaspora in Israel, 1965–2011," http://www.blackpast.org/perspectives/black-diaspora-israel-1965-2011, accessed April 30, 2015.

23 Galia Sabar, "African Christianity in the Jewish State: Adaptation, Accommodation and Legitimation of Migrant Workers' Churches, 1990-2003," *Journal of Religion in Africa* 34:4 (2004), 419.

24 Galia Sabar, "The Rise and Fall of African Migrant Churches: Transformations in African Religious Discourse and Practice in Tel Aviv," in Sarah S. Willen, ed., *Transnational Migration to Israel in Global Comparative Context* (New York: Macmillan Palgrave, 2013), 190–196.

25 Bina Fernandez, "Degrees of (Un)Freedom: The Exercise of Agency by Ethiopian Migrant Domestic Workers in Kuwait and Lebanon," in Bina Fernandez and Marin de Regt, eds., *Migrant Domestic Workers in the Middle East: The Home and the World* (New York: Palgrave Macmillan, 2014), 51, 57–61, 64–68.

26 "Mission Atlas Project: Jordan," www.worldmap.org/Jordan.html, accessed January 31, 2016.

27 J. Boozee, "Syria," in Stanley M. Burgess and Eduard M. Van Der Maas, eds., *The New International Dictionary of Pentecostal and Charismatic Movements* (Grand Rapids: Zondervan, 2002), 9–10.

28 Pardis Mahdavi, "Immobilized Migrancy: Inflexible Citizenship and Flexible Practices among Migrants in the Gulf," in Bina Fernandez and Marin de Regt, eds., *Migrant Domestic Workers in the Middle East: The Home and the World* (New York: Palgrave Macmillan, 2014), 75–93.

29 David B. Barrett, George T. Kurian, and Todd M. Johnson, eds., *World Christian Encyclopedia* vol. 1, 2nd ed. (Oxford: Oxford University Press, 2001), 437–438.

30 Patrick Johnstone and Jason Mandryk, *Operation World* (Cumbria, UK: Paternoster Lifestyle, 2001), 92–93.

31 Johnstone and Mandryk, *Operation World*, 647–649.

32 Johnstone and Mandryk, *Operation World*, 498; Barrett et al., eds., *World Christian Encyclopedia*, 568–69.

33 "Mission Atlas Project: Middle East – Qatar," www.worldmap.org/qatar.html, accessed December 29, 2015; Johnstone and Mandryk, *Operation World*, 532-33.

34 Marina de Regt, "Ethiopian Women in the Middle East: The Case of Migrant Domestic Workers in Yemen," (African Studies Center Seminar, University of Amsterdam, February, 2007), 7.

35 Barrett et al., eds., *World Christian Encyclopedia*, 810–811.

36 Thomas, "South Asian Diaspora," 119.

37 Gina A. Bellofatto and Todd M. Johnson, "Key Findings of Christianity in its Global Context, 1970-2020," *International Bulletin of Missionary Research* 37:3 (2013), 158; Julie Ma and Allan H. Anderson, "Pentecostals (Renewalists), 1910–2010," in Todd M. Johnson and Kenneth R. Ross, eds., *Atlas of Global Christianity*, 1910–2010 (Edinburgh: Edinburgh University Press, 2009), 102.

38 "Global Christianity—A Report on the Size and Distribution of the World's Christian Population," Pew Research Center, 63, http://www.pewforum.org/files/2011/12/Christianity-fullreport-web.pdf, accessed January 30, 2016.

21 Spirit-Empowered Apostolic Ministry to the Poor: Through the Lens of Three Ministries

John Thompson

Abstract

Apostolic leaders are "sent ones" who also lead the body of Christ as a "sent" people into the world. The apostles in Jerusalem reminded the Apostle Paul in his ministry to the Gentiles to "remember the poor." This chapter examines the nature of the apostolic calling, its intersection with ministry to the poor, and the role of the Holy Spirit in ministry to the poor. The life stories and observations of three Spirit-empowered apostolic leaders actively engaged in caring for the poor are presented as lenses for examining the role of the Holy Spirit in ministry to the poor, the role of church leadership in serving the poor, and the challenges facing Spirit-empowered ministry to the poor. These apostolic leadership describe how the Holy Spirit initiates ministry to the poor, does the miraculous in the midst of ministry to the poor, and gives discernment for effective ministry to the poor.

Introduction

A convergence of ministry trends places the poor at the epicenter of apostolic ministry today. The emphases on unreached peoples, church planting, missional ministry, and holistic ministry are initiatives from the heart of God in recent decades and today. Almost 6,000 unreached people groups and the fifty least evangelized megacities reside in the 10/40 window, and this is where over eighty percent of the most desperate poor of the world live who earn less than a dollar a day.[1] Consequently, reaching the least reached necessitates engagement with the poor. "Missional" terminology has dominated ministry literature in the past two decades. As churches in the affluent West experiment with a missional ministry, there seems to be a maturation of understanding moving from benign community projects to a deeper engagement of meeting real needs, caring for people in poverty, and a rising passion for social justice.

The missional emphasis in church ministry in the West coincides with a healing of the great divorce in mission work. The first half of the twentieth century witnessed a great rift between evangelism and social action along the divide between evangelical and liberal Protestant communities. The tectonic plates have been coming back together over the past half century so that today holistic ministry and the call for social justice is being championed in evangelical and charismatic circles. Ministry to the poor is taking center stage again as it was in the early centuries of the church and at various moments and places throughout church history. The Spirit of God seems to be reviving and deepening the call and commitment of the body of Christ to care for the poor.

Apostolic leaders play an important role in leading the body of Christ to serve the poor. Apostolic ministries and leaders push and pull the church beyond natural socio-economic and geographic boundaries to extend the kingdom of God across typical human barriers. An apostle is a "sent one." Consequently, apostolic leaders instinctively call the body of Christ to missional (sent) ministry. These leaders and their ministries in the body of Christ embrace and often embody a missional ecclesiology. God is a sending God who sent himself into the world. Likewise, through the empowerment of His Spirit, God sends His people into the local community, the national landscape and to the far reaches of the earth. In this mission of "going," many apostolic leaders are heeding the words of the apostolic leadership core in Jerusalem (James, Cephas, and John) to the apostle Paul. They charged him to "remember the poor" in fulfilling his apostolic ministry to the Gentiles (Gal 2:7–10).[2]

This command to "remember the poor" is being pursued in dynamic ways by three Spirit-empowered apostolic leaders interviewed for this article.[3] While numerous Spirit-empowered apostolic ministries serve the poor around the world, these three ministries are connected to the author through personal relationships and ministry networks. The interview questions sought understanding of each leader's ministry calling to the poor, their understanding of how the Holy Spirit informs and shapes their work with the poor, and their observations about Spirit-empowered ministry to the poor. Through the lenses of these three Spirit-empowered ministries to the poor, the reader will encounter the observations and reflections of these apostolic ministry practitioners and the present author on the role of the Holy Spirit in ministry to the poor, the role of church leadership in serving the poor and the challenges facing Spirit-empowered ministry to the poor.

Three Apostolic Ministries
Martyn Dunsford – Care and Relief for the Young

Martyn Dunsford is an apostolic leader in Newfrontiers and founder of Care and Relief for the Young (CRY), a ministry to the poor among unreached peoples. Newfrontiers is a Spirit-empowered team of apostolic leaders fostering networks of churches around the world. Martyn works with Newfrontiers in over fifty nations and is a spiritual father to many churches and pastors. His charity organization, CRY, has thirty-six projects in twenty-eight nations seeking "to rescue and restore children and young people broken by poverty, oppression, exclusion, and abuse."[4] CRY projects provide food, water, shelter, and education to children and youth. CRY comes alongside local churches and local individuals who facilitate and lead these ministry projects to the poor.

CRY was founded in 1992, shortly after the fall of communism in Romania. Before the fall of communism in Eastern Europe, Martyn traveled extensively across Eastern Europe, Ukraine, and Russia engaging in apostolic work. After the fall of communism, in response to seven thousand children living on the streets of Bucharest, Martyn began distributing food to kids on the streets and in the heating canals of the city. With the collapse of social services in the early days of post-communism, local officials observed the compassionate action for these refugee children in post-communist Romania and gave Martyn a dilapidated building to house kids. In this moment, CRY was born. CRY renovated the building so that it could house sixty to seventy kids at a time. With a ten-year lease, it took three years to renovate, and over the next seven years, 200 kids resided in the home. As the lease expired, CRY discerned that many of the kids had parents and decided to shift their strategy to get kids back with their parents or into Christian homes. A social services team and fostering agency was formed by CRY, and they worked to integrate the kids into families. Today, many of these kids have grown up and started families of their own. This model was subsequently replicated in Ukraine in partnership with local Ukrainian churches to serve abandoned kids in Ukraine as well.

Meanwhile, at the end of the 1990s, the Kosovo war fostered a refugee crisis in the Balkans. The churches that Martyn had been working with in Albania asked him to help them care for refugees flooding into Albania.

He and his team gathered clothes, hygiene products, food, medical supplies, and tents in the local community of the church he was pastoring in England. CRY sent seven twenty-eight-ton vehicles filled with aid to Albania. CRY and King's Community Church, the church Martyn was pastoring in Southampton, are legally separate entities. However, there is much overlap. His church, through CRY, mobilized the whole village community into social action to serve Kosovo refugees. Stores, clubs, and the local council, all joined in the effort. CRY facilitated their humanitarian work through local churches in Albania. Receiving loving help from Christians, a number of the Kosovo refugees came to faith in Christ and, after returning to Kosovo, started churches. Furthermore, back in England, King's Community Church gained notoriety in the community for its work serving the Kosovo humanitarian crisis. This positive visibility contributed to its own church growth.

CRY was registered separately from the local church so that funds could be raised from non-Christian sources. Today most of CRY's funding comes from outside churches. CRY developed a very creative revenue stream. Fifty percent of the funding for all of the CRY projects is generated from ten resale stores called CRYSHOP located in southern England and the Channel Islands. These stores created a way for people to help those who are far removed geographically from these desperate places of poverty. Individuals can shop in the resale stores, they can donate items for resale, and they can volunteer to work in the stores.

CRY continues to grow. In 2018, they expanded into four new countries (Kenya, Nepal, Greece, and Haiti) with a total of thirty-five projects in twenty-eight nations. In the first quarter of 2019, they began work in two additional countries (Somalia and Kurdistan) and expanded their work in Iraq (providing care packages to families).

Agnes Bangura – Rabboni Missions International

Agnes and the late Gregory Bangura lead Rabboni Missions International, an apostolic ministry serving the poor and expanding the kingdom of God in West Africa. They met in the Ivory Coast in 2003. Before they met and married, Agnes led a ministry called Mission in Jesus' Name. She organized a distribution center for food, clothing, and medicine for the poor. Pastoring a church, she handed out food packages every Sunday to congregants who had no food available at home. She networked with all of the churches in the area as well, asking them to provide names of their members in need so that she could also provide food, clothing and medicine to suffering congregants of other churches. When she met Gregory, he was leading a ministry called Christ Outreach Ministry. He too assisted the poor, but also engaged in church planting work. In fact, by 2009, he had one hundred churches under his care. However, he relinquished oversight of all of them except one so that he could focus on training church planters and raising up new churches. Agnes and Gregory were married in 2004, and together they formed Rabboni Missions International. Rabboni facilitated their mutual apostolic callings with focused work in church planting, literacy, leadership training, and community development.[5]

Ten years ago, in 2009, Agnes and Gregory began to shift their focus from ministry in the relatively more prosperous West African nation of Ivory Coast to the significantly poorer nation of Sierra Leone. They moved to Sierra Leone in August 2010. The poverty in Sierra Leone was and is overwhelming. In April 2019, Sierra Leone was ranked as the eleventh poorest nation in the world.[6] Agnes estimates that seventy percent of the population cannot afford two meals a day, and sixty percent of the population cannot afford the cost of schooling their children, or even the cost of a bed to sleep on. She notes that people are dying simply because they cannot afford to go to the hospital or even to check if their fever is caused by malaria.

Sierra Leone's eleven-year civil war, lasting from 1991–2002, destroyed the infrastructure of the country, and everything came to a standstill for a decade. Children did not go to school, and people did not work. Seventeen years after the conclusion of the civil war, many people still do not have electricity nor running water and cannot even afford the right containers to put their water in, according to Agnes. Only forty-eight percent of the total population is literate today.[7] Agnes observes that the differences between Sierra Leone that other West African nations like Liberia or Ivory Coast is visible (even though Liberia is currently listed as the seventh poorest nation in the world).[8] One can see the suffering caused by poverty in villages and cities across Sierra Leone.

To date, Rabboni Missions International has planted three hundred churches in this Muslim-majority nation (over seventy-eight percent Muslim),[9] facilitated numerous feeding projects, engaged in educational initiatives for children, provided medical assistance, and served villages during the Ebola crisis. Feeding projects include an annual Christmas lunch feeding thousands of children on Christmas day, distributing bags of rice to village imams and pastors, and giving gifts of food to villages. Educational initiatives include running two preschools with ninety-eight children and assisting twelve Christian schools sponsoring some of the school fees for poor children, donating supplies, and even paying some of the teacher salaries. Medical ventures comprise hosting medical mission teams, training clinics for nurses and doctors, and building a nursing and midwifery school. During the Ebola crisis, Rabboni trained whole villages in Ebola prevention methods and distributed disinfectant supplies and food to villagers. They currently host a weekly medical awareness program on the radio called Rabboni Health Talk.

In the early morning hours of January 12, 2019, Gregory Bangura unexpectedly passed into eternity. In the wake of such a great loss for the people of Sierra Leone and all who knew Gregory, Agnes remains steadfast. She shares the same apostolic calling as her late husband and continues to carry the leadership torch of Rabboni Missions International into the future. May Gregory's passion to love and serve the poor be perpetuated and multiplied by all those who had the honor to intersect with his life and ministry.

Stavros Ignatiou – Created Equal

Stavros Ignatiou is an apostolic leader serving refugees and Gypsies around Athens, Greece, and a spiritual father to churches and pastors in Greece, Cyprus, Albania, and several other nations. He pastors two churches (one in Athens and one in Cyprus) and leads a ministry called Created Equal that facilitates his apostolic work with the poor. Stavros was born and raised in Cyprus and came to Athens in 1989, and began working with youth in the church. In the early 1990s, he got involved in refugee ministry when two young Albanian boys showed up in his youth meeting. Albanian refugees flooded all of Greece in the 1990s. By 2001 almost a half million Albanians resided in Greece with a total population of less than 11 million people.[10] According to Stavros, at one point, Athens had the second largest Albanian population for a city after Tirana, Albania. Many are second and third-generation Albanians living in Greece who have never been to Albania. Many Albanians came through the church Stavros served in and became followers of Jesus. Stavros started making trips to Albania, taking humanitarian aid, and through these trips, many people got saved, and churches were started. Most of Stavros' ministry in Athens over the last three decades has focused on serving immigrant peoples.

Five years ago, a new flood of immigrants began to pour into Greece from Syria and other Middle Eastern nations. This immigration flow was different in that they came with nothing, no food, no blankets, and no place to stay. Mass numbers of people were living on the streets seeking to go north into other parts of Europe. Soon the borders closed, and many were stuck in Greece. Stavros immediately began helping these new refugees distributing clothing, feeding people, cooking for them, and bringing doctors to help them. He started a distribution center to receive and distribute donated items from Christian communities in other parts of Europe. He hosts teams throughout the year that serve refugees. In 2018, his ministry distributed thirty-two pallets of baby food, prepared and served 2,550 meals, gave out 400 family food bags, hosted eleven volunteer groups, held two medical clinics, facilitated kids programming for 7,300 kids, and delivered a wide assortment of basic necessities to people in poverty.[11] As the love of Jesus has been expressed to refugees through acts of kindness and gifts of provision, some of these refugees have become followers of Jesus as well. Witness is not intentional nor forced; it just happens naturally. In fact, Stavros asks his team not to come with an agenda to witness, but to come to just express and show love to people. God is blessing this beautiful expression of his own heart for hurting humanity.

Hearing about his service to refugees, the Roma (Gypsy) community contacted Stavros and asked if he could provide them medical help. When he visited their camp of 1,000 Roma people outside of Athens, he was shocked by the level of poverty. The people live in self-made shacks with dirt floors, no electricity, and no running water. Consequently, people are dirty and wear unwashed clothing. Many are sick and have skin infections. Domestic violence is rampant. The government has classified this camp as dangerous with criminal activity. Since the average starting marital age is twelve years old, they met a thirty-five-year-old mother with five grandchildren. Stavros asserts that this is the worst camp in Greece. He goes there because no one else goes there. His stated passion is to go where no one else wants to go. He serves this Roma camp through periodic medical clinics, distribution of food and blankets, playing with the kids, and trying to raise up leaders.

All of this apostolic ministry to the Roma, to refugees, and to churches in Southeastern Europe and the Middle East operated organizationally under the umbrella of the local church he founded and pastors in Athens. However, in 2019 Stavros launched an NGO called Created Equal to carry out these compassion ministries and apostolic functions. The vision of Created Equal is "to see a world where the worth of every human being is seen as equal." The mission is "to promote equality through activities of social justice, education, awareness, and solidarity."[12] This organizational structure separate from the local church provides a more neutral platform enabling Stavros to network more freely with secular organizations, just as CRY does for Martyn.

Considering the Nature of Apostolic Ministry

The stories of Stavros, Agnes, and Martyn all share common elements that will be explored throughout this chapter. The first commonality is that each of them pastored local churches but also established a separate organization for their apostolic work. Though they served as pastors, all three leaders were driven by an overriding external focus to serve hurting people in the surrounding community beyond their local congregations. Their churches were exceptional in engaging the community and gained positive reputations for doing so. Yet, all three saw the need to found independent ministries from their local church to facilitate their apostolic calling.

The Tension Between Apostolic and Local Church Ministry

All three have had to manage the tension between pastoring a local church and leading in the community, nationally, and internationally. Stavros merged his local church with another Athenian congregation whose leader had a strong shepherding gift, thus enabling Stavros to focus primarily on the apostolic work. Martyn eventually stepped out of the lead role in his church but remains there today as an elder. Agnes continues to pastor a local congregation, but for most of the decade of their ministry in Sierra Leone, Gregory did not pastor a local congregation as he poured his life into impacting the local chiefdom and the entire nation. He often remarked, "Agnes is pastoring me!"

This tension between apostolic ministry and local church ministry is exasperated by the Protestant emphasis on local churches. Ralph Winter made a strong historical case for two separate but equal structures in the body of Christ in his seminal article, "The Two Structures of Redemptive Mission," that appeared in the January 1974 issue of *Missiology: An International Review*.[13] Local churches and Paul's missionary band are seen in the New Testament working independently and interdependently. Winter contended that these two structures mirrored the Jewish tradition of both synagogue and Jewish proselytizers at work across the Roman Empire in the first century.[14] The dyadic structure was perpetuated in subsequent centuries in the rise of monasticism in addition to the local parish. The monastic movements spread the good news to distant lands, not local parishes.[15] Winter used the term modalities to refer to the local church/parish structure. He called the second structure, Paul's apostolic band, and the later monastic movements, sodalities. Winter observed that "the Protestant movement started out by attempting to do without any kind of sodality structure."[16] He lamented, "This omission, in my evaluation, represents the greatest error of the Reformation and the greatest weakness of the resulting Protestant tradition."[17] Not until the proliferation of mission societies in the nineteenth century, a sodality structure, did Protestantism began to make great strides in global expansion.

Sam Metcalf described these two redemptive structures of the church as the two legs of the body of Christ.[18] Both are essential and must function independently and interdependently. When the body of Christ is local-church centric, demanding all missionary and community activities to be under the umbrella and control of the local church,[19] the body of Christ hops on one leg. But when both structures are embraced, organized separately, and yet work in concert, the body of Christ leaps, not limps.[20] Alan Hirsch suggested the consequences of a local-church centric ecclesiology is that the gifts of shepherd and teacher have taken center stage, and the other gifts of apostle, prophet, and evangelist were exiled. Thus, the body of Christ cannot come into maturity and fullness.[21]

Individuals gifted to serve as apostles, prophets, and evangelists often struggle with an identity crisis in ministry today. Ministry legitimacy is often tied to pastoring a local church in Spirit-empowered and evangelical

Protestant circles. It seems that the three apostolic leaders interviewed for this article have each been on a journey to break out of the pastor-centric worldview of their faith traditions. Unfortunately, this has even shaped the dominant models for church planting in the West. Church planters usually have apostolic giftings. However, the process of church planting is often rushed because ministry respectability is achieved by pastoring a local congregation. The New Testament and historic model of a three-step church planting process[22] have been compressed to a one-step process of launching Sunday worship as quickly as possible.[23] The unintended consequence is that evangelism, discipleship, and community formation that make up the first two steps are never deeply formed in the DNA of the church, and these three elements then become the perennial struggle for the new church. Apostolic ministry should not be confined to a narrow contemporary approach to church planting. The Apostle Paul engaged in the broader activity of "gospel planting," not the narrower contemporary fixation on "church planting." Paul established many local churches, but it was a byproduct of planting the gospel. Paul speaks of planting and sowing a number of things (1 Cor 9:11; 15:36–37; 42–44; 2 Cor 9:5–9; Gal 6:6–10; 1 Cor 3:5–16), but none of them are the local church. Paul's focus is on planting the good news of Jesus and laying a foundation of Jesus Christ. Paul does establish local churches, appoints elders, gives instructions on the worship gatherings, etc. So, he does work to establish local congregations. However, it is the good news of Jesus and his kingdom that Paul plants/sows. Today, the tail may be wagging the dog. Apostolic ministers (as well as prophets and evangelists) need to break free from skewed expectations within their faith communities.

The Apostolic Calling

To explore apostolic ministry to the poor, first, one must define the apostolic role. The New Testament uses the word apostle eighty times. There are twenty specific individuals called apostles in the New Testament. The twenty include the twelve apostles appointed by Jesus during his earthly ministry as well as Matthias (chosen to replace Judas), Paul, Barnabas (Acts 14:4, 14), Adnronicus (Rom 16:7), Junia (Rom 16:7), Epaphroditus (Phil 2:25), Silvanus (1 Thes 1:1, 2:6) and Timothy (1 Thes 1:1, 2:6). Paul mentions apostles in Corinth without providing individual names (1 Cor 9:5; 12:28). Apostles are listed first in the five-fold ministry gifts in Ephesians 4:11–12. The apostle, prophet, evangelist, shepherd, and teacher are given by Christ "for the equipping of the saints for the work of service, to the building up of the body of Christ." Their purpose impacts the saints and the body of Christ. Paul does not say specifically the local church though there is an indirect relationship since saints are found in local churches, and local churches are part of the body of Christ. Certainly, these leadership gifts can function in the local church, but that is not dealt with directly in Ephesians chapter four. We do see that the church at Antioch had prophets and teachers on the leadership team, so these five can serve in local church leadership (Acts 13:1). Paul was not on this team. Apostles were not listed because he and Barnabas had not yet been sent out to begin their apostolic work. Paul likely was one of the "teachers" on the list. Interestingly, shepherds (pastors) are not mentioned in the Antioch church.

What type of leadership does the apostolic ministry gift provide the body of Christ? According to Mike Breen, an apostle is "One who is sent out. Apostles are visionary and pioneering, always pushing into new territory. They like to establish new churches or ministries. They come up with new, innovative means to do kingdom work."[24] The apostle is entrepreneurial. He/she seeks to extend and mobilize others to extend God's kingdom to new places and new people. They are adventurous and comfortable with risk.

Alan Hirsch proposed two kinds of apostles based on Paul and Peter. Paul served as an apostle to the Gentiles, leading an apostolic team across the eastern part of the Roman Empire, planting the gospel and subsequently establishing churches in cities where the gospel had not yet gone. Peter served as an apostle to the Jews. Whereas Paul extended and established Christianity in new places, Peter went to Joppa and Lydia, predominantly Jewish cities. Then through his encounter with Cornelius in Caesarea, Peter "reframes the identity and mission of the church."[25] Peter reshaped the church's understanding of their mission and identity. There was an evangelist already in Caesarea. Philip was living there. But God sent for Peter at Joppa because it was not just about winning the centurion to the Lord. God would use this event through Peter to reshape the thinking of the body of Christ. Consequently, a key apostle was needed. "Whereas Pauline apostles tend to cross cultures to pioneer new missional communities, Petrine apostles tend to mobilize existing communities to become and remain missional."[26] So Petrine type apostles focus more on innovation in the existing church, and Pauline type apostles focus more on new fields of ministry.

In addition to the "going" nature of apostolic ministry, apostles lay a foundation. This task is shared with the prophetic ministry gift as well. Paul instructed the Ephesians that God's household had been "build on the foundation of the apostles and prophets" (Eph 2:19–20). To the Corinthians, Paul referred to his personal calling to lay foundations: "According to the grace of God which was given to me, like a master builder I laid a foundation, and another is building on it" (1 Cor 3:10). A master builder envisions the end product and lays the right foundation. In laying a foundation, apostles appoint leaders for local congregations and for the body of Christ. Jesus selected, developed, and deployed twelve disciples. Later these twelve, set up guidelines for selecting leaders for the ministry of feeding widows. Peter set guidelines for filling the vacant leadership spot left by Judas' defection. Paul and his apostolic team appointed elders in local congregations in numerous cities. If ministry to the poor is an essential for the believer, the local church, and the body of Christ, then the apostle should pioneer ministries that serve the poor globally, encourage local church ministry to the poor, and set the heart of compassion in the foundation of new local churches.

Local Church Leadership and the Apostolic Leadership Gift

When the New Testament speaks specifically about local church leadership, it uses four terms: overseers, elders, leaders, and deacons. "Elders" is used twenty times to refer to church leaders in the local church setting are always mentioned in the plural. Paul appointed elders to lead local churches sometime after converts had been won and a gathering established. "Overseer" is used six times and is synonymous with the elder role and yet distinct from deacons. "Leaders" appears four times, but only in two places (Heb 13 and Luke 22). Similarly, "deacons" appear six times, but only in two places (1 Tim 3 and Phil 1:1). The scriptures say the least about what deacons do, only that they serve. Elders, overseers, and leaders are all generic terms for local church leadership. They are interchangeable terms, and all are listed in the plural. Along with deacons, these four terms are the titles used for leadership in the local church.

Ephesians 4:11 speaks of five leadership gifts or types, and none of the four generic terms listed above are included. One difference between these two categories of leadership is that elders, overseers, leaders, and deacons are appointed by people, but these five gifts are given by Christ. The five ministry gifts are given to equip individuals for service and to build up the body of Christ. That could happen in a local congregation but is not bound to that context. Certainly, local church leadership teams include people with these giftings. The leadership team in Antioch had both prophets and teachers.

Unfortunately, in many contemporary Protestant circles, the pastor is the dominant generic term used to refer to key church leaders. "Pastor" only occurs once in New Testament translations, and it is in the Ephesians fivefold ministry gifts list. Everywhere else in the New Testament, the same word is translated "shepherd," which is more descriptive and helpful in understanding the type of leadership this gift provides to the body of Christ.

It seems then that God gifts individuals to serve the body of Christ. These five gifts, and possibly other gifts, are recognized by the faith community and consequently are appointed to leadership teams in local churches. Therefore, local churches are led by people who possess some of the Ephesian four ministry gifts. Mega churches, for example, are often led by individuals with the gifting of the apostle, prophet, or evangelist, but not the shepherd gift. Yet, these giftings can frustrate local churches in which relational shepherding of the congregation is needed. Apostolic leaders seem to chafe against the confines of local church ministry.

Serving the Poor

Having established a description of the apostolic leadership gift as well as the importance of both sodalities and modalities in the body of Christ, we can now explore the contours of apostolic ministry to the poor. Inherent in the Christian faith is the necessity to love our neighbor, especially the poor and abused. This is not an option, but a given of the Christian faith. God "executes justice for the orphan and the widow and shows his love for the alien by giving him food and clothing," and therefore, his people must also "show . . . love for the alien," and help the desperately poor (Deut 10:18). James succinctly states, "Pure and undefiled religion in the sight of our God and Father is this: to visit orphans and widows in their distress, and to keep oneself unstained by the world" (James 1:27). Jesus declared in the parable of the sheep and the goats that the Son of Man would judge people based on what they did or did not do for the hungry, the thirsty, the naked, the stranger, and the prisoner (Matt 25:31–46). In congruence with these biblical injunctions, the book of Acts described the early church with a robust feeding program for widows (Acts 6:1–7), and 2 Corinthians detailed the coordination of local congregations sending aid to those suffering from famine in Palestine (2 Cor 8–9). The Church Fathers also describe a church dedicated to helping the poor.[27] Rupen Das contends that in the first six centuries of the church, "the central truth through all the teaching was that the only way one could demonstrate that they were true followers of Christ, was if they showed mercy and compassion towards the poor." If the church today is to follow the biblical mandate and early church example of ministry to the poor, church leaders must teach and organize believers for this Godly orientation toward serving those in need.

"Remember the Poor"

The three apostolic leaders interviewed for this article and the local churches they pastored believe deeply in a biblical mandate for the body of Christ to care for the poor. These three apostolic leaders also personally embrace the charge given to the Apostle Paul to "remember the poor" in Galatians 2:10. Agnes Bangura recounted:

> One thing that God spoke to us about was in the book of Galatians chapter two and verse ten. God seriously spoke to us about that. So, what we do when we come in a place, like Sierra Leone, is to identify things that people always come to ask us for. And we would investigate what the real needs of the people are. So, in Sierra Leone, we identified hunger. We identified education. We identified health. We identified three areas where . . . the Lord drew our attention. . . . Also, we saw this as an opportunity because we are in [a] Muslim dominated area. We saw it as a way for us to be able to . . . meet and to live with the Muslims. And it's an opportunity for us to show the love of Christ. So, we opened ourselves up to the people in need.[28]

Likewise, Martyn Dunsford wrote a book chapter titled, *Apostolic Ministry with Respect to the Poor*. He insisted, "Surely this apostolic injunction was given to emphasize the fact that a significant aspect of apostolic ministry is to care for the poor."[29] In addition to remembering the Jewish poor of Jerusalem, "it indicates an apostolic responsibility to care for the poor cross-culturally and trans-nationally as well as for the poor in their own localities."[30] Martyn suggests that the apostles' primary role in ministry to the poor is teaching the church about its responsibilities toward the poor, as well as modeling ministry to the poor through their own personal example. The church responsibilities would include "a basic minimum to seek to provide daily for the daily necessities of life for its 'poor' members" as well as responding "to the needs of the saints, and then all other people, in other regions or nations as God directs and enables."[31] However, he feels that "apostles don't have to be experts on setting up and managing social care projects for the poor."[32] Martyn's advice is in alignment with the apostles' response to the problem with the distribution of food to the Hellenistic widows in Jerusalem. They appointed others to facilitate the feeding program so that they could remain devoted "to prayer and to the ministry of the word" (Acts 6:4). They affirmed the importance of feeding the widows and restructured the ministry to accommodate the growing demand. But they did not allow their time to be consumed with the daily program activities of caring for the poor.

Perhaps Paul and Barnabas were reminded to "remember the poor" as they went to the Gentiles because ministry to the poor is centered more in the gift of the prophet rather than the gift of the apostle. Apostles constantly look to the horizon to see where they can go next with the gospel. But prophets are tuned into the heart of God and exhibit prophetic passion. The Old Testament prophets demanded that the people of God defend the widow and the orphan. The prophet is a "seer" who has spiritual insight into the way things are. They challenge people to make things right with God and with the world. They call people to purity and intimacy with God. They also speak against social injustices in our world and call God's people to be people of justice and righteousness in our world. They feel God's heart for the hurting and call people to action on behalf of the suffering. Apostles know the great importance of ministry to the poor, but their apostolic nature pulls their attention toward expanding the kingdom of God. Paul was eager to remember the poor, but Peter and James felt it necessary to remind him as they innately understood the apostolic nature.

Martyn, Stavros, and Agnes all had personal experiences that influenced their personal passion for ministry to the poor. Without those experiences, they too might have needed a reminder to remember the poor in the midst of their apostolic activities. Agnes has been immersed in a ministry context where poverty is an overwhelming reality. Similarly, James and Peter served in Jerusalem, so they were confronted daily with the suffering of believers. Paul may have been more removed from pervasive poverty as he traversed the economic and cultural centers of the Roman Empire. Martyn described two defining moments visiting orphanages in Romania that turned his heart toward caring for the poor:

> The defining moment for me was when in one orphanage all these kids come running jump into our arms. They were all naked, with things crawling around all over them and excrement was everywhere. My wife was totally comfortable with that. For me, it horrified, shocked, and repelled me. I realized how cold and hard my heart was and how incredible it was that Jesus so often reached out and touched the leper. Yet, here I was being afraid of being touched or touching these children. It was a real moment for me before God. I saw how pathetic and superficial I really was. I felt God really challenging me. My wife and I decided we had to do something.
>
> Another point in that whole journey was when we saw the orphanage care worker cleaning a child's face. The child was screaming. My wife is a nurse, so we went to see what was wrong. She saw that the care worker was cleaning the face of this orphaned kid with bleach and causing a lot pain. We recognized that there is all this aid that had been brought over from the UK through different agencies, but there was no training. There was no thought about the ongoing care of the children or how to do something that would substantially change children's lives. [33]

Stavros' experience as a teenager makes him very attuned to the suffering of refugees. Stavros grew up in Cyprus, and at the age of thirteen, his city of Kerynia (now renamed Girne), was invaded by the Turks. For two weeks, he and his family fled from city to city. They arrived at his uncle's house, where they took up temporary residence for a month and a half. They then had to move to a village in the mountains for a year and a half. Finally, they moved to the capital of Nicosia and settled there. These life experiences sensitized these three apostolic leaders to the plight of the poor.

Spirit-Empowerment in Ministry to the Poor

The testimonies of these three apostolic leaders expressed in each of their interviews suggest that the power of the Holy Spirit is released in greater measure in ministry to the poor in the community during the week than in worship on Sunday mornings. Miracles happen when people serve the needs of others outside the walls of the church. Stavros observed from his own experience that usually, people are not instantaneously healed when prayed for in the church. However, he has seen more instantaneous healings ministering to the poor outside of Sunday morning. Once, even a paralyzed person got up and walked. He longs to see more miracles and believes there will be an increase of miracles the more God's people engage in meeting the needs of suffering people. Martyn pointed out that two things drove church growth in the book of Acts: the supernatural and care for the poor. In light of Stavros' observations, perhaps the reason so much supernatural activity happened in the book of Acts was because believers served the poor and sought to expand the kingdom of God into new places. Miracles were not confined to times of gathered worship in Acts. Rather, they primarily happened outside the synagogue and worship gatherings. For Spirit-empowered communities to see a greater release of the power of the Holy Spirit, it seems that it will naturally happen as believers engage more with hurting people beyond the Sunday worship experience.

Stavros identified other important types of miraculous manifestations of the Holy Spirit as well in ministry to the poor. One miracle is the provision to feed large crowds and provide numerous items to people in need. The amount and magnitude are, to him, a tremendous miracle. Like Jesus feeding the five thousand, God has miraculously provided for each of these ministries as they serve the poor. Second, Stavros experienced other gifts of the Spirit while ministering to the poor that have included the prophetic, gifts of discernment, words of wisdom, and words of knowledge. Third, Stavros identified the important role of the Holy Spirit as the comforter in working with the poor. He stated, "It's also another miracle that a very sensitive person like me can hold it together. As one comforts those who are suffering, you want to cry all the time. But you become strong because the Holy Spirit is the comforter. I have never seen the Holy Spirit comforting me so much in my life as when I minister to the poor."

Stavros cautioned though that the Holy Spirit loves to work in private and respectful ways. Prophetic words should not be delivered as "thus says the Lord…" Healings should not be for show where a believer says, "Ok guys, watch me now as I'm going to heal this person." Jesus warned his followers as well to not get caught up in the temptation to do acts of righteousness "before men to be noticed by them" (Matt 6:1).[34] He went on to say, "So when you give to the poor, do not sound a trumpet before you, as the hypocrites do in the synagogues and in the streets" (Matt 6:2).[35] Stavros felt that the more he sought to do the work of the ministry in a private, low-key manner, the more he was able to achieve.

Interestingly, it seems that this reflects the nature of the Holy Spirit and his role in the Trinity. Jesus is the one who is to be lifted up. The Holy Spirit is the unseen partner of the Trinity. The Holy Spirit seeks to glorify Jesus and empowers his people to be witnesses of Christ. The gentle, quiet caring work of the Holy Spirit through the compassionate care of God's people is a powerful witness. Stavros related a story of a Muslim woman who attended one of his medical clinics for two days. She approached a volunteer from Haifa who came to serve as a translator at the clinic. The woman said to this translator, "I've been watching you for two days. . . . I've been sitting there in the corner, and I've been watching you. And I've never met anyone in my country and especially Muslims who treat people the way you do. You treat the kids with care. You treat the women with care. You love us all. What is behind this?"[36] That led to a long discussion through which she led this woman to Jesus. Through the actions of Christ's followers loving the poor, the Holy Spirit empowers his people for witness. But this is often not in a loud public way, but in a low-key, caring, relational way.

Spirit Leading for Ministry to the Poor

Apostolic leaders are strategists always on the lookout for ways to expand the kingdom of God. The apostolic leaders interviewed for this article all exemplify that trait. However, they also warned against using ministry to the poor as a strategy for kingdom expansion. They emphasized a holistic gospel that places love at the center. Because of love for people, the body of Christ must act on behalf of the poor. Because of love for people, it will be natural in the process to share Christ. However, ministry to the poor is not a means to an end. It is obedience to Jesus who instructed us to feed the hungry, clothe the naked, welcome the stranger, and visit the prison. It is rooted in the heart of God to bring good news to the poor that is practical as much as spiritual.

Martyn argued that Paul never used the ministry to the poor as a strategy to expand the kingdom of God. "There is no suggestion in Acts that a particular apostolic strategy to reach into a new area was to identify and focus on bringing the gospel primarily to a particular poor group of people. In fact, Paul seems to prioritize reaching major regional cities, rather than poorer rural areas."[37] Often prominent people were the first who responded to the gospel message.[38] Care for the poor happened as local churches formed and began to serve people in their community. It is simply what believers do. It is not a strategy for witness. But when believers live this kind of Christ-like life, the witness is compelling. In the early chapters of Acts, the believers had everything in common and, in radical generosity, sold property and possessions in order to share with anyone who had need. It is no surprise that given that kind of deep love for one another, "the Lord was adding to their number day by day those who were being saved" (Acts 2:44–47). After the apostles expanded the feeding program to care for all of the widows, Luke again remarked, "the number of the disciples continued to increase greatly in Jerusalem" (Acts 6:7). When ministry to the poor is an evangelism strategy, there is a danger of manipulation of the poor. But when it is centered in love for people, it is a compelling apologetic.

Ministry to the poor should be initiated from the heart of God and the leading of the Holy Spirit. The Holy Spirit prompts people to engage in ministry to the poor. The lame beggar was placed at the temple gate every day. Jesus likely walked past this beggar a number of times during his Jerusalem visits. But on the day Peter and John entered the temple, the Spirit of God prompted them to do something (Acts 3:1–10). Martyn noted that in his church, the leadership does not decide what poverty projects should be undertaken. Rather, God gives a ministry idea to people in the congregation, and those ministries then develop through the person the Holy Spirit spoke to. Consequently, it is not the leadership putting together the strategy for poverty care. It is the Holy Spirit who touches people's hearts. Stavros mentioned walking down the street one day with his wife Lois and feeling an impression by the Holy Spirit to start a distribution center. Looking back, it was clear to him that this was the voice of God because on his own he feels he could never have recruited so many teams of people to serve, acquired such large quantities of donated supplies, nor raised funds necessary to serve all the refugees and gypsies that have been served the last four years.[39] The Holy Spirit leads those who will listen and obey.

Discernment for Ministry to the Poor

Not only does the Holy Spirit initiate ministry to the poor, but the Holy Spirit also gives discernment for this difficult type of ministry. Agnes identified several ways that the gift of discernment is needed. First, apostolic leaders need discernment regarding what to invest in. In the West African context, the needs are immense. Ministry to the poor requires setting priorities because the needs are endless. Furthermore, there is a tension between helping build long-term sustainability and the immediate short-term needs of people. Agnes recalled setting up bank accounts for twenty women and giving each of them funds to develop small businesses. Only two of the twenty succeeded. All the others used the money for their daily needs. In hindsight, she recognized the need to study their lives first and discern how best to help.[40]

Agnes' late husband, Gregory, lived a life permeated by the leading and discernment of the Holy Spirit. Many mornings he would wake up early and hear the Lord whispering, "take some money and put it in your pocket." He would do so and then go outside and sit by the road. He would watch the people passing by until he sensed the Lord identifying a particular person. He would greet the person and give them the money. Often people would break out in tears as this was just the miracle provision, they needed that morning. Sometimes he and Agnes felt a prompting to buy bags of rice, divide them up into smaller packets and distribute them in the community door to door. On the flip side, Agnes pointed out that discernment is also needed regarding people who would try to take advantage of one's generosity.

Martyn discussed the essential elements of discernment necessary for establishing poverty projects outside the local context. He prays for God to bring him to the right people to work with. The best indicator, according to Martyn, is not their religious passion but rather their care for people. Are they compassionate, caring people who have hearts like Jesus? Martyn confidently asserts, "I find it very easy to know who to work with and who to avoid. I can tell within five minutes if this is someone God is joining me to in order to help, to serve, and to get behind. And I would say almost invariably it's right. So, I think the Holy Spirit does lead you to people. And I'm praying that all the time." This leading is further solidified by confirmations of the Holy Spirit when one goes to a particular place. He looks for "little touches from God," indicating that the Holy Spirit is orchestrating the connection.[41]

Revelation and Formation from Serving the Poor

Not only does the Holy Spirit lead apostolic leaders regarding ministry to the poor, but there is also a powerful process released in the life of the leader and every believer who blesses the poor. That process includes both revelation and formation. One of the functions of the Holy Spirit is to help us by teaching us. Jesus promised that that "the Helper, the Holy Spirit, whom the Father will send in My name, He will teach you all things" (John 14:25–27). Stavros spoke of how engagement with the poor helped him understand the cross. Sometimes people are ungrateful and even hostile to those offering help. Stavros has experienced this working in the Gypsy camp. His natural response was to get upset. But upon further reflection, he felt the Holy Spirit showing him how much he, himself, is forgiven, and the cross has taken on new significance. Furthermore, these experiences have pushed him to seek an understanding of the people he is working with at a deeper level. What is behind their behavior? Why are they getting upset at us? Why are they so anxious? The Holy Spirit uses these ministry experiences to teach the one serving. Stavros referred to this as a revelation.[42] The Apostle Paul touched on this principle of ministry, forming an understanding. He wrote to Philemon, "I pray that the sharing of your faith may become effective for the full knowledge of every good thing that is in us for the sake of Christ" (1:6 ESV). Sharing the faith fosters a deeper understanding of the faith.

Not only does the Holy Spirit give his followers a deeper understanding of their faith as they serve, he also shapes their lives through these experiences. The Holy Spirit uses these ministry experiences to grow the fruit of the Spirit in believers' lives. He drives out judgmentalism through engagement with suffering humanity. The Spirit teaches the minister about his/her own heart and faith. Exposure to the pain of others sensitizes the believer and minister. Stavros described this as almost a physical pain that one feels in their heart for people as they lean into the suffering of others. Ministry to the poor is a two-way street. Not only does God use his people to be conduits of blessing, He, in turn, blesses the giver.

Conclusion

Spirit-empowered apostolic leaders who serve the poor know first-hand that the Holy Spirit permeates ministry to the poor. The Spirit leads the people of God into acts of service. Discernment for this engagement with the poor is needed in multiple ways. Amazingly, miracles happen in greater measure when believers step into the lives of hurting people in the world around them. "Remember the poor" is a clarion call for every believer, every local church, and every apostolic leader.

Notes

1. "What is the 10/40 Window?" Joshua Project, https://joshuaproject.net/resources/articles/10_40_window, accessed May 15, 2019.

2. Unless otherwise specified, all scripture references in this chapter come from the New International Version (NIV) (Grand Rapids, MI: Zondervan, 1984).

3. Interview with Martyn Dunsford, February 12, 2019. Interview with Agnes Bangura, February 15, 2019. Interview with Stavros Ignatiou, February 19, 2019. All interviews were conducted by Zoom. The interviewer conducted the interview from Tulsa and the interviewees were each in their home countries: Dunsford in England; Bangura in Sierra Leone; Ignatiou in Greece. The interviews were approximately one hour and fifteen minutes in length. The interviews were transcribed.

4. "About," CRY, https://www.cry.org.uk/about, accessed May 16, 2019.

5. The four components are listed as their mission on their Facebook page. See "About," Rabboni Missions International, https://www.facebook.com/pg/rabbonimissionsinternational/about/?ref=page_internal, accessed on May 17, 2019.

6. This figure is based on the International Monetary Fund, World Economic Outlook Database, April 2019, and was reported by Luca Ventura. See Luca Ventura, "Poorest Countries in the World 2019," *Global Finance Magazine*, April 17, 2019, https://www.gfmag.com/global-data/economic-data/the-poorest-countries-in-the-world, accessed May 17, 2019.

7. The CIA World Factbook reports 48.1% of the total population are literate. "Sierra Leone," *CIA World Factbook*, last updated May 13, 2019, https://www.cia.gov/library/publications/resources/the-world-factbook/geos/sl.html, accessed May 17, 2019.

8. Ventura, "Poorest Countries," https://www.gfmag.com/global-data/economic-data/the-poorest-countries-in-the-world, accessed May 17, 2019.

9. The CIA World Factbook reports the religious makeup of the population: 78.6% Muslim, 20.8% Christian, 0.3% Other, 0.2% Unspecified, "Sierra Leone," https://www.cia.gov/library/publications/resources/the-world-factbook/geos/sl.html, accessed May 17, 2019.

10. According to the 2001 Greece Census, 443,550 Albanians were living in Greece. There were a total of 797,091 immigrants at the time in a total population of 10,964,020. See Martin Baldwin-Edwards, "Immigration into Greece, 1990-2003: A Southern European Paradigm?" *European Population Forum 2004*, Table 2, https://www.unece.org/fileadmin/DAM/pau/_docs/

pau/2004/PAU_2004_EPF_Sess4PresnBaldwinEdwards.pdf, accessed May 21, 2019.

11 Information reported in the "Athens Christian Center Yearly Report 2018," an internal organizational report written annually by Stavros Ignatiou. This is the church Stavros founded and pastored.

12 Information reported in the Created Equal newsletter distributed by email on July 9, 2019, to partners and friends of Stavros' ministry.

13 Ralph D. Winter, "The Two Structures of God's Redemptive Mission," *Missiology: An International Review* 2:1 (January 1974), 121.

14 Winter, "Two Structures," 122.

15 Winter, "Two Structures," 125–126.

16 Winter, "Two Structures," 131.

17 Winter, "Two Structures," 131.

18 Sam Metcalf, *Beyond the Local Church: How Apostolic Movements Can Change the World* (Downers Grove: IVP, 2015), 13–14.

19 Metcalf, *Beyond*, 65–69.

20 Metcalf, *Beyond*, 43.

21 Alan Hirsch and Tim Catchim, *The Permanent Revolution: Apostolic Imagination and Practice for the 21st Century* Church (San Francisco: Jossey-Bass, 2012), 15–17.

22 Stefan Paas defines the classic model as "evangelism (conversion), gathering (baptism and community formation), and planting (constitution)." See Stefan Paas, *Church Planting in the Secular West: Learning from the European Experience* (Grand Rapids: Eerdmans, 2016), 31.

23 Paas, *Church Planting*, 38–39. Paas contends that this compression happened over the last one hundred years as a result of the concepts articulated by Roland Allen and Donald McGavran.

24 Mike Breen from www.fivefoldsurvey.com. Material online is excerpted from his and Steve Cockram's book, *Building a Discipling Culture* (Greenville: 3DM International, 2014).

25 Hirsch, *Permanent Revolution*, 122.

26 Hirsch, *Permanent Revolution*, 124.

27 See Rupen Das, *Compassion and the Mission of God: Revealing the Invisible Kingdom* (Cumbria: Langham Global Library, 2015), 87–103. Helen Rhee also provides a reader of primary sources for teachings on wealth, poverty,

and charity in the Church Fathers. See Helen Rhee, Wealth and Poverty in Early Christianity (Minneapolis, Fortress Press, 2017).

28 Interview with Agnes Bangura.

29 Martyn Dunsford in "Apostolic Ministry with Respect to the Poor," 46. This was a discussion paper written by Martyn and part of a larger unpublished book. This chapter was sent to the present author. The details of book it was included in are unknown.

30 Dunsford, "Apostolic Ministry," 46.

31 Dunsford, "Apostolic Ministry," 49

32 Dunsford, "Apostolic Ministry," 50.

33 Interview with Martyn Dunsford.

34 Interview with Stavros Ignatiou.

35 Interview with Stavros Ignatiou.

36 Interview with Stavros Ignatiou.

37 Dunford, *Apostolic Ministry*, 54.

38 Dunsford lists examples from Acts: Sergius Paulus, Lydia, prominent women in Thessalonica, Dionysius, Demaris, Erastus, and Gaius. See Dunford, *Apostolic Ministry*, 54.

39 Interview with Stavros Ignatiou.

40 Interview with Agnes Bangura.

41 Interview with Martyn Dunsford.

42 Interview with Stavros Ignatiou.

22 "I Tried Poverty": Exploring the Psychological Impact of Poverty and Prosperity in the Life of Oral Roberts

Daniel D. Isgrigg

Abstract

The origin of the prosperity gospel is most often linked to the influence of American Pentecostal Christianity, particularly to Oral Roberts and his concept of "seed faith." In light of this, this study seeks to understand Oral Roberts' concepts of poverty and prosperity by exploring the psychology of his own experience of poverty. It will suggest that the biology of inequality he experienced as a child shaped the development of his prosperity teaching.

Introduction

As a tradition whose first adherents were from poor and minority classes, Pentecostals have always been interested in the interplay between poverty and their Pentecostal faith.[1] Today, Pentecostals have become increasingly interested in the extent to which Pentecostals were engaged in social issues such as poverty.[2] As Donald E. Miller and Tetsunao Yamamori have documented, the global Pentecostal church is a progressive form of Pentecostalism that is engaging social issues, especially work among the poor.[3] The emphasis on personal transformation inherent in the Pentecostal message has been directly linked to upward social mobility as converts become honest, faithful, and hardworking citizens. As Miller and Yamamori recognize, "financial gain is an unintended consequence of a changed life."[4] Thus, for many global Pentecostals, the gospel truly has become "good news to the poor" not just in a spiritual sense, but in a this-worldly sense that can affect a person's economic situations.

In placing a focus on the benefits of faith to lift believers out of poverty, a stream of Christian teaching has emerged in Pentecostal and Charismatic circles known as the "prosperity gospel." As Jacob Ayantayo defines it, the "prosperity gospel" is the teaching that emphasizes the benefits of the faith primarily in terms of "material possession or acquisition."[5] Emphasis is often placed on the gospel's ability to give believers success, health, and wealth through the principles of faith and divine economics. In this theology, it is not just that the gospel leads people out of poverty through neo-liberal economic uplift; it is God himself who provides financial resources to those who believe in him.[6] Critics of this form of "health and wealth" teaching point out that often this spiritualized materialism commercializes religion and turns faith into little more than an economic transaction.[7] Worse, it has too often been used as a litmus test for divine approval, implying that material blessing equals favor from God, and poverty equals the opposite.

Originally a North American phenomenon, the prosperity gospel has expanded its influence globally, especially in the Majority World. In many of the poorest global contexts, such as Africa, preachers emphasize "the spirit of prosperity in order to counter the spirit of poverty, which is claimed to be the cause of African problems."[8] The message is so popular that many "prosperity churches" have become some of the largest Pentecostal and Charismatic churches in Africa. Critics of the prosperity gospel have argued that the pastors of these megachurches have used the prosperity message to enrich the preacher more than uplift the poor. Further, it is often the churches in urban settings that have benefitted most, which has done little to uplift the poor outside the already middle class in these communities.

The origin of the prosperity gospel is most often linked to the influence of American Pentecostal Christianity in the last few decades, particularly to Oral Roberts and his concept of "seed faith." Kate Bowler labels Oral Roberts as the "major architect of the prosperity gospel."[9] Furthermore, the spread of prosperity in Africa was primarily through Archbishop Benson Idahosa, who is considered the "pioneer of prosperity gospel" in Africa and was a close friend of Oral Roberts, who exported his ideas of God's blessings and "seed-faith" into his African context and gave rise to current prosperity leaders such as David Oyedepo in Nigeria.[10] In light of the blame placed on Roberts for the negative effects of the "prosperity gospel" in the Majority World, this study seeks to understand Oral Roberts' concepts of poverty and prosperity by exploring the psychology of his own experience of poverty. It will use Roberts as a case study on the psychological effects of poverty and how his experience shaped his concept of God and the promise of material provision.

"I Tried Poverty"

Kate Bowler's examination of prosperity teaching in America notes that Oral Roberts once quipped, "I tried poverty; I didn't like it."[11] This is a fitting quote to illustrate how Oral Roberts' prosperity teaching cannot be understood apart from his impoverished upbringing. Roberts was born in 1918 in rural Oklahoma, where his father, Ellis, and mother, Claudius, made their home prior to statehood. Ellis was a tenant farmer who owned a 160-acre farm in Pontotoc County, Oklahoma. Originally Methodists, the Roberts were saved, sanctified, and filled with Holy Spirit when pioneer Pentecostal revivalists came to Ada, Oklahoma in 1914.[12] So impacted by his conversion and call to the ministry, Ellis sold his land and launched into pastoral and evangelistic ministry. Shortly after he sold it, oil was discovered on his land, and the new owners were becoming wealthy. But Ellis did not regret it. He said, "You can have your oil money. I've got an oil well in my soul. Many people are getting saved in my meetings. That's worth more than all the oil fields in the world."[13]

This decision to sell all for the sake of the gospel ministry led the Roberts family into a life of poverty that deeply affected Oral. Despite Ellis pioneering twelve churches as an evangelist, the ministry did little to provide for the Roberts family, who did not own a home or a car. On one occasion, Ellis was invited to preach in a town fourteen miles away. To save money on the bus fare, he walked to and from the church in the dead of winter, arriving home in the middle of the night. When Claudius asked why the church did not drive him home, Ellis replied as Oral listened in from his bed, "They knew I had no way except to walk, but no one volunteered."[14] On another occasion, while Ellis was at a revival, Oral's mother announced to her children, "We're out of groceries and I'm sorry, but we'll have no supper tonight."[15] Events like this shaped Oral's remembrance of the church and ministry. He lamented that church members took advantage of Ellis's love and care for them by intentionally keeping him in need in order to "be poor like Jesus." Oral famously recalls that the deacons would say, "God, you keep Rev. E. M. Roberts humble, and we'll keep him poor."[16]

Oral's accounts of how the strain of poverty tore his father apart "emotionally and spiritually" demonstrate how much his experience as a young child traumatically impacted him even later in life.[17] His father's decision to choose ministry over stability meant that Oral would be destined to be poor and made him angry with God and with his parents. Ellis, who was once a tenant farmer, turned to sharecropping to make ends meet and would move to various farms to pick cotton during harvest seasons.[18] Oral just could not understand why his father had given up being a successful farmer for a life of suffering in ministry.[19] He and his brother would ask, "Why did papa have to preach? We hardly ever had enough to eat."[20] He knew the calling to serve God should be an honorable calling, yet he could not understand why serving God meant poverty, hunger, depression, and suffering. He recalls, "Why was it that we were 'supposed to be poor'? The doctors lived in good houses, so did the lawyers and merchants, and many others."[21] The only reward his family received for sacrificing for the ministry was "stinking poverty."

The suffering Roberts experienced as a child led him into a deep sense of hopelessness. He was a bright student who loved school and hoped one day to be a lawyer or Governor of Oklahoma, but often missed school because he was expected to join his father in the fields until the harvest was finished. By his teen years, Roberts had come to the conclusion that if he stayed in his parents' house, he would never achieve his educational and life goals. So, at the age of sixteen, he ran away to live with the basketball coach at Atoka High School, nearly fifty miles away, hoping to elevate himself by playing basketball. He quickly realized that life was not any better there. At sixteen, he had to support himself by working several jobs. He recalls, "I couldn't make enough to eat on. Many times, I didn't have enough to eat or the right place to sleep."[22] To add to his misery, he was beginning to grow sick and developed tuberculosis, which left him bedridden and dying after collapsing during a basketball game. Roberts' coach drove him home to Ada, which for Oral meant "back to poverty, back to a religious faith that found no place in me, back to dreaming with no way out."[23] After struggling for several weeks, Oral was saved and later received his healing in the tent of George Moncey.[24]

The Poor Evangelist

Following his healing, the effects of his sickness and poverty were still very much with him. The months of weakness he endured kept him from finishing high school and left him with few options for a career path moving forward. As a result, Roberts felt called to follow his father in the same path of ministry, which he also knew meant choosing a life of poverty. Yet, Roberts believed in his ability to be successful in ministry. He jumped in wholeheartedly and quickly became a sought-after speaker in the Pentecostal Holiness Church (PHC) denomination.[25] For the first couple years, while traveling and preaching, Oral and Evelyn often lived in the homes of other families, sometimes weeks at a time or until Evelyn would get fed up and take the kids to her parents' house. Evelyn recalls, "[We] never really knew what a home was like. Rebecca Ann, our oldest child, was carried from place to place until she was past two years old."[26]

Although a successful revival speaker, Oral suffered from the same challenges of poverty and instability as his father. To supplement his income during revivals, Oral would do side jobs such as hanging wallpaper in the town where he was ministering.[27] Worn to the point of exhaustion and in search of more financial provision, Oral decided to turn to pastoral ministry, taking his first church in Fuquay Springs, North Carolina, in 1941. In 1942, he moved his family back to Oklahoma to pastor the Shawnee PHC. The Shawnee PHC was a sacrifice at first. Still, by the time Roberts had been there a year, he had already seen several wage increases and even noted his salary was the highest in the area among PHC churches at forty dollars per week.[28] Roberts also enrolled at Oklahoma Baptist University.[29] Although he enjoyed a living wage, he was uncomfortable staying in one place. In 1943 he returned to evangelistic ministry and, for a short time in 1945, considered becoming a missionary to Palestine.[30]

In 1946, after several more years of successful evangelistic ministry, Roberts was once again looking for stability and came to Enid, Oklahoma, to pastor the Enid PHC. Although he was successful in the new church, he was suffering psychologically beneath the surface and admitted that he was miserable.[31] Roberts' struggle in ministry went beyond simply not having God's power in his life; he lamented that although he preached the abundant life, he suffered from depression and the constant torment of not having enough.[32] He recalls that his family did not have enough clothes and that sometimes Evelyn had to leave items at the checkout stand in the grocery store when she did not have enough money.[33] Roberts resented his church board for not doing more to supply for the needs of his family, and like his father before him, concluded that the church was simply unconcerned. It was in this struggle that he discovered 3 John 2, the verse that would change his life and set him on a course toward making a name for himself in healing evangelism.

The Biology of Inequality

"I have never been a person who can live with a need. Something has to give—me or the need."[34]

Research concerning the biological effects of socioeconomic status is just beginning to catch up with the social effects on health, education, and emotional development.[35] Researchers are beginning to understand that the stress of poverty has a significant impact on brain development. The stress of "not enough" handicaps the whole person to where people are continually hindered by unmet basic needs. Lucy Jewell has identified this as the "biology of inequality." The awareness of poverty and lack actually changes a person's brain in a way that limits their cognitive wellbeing and makes them more susceptible to a number of psychological inequities.[36] She says:

> Structural violence and status syndrome are not just abstract theories. We are now beginning to understand the mechanics of how this happens in the body. Through the mechanism of stress, social and economic inequality produces measurable changes in the human body at the genetic and synaptic level. . . . Growing up in a disadvantaged environment correlates with greater social and psychological problems, such as anxiety, impulsiveness, and depressiveness.[37]

In this way, poverty is more than psychological; it is biological even to the genetic level, affecting cognition, development, and health. Jewell says, "These factors of inequality manifested in poor health and scarcity mentality become encoded into the DNA and can be passed on to the next generation, continuing the cycle of poverty."[38]

The concept of the "biology of inequality" is instructive to understanding Roberts' story. Each of his autobiographies tells of his own family's food insecurity, lack of education, and poor health. Though a brilliant man, his upbringing of poverty and disease affected his educational life. His childhood dreams of being a lawyer and Governor of Oklahoma seemed destined for disappointment because he missed school so often due to his father's seasonal farming. By the time he was a sophomore, he had been in ten different schools.[39] Even when he attended school, his issues with stuttering affected his reading skills and made him the target of bullying.[40] His socioeconomic status also made him susceptible to disease; he contracted tuberculosis at age sixteen. His poor health once again kept him from attending and graduating from high school, opting some years later for a GED. His experience as an adult was not much different. In 1943, he enrolled for a year and a half at Oklahoma Baptist University and later enrolled in Phillips University in Enid, Oklahoma in 1946.[41] In both cases, his proclivity to endure only short tenures in ministry appointments—a trait highly characteristic of children from impoverished backgrounds—hindered his ability to stay focused on his education, and he never finished.[42]

Experiencing poverty during early adolescence can alter the human psyche with feelings of insufficiency and insecurity that manifest as the constant sense of "never enough." The stress of watching his parents struggle as a child and his own struggles with his family greatly impacted the psychology of Roberts. No matter how successful he became in ministry, he still struggled with having enough. In fact, it was this feeling of dissatisfaction that led him, in 1947, to search for greater fulfillment in ministry through launching into healing evangelism.[43] Even still, at the height of his popularity as America's healing evangelist, he admitted, "No matter how large the crowds grew or how many thousands were healed, or how many souls were saved, I still felt a certain emptiness that would not go away."[44] Statements like this suggest that Roberts may have never been able to recover fully from his compulsion to achieve to compensate for his feelings of inadequacy as a child.

God's Sufficiency for Roberts' Poverty

At the lowest point in his emotional health, while pastoring in 1946, Roberts discovered 3 John 2. Prior to this discovery, Roberts struggled with the attitude among Pentecostals that poverty was good for Christians. Depression-era Pentecostals were critical of wealth and often taught that Jesus was poor, and therefore those who followed Jesus should also be poor, especially pastors.[45] For Roberts, this attitude was nothing more than a justification for the church to place a low priority on the pastor's family and their needs. Beyond that, it ingrained in him the idea that God was not concerned with physical and financial needs. But the discovery of 3 John 2 changed all that in his mind. In it, he discovered that God desired not for people to be poor, as his childhood had conditioned him, but "to prosper and be in health." He said, "I found that there was a true scriptural basis for believing that God wants man to be happy, normal, healthy, strong and prosperous."[46] Poverty, like disease, then, was an enemy that Jesus came to conquer.

It is no coincidence that Roberts developed his view of prosperity alongside his view of healing. Like sociologists today, he recognized the correlation between disease and poverty. Roberts understood the role stress could play in the psychology of poverty as a root cause of poor health.[47] Similarly, he recognized, no doubt by his own experience, that those who live in poverty are more susceptible to societal disadvantages that bring disease. He says, "Poor housing tends to breed disease, and disease among the poor affords little opportunity for adequate medical care."[48] The theological connection between healing and divine provision was a logical one in his mind. In Roberts' mind, the gospel was good news for both. If God was a healing God who could address the symptoms of poverty, then addressing poverty with God's provision was also part of the healing gospel. He also recognized that it was the worry and stress created by poverty that caused sickness.

Poverty and the Origin of "Seed Faith"

What Roberts accomplished over the next four decades was nothing short of remarkable. Through his healing ministry, millions of people came to faith in Christ and were healed in his crusades. Roberts' televised tent crusades brought Pentecostalism into the mainstream, and he also had a prolific radio and print media ministry.[49] In the early 1960s, Roberts made the transition from evangelist to the founder of the nation's first Charismatic university, Oral Roberts University (ORU). In the 1980s, he launched into the field of Christian medicine by opening the medical school at ORU and building the City of Faith Medical and Research Center.[50] In each successive decade, Oral Roberts continued reinventing himself and his ministry to push the envelope of what was possible for Christian ministry. Although there is no doubt that Roberts was a man of unique faith and vision, there was certainly more to his accomplishments than simply talent and personality. He was driven by an intense sense of mission to accomplish impossible goals that required God to be a God who provided.

During this first decade as a healing evangelist, Oral Roberts Ministries required a large donor base to fund his healing crusades, television ministry, nationwide radio programs, and distribution of hundreds of thousands of magazines around America and to 154 foreign countries. To help him fund this, Roberts discovered the practical value of wealth by befriending a number of wealthy Pentecostal businessmen who supported his ministry and whom he organized into the Full Gospel Businessmen's Fellowship with Demos Shakarian. These wealthy men became the backbone of his support and acquainted him with the power of wealth for accomplishing big things. Even so, during the evangelistic era, Roberts kept his own wealth private and continued to project the image of a flashy, but not materialistic, evangelist.[51]

The first development in Roberts' teaching of prosperity came in 1957 with the introduction of the "blessing pact," a special giving arrangement he created for his partners to join with him in meeting the financial demands of ministry. Connected with the "blessing pact" was the idea that God would reward believers who invested in worthy ministries. Roberts also began to emphasize God's abundance and surplus for believers who faithfully gave. In 1958, he commented:

> GOD DEALS IN SURPLUSES! God is not interested in your starving to death. He is not interested in your being so stricken with poverty that you cannot clothe, house, and feed yourself and your family or find your useful place in society. God knows that you're in a material world. He *knows* that you have needs, and he has promised to add all these things unto you if you put his kingdom first.[52]

The surplus rested in God's goodness as the hope that one does not have to live in poverty. However, the key to experiencing God's abundance was also linked to one's generosity. As one blessing pact partner declared, "Since I received this blessed supply from God, I joyously pass a portion on to you to use for God's work."[53] At this point, giving originated out of abundance—such as was the case with his wealthy business friends—rather than giving out of needs.

Over the next decade, Roberts' drive to achieve meant his demand for support needed to grow exponentially as he maintained his previous ministry initiatives while launching his newest venture: Oral Roberts University. Between 1962 and 1985, Roberts built a 500-acre university campus with twenty-five state-of-the-art buildings—fourteen of which were built during the decade of the 1970s.[54] Just as soon as one building was going up, the next campaign would launch. His pace was relentless.[55] Each building required massive fundraising campaigns to solicit contributions from his base.

As the demands of building the university increased, the amount of provision needed for the ministry was growing exponentially. The previous emphasis on God's abundance through the "blessing pact" began to morph into the idea of "seed-faith" in 1969, through the three keys to the "blessing pact": recognize God is your source; give a seed that represented your faith; and then expect a miracle.[56] The key, however, was no longer that you gave out of your abundance but out of your need. Roberts says, "Your Blessing Pact giving is a higher law of faith. You give BEFORE you have received; you give as seed money for God to multiply back to you."[57] The emphasis on giving out of your need was a crucial step that fueled the idea of the prosperity gospel. Rather than giving because one has prosperity, one gives as a way to achieve prosperity.

Each phase of his ministry, from the tent to the university, was to some degree motivated by the biology of inequality in which he was constantly revisiting his feelings of insufficiency and insecurity rooted in his impoverished childhood. At each stage in his ministry, the demands to achieve tested his own adequacy and his belief in the sufficiency of God to provide for his needs. This is particularly seen in the development of his prosperity teachings, which slowly developed as the demand for funds increased.

From Sufficiency to Prosperity

In 1970, Roberts released what is perhaps his most famous book, *The Miracle of Seed Faith*.[58] Up until 1970, Roberts' emphasis on blessing was primarily focused on God's abundance to help believers and meet their needs. The idea of using giving to God as a means to gaining wealth was largely absent from his preaching and teaching. Like healing, God's provision flowed out of his goodness and his desire to bless people who had faith in him. However, the financial demands of the university led

"I Tried Poverty" 415

Roberts to emphasize that "sowing" into God's ministry through the blessing pact was a way to "reap" a harvest for a person's own need. Thus, the message of "seed faith" became the primary way to maintain his financial base that now included the university, the Hollywood style prime-time television specials, and worldwide ministry through the World Action Teams. The university alone required a budget of several million dollars per month to expand the buildings on-campus and create the new Graduate Schools of Theology, Medicine, Law, and Dentistry in the mid- to-late 1970s. A significant factor that also led to a change in Roberts' giving message was related to his base. In the years after starting ORU, Roberts' financial situation was changing from classical Pentecostals and Full Gospel Businessmen in the 1950s to Christians from mainline Charismatic communities, particularly the United Methodist Church. By the late 1970s, in a time when the American economy was struggling and Roberts' many initiatives had overtaxed his support base, many of Roberts' earliest Pentecostal supporters had moved on.

Things came to a head in 1977 with the announcement that Roberts would build a 120 million dollar, three-tower City of Faith Medical Complex and Research Center. This decision, however, was not made because of the tide of success as a ministry; it was born out of a "desert" experience following the death of daughter Rebecca and son-in-law Marshall Nash in a plane crash in 1977.[59] Behind the scenes, Roberts was also dealing with the deteriorating marriage of his son Richard and his wife Patti, who divorced officially in 1978. On top of that, Oral's brightest son, Ronnie, had been caught up in years of drug abuse and self-destruction that eventually led to his suicide in 1982.[60] After years of declaring "God is a good God" and seemingly having success in everything they put their hands to, the Robertses were once again emotionally placed in a place of powerlessness. No amount of fame or fortune he had achieved could bring Rebecca back, save Richard's image, or restore Ronnie.

What I am suggesting is that the personal emotional trauma of 1977 awakened in Oral Roberts the "biology of inequality" to the point that he had a compulsive need to build the City of Faith, despite the enormous cost and difficulty. To do this, it would test his fundamental assumptions about God's goodness and sufficiency. How could a minister with a ten million dollar per month budget possibly feel poor? The answer may lie in the "Relative Income Hypothesis," which posits that perceptions of poverty are relative and contextual.[61] Helen Rhee points out often the idea of income sufficiency and wealth is a relative concept.[62] While the secular press believed his appeals for millions were motivated by self-enrichment, I suggest that it was more plausible that Roberts' trauma re-awakened his biology of inequality. For Roberts, it did not matter how many millions God had provided in the past. Psychologically, he was still the struggling minister who did not have enough to do what God was demanding of him. In these moments, Roberts was faced with the questions of his earliest years: Does serving God mean suffering lack? Will God provide what he demands?

The emotional responses to Roberts' lack in funding the City of Faith quickly became more controversial in early 1981, when the stress of raising the final forty-five million was fully upon him, and he claimed that he saw a vision of a "900-foot Jesus" that held the City of Faith in his hands.[63] Dismissed as emotional manipulation by outsiders, Roberts' psychological trauma seems apparent in his appeals. Roberts even went on television on *Larry King Live* and the *Donahue* show to defend his vision.[64] To his critics, he said, "Yes, I have always seen Jesus, by the eyes of faith, as he has met the needs of the people through the years. But I also saw Jesus, just as I reported, lifting up the City of Faith. I hope I will see him again."[65] But the reality was, God had already provided Roberts with seventy-five million in cash to that point to build the hospital.

Over the next year, Roberts began to promise that if his supporters would help him build the hospital debt-free, that God would also give "the money you need for your bills and debts."[66] To do this, nothing less than a full-on commitment to "seed-faith" and prosperity teaching would be necessary to accomplish his goals. Thus, his message of prosperity was solidified, evident in the books he released during this time, including *Flood Stage: Opening the Windows of Heaven* in 1981, *If You Need to Be Blessed Financially Do These Things* in 1982, and *Attack your Lack* in 1985.

While the City of Faith opened debt-free in 1981 (although somewhat unfinished), the expenses of running the hospital and medical school kept Roberts in a constant place of need. His pleas for funding and the resulting emotional turmoil continued. Roberts often mentioned the strain he was under in his articles about the City of Faith in the *Abundant Life* magazine.[67] During the financial crisis in 1985, Roberts opened up about his struggles on national television:

I have asked God why this emergency happened to us.... You know, "What have we done to deserve this thing? Haven't we obeyed you, Lord? There's no other man in the twentieth century who has built a university, a medical school, and a medical center. And I did it because God commanded me to. Now, why have you brought us this far?[68]

Within this appeal, one can hear the echoes of the same questions he expressed as a little boy about his father's experience. Why does obedience to God lead to insufficiency?

Roberts' New Friends: The Word of Faith

Before the City of Faith and the controversies, Roberts was one of the most influential figures in American culture. But now, his financial base was abandoning him, and the American public was turning on him, leaving him friendless and searching for a new support base. Stepping into this vacuum, the leaders of the burgeoning Word of Faith movement welcomed him into their family, led by Kenneth E. Hagin and his protégés Kenneth Copeland and Fredrick K. C. Price. Up until this point, despite their similar Pentecostal origins and close proximity in Tulsa, Roberts and Hagin were not closely associated. In the first decade and a half, the "Faith Movement" was not well received by the primarily mainline Charismatic faculty and students on the campus of Oral Roberts University.[69]

In 1979, in the midst of Roberts' declining support and greatest fundraising demands, Kenneth Hagin invited Roberts to attend his annual Campmeeting in Tulsa. During one of the services, Hagin shared his deep appreciation for Roberts and surprised him by taking a love offering to help him with his vision.[70] That night, Hagin, Kenneth Copeland, John Osteen, and Pat and Debbie Boone led the way as the audience overflowed with pledges to save the City of Faith. This gesture deeply moved Roberts, and he commented, "I sat with my head in my hands, tears flowing down my cheeks, realizing that nothing like this had ever happened on my behalf."[71] Roberts found new friends that would walk with him through his most difficult times. In fact, three years later, it was Hagin who stepped in to comfort the family when Ronnie committed suicide in 1982, and assured Roberts that Ronnie "has not gone to hell" but that he was actually saved through his death.[72]

Over the next few years, Roberts was a regular speaker at Hagin's Campmeeting, and his rhetoric about prosperity followed suit. He was still careful about the "faith" principles around campus, but he could not deny that God was providing through this new constituency. Speakers at ORU chapel services began to shift from mainline Charismatics and Hollywood celebrities to Word of Faith preachers. The introduction of Word of Faith messages on campus caused controversy among some of the storied faculty, including Howard Ervin and Charles Farrah.[73] This alliance was also problematic for the United Methodists, who removed their affiliation with the seminary, which hurt Roberts deeply. However, this gave him the opportunity to initiate his own ministerial fellowship called "International Charismatic Bible Ministers," filled largely with independent Charismatic and Word of Faith ministers including Copeland, Jerry Savelle, Mike Murdock, Earl Paulk, and other emerging independent Word of Faith Charismatic ministers.[74] Many of these same ministers joined the Board of Regents at ORU as well.

These new prosperity influences were the final step in the process of transforming Roberts' theology of simply God's ability to supply basic needs into a full-blown prosperity message that promised financial blessings through giving. His new Word of Faith friends landed him the reputation as not only a "health and wealth" charlatan who used God to "pickpocket" gullible Christians, but the leader of them.[75] Criticism over his financial excesses increased for decisions such as purchasing their 2.4-million-dollar home in Palm Springs in 1982.[76] Worse, Roberts was being lumped in with his fellow televangelists, Jim Bakker and Jimmy Swaggart, who were embroiled in financial and sexual scandal.

The image of Roberts as the worst of all prosperity preachers was solidified when in July 1986, Roberts announced that if he did not raise eight million dollars, God would "call him home."[77] While Roberts' plea was intended to raise the money to continue to scholarship the students in his medical school, this brazen statement seemed to be the final straw for those in the mainline churches who had supported him.[78] The public ridicule only added to his feeling of abandonment. He commented, "Few people have had their losses and failures trumpeted by the media. . . I stopped reading the ridicule after I saw there was no end to it. It hurt so bad I sometimes felt as King David did: 'Oh that I had wings like a dove! for then I would fly away and be at rest.'"[79]

In 1987, the United Methodist Church withdrew its support from Roberts, the ORU seminary, and several of the Methodist faculty left.[80] Two years later, in 1989, heartbroken, Roberts closed ORU Medical School and City of Faith in defeat. Roberts called this "a disaster" that "took away a part of my soul."[81] Roberts eventually stepped down as president in 1991, and moved to his home in California, where he could find some distance from his own pain.[82]

Conclusion

Considering the development of Roberts' view of prosperity in the late 1970s and 1980s, critics of the so-called "health and wealth" gospel are rightly justified in their critiques and in pointing to Roberts as a source. He was certainly responsible for concepts of "seed faith" that have been used by prosperity teachers globally as justification for self-enrichment. However, his view of prosperity did not begin this way. Roberts' view of prosperity began as the "sufficiency gospel" rather than "prosperity gospel." Through faith and the scriptures, especially 3 John 2, he overcame his own anxiety of insufficiency by believing in a God who desired to meet basic human needs. Roberts was able to reprogram the biology of inequality in ways that provided him hope that things could get better by believing in a God who cared about his needs. Roberts' orientation was not toward worldly abundance but toward God's sufficiency. He did not advocate for believers to enjoy boundless riches, only that God would supply their needs and enable people to live "the abundant life" and to accomplish what God had set before them. Because of this, he was able not only to overcome decades of poverty but also to believe that he could ultimately accomplish anything God asked him to do.

Roberts' development of prosperity teachings was also rooted in his experience of poverty. His need for a further developed "prosperity gospel" was ultimately governed by psychological factors of lack of security rather than theological or materialistic factors. At the end of the day, he was not self-enriching; he was coping with an acute sense of loss related to the two highly debilitating forms of personal trauma: a child's premature death and a child's suicide.[83] In Roberts' case, his religious views helped him find meaning in order to make sense of his loss. The City of Faith represented Roberts' reconstruction of meaning as a coping and recovery mechanism out of his grief.[84] He could not save his children, but he could save others through a hospital, a place of healing and recovery. The only way to do that was to raise money and go all-in on God's ability to provide in a time when he was also coping with the abandonment of his support structure. Into this space, ministers from the prosperity wing of his movement enabled him to focus on the material aspects of God's blessings to accomplish his vision.

As we consider the doctrine of prosperity as it has advanced into the world, it is necessary to recognize that Roberts' view of prosperity originated in the simple concept of God's goodness and provision for believers. That belief allowed Roberts to escape his own poverty by moving him into a sphere of sufficiency and security that counteracted the biology of inequality. Roberts' experience is proof that belief in God's sufficiency has a powerful effect on poverty by alleviating psychological stress and regulating the biological and emotional states. But Roberts' story also illustrates the dangers of turning God's sufficiency into a means to an end. For Roberts, his emotional trauma triggered a sense of overcompensation that resulted in Roberts' overemphasis on God's abundance. This has resulted in others who used Roberts' views of seed faith as means for self-enrichment.

While the abuse of prosperity theology is problematic for global Christianity, it should not negate the powerful impact of belief in a God who provides for those in difficult socioeconomic situations. As Amos Yong notes, the social uplift that faith in God brings should not be the privilege of Western societies. He says, "Why is it implausible that God should transform the poverty of his people into affluence across the southern hemisphere as God has done so in the Western world?"[85] Indeed, if God can provide for an impoverished Pentecostal Holiness preacher in depression-era Oklahoma, why would he be so limited in impoverished systems globally? As Yong points out, "Minimally, I suggest that in impoverished situations, such a prosperity message will engender hope and perhaps motivate a certain course of action that anticipates the gradual, if not more efficient, overcoming of poverty."[86] When hope is coupled with other values such as hard work, resiliency, community responsibility, and innovation, it fuels possibility thinking and enables one to overcome the biology of inequality. Perhaps if this idea of faith in God to provide as a form of sufficiency gospel could supplant the prosperity gospel, the work of elevating the poor could be more effective in the type of social uplift that the gospel requires of the church.

Notes

1 This research was originally presented at the 2019 Scholars Consultation of Empowered21 held June 3–4, 2019, in Bogota, Colombia, where the theme was "Poverty, its impacts, and the responses of Spirit-empowered communities."

2 The theme of social engagement among Pentecostals was front and center in the 2018 Annual Meeting of the Society for Pentecostal Studies.

3 Donald E. Miller and Tetsunao Yamamori, *Global Pentecostalism: The New Face of Christian Social Engagement* (Berkley, CA: University of California Press), 2007.

4 Miller and Yamamori, *Global Pentecostalism*, 165.

5 Jacob K. Ayantayo, "Prosperity Gospel and Social Morality: A Critique," in Akintude E. Akinade and David O. Ogubile, eds., *Creativity and Change in Nigerian Christianity* (Lagos: Malthouse Press, 2010), 202–203.

6 Asoneze Ukah, "The Deregulation of Piety in the Context of Neoliberal Globalization," in Vinson Synan, Amos Yong, and J. Kwabena Asamoah-Gyadu, eds., *Global Renewal Christianity* (Lake Mary, FL: Charisma House, 2016), 362–378.

7 Ayantayo, "Prosperity Gospel and Social Morality," 208–209.

8 Clifton Clarke, *Pentecostal Theology in Africa* (Eugene, OR: Wipf and Stock Publishers, 2014), 139.

9 Kate Bowler, *Blessed: A History of the American Prosperity Gospel* (Oxford: Oxford University Press, 2012), 48.

10 Clarke, *Pentecostal Theology in Africa*, 139; E. Kingsly Larbi, "The New Face of African Christianity: David Oyedepo's Winners Chapel and the Pentecostal Message of Salvation," in Vinson Synan, Amos Yong, and J. Kwabena Asamoah-Gyadu, eds., *Global Renewal Christianity* (Lake Mary, FL: Charisma House, 2016), 19–38.

11 Bowler, *Blessed*, 234. The actual origin of this phrase Bowler does not identify. While I cannot confirm this phrase, it was certainly consistent with his attitude.

12 Ellis Roberts, "God's Hand on My Life," *Healing Waters* 5:9 (August 1951), 6. Ellis and Claudia attended a brush arbor revival hosted by Luther Dryden, Dan York, and Dan Evans four miles from their home.

13 Roberts, "God's Hand on My Life," 7.

14 Oral Roberts, *How I Know Jesus Was Not Poor* (Altamonte Springs, FL: Creation House, 1989), 14.

15 Oral Roberts, *Expect a Miracle* (Nashville: Thomas Nelson, 1995), 14.

16 Roberts, *How I Learned Jesus Was Not Poor*, 7.

17 Roberts, *How I Learned Jesus Was Not Poor*, 5.

18 Louis M. Kyrakoudes, "'Lookin' for Better All the Time': Rural Migration and Urbanization in the South, 1900–1950," in R. Douglas Hurt ed., *African American Life in the Rural South*, 1900–1950 (Columbia: University of Missouri Press, 2003), 16, points out that both blacks and whites in the South were stuck in the cycle of yearly moving from farm to farm in search of lower rent or better yields to improve their economic status.

19 Roberts, *How I Learned Jesus Was Not Poor*, 14.

20 Roberts, *Expect a Miracle*, 14.

21 Roberts, *How I Learned Jesus Was Not Poor*, 6.

22 Oral Roberts, *Oral Roberts' Life Story* (Tulsa: Oral Roberts, 1952), 42–43.

23 Roberts, *Expect a Miracle*, 22.

24 Daniel D. Isgrigg and Vinson Synan, "An Early Account of Oral Roberts' Healing Testimony," *Spiritus: ORU Journal of Theology* 3:2 (Fall 2018), 169–177.

25 Isgrigg and Synan, "An Early Account of Oral Roberts' Healing Testimony," 170–173, gives the account of Roberts' early success, preaching six hundred times in the first four years of his ministry.

26 Evelyn Roberts, "I Married Oral Roberts," *Abundant Life* 7:1 (December 1952), 4.

27 David E. Harrell, Jr., *Oral Roberts: An American Life* (Bloomington, IN: Indiana University Press, 1985), 50.

28 Roberts, *Expect a Miracle*, 54; *The East Oklahoma Conference News* (October 1943), 4.

29 "Editor Speaks at O.B.U.," *Pentecostal Holiness Advocate*, April 4, 1946, 10.

30 "Foreign Missions," *Pentecostal Holiness Advocate*, November 18, 1945, 10, notes, "Rev. G. Oral Roberts came before the Board having been called to labor in Palestine." "Editors Mail," *Pentecostal Holiness Advocate*, January 10, 1946, 2, reports Oral Roberts first enrolled in East Central State College in Ada, while preparing for missionary service in Palestine.

31 Roberts, *Oral Roberts' Life Story*, 62–63.

32 Roberts, *Oral Roberts' Life Story*, 62–63.

33 Oral Roberts, *Miracle of Seed-Faith* (Tulsa, OK: Oral Roberts Evangelistic Association, 1970), 16.

34 Roberts, *Miracle of Seed-Faith*, 6.

35 An example of clinical studies that compare early life stress with brain development and epigenetics is John Mclean, Rajeev Krishnadas, G. David Batty, et al., "Early Life Socioeconomic Status, Chronic Physiological Stress and Hippocampal N-acetyl Aspartate Concentrations," *Behavioral Brain Research* 235:2 (December 2012), 225–30, https://doi.org/10.1016/j.bbr.2012.08.013, accessed January 16, 2020.

36 Lucy A. Jewell, "The Biology of Inequality," *Denver Law Review* 93:3 (2018), 611–612, points out, "one's material environment can get under one's skin and into one's genetic and brain pathways."

37 Jewell, "The Biology of Inequality," 610.

38 Jewell, "The Biology of Inequality," 618.

39 Roberts, *Expect a Miracle*, 18.

40 Roberts, *Oral Roberts' Life Story*, 35.

41 Roberts received enough life experience credits from his years in ministry to apply for and received his B.A. and M.Div. from Oral Roberts University in 1989. He was awarded an honorary doctorate from Centenary College in 1975.

42 Jewell, "The Biology of Inequality," 631, points out that children from poverty show reduced ability to filter distractions and hindered achievement because of short attention spans.

43 Roberts, *Expect a Miracle*, 64.

44 Roberts, *Expect a Miracle*, 157.

45 See, Daniel D. Isgrigg, "Interpreting the Signs of the Times: How Eschatology Shaped Assemblies of God Social Ethics," (47th Annual Meeting of the Society for Pentecostal Studies, Cleveland, TN, March 2018), 4–5.

46 Roberts, *Oral Roberts' Life Story*, 73.

47 Oral Roberts, "God's Three Ways to Stop Being Afraid," *Abundant Life* 12:3 (March 1958), 4–7.

48 Roberts, *How I Know Jesus Was Not Poor*, 15.

49 Jim Hunter, Jr., "Where My Voice Is Heard Small: The Development of Oral Roberts' Television Ministry," *Spiritus: ORU Journal of Theology* 3:2 (2018), 239–257.

50 John R. Crouch, Jr. "Healing through Prayer and Medicine: How Oral Roberts' Healing Vision Was— and Continues to Be—Fulfilled," *Spiritus: ORU Journal of Theology* 4:2 (2019), 191–203.

51 Harrell, *Oral Roberts*, 193. Roberts certainly enjoyed a significant level of personal wealth, becoming a shrewd businessman and owning various properties and land investments in addition to his own ranch in Bixby, Oklahoma.

52 Oral Roberts, "God has a Divine Abundance for You," *Abundant Life* 12:11 (November 1958), 2.

53 "Finds Blessing-Pact Brings Totally Unexpected Blessings," *Abundant Life* 12:5 (May 1958), 23.

54 The order of buildings are as follows: Timko-Barton Hall, Braxton Hall, Shakarian Hall (1962); EMR Hall, Claudius Hall, Health Resources Center, Learning Resources Center (1965); Prayer Tower (1967); University Village, Student Activity Center (1969); Mabee Center (1972); Susie Residence Tower, Wesley Residence Tower (1972); Howard Auditorium (1973); Athletic Residence Hall, Christ Chapel (1975); Francis Hall, Susie Hall, School of Medicine (1976); Baby Mabee, J. L. Johnson Baseball Stadium (1977); Student Apartment Complex, Graduate Center (1978); City of Faith (1978–1981); Grandview Hotel (1981); Journey through the Bible (1986).

55 An anecdotal story often told around the university that on the day Oral Roberts died, he called out to God, "Not yet, Lord! Just one more building!"

56 Oral Roberts, "An Exchange of Letters," *Abundant Life* 23:10 (November 1969), 18–19.

57 Roberts, "An Exchange of Letters,"18–19.

58 Roberts, *Miracle of Seed-Faith*, 8.

59 Oral Roberts, "I Will Rain upon Your Desert," *Abundant Life* 31:10 (October 1977), 1–13.

60 Harrell, Oral Roberts, 337; Roberts, *Expect a Miracle*, 206–210.

61 Barbara Wolfe, William Evans, and Teresa E. Seeman, eds., *The Biological Consequences of Socioeconomic Inequalities* (New York: Russell Sage Foundation, 2012), 21.

62 Helen Rhee, *Loving the Poor, Saving the Rich: Wealth, Poverty, and Early Christian Formation* (Grand Rapids: Baker Academic, 2012), 73–101.

63 Oral Roberts, "Who Hath Believed Our Report," *Abundant Life* 35:2 (February 1981), 1–7.

64 The critiques of Roberts' vision were numerous, especially in Tulsa. See "Oral Roberts tells of talking 900-foot Jesus," *Tulsa World*, October 16, 1980, https://www.tulsaworld.com/archive/oral-roberts-tells-of-talking-

to--foot-jesus/article_bbe49a4e-e441-5424-8fcf-1d49ede6318c.html, accessed November 5, 2019; David Avril, "Roberts says 900-foot Jesus Appeared Before My 'Inner Eyes,'" *Tulsa World*, May 7, 1982, https://www.tulsaworld.com/archive/oral-roberts-says--foot-jesus-appeared-before-my-inner/article_5f277265-a4d8-5647-86b3-6db313dd0f23.html, accessed November 5, 2019.

65 Oral Roberts, "Who Hath Believed Our Report," 7.

66 Oral Roberts, "Everything in Ministry Has Pointed to this Moment of God's Time," *Abundant Life* 35:11 (November 1981), 1–4. Cf. Oral Roberts, "How to Let God Put His Hand on Your Hands," *Abundant Life* 35:5 (May 1981), 13.

67 Oral Roberts, "The Master Plan God Has Given Me," *Abundant Life* 31:11 (November 1977), 6; "The Time Has Come," *Abundant Life* 38:3 (March 1984), 14–18; Oral Roberts, "People Are Experiencing a Major New Offensive Mounted by the Enemy," *Abundant Life* 38:7 (July 1984), 9.

68 "There's Healing for You and There's a Faith-Walk for You in the Emergencies of Life," *Abundant Life* 39:6 (August 1985), 3–4.

69 Harrell, *Oral Roberts*, 423.

70 Harrell, *Oral Roberts*, 424.

71 Oral Roberts, "The Night I Found Out That God Hadn't Forgotten Me in My Struggle," *Abundant Life* 33:10 (October 1979), 6–13.

72 Roberts, *Expect a Miracle*, 209–210.

73 Harrell, *Oral Roberts*, 424–425.

74 "Charismatic Bible Ministries," *Abundant Life* 40:2 (March/April 1986), 10–13.

75 Henry Fairlie, "Evangelists in Babylon," *The New Republic* 196:17 (April 27, 1987), 22–24.

76 Harrell, *Oral Roberts*, 355.

77 Roberts, "God Says: It's Action Time," *Abundant Life* 41:2 (March/April 1987), 3.

78 It is important to understand that Roberts' commitment to begin the medical school was attached to the idea that he would raise the money to scholarship all of the ORU Medical School students so that they were not hindered by debt after graduation. The goal was to scholarship doctors to serve as healing agents in medical missions around the world. This was the obedience to which Oral Roberts felt God had called him. He felt that if he could not obey God to raise the money to keep the medical school going, he had no more assignment here on earth. See John R. Crouch, Jr.,

"Healing through Prayer and Medicine," 191–203; Thomson K. Mathew, "Oral Roberts' Theology of Healing: A Journey from Pentecostal 'Divine Healing' to Charismatic 'Signs and Wonders' to Spirit-empowered 'Whole Person Healing,'" *Spiritus: ORU Journal of Theology* 3:2 (2018), 303–23.

79 Roberts, *Expect a Miracle*, 300.

80 Roberts, *Expect a Miracle*, 327–329.

81 Roberts, *Expect a Miracle*, 298.

82 The story of the devastation of the City of Faith decisions does not end in 1991. Over the next decade, Richard Roberts attempted to navigate a university and ministry saddled with fifty million dollars in debt and declining enrollment. These tensions eventually led to a crisis in 2007, when the University almost went under. The story of the university's recovery after 2007 is told in Neil Eskelin, *The New ORU* (Tulsa, OK: Oral Roberts University, 2018).

83 Roberts A. Neimeyer and Diana C. Sands, "Meaning Reconstruction in Bereavement: From Principles to Practice," in Robert A. Neimeyer, Darcy L. Harris, et al., eds., *Grief and Bereavement in Contemporary Society: Bridging Research and Practice* (New York: Routledge, 2011), 12.

84 Neimeyer and Sands, "Meaning Reconstruction in Bereavement," 9–10.

85 Amos Yong, "A Typology of Prosperity Theology: A Religious Economy of Global Renewal or a Renewal Economics," in Katherine Attanasi and Amos Yong, eds., *Pentecostalism and Prosperity: The Socio-Economics of the Global Charismatic Movement* (New York: Palgrave MacMillan, 2012), 24.

86 Yong, "A Typology of Prosperity Theology," 19.

23 A DREAMer's Journey and the Holy Spirit's Comfort: A Personal Reflection

Lemuel J. Godinez and Yasmine A. Godinez

Abstract

DREAMERs, as colloquially known, are undocumented immigrants brought to the United States as children. Differed Action for Childhood Arrivals (DACA) passed by executive action in 2012 has granted a measure of impermanent relief for thousands of them. DREAMERS live as "foreigners" and "aliens" in the only land most of them have known as home. Like most immigrants, they will have to overcome emotional and psychological distress. However, DREAMer Distress is a qualitative form of poverty unique to the young, undocumented immigrant. Apart from lacking the benefits afforded by legal status, DREAMers are confronted with forming a unique socio-cultural identity that can leave them living in the emotional gap of *Ni de aqui, Ni de aya* (neither from here nor there). The Holy Spirit is not deaf to the DREAMer's plight but is able to be an ever-present help, making a way where there was none. The DREAMer's journey can be seen as a prophetic call and reminder to the church of her true DNA as sojourners on earth. Not unlike DREAMers, the church, too is in a gap, having its real citizenship in its promised spiritual homeland.

Introduction

The term immigrant has become a buzzword provoking varied sentiments. In the United States, immigrants increasingly make many news headlines and are continuously the subject of debate. It is far easier to talk about immigrants as a subject in abstract form without remembering that they are humans. Humans that endure a great deal to come to the United States and often continue to pay a multifaceted price to remain. The plight is perhaps most evident for undocumented immigrants,[1] towering over them as a daily stressor. The mental and emotional distress riddling their lives can be called a form of poverty. This chapter focuses on the mental and emotional distress of one such group of immigrants, the DREAMers. DREAMer distress, as this article will describe, is cause for concern. Even with the most positive outlook and hope for the future, a DREAMer's distress cannot be all at once resolved by granting them legal status. This article is not a political commentary on immigration in the United States today, a biblical theology on immigration, nor an attempt at a persuasive homily on how the church ought to treat immigrants. Works such as these abound.[2] Instead, it is a story of a single DREAMer and a testimony of what the guidance and power of the Holy Spirit can do amid hopelessness. Our DREAMer's journey and experience will be interwoven with the various psychological and emotional factors that research shows can contribute to poverty among undocumented immigrant families and DREAMers in particular. His first-person narrative will unfold and provide clear examples of the DREAMer Distress this article aims to explain. The work will conclude with some reflections on the Dreamers' journey and theological points of contact between Dreamers and Christians today.

Immigration in the United States

Of the roughly 40 million immigrants in the United States, about three-quarters are legally here, while one-quarter are here unauthorized.[3] Estimates of the number of unauthorized immigrants range from 10.5 million to 12 million people.[4] Some immigrants arrived as children with little knowledge of the land left behind or understanding of the situation in the United States. In 2012 President Barack Obama passed Deferred Action for Childhood Arrivals (DACA) by executive order. At the time this work is written, about 649,000 young immigrants have work permits under the DACA program, which protects them temporarily from deportation.[5] DACA beneficiaries are sometimes called Dreamers, as a colloquial catchphrase, after the Development, Relief, and Education for Alien Minors (DREAM) Act was first proposed in Congress in the early 2000s.[6] However, DACA remains an impermanent solution for thousands of DREAMers who must still wait for the U.S. Congress to pass legislation on their behalf.

All DACA recipients are DREAMers, but not all DREAMers are DACA. To qualify for DACA, they needed to have met specific requirements, including having immigrated to the United States before their sixteenth birthday, be either in school or have graduated from high school, and have no felony charges.[7] As of September 2019, DACA recipients hail from over 158 countries and reside in all fifty U.S. states and territories. The top ten countries from which DACA recipients come are Mexico (eighty percent), El Salvador, Guatemala, Honduras, Peru, South Korea, Brazil,

Ecuador, Colombia, and Argentina. About eighty percent have lived in the United States for more than fifteen years, and half of them have lived here for twenty years or more.[8]

Beginning in June 2017, the DACA program stopped accepting new applicants.[9] On June 28, 2020, the U.S. Supreme Court blocked the Trump administration's attempt to terminate the DACA program for existing beneficiaries, requesting the administration do so in a proper way.[10] Adding to the saga, on December 4, 2020, a U.S. District Court judge ordered the Trump administration to restore the program to pre-2017 status.[11] According to a Pew Research Center survey, about three-quarters of adults in the United States say they favor granting permanent legal status to immigrants who came illegally to the United States as children.[12] Despite evidence of this positive popular opinion, DREAMers and DACA's future remains bleak in the political arena.

The Plight of Immigrants to the United States

Some immigrants feel forced to migrate, but many immigrants choose to come to America seeking a dream, better opportunities, or to rejoin the family. Some can find a better home, find a stable job, and give their family a better life. Undocumented immigrants, however, can have a more tortuous path to a better life. Research shows that undocumented immigrants have lower educational attainment and higher poverty rates in the United States compared to the general U.S.-born population.[13] Although having reached a new land and context, they can continue to face recontextualized forms of poverty that were unanticipated or largely unconsidered when opting to migrate. This recontextualized poverty includes socioeconomic disadvantages, marginalization, exploitation, and unmet basic physical and mental health needs.[14]

My family left Mexico a few years before the Peso collapse of 1994. They had heard anecdotes of the overflowing prosperity in the United States, and with so many of their loved ones finding steady work, the anecdotes seemed credible. Dreaming of a better quality of life, they sacrificed cultural and familial ties and migrated North. My family could have never known that the quest for the famed "American Dream" did not come without vexing and pervasive costs; that even after paying a high material price to get to the United States, other challenges of a more lasting kind were ahead. In my case, no part of me was untouched by the decision to immigrate; my early sense of identity, thinking process, and emotional development were all impacted.

Emotional Distress as a Form of Poverty

The Oxford Dictionary defines poverty as "the state of being extremely poor; the state of being inferior in quality or insufficient in amount."[15] Though emotional distress and mental illness are not typically viewed as poverty, they certainly are a qualitative form of poverty. Studies have shown a correlation between emotional health and quality of life.[16] Being undocumented does not always equate with financial poverty, but will be linked to varying degrees of emotional and mental hardships to overcome.

Emotional distress resulting from chronic stress over time is a critical unifying, and prevalent theme among research studies on undocumented individuals.[17] It is understood as relating to the manifestation of depressive and anxiety symptoms. Depressive symptoms common in undocumented immigrant populations may appear as low self-esteem, feelings of helplessness, loss of motivation, and powerlessness. Physical symptoms may include fatigue, decreased sleep, and appetite. Anxiety-related symptoms include *ataque de nervios* (panic attacks), excessive worry, racing thoughts, and uncertainty.[18] In a young immigrant, these symptoms may come to overshadow the self-actualization process, decrease productivity, and dwarf the development of imagination, increasing the probability of financial poverty.

Reflecting on my early years, I realize that most of my thinking was centered on how uncomfortable I felt and, at times, how different I was. Those years were emotionally turbulent. It is as if I were always in a mental fog. Questions such as, "why must I work harder to be heard than my American peers," "why do some look at me like I am a threat," "why do I often feel the need to prove myself when my American peers seem so relaxed," and others such as these began to haunt me. I remember very few vivid dreams before my adolescence. My American friends would talk about growing up to be astronauts, doctors, and teachers, but I had faint ideas for myself. Perhaps my focus was obscured by this mental fog that clouded my ability to visualize my future. I simply could not dream of my tomorrow.

Moreover, in my home, the focus was on how to alleviate short-term deficits and needs. Retirement, asset building, and wealth management were not conversations at our dinner table. Additional complications were that my family did not speak the language, were unfamiliar with the ins and outs in the United States, had no access to welfare assistance, and lived under constant fear of deportation. We did not have the mindset nor the security to create long-term financial plans. At a very young age, I was beginning to follow that pattern of thinking that can only concentrate on today's wants rather than looking towards the future of who I could be, what I could do, and how I could go about it.

In Pursuit of the American Dream

Before stepping foot in the United States, some immigrants have already experienced stressors that warrant concern for future emotional and mental health ranging from financial hardship, crime in their community and/or family, or political and social instability. When deciding to emigrate, some carry the weight of unprocessed grief from leaving behind family, friends, career, or class/status held in their home country. Later, though this weight may be undefined for young DREAMers, it becomes very present in their parents' focus and perspectives. It is important to note that though many DREAMers may not recall experiencing these pre-migration stressors themselves, their restless state of mind, lack of connectedness, or a general sense of instability may be influenced by the stressors, spoken or unspoken, of their parents' past.

At their crossing, undocumented immigrants face another myriad of possible dangers and stressors. Entering the United States unauthorized has been associated with various negative experiences, including the possibility of detainment, experiencing or witnessing violence, extortion from immigration authorities or organized crime, environmental hazards, abandonment by *coyotes* (border crossing guides), sexual abuse, physical injury, or death.[19] These events may shatter a person's sense of safety and contribute to the development of Post Traumatic Stress Disorder (PTSD) symptoms years after the episode. Furthermore, research shows that feelings of guilt or shame may not be uncommon even years later, due to the dominant rhetoric criminalizing them and their parents for entering the country illegally.[20] This shame can lead many young immigrants to internalize the judgment and feel somehow defective.

   I arrived in the U.S. when I was three. I first discovered I was an undocumented immigrant in school when I was nine. I remember the episode well: a teacher had spoken to the principal about my lunch form missing "some information." I could not provide the information, not because I wanted to conceal anything, but I was unaware I did not have it. I remember the feeling of wanting to hide my face, though I did not understand why. That was the beginning of a sense that would come to overshadow me at times, the feeling that I was doing something wrong or that I was somehow flawed, afraid of being exposed, or called out to face the law. It soon became nerve-racking to turn in any administrative school document because they always lacked complete information. To this day, having to fill out personal information forms, at a bank, for example, strikes a hint of uneasiness in me.

   In the United States, undocumented immigrants can expect ongoing adjustment and adaptation difficulties. DREAMers learn to live as "Americans" without being fully recognized as such, nor offered the legal rights the United States affords its citizens. They are considered to be "illegal aliens" in the United States, and "strangers" in the only land they know as home. The undocumented experience can include low wages, strenuous jobs, working without benefits, and language and cultural differences, and these feed into a feeling of marginalization and invisibility. These adverse effects are exacerbated in the United States, where racial and ethnic tensions exist. According to the Pew Hispanic Center, thirty-eight percent of Latinos reported personal experiences with discrimination in the United States. About half said they had serious concerns about their place in the country.[21] Experiences associated with discrimination among Latino/a youth have been linked to lower self-esteem, self-blame, and problem behaviors.[22]

   Feeling like a vulnerable outsider can have strange effects on the mind. Apprehension and a sense of thought-paralysis with unfamiliar places, people, or conversations were some of the earliest stressors I experienced. In elementary and middle school, I recall feeling a sense of vulnerability and lack of comprehension. Managing language barriers, cultural differences, and academic expectations, while needing to belong wore my mind thin. I would burst into defiance in moments of distress, finding myself in physical altercations, regularly "ditching" classes, and getting suspended. By the age of ten, I had experienced racial slurs, prejudice, and demeaning stares. Having both brown skin and an undocumented status, I often felt unsafe and socially incompetent around non-Latinos. Over the years, I learned to nod, smile, and nervously laugh with people, unable to express what I was thinking or how to be myself fully. How could the land my parents dreamed of become such an emotionally challenging place to live? Even though our family did have so much more to be grateful for, the anxiety and fear always had me asking: Is this not the "land of milk and honey," and if not now – when?

Most regrettably, research shows that despite adaptive and acculturation processes, this experience does not improve with more extended residence in the United States, finding instead that a longer period in the United States increased psychological distress rates through increased perceived discrimination.[23]

DREAMer Distress

As exemplified, emotional distress and the onset of depressive or anxiety-like symptoms are perpetuated by multiple experiences on an undocumented individual. At every stage, undocumented youth face various degrees of risk making them vulnerable to suffer from such symptoms. Over time, these undocumented-related stressors on the individual and the family accumulate into a general trauma experience or what the authors call DREAMer Distress.

Moreover, DREAMer Distress includes a particular stressor that is unique to the young undocumented immigrant. DREAMers are confronted with forming a unique socio-cultural identity distinct from that of their parents. They encounter various challenges that their parents have not experienced (e.g., going to primary school in a non-native tongue, carrying the weight of translating for their parents, or parentification whereby they become more responsible for family matters not normative for their age).[24] This gap in parental know-how puts DREAMers at a greater risk for more significant stress in their acculturation and identity formation process. Moreover, DREAMers are left to rely primarily on themselves or seek help from those outside their immediate family system. Negative consequences of these added stressors may manifest as chronic anxiety, apathy, decreased academic functioning, and other adverse long-term outcomes.[25] Adult immigrants typically are more insulated from possible negative consequences from acculturation stress by their strong ethnic identities and continued use of their home country as a point of comparison for assessing their quality of life.[26]

Like all immigrant children, I was growing up in the divide of several "worlds." Although I came to the United States at a relatively young age, the substantial cultural and social differences between home and school by age ten were enough to complicate my sense of identity. Like my parents, I was a physical stranger in America, but unlike my parents, I was an outsider to the Mexican culture. This difference played a significant role during family and church gatherings, holidays, and birthday parties. I would come to develop my own composite culture, drawing a "second-hand" Mexican culture from my family, and honing some form of American culture at school. English was for school, Spanish was for home, but my native tongue would always be *Spanglish*. Those I mostly related to were second-generation immigrants like me who were *Ni de aqui, Ni de aya* (neither from here nor there). In the formative years of ages ten to fifteen, there was no one around me who could tutor me academically, mentor me on the importance of education, nor provide a mature perspective on my burgeoning needs for solidarity and desire to belong to a land.

I spent many of my pre-adolescent years wrestling to uncover "roots" of which I could be proud. My quest for identity was perpetually plagued by the visceral sense of being an alien in the United States – the only place I called home. As a young kid, I wondered if it would be easier to go back to Mexico and avoid this entire predicament. At times, I would close my eyes and yearn for a land for people like me, so those unconnected to a homeland could find a place of relief and rest. A land where I naturally fit, a place of opportunity like the United States; a place where I had deep roots but was no "alien." A land where I would not be judged by "the color of my skin" or my lack of documentation, but as Martin Luther King Jr. put it, by "the content of my character." It felt overwhelming to be a young person of color and encounter prejudice and at the same time not have the confidence of residing legally in "my own land."

As I grew older, I learned the importance of a Social Security number (a national identification number). I would continue to be reminded of how much my "identity" lacked validation due to the absence of an I.D. (identification card) and rights not afforded to me. I could not get a legal job, a bank account without having to pay strange fees, a driver's license or state I.D., travel domestically or internationally, vote, get health insurance, apply for a mortgage or car loan, and many other "privileges" like these. Being unable to enjoy so much of what the United States offers its youth, I began to live a life in the "shadows," doing the best I could with what I had.

The Holy Spirit and My Undocumented Plight

The question often comes to those far removed from the immigrant plight, even if unvoiced, "Why migrate or stay in such a situation? Why don't they go back to their country?" The question is insensitive, even crass. There are no easy answers; families worldwide do their best to survive, and mine was no different. What did make a difference in my life was the presence of God.

I grew up in a Christian home but did not immediately embrace the faith. When I was twelve, during a Saturday church service, I felt the love of God so strongly on my body that I began to cry. For the first time, I felt protected. Although he did not immediately remove fear, the Holy Spirit began to systematically dissolve my mental fog. I would come to know that hidden behind the fog was always a dynamic passion and a desire to run after my dreams. That is what began to visibly rise within me as my interest levels and motivational drive were unleashed. I began to think more clearly about my future and became little constrained by the limited options DREAMers were portrayed to have. And so, in the early 2000s, before the passing of DACA, I began to use my imagination to chart out my aspirations and goals by faith. The more I dreamed about what my future held, the more vivid my hope became, and the more confident I became God would always reward that hard work - even if in unexpected ways.

From seventh grade until my final year in high school, I poured myself relentlessly into my studies. That was my strategy: seek God in my heart, dream big with my mind, and work hard with what was before me. I found that concentrating on my hope and leaving everything else to God gave me the same confidence as if I had a social security number. By high school, I was involved in sports, extracurricular activities, community service, led a weekly Bible study amongst my peers, and began to investigate some of the best colleges in the country. I was officially dreaming. There was no guarantee I would be able to go to university after I finished high school, but the hope within me promised otherwise.

As my final year in high school approached its end, I applied to an engineering program at Colorado School of Mines (CSM). Unfortunately, a fellow DREAMer and I were both denied because of our undocumented status. I remember the sense of devastation and powerlessness I felt, and my mother's disappointment when she realized there was a unexpected ceiling on her son's academic future. A giant obstacle had confronted me, a Goliath much more able, potent, and experienced than I (1 Sam 17:4–7), but he would not have the final word. The next chapter of my life can only be described as a series of supernatural miracles.

In 2007 a group of us high schoolers were invited to a Rotary International lunch where coincidentally (or by design), the President of CSM would be speaking. Knowing that I was interested in the university, but unaware I had already been denied, our Rotary sponsor introduced us to the president. Up to this point, admission to this university was no longer a viable option, yet the Holy Spirit never allowed me to despair. At that moment, it was as if a window of palpable grace opened over a DREAMer friend and I, and the president took an interest in us. From this moment on, the President's affiliate would consistently reach out to us, and because of our strong academic standing, we were eventually granted provisional admission with the caveat that we would pay international tuition (which was, at the time, three times that of in-state tuition). Goliath had been struck with a stone but was only half dead (1 Sam 17:48–50); the next challenge would be how to pay out-of-state tuition without traditional access to financial assistance or federal aid.

This journey with the Holy Spirit taught me so much. I found there is something contagious about passion. Those with little reason to help found themselves inexplicably needing to help us. The Holy Spirit's presence consistently safeguarded my hope in my final year of high school, leading me to know that provision was headed our way. My DREAMer friend and I found favor and began to be introduced to potential sponsors within the city. Our high school counselor became a relentless advocate. We met several donors that pledged a portion of the exorbitant tuition, and by the time I graduated high school, I had my first year's tuition fully pledged for by generous donors. Goliath was now dead (1 Sam 17:51), but would he stay dead for the remaining three years of tuition? It would prove to be so. I would see the faithful provision of God for four years.

These were exciting and difficult years. Like many DREAMer, I was the first in my family to go to University. It was a challenging Engineering program. I spent most of those years in study or lost somewhere in the library. Though sponsors had been generous, I was navigating the concerns common to my undergraduate peers stepping out into the responsibilities of adulthood (e.g., rent) but without parental know-how or financial aid access. This was compounded by the challenge of not being able to legally work or drive. God remained faithful. In 2011, when the final semester of our undergraduate degree was drawing to an end, my DREAMer friend and I began to wonder about the benefit of staying in school with the hope of buying time for an immigration policy change that would allow us the possibility to work in our field. This idea, however, was expensive. It seemed like Goliath's brother was picking a fight, making me wonder how many giants we would have to ultimately kill in this land (2 Sam 21:22). But this giant, too, would not have the last word.

That spring, one of our donors pledged our graduate school tuition. By the Fall of 2011, I became the first in my family to pursue a graduate degree. When DACA was passed in 2012, I felt a sense of relief, but it did not give me a reason to hope for the first time. By this point, I had learned that God opens doors where we only see a wall. With the Holy Spirit's leadership, and the help of so many incredible people, I dreamed-of and pursued my academic goals. God was indeed faithful, and I finished my Master of Science degree in 2014. I finished this degree with high honors, having grown not only as a thinker, but as a man. During this time, the Holy Spirit taught me how periods of our lives that seem full of routine and monotony can be used to work on our character and vision. In this season, he sowed seeds for dreams that are still to be uncovered.

Reflection of a DREAMer

The story, of course, does not end there. So much has happened between the end of my graduate degree and where I stand today. Time and space would fail, however, to enumerate the many challenges and blessings that followed, and I live still today. No part of me was untouched by my parent's decision to migrate from Mexico to the United States. There are many anxieties and fears from the early years that still plague me. Some are small but are very much still there. At times, I had no idea how to navigate or rid myself of these. Today, with the help of the Holy Spirit, I am overcoming them day-by-day. It is, perhaps, ironic that those called DREAMers can, in many ways, be held back from dreaming; that certainly was my case without the Holy Spirit.

When I reflect on my story as an immigrant, and as a child of immigrants, I am nothing but thankful. Thankful because an immigrant's life is so often limited in options, and it is because of those lack of options that I was cast upon the mercies of the Lord, and my heart learned to trust in God. I was reminded time and time again of the Psalmist:

> On you was I cast from my birth, and from my mother's womb you have been my God. Be not far from me, for trouble is near, and there is none to help. Many bulls encompass me; strong bulls of Bashan surround me; they open wide their mouths at me, like a ravening and roaring lion (Ps 22:10–13) [27]

I am grateful for the United States. I am thankful for the courage my parents showed to migrate. I have benefited tremendously from the opportunities in the U.S.; I would not have had the same opportunities and resources in Mexico. However, it is my conviction that regardless of the origin of one's plight, one can be reminded that God can make a way when there is no way. It is not in God's nature to overlook our pain or hopelessness. Here too, I am reminded of the Psalmist:

> For he has not despised or abhorred the affliction of the afflicted, and he has not hidden his face from him, but has heard, when he cried to him. From you comes my praise in the great congregation; my vows I will perform before those who fear him. The afflicted shall eat and be satisfied; those who seek him shall praise the LORD! May your hearts live forever! (Ps 22:24–26)

It is my experience that when God is in the picture, no matter the starting point, the hand we are dealt, or the obstacles in our way, we can reach our destination. Where we place our hope is just as powerful as the resources and assets we count on; and so regarding our difficulties and obstructions, again the psalmist is poignant: "Some trust in chariots and some in horses, but we trust in the name of the LORD our God. They collapse and fall, but we rise and stand upright" (Ps 20:7–8).

My story is not without parallel among DREAMers. DREAMers come from many different paths and face various challenges, but one thing is common among them all: Dreamers are resilient, and their stories are inspiring. If you are fortunate to win the trust of a Dreamer and hear the intricate details of their story, one thing would be clear: an unexplainable grace has consistently followed them. Though the journey has been challenging, and many still deal with Dreamer Distress, not a single Dreamer I know is willing to give up. Though the DACA program's future is uncertain, I do not doubt that DREAMers can continue to dream big and that the unexplainable favor of God can make way for them.

DREAMers as a Prophetic Call and Reminder to the Church

"He executes justice for the fatherless and the widow, and loves the sojourner, giving him food and clothing" (Deut 10:18).

"You shall not wrong a sojourner or oppress him, for you were sojourners in the land of Egypt. You shall not mistreat any widow or fatherless child. If you do mistreat them, and they cry out to me, I will surely hear their cry" (Exod 22:21–13).

The Holy Spirit's activity is powerfully attentive to the undocumented immigrant's distress. Rarely are the stories and challenges of DREAMers heard beyond the political arena, much less understood with empathy. Their future, present, and past become mere talking points for skilled politicians. Often, DREAMers' humanity is lost in such spaces. We hope that amid such debates, with polarized opinions on undocumented immigrants' future, this work can stand as a source of understanding and a beacon of hope. The Holy Spirit is not deaf to the DREAMer's plight; He is an ever-present help. As described by our DREAMer's testimony in this work, the fear, anxiety, and fog lift as the Spirit of God guides, reveals, and comforts those who depend on him.

Furthermore, we would like to bring the church's attention to how the DREAMer journey is not unlike that of every believer as sojourners on this earth. The hardships Christians face in this world are marked by future uncertainty, analogous to DREAMers. In many ways, there may be a parallel in the immigrant's journey to the United States to reflect believers' hope of sojourning towards a heavenly "land flowing with milk and honey." DREAMers know the value of U.S. citizenship; many of their important decisions are impacted by its absence. The church that treasures its heavenly citizenship (Phil. 3:20) will live its life in light of that promise – its present decisions influenced by what is to come. Christians are the "pilgrim people of God,"[28] traveling through the temporary things we now see towards a clear destination – a kingdom that cannot be shaken (Heb 12:27–28, 13:14). They must not grow weary of being sojourners but take Abraham's outlook and continue toiling in hope for the spiritual homeland promised to the traveling people of God (Heb 11:9–10).

Finally, we would like to bring attention to the role of DREAMers as a population with a prophetic call and role in our day and age. From its foundation, the United States is the land that evokes inspiration for freedom, opportunity, and prosperity to a grand majority of immigrants from around the world. Every year, the United States celebrates a holiday that commemorates a group who sat around their first harvest at a table with Native Americans and themselves, the pilgrims, the immigrants of the time, and thanked God. A historian of the Pilgrims who first emigrated to the United States wrote, "But they knew that they were pilgrims and strangers here below, and looked not much on these things, but lifted up their eyes to heaven, their dearest country, where God hath prepared for them a city (Heb 11:16), and therein quieted their spirits."[29] Four hundred years later, since Native Americans and pilgrims sat at a table together, the United States leadership now sits divided and confused about what to do with some of the pilgrims of the day—the DREAMers.

Could it be that God has brought up a generation of young DREAMers to be emblematic of those who learn not to lean on what is temporary? Could it be that God is raising a new generation of "pilgrims" who know all too well how to overcome the perils of living in the distress of uncertainty, and remind the church to keep her heart filled with dreams and hope? Even with the most recent pandemic, where the entire world is vexed with uncertainty due to the challenges brought upon by COVID-19, it seems as if for DREAMers, a new platform has arisen. Their familiarity with uncertainty and distress might speak loudly to those who have less familiarity with these emotions. Similar to the first immigrants, Spirit-empowered DREAMers keep their eyes above, on their dearest country. The DREAMer cries out for the feeling of "home," their eyes cannot help but look for it. Spirit-empowered DREAMers depend on the only thing that is certain to them: The word of God, the promises of a helper, and the comfort of belonging to a lasting homeland. May the church worldwide see in the DREAMer's journey a reminder to hope for a land whose foundation is built by God (Heb 11:10) and remember that true and lasting prosperity is found in their spiritual homeland – the city of God:

> These all died in faith, not having received the things promised, but having seen them and greeted them from afar, and having acknowledged that they were strangers and exiles on the earth. For people who speak thus make it clear that they are seeking a homeland. If they had been thinking of that land from which they had gone out, they would have had the opportunity to return. But as it is, they desire a better country, that is, a heavenly one. Therefore, God is not ashamed to be called their God, for he has prepared for them a city. (Heb 11:13–16).

Notes

1. The Oxford Dictionary defines undocumented as not having appropriate legal documents, being used to reference an immigrant's legal status in the United States. See "Undocumented," *Oxford Dictionary of English* (Oxford: Oxford University Press, 2012), MSDict Viewer Version 2.2.0.7.

2. See, for example, James K. Hoffmeier, *The Immigration Crisis: Immigrants, Aliens, and the Bible* (Wheaton: Crossway Books, 2009); Ana T. Bedard, "Us Versus Them?: U.S. Immigration and the Common Good," *Journal of the Society of Christian Ethics* 28:2 (2008), 117–140; Benjamin R Knoll, "'And Who Is My Neighbor?': Religion and Immigration Policy Attitudes," *Journal for the Scientific Study of Religion* 48:2 (June 2009), 313-331; Charles Edward Van Engen, "Biblical Perspectives on the Role of Immigrants in God's Mission," *Journal of Latin American Theology* 3:2 (2008), 15–38.

3. This work will use "unauthorized," "irregular," and "illegal" as broad synonyms for undocumented immigrants.

4. Abby Budiman, "Key Findings about U.S. Immigrants," Pew Research Center, August 20, 2020, https://www.pewresearch.org/fact-tank/2020/08/20/key-findings-about-u-s-immigrants/, accessed October 1, 2020.

5. Jens Manuel Krogstad, "Americans Broadly Support Legal Status for Immigrants Brought to the U.S. Illegally as Children," Pew Research Center, June 17, 2020, https://www.pewresearch.org/fact-tank/2020/06/17/americans-broadly-support-legal-status-for-immigrants-brought-to-the-u-s-illegally-as-children/, accessed September 18, 2020.

6. Daniela Alulema, "DACA and the Supreme Court: How We Got to This Point, a Statistical Profile of Who Is Affected, and What the Future May Hold for DACA Beneficiaries," *The Center for Migration Studies of New York* (CMS), last modified November 11, 2019, https://cmsny.org/publications/daca-supreme-court-alulema-111119/, accessed October 1, 2020.

7. "Consideration of Deferred Action for Childhood Arrivals (DACA) | USCIS," *U.S. Citizenship and Immigration Services*, last modified February 14, 2018, https://www.uscis.gov/archive/consideration-of-deferred-action-for-childhood-arrivals-daca, accessed October 1, 2020.

8. Alulema, "DACA and the Supreme Court."

9. Chad. F Wolf, "U.S. Department of Homeland Security Memorandum," Memorandum, July 28, 2020, https://www.dhs.gov/sites/default/files/publications/20_0728_s1_daca-reconsideration-memo.pdf, accessed September 1, 2020.

10 Wolf, "U.S. Department of Homeland Security."

11 Jane Wester, "Brooklyn Federal Judge Orders Trump Administration to Remove Limits on DACA," *New York Law Journal*, last modified December 4, 2020, https://www.law.com/newyorklawjournal/2020/12/04/brooklyn-federal-judge-orders-trump-administration-to-remove-limits-on-daca/, accessed October 1, 2020.

12 Krogstad, "Americans Broadly Support."

13 Jeffrey S. Passel and D'Vera Cohn, "U.S. Unauthorized Immigrants Are More Proficient In English, More Educated than a Decade Ago," Pew Research Center, May 23, 2019, https://www.pewresearch.org/fact-tank/2019/05/23/u-s-undocumented-immigrants-are-more-proficient-in-english-more-educated-than-a-decade-ago/, accessed September 18, 2020.

14 Omar Martinez, Elwin Wu, and Theo Sandfort, et al., "Evaluating the Impact of Immigration Policies on Health Status Among Undocumented Immigrants: A Systematic Review," *Journal of Immigrant and Minority Health* 17:3 (2015), 947–970.

15 "Poverty," *Oxford Dictionary of English* (Oxford: Oxford University Press, 2012), MSDict Viewer Version 2.2.0.7.

16 Amy C. Butler, "Poverty and Adolescent Depressive Symptoms," *American Journal of Orthopsychiatry* 84:1 (2014), 82–94.

17 L. M. Garcini, K. E. Murray, and A. Zhou, et al., "Mental Health of Undocumented Immigrant Adults in the United States: A Systematic Review of Methodology and Findings," *Journal of Immigrant & Refugee Studies* 14:1 (2016), 1–25.

18 Luz M. Garcini, Thania Galvan, and Vanessa Malcarne, et al., "Mental Disorders Among Undocumented Mexican Immigrants in High-Risk Neighborhoods: Prevalence, Comorbidity, and Vulnerabilities," *Journal of Consulting & Clinical Psychology* 85:10 (2017), 927–936.

19 Stephanie A. Torres, Catherine DeCarlo Santiago, and Katherine Kaufka Walts, et al., "Immigration Policy, Practices, and Procedures: The Impact on the Mental Health of Mexican and Central American Youth and Families," *The American Psychologist* 73:7 (2018), 843–854.

20 Duhita Mahatmya and Lisa M. Gring-Pemble, "DREAMers and Their Families: A Family Impact Analysis of the DREAM Act and Implications for Family Well-Being," *Journal of Family Studies* 20:1 (2014), 79–87.

21 Ana Gonzalez-Barrera and Mark Hugo Lopez, "Before COVID-19, Many Latinos Worried about Their Place in America and Had Experienced Discrimination," Pew Research Center, last modified July 22, 2020, https://

www.pewresearch.org/fact-tank/2020/07/22/before-covid-19-many-latinos-worried-about-their-place-in-america-and-had-experienced-discrimination/, accessed September 10, 2020.

22 Torres et al., "Immigration Policy, Practices, and Procedures."

23 Krista M. Perreira, Nathan Gotman, and Carmen R. Isasi, et al., "Mental Health and Exposure to the United States: Key Correlates from the Hispanic Community Health Study of Latinos," *The Journal of Nervous and Mental Disease* 203:9 (2015), 670–678.

24 Kim M. Tsai, Nancy A. Gonzales, and Andrew J. Fuligni, "Mexican American Adolescents' Emotional Support to the Family in Response to Parental Stress," *Journal of Research on Adolescence: The Official Journal of the Society for Research on Adolescence* 26:4 (2016), 658–672.

25 Anne Bridgman, "How the Threat of Deportation Affects Children in Latino Immigrant Families," *Social Policy Report Brief* (Society for Research in Child Development, 2018), 3, https://eric.ed.gov/?id=ED592341, accessed October 1, 2020.

26 Nancy S. Landale, Jessica Halliday Hardie, and R.S. Oropesa, et al., "Behavioral Functioning among Mexican-Origin Children: Does Parental Legal Status Matter?" *Journal of Health and Social Behavior* 56:1 (2015), 2–18.

27 All scriptures in this paper use *The Holy Bible: English Standard Version* (Wheaton, IL: Crossway Bibles, 2016).

28 I. Howard Marshall, "Soteriology in Hebrews," in Richard Bauckham, Daniel R. Driver, and Trevor A. Hart, et al., eds., *The Epistle to the Hebrews and Christian Theology* (Grand Rapids, MI: Eerdmans, 2009), 257.

29 lexis de Tocqueville, *Democracy in America*, 4th ed., vol. 1, trans. Henry Reeve (Cambridge: Sever and Francis, 1864), 40.

The Kingdom Comes: Postscript

Rebekah Bled

Introduction

"There are stories that distort, and stories that form."[1]

As humans, our own shared origin story begins with a purposeful universe. Our story is one of human, relational, and ecological flourishing in a shared community with the Creator himself. But the furious dragon from the book of Revelation whose ambition is to make war on the earth (Rev 12:17) prowled in the form of a serpent, who slithered up to Adam and Eve, and distorted the story. Soon, all was not well. Shame, banishment, broken relationships, fratricide: these and more spiraled into a world whose chaos has returned. Where Adam and Eve's son Cain would be avenged seven times, seven generations later, Lamech is boasting that he will be avenged seventy-seven (Gen 4:23–24). The growth of violence and grandiosity is exponential. The dragon continues to prowl. Now there is a pain in work, pain in childbirth, death, and death's legacy. But there is a promise. The serpent, though it slithers, does not triumph. The dragon's time is limited (Rev 12:12). All will be made well again, sorrow and sighing will flee (Isa 51:11), and the tears will be wiped from all faces (Isa 25:8). Indeed, "It takes nothing from the loveliness of the verse to say that is exactly what will be required."[2]

The promise of comfort in the form of wiped tears serves as an indicator that tears are present, that there is much for which to weep. Among the effects of the curse, poverty is particularly insidious, taking a multitude of forms, devastating in its effects, pervasive in its hold. In between now and the full realization of the promise, how do we live? What is our role as Christ's beloved bride as we wait for his return? This is the question that this postscript will explore using a framework from an allegorical work of fiction, in other words, from a story that forms. This framework separates into categories the world's brokenness and the coming kingdom at work in those broken places, naming them "the world goes not well," and "the kingdom comes," respectively. I go to allegorical fiction for this framework because it holds space for the overlap of the world's deep pain, and of God's deeper goodness. As Doreen Benavidez and Edwardneil Benavidez point out, distorted stories lead to deformed identities, and require a dynamic and robust narrative of restoration in response.[3]

A Story that Forms

The framework of this postscript finds its source in the following story, taken from *Tales of the Kingdom* by David and Karen Mains.[4] It is about a boy who has stumbled into a place called Great Park, a place very different from where he was born. There, he was always called Scarboy after the result of a disfiguring accident at the hands of tormenters when he was young. But in Great Park, he is called Hero, though in his own mind, he has done nothing to earn this name. Though he doesn't know it yet, Hero has found the kingdom; that is, "anywhere the king is and is obeyed."[5] Disoriented to this new way of being in the world, Hero goes out to explore Great Park and meets a girl his age:

> "Welcome to the kingdom," she said with a smile.
> "The kingdom?" Hero echoed. Everyone knew there was no such thing. Then he stopped; of course, the girl must be pretending. He could play along. "Oh, I suppose your father is the king."
> "Oh, no," she answered. "The king is my older brother, as he is a brother to all."
> Hero tried not to show his doubts. "Then you must be a princess," he teased, looking at her much-washed pants and shirt.
> "Yes" .... "Welcome, Hero."
> Hero choked back a laugh and was surprised she knew his new name.... He was pleased when their conversation was interrupted.
> A cry echoed through the woods, "How goes the world?"
> An answer came back, "The world goes not well."
> Then another answer, "The kingdom comes."
> "That's the watch cry," (the girl) explained. "It goes from tower to tower."

The princess continued, explaining the watchtower call, saying that when something goes wrong, and the citizens of the kingdom are called to action, they shout with one voice, "To the king! To the restoration!"[6]

Within the pages of this book, I see a world that "goes not well." But I also see the bold response of Spirit-empowered scholars and practitioners who stand, as if in a watchtower, in the places of human suffering caused by poverty and cry out the good news, "The kingdom comes." These chapters declare the coming kingdom in three categories. The first is through the local church's undergirding of their proclamation with their faithful social engagement. Proclamation alone is not sufficient for salvation that begins in the present. Declarations of Christ as unique savior and king must be followed up with actions bearing witness to his kingdom among all of us. What begun in Pentecost was immediately followed by the early church's self-sacrificial meeting of practical needs in the community (Acts 2, 4:32–36). Today's church must do no less.

Second, the kingdom comes in part through the contextualized responses of scholars and practitioners to the different demands of urban and rural poverty. Urban and rural poverty both hold people captive in issues of survival; however, each setting demands a unique response. As Joel Tejedo notes, a contextualized ministry seeks to discern the questions the people in a given context are asking, and then respond to those questions. This chosen position of learner allows for the appropriate stewardship of power when the wealthy seek to serve the poor. In contextualizing responses to the specific issues each urban or rural context faces, those who seek to respond to the issues of poverty must never stop listening to those who are themselves poor.

Third, the kingdom comes through the Spirit-empowered affirmation of the prophetic narrative of restoration in the present, which points to the fullness of our promised hope. "Words create worlds,"[7] and the stories we tell and listen to shape our identity, relationships, and sense of both urgency and agency in the world. Jocabed Solano and William Lyons discuss the narrative of restorative justice through the lens of the Year of Jubilee.[8] Doreen Benavidez and Edwardneil Benavidez, Alfred Cooper, Mary Kathleen Mahon, Makonen Getu, Lemuel and Yasmine Godinez, Daniel Isgrigg, Younghoon Lee, and Marcelo Vargas talk about the transformation of identity that comes to those in poverty through a new story; one not of voicelessness, but of empowerment, hope, and agency through the Holy Spirit.[9]

Though the world goes not well, through these and other watchtowers, the kingdom comes. May this book serve as an invitation to lift your head and join the call, "To the king! To the restoration!" For, indeed, there is much to be restored.

Proclamation Proved by Social Engagement

Throughout scripture, the verbs of God's tenderness are frequently directed towards the poor. He is near (Ps 34:18; 109:30–31), attentive (Exod 2:24–25), responsive (Ps 12:2; 140:12), a refuge (Ps 9:9, 14:6; Isa 25:4), and takes pity on and calls the poor precious (Ps 72:12–14). He names himself father, defender, and advocate of the poor (Ps 68:5; Prov 13:23) and seems to take it personally when the poor are mocked, calling it an insult to himself (Prov 17:5). Even the most cursory reading of scripture demands the reader to reckon with the engagement of poverty as a critical component of discipleship (Prov 21:13; 29:7). God acts for, with, and among the poor. Theologian Udo Middlemann notes that from the first moment of distortion God:

> . . . Explains himself to a spoiled creation of which he is not the author. Yet he does not withdraw from it. . . . He ran after Adam and gave instructions on how to limit the effects of the fall, how to resist death with another generation of children, and how to continue in hope of the salvation that would come in the future through a woman's child, the promised Messiah.[10]

Social Engagement as the Fruit of Repentance

God acts and calls us to act with him to see his kingdom come (Matt 6:9–10), to bear fruit worthy of our repentance (Matt 3:8; Luke 3:8). What are these fruits? David Bosch suggests that they are different for the poor and for the rich:

> In Luke's gospel, the rich are tested on the ground of their wealth, whereas others are tested on loyalty to their family, their people, their culture, and their work (Luke 9:59-61). . . .Luke wishes his reader to know that there is hope for the rich, insofar as they act and serve in solidarity with the poor and oppressed. In their being converted to God, rich and poor are converted toward each other.[11]

John the Baptist makes it clear in the book of Luke that the fruit the rich are to bear is both economic and relational in scope (3:10–14).[12] Economic, because he goes straight to the place of power and possession, first in domestic life, then civically, then in the military. Relational, because as power and possession increase, so too do the instructions on how to wield it. While those with two coats and food are urged towards generosity of as much as fifty percent of their possessions, those with the power of the government behind them have scrupulous honesty added to the list (Luke

3:12–13). Soldiers with increased power and influence were instructed to refrain from lying, defamation, and extortion, and were instructed to be content with their wages (Luke 3:14). Further, there is also the significant point that in order to give a coat or food away, one needs to have to have at least a modicum of awareness of who is without these things. Bosch emphasizes the relational and economic responsibility of the wealthy to their neighbor, and drawing from the parable of the good Samaritan, defines neighbor as "the one in need who makes a demand of me and whom I dare not leave by the roadside."[13]

Justice Arthur expands on this theme, emphasizing that the risks in ignoring the material needs of as well as relational fellowship with the poor are not for the poor alone. When believers with more than one coat in their closet leave their neighbors "by the roadside," their own discipleship is stunted.[14] Trevor Grizzle emphasizes the dangers that await the wealthy when money becomes an object of affection. "For Luke, distribution of wealth in the service of the poor not only serves a humanitarian purpose, attachment to it is a detriment to Christian discipleship, hence a call for its renunciation."[15] While salvation lasts into eternity, the fruits of our salvation repentance take root immediately, among our neighbors.

Urban Poverty

When considering social engagement, notable differences emerge between rural poverty and urban poverty. For example:

> At the neighborhood level, research shows that those living in urban poverty often cluster in inner-city neighborhoods with substandard and crowded housing, high crime rates, excessive noise levels, and inadequate services. Psychological disorders, divorce, and other social pathologies are higher among those living in low-income urban neighborhoods than rural ones.[16]

Harvard professor of economics Edward Glaeser unapologetically advocates for urban centers as hubs of poverty relief and alleviation, calling cities "our greatest invention."[17] Here, Floyd McClung adds that creation begins in a garden and ends in a city, making urban centers part of God's original design for humanity.[18] Further, to paraphrase Glaeser, urban areas don't cause poverty; they attract the poor.[19] Jesus said to his disciples, the poor you will always have with you (Matt 26:11). According to Glaeser, these should not be the same poor. "If a city is attracting continuing waves of the less fortunate, helping them succeed, watching them leave, and then attracting new disadvantaged migrants, then it is succeeding at one of society's most important functions."[20]

But, to phrase it mildly, this can be exhausting. Cities attract diversity and bring discrepancies up close, increasing the potential for polarization and misinterpretation. It is exhausting to be misunderstood, as Lemuel Godinez and Yasmine Godinez note,[21] as it is exhausting to misunderstand. Discussing the experience of those who have immigrated to another country or urban center in pursuit of a better life, Godinez and Godinez point out that, "having reached a new land and context, they can continue to face recontextualized forms of poverty that were unanticipated or largely unconsidered when opting to migrate."[22] On the receiving end, the wealthy and less-poor can experience compassion fatigue, and be tempted to disengage, saying with words or actions, "I've already done my part." It is perhaps precisely because of the continuous and pervasive presence of poverty, that Moses warns the recently emancipated Israelites, "the poor you will always have with you. Therefore, I command you to be openhanded toward your fellow Israelites who are poor and needy in your land" (Deut 15:11).

Again, McClung is helpful: "There is much evidence of urban theology in the Bible. A clear urban tradition is found throughout the scriptures that is both positive in nature and points to God's esteem for the place where he calls his people."[23] Spirit-empowered believers in urban contexts face both unique and tremendous challenges, but also an enormous opportunity. In an urban setting where the dominant narrative can be, "I am being crushed," Spirit-empowered believers proclaim the narrative of resurrection. When Peter stood in the power of the Holy Spirit, proclaiming Christ in Jerusalem, about three thousand people in the city believed (Acts 2:14, 41). Grizzle notes the book of Acts follows Peter's proclamation with equally Spirit-empowered social engagement.[24] Thus, the proclamation of salvation through Christ was proved credible through the daily witness of the Christian community in the city. Ivan Satyavrata illustrates this undergirding of social engagement in the modern urban context of Kolkata, saying that the "hub of this holistic social ministry wheel" is the local, Spirit-empowered, urban church.[25]

In describing the reactions of natives of Baguio City, Philippines, to the waves of impoverished "squatters," Joel Tejedo notes that the frustration many city dwellers feel has turned to blaming these squatters for national economic disappointments.[26] Tejedo contrasts this attitude with that of the churches and other NGO's, who instead of blaming the squatters "sympathize with their miseries and advocate their rights through various interventions."[27] Donald Miller and Tetsunao Yamamori extend this attitude of advocacy, writing about Spirit-empowered believers worldwide:

> As Pentecostals have become upwardly mobile, better educated, and more affluent, they have begun viewing the world differently. Pentecostals no longer see the world as a place from which to escape— the sectarian view— but instead as a place they want to make better. Reading the Bible from this perspective, Pentecostals have begun to model their behavior after a Jesus who both preached about the coming kingdom and healed people and ministered to their social needs.[28]

In this view, the poor become less poor as they are able to access new opportunities, and then turn to help the ones following in their footsteps. The rich are promised the continual presence of the poor (Matt 26:11), instructed to love God and their neighbor (Matt 22:37–39; Luke 10:27), and are judged according to how they helped with, or hoarded their wealth[29] (Prov 19:17; Luke 12:16–21; 16:19–31; 1 Tim 6:18). To paraphrase and reiterate Bosch, as each is converted to God, they move towards each other.[30] This is not to gloss over the extreme difficulties of urban poverty, rather to point to a hope within it. The world goes not well, but even in the crush of urban slums, the kingdom comes.

Rural Poverty

Glaeser suggests that "urban poverty should be judged not relative to urban wealth but relative to rural poverty." [31] He notes that the extreme poverty rate in Lagos, Nigeria is less than half the rate of extreme poverty in rural Nigeria. Comparing urban megacity, Kolkata, to the rest of the West Bengal region finds a poverty rate of eleven percent in Kolkata, and a rate of twenty-four percent in rural West Bengal.[32] Michele Tine also gives helpful insight into differences between urban and rural poverty, saying:

> Rural poverty brings a host of its own stressors. Rural poverty is associated with higher infant mortality, lower quality housing and health care, and fewer formal support services than urban poverty. . . . And in direct contrast to the overcrowding and excessive noise levels of low-income city neighborhoods, individuals living in rural areas face great isolation—from people, technology,

and institutions. Importantly, research suggests this isolation often prevents the rural poor from utilizing social support networks. Indeed, rural families receive, give, and expect significantly less help from others in their "town" than do urban families. This is relevant because social support is thought to buffer individuals from stress. Such social support may protect those living in impoverished urban neighborhoods from some of the negative consequences of urban poverty.[33]

Again, the world goes not well, and close to one billion people globally live in a daily reality reminiscent of the middle ages, many of them in rural contexts.[34] The core issues of urban and rural poverty alike are that of life and death. However, responses to these issues must be contextualized for urban or rural landscapes.

Irene Banda Mutalima sees the local church in Zambia, which has a rural poverty rate of more than seventy-six percent, as the best fit through which impoverished rural communities are resourced. As experts in the local context, churches are able to define what assets and capabilities exist within a community. When partnered with the guidance and funding of micro-finance organizations, Banda hypothesizes that the rural poor can be empowered to author their own livelihood improvements.[35] Churches can serve the rural poor by functioning as hubs of equipment and empowerment. Similarly, schools are places people come together to be equipped through the increase of knowledge and practical, marketable skills. Education becomes even more critical in a rural environment, where opportunities are scarce. Churches and schools are, if you will, watchtowers within communities from which to declare, "the kingdom comes."

In impoverished rural areas which have a lack of access to networks and resources as one of their primary negative identifiers, the dominant story can easily be, "I'm alone, I'm powerless, I'm stuck." Spirit-empowered education speaks to the whole person in this context, transforming the identity through a new story. This new story finds its credibility in the experience of the nearness of God through his Spirit, combined with the attainment of practical skills, all taking place within a gathered, supportive community.[36] As Mahon describes, agency is unleashed when children begin to believe the narrative of God with and for them, empowering them to "do all things through Christ who strengthens me."[37]

Liberation Theology and Prosperity Gospel

Contextual theology necessarily takes into account the context in which the theologizing unfolds, including what day-to-day struggles people in a particular context rely on their theology to address. The prosperity gospel is one such theology; Liberation Theology is another. Though both Liberation Theology and the prosperity gospel represent contextual theologizing addressing the "materiality of salvation,"[38] they falter if the savior within the theology becomes interchangeable. For example, in Liberation Theology, the role of savior may theoretically be played by those who change the fortunes of the poor through revolution resulting in top-down economic justice reform. The savior in the prosperity gospel may be the reductionist and magical thinking often espoused through a leader who invites adherents to essentially create their own reality. However, the soaring arc of scripture is one of specificity. It is both linear and contextual, serving as a protection against these vulnerabilities. The linear nature of scripture assures us that God's story is progressing towards a good resolution in which the coming kingdom will be consummated and the promise of death's eradication will be fulfilled. The contextual nature of scripture wraps us into the story, weaving our context and choices into the grand narrative of reconciliation whose telling began at the story's first distortion. In describing the root longings within adherents of the prosperity gospel, Opoku Onyinah describes the hunger of the human heart for identity, belonging, and genuine encounter with what Allan H. Anderson calls "primal spirituality."[39] The scriptural narrative of restoration that wraps even the most destitute into its embrace finds its footing, not in material gifts alone, but in the presence of the giver himself. César Garcia's reflection is poignant here:

> . . . A consequence of been filled with the Holy Spirit is financial sharing in the community of the Spirit. In addition to prophecy, miracles, and other mystical experiences, a life of generosity and sharing of wealth has to be a fruit of the Spirit. Only God's presence can overcome the natural human tendency towards egocentrism and self-satisfaction. Only God's presence overcomes consumerism and materialism, creating in that way, an alternative community to the society.[40]

The Prophetic Narrative of Restoration

As God through Moses taught the ways in which his newly emancipated people should live, he built into the fabric of their self-understanding a year of restoration. This is the year of Jubilee.

Year of Jubilee

Though the world goes not well, according to the year of Jubilee, the slave, the indebted, even the land were never more than a generation away from respite and celebration (Lev 25:8–55; Deut 15).[41] In discussing the year of Jubilee, Solano notes that "the implications of what is not being done are present when one hears what one has to do."[42] Like the Israelites who were so often unfaithful to their identity as bride and beloved and thus turned away from their neighbor (Ezek 22:29), the prophetic call to return to our first love (Rev 2:4) and to our neighbors, comes to the church again.

When the Church Does Not Respond

If the primary commandments are to love the Lord your God, and to love your neighbor as yourself (Mark 12:30–31), and neighbor can be defined as "the one in need who makes a demand on me and whom I dare not leave by the roadside,"[43] then it seems a necessary corollary is that a community of believers who fails to respond to the poor cannot be found faithful. The following is a personal story illustrating what is at stake when the church fails to respond.

I had a dream one night, in which I was working at an upper-class church in North America and had to walk from one end of a large building to another in a limited amount of time. As I walked, people kept tugging on my sleeve and asking about institutional programming. I answered, feeling increasingly harried and harassed. In wondering how to take a break, an idea occurred to me with startling clarity: pretend to be homeless. I then lay down on the floor in the busiest hallway, with a trash bag as a blanket, and was astounded to see that I was totally ignored, though my face was still visible. In this dream, I slept in the hallway until the church was emptied and locked. Not once did someone pause on their way. I had discovered how to become invisible.

Sadly, upon waking, I did not immediately realize I had been dreaming, so plausible did it seem. When we, as believers, fail to pay attention to our neighbor on the roadside, it does not mean that our neighbor has failed to pay attention to us. The parable of the good Samaritan clearly notes the ones who walked by on the other side of the road, stepping around the injured man (Luke 10:31–32). The injured man saw them choose to disengage. The injured man knew, too, that they professed to bear Christ's name. Middlemann is incisive in his word to the church. The world goes not well. Our neighbors have a need. "We stand before God and in the middle of history where judgment will take place. Individual life has significance, and all actions matter."[44] The Old Testament prophets were clear in their word to a people of God who had become inwardly focused: "Return." The wealthy find their way back to God, in part, through friendship and support of their non-wealthy neighbors. The poor are waiting and watching. The response of the church matters. May the kingdom come.

Reading Scripture from the Margins

For those in poverty, salvation must not be just a promise for the future. The poor do not have time or margin for their religion to fail. If you are running for your life,[45] for example, you must be very sure that the one to whom you are praying hears and responds to your prayers. For many Pentecostals, including David Yonggi Cho and Oral Roberts, this assurance comes in the form of divine healing.[46] Philip Jenkins describes how those in impoverished situations may read certain parts of the Bible, "almost as an unfolding documentary,"[47] as those passages regarding struggles with disease and poverty find familiarity in lived experience. Divine healing then provides proof that Christ can be believed.

Evangelist Oral Roberts experienced the entire trajectory of his life-changing when he read 3 John 2 and believed it.[48] David Yonggi Cho, the founding pastor of the largest church in the world, experienced divine healing from tuberculosis after an encounter with God's word. Yonggi Cho also experienced healing from a worldview of hopelessness as he continued to pursue and believe scripture.[49] Both men had an initial intimate experience with God which resulted in healing, as well as the ongoing experience of God's presence through Spirit-empowered reading, and thus, Spirit-empowered living. From this place of experience, they concluded that God is who scripture says he is, and he can and should be believed. Both men championed hope as a solid thing, whose foundation is Christ, which rich and poor alike can build their lives on. Indeed, "since we have such a hope, we are very bold" (2 Cor 3:12) in holding onto the prophetic narrative of restoration, which both speaks to our immediate circumstances and echoes into eternity.

Areas of Further Research

The poor you will always have with you, is, in part, an encouragement to ongoing research in poverty alleviation, so that the poor are not always the same poor. Further research is needed, for example, on how to scale and sustain effective outreaches to urban populations in poverty, particularly related to issues stemming from proximity, such as sanitation, housing, and violence. Additionally, if Glaeser is correct that urban centers' success leads to the continual attraction of the poor to these cities, then Spirit-empowered believers within these cities must embrace both an ethic of welcome as well as practices of renewal so that engagement does not turn to bitterness, and welcome to resentment, as the needs keep mounting. How, in under-resourced communities with ever-increasing need, do the emotions of overwhelm threaten to paralyze the very ones who give their life to responding? Further research is needed to know how to scale and sustain both the outreaches and the ones reaching out.

Additionally, many wealthy Christians have their first exposure to poverty on a short-term mission trip. Though short-term missions are beyond the scope of this work, further research is needed into helping short-term exposure to poverty turn into long-term advocacy on the part of the short-term teams, as well as the team's sending churches.

Conclusion

Middlemann states, "we are not called to politely accompany people through the tragedy of their lives, to hold their hands in their pain, but to enable them to change their physical and intellectual/spiritual environments in order to diminish that tragedy."[50] He continues, "servanthood is a choice to act from strength in the midst of much tragedy."[51] In the midst of human suffering, the Spirit-empowered body of Christ on the margins draws strength from scripture, which they not only ingest, but which they act upon. They draw strength from the intimacy of shared experience with the one who is near to the brokenhearted (Ps 34:18); the one who also weeps

(John 11:35). With this strength, they thus serve the wealthy, whose access to this way of understanding the heart of God is only through an authentic relationship with the poor. Without the poor's help, the rich are unable to grasp a fuller, more robust understanding of God. Where the rich are called and judged according to how they steward their resources to help diminish the physical tragedy of poverty, the poor act from a position of strength towards the rich, diminishing the tragedy of self-obsession the worship of wealth engenders. From this place of strength, the poor remind the wealthy that God is both accessible and powerful, that his word is active and alive, and that we belong to him. The Spirit-empowered poor remind the wealthy: the kingdom comes.

Notes

1. See chapter 10.
2. Marilynne Robinson, *Gilead* (New York: Farrar, Straus, and Giroux, 2004), 246.
3. See chapter 3.
4. David Mains and Karen Mains, *Tales of the Kingdom* (Mount Morris, NY: Lamplighter Publishing, 1983).
5. Mains and Mains, *Tales of the Kingdom*, 32.
6. Mains and Mains, *Tales of the Kingdom*, 32.
7. Personal communication with W. Jay Moon, Professor of Church Planting and Evangelism at Asbury Theological Seminary (2017).
8. See chapters 10 and 1 respectively.
9. See chapters 19, 11, 12, 16, 23, 22, 17, and 9 respectively.
10. Udo Middlemann, *Christianity Versus Fatalistic Religions in the War Against Poverty* (Colorado Springs: Paternoster, 2007), 34.
11. David Bosch, *Transforming Mission: Paradigm Shifts in Theology of Mission* (Maryknoll, NY: Orbis, 1991), 105.
12. Bosch, *Transforming Mission*, 99.
13. Bosch, *Transforming Mission*, 104.
14. See chapter 2.
15. See chapter 3.
16. Michele Tine, "Growing Up in Rural vs. Urban Poverty: Contextual, Academic, and Cognitive Differences," in ed., Gabriel Staicu, *Poverty, Inequality, and Policy* (n.p.: IntechOpen, 2017), section 3.1.
17. Edward Glaeser, *Triumph of the City: How Our Greatest Invention Makes Us Richer, Smarter, Greener, Healthier, and Happier* (New York: Penguin Books, 2011).
18. Floyd McClung, *Seeing the City with the Eyes of God* (Tarrytown, NY: Chosen Books, 1991), 64–66.
19. Glaeser, *Triumph of the City*, 9, 70.
20. Glaeser, *Triumph of the City*, 81.
21. See chapter 23.
22. See chapter 23.
23. McClung, *Seeing the City*, 68.

24 See chapter 3.

25 See chapter 5.

26 See chapter 18.

27 See chapter 18.

28 Donald E.Miller and Tetsunao Yamamori, *Global Pentecostalism: The New Face of Christian Social Engagement* (Berkley: University of California Press, 2007), 30.

29 See chapter 2.

30 Bosch, *Transforming Mission*, 107.

31 Glaeser, *Triumph of the City*, 10.

32 Glaeser, *Triumph of the City*, 73–74.

33 Tine, "Growing Up," section 3.1.

34 Paul Collier, *The Bottom Billion: Why the Poorest Countries are Failing and What Can Be Done About It* (Oxford: Oxford University Press, 2007), 3.

35 See chapter 15.

36 See chapters 12 and 16.

37 See chapter 12.

38 Miroslav Volf, "Materiality of Salvation: An Investigation into the Soteriologies of Liberation and Pentecostal Theologies," *Journal of Ecumenical Studies* 26:3 (1989), 447–467.

39 See chapter 4.

40 See chapter 8.

41 See chapter 1.

42 See chapter 10.

43 Bosch, *Transforming Mission*, 104.

44 Middlemann, *Christianity Versus Fatalistic Religions*, 79.

45 See chapter 14.

46 Candy Gunther Brown, ed., *Global Pentecostalism and Charismatic Healing* (Oxford: Oxford University Press, 2011).

47 Philip Jenkins, *The New Faces of Christianity: Believing the Bible in the Global South* (Oxford: Oxford University Press, 2006), 172.

48 See chapter 22.

49 See chapter 17.
50 Middlemann, *Christianity Versus Fatalistic Religions*, 121.
51 Middlemann, *Christianity Versus Fatalistic Religions*, 120.

Contributors

Babatunde Adedibu holds a Ph.D. in Missiology from North West University, South Africa. He is the Provost of Redeemed Christian Bible College, an affiliate of Redeemer's University, Ede, Nigeria where he is an Associate Professor in the Department of Christian Religious Studies. Babatunde's research interest includes interrogating new dynamics of religious experience(s) and expression(s) in Africa and the African Diaspora, with a particular focus on non-Western Christianity.

Justice A. Arthur is the head of the Theology Department and the Graduate Studies Coordinator, School of Theology, Mission and Leadership, Pentecost University in Accra, Ghana. He previously served as a research fellow at the Chair of Religious Studies (Religionswissenschaft I) with a special focus on Africa at the University of Bayreuth in Bavaria, Germany.

Irene Banda Mutalima is the founder and CEO of TUCUZA Associates Limited, a social business in Zambia. Irene has a corporate background in retail banking and microfinance with international exposure in Africa, Latin America, Asia and Eastern Europe. She has an M.A. in Theology and Development Studies from Leeds University/Oxford Centre for Mission Studies.

Doreen Benavidez is a Filipina Pentecostal serving as the Head of the Research Department at Asian Seminary of Christian Ministries, Makati City, Philippines. She leads Mindoro Missions Team, a mission organization ministering to the Mangyan tribes in the Philippines. She is married to Edwardneil.

Edwardneil Benavidez, a Filipino Pentecostal, serves as Dean for Religious Education at Bethel Bible College, Valenzuela City, Philippines. He is an adjunct faculty member of Asian Seminary of Christian MInistries, Makati City, and a pastor of Precious Cross Christian Church, Makati City, Philippines.

Rebekah Bled is an ordained minister and a Ph.D. student in Contextual Theology at Oral Roberts University.

Alfred Cooper a fourth-generation Anglo-Chilean, has served with South America Mission Society in Chile since 1975. He pastors the church,

La Trinidad de Las Condes. He pursued an M.A. from Azusa Pacific University and a Ph.D. at Oxford Centre for Mission Studies. In 2010 he was invited by the President of Chile, Sebastián Piñera, to be Chaplain in the Presidential Palace. His book, *Inside the Palacio* (2019) tells the story of the 33 rescued miners during this time.

David D. Daniels III joined the faculty of McCormick Theological Seminary in 1987 and was inaugurated Professor of Church History in 2003. David has been a member of the American Academy of Religion since 1989, the Society for the Study of Black Religion since 1993, and the Society for Pentecostal Studies since 1979. He is the author of various articles and book reviews on the history of Christianity and serves as a member of several research projects.

César García is general secretary of the Mennonite World Conference (MWC), a global communion that serves some 1.5 million members around the world. César is from Bogotá, Colombia. He has been a church planter, pastor, and professor of Bible and Theology. Prior to his current position, César was chair of the *Iglesias Hermanos Menonitas de Colombia* (Mennonite Brethren Churches of Colombia) and secretary of the MWC Mission Commission.

Makonen Getu serves as Vice President of Transformation and Training at Edify. He has forty years of experience as an international development practitioner. He has taught at University of Stockholm and the Oxford Centre for Mission Studies. His Ph.D. is in Economic History with a concentration in Development Studies from the University of Stockholm. Makonen has published several books, pamphlets and articles on topics related to development, foreign aid, microfinance, HIV/AIDS, human trafficking, and faith.

Lemuel J. Godinez, a DREAMer, holds a Master of Divinity and Master of Biblical Literature from Oral Roberts University. In 2018 he was awarded the Graduate School of Theology and Ministry Dean's Fellowship. Lemuel has a B.S. and M.Sc. in Petroleum Engineering from Colorado School of Mines. He felt a call to ministry in 2016. Before coming to ORU, Lemuel served as a youth pastor in San Antonio.

Yasmine A. Godinez works as an addictions and trauma therapist at a prison diversion program for women in Tulsa, Oklahoma. She holds an M.A. in Professional Counseling in Marriage and Family Therapy from

Oral Roberts University. While at ORU, Yasmine was awarded "Most Outstanding Graduate Student" for the College of Theology & Ministry. Prior to ORU, Yasmine served as a missionary in North Africa, the Middle East, Haiti, and Spain.

Trevor Grizzle is Professor of New Testament in the Graduate School of Theology and Ministry at Oral Roberts University in Tulsa, Oklahoma. He holds a Ph.D. from Southwestern Baptist Theological Seminary. In addition to several book chapters and published scholarly articles, he has written *Church Aflame* (Pathway Press, 2001), and *Ephesians* (Deo Publishing, 2013). A former missionary to Ghana, West Africa, he is founder and Lead Pastor of Hope International Ministries in Tulsa.

Daniel D. Isgrigg is Assistant Professor and the Director of the Holy Spirit Research Center at Oral Roberts University, Tulsa, Oklahoma, USA.

Médine Moussounga Keener is Community Formation Pastoral Care Coordinator at Asbury Theological Seminary in Wilmore, Kentucky. Originally from Congo Brazzaville, she holds a Ph.D. from University of Paris 7. She has published articles in *Dictionary of African Christian Biography, Africa Study Bible* among others. She coauthored with her husband Craig, *Impossible Love* (2016), and "Reconciliation for Africa," a booklet on ethnic reconciliation. She has shared her experiences of war and reconciliation both in Francophone Africa and in the United States.

Younghoon Lee is Senior Pastor of Yoido Full Gospel Church. He emphasizes the absolute sovereignty of God and faith of absolute positivity and absolute thanksgiving according to the cross of Jesus Christ. He graduated from Yonsei University, Hansei University, and United Graduate School of Theology at Yonsei University in Korea. He completed his master's course work at Westminster Theological Seminary and received his M.A. and Ph.D. in Historical Theology from Temple University in the United States.

William L. Lyons is Professor of Old Testament and Semitic Languages in the College of Theology and Ministry at Oral Roberts University. He holds a Ph.D. in Religions of Western Antiquity from Florida State University, an M.A. in Hebrew and Semitic Languages from the University of Wisconsin, and a M.A. and B.A. in Biblical Studies from ORU. He has taught at Regent University (Virginia), Florida A&M University, Florida

State University, and in India, Guatemala, Russia, South Africa, Israel, United Kingdom, and Colombia.

Wonsuk Ma, A Korean Pentecostal, serves as Dean and Distinguished Professor of Global Christianity at Oral Roberts University, Tulsa, Oklahoma. He previously served as Executive Director of the Oxford Centre for Mission Studies, Oxford, UK. He serves as Co-chair of Scholars Consultation, Empowered21.

Mary Kathleen Mahon is Executive Director and President of ChildHope (formerly Latin America ChildCare) and has served in Costa Rica and Venezuela with Assemblies of God World Missions for more than 25 years. She received her undergraduate and graduate degrees from Vanguard University of Southern California. Her Ph.D. in Intercultural Education is from Biola University. She is an ordained Assemblies of God minister with the Southern California Network and resides in Costa Rica.

Eric N. Newberg is Professor of Theological and Historical Studies and Associate Director of the PhD program in Theology, Oral Roberts University. Prior to his current position, he served as Head of Pastoral Theology at Alphacrucis College in Sydney, Australia. He is the author of *The Pentecostal Mission in Palestine: The Legacy of Pentecostal Zionism* (Wipf and Stock, 2012) and *Charles Finney and the Civil War: How Evangelical Religion Changes American Politics* (Edwin Mellen, 2018).

Opoku Onyinah is the immediate past president of Ghana Pentecostal and Charismatic Council, Ghana, and the immediate past chairman of the Church of Pentecost, Ghana, with branches in 102 countries. Currently, he lectures at Pentecostal University, Accra, Ghana, and is the president of the Bible Society of Ghana. He also serves as co-chair of Scholars Consultation, Empowered21.

Sylvia Owusu-Ansah is Lecturer at Central University, Ghana, and the head pastor of Revival Temple, Perez Chapel International, Accra, Ghana. Her research interests include missions-related studies, cross-cultural communication, gender studies, interreligious conflict mediation and dialogue. Among her publications are the book chapters, "The Role of Interrelegious Collaboration in Conflict Prevention and Peaceful Multi-Religious Co-Existance: A Case Study of Northern Ghana" (2018), and "Neo-Pentecostalism in Postcolonial Ghana" (2018).

Ivan Satyavrata serves as Senior Pastor of the Assembly of God Church in Kolkata, an ethnically diverse congregation of eight language sections, with a weekly attendance of around 5000 people, and a social outreach providing education and basic nutrition for several thousand children. He has a Th.M. degree from Regent College, Vancouver, Canada, and a Ph.D. through the Oxford Centre for Mission Studies. His publications include many articles and four books, including, *Not to Destroy, but to Fulfil* (Regnum, 2019).

Jocabed R. Solano Miselis was born in the Gunayala region in Panama. She holds an M.A. in Interdisciplinary Theology for Integral Mission granted by CETI in Alliance with the University of Carey University in Canada. She is Director of the NGO *Memoria Indígena*, is part of the Steering Committee of the FTL (Latin American Theological Fraternity) and is a member of the Evangelical Coalition for Climate Justice. She is from the indigenous Gunadule nation in Panama.

Joel A. Tejedo is a research professor at Asia Pacific Theological Seminary (APTS) and currently a member of post-graduate studies of the seminary where he teaches the Church and Community and other related ministry courses. Prior to his current post in the seminary, Joel served for twenty-four years as a pastor in the rural areas in Northern Philippines. He and his wife have three children and have served as missionaries at APTS since 2009.

John Thompson is Professor of Global Leadership at Oral Roberts University and serves as a Billy Graham Center Fellow. He is also the president and founder of Global Equip, an organization that trains and resources leaders in developing nations.

Marcelo Vargas lives in La Paz, Bolivia. He is Director of *Centro de Capacitacion Misionera*, which gives an Integral Mission focus to a yearly post-graduate program. Most of his time is spent working with churches with Aimara indigenous background in suburb areas. He has lived and worked in Brazil and England and traveled to all continents, presenting published papers about Globalization, Contextual Theology, and Integral Mission.

Select Bibliography

Addae-Korankye, Alex. "Cause of Poverty in Africa: A Review of Literature." *American International Journal of Social Science* 3:7 (2014): 147-153.

Alkire, Sabina, Pedro Conceição, Ann Barham, Cecilia Calderón, Adriana Conconi, Jakob Dirksen, Fedora Carbajal Espinal, et al. "Global Multidimensional Poverty Index 2019: Illuminating Inequalities." *Oxford Poverty and Human Development Index* and UNDP, n.p.:2019.

Anderson, Allan H. *Spreading Fires: The Missionary Nature of Early Pentecostalism.* New York: Orbis, 2007.

Anderson, Allan H. "Spreading Fires: The Globalization of Pentecostalism in the Twentieth Century." *International Bulletin of Missionary Research* 31:1 (January 2007).

Armitage, David J. *Theories of Poverty in the World of the New Testament.* Gomaringen: Mohr Siebeck Tubingen, 2016.

Arthur, Justice A. "The Gospel of Prosperity and its Concept of Development: A Ghanaian Pentecostal-Charismatic Experience." *Religion* 51:1 (2020).

Attanasi, Katherine, and Amos Yong, eds. *Pentecostalism and Prosperity: The Socio-Economics of the Global Charismatic Movement.* New York: Palgrave MacMillan, 2012.

Autero, Esa. *Reading the Bible Across Context: Luke's Gospel, Socio-Economic Marginality, and Latin American Biblical Hermeneutics.* Leiden: Koninklijke Brill, 2016.

Beltran Cely, William Mauricio. *De Microempresas Religiosas a Multinacionales de la Fe: La Diversificación del Cristianismo en Bogotá.* Bogotá: Universidad de San Buenaventura, 2006.

Bowler, Kate. *Blessed: A History of the American Prosperity Gospel.* Oxford: Oxford University Press, 2012.

Brouwer, Steve, Paul Gifford, and Susan D. Rose. *Exporting the American Gospel: Global Christian Fundamentalism.* London: Routledge, 1996.

Burgess, S. M. "Pentecostalism in India: An Overview." *Asian Journal of Pentecostal Studies* 4:1 (2001).

Butler, Amy C. "Poverty and Adolescent Depressive Symptoms." *American Journal of Orthopsychiatry* 84:1 (2014): 82–94.

Chambers, Robert, Deepa Narayan, Meera Shah, and Patt Petesch. *Voices of the Poor: Crying Out for Change.* Oxford: Oxford University Press, 2000.

Chambers, Robert. *Rural Development: Putting the Last First*. London: Longman and Group, 1983.

_____. *Whose Reality Counts? Putting the First Last*. West Yorkshire, England: Intermediate Technology Publications, 1999.

Cho, Yonggi David. *Five-fold Gospel and Three-fold Blessing*. Seoul: Seoul Press, 1997.

Christian, Jayakumar. *God of the Empty Handed: Poverty, Power, and the Kingdom of God*. Monrovia, CA: MARC, 1999.

Clark, John F. *The Failure of Democracy in the Republic of Congo*. Boulder: Lynne Rienner Publishers, 2008.

Coles, Robert. *The Spiritual Life of Children*. Boston: Houghton Mifflin, 1990.

Daniels, David D. III. "Against Poverty: The Holy Spirit and Pentecostal Economic Ministries." In *The Mighty Transformer: The Holy Spirit Advocates for Social Justice*. Edited by Antipas Harris. Irving, TX: GIELD Academic Press, 2019.

_____."Economic Democracy, Martin Luther King, Jr., and the Black Church Tradition." *Telos: Critical Theory of the Contemporary* (Spring 2018): 29-45.

_____. "Future Issues in Social and Economic Justice: The Social Engagement of Pentecostals and Charismatics." In *Spirit-Empowered Christianity in the 21st Century*. Edited by Vinson Synan. Lake Mary, FL: Charisma House, 2011.

_____. "Prosperity Gospel of Entrepreneurship in Africa and Black America: A Pragmatist Christian Innovation." *In Pastures of Plenty: Tracing Religio-Scapes of Prosperity Gospel in Africa and Beyond*. Edited by Andreas Heuser. Frankfurt am Main: Peter Lang, 2015.

Das, Rupen. *Compassion and the Mission of God: Revealing the Invisible Kingdom*. Cumbria: Langham Global Library, 2015.

Dempster, Murray A., Byron D. Klaus, and Douglas Petersen, eds. *Called and Empowered: Global Mission of Pentecostal Perspective*. Peabody: Hendrickson Publishers, 1991.

Driver, John. *Contra Corriente: Ensayo Sobre Eclesiología Radical*, 3rd Ed., Colección Comunidad En Compromiso. Santafé de Bogotá, Colombia: CLARA, 1998.

Dyck, Bruno. *Management and the Gospel: Luke's Radical Message for the First and Twenty-First Centuries*. New York: Palgrave Macmillan, 2013.

Fernandez, Bina. "Household Help? Ethiopian Women Domestic Workers' Labor Migration to the Gulf Countries." *Asian and Pacific Migration Journal* 20:3-4 (2011): 433-457.

Fernandez, Bina, and Marin de Regt, eds. *Migrant Domestic Workers in the Middle East: The Home and the World*. New York: Palgrave Macmillan, 2014.

Frank, Arthur W. *Letting Stories Breathe: A Socio-Narratology*. Chicago: University of Chicago Press, 2010.

Garcini, L. M., K. E. Murray, A. Zhou, E. A. Klonoff, M. G. Myers, and J. P. Elder. "Mental Health of Undocumented Immigrant Adults in the United States: A Systematic Review of Methodology and Findings." *Journal of Immigrant & Refugee Studies* 14:1 (2016): 1–25.

Gnuse, Robert. "Jubilee Legislation in Leviticus: Israel's Vision of Social Reform." *Biblical Theology Bulletin* 15:2 (1985): 43–48.

Harrell, Jr., David E. *Oral Roberts: An American Life*. Bloomington, IN: Indiana University Press, 1985.

Hay, David, and Rebecca Nye. *The Spirit of the Child*, rev. Ed. London: Fount, 2006.

Hoover, Willis Collins. *History of the Pentecostal Revival in Chile*. Translated by Mario G. Hoover. Santiago: Ebenezer Publishing House, 2000.

Igboin, Benson Ohihon. "Karl Marx on Religion: The Perspective of Boko Haram in Nigeria." *Journal of Religious Culture* 183 (2014): 4.

Im, H. Chandler, and Amos Yong, eds. *Global Diasporas and Mission*. Eugene: Wipf & Stock, 2014.

Jewell, Lucy A. "The Biology of Inequality." *Denver Law Review* 93:3 (2018).

Keener, Craig. *Acts: New Cambridge Bible Commentary*. Cambridge: Cambridge University Press, 2020.

Keener, Craig, and Médine Moussounga Keener. *Impossible Love*. Grand Rapids, MI: Baker Publishing Group, 2016.

Keener, Médine, Moussounga. "How Subjection Harms Congolese Women." *Priscilla Papers* 21:3 (Summer 2007).

_____. "7 Things Christians Should Know About Refugees." Seedbed.com, June 20, 2016. https://www.seedbed.com/7-things-christians-should-know-about-refugees/.

Lanndale, Nancy S., Jessica Halliday Hardie, R. S. Oropesa, and Marianne M. Hillemeier. "Behavioral Functioning among Mexican-Origin Children: Does Parental Legal Status Matter?" *Journal of Health and Social Behavior* 56:1 (2015): 2–18.

Lee, Younghoon. *The Cross on Calvary: The Theological Foundations of the Full Gospel Faith*. Seoul: Church Growth Institution, 2011.

_____. *The Holy Spirit Movement in Korea*. Oxford: Regnum Books International, 2009.

_____. *60th Anniversary of The Assemblies of God of Korea*. Seoul: Yoido Full Gospel Church Press. 2018.

_____. *60th Anniversary of the Assemblies of God of Korea with the Holy Spirit.* Seoul: The Assemblies of God of Korea, 2013.

Lyons, William L. "Extending the Right Hand: An Important Yet Overlooked Defining Action of the Nascent Church." In *We, the Church: Studies in Mission & Evangelization. Essays in Honor of Bishop Dr. B. S. Moses Kumar.* Edited by Smitha P. Coffee and Donna Tracy Paul. New Delhi, India: Christian World Imprints, 2017.

Mahatmya, Duhita, and Lisa M. Gring-Pemble. "DREAMers and Their Families: A Family Impact Analysis of the DREAM Act and Implications for Family Well-Being." *Journal of Family Studies* 20:1 (2014): 79–87.

Malik, Charles. *A Christian Critique of the University.* Downers Grove, IL: Intervarsity Press, 1982.

Martin, David. *Tongues of Fire: Explosion of Protestantism in Latin America.* Oxford: Basic Blackwell Ltd, 1990.

Miller, Donald, and Tetsunao Yamamori. *Global Pentecostalism: The New Face of Christian Social Engagement.* Berkeley: University of California Press, 2007.

Myers, Bryant. *Walking with the Poor: Principles and Practices of Transformational Development.* Maryknoll, NY: Orbis Books, 2000.

Ng, Alex Hou Hong, Abdul Ghani Farida, Fock Kui Kan, Ai Ling Lim, and Teo Ming Ting. "Poverty: Its Causes and Solutions." *International Journal of Humanities and Social Sciences* 7:8 (2013): 2471–2479.

Ngbea, Terwase, and Hilary Chukwuka Achunike. "Poverty in Northern Nigeria." *Asian Journal of Humanities and Social Studies* 2:2 (April 2014).

North, Douglas, and Robert Thomas. *The Rise of the Western World.* Cambridge: Cambridge University Press, 1973.

Obasanjo, Olusegun. "Liberation Theology and the Crisis in North Eastern Nigeria." In *African Christianity in Local and Global Context.* Edited by Samson Adetunji Fatokun. Ibadan, Nigeria: University of Ibadan, 2019.

Obiorah, Mary J., and Favour C. Uroko. "'The Spirit of the Lord God is Upon Me' (Is 61:1): The Use of Isaiah 61:1–2 in Luke 4:18–18." *HTS Teologiese Studies/Theological Studies* 74:1 (2018): 1–6.

Olabimtan, Apuwabi. "The Effects of Religious Crisis on Economic Development in Nigeria." *International Journal of Academic Research in Business and Social Sciences* 8:6 (2018): 325-326.

Orellana, Luis. *El Fuego y la Nieve,* Vol. 1. Hualpén, Chile: CEEP Ediciones, 2006.

Onwumah, Anthony C. "Communal and Ethno-Religious Crises and their Implications for National Development in Nigeria." *Developing Country Studies* 4:17 (2010): 118-125.

Peterson, David. *The Acts of the Apostles: Pillar New Testament Commentary.* Grand Rapids: Eerdmans, 2009.

Petersen, Douglas. *Not by Might, Nor by Power: A Pentecostal Theology of Social Concerns in Latin America.* Oxford: Regnum Books International, 1996.

Phillips, Thomas E. *Reading Issues of Wealth and Poverty in Luke-Acts.* New York: Edwin Mellen Press, 2001.

Pleins, J. David. "Poor, Poverty." In *Anchor Yale Bible Dictionary.* Edited by David N. Freedman, et al. Vol. 5. New Haven, CT: Yale University Press, 2007.

Polhill, John. Acts: *The New American Commentary,* Vol. 26. Nashville, TN: Broadman Press, 1992.

Rhee, Helen. *Wealth and Poverty in Early Christianity.* Minneapolis: Fortress Press, 2017.

Rosik, Mariusz, and Victor Onwukeme. "Function of Isa 61:1–2 and 58:6 in Luke's Programmatic Passage (Luke 4:16–30)." *Polish Journal of Biblical Research* 2 (2002): 67–81.

Roth, John D. *Where the People Go: Community, Generosity, and the Story of Everence.* Harrisonburg, VA: Herald Press, 2020.

Salinas, J. Daniel, ed. *Prosperity Theology and the Gospel: Good News or Bad News for the Poor?* Peabody: Hendrickson Pub Marketing, 2017.

Satyavrata, Ivan. *Pentecostals and the Poor: Reflections from the Indian Context.* Baguio: APTS Press, 2017.

Schneider, John R. *The Good of Affluence: Seeking God in a Culture of Wealth.* Grand Rapids, MI: Eerdmans, 2002.

Sepúlveda, Juan. "Another Way of Being Pentecostal." In *Pentecostal Power: Expressions, Impact, and Faith of Latin American Pentecostalism.* Edited by Calvin L. Smith. Leiden: Brill, 2011.

Sider, Ronald J. *Evangelism and Social Action: Uniting the Church to Heal a Lost and Broken World.* London: Hodder and Stoughton, 1993.

Solano, Jocabed, "Las Narrativas Como Resistencia Política. La Experiencia de la Nación Guna." In *Juventudes: Otras Voces, Nuevos Espacios: Confrontando la Teología y la Misión.* Edited by Priscila Barredo Pantí and Nicolás Panotto. N.p.: Fraternidad Teológica Latinoamericana, 2018.

———. Voces Indígenas: "Fortaleza Espiritual de los Pueblos de Abya Yala," https://theglobalchurchproject.com, October 7, 2018. https://theglobalchurchproject.com/jocabed-spanish/.

Sørenson, Ninna Nyberg, and Ida Marie Vammen, "Who Cares? Transnational Families in Debates on Migration and Development." *New Diversities* 16:2 (2014): 89-108.

Stark, Rodney. *The Rise of Christianity: A Sociologist Reconsiders History.* Princeton: Princeton University Press, 1996.

Stearns, Jason K. *Dancing in the Glory of Monsters: The Collapse of the Congo and the Great War of Africa.* New York: Public Affairs, 2011.

Stivers, Laura A., Christine E. Gudorf, and James B. Martin-Schramm. *In Christian Ethics: A Case Method Approach*, 4th Ed. Maryknoll: Orbis Press, 2012.

Stott, John. *The Message of Acts.* Downers Grove, IL: Intervarsity Press, 1990.

Torres, Stephanie A., Catherine DeCarlo Santiago, Katherine Kaufka Walts, and Maryse H. Richards. "Immigration Policy, Practices, and Procedures: The Impact on the Mental Health of Mexican and Central American Youth and Families." *The American Psychologist* 73:7 (2018): 843–854.

Tsai, Kim M., Nancy A. Gonzales, and Andrew J. Fuligni. "Mexican American Adolescents' Emotional Support to the Family in Response to Parental Stress." *Journal of Research on Adolescence: The Official Journal of the Society for Research on Adolescence* 26:4 (2016): 658–672.

Tsele, Molfe. "The Role of the Christian Faith in Development." In *Faith in Development: Partnership Between the World Bank and the Churches of Africa.* Edited by Deryke Belshaw, Robert Calderisi, and Christopher Sugden. Oxford: World Bank and Regnum Books, 2001.

Ventocilla, José, Heraclio Herrera, and Valerio Núñez. *El Espíritu de la Tierra: Plantas y Animales en la Vida del Pueblo Kuna.* Quito: Ediciones Abya-Yala, 1999.

Volf, Miroslav, and William H. Katerberg. *The Future of Hope: Christian Tradition Amid Modernity and Postmodernity.* Grand Rapids: Eerdmans, 2004.

Wagle, Udaya. "Rethinking Poverty: Definition and Measurement." *International Social Science Journal* 54 (2002): 155–165.

Wagua, Aiben. *En Defensa de la Vida y su Armonía.* Panama: Proyecto EBI Guna / Fondo Mixto Hispano Panameño, 2011.

Weber, Max. *The Protestant Work Ethic and the Spirit of Capitalism.* New York: Scribner, 1958.

———. *Sociology of Religion.* Translated by Ephraim Fischoff. Boston: Beacon Press, 1963.

Weaver, Alain Epp. *States of Exile: Visions of Diaspora, Witness, and Return.* Scottdale, PA: Herald Press, 2008.

Willen, Sarah E., ed. *Transnational Migration to Israel in Global Comparative Context.* New York: Palgrave Macmillan, 2013.

Winter, Ralph D. "The Two Structures of God's Redemptive Mission." *Missiology: An International Review* 2:1 (January 1974): 121-139.

Wolfe, Barbara, William Evans, and Teresa E. Seeman, eds. *The Biological Consequences of Socioeconomic Inequalities.* New York: Russell Sage Foundation, 2012.

Wright, Christopher J. H. *Old Testament Ethics for the People of God.* Downers Grove: InterVarsity Press, 2004.

Name and Subject Index

A

Aaron, 13
Abrams, Minnie, 88
Absolom, 13
absolute poverty, 124, 127, 237–238
abundance, generosity and, 413
Abya Yala people, 178, 179, 180–183, 187n2
Acquaye, Hannah Emma, 105
Acts (book), poverty writings within, 48
Adam, 283, 447
Addae-Korankye, Alex, 125
Addis Kidan Baptist Church, 302
Adelaja, Sunday, 112
Adeyemi, Samuel, 106, 112–114
Adnronicus, 388
Adventist Development and Relief Agency, 283
affluence, 30
Africa
   Anabaptists in, 152
   Edify within, 286
   migrants from, 370–371
   ministry in, 383
   Pentecostalism within, 69–70, 75
   poverty within, 282
   prophets within, 71
   prosperity gospel within, 72
   West, 398
   witchcraft within, 294–295
Africa Initiated Churches (AICs), 69–70
African Americans, Holy Spirit baptism on, 65
African Christianity, Pentecostalism within, 70
African Initiated Christianity (AIC) movement, 370–371
African migrant churches, 370–371, 374
African Traditional Religion, 71
agency, 210–211, 214–215, 454
agriculture, 332

Aimara, 157–159, 169–171, 172, 174n1. *See also* Power of God (PoG) Church
Albania, 381–382, 384–385
Albó, Xavier, 158
Alexander, Frank, 149
Algeria, 368
alienation, 325
Allatog, Byron, 355–357
Allen, A. A., 66
amnesia, within Colombia, 141–142
amphetamine, 245n10
Anabaptism, 146–149, 150–152
ancestral models, 178–179
Anderson, Allan H., 86, 301, 455
Anderson, Robert, 302, 313
Anim, Emmanuel, 70–71
Ankrah, Samuel Korankye, 32
Anmar Dadgan an Nangan Daniggid, of the Gunadule nation, 179
anoint/anointing, 11–19, 21
Ansan, South Korea, multicultural center within, 310
anti-intellectualism, Holy Spirit *versus*, 54–55
Antioch church, 48
apostles, 380, 388–390, 393
Apostolic Christian World Relief, 100
apostolic ministry. *See also specific ministers*
   calling within, 388–390
   leadership within, 388–391
   local church ministry tension with, 386–388
   nature of, 386–391
   overview of, 379–380
   serving the poor within, 391–399
Arabian Gulf, 372–373
Arabian Peninsula, 367–368
Argentina, 69
Armanios, Febe, 369
Arroyo, Gloria, 322–323
Arthur, Justice, 451
Ashmore, Kathy, 108

477

Asia, 68–69, 152, 286
Assemblies of God
　in Egypt, 369
　in India, 88, 89–94
　in Jordan, 372
　in Lebanon, 371
　in the Middle East, 366
　Pentecostal movement and, 313
assets, 263, 264
Attack Your Lack (Roberts), 416
Attanasi, Katharine, 31
Avanzini, John, 66
awareness-sensing, 213
Ayantayo, Jacob, 405
Azusa Street revival, 64–65

B
Bab Igala, of the Gunadule nation, 179
Baer, Hans, 101
Baguio City, Philippines, ministry in, 321–322, 333–335, 336–337, 340n3, 452–453
Bahrain, Pentecostalism within, 372
Bakker, Jim, 418
Balewa, Alhaji Tafawa, 230
Balisacan, Arsenio, 329
Balu Wala, of the Gunadule nation, 177, 180–183, 184–185
Bangura, Agnes, 382–384, 386–387, 392, 393–394, 398
Bangura, Gregory, 382–384, 386–387, 398
baptism of the Holy Spirit, 84, 86, 92, 193
Barnabas, 57–58, 275, 388, 393
barong barong (squatter areas), 322–324, 452–453
Bartleman, Frank, 86
basic security, focus of, 102
believers/Christians, unity of, 49–50, 56. *See also* church/early church
Benavidez, Doreen, 448
Benavidez, Edwardneil, 448
Berg, George, 88
Berger, Peter, 102
Bessler, David A., 128
Bethel Healing Home, 85–86
Biler, 180, 187n6, 187n13
biology of inequality, 410–411, 415, 419
blessing, 1, 33, 102, 311–312
blessing pact, 413, 414, 415
body of Christ, 387. *See also* church/early church
Bogo City, Philippines, war on drugs within, 355–357
Bogota Consultation (2019), 2–4
Boko Haram, 235–236
Bolivia, 157–159, 169–171, 172, 174n1. *See also* Power of God (PoG) Church
Bonhoeffer, Dietrich, 149
Bonilla, Coralia, 218, 219
Bonilla, Jaime Laurence, 143
Bonnke, Reinhard, 232
Bono, 281–282
Boone, Pat and Debbie, 417
Bosch, David, 450, 451
Bowler, Kate, 73–74, 406
Boxing Day, 309
Branham, William, 66
Bravo, Juan Arias, 194
Brazil, 69
breaking of bread, within the early church, 55–56
Breen, Mike, 389
Brenes, Luis Gonzalez, 216–217
Brethren in Christ, as Anabaptists, 146
Brouwer, Steve, 72
Bruce, F. F., 56
Buddhism, work ethic concept within, 133
Bueno, John, 215
Bulumkutu, Nigeria, 231
Buntain, Mark and Huldah, 89–90
Bursod, 180, 187n7
business, witchcraft and, 294–295
Business As Mission, 283

C

Cain, 447
Canada, Anabaptists in, 152
capabilities, 263, 264
capitalism, 115
capital sector, injustice within, 115
Care and Relief for the Young (CRY), 381–382
case poverty, 127
Castaldo, Adriana, 363–364
Catholicism, Populist, 158
Catholic Relief Services, 283
Center for Family Ministries (CEFAM), 357
center-on-God response, 149
center-on-the-church response, 150–151
center-on-the-poor response, 151–152
Central University, 105
Cerullo, Morris, 66
Channel Islands, CRYSHOP within, 382
character development, 292–295
child development, holistic, 336
ChildHope, 207, 211, 213–214, 215–220
children
   agency of, 214–215, 454
   emotions of, 214
   identity construction of, 209–211, 218–219
   within poverty, 214–215
   powerlessness of, 218–219
   spiritual development of, 211–214
   as violence victims, 346
Childs, Brevard, 12
Chile, 69, 193–195
Cho, David Yonggi, 301, 304, 305, 311, 312, 457
Cho, Paul Yonggi, 69
Christ for all Nations, 366
Christian Aid, 283
Christian Greenmovement Mission (C.G.M.), 313
Christianity. *See also* church/early church

civic engagement within, 324–325
in Congo Brazzaville, 249–250
education response of, 282–285
poverty and, 1–2
Christ Outreach Ministry, 383
church-based learning centers, 332
church/early church. *See also specific denominations/churches*
   breaking of bread within, 55–56
   center on, 150–151
   Christ's role within, 314
   in Colombia, 142–143
   donations to, 33
   expressive strategy of, 101
   fellowship within, 55
   generosity within, 49, 58
   growth of, 53, 54, 58, 74, 395
   holistic mission of, 338
   instruction in, 54–55
   integral mission of, 175n8
   lack of response by, 456–457
   leadership within, 390–391
   mass empire culture within, 144
   mission of, 46
   mission of God and, 1
   poverty role of, 4, 52–53, 143, 331, 393, 454
   prayer within, 56
   role of, 152
   sharing within, 56–57
   social action role of, 267–268
   social engagement of, 302–304
   socio-economic life of, 49
   Spirit-empowered, 265–267
   Spirit-inspired response to destitute by, 48–51
   as two legs of the body of Christ, 387
   unity within, 50
   wealth within, 33
Church of God (Cleveland), 366, 372
Church of Pentecost (Ghana), 103–106
Church of Pentecost Social Services (PENTSOS), 104–105, 106
church planting, 388

"Church With the Open Arms" (India), 90–91
citizenry, 115–116, 284
City of Faith Medical and Research Center, 412, 415, 416, 420, 427n82
civic engagement, 324–327, 333–335, 339, 340n2
civil war, 250–251
Classical Pentecostalism, 213–214
COGIC Charities, 100
Coleman, Rachel, 48, 50, 53
Coles, Robert, 212
collaboration, 273, 290–291
collective poverty, 127
Collier, Paul, 251
Colombia
 amnesia within, 141–142
 Anabaptism within, 146–152
 church role within, 143–144
 historical problems within, 142
 Liberation Theology within, 144–146
 Marxism within, 145
 Mennonites within, 151
 pastor viewpoint within, 141
 prosperity gospel within, 143–144
 violence within, 142
comfort, promise of, 447
Commonwealth Education Hub, 284
communal blessing, 311–312
communalism, 56–57
communism, 56–57
community, 93, 151, 177–178
compassion, 48, 49, 83
Conference on Faith, Science, and the Future, 2
confession, faith through, 67
conflict, biblical example of, 266–267
Congo Brazzaville, 249–257
connection, 268
Constantinian synthesis, 145, 154n16
consumption, to entrepreneurship, 113–114
contextual theology, 455
conventional logic systems, 172

conversion, PoG church viewpoint of, 164–165
Convoy of Hope, 99
Cook, Robert, 89
Cooperative Mutual Support and Social Services Society Limited of the Church of Pentecost (PENCO), 105
Copeland, Kenneth and Gloria, 66, 67, 417
copper industry (Zambia), 269–270
Cordilleran Pentecostals, 327, 329–330, 331, 332
Cornelius, 312
corruption, 128, 228, 293–294
cosmic level warfare, 68
covenant, breaking of, 326
Crane, Chris, 286
Created Equal, 386
creation, abundance within, 1
credit unions, micro-financing by, 105
cross, theology of, 151
CRY (Care and Relief for the Young), 381–382
CRYSHOP, 382
culture, spirituality within, 214
cyclical poverty, 127
Cyprus, 384
Cyrus, 15, 24n19–20

D
DACA (Deferred Action for Childhood Arrivals), 430–431
Daejo-Dong, South Korea, YFGC church within, 301
Dalits, empowerment of, 89
Das, Rupen, 392
Daughtry, Herbert, 114
David, 13, 16–17
Davis, Mike, 99
Dawson, Tiger, 286
Day, Keri L., 114, 116
Daystar Christian Centre, 112
Daystar Leadership Academy, 112–114
deacons, leadership of, 390

death, in Congo Brazzaville, 254–255
Deebat, Uztas Ahmed, 232
Deferred Action for Childhood
    Arrivals (DACA), 430–431
demonology, 68
depression, symptoms of, 432
destitution, 47–48
development, 178
Development, Relief, and Education
    for Alien Minors (DREAM) Act,
    430
discernment, 398–399
disciples, 30, 266–267
discipleship, 47–48, 52
disconnection, within migration, 364
discrimination, 127
disease, 254–255, 412
disobedience, 72
distress, emotional, 432–433
distribution of resources, inequity
    within, 208
divine agency, 101
divine healing, 305–306, 457
domestic workers, 365
Dominican Republic, 286
Donaldson, Margaret, 213
Dorcas, 312
DREAM (Development, Relief, and
    Education for Alien Minors) Act,
    430
DREAMer Distress, 429, 435–437
DREAMers
    American Dream and, 433–435
    emotional distress of, 432–433
    overview of, 429–430
    personal story of, 437–441
    plight of, 431–432
    as prophetic call, 441–443
Driver, John, 152
drugs, within the Philippines,
    345–351, 355–357
Duncan-Williams, Nicholas, 32
Dunsford, Martyn
    ministry of, 386
    overview of, 381–382
    quote of, 392–393, 394, 398–399
    viewpoint of, 395, 396–397
Duterte, Rodrigo, 345, 348–351

E
early church. *See* church/early church
Ebola crisis, 384
ecology, 200
economic democracy, 114–116
economic fruit, 450
economic justice, 114–116
economy on the margins, 99, 100–101
Ecumenical Church Loan Fund, 283
Edify
    benefits of, 291
    history of, 286
    lending within, 290–291
    overview of, 296–297
    partnerships of, 290–291
    products and services of, 286
    projects and school income of,
        289–290
    response and contribution of,
        285–286
    school entrepreneurs of, 288–290
    school loans from, 287
    teacher and support staff of, 290
Educate A Child, 284
education
    access to, 287–288
    church-based learning centers as, 332
    higher education, 105
    HONEY Project and, 104
    importance of, 284
    in India, 90
    low-fee independent schools (LFIS),
        286
    poverty and, 127–128, 208–209,
        282–285, 454
    within pragmatic prosperity gospel,
        107
    quality of, 287–288
    school entrepreneurs within,
        288–290
    support staff within, 290
    teachers within, 290
    as tool, 128–129

Edwards, Robert and Doris, 88
Egypt, Pentecostalism within, 369
elders, leadership of, 390
Elijah, 14–15
Elim Welfare Town, 307
Elisha, 14
El Salvador, 215
emotional distress, 432–433, 435–437
emotions, of children, 214
Empowered21, 2–3
End Poverty campaign, 281–282
England, CRYSHOP within, 382
entrepreneurial talents, 101
entrepreneurship, 106–107, 113–114
environmental concerns, 263–264
Epaphroditus, 388
epistemicide, 178
epochs, Gunadule nation and, 187n2
Ervin, Howard, 418
eschatological hope, 94
Estep, William R., 148
Ethiopia, 302, 370
Ethiopian Cultural Center (Yemen), 373
Europe, Anabaptists in, 152. See also specific locations
evangelism, 167–169, 193–194, 379–380
Eve, 283, 447
extrajudicial killings (EJKs), within the Philippines, 346–347
extreme poverty, 127

F

faith, through confession, 67
faith development theory, 212, 224n32
faith of sharing, 312
the fall, 1, 325
famine, 325
farming, 270–273, 332
Farrah, Charles, 418
fatherless, provisions for, 132
Faupel, William, 65
feeding program, in India, 90
fellowship, 55
female poverty, 125. *See also* women
Fernandez, Bina, 371
Fertile Crescent, 24n19–20
FHI, 284
fiestas/festivals, of Bolivia, 158
Figueroa, Daniel, 189
financial blessing, 102
Five-Fold Gospel, 318n50
Flood Stage: Opening the Windows of Heaven (Roberts), 416
Forbes, James, 100
formation, from serving the poor, 399
Fosu, Augustin Kwasi, 126
Foursquare Gospel Church, 366
Fowler, James, 212
Fox, Calvin, 125–126
freedom, safeguarding of, 147
freelancing, within domestic work, 365–366
Frodsham, Stanley H., 86
frugality, 199
fruit of the Spirit, 148
Full Gospel Businessmen's Men Fellowship, 67, 366
Full Gospel Medical Center, 308

G

Garcia, César, 455
gardening, as livelihood, 337
Gaza, 376n17
Geldoff, Bob, 282
gender inequality, 125
generalized poverty, 127
generosity
　abundance through, 413
　of Barnabas, 57–58
　within the church, 49, 58
　effects of, 397
　examples of, 312
　as fruit of the Spirit, 148
　as intercession, 307–308
　personal conviction of, 147
Gerasene demoniac, 351–355
Ghana, 103–104, 286
Ghanian Pentecostal-Charismatic Christianity, 27–28, 31–32, 38, 39

Gifford, Paul, 72
giving, 147, 161–162
Glaeser, Edward, 451–452, 453
gleaning, provisions within, 132
Global Pentecostalism (Miller and Yamamori), 100, 306–307
Global South, prosperity gospel within, 63. *See also specific locations*
Global Terrorism Index (GTI), 228
God
    anointing and, 16
    anti-poverty response of, 283
    character of, 146
    mission of, 1
    as multiplier, 33
    poverty provision from, 131–133
    as a sender, 380
    tenderness of, 450
Godinez, Lemuel, 452
Godinez, Yasmine, 452
Godoy, Daniel Figueroa, 196
gold, 308
Gonzalez, Justo, 53–54
Goodpeople, 309–310
Goodpeople Emergency Relief Organization, 310
Good Samaritan, 30
gospel planting, 388
governance, responsibility of, 129
Grant, Walter V., 66
Great Commandment, 59
Great Commission, 59
Greece, 382, 384
greed, 51
Grizzle, Trevor, 451
ground-level warfare, 68
Guachalla, Pastor, 160–161
Guarilihue (Pearl of Itata), Chile
    gospel arrival within, 197–198
    history of, 190–192
    Iglesia Evangélica Pentecostal within, 192
    overview of, 189
    poverty in, 196–197
    prophecy regarding, 192
    study focus of, 190
    wine within, 191–192, 202
Guelich, Robert, 52
guilt, 433–434
Gumi, Sheikh, 231
Gunadule nation
    Balu Wala story within, 177, 180–181, 184–185
    epochs of, 187n2
    overview of, 177–178, 187n1
    songs of, 180
    stories within, 179–180, 184
Guti, Ezekiel, 102, 103
Gutiérrez, Gustavo, 145

H

Habitat for Humanity, 308–309
Hackett, Rosalind, 72
Hagin, Kenneth E., 66–67, 69, 107, 417, 418
Haiti, CRY within, 382
Hanks, Thomas, 326
Hannah, Song of, 15
harvest, 25n26
Hauerwas, Stanley, 150
Haughton, Jonathan, 125
Hausa-Fulani crisis (Nigeria), 232
Hay, David, 213
Hazael, 14–15
healing
    assurance from, 457
    blessing of, 305–306
    example of, 395
    overview of, 92–93
    Pentecostal belief regarding, 65
    poverty and, 412
    televangelists and, 66–67
health and wealth gospel, 405–406, 419. *See also* prosperity gospel
health care, 308, 310
Heward-Mills, Dag, 107
higher education, business within, 105. *See also* education; specific institutions
Hillsong Church (Australia), 74
Hinn, Benny, 66

Hinojosa Venegas, Froilán, 195–198, 201
Hirsch, Alan, 387, 389
Hispanic Americans, poverty statistics of, 130
History Makers Training, 112
Hodges, Melvin, 86–87
holiness, of Iglesia Evangélica Pentecostal (Guarilihue, Chile), 199
Holistic Child Development program, 336
holistic mission, 338
holistic salvation, 312–313
Holy Spirit
  Azusa Street revival and, 64–65
  baptism of, 84, 86, 92, 193
  as comforter, 395
  community through, 93
  discernment from, 398–399
  outpouring of, 50–51
  prosperity from, 111
  revelation from, 399
  role of, 396–397
  spiritual transformation from, 91
  supernatural power of, 199
  as truth, 54–55
  undocumented immigrants and, 437–439, 441
  work of, 4, 53
homicides under investigation (HUI), within the Philippines, 346
HONEY Project, 104
HONEY Project Global Outreach, 106
Hoover, Willis, 193, 194
hope, 94, 116, 220
Hope International, 283
hopelessness, 207
housing, Habitat for Humanity and, 308–309
human agency, 101, 102
human resource (HR) management, 288–289
humble poor, 327
Hungary, 381
hunger, 253–254

I
Ibeler, 180–181, 187n8, 188n14
Idahosa, Benson Andrew, 70, 107
identity, 209–211, 218–219
If You Need to Be Blessed Financially Do These Things (Roberts), 416
Iglesia Evangélica Pentecostal (Guarilihue, Chile), 192, 193, 194–196, 198–201
Iglesia Metodista Pentecostal (Guarilihue, Chile), 193
Ignatiou, Stavros
  ministry of, 386, 394, 395
  overview of, 384–386
  quote of, 395–396
  viewpoint of, 397, 399
igubwala, 180–181, 187n12
illegal settler, 322
Ilocano Pentecostals, 327, 330, 331, 332
image of God, 1
immigrants/immigration
  DREAMer Distress within, 435–437
  overview of, 429
  personal story of, 431–432, 434–435, 436–439
  plight of, 431–432
  unauthorized, 430, 433
  undocumented, 431–432, 444n1
  in the United States, 429–431
income, 130, 133, 209, 288–290, 367–368
income poverty, 124, 130, 262
India
  church social engagement within, 303
  conditions of, 89
  Kolkata Assembly of God within, 303
  Kolkata [Calcutta] experience, 89–94
  Pentecostal social engagement in, 88–89
  poverty within, 453
Indian Pentecostalism, social engagement in, 88–89

indigenous business, penny capitalism and, 106
Indigenous people, 178–179
Industrial Revolution, 280
inequality, 2, 410–411
injustice, as oppression form, 326
instruction, within the early church, 54–55
intercession, generosity as, 307–308
International Monetary Fund (IMF), 307–308
International Praise Center, 334
Iraq, 382
Islam, 133, 230, 243–244
Israel, 150, 183–184, 369–371, 376n17
Israelites, 325
Ivory Coast, 383

J

Jacob, 13
Jakes, T. D., 73
James, 51, 394
Jenkins, Philip, 457
Jeon, Paul, 55, 58
Jesus
 compassion of, 48
 financial teachings of, 27, 28, 35
 as fulfillment, 15
 Gerasene demoniac and, 351–355
 ministry of, 311, 395–396, 397
 Pentecostal belief regarding, 65
 poverty lifestyle of, 18, 311
 as Son of Man, 155n33
Jewell, Lucy, 410
Jimeta, Nigeria, riot in, 231
Joash, 14
John, 51, 397
Johnson, Luke Timothy, 53
John the Baptist, 18, 450
Jones, Randolph L., 114
Jordan, Pentecostalism within, 372
Jos, Nigeria, conflict in, 235–236
Joseph Business School, 107–112, 114
Joseph Business School Global Network, 110–111
Joseph Center, 109–110
Josephus, 57
Jotham's fable, 13
Jubilee Year, 19–20, 21–22, 132, 183–185, 456
Julian the Apostate, 21
Junia, 388
justice, 2, 103, 133, 149

K

Kafanchan riot (Nigeria), 232
Kano, Nigeria, riot in, 231
Keener, Craig, 49
Kenya, 382
Khandker, Shabidur R., 125
kibock sinang (seeking blessings) theology, 305–306
Kim, Sebastian C. H., 305
Ki-Moon, Ban, 262
King, Coretta Scott, 74
King, Martin Luther, Jr., 114
kingdom of God, 447–449
kings, anointing of, 13–14
King's Community Church, 382
kinship rules, 125
Koch, Bradley, 73, 74
Kolkata, India, 303, 453
Kolkata Assembly of God, 303
Kolkata [Calcutta] experience, 89–94
Korankye-Ankrah, Sam, 29
Kornegay, Eddie, 111
Kosovo, 381–382
Kraft, Charles, 68
Krayhill, D. B., 49
Kurdistan, 382
Kuwait, 372
Kwarteng, Charles O., 105

L

labor, exploitation of, 115
La Casa de Dios in Riosiño square (La Paz), 159
Lagos, Nigeria, poverty within, 453
lame beggar, story of, 397
Lamech, 447
lament, 185–186

La Paz, Bolivia, PoG church within, 157–159, 159–163
Lapiz, Ed, 324
large deficit of decent work (LDDW), 363
Latin America
  economic disparity within, 207
  Edify within, 286
  Pentecostalism within, 69, 157–158
  poverty within, 208–209
  salaries within, 209
Latin America ChildCare (LACC), work of, 99. *See also* ChildHope
Latter Rain Movement, 66
Lazarus, 30, 36–38
laziness, 256–257, 326
leadership, 273, 390–391
Lebanon, 371
legitimacy, ministry, 387–388
Levant (Israel, Lebanon, Jordan, Syria, and Iraq), Pentecostalism within, 369–372
Levi, 51–52
liberation, 92
Liberation Theology, 144–146, 455
Liberia, 383
Libya, 368
life expectancy, 262
Liñan, Hernán, 191
Lindsay, Gordon, 66
Lipton, Michael, 129
literacy rates, 240, 262
livelihoods, 263–265, 336–338
living wage, 130
loan capital, 287–288
Long, Eddie, 73–74
Lord's Supper, 55
The Lost Sheep Initiative (TLSI), 357
love, baptism of the Holy Spirit and, 86
"Love Rice," 309
Lower Rock Quarry (LRQ), Philippines, ministry in, 321–322, 333–335, 336–337
low-fee independent schools (LFIS), 286, 287–288

Luke, Gospel of, 29–31, 38–39, 47–48, 51–52
Lutheran World Federation, 283
Lynn, Elizabeth, 103

M

Ma, Julie, 324
Ma, Wonsuk, 303, 324
Maasai people, 310
Macedonian churches, generosity of, 312
Maggay, Melba, 324
Maghreb (North Africa), 368–369
Magnificat, 30
Mains, David and Karen, 448
Maitatsine sect (Nigeria), 230–231
malaria, 254, 255
Mallams (Nigeria), 241–242
Mandela, Nelson, 281
Manila, Philippines, 323
manipulationist orientation, 101
Martel, Don José, 192
Martel, Hector Neira, 201–203
Martel, María José Sanhueza, 202–203
Martel, Valentina Sanhueza, 202
Marwa, Mohammadu, 230–231
Marxism, 145, 229
Mary (mother of Jesus), 30
material possessions, significance of, 29–30
Matthew, 52
Matthew, Thomas K., 69
Matthias, 388
Maxwell, David, 102
McCain, Danny, 112
McClung, Floyd, 451, 452
McPherson, Amy Semple, 302
"Medical Service of Love," 310
mega churches, leadership within, 391
Mennocostals, 153n3
Mennonites, 146, 151–152
mental illness, as poverty, 432–433
Menzies, William W., 305–306
Mercy Hospital (India), 90

Metcalf, Sam, 387
Methodist Church, 193, 418, 419
Microfinance Institutions (MFIs), 290–291
micro-financing, 105, 332
Middle East, Pentecostalism within, 366–374. *See also specific locations*
Middlemann, Udo, 450, 457, 458
migration
   within the Arabian Gulf, 372–373
   disconnection within, 364
   of domestic workers, 365
   global poverty and, 363–366
   within Levant, 369–370
   research regarding, 364
   temporary, 367–368
   voluntary, 364
Millennium Development Goals (MDGs), 126, 208, 262–263, 280–281
Miller, Donald E., 86, 91, 94–95, 302, 306–307, 405, 453
minimum wage, 130
mining industry, within Zambia, 269–270
ministry. *See also* church/early church; *specific ministries*
   discernment within, 398–399
   formation from, 399
   legitimacy within, 387–388
   revelation from, 399
   Spirit leading within, 396–397
minorities, violence against, 178–179
The Miracle of Seed Faith (Roberts), 414
miracles, 395
mission
holistic, 338
   within neo-Pentecostalism, 172
   PoG church viewpoint of, 165–167, 169–171
   reality and, 324
missional ministry, 379–380
missionaries, 86–87. *See also specific people*
Mission in Jesus' Name, 382–383
mission of God, 1
modalities, 387
Moise, Ngoma, 252
monetary poverty, 124
money, love of, 36. *See also* wealth
Montgomery, George and Carrie (Judd), 86
morality, of Iglesia Evangélica Pentecostal (Guarilihue, Chile), 200
mortality rates, 262
Moses, 13
Motyer, J. A., 15
Muindi, Florence, 302–303
Mukti Mission revival (India), 88–89
multidimensional poverty, 124
Muñoz, Aldo Exequiel Córdoba, 195
Murdock, Mike, 418
Muslim Background Believers, 371
Mutalima, Irene Banda, 454
Myers, Bryant, 329
Myers, Clay, 33–34
Myers, Diana, 363
Myles Munroe Bahamas Faith Ministry International (Bahamas), 74
mystery-sensing, 213

N

Nabgwana, of the Gunadule nation, 179–180
Nadu, Tamil, 88
narrative, role of, 219–220
Nash, Marshall and Rebecca, 415
Nathan, 13, 16–17
natural disasters, 125, 129–130, 263, 329–330
Neira, Apolonides Exequiel Sanhueza (Pastor Polo), 194–195, 196
Neira, José Miguel, 191
Nepal, 382
Newfrontiers, 381–382
Nigeria
   Boko Haram in, 235–236
   Daystar Leadership Academy within, 112–114
   economic status of, 236–237

Hausa-Fulani crisis of, 232
Islam in, 230, 243–244
kidnapping incident within, 235, 242
literacy rates of, 240
Maitatsine sect of, 230–231
Mallams in, 241–242
overview of, 227–229
poverty and wealth within, 236–241, 282, 453
religious crisis within, 229–236, 240–244
Shariah Law in, 232
statistics of, 243
Zango Kataf crisis of, 232
North-Western Province (Zambia), 269–275
Nye, Rebecca, 213

O

Obama, Barack, 430
Obasanjo, Olusegun, 232
obedience, 72, 144
oil of gladness, 13
Oman, 373
Onoja, Adoyi, 100
Onyinah, Opuku, 104, 455
Operation Blessing International Relief and Development Corporation, 99–100, 118n2
Opportunity International, 283
oppressed/oppression
 within development, 178
 examples of, 125–126
 overview of, 17–19, 292–293
 within poverty, 326
 story of *Balu Wala* and, 183
Oral Roberts Ministries, 413
Oral Roberts University (ORU), 412
Organization for Economic Cooperation and Development (OECD), 124
orphanages, Indian, 88
orphans, 19, 132
Osborn, T. L., 66
Osses, José Morales, 196

Ossom-Batsa, George, 38
Osteen, John, 417
Otabil, Mensa, 29, 32, 39
out-grower scheme, within the farming pilot project, 270–273
overseer, leadership of, 390
Oyedepo, David, 406

P

Padilla, René, 144, 175n8
Palacios, Marco, 142
Palestine, 376n17
Palestinian Intifada (Uprising), 369–370
Panotto, Nicolas, 178
Parable of the Rich Fool, 51
parables
 of Lazarus, 30, 36–38
 Parable of the Rich Fool, 51
 of rich man, 30, 36–38
 of rich young ruler, 30
 sheep and goats, 392
 of talents, 31
 unjust steward, 34–36
Paraguay, 151–152
Parham, Charles F., 85–86
participatory interventions, 335
pastors, 141, 275, 391
Paul
 as apostle, 388, 389
 calling of, 390
 generosity teachings of, 55
 as gospel planter, 388
 ministry of, 393, 394, 396–397
Paulk, Earl, 418
penny capitalism, 106
Pentecost, event of, 50, 51, 53, 266
Pentecostal Assemblies of God (PAG), 334, 335
Pentecostal-Charismatic Christianity, 33. *See also* Ghanian Pentecostal-Charismatic Christianity
Pentecostal churches, social engagement of, 302–304
Pentecostal Holiness Church (PHC), 88, 409

Pentecostalism
  in Africa, 69–70, 75
  African Christianity and, 70
  in Asia, 68–69
  attraction of, 71–73
  beliefs of, 303
  in Chile, 193–195
  core message of, 65–68
  experience of God within, 158
  focus of, 94–95
  healing viewpoint of, 66–67
  historical considerations for, 302
  influences of, 84
  in Latin America, 69
  Latter Rain Movement within, 66
  in the Middle East, 366–374
  missiological implications of, 338–339
  missionary nature of, 86–87
  overview of, 64–65
  pragmatic progressive wing of, 100
  Progressive, 99
  prosperity gospel and, 71–75
  as reconstruction, 158
  as revival movement, 85
  social engagement of, 83–84
  as socio-religious expression, 157
  spirituality of, 91
  spiritual warfare within, 68
  televangelists and, 66–67
  themes within, 85
  witchdemonology and, 70–71
  youth viewpoint regarding, 201–203
Pentecost University, 105
Pentvars Business Journal, 105
Persia, 24n19–20
personal money management program, 337
Peter
  as apostle, 389
  boldness of, 266
  calling of, 390
  as disciple, 51
  ministry of, 397
  sermon of, 54, 452

Petersen, Doug, 83
Peterson, David, 53
Pharisees, 35, 36
Philippines
  challenges within, 328
  combating poverty within, 330–331
  Holistic Child Development within, 336
  illegal settler within, 322
  law-abiding citizens of, 349
  means of fighting poverty within, 332–333
  ministry impact within, 337–338
  missiological implications of, 338–339
  municipal hospital within, 310
  nature of poverty within, 329–330
  participatory interventions within, 335
  personal story within, 321–322
  poverty causes within, 330
  Sambayanihan Ministries International Inc. (SMII) within, 333–335
  skills and livelihood training within, 336–337
  squatter areas within, 322–324
  study methodology within, 327–328
  unemployment within, 338–339
  war on drugs within, 345–351, 355–357
pilgrims, significance of, 442
Pneuma Youth Mission, 309
Polhill, John, 50
police, within the Philippines, 346
political capital, squatters as, 324
Polman, Gerrit, 86
poor/poverty
  biblical definitions for, 125
  biblical treatment of, 131–132
  causes of, 127–131, 134, 296, 325, 329, 330
  center-on, 151–152
  challenges of, 262
  Christianity and, 1–2
  church and, 4, 46, 52–53, 143

classification of, 262
culture of, 130
as curse, 38
defined, 124, 236, 279, 341–342n29, 432
economic democracy and, 115
economic disparity within, 207
entitlements of, 342n31
eradicating, 134
extreme, 127
factors of, 125
generalized, 127
geography of, 282
global effort regarding, 280–282
God's aid/concern for, 37, 46
God's provision for, 131–133
within the Gospel of Luke, 29–31
government role within, 129
helplessness within, 275
humble, 327
identification of, 124–127
images of, 325
impact of, 4
manifestations of, 236
means of fighting, 332–333
micro-financing for, 105
modern response to, 20–21
nature of, 329–330
overview of, 17–19, 123, 261–262
as positive, 38
powerless, 326–327
prosperity gospel and, 31–33, 39
reduction as global agenda, 126
roots of, 3–4
solutions to, 279–280
stereotypes of, 256–257
treatment of, 128
types of, 126–127
who they are, 46–47, 52
Populist Catholicism, 158
Post Traumatic Stress Disorder (PTSD), 433
powerlessness, 207, 210–211, 218–219, 255–257
powerless poor, 326–327
Power of God (PoG) Church
conversion viewpoint within, 164–165
cultural context of, 158–163
evangelism viewpoint of, 167–169
giving response within, 161–162
leader and member interviews of, 163–171, 174–175n8
mission viewpoint within, 165–167, 169–171
overview of, 157–159, 171–173
radio stations of, 162–163
worship experience within, 160–163
pragmatic prosperity approach, 102–103, 106–107, 113–114
praxis, reflection on, 144–145
prayer, 49–50, 56, 92
Price, Fredrick K. C., 66, 417
primal spirituality, 455
Professional and Business Network, 103
Program for Acquiring Competence and Entrepreneurship, the Center on Education and Training for Employment, and Ohio State University (PACE-CETE/OSU), 109
Progressive Pentecostalism
defined, 99
economic ethic of, 101–103, 117
economic justice and democracy and, 114–116
economic ministry of, 103–114, 116–117
economy on the margins and, 100–101
focus of, 100
ministries of, 306–307
penny capitalism and, 106
prophetic ministry, civic engagement within, 325–327
prophetism, witchdemonology and, 70–71
prophets, role of, 326–327, 393
prosperity, 102, 414–417, 420–421
prosperity gospel

abuse of, 420
within Colombia, 143–144
defined, 405–406
expansion of, 406
Liberation Theology and, 455
negative aspects of, 75
origin of, 406
overview of, 63–64
Pentecostalism and, 71–75
reality of, 38–39
wealth and poverty issues within, 31–33
Protestant ethic, 102
Protestants, 193
Puritans, 102

Q
Qatar, 373
quality of life, within poverty, 265
"quasi-prophets," 71
Quimby, Phineas Parkhurst, 66–67

R
Rabboni Health Talk, 384
Rabboni Missions International, 382–384
Radical Reformation, 147
Ramabai, Pandita, 88–89
reality, mission and, 324
The Redeemed Christian Church of God (Nigeria), 74
Regent University College, 105
rehabilitation, of drug addicts, 355–357
relational fruit, bearing of, 450
relationships, broken, 285, 292–293, 296
Relative Income Hypothesis, 415–416
relative poverty, 124
"remember the poor" command, 380, 392–394
repentance, 450–451
Republic of Congo. See Congo Brazzaville
restoration, 285, 456–458
revelation, from serving the poor, 399

Rhee, Helen, 416
Richard, Pablo, 184
Rich Christians in an Age of Hunger (Sider), 45–46
rich man, parable of, 30, 36–38
rich-poor gap, 314
rich young ruler, 30, 48
Robeck, Cecil, 86
Roberts, Claudius, 407
Roberts, Ellis, 407–408
Roberts, Oral
  Attack Your Lack, 416
  biology of inequality and, 410–411, 415, 419
  criticism of, 418
  as evangelist, 408–410
  financial base of, 415
  Flood Stage: Opening the Windows of Heaven, 416
  If You Need to Be Blessed Financially Do These Things, 416
  influence of, 69
  inspiration of, 457
  ministry of, 66, 67
  The Miracle of Seed Faith, 414
  overview of, 419–420
  personal life of, 415
  poverty life of, 407–411, 419
  prosperity viewpoint of, 411–412
  quote of, 413, 417
  seed faith concept of, 406, 412–414, 416
  supporters of, 417–419
Roberts, Patti, 415
Roberts, Richard, 415
Roberts, Ronnie, 415, 417
Robertson, Pat, 66
Roma (Gypsy) community, 385–386, 399
Romania, 381
rural poverty, 126, 453–454

S
Sabates, Ricardo, 363–364
Sabates-Wheeler, Rachel, 363–364
Sabbatical Year, 19–20, 21–22

Sacks, Jeffrey, 282
sacred stories, role of, 219–220
salaries, 130, 133, 209, 288–290, 367–368
salvation, 31–32, 65, 312–313
Salvation Army, 86
Sambayanihan Ministries International Inc. (SMII), 333–335, 336, 337
Sandoval, don Miguel, 198–199, 201
Sanhueza, Miguel, 192
Sanneh, Lamin, 366
Santos, Kian delos, 346
Satan, 447
Satyavrata, Ivan, 303
Saudi Arabia, 372
Saul, 13
Save Africa's Children, 99
Savelle, Jerry, 418
Schmoll, Pamela, 72
school entrepreneurs, income/wealth generation through, 288–290
School of Business (Pentecost University), 105
schools, poverty role of, 454. See also education
Scripture Union, 67
Second Coming, 94
security, basic, 102
seed faith concept, 406, 412–414, 415, 416
seeking blessings (kibock sinang) theology, 305–306
self-concept, 209–210, 224n45
self-denial, 147
Sen, Amartya, 210
Señor del Gran Poder Fiesta, 159–160
Seoul, Korea, 308, 309. See also Yoido Full Gospel Church (YFGC)
servanthood, 458–459
serving, function of, 268
sex trafficking, in India, 90
Seymour, William J., 64–65, 86
Shakarian, Demos, 413
shame, 433–434
Shariah Law, 232

sharing, 49, 55
sheep and goats parable, 392
shepherd, 387, 391
shields, anointing of, 13
Sider, Ronald, 45–46, 267–268
Sierra Leone, 383
Silvanus, 388
sin, 285, 292–293, 296
Singer, Merrill, 101
skills training, 336–337
slothfulness, 326
Small Business Development Center (SBDC) (Joseph Center), 109–110
social action, 267–268, 379–380
social capital, 339
social engagement, 88–89, 94, 302–304, 450–451
social gospel movement, 85
social impact, 84–87, 91
social justice, 143–144
social ministry, 99, 103–106, 311–313
social needs, 304
socioeconomic status, biological effects of, 410–411
Solomon, 13–14
Somalia, 382
Song of Hannah, 15
Son of Man, Jesus as, 155n33
soul, salvation of, 312
South Asia, 286
South Korea. *See also* Yoido Full Gospel Church (YFGC)
  Elim Welfare Town within, 307
  food distribution within, 309
  gold value within, 308
  intercultural ministry in, 310–311
  kibock sinang (seeking blessings) theology within, 305–306
"South-North Sharing Campaign," 309
sowing and reaping, 32, 33
Soyinka, Wole, 228–229
Spanish conquistadores, 142
Spirit-empowered church, 265–267, 296. *See also* church/early church
Spirit-empowered ministry, 394–396

Spirit-empowerment, 215–216, 219
spiritual development of children, 211–214
Spiritual Formation Leadership Seminars (SFLS), 314–315
spiritual gifts, 65, 387–388
spiritual growth, 268
spirituality, 91, 214, 217–218
spiritual sensitivity, 213
spiritual warfare, 68
squatter areas (barong barong), 322–324, 452–453
standard logic systems, 172
stewardship, 58
storytelling, power of, 348
strangers, provisions for, 132
strength, from servanthood, 458–459
structural causes of poverty, 127–131
Sub-Saharan Africa, poverty within, 282. *See also specific locations*
success, within the prosperity gospel, 32
sufficiency, to prosperity, 414–417, 420–421
sufficiency gospel, 419
"Super-Charismatic" prophetic movement, 71
supernatural, growth of the church and, 395
support staff, within education, 290
Susan, Rose D., 72
sustainability, justice and, 2
Sustainable Development Goal (SDG), 123, 134, 280–281, 284
sustainable livelihoods, 263–265, 275
Swaggart, Jimmy, 418
Sweetland, D., 49
Synan, Vinson, 69
Syria, 372, 385

T

tabernacle, anointing within, 13
talents, parable of, 31
Tales of the Kingdom (Mains), 448
Tapia, Luis René Zambrano, 195
tax income, generation of, 291
Taylor, Michael, 325
Taylor, William, 193
teachers, 290, 387
Tearfund, 283
Tejedo, Joel and Carolyn, 334, 452–453
televangelists, 66–67
temporary migrants, 367–368
tenderness of God, 450
terrorism, within Nigeria, 228
testimonies, role of, 219–220
thaumaturgical concept, 101
A Theology of the Church and its Mission (Hodges), 86–87
theory of change, 271–273
Thomas, Deloris, 108, 109
Thomas, V. V., 89
Timothy, 388
Tine, Michele, 453–454
tithes, 326
Tomlinson, A. J., 86
Torres, José Martel, 197, 198, 199
training, skills and livelihood, 336–337
transformation, power of, 198–199
transnational migration
    within the Arabian Gulf, 372–373
    disconnection within, 364
    of domestic workers, 365
    global poverty and, 363–366
    within Levant, 369–370
    research regarding, 364
    voluntary, 364
Trasher, Lillian, 369
Trump, Donald, 73
truth, Holy Spirit and, 54–55
Twelftree, Graham, 55–56

U

Ukraine, 381
Ulloa, Edith, 200–201
unauthorized immigration, 430, 433
undocumented immigrants, 431–432, 444n1
unemployment, in the Philippines, 328, 338–339

United Arab Emirates, 372–373
United Methodists, 193, 418, 419
United States
   American dream within, 433–435
   Anabaptists in, 152
   DREAMer Distress within, 435–437
   DREAMers within, 429–430
   immigration within, 429–432
   inspiration of, 442
unity, 49–50, 56
Universal Church of the Kingdom (Brazil), 74
Universal Church of the Kingdom of God (IURD), 69, 73
unjust steward, parable of, 34–36
urban modernity, 158
urban poverty, 451–453
urban theology, 452
useful citizen, 284

V

value-sensing, 213
violence, 125, 142, 178–179
Vision 2018 (Church of Pentecost), 104
Volf, Miroslav, 94, 145–146
voluntary migration, 364
voluntary society, 148

W

Wacker, Grant, 302
wages, 130, 133, 209, 288–290, 367–368
Wagner, Peter, 68
water, need for, 257–258
wealth
   within churches, 33
   as evidence of Christian faith, 38
   generation of, 288–290
   as gospel impediment, 30
   within the Gospel of Luke, 29–31
   governmental power within, 46
   love of, 36
   negative view of, 27, 28–29, 39–40
   opinions regarding, 1
   oppression by, 18
   perils of, 51–52
   as positive, 40
   proper use of, 30–31
   prosperity gospel and, 31–33, 39
   redistribution of, 29, 147
   reversal of, 37
Weaver, Alain Epp, 150
Weber, Max, 106
Weberian concept of development, 190
West Africa, 398
West Bank, 376n17
West Bengal, 453
White, Paula, 73, 107
widows, 19, 132, 393
Wilkinson, Michael, 63, 367
Williams, Smallwood, 114
wine, 191–192, 202
Winston, William "Bill," 106–108, 111
Winter, Ralph, 387
Wisely, Susan, 103
witchcraft, 294–295
witchdemonology, 70–71
Witte, John, 149
Wolfensohn, James D., 123
Wolterstorff, Nicholas, 149
women, 125, 322, 365
Wood, George O., 83
Woodberry, Robert, 74
Word of Faith movement, 417–419
work ethic, 133
World Assemblies of God Relief and Development Agency, 100
World Bank, 124, 126
World Vision, 283, 294
worship, 92, 160–163, 268
Wright, Christopher J. H., 20
Wyatt, Thomas, 66

Y

Yamamori, Tetsunao
   quote of, 91, 94–95, 453
   viewpoint of, 302
   work of, 86, 405

writings of, 306–307
yatiri, 162, 173
Yemen, 373
Yerima, Alhaji Sani, 232
Ylvisaker, Paul, 103
Yoder, John Howard, 148
Yoido Full Gospel Church (YFGC)
   Christian Greenmovement Mission (C.G.M.) of, 313
   Elim Welfare Town and, 307
   faith of sharing theory of, 312
   food distribution by, 309
   Full Gospel Medical Center of, 308
   Habitat for Humanity and, 308–309
   intercultural ministry of, 310–311
   International Monetary Fund (IMF) and, 307–308
   overview of, 301, 313–315
   prosperity gospel within, 74
   social engagement legacy of, 313
   social needs response of, 304
   Spiritual Formation Leadership Seminars (SFLS) of, 314–315
   theological response of, 305–311
Yoido Full Gospel Global Network (YFGN), 314
Yong, Amos, 420
Youth with a Mission (YWAM), 366
Yung, Hwa, 68, 324
Yusuf, Mohammed, 235

Z

Zacchaeus, 31
Zadok, 13
Zambia
   church action within, 269
   North-Western Province of, 269–273
   poverty within, 269, 454
   Spirit-filled church within, 273–275
   theory of change within, 271–273
   witchcraft within, 294
Zango Kataf crisis (Nigeria), 232

Scripture Index

Old Testament

Genesis
12:10	325
19:24–29	325
26:1	325
28:18	13
3:7, 21	283
4:23–24	447
41	337
45:1	325
47:20–26	325

Exodus
15:26	72
15:27	307
2:24–25	450
22:21–23	441
22:22–23	37
22:25	132
23:10–11	19, 179, 183
23:24	72
23:6	131
29:2	13
29:7	13
30:33	24n8
31	108
7–12	325

Leviticus
19:13	133
19:9–10	17, 25n26, 46, 132
2:4	13
23:22	25n26, 132
23:35	17
25	26n34
25:1–7	19
25:2	19
25:23	20
25:23–55	19
25:35	46
25:35–38	132
25:39–41	132
25:54	132
25:55	20
25:8–17	19
25:8–55	456
27:16–25	19
7:12	13
7:36	24n10
8:10	13
8:12	13

Numbers
36:4	19
6:15	13
7:10	13

Deuteronomy
10:18	37, 132, 391, 441
11:26–32	72
14:28–29	37
15	456
15:1–11	19
15:1–9	132
15:11	46, 131, 258, 452
15:4	59, 261, 266
15:7–11	20–21, 26n34
16:19	326
16:20	133
24:10–11	132
24:14	326
24:14–15	133
24:19–22	132
28–30	32
28:15–68	72
4:5–8	150

Judges
9:7–20, 57	13

Ruth
1:6	325
3:3	12

1 Samuel
10:1	14
10:1, 9	14
12:3, 5	15
15:22	25n22
16:13	14
16:3	14
16:6	15
17:4–7	438
17:48–50	438
17:51	439
2:10	15
2:35	16
24:6	13, 15
9:16	13

2 Samuel
1:21	13
12	16–17
19:10	13
19:21	15
2:4–7	13
21:22	439
23:1	15
5:3	13

1 Kings
1:34, 35	13
1:39	13, 14
17:1–16	325
18	14
19:15	14
19:16	14

2 Kings
11:12	14
14:17	326
14:26	326
21:1–10	327
21:1–18, 24–25	326
23:25	16, 17
23:30	14
4:1–7	325
6:24–7:20	325
9:4–13	24n13
9:6	14

1 Chronicles
29:22	14

2 Chronicles
8:9	311

Nehemiah
10:31	19
13:15–18	326
5	325

Job
1:16, 18–19	325
29:12, 16	18

Psalms
1:3	32
105:12–13	24n14
105:15	14, 24n14
109:30–31	450
12:2	450
14:6	450
140:12	450
19:18	327
2, 18, 20, 21, 45, 72, 89, 101, 110, 132, 144	25n21
20:7–8	440
22:10–13	440
22:24–26	440
22:26	18
23:5	14
24:1	184
27:4	266
34:18	450, 458
41:1	132, 133, 327
48:6–8	13
5:6	327
72	149
72:12–14	450
84:11	32
9:9	450
92:10	14

Proverbs
10:4	326
10:4, 15	18
13:18	131, 326
13:22	39
13:23	450
14:23	131
14:31	327
17:5	450
19:15	326
19:17	453
20:13	326
21:13	450
21:17	326
21:5	131, 326
22:9	46, 132
23:19–21	326
23:20–21	131
24:30–34	326
28:19	326
28:27	132
29:7	450
3:9–10	326
6:10–11	18
6:6–11	326
6:9–11	131

Ecclesiastes
5:8	325
9:16	128

Isaiah
1:6	12
10:1–4	128
10:2	18
2:1–5	325
21:5	13
25:4	450
25:8	447
40–55	12
41:1	24n19
41:17–18	132
41:25	15
44:28	15
45:1	14
45:1–3	15
45:1–7	15
45:13	15
47	15
48:17	108
49:13	327
5:8	18
51:11	447
58:13–14	326
58:6	12, 23n3
61	5, 11, 12, 14, 19, 21
61:1	14, 17, 23n5
61:1–2	23n3, 23n5
61:1–3	11, 23n2, 25n24
61:2	19
61:3	13
61:8	149
66:2	327

Jeremiah
22:14	13

Lamentations
4:20	16

Ezekiel
22:23–31	325
22:29	456
22:34	325
46:1	19

Daniel
4:27	312

Hosea
4:6	129

Joel
1	325

Amos
2:6	327
2:7	18
4:1	18
5:1	327
5:11	18
6:6	12

Micah
3:1–4, 9–12	325
4:1–4	325
6:8	134, 286

Habakkuk
3:13	16

Zephaniah
2:3	327
3:12	327

Zechariah
4:1–14	14
7:10	128

Scripture Index

Malachi
3:6–12   326

New Testament
Matthew
11:5   134
19:21   48
2:13–15   257
22:37–39   453
25   104, 283
25:31–46   392
26:11   451, 453
26:12   12
26:6–9   48
28:19–20   54
3:8   450
5:13   314
5:3   18
5:7   327
6:1   396
6:10   92
6:2   396
6:33   32
6:9–10   450

Mark
1:24   353
1:27   354
11:23   67
11:23–24   67
12:30–31   456
12:42   47
16:1   12
4:35–41   352
5:1   352
5:1–20   351–355, 358
5:11   352
5:15   353–354
5:18   354
5:19   355
5:20   355
5:3   352
5:4   352
5:9   353

Luke
1   30
1:5–44   47
1:52–53   23n4
10:1–12   30
10:25–37   30, 35
10:27   453
10:31–32   457
10:34   12
12:13–21   23n4, 35
12:13–31   29
12:15   51
12:16–21   0, 51, 453
12:33   48, 51
12:33–34   46
14:12–14   48
14:13   131
14:13–14, 21   23n4
14:13, 21   47
14:25–33   31
14:33   52
15   35, 36
15:11–32   35
16   27, 33–34, 36, 38–39
16:1   35
16:1–13   23n4, 27, 28, 29, 30–31, 34–36, 35, 36, 39
16:1–2   34
16:1–31   29
16:1–8   33
16:1–9   36
16:13   36, 39
16:14   35, 36
16:14–18   36
16:19–21   37
16:19–26   36
16:19–31   23n4, 28–29, 30, 33, 35, 36, 39, 453
16:20, 22   47
16:22   37
16:22–23   37
16:24–31   37
16:25–26   37
16:27–31   36, 37
16:3   34
16:4   34
16:5–7   34
16:8   34, 36
16:9–13   33, 35
16:9–14   33
18:18–23   29
18:18–25   30, 31
18:18–30   35
18:22   1, 23n4, 47, 51
18:22, 23   48
18:25   30
19:1–10   28, 31, 35
19:1–9   27
19:11–27   31, 35
19:8   23n4, 47
2:44–45   56
2:44b   56
2:45   56
21:1–4   23n4
21:2   47
21:3   47
22   390
22:19   55
23:56   12
24:30   55
24:30, 35   55
24:49   265
3:10–14   450
3:12–13   450–451
3:14   451
3:8   450
4   12, 17, 21, 30
4:16–18   48
4:16–30   23n3
4:18   14, 23n5, 47, 129, 134
4:18–19   12
5:11   51
5:28   51–52
6   30
6:10   134
6:20   18, 28, 38, 47
6:20–24   29
6:20–49   23n4
6:38b   67
7:22   23n4, 47
7:46   12
9:1–6   30
9:16   55

9:51–19:27	35	2:44a	56	9:11	388
9:57–62	35, 61	2:45	18, 51	9:5	388
9:59–61	450	2:46	50, 57		

John

2 Corinthians

10:10	32	2:8–11	53	10:3–5	xii
11:35	459	2:9, 11	366	13:14	93
12:5–8	48	20:32–35	49	3:12	458
13:29	48	3:1–10	19, 397	3:16	266
13:34–35	59	4:23	49	3:3	314
14:25–27	399	4:24	50	5:17–19	152
21:17	77	4:26	50	8–9	18, 392
3:8	64	4:31	51	8:1–5	312
8:32	129	4:32–35	49	8:1–6	53
9:6, 11	12	4:32–36	449	8:4	55
		4:32–37	45, 49, 52, 53, 57, 266, 275, 312	8:9	32, 132
				9:13	55

Acts

1:14	49, 50, 54	4:32–38	49	9:5–9	388
1:14a	50	4:33	58		
1:15	50	4:34–35	261	**Galatians**	
1:8	53, 91, 265	4:37	57	2:10	18, 46, 392
10:2	312	4:39	199	2:7–10	380
10:38	14	5:1–11	267	6:10	59
11:27–30	48	5:12–16	53	6:6–10	388
11:29	48	5:4	57		
12:12	57	5:42	93	**Ephesians**	
13:1	389	6	275	1:14	94
14:4, 14	388	6:1–6	48, 49, 267	2:19–20	390
2	265, 268, 366, 449	6:1–7	261, 392	4:11	391
2, 4	50, 52	6:4	393	4:11–12	66, 389
2:1	50, 51	6:7	267, 397	4:28	46
2:1–4	265	9:36	312		

Philippians

2:1, 44–47	50	**Romans**		1:1	390
2:14, 41	452	15:25–28	53	2:1	93
2:17	94	15:26	18	2:25	388
2:36	266	16:7	388	3:20	442
2:38	54	8:21	94	4:13	217
2:39	54			4:19	67
2:4	84	**1 Corinthians**			
2:41	54	10:16	55	**Colossians**	
2:41–47	45, 49, 52–53	12	93	1:13–14	1
2:42	49, 54, 55	12:28	388		
2:42–46	49, 93	15:36–37	388	**1 Thessalonians**	
2:42–47	49, 52, 57, 268	15:42–44	388	1:1	388
2:43	51, 56	16:1	53	2:6	388
2:44–45	56	3:10	390		
2:44–47	397	3:11	149	**1 Timothy**	
		3:5–16	388	3	390
				6:18	453

Philemon
1:6	399

Hebrews
1:9	13
11:10	443
11:13–16	443
11:16	442
11:9–10	442
12:27–28	442
13	390
13:14	442

James
1:26	20
1:27	18, 46, 392
2:5	134
2:6	18
4:13–17	18
4:2	32
5:14	12

1 John
2:20, 27	14

3 John
1:2	304
2	32, 304, 305, 410, 411, 412, 419, 457

Revelation
12:12	447
12:17	447
2:4	456

Ancient Sources
Josephus
Antiquities
3.280.3	19

Sifra
8:2	19

www.ingramcontent.com/pod-product-compliance
Lightning Source LLC
Chambersburg PA
CBHW071948110526
44592CB00012B/1035